From Viking to Crusader

From Viking to Crusader

The Scandinavians and Europe 800–1200

General Editors:
Else Roesdahl and David M. Wilson

RIZZOLI
NEW YORK

First published in the United States of America in 1992 by
RIZZOLI INTERNATIONAL PUBLICATIONS, Inc.
300 Park Avenue South, New York, NY 10010

Editorial committee: Else Roesdahl, Lilja Árnadóttir, Torsten Edgren, Erla B. Hohler, Niels-Knud Liebgott, Göran Tegnér

Catalogue coordination: Björn Fredlund, Per Malmberg, Birgitta Schreiber

Translation from Danish, Norwegian, Swedish and German by Helen Clarke, with additional translations by Joan F. Davidson, David Liversage, Clifford Long, Kirsten Williams (Russian texts were translated from the Swedish translation of Ingmar Jansson)
Translation from French by Joan F. Davidson, Gillian Fellows-Jensen

Design: Gösta Svensson

Front cover: Animal-head post from a Viking chieftain's bed, Gokstad, Norway (cat. no. 167)

Back cover: The Åby crucifix, Denmark. C. 1100 (cat. no. 460)

Illustration p. 2: Picture-stone from Ardre, Gotland, Sweden. 8th–9th century (cat. no. 1)

Illustration p. 5: The Halikko hoard, Finland. 12th century (cat. no. 496)

Illustration p. 6: The Lisbjerg altar, Denmark. Mid-12th century (cat. no. 467)

ISBN 0-8478-1625-7
LC 92-50205

Printed and bound by Bohusläningens Boktryckeri AB, Uddevalla, Sweden, 1992

Catalogue published with support from The Tuborg Foundation (Tuborgfondet)

Patrons

H.M. Queen MARGRETHE II of Denmark

H.E. Mauno KOIVISTO, President of the Republic of Finland

H.E. Vigdís FINNBOGADÓTTIR, President of the Republic of Iceland

H.M. King HARALD V of Norway

H.M. King CARL XVI GUSTAF of Sweden

H.E. François MITTERRAND, President of the French Republic

H.E. Dr. Richard von WEIZSÄCKER, President of the Federal Republic of Germany

This book is published in conjunction with the exhibition organized by
The Nordic Council of Ministers in collaboration with The Council of Europe

The 22nd Council of Europe Exhibition

Les Vikings... Les Scandinaves et l'Europe 800–1200
Grand Palais, Paris, 2 April—12 July 1992

Wikinger, Waräger, Normannen. Die Skandinavier und Europa 800–1200
Altes Museum, Berlin, 2 September—15 November 1992

Viking og Hvidekrist. Norden og Europa 800–1200
Danmarks Nationalmuseum, Copenhagen, 26 December 1992—14 March 1993

Honorary Committee

Scandinavia

Grethe ROSTBØLL
Minister of Culture, Denmark

Tytti ISOHOOKANA-ASUNMAA
Minister of Culture, Finland

Ólafur G. EINARSSON
Minister of Education and Culture, Iceland

Åse KLEVELAND
Minister of Culture, Norway

Birgit FRIGGEBO
Minister of Culture, Sweden

France

Roland DUMAS, Minister of Foreign Affairs

Jack LANG, Minister of Education and Culture

Catherine TASCA, Secrétaire d'Etat chargée de la Francophonie et des Relations Culturelles Extérieures

Alain DECAUX, de l'Académie Française, Président de l'Association Française d'Action Artistique

Germany

Eberhard DIEPGEN, Governing Mayor of Berlin

Professor Dr. Werner KNOPP, President of the Stiftung Preussischer Kulturbesitz

Ulrich ROLOFF-MOMIN, Senator for Cultural Affairs

The Council of Europe

René FELBER, Chairman, Committee of Ministers

Sir Geoffrey FINSBERG, Chairman of the Parliamentary Assembly

Catherine LALUMIÈRE, Secretary General

The Council of Europe Organizing Committee

Else ROESDAHL, Reader in Medieval Archaeology, University of Aarhus. *Academic coordinator of the exhibition*

Niels-Knud LIEBGOTT, Deputy Director, Danmarks Nationalmuseum, Copenhagen

Dr. Torsten EDGREN, Director, Head of Research Department, Museiverket, Helsinki

Thór MAGNÚSSON, State Antiquary, Director of Thjóðminjasafn Íslands, Reykjavík

Erla B. HOHLER, Keeper of the Medieval Department, Universitetets Oldsaksamling, Oslo

Göran TEGNÉR, Deputy Keeper of Medieval and Later Antiquities, Statens historiska museum, Stockholm

Jean-Pierre MOHEN, Conservateur Général du Patrimoine, Adjoint au Directeur des Musées de France

Max MOULIN, Chargé de mission, Association Française d'Action Artistique, Services des Arts Plastiques, Paris

Professor Dr. Wolf-Dieter DUBE, Director General, Staatliche Museen Berlin—Preussischer Kulturbesitz, Berlin

Professor Dr. Wilfried MENGHIN, Director, Museum für Vor- und Frühgeschichte, Berlin

Professor Dr. Kurt SCHIETZEL, Director, Archäologisches Landesmuseum, Schleswig

Dr. Patrick WALLACE, Director, National Museum of Ireland, Dublin

Sir David WILSON, sometime Director, The British Museum, London

The Council of Europe, Secretariat

David MARDELL, Head of Division, Directorate of Education, Culture and Sport, The Council of Europe, Strasbourg

Birgitta BJÖRNBERG-PARDO, Administrative Assistant, Directorate of Education, Culture and Sport, The Council of Europe, Strasbourg

Irène HERRENSCHMIDT, Administrative Assistant, Directorate of Education, Culture and Sport, The Council of Europe, Strasbourg

Nordic Council of Ministers, Secretariat

Dr. Björn FREDLUND, Special Projects Director, Nordic Council of Ministers, Copenhagen

Birgitta SCHREIBER, Administrative Assistant, Nordic Council of Ministers, Copenhagen

Exhibition design

Vincen CORNU and Benoît CRÉPET, Atelier Onze, Paris
Grafikbüro Damm, Berlin

The Scandinavian Organizing Committee

Else ROESDAHL, Reader in Medieval Archaeology, University of Aarhus. *Academic coordinator of the Exhibition*

Niels-Knud LIEBGOTT, Deputy Director, Danmarks Nationalmuseum, Copenhagen

Jørgen NORDQVIST, Director of Conservation, Danmarks Nationalmuseum, Copenhagen

Torsten EDGREN, Head of Research Department, Museiverket, Helsinki

Pirkko-Liisa LEHTOSALO-HILANDER, Associate Professor, University of Turku

Jónas KRISTJÁNSSON, Professor, Director of Stofnun Árna Magnússonar, Reykjavík

Thór MAGNÚSSON, State Antiquary, Director of Thjóðminjasafn Íslands, Reykjavík

Erla B. HOHLER, Keeper of the Medieval Department, Universitetets Oldsaksamling, Oslo

Sigrid H. H. KALAND, Keeper of Prehistoric Antiquities, Historisk Museum, Bergen

Ingmar JANSSON, Reader in Archaeology, University of Stockholm

Göran TEGNÉR, Deputy Keeper of Medieval and Later Antiquities, Statens historiska museum, Stockholm

Nordic Council of Ministers, Secretariat

Björn FREDLUND, Special Projects Director, Nordic Council of Ministers, Copenhagen

Birgitta SCHREIBER, Administrative Assistant, Nordic Council of Ministers, Copenhagen

Reconstruction of the second wreck found at Skuldelev, Denmark. The ship was about 30 m long and built in Ireland.

Catalogue of exhibition

Foreword

Olaf Olsen

Most museum curators have an ambivalent attitude to the large-scale touring exhibitions of masterpieces of internationally-renowned art or of archaeological treasures which in recent years have come to occupy an important position in the exhibition programmes of the major museums. They are often cultural events of high quality and attract a large public attendance.

But—to be totally frank—how many of us in fact really like lending our own museum's treasures to exhibitions of this kind? One is always hesitant to subject them to the dangers of travel, and there is always the fear that they might suffer damage through being kept for months in climatic conditions different from those at home. One can only relax and rejoice on the day when everything has returned home safely and been restored to its usual place in the collections.

It is therefore remarkable that the exhibition *From Viking to Crusader*—initiated by the Nordic Council of Ministers and subsequently integrated by the Council of Europe into its series of international exhibitions—has received assent to borrow virtually all the objects requested for it, from no less than 85 lenders in 15 countries. The reason for this is undoubtedly that the major historical museums in the Scandinavian countries have unanimously supported the exhibi-tion, inspired by a programme devised by Else Roesdahl and the Scandinavian Organizing Committee. This is the largest and most ambitious Viking exhibition ever arranged, and it is more than that, since it goes beyond the Viking Age into the period when Scandinavia developed into a fully recognised part of Christian Europe.

In the Scandinavian museums we each feel that this has become *our* exhibition—a common Scandinavian presentation of what the North had to offer and of what it received in the course of the period during which Scandinavia became part of Europe.

At the same time we would wish to thank most warmly our neighbours in Europe, who have also lent—in a spirit of true academic co-operation—to this exhibition. Particularly we would thank our colleagues in Great Britain, Ireland, Russia, Schleswig, Poland, Estonia and Latvia.

We are extremely grateful to *Skibsreder A.P. Møller og hustru Chastine Mc-Kinney Møllers Fond til almene Formaal* for a most generous subvention to enable the exhibition to be mounted in the Danish National Museum in Copenhagen after the displays in the Grand Palais in Paris and the Altes Museum in Berlin. The National Museum acknowledges this help with deepest gratitude.

Lenders to the exhibition

Scandinavia

Denmark

Danmarks Nationalmuseum, Copenhagen 11, 17, 30, 32, 34–38, 46, 58, 65, 67–68, 76–79, 93, 106–107, 109, 113, 116, 122, 124, 131, 140, 142, 144–149, 152–153, 170, 173–174, 180, 188, 191–195, 198, 266–267, 338–341, 343–344, 415, 422–423, 425, 448, 456, 460, 466–468, 470–471, 475, 478–482, 487–488, 493, 514, 539–544, 556, 565, 601, 604–607, 610, 612

Den Antikvariske Samling, Ribe 102, 178, 184

Den Arnamagnæanske Samling, Copenhagen 337, 521, 523, 525, 527

Det Kongelige Bibliotek, Copenhagen 509, 513, 528–530, 538

Forhistorisk Museum, Moesgård, Århus 183

Kulturhistorisk Museum, Randers 112

Langelands Museum, Rudkøbing 45, 172

Nørre Snede kirkes menighedsråd 451

Roskilde Museum 100

Svendborg og Omegns Museum, Svendborg 580

Sydhimmerlands Museum, Hobro 111, 117

Vejle Museum 20, 59, 81–83

Viking Ship Museum, Roskilde 2, 6, 9, 559

Zoologisk Museum, Copenhagen 591

Finland

Satakunnan museo, Pori (Björneborg) 21

Suomen kansallismuseo – Finlands nationalmuseum Helsinki 22, 39, 200–215, 217–237, 240, 495–496, 536, 558

Suomen merimuseo – Finlands sjöhistoriska museum, Helsinki 7

The Faroe Islands

Føroya Fornminnissavn, Tórshavn 315–323

Greenland

Grønlands Nationalmuseum og Arkiv, Nuuk 342, 434

Iceland

Byggðasafn Rangæinga og V. Skaftfellinga, Skógum (Skógar museum) 331

Landsbókasafn Íslands, Reykjavík 526

Stofnun Árna Magnússonar, Reykjavík 336, 510, 519–520, 522, 524

Þjóðminjasafn Íslands (Islands Nationalmuseum), Reykjavík 16, 71, 246, 324–330, 332–335, 433, 454, 483, 563, 588, 590

Norway

Historisk Museum, Universitetet i Bergen 41, 50, 52–54, 64, 75, 90, 123, 128, 130, 139, 150, 410, 465, 502, 506–507, 533, 574, 616–617

Nidaros Domkirkes Restaureringsarbeider, Trondheim 444–447

Riksarkivet, Oslo 516, 518

Skimuseet, Oslo 23

Tromsø Museum 28, 74, 99, 114, 154, 238–239, 348, 494

Universitetets Myntkabinett, Oslo 545–551

Universitetets Oldsaksamling, Oslo 3, 5, 8, 10, 15, 25–26, 29, 33, 40, 42, 63, 84–85, 89, 91–92, 94, 101, 108, 110, 115, 118, 129, 137–138, 141, 155–169, 241, 417, 441–443, 457, 459, 472, 489, 499, 517, 557, 587

Vitenskapsmuseet, Universitetet i Trondheim 13–14, 88, 136, 197, 421, 476, 484, 501, 504, 534, 564, 567–572, 579, 592

Sweden

Danderyds församling 464

Domkyrkoförsamlingen, Skara 477

Göteborgs arkeologiska museum, Gothenburg 4

Gotlands fornsal, Visby 485

Kulturen, Lund 18–19, 24, 61–62, 69–70, 419, 435, 561–562, 573, 577, 586, 589, 596–597, 602, 613

Kungliga myntkabinettet, Stockholm 143, 153, 307, 423–424, 426, 552, 554–555

Lunds universitets historiska museum 423, 474

Riksarkivet, Stockholm 508, 515

Sigtuna museums 498, 505, 531, 553, 560, 576, 578, 582–584, 598

Skara stifts- och landsbibliotek 511

Statens historiska museum, Stockholm 1, 12, 27, 31, 43–44, 47, 49, 51, 72, 80, 95, 101, 103–104, 119–121, 125–127, 132–135, 143, 151, 175–177, 179, 181–182, 185–186, 190, 196, 242, 244–245, 313–314, 411, 414, 440, 449–450,

Preface — Vikings and sagas

Jónas Kristjánsson

Documentary sources for the Viking Age fall into two categories according to their origin. There are the written sources from the homelands of the Vikings and those from the countries they visited. In the latter they were usually not welcome. Churches and monasteries were often the goals of these Scandinavian raiders and, since the writers of history were usually men of the cloth, they found it hard to describe in sufficiently vigorous terms the viciousness and destructiveness of the Vikings. These latter sources are mostly brief entries in annals, but towards the end of the Viking Age some of the foreign sources become slightly more expansive.

Most Scandinavian stories about Vikings come from Iceland, but there are also some which are Norwegian and Danish. These are in poetry and prose (from Sweden we only have brief runic inscriptions). The poems are attributed to named scalds who lived during the Viking Age and it is thought that most of the attributions are correct. The date of some of the stanzas, however, is not certain and some are demonstrably much later than they pretend to be. The old Scandinavian poems are, like the foreign annals, short and pithy—hardly more than enumerations of battles and other acts of war, and the actual information is often enmeshed in a richly ornamented scaldic language. Old Scandinavian poetry is, however, a valuable contemporary source, as far as it goes. Indeed the poems survive because the saga writers used them as sources and absorbed them into their works as proof of historical veracity. A famous example of this is Snorri Sturluson's comment on the value of scaldic poems as source material in the prologue to his history *Heimskringla* (The Circle of the World) from *c.* 1230 AD.

But the Icelandic sagas are by far the most extensive and colourful stories we have about Viking exploits and Viking life. They fall into several categories according to literary style as well as historical value. Those sagas which take place in the Viking Age itself—the so-called *sagas of the Icelanders* and *kings' sagas*, which describe events in the tenth century and in the beginning of the eleventh—were, however, not written down until the thirteenth and fourteenth centuries. And although many sagas are based on old poetry and tales which were passed on through generations, it is clear that much may have changed along the way.

A third group comprise the so-called *fornaldarsögur*. They take place in legendary times, mainly before the settlement of Iceland—that is if it is possible to date the action at all. In

Fig. 1. Kringla, *written c. 1260, the earliest surviving manuscript of the Icelander Snorri Sturluson's* Heimskringla *with sagas of Norwegian kings. Cat. no. 526.*

many of these sagas the heroes 'go viking' and today scholarly literature often calls them *Viking sagas*. The *fornaldarsögur* were intended as entertainment—veracity was not of primary importance. They are branches on the great tree of Icelandic saga literature and they have had an immense influence in shaping the popular conception of the Viking Age.

Naturally the Icelandic sagas tell of many things other than Viking raids. They also tell of the lives of people at home in the Scandinavian countries; in Iceland and Norway, in Sweden and Denmark, on the Faroes, the Orkneys and in Greenland. Taken as a whole, the sagas paint a rich and varied picture of the Scandinavian past. In this picture one of the distinctive features is the description of daring Viking expeditions, seen in the golden glow which distance lends to time and space.

Fig. 2. 8th–9th cent. Hiberno-Saxon mount found in a Viking Age grave at Myklebostad, Norway. Cat. no. 128.

Fig. 3. Viking raiders. Page from French manuscript of the Life of St Aubin. C. 1100. Cat. no. 439.

A short tale in *Egil Skallagrímssons saga* encapsulates the view from the High Middle Ages, looking back to the glorious Viking Age. Egil was an early developer and of a revengeful disposition and when he was seven years old he became angry with a playmate and hit him on the head with an axe, so that it stuck in the brain. His father was displeased, but his mother said that there were the makings of a Viking in Egil. He then spoke this verse:

> My mother told me men
> must and would buy me a good
> fast ship and finest oars
> to fight with Viking men;
> to stand tall in the prow,
> to steer the vessel well,
> to hold for harbour and
> hack down man after man.   (Transl. C. Fell and J. Lucas)

Njáls saga is the greatest and most famous of all the sagas of the Icelanders. The first part of the saga tells of Gunnarr from Hlidarendi. He excelled in all sports; he could jump his own height in full battle array, backwards no less than forwards. The story of such a hero would, naturally, be incomplete if it did not tell of his exploits on Viking expeditions. At an early age he travelled, together with his brother Kolskeggr, from Iceland with a Norwegian sea captain called Hallvarðr. When they reached Norway Gunnarr said that he wanted to go raiding and get wealth. They obtained two longships from Hallvarðr's kinsman Olvir, who lived out east by the Gota river. When they set course down the river they met two brothers, Vandill and Karl, who were also steering each his ship, and these brothers at once prepared to attack:

Fig. 4. Part of the great Gnezdovo hoard, Russia, with jewellery, a sword and 2 oval brooches. 10th cent. Cat. no. 304.

"Gunnarr drew his sword—it was a fine weapon that Olvir had given him—and without pausing to put on his helmet he jumped on to the prow of Vandill's ship and cut down the first man he met. Meanwhile, Karl had laid his ship against Gunnarr's on the other side, and now he hurled a spear directly across it, aiming at Gunnarr's waist. Gunnarr saw the spear coming, whirled round faster than the eye could follow, caught the spear in flight with his left hand, and hurled it back at Karl's ship. The man who was in its way fell dead. Kollskeggr took hold of an anchor and heaved it into Karl's ship; one of the flukes smashed through the hull, and the dark-blue sea came pouring in. The crew had to scramble off their vessel into the other ships. Gunnarr now leapt back to his own ship, and Hallvarðr drew along-side him. A tremendous battle developed. The men had seen their leader's courage, and each one fought as hard as he could. Gunnarr laid about him, hacking and hurling, killing men on all sides, and Kolskeggr gave him brave support. Karl had joined his brother Vandill on his ship, and there they fought side by side all day. At one stage, Kolskeggr was taking a rest aboard Gunnarr's ship. Gunnarr noticed this and said to him, 'You have been kinder to others than to yourself today, for you have quenched their thirst forever.' Kolskeggr took a bowl full of mead, drained it, and returned to the fight. Eventually Gunnarr and Kolskeggr boarded the ship defended by Vandill and Karl. Kolskeggr worked his way down one side of it, Gunnarr down the other. Vandill came to meet Gunnarr and struck at him, but the sword hit his shield and stuck there fast; with a wrench of the shield, Gunnarr snapped the sword at the hilt. Then Gunnarr

Fig. 5. Bamberg casket. Scandinavian shrine from c. 1000. Now in Bayerisches Nationalmuseum, Munich, Germany. Cf. cat. no. 267.

struck back; to Vandill it seemed as if there were three swords coming at him at once, and he did not know where to defend himself. The sword sliced through both his legs. Then Kolskeggr ran Karl through with a spear. After that they seized much booty."

(Transl. M. Magnusson and H. Pálsson)

After this Gunnarr and Hallvarðr spent two summers on Viking raids. The saga describes a great battle which they fought out east near Estonia. They won a glorious victory and later went to Norway with a large booty.

The kings' sagas and the sagas of the Icelanders are history writing by the yardstick of their age. But the Viking Age became more and more distant, and the taste of the Late Middle Ages demanded increasingly exaggeration and

courtly romance. *Njáls saga*, which was written shortly before 1300, lies on the threshold between the older historical sagas and the wildly exaggerated sagas of the fourteenth century. Its author has made use of many older written sources and has to some extent sought to tell of actual events. The saga seems realistic on the surface, but, if read carefully, it turns out that much in it is unlikely and could hardly have taken place in real life—the stories of Gunnarr's and Kolskeggr's Viking expeditions demonstrate this clearly. But many of the sagas are great works of literature, and it was widely believed that their contents were probably true.

Later ages became even more certain of the veracity of the sagas, although dissenting voices were sometimes heard, not least in the age of enlightenment in the eighteenth

Fig. 6. Madonna from Mosjö, Sweden. Mid 12th cent. Cat. no. 462.

century. In the nineteenth century, however, the romantic cultivation of the sagas came into full bloom. Young Norwegians and Icelanders read the sagas with enthusiasm, and sought strength from them in their struggle for their peoples' national independence. In Denmark Saxo's *Gesta Danorum* ('The Deeds of the Danes') was also read. Poets, authors and painters sought in this literature motives for their books and paintings—N.F.S. Grundtvig wrote *Scenes from the Decline of Heroism in Scandinavia* (1809), Elias Tegnér wrote *Frithiofs saga* (1825) and Henrik Ibsen wrote *The Warriors at Helgeland* (1857).

But with the new and rigorous critical approach to sources in the second half of the nineteenth century, the belief in the high historical value of the Icelandic sagas began to falter, and in the early twentieth century it received its death blow. Historians today use sagas with great caution and prefer not to believe them unless they are supported by other, more reliable, sources.

The same applies to several other groups of sources about Vikings. For example, it has been observed that foreign accounts of the Vikings' raids and the size of their armies are wildly exaggerated. So, while the sagas give a highly idealised picture of the Vikings, the foreign annals often do the opposite. Scholars today try to balance the various sources against each other and to evaluate each piece of information concerning the situation which caused it to be written down in the first place. Further, archaeology has provided a whole new group of evidence, which tells of other aspects of the Viking Age—technology, for example, and trade and daily life.

But the Icelandic sagas are still of great importance for our view of the Vikings and the Viking Age. This literature, which so splendidly dramatizes the events of the Viking Age, is to many the essential basis for their conception of the period. Without them what would we make of the discovery of Iceland and Greenland and the journeys to America? What would we believe about the unification of Norway? What would be left of scaldic poetry?

The great narrative art of the sagas created the picture of the Scandinavian Viking Age and carried it forward through the centuries. This picture has provided Scandinavia with a national heritage and has made an impact far beyond its borders. It is a part of the national consciousness and it has lent strength in adversity and inspiration to new literary masterpieces. The portrait of the Vikings, as presented by the sagas, is exaggerated and embellished, but it is imbued with its own vigour and it is a part of a distinctive and outstanding literature.

Fig. 7. Portal of the stave-church at Ål, Norway. Mid 12th cent. Cat. no. 441.

Introduction

Else Roesdahl and David M. Wilson

The Exhibition

This exhibition tells a story of Scandinavia and its European connections from *c.* 800 to 1200: a period which starts with the Viking Age and leads into the full medieval period. It depicts the culture and society of the North and also shows how this vast geographical area, which at the beginning of the period was almost unknown by other peoples, came to influence Europe, until it itself became a part of Christian Europe.

This period and its problems have never previously been dealt with as a whole. The exhibition and its accompanying book are intended to present a dramatic history and to show those important objects which shape our perception of the period. These objects come from Scandinavia and from all the places with which it had contacts. They comprise rune-stones, weapons, jewellery, gold hoards, coins, iron bars, parts of ships, animal bones, manuscripts of poems and narrative history, pagan burials, baptismal fonts, carved portals from stave churches, and much besides. Each object has its own historical significance, but can also be appreciated in its own right.

There have been many exhibitions and books about the Vikings, but this exhibition is something more than those. It depicts the history of the foreign exploits of the Vikings, but also shows the Vikings and their successors in their homeland; that part of Europe which lay in the far north, balanced between east and west, and which had its own identity, imagination and traditional culture. The history of Scandinavia is the history of influences from all parts of the known world—from Arabia to Greenland, from the Shannon to the Volga—and its reactions to them. Scandinavia possessed valuable economic resources, virtually all the necessities of life: cattle, grain, fish, wool, iron, timber, furs and so on, many of which were exported. This strong economic base enabled the countries of the North to absorb impulses from other lands and cultures which renewed and developed their own culture.

The exhibition illustrates the formation of large nation states in Scandinavia through the combining and restructuring of chieftainships and small kingdoms. It tells of technical, economic and social developments, of the introduction of Christianity, of the establishment of a literate culture, and of a world-renowned Scandinavian poetry and literature—the eddaic poetry, scaldic poetry, sagas, and histories. It also tells of pre-Christian religion and of the lively and imaginative decorative art which adorned so many utilitarian objects of everyday life. This art had its origins in a common north-European animal ornament which had its roots in the late Roman Iron Age, but it developed its own character in Scandinavia. It attracted many European influences and in the course of the 12th century was absorbed into the Scandinavian versions of Romanesque styles, best seen in wood carving in Norway and stone sculpture in Sweden and Denmark.

The exhibition does not underplay the drama of the Vikings' military and political exploits in foreign lands, nor their significance. It deals with the take-over of Normandy, the conquest of England, the settlement of completely new lands in the north Atlantic, the first Europeans in America, the trade routes through Russia and regular contacts with Byzantium. This is a history of close connections with alien political systems and religions, also of 12th-century conquests and crusades whereby Christianity was violently imposed upon the Slav and Baltic countries.

Natural environment

It is impossible to understand Scandinavia without realizing its enormous size and colossal natural resources. The distance between the North Cape and the Danevirke—between northernmost Norway and Denmark's southern boundary—is roughly the same as the distance from the Danish border to Africa. Denmark is a green and rolling land with many islands, large and small. Modern Norway and Sweden are separated by high mountains. Norway to the west is deeply cut by fjords, and along most of its coast a fringe of islands and skerries provide sheltered waters for shipping; green valleys relieve the mountain ridges. To the east, in what is now Sweden, there is almost impenetrable forest interspersed with great tracts of rich agricultural land. Finland is also covered by enormous forests, dotted with innumerable lakes but also with good agricultural land. Iceland, far to the west in the Atlantic Ocean, has active volcanoes, warm springs and geysers, and barren mountains, but, as in the Faroes, there are rich pastures. For the most part Greenland is covered by glaciers, but animal husbandry is possible on the shores of the fjords of the south-west coast.

The climate varies dramatically. Norway, Sweden and Finland are cut by the Arctic Circle. The Gulf Stream modifies the climate of the Norwegian coast and the Atlantic islands, but in winter large parts of Finland and Sweden, the Norwegian valleys and the whole of northern Scan-

Fig. 1. The Gokstad ship, Norway. The ship is 23.3m long and 5.25m wide.
Displayed in the Viking Ship Museum, Bygdøy, Oslo.

Fig. 2. The town of Ribe on the west coast of Denmark, from the sea.

dinavia are covered in snow. So in winter, overland travel by
sledge, ski and skates was easy and rapid, but ships were the
most important means of summer transport throughout the
North as a whole, and the sea bound the countries together.
Outstanding ships and skilful sailors enabled Nordic merchants, warriors and farmers to travel the seas, both east and
west, in search of rich markets, great wealth and new land.
It is for good reason that the ship has become the symbol of
the Viking age.

The Sources

Throughout the Viking age some of the foreign exploits of
the Northmen were recorded in chronicles and other works
compiled in France, Germany, England, Ireland, Russia,
Byzantium and the Islamic Caliphate. But they tell us very
little about conditions in Scandinavia itself. Frankish
sources mention military confrontations between Charlemagne's Franks and the Danes along the Danish borders.
Economic and social structures in north Norway and a
journey in the Baltic Sea were briefly described to King
Alfred the Great of Wessex c. 890. There are also stories of
Christian missionaries in Sweden and Denmark, and a general description of the North in about 1070 written by the
German cleric Adam of Bremen. There are scattered references to dynasties, kings, and dramatic events, but no com-

prehensive history. Scandinavia's own Viking age must
primarily be understood from other sources: archaeological
discoveries of houses, farms, towns, fortresses, household
equipment, provisions, tools, imported goods, burials and so
on; and from place-names and oral traditions which were
first written down in the 12th and 13th centuries.

With the arrival of Christianity in the 10th and 11th
centuries, and through the influence of the Church by
means of literacy and closer international contacts, Scandinavia at last began to reveal itself. It does so particularly in
written sources, culminating c. 1200 in the Latin work *Gesta
Danorum* (The Deeds of the Danes) by Saxo Grammaticus,
and, slightly later, in the Icelander Snorri Sturluson's works
on Nordic poetry, mythology and Norwegian kings: the
Edda and *Heimskringla*. The development of the church also
stimulated the production of charters, laws, lives of saints
and other documents.

The Scandinavians had their own script, the runic
alphabet, with its roots in the centuries immediately after
the birth of Christ. Runes are best known from stones with
commemorative inscriptions, dating from the 10th to 12th
centuries. From these we gain glimpses of individuals and
their exploits, of the structure of society and the way of life.
Finds from excavations in Bergen, Sigtuna and other towns
show that from about 1000 runes were also commonly used

Fig. 3. *The 12th-cent. church at Kinn, Nordfjord, in the diocese of Bergen, Norway.*

in daily life—carved on sticks—for short messages, trade agreements, curses, and poems. Nevertheless, written information about most of Scandinavia is very scarce from before 1200, and historical developments in the separate countries were by no means similar. Without material remains our knowledge of the North would be one-sided and very limited. The steadily increasing number of excavated finds and, from the later part of the period, churches and other buildings together with many decorated objects preserved in churches, illuminate our knowledge immeasurably.

800–1200

The Vikings shook Europe, but the reasons for their spectacular expansion will probably never be satisfactorily explained. There must have been many reasons. Even before the Viking Age, Scandinavians were in contact with the outside world, particularly as merchants. They saw great opportunities for plunder and seized the chance to gain profit, at first from the monasteries scattered along the coasts of western Europe. Then came devastating plunder and ransom exacted from markets, towns and kingdoms. This led to the acquisition of power over whole regions; to settlement, and to the establishment of international trading stations. Part of the background of the individuals who took part in raids and emigrations may have been condi-

tions at home: threat of famine, political problems, exile, poverty, lack of land. We know but little of these. A large part of the world lay undefended, presenting opportunities for power and glory, gold, adventure, new lands. Unpopulated islands in the North Atlantic—Iceland, Faroes, Greenland—were also attractive to some, and historians about 1200, living at a time of massively increasing central power, thought that they knew the reason for the emigrations to Iceland three-hundred years earlier: reaction to Harald Fairhair's unification of Norway.

The Scandinavians not only took, they also gave. The Viking raids brought enormous wealth to the North along with new impulses which were to provide the background for radical changes in Nordic society in the following period. Their influences on Europe include their language, personal names, and place-names, all of which modified those of England, Ireland and Normandy. Normandy acquired a Scandinavian ruling dynasty and a political system from which base it became one of the greatest powers in 11th- and 12th-century Europe. The rulers of the Russian kingdom with its capital in Kiev—to become the centre of the early Russian state—were also of Nordic origin. England's unification into one kingdom in the mid-10th century was due to the southern English kings' systematic political struggle against the Scandinavian kingdoms which were estab-

Fig. 4. The Piraeus lion. On the shoulders of this marble lion from the Athenian port of the Piraeus a Scandinavian traveller inscribed long looping bands of runes, as on the Swedish rune-stones. The text is illegible, and both runes and bands are hardly visible today. The lion was brought to Venice as loot in 1687. Photograph from c. 1854.

Fig. 5. The stone from St Paul's churchyard, London, is decorated in Scandinavian style and has a runic inscription on one side. The paint is preserved: dark red, black-blue and white on a gesso base. This watercolour records these colours. Early 11th cent. Cf. cat. no. 416.

lished there a hundred years before. Many places where Scandinavians settled are still distinctive through their structures of ownership, land-use, or political systems; Normandy, for example, was an administrative unit of France up to the Revolution, and the Isle of Man still has its own parliament. In Ireland most of the large towns, such as Dublin, Wexford, Waterford and Limerick, were founded by the Vikings.

The last great Viking raid on western Europe was the Norwegian king Harald Hardråda's attempt to conquer England. He was defeated and killed at the battle of Stamford Bridge in 1066. After this, the Nordic kings were fully occupied in organizing their own kingdoms and also in waging wars in Scandinavia and around the Baltic Sea, wars which differed little from the Viking raids. The kingdoms of the North were finding the form and structure which would serve throughout the rest of the Middle Ages, with kings and churches, privileged great landowners, farmers, merchants, craftsmen, and towns and monasteries, but also with many landless peasants.

The dramatic reports of the sudden descent on western Europe in the years around 800 have long signified the beginning of the Viking Age, but for its true origins we must look back into the previous century. The year 1200 does not have the same mystical significance as 800, but it does mark the end of an era and a new beginning. By then much of the old Scandinavian culture had become history, and European ideals were gaining ground at an increasing

rate. Denmark, Norway and Sweden were rapidly becoming kingdoms of a European type. The Christian church, an international economy and many towns were increasing factors in society. By 1200 Iceland had been a republic for 300 years, and had laid the ground work for its own vernacular written history. The farming community in distant Greenland was also politically independent. The Faroes belonged to the Norwegian kingdom, as did the Northern and Western Isles off the Scottish coast. Finland was becoming linked to the west, but continued to have its own culture and language.

The romantic view of the Vikings, based on foreign written sources and native heroic literature, played an important role in Nordic and German national ideologies in the 19th century and later, and still colours the picture of Scandinavia's past. This exhibition tries to give a more balanced picture, showing that, between 800 and 1200, the Nordic countries developed in ways which were really not so different from those of other lands. At the beginning of this period the Scandinavians were pagans but this does not mean that they were barbarians; they were just as cultivated and just as brutal as their contemporaries elsewhere. The achievements of the period in literature, in art, technology and politics can today be easily appreciated both in themselves and as reminders of an important and dramatic period in the history of Scandinavia, a time when the people in the North were influential in changing Europe, and a time when the northern lands became Scandinavia.

Coin bearing the name and head of Sven Forkbeard, struck in Denmark c. 995 on the model of English silver coins which were used in massive quantities in payment of Danegeld to the Vikings. Similar coins were also struck by King Olaf Tryggvasson of Norway, by King Olof Skötkonung in Sweden and by the Scandinavian King Sigtryg Silkbeard in Dublin. Cat. no. 423.

Scandinavia and Europe

The Scandinavian kingdoms

Else Roesdahl

The homelands of the Vikings lay in the far north of Europe, in the vast and widely differing lands which today make up the kingdoms of Denmark, Norway and Sweden. It is a vast area, encompassing rough mountainous regions, fertile valleys, large forests, lakes and green plains. In summer there are long light nights and the north of Scandinavia experiences the midnight sun. The winters, however, are long and dark. In mid-winter the sun does not even rise in the north of Scandinavia, but the darkness is tempered by the whiteness of the snow (cf. maps pp. 430–2).

Ever since the Stone Age the whole of Denmark and large parts of present-day Norway and Sweden have been inhabited by people whose economy has chiefly been based on agriculture and livestock in various combinations. In Norway's coastal and fjord areas the farming settlements reached a latitude of about 70°, more or less where Tromsø is now situated. The Saami (Lapps) lived to the north of this; they also lived inland further to the south and in northern Sweden. They had their own culture and language, and also—in part at least—their own economic structure which was essentially based on hunting and fishing. In these areas the borders were indistinct and central authority was weak for many centuries after the rest of Norway and Sweden had become kingdoms. But there was always contact between the Saami and the Scandinavian farmers. In the south, where Denmark shared its borders with the Frisians and the Saxons, Scandinavia was clearly limited and defended by the great linear fortifications known collectively as the Danevirke (fig. 2); this same border was maintained until 1864. The Saxons and the Frisians in the course of the eighth century had been incorporated into the mighty Frankish realm and forced to adopt Christianity.

Denmark, Norway and Sweden gradually came into being and their boundaries began to be defined in the period from approximately 800 to 1200. Their formation took place in a time of cultural, economic and political ferment, and the development advanced separately and at different rates depending for example on the very different scale of the countries concerned and the natural conditions prevailing in them, as well as on their interface with other regions, conditioned by geography. Denmark is placed like a gateway between western Europe and the Baltic region, and is open both to the south and west—to the Slav areas of the southern Baltic, to Germany and to England. Norway turns to the west and south—to the Atlantic Ocean, the British Isles and the coastal areas of western Europe. Large parts of Sweden, however, are more closely related with the east—with the Baltic, Finland and Russia.

Viking raids, trade expeditions and migrations from Denmark, Norway and Sweden were directed chiefly towards these different areas. Innovations from western Europe, such as Christianity, Latin writing, towns, the creation of kingdoms and the use of coinage usually reached Denmark, which was closest, first. Then Norway. Sweden was situated further away and came last in line; but it, on the other hand, had closer connections with eastern Europe, Byzantium and the Caliphate. This involved contact with mighty realms and cultures, and access to even greater riches than those of western Europe. In the East there were many religions, and when Christianity was introduced into Russia in 988 it came in the Greek Orthodox version. Sweden did not become Christian until around 1100 (from western Europe), Norway in the early decades of the eleventh century, and Denmark earlier, about 965. In each case royal power within the kingdom was consolidated in close interaction with the new, decisive, element in society—the Christian, Roman Catholic Church. By the year 1200 Denmark, Norway and Sweden were all established as national states in accordance with western European patterns. The Finnish, Baltic and Slav tribes living on the other side of the Gulf of Bothnia and the Baltic almost all subscribed to heathen religions during the Viking Age; they were converted to Christianity during the twelfth and thirteenth centuries, in part as a result of Scandinavian crusades.

In the Viking Age the Scandinavians spoke more or less the same language, "the Danish tongue", which along with a sizeable collection of personal names was carried to Iceland, the Faroe Islands and Greenland, as well as to the Orkneys and Shetlands, when those regions were settled or conquered by Scandinavians in the course of the ninth and tenth centuries. The sea, ships of outstanding quality, capable seamen and traders and many natural resources which provided the raw material for trade, all contributed to bind this enormous area together. It provided the basis for what was in many respects a common culture shared by Scandinavia and the new territories in the North Atlantic, which throughout most of the Viking Age was clearly differentiated from that of the rest of Europe. This common culture is seen not only in language, but also in religion, writing, art, scaldic poetry, women's clothing, ornaments and more.

During the Viking Age and early Middle Ages, the differences between the Scandinavian lands and the rest of

Fig. 1. Satellite photograph of Denmark, Norway, Sweden and the Baltic region with Finland.

Fig. 2. The Danevirke, Denmark's southern boundary. The town of Schleswig can be seen in the background.

Europe, as well as many of the distinctions within Scandinavia between the different countries themselves, were gradually reduced as a result of the dramatic expansion of contacts with the rest of the world. The introduction of Christianity, and all that accompanied it, became the distinguishing and decisive feature of "Europeanization", but the Viking military expeditions and the rapid expansion of trade were also of great significance. Christianity, in all these countries, was not imposed from outside, and its practices, including its organization, was adapted as it developed in order to fit local customs and traditions and new needs and opportunities. This also applied to other forms of influence from Europe. Throughout the whole of the Viking Age, and also into the first centuries thereafter, Scandinavia and the Atlantic territories had the political, economic and cultural strength to choose and adapt what was new to suit their own conditions.

The cultural expressions of the time were based on a strong consciousness of their own distinctive qualities and a pride in them. This is clearly expressed in the preface to

Saxo's major Latin work from about 1200, *Gesta Danorum* (The Deeds of the Danes) (cat. no. 529–30). It begins: "Because other nations are in the habit of vaunting the fame of their achievements and joy in recollecting their ancestors, Absalon, Archbishop of Denmark, had always been fired with a passionate zeal to glorify our fatherland. He would not allow it to go without some noble document of this kind . . ." (translation: P. Fisher).

A little later, about 1220, the Icelander Snorri Sturluson wrote a text-book on scaldic poetry, *Edda* (cat. no. 521). Scaldic poetry was a particular Nordic form of poetry with very complicated rules and a stock of words which was based *inter alia* on a knowledge of the old Scandinavian gods. Snorri wrote in his mother-tongue, Saxo in Latin, but in both cases the impetus for their writing was their feeling that they were living though a time of great change. As the new ideas flowed in, so the great events of the past and the qualities of the home culture had to be maintained and cultivated, and demonstrated to the surrounding world. It is in large measure through the great literature which was

Fig. 3. The chieftain's centre, Borg, Lofoten, Norway. The excavation of the 81m-long house shows as a brown patch on the left. The Atlantic is in the background. Cf. cat. no. 154.

created in Denmark, Norway and Iceland in this time of ferment that our knowledge of the old Scandinavian culture (including that of the pre-Christian culture) has been preserved.

The kingdoms

Very little is known about the political geography of Scandinavia at the beginning of the Viking Age, but it is clear that as elsewhere in Europe there were many kingdoms in fluctuating power-constellations and without fixed borders. Unification and stabilization took place by means of many internal conflicts between kings, chieftains and regions, and in each place the Church came to play a central role.

Denmark (that is present-day Denmark together with German South Schleswig and the present Swedish provinces of Skåne and Halland) was possibly unified under a single king even before 800. There is virtually no evidence as to how unification took place, but by the middle of the tenth century, in the reign of Harald Bluetooth, Denmark had emerged clearly as a single realm with a single king. The

country had taken the name of its people, the Danes, but the meaning of the second component (-mark) is contested.

Scaldic poetry and sagas relate that important parts of Norway were united under one king, Harald Hårfager (Finehair), at the end of the ninth century. The decisive event in this process was his victory in the sea-battle of Hafsfjord, near present-day Stavanger. The stabilization and expansion of the Norwegian kingdom was extremely lengthy and dramatic. In this process King Olaf Haraldsson (later St. Olaf, killed in 1030) occupied a key position. The name Norway means "north-way", and owes its origins to the sailing-route along the length of the country's west coast.

The unification of Sweden came late, in the course of the eleventh and twelfth centuries. It happened as a result of lengthy power-struggles between leading families in two of the largest 'regions', Östergötland and Västergötland. But the basis of royal power came to be the rich Svealand in the Mälar region; it was from here that Sweden took its name.

In none of these cases did the course of creation of a kingdom run smoothly. There were periods when one king-

Fig. 4. Burial mounds, Borre, Norway. Scaldic poetry and sagas associate Borre with Viking Age Norwegian kings. Cf. cat. no. 169.

dom or another was again split up into several parts, and there were many wars between kings and many civil wars; in the period 1134–67 four Danish kings, eight Norwegian kings and three Swedish kings were killed. At times a kingdom or a part of it had to submit to a king or an overlord from another Scandinavian country or, in the case of Denmark, from Germany. But throughout the Middle Ages Denmark tended to be the dominant power in Scandinavia. It was the smallest country, the most densely populated, and it was where central power was at its strongest.

Around the year 1200, however, the borders began to be fixed. National identity was by then so rooted in all three countries, and internal conditions so stable, that each had acquired an archbishopric—respectively in Lund (1103), Trondheim (1152/53) and Uppsala (1164). Each country by then also had a royal saint—a canonised king: St. Knut in Denmark, St. Olaf in Norway and St. Erik in Sweden (fig. 8). The Orkney Islands, which were formally an earldom under Norwegian rule, had a canonised earl, St. Magnus, while the republic of Iceland had two bishop-saints, St. Thórlak and St. Jón (cf. cat. no. 483, 534–7). Denmark, Norway, Iceland and Orkney also had written national histories (cat. no. 520, 525, 529–30).

The Viking raids in Europe in the ninth century and the beginning of the tenth century were not national ventures. As a rule they were carried out by independent and loosely-organized groups, often led by members of the royal family or by other chieftains who had lost their support in their home territory. Nor were the independent Viking kingdoms

which were established after the conquests in England and Ireland stable. Gradually they fell under the rule of English or Irish kings. Alone among the Viking territories in western Europe, Normandy developed strongly. In 1066 Duke William conquered the whole of England and proved able to maintain his rule there.

When a king conquered a neighbouring country or a part of it his new subjects had to pay taxes and to undertake military service—as long as his reign lasted. But, as the Scandinavian kingdoms progressed towards unity and greater internal organization, the opportunities for national expansion and the consolidation of conquests grew. For short periods, 1018–35 and 1040–42, after the Danish conquest of England, the two countries had a joint king, and as a consequence of the Viking Age settlements and conquests the Faroe Islands, the Orkney and Shetland Islands, the Hebrides and the Isle of Man came under the Norwegian crown. But Greenland and Iceland remained republics until those countries, in 1261 and 1262–64 respectively, recognized Norwegian sovereignty and accepted allegiance to the Norwegian crown.

After the Viking Age, expansionist aims were chiefly directed towards the Baltic region. The expeditions to a great extent followed the pattern of earlier ones, but often bore the title of crusades and were led by King and Church. In the second half of the twelfth century large parts of the southern Baltic coast came under Danish rule for a while, as did Estonia (in 1219). Sweden made no territorial conquests at that time, but Swedish interests in Finland grew and

Fig. 5. Harald Bluetooth's great rune-stone at Jelling, Denmark, c. 965. The inscription on one face, which says, among other things, that he had won Denmark for himself, continues beneath the Great Beast with 'and

Norway'. The third face of the stone is illustrated on p.153. Cf. cat. no. 193. The stone on the right was raised by King Gorm in memory of his queen, Thyre.

became the basis for crusades and later conquests which were to have lasting significance. Norway consolidated its formal sovereignty over the Atlantic and Scottish islands. King Magnus "Barefoot" himself went on several expeditions in these regions, seeking silver, glory and adventure and consolidating his power over them. In 1103 he was killed in Ireland at the age of about 30; according to the saga he said: "Kings are for glory, not for long life".

Kings and the organization of their realms

Throughout the Viking Age and the early Middle Ages royal power and the organization of kingdoms underwent rapid development, but it would be wrong to conceive of the Viking kings purely as leaders of the army. Their chief responsibility was to maintain order in the country. Without order society could not function. This was the reason why royal power was accepted.

Fig. 6. The Viking fortress of Trelleborg, Denmark. C. 980. Cf. cat. no. 113.

The king was the military leader of the country when there was a threat of attack from outside, and the people had a common duty to defend the country; a levy, or *leidang*, was raised in time of trouble and an organized military force with ships, crews, equipment and provisions, was thus provided to defend the country. The levy was based on a systematic sub-division of the kingdom, and on land-ownership. Gradually the duty of providing ships and manpower was replaced by taxes, and the military forces were transformed into a professional warrior-class with tax-exemption. A king normally fought at the forefront of the army, surrounded by his own chosen warriors.

The construction and growth of large military fortifications, such as Denmark's border-rampart, the Danevirke (fig. 2), Torsburgen on Gotland and the ramparts around Hedeby, Ribe, Birka and many other towns must also have been based on a universal obligation of defence, often controlled by the king. The fortifications of the Viking Age were collective defence-works, with the specific exception of the four characteristic geometric ring-fortresses in Denmark, which were constructed by the king around the year 980 (fig. 6) and had a very short life.

The king was also seen as head of state in dealings with other powers, and it was the king that the Christian missionaries first approached in order to conduct their activities in a country. The king had his own men—agents—placed throughout the kingdom to carry out his commands, to look after his interests and to ensure the continuity of his revenue, including that from large and far-flung estates. This system, together with an administration closely associated with the king, was developed in parallel with the growth of state power. As early as the Viking Age there were royal representatives in towns and at markets, where peace had to be maintained and duties were levied in return. But

Fig. 7. *Full-scale reconstruction of a building at the Viking fortress of Fyrkat, Denmark. C. 980. Cf. cat no. 111, 117.*

Denmark, Norway and Sweden continued to be split up into 'lands', each with its own *ting* (assembly), where all important decisions were agreed.

The real economic basis of royal power was landed property, but the revenue was supplemented by taxes from towns and markets and probably tolls. There are also cases where kings took part in actual trading enterprises, and towns such as Lund, Sigtuna, Trondheim and many others were founded by kings. Throughout the Viking Age the products of plunder and taxes levied abroad constituted an important source of income, and a number of kings acquired their thrones by means of wealth gathered from expeditions to the east or west. This was true, for example, of the Norwegian kings Olaf Tryggvason (c. 995–1000) and Harald the Hardruler (1047–66). Their silver had come respectively from England and from the East. With the close of the Viking Age and the drastically reduced opportunities for acquiring income in this way the kings' expenses had to be covered to an increasing degree by domestic taxes, levies and fines, as in the rest of Europe.

A king had to be of royal descent. This was the foundation of legitimacy, but there were no strict rules of succession. He had to be elected. Normally the choice would fall on one of the dead king's sons, never on a woman, but there could be several kings at one time. The power-base was support from the chieftains and the 'lands'. Not until after the middle of the twelfth century was there any attempt to establish a fixed line of succession, an idea strongly supported by the Church. In 1163/64 the child-king Magnus Erlingsson was crowned as Norway's king by Archbishop

Øistein. This took place in Bergen, and a law of succession to the throne was passed, setting out for the first time the principle of sole rule. The coronation was the first of its kind in Scandinavia and emphasized the concept that the king was enthroned by God. In 1170 Valdemar the Great of Denmark sealed his extensive new royal power with a large-scale assembly in his new church in Ringsted. There his father, Knut Lavard, was enshrined as a saint, and his 7-year-old son Knut was crowned by Archbishop Eskil. The first Swedish coronation probably took place in 1210.

The participation of the Church in the coronation of kings underlines the fact that it had by then become as

Fig. 8. *St Erik's funerary crown from his shrine in Uppsala cathedral, Sweden. ?1160. Photo: 1946. Cf. cat. no. 535.*

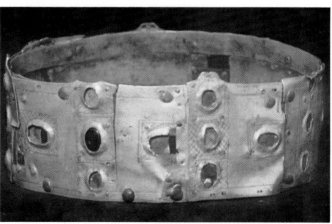

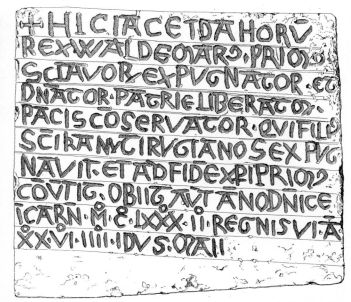

Fig. 10. Lead plaque from King Valdemar the Great's grave at Ringsted, Denmark. The Latin inscription reads 'Here lies the king of the Danes, Valdemar, the first conqueror and ruler of the Slavs, liberator of the fatherland, preserver of the peace. He, son of Knut the Holy [duke Knut Lavard], subdued the dwellers on Rügen and was the first to convert them to the Christian religion. He died in the year of Our Lord 1182, in the 26th year of his reign, on 12 May'. The other face of the plaque carries a slightly longer inscription, probably early 13th cent.

Fig. 9. Marble head of the Norwegian king Eystein Haraldson. Probably from Munkeliv Monastery, Bergen. First half of the 12th cent. Cat. no. 533.

powerful a force in Scandinavian society as it was elsewhere (cf. cat. no. 514–6). With its bishoprics and parishes it had its own territorial divisions; with tithes and Peter's pence (a tax paid direct to the Pope) it had its own tax system; in certain matters it had its own legal authority. In Norway this gave rise to bitter conflict between the Church and King Sverre (1177–1202). The Archbishop was driven into exile, the King was excommunicated, and only on his death-bed did he advise his son to make peace with the Church.

The real power of a monarch resided in his ability to collect men around him, provide for his own safety, lead, achieve results and reward his people well. A good reputation, great glory and abundant silver were preconditions for gaining the support of his people. Kings and chieftains were surrounded by splendour and symbols of prestige; they held large feasts, gave fine gifts, scalds told of their glory, large buildings and splendid objects of art were created to promote their fame (cat. no. 119–74, 191–3, 413–8, 525–38).

This is the background, for example, to the 81 metre-long chieftain's house excavated in Borg on Lofoten in Northern Norway (fig. 3), and the royal hall, 500 square metres in area, at Lejre in Denmark, both of which date from the Viking Age. It is also part of the background to the Danish geometrical fortresses and their large halls (figs 6–7), and of such dynastic monumental constructions as the burial mounds at Borre in Southern Norway (fig. 4). The most distinguished monument-complex of the Viking Age, with large mounds, a church and a runic stone with pictorial decoration is to be found at Jelling in Central Jutland, and was constructed at the period of the Conversion of Denmark (fig. 5 and pp. 153–4, figs 2–3).

After the advent of Christianity many prestigious elements became linked to the Church—church buildings, the establishment of monasteries and donations or furnishings for them—(cf. pp. 152–61 and cat. no. 440–84, 508–13). From the twelfth century onwards the kings and the leading noblemen of the country began to build fortifications for their residences: castles on the western European pattern.

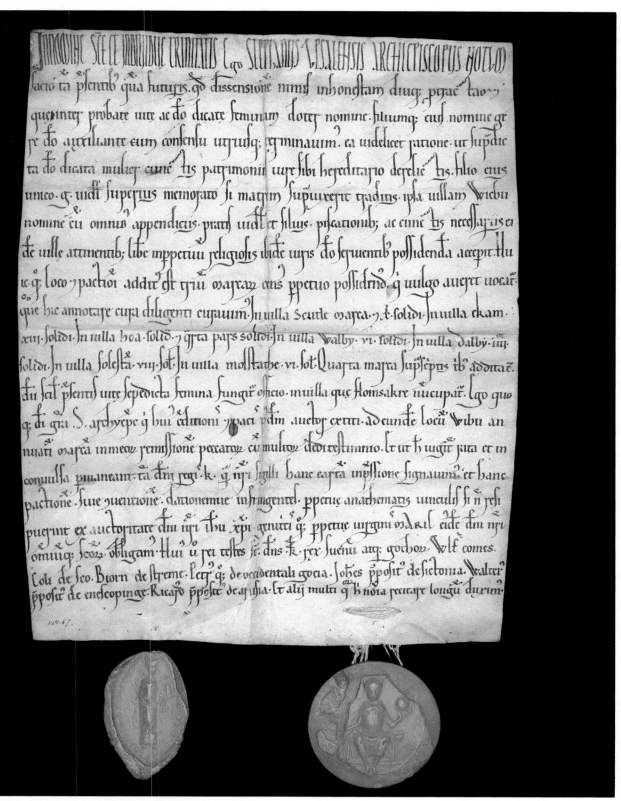

Fig. 11. Sweden's earliest surviving charter, with seals of the archbishop and the king. C. 1165. Cat. no. 515.

Ships and travel

Ole Crumlin-Pedersen
Mogens Schou Jørgensen
Torsten Edgren

Seafaring and ships

The ship brought the Vikings to the forefront of European history in the ninth century.

West European chronicles record the arrival of the Scandinavians, in fleets of speedy warships, in England, France, Spain and the western Mediterranean. The Norwegian Ottar (Ohthere) visited the court of King Alfred *c.* 890 and described his journeys with trading goods collected as far north as the White Sea. Other sources tell of voyages of discovery in the Atlantic, the settlement of Iceland and Greenland, and expeditions to Vinland. In the East, the Nordic Vikings and merchants travelled along the Russian rivers to the Caspian Sea, and by way of the Black Sea, to Byzantium where the emperors surrounded themselves with a bodyguard of Scandinavian warriors.

Behind these events lies the fact that without the Viking sailing-ship there could have been no Nordic expansion in this period. The ship was the indispensable means of transport whereby the Vikings advanced, not only abroad but also in Scandinavia itself with its long coastline, many sounds, fjords and rivers.

Scandinavian shipbuilding of the period 800–1200 is therefore worthy of detailed study. It not only tells of the maritime technology of the Scandinavians, but it also illuminates many other aspects of society, for the ship had a central place in the imagination of the Vikings. It was a tool in the struggle to achieve wealth and honour, but it was also admired like a toy (cf. cat. no. 13, 73, 315).

It is, therefore, very fortunate that, particularly in south Scandinavia and the west Baltic area, many ships of this period have been preserved in graves or as wrecks. Most of them belong to the Scandinavian ship-building-tradition, displaying such characteristic features as the double-ended shape built of overlapping planks (cf. cat. no. 2, 4, 6); but one Frisian, and a number of Slav ships have also been found. Further east, along the south coast of the Baltic, other Slav ships of this period have been excavated, and a river boat with its sewn hull is known from Finland (cat. no. 7). There are, however, remarkably few discoveries from the North Sea area—there is little evidence, therefore, of Frisian, Frankish and Anglo-Saxon ships to compare with those from Scandinavia and their Slav contemporaries.

The Vikings' warships were propelled by oars and sail (cf. cat. no. 5), which could have been used independently or together. Rowing had been known to the Scandinavians for many centuries before the sail was introduced just before the beginning of the Viking Age (although sails had long been in use in western Europe). There are few finds to illustrate the development from oars to sail, but it can be broadly followed on the representations of ships on Gotland picture-stones (cf. cat. no. 1, 175). It seems clear that until the seventh century, ship-building developed in accordance with the hull-shape designed for propulsion by oars. The Nydam ship in Schleswig, Germany, and the Sutton Hoo ship in East Anglia, England, are examples of this pre-Viking tradition, which can also be traced in various finds from Norway, Sweden and Denmark.

Sails were first introduced when the rowing boat had reached its perfect form in vessels up to 30m long. Boat-builders then undoubtedly found that they had problems. The two means of propulsion made different demands on the shape of the hull: rowing boats were narrow with low sides whereas sailing ships needed greater beam in order to achieve stability; they, therefore, had to have a deep or long keel to prevent drift. Furthermore, the Nordic rowing boats were also designed so that the crew could pull them up on land, even in rough weather. So they had to be light. In contrast, the west-European tradition of sailing ships was based on comparatively heavy vessels.

Nevertheless, the Scandinavian boat-builders, probably at the end of the eighth century, managed to find a compromise between these different requirements, and produced a new type of vessel—the Viking ship. This light and fast ship could sail for long distances over the open sea in order to arrive suddenly on a foreign shore using oars or sail; it could beach on the open shore and leave equally rapidly. With this type of vessel, Norsemen had a means of transport akin to the vessels on which the Greek argonauts roamed throughout the Mediterranean and the Black Sea some 1200–1500 years earlier.

Only a few ships of the ninth century have been found, but among them the great ship from Oseberg, southern Norway, is outstanding, with its magnificent decoration of stem and stern. A more utilitarian ship has been found not far away at Kålstad, near the trading centre of Kaupang; this vessel demonstrates that even at the beginning of the Viking age some form of specialization was developing between merchantmen and long-distance sailing in warships. The tenth century has few ship-finds, those which are known

Fig. 1. 'Saga Siglar' and 'Roar Ege' under full sail in Roskilde fjord. Roskilde cathedral in the background. The two ships are full-scale reconstructions of the Viking Age ships nos. 1 and 3 from Skuldelev, Denmark. Cf. cat. no. 2.

coming mainly from chieftains' burials. Such, for example, is the Gokstad ship, also from southern Norway—it is 23.3 m long and 5.25 m wide, with seats for 32 oarsmen (p. 25, fig. 1).

The discovery of the Gokstad and Oseberg ships in 1880 and 1904 (fig. 2) respectively, and their subsequent display at Bygdøy near Oslo, stimulated in no mean fashion the study of shipbuilding traditions; and they were to influence the opinions of many generations of archaeologists concerning the character of Viking ships. The Gokstad ship possibly represents the type of chieftains' ship which was part of the fleets which set sail from Norway to the British Isles in the first phase of the Viking raids. The excavation of the Ladby ship, Fyn, in 1935, on the other hand, showed that ships of a completely different type were built in Denmark. They were narrower and of shallower draught, suitable for the shallow waters of Denmark and for sailing along the south coast of the Baltic.

There is much more evidence for ship-building in the eleventh century, thanks to the many ships found as wrecks or as part of blockades. Of these the most important are the Äskekärr ship (cat. no. 4), from the Göta river in west Sweden, and the five ships from the blockade at Skuldelev, now displayed at the Viking Ship Museum, Roskilde in Denmark. The Äskekärr ship is some 16 m long and is a merchantman, but the Skuldelev ships are of five different types and enable us to gain a good impression of shipbuilding in the the eleventh century.

Wreck 1: 16.5 m long, wide-bodied, sea-going merchantman built of pine and probably from west Norway

Wreck 2: *ca.* 30 m long, sea-going warship; dendrochronological analysis of the oak timbers suggests that it was built in Dublin

Wreck 3: 14 m long, narrow, all-purpose ship of oak, probably built locally in Roskilde Fjord (cat. no. 2)

Wreck 5: 18 m long, narrow warship for 26 oarsmen, of

Fig. 2. The Oseberg burial mound on the Oslo fjord, Norway, during excavation in 1904. The mound covered a ship in which a wealthy woman, perhaps a queen, was interred in the first half of the 9th cent. together with rich grave-goods. Cf. cat. no. 5, 10, 155–66.

oak, pine and ash, probably a local ship manned by the local levy

Wreck 6: 12 m long, built of pine, probably a fishing boat from the Baltic.

Important ship finds have also been made in the harbour of Hedeby. Three vessels have been found, each of which illustrates different aspects of Viking Age seafaring. These comprise a very long and narrow warship, a large and bulky merchantman (both of Nordic type), and a small vessel combining Scandinavian and Slav features. These ships were salvaged in fragments and are displayed at Hedeby.

The same mixture has been found among timber re-used from broken-up ships at the shipyard on the Fribrødre river, Falster, where shipbuilding in the Slav manner seems to have flourished about 1100 (cat. no. 6).

These and other finds enable us to trace the development of cargo vessels up to the fourteenth century, during which time there was increasing specialization between merchantmen designed for long-distance travel and smaller freighters for local trade. Large ships, which would carry as much as forty tons, are found as early as the eleventh century, this rose to sixty tons in the twelfth century, whilst a ship dated c. 1250, of which parts were found in the harbour at Bergen, Norway, must have carried at least a hundred-and-fifty tons.

Fewer Scandinavian warships are found after the eleventh century; for these we have to rely on written sources and wall paintings, which tell of the development of increasingly larger vessels up to and in the thirteenth century.

By building replicas of the Oseberg, Gokstad, Ladby and Skuldelev 1, 3 and 5 ships in recent years it has been possible to test their true characteristics. The greater part of our knowledge of the construction of eleventh-century ships derives from these attempts to re-create their original

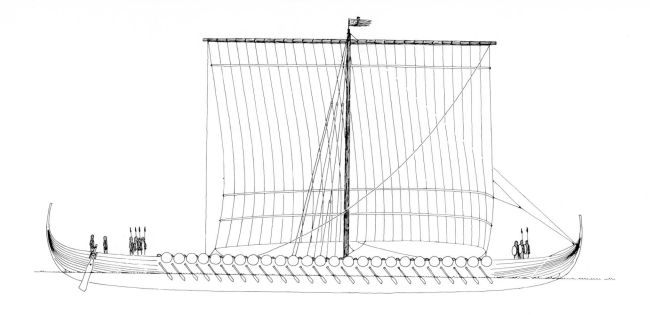

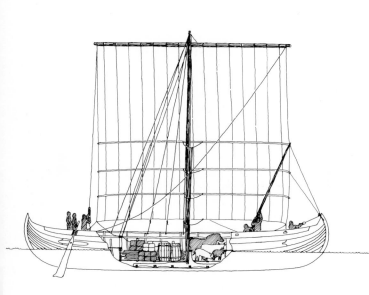

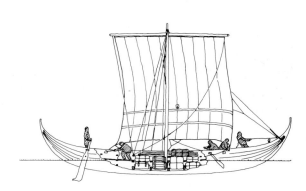

Fig. 3. Four 11th-cent. ships found at Skuldelev, Denmark: two warships (above and below), two merchantmen (centre). Reconstructions drawn at the same scale.

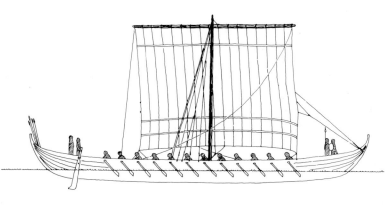

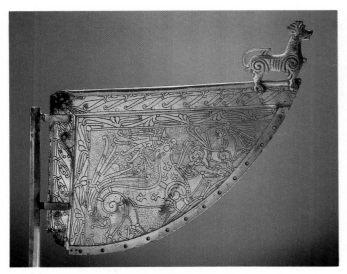

Fig. 4. Weather-vane from Heggen, Norway, which embellished the prow of a Viking ship. C. *1000–1050. Cat. no. 417.*

methods of construction, showing that lightness and strength were dependent on the choice of high quality split timber. Although the merchantmen were built more sturdily, wider and higher, they did not lose contact with traditions which have been kept alive up to the present day in the boat-building yards of west and north Norway.

About 1200 a 'new' type of ship appeared, in competition with the Scandinavian ship. This was the *cog*, first recorded in written sources from the ports of the Baltic and the North Sea, which in the course of the fourteenth century dominated the sailing routes as part of the means of transport used by the Hanseatic merchants. The cog has previously been assumed to have been a new development, a particularly capacious freight ship which replaced the Scandinavian vessels because they could not fulfil the demands of later medieval trade.

Ship discoveries show, however, that this is not so. The medieval cog developed from an earlier type of ship used on the Rhine and around the Frisian coast. It borrowed constructional elements from the Scandinavian building tradition and developed into a true sea-going vessel. The early form of river vessel is known from a boat which is dated about 1200, found stranded at Kollerup on the Jutland coast. An example of a complete specimen of the fully-developed Hanseatic cog (c. 1380) was found at Bremen. Both these ships would carry less freight than the largest Nordic ships of the period.

Throughout the whole period 800–1200 seafaring in the North was based in most cases on passage in sight of land. Ships usually anchored overnight in natural harbours. A journey of this nature was described by Ottar to Alfred the

Great; it took five days from Kaupang in Oslo Fjord to Hedeby on the Schlei. This is quite different from the Atlantic journeys undertaken by the Vikings to reach the Faroes, Iceland and Greenland. The sagas tell us that the voyagers followed the Norwegian coast until they reached a point near Bergen whence they set sail westwards. By using their knowlege of the currents, and the habits of sea mammals and sea birds, they could find their way to the Shetlands, the Faroes, Iceland and Greenland.

What the sagas do not tell us is how sailors could sail due west without the help of compasses (which only came into use in northern Europe after 1200). It can only be assumed that the Vikings had a good enough knowledge of the stars (and the sun during the summer months) for them to hold a course. If the sky was partly overcast, the bearing of the sun might have been found through a 'lodestone', but if it were foggy this would have been of no help, and if such weather lasted for a long time the ships could have been driven off course.

A ship which was fortunate enough to make landfall in one of the Atlantic settlements would have been the cause of great celebration, both on land and onboard, for the ship brought such provisions as iron and timber, as well as news from Scandinavia and the rest of Europe. When it returned homewards its hold was filled with goods from the far North, ropes made of walrus hide, costly furs, and ivory from walrus and narwhal. Thus, by means of ships the farthest outposts of the North were kept in touch with the centres of European culture.

O C P

Land transport

Whereas the sea gave boundless opportunities for travel, progress by land was more limited. Viking Age roads did not consist of clearly defined lines through the countryside, rather they were corridors some kilometres in width defined by features in the landscape. They ran along natural routes: ridges and watersheds, rivers and lake systems. They were routes of varying importance: local, regional or international. Nodal points in a network of communication grew up where land and water routes crossed at depots, market-places and trading centres.

Most routes had alternative parallel courses, along rivers or through lakes, and the same route may have had several courses depending on the purpose of the journey, the time of year or the means of transport. The needs of riders, carts, military transports and cattle drovers were different; winter was used for transport and travel by sledge.

In difficult terrain the normal means of transport was by foot or on horseback; easily passable routes were used by carts or sledges which were especially adapted to local condi-

Fig. 5. Part of the Oseberg tapestry, Norway. Reconstruction. The scene probably shows a ceremony but also illustrates everyday transport—on foot, on horseback, and by waggon. C. 800–850.

tions. Tracks were followed, and if a route proved impassable, a new path would be taken alongside it. The road may then have become a broad belt of deep and parallel ruts. True road-building only took place where the terrain demanded it, as through marshy areas or across fords or over bridges which spanned rivers or narrow fjords.

The building of roads in the Viking Age did not differ greatly in technique from that of earlier periods. The simplest roads were made of branches and brushwood, but many sorts of timber-built roads are found, from closely-set tree trunks to carefully carpentered structures. Stone-paved roads, known in the North as early as the late Bronze Age, occur in numerous forms, often as stone pavings edged by stones of up to a metre in size. Kerbstones defined the course of the road and at times in effect served as stepping stones for those travelling on foot.

The different types of roads were seldom expressions of architectural thought. The suitability of the subsoil and the

Fig. 6. The 50m-long ford across the Nyköping river at Släbro, Södermanland, Sweden, is usually submerged, but a day of very low water in 1984 showed its Viking Age appearance. Hollow ways led through cemeteries on each side of the crossing. The route was marked by two rune stones.

Fig. 7. Excavation of the bridge at Ravning Enge, Denmark. The bridge was more than 700m long and was built c. 980. In the fore-ground are the remains of a group of four vertical piles; the locations of others are shown by white markers. Cf. cat. no. 20.

most functional surfacing were aimed at; a single stretch could consist of a number of different types of paving. The carriageway itself may have been covered with gravel or sand to give a smoother surface, and much of the road was visible only in the driest periods.

Shortly before 1000 the first real free-standing bridges were built in Scandinavia. Earlier smaller bridges were incorporated into the construction of a road or causeway when it passed over a stream, but now longer bridges began to be built. Little is known concerning their true appear-ance, for remains of their superstructure seldom survive. But their foundations show that there were bridges of vari-ous types, from the simple to the very sophisticated. There were, however, few bridges. When they were built they were either the only way of making a crossing, or were intended to solve a specific problem.

A group of Danish bridges from the end of the 10th century seem to have been built with a similar purpose in mind. One such belongs to the most impressive engineer-ing-works of the time. Seven-hundred metres long, it crosses the wide valley of the river Vejle at Ravning Enge, 10 km south-west of Jelling. With a carriageway area of at least 3500 m² it is carried on more than a thousand supporting posts (cat. no. 20), the bridge was a great technical achieve-ment and represents an enormous outlay of both timber and manpower. It is unique as a piece of engineering, but it had, like certain smaller and simpler bridges, only a short life.

A construction of the size of the Ravning Enge bridge must have been the responsibility of a central power. It was built *c.* 979, in the reign of Harald Bluetooth, at the same time as the geometric ring-forts (p. 38, fig. 6). It was pre-

sumably part of the same national master plan; the quantity of work and the amount of material used seem unnecessarily lavish in relation to its economic and utilitarian poten-tial. But, apart from being a practical feature in an overall military strategy, this bridge was undoubtedly a prestigous structure—a symbol of power.

A central initiative also resulted in the construction of about a dozen wooden-paved bridleways which, between 1000–1200, were laid through the marshy areas of central Norway. Many kilometres of track were built which were the main roads—here organised for the first time.

Two rune-stones at the side of Tjuvstigen, an ancient track near Stockholm, are inscribed, 'Styrlög and Holm/ raised this stone/ in memory of their brothers/ close to the road...' and 'Ingegerd had raised/ another stone/ in memory of her sons/ visible memorials...' Memorials were erected where people travelled so that they could be seen by many. Burial mounds on high ground could be seen from afar, but standing stones and rune stones stood beside the roads themselves and also had a practical purpose as signposts at times when the weather was bad or the countryside was covered with snow.

Such memorials could assume a monumental character. Thus, rows of standing stones line the routes from Husby-Långhundra and Läby in Uppland, Sweden, and a rune stone is included in similar rows of standing stones at Lunda, Anundshögen and Årby in Sweden, and on Gimsøy in north Norway. A single uninscribed stone without inscription may have marked each crossing, and one or more opposed rune stones greeted those who came to such cross-roads as Ulunda, Lingsberg and Släbro in Sweden.

Fig. 8. One of 4 rune stones from Jarlabanke's 'bridge' in Täby, Uppland, Sweden. This stone is 2.2m high and was erected in the second half of the 11th cent. The inscription reads, 'Jarlabanke had these stones raised in memory of himself in his lifetime. And he made this bridge for his soul. And alone he owned the whole of Täby. God help his soul'.

Gullbron, Broby bridge and Jarlabanka's bridge in Uppland are magnificent monuments, each place has two large, decorated rune stones where the road reached a firm path of land. Jarlabanka's stones marked a bridge which formed part of a route which can be traced for over 40 km between Lunda and Lake Mälar. The road led to the site of the local 'thing' and was probably established during the eleventh-century reorganization of the settlements and administrative divisions of the area.

The runic inscriptions also tell of other notable examples of road-building in the transitional period between paganism and Christianity. A few rune stones in Denmark and Norway, and more than a hundred and twenty-five stones in Sweden record the 'building of a bridge'. Linguistically, the word 'bridge' could mean either a free-standing bridge

(a bridge in the modern sense of the word) or, more usually in this context, a ford or a causeway over marshy ground. The clearing of roads is also mentioned, and this would have included work to rebuild or repair existing roads, some of which may have dated back to the beginning of the 1st millennium AD.

Some inscriptions define the precise reason for building a bridge, as, for example, on the Morby stone (cat. no. 497), when the person who raised it did so, 'for the soul of her daughter Gillög'. Two causeways at Näs may be those mentioned on a nearby rock-face, 'Livsten had the bridges made for his soul's sake and for that of Ingerun his wife, and of his sons ...'. The Årby stone was raised by brothers in memory of their father, '... and they made the bridge to please God ...'.

These bridges were 'soul gifts', donations which would help the salvation of the donor or of the commemorated person. The growth, work and economy of the Church depended on a well-organized road network, upkeep and repair of which could be regarded as a suitable offering to God. The symbolic character of the work was understood by everyone, not just in the transition from paganism to Christianity, but in the Christian period itself. In the future life of both pagans and Christians, the dead set out on a long journey, a dangerous voyage, which could be alleviated

Fig. 9. The stone-paved road in the Risby Valley on Sjælland, Denmark. In the background is the timbered construction over the river. Late Viking Age.

Fig. 10. Sledge from the Oseberg grave, Norway. 9th cent.

in practical ways. It was, as we can see from the rune-stones, often the women who had the bridges built. One reason for this must be that women were the first to interest themselves in the new religion.

The ecclesiastically inspired road system, undoubtedly supported by secular power, was presumably the basis for the provision of roads mentioned in the earliest laws—a duty which was laid on people throughout the Middle Ages. A functioning road-network was needed, for various reasons, by all strata of society: it was the basis for some of life's most important activities.

M S J

Winter transport

Because of their geographical position, the countries of the North were part of a region where the need for winter transport and communications was always of great importance. This holds for the whole of northern Eurasia, from Norway in the west to the Bering Strait in the east, where the land was covered in snow for long periods of the year. Certainly, the written sources record some exceptionally hard winters in northern Europe as a whole, but generally coastal shipping, which was of such great importance to the populations of the Danish and Norwegian coasts and the south coast of the Baltic, could continue for much of the year. This is in contrast to the Bay of Finland and the Gulf of Bothnia, where ice and snow regularly prevented foreign contacts and trading ventures throughout the winter. Heavy snowfalls and low temperatures sometimes stopped land transport even in south Scandinavia, but—when they iced over—waterways, lakes and marshes could be used. In Eurasia, many means of winter transport and communication had been developed as early as the Stone Age in order to maintain settlement and subsistence.

Apart from the sledges found in the Norwegian ship-burials of Oseberg and Gokstad, most archaeological evidence for transport and communications comes from the marshlands and bogs of northern Finland, Sweden and Norway. Such evidence can be supplemented by illustrations and information of a general character in medieval written sources, and in later literature such as Olaus Magnus' *Carta Marina* (1539) and *Historia de gentibus septentrionalibus* (1555).

The earliest and simplest type of sledge in the late Iron Age and Middle Ages (although rooted deep in prehistory) was the 'ski-sledge', a low sledge pulled by hand along flat ground. The runners had upturned points which could push a way through snow drifts. These sledges were mainly used for hunting in the northern districts, where this was either the only means of subsistence or a welcome supplement to stored summer crops. It was sledges of this type that transported furs, a leading element in summer trade. Heavy and bulky goods would demand stronger and heavier sledges —particularly for use over waterlogged ground in the summer. Some of these, where their parts were lashed together, are reminiscent of ski-sledges in their construction, but others for example the Oseberg sledges were of jointed timbers, secured by rivets or nails. These were drawn by horses or oxen.

Sledges were not only used for carrying cargo, they were also personal transport, as were the three decorated sledges from Oseberg. Such sledges are also depicted on several eleventh-century picture-stones from Gotland, and we have written mention of journeys by sledge from the Swedish mainland to Gotland, and from Estonia to Sweden in 1293. Ice undoubtedly eased communication. Travellers over ice needed to appreciate its characteristics, a knowledge gained over generations. Despite this knowledge and experience there were accidents. Well known, for example, was the death of the Norwegian king Halfdan Svarte and his followers when they travelled across the ice of Rands fjord one spring in the ninth century.

Skates were also used to traverse the ice of the bays, rivers and lakes; they were made of the long-bones of elk, horse or cattle and tied to the foot (cat. no. 24). Many Viking Age and early medieval skates have been found (cat. no. 25). They were not skates in the present sense of the term, for the traveller propelled himself on them by using sticks with iron tips.

Skis were very important for winter travel and for hunting, and many have been found in Finland, central and north Sweden, Norway and north-west Russia (cat. no. 21–23). In Finland alone, more than a hundred skis have been recovered from bogs and a third of these have been dated before 1200 by radiocarbon methods—many of them to as early as the Stone Age. Skis are also depicted on rune-stones and rock engravings in Scandinavia and round the White Sea. They are also mentioned in early Scandinavian literature.

Early skis, mostly found accidentally, can be divided into a number of regional types of different ages although they may overlap in date. They are categorized according to their shape and the way they were attached to the foot. Most are

Fig. 11. Decorated ski from Laitila, Finland. Cat. no. 22.

made of pine (*Pinus silvestris*), an elastic and tough wood, the gliding potential of which was enhanced by its resin. The so-called Bothnian ski was distributed throughout the North. Skis of this type are characterized by their short lanceolate shape, (up to 165 cm in length), polished gliding face, raised foot plates, and horizontal attachment holes. As early as the stone age, Finnish skis had a groove on their under sides —as they do today. The groove gave added pace and eased steering. Late Iron-Age and early medieval skis could be as much as three metres in length. In south-west Finland they were extremely broad and often decorated with linear ornament and interlace.

A particular type was the unmatched ski, which consisted of one long ski for the left foot with groove and a much shorter ski for the right foot with a fur-covered surface. This central Nordic ski-type involved a technique different from that of the paired skis: the long left ski slid forward when propelled by the shorter ski, the skier balancing himself with a stick. Unmatched skis were mainly used for hunting elk. Their date is uncertain, but they must already have been in use in the prehistoric period. Ski sticks are also difficult to date. Skiing without sticks or with a single stick must have been common; the adoption of two ski sticks is a recent development.

The winter with its harsh climate—frost, snow and cold —meant that there were only few trading and external contacts, but it was by no means a time of isolation. Winter was the time for social contact, when people visited each other, exchanged news and made plans for the coming spring and summer.

T E

New lands in the North Atlantic

Thór Magnússon, Símun V. Arge, Jette Arneborg

The discovery and settlement of Iceland

It seems certain that Iceland was largely settled by Norwegians in the latter part of the ninth century. Accounts of this in medieval Icelandic literature tell of many chieftains who fled from Norway after Harald Fairhair brought the whole country under his rule in 872. The chieftains could not accept his role, and, as a new, unknown and fertile land had been discovered far to the west, many of them set out for it. Most of these emigrants came from western Norway; some are said to have been settled for various periods in Scotland, the Western Isles or Ireland on their way to Iceland, and to have captured slaves—both male and female—to bring with them. Thus, there is an academic controversy about the proportion of the Icelandic population which might be of Celtic origin; some think that the proportion may be high, others think it insignificant.

The priest Ari the Wise lived in the twelfth century and wrote *Islendingabók* (cat. no. 520), a short account of the first settlement of Iceland and its subsequent history. He says that, when the Scandinavian settlers arrived, they found Christian men there who fled when the Norse heathens came. These men left behind them books, bells and croziers, which showed that they must have been Irish monks. Most scholars believe Ari's account to be reasonable, although no remains attributable to the monks have been found. They may have been poor in worldly wealth, and had probably not lived in Iceland for long.

So far nothing has have been discovered in Iceland which contradicts Ari's account of the settlement, its date, the people who settled there, or where they came from.

At the beginning of the Viking Age, Iceland must have been the world's largest unpopulated country. It has an area of 103,000 square kilometres; and its situation, in the middle of the Atlantic eight-hundred kilometres from the nearest land, means that it could not have been reached before shipbuilding and navigation had become fairly well developed. It would seem that it was not until the Viking Age that ships capable of sailing on the open ocean were built; it was only then that the ships themselves, their sailing equipment and the art of navigation were sufficiently developed to reach the North Atlantic. Finds of ships in Norway, Denmark and elsewhere in the North indicate that before that time ships were ill-suited to long sea voyages.

Before discovering Iceland, the Norsemen had sailed westwards from Norway, particularly to the Shetlands, the Orkneys and the Hebrides, venturing further and further to the west as their skill, ability and daring allowed. Archaeological remains demonstrate their settlements in these regions, either as Viking raiders or as peaceful traders and farmers who sought in the west better living conditions than they had at home. From the Orkneys it is only a short sailing time to the Faroes, which seem to have been settled in the ninth century. The sailors who first discovered Iceland may have been driven off course on their way to the Faroes, thus arriving in this unknown land.

Iceland provided good living conditions for the first settlers. The fertility of the country is certainly variable, but in *Islendingabók* Ari emphasizes the wealth which it provided. He says that the countryside was covered with woodland between the mountains and the coast. Many places had excellent agricultural potential, fish were abundant and the birds were so tame that they could often be caught by hand. Even though Ari may have been indulging in some exaggeration, it is clear that the country was very fertile. The land had always been free from all forms of livestock, so the flora was neither threatened nor damaged. The woodland mentioned by Ari was probably birch—low-growing mountain birch of a type which can still be seen today in those few places in Iceland where the woods have not been destroyed. Erosion, largely caused by grazing sheep, which has so damaged Iceland in recent times had then not begun. The plant cover presumably varied from place to place, but we may assume that, for example, the woodland was ideal for the winter grazing of sheep as it was until well on into the present century. The fish were probably caught on shallow fishing banks, as they still were until the introduction of modern fishing methods and equipment; birds and sea mammals were fearless because they were not used to mankind.

The written sources indicate that settlement began about 874, and this is usually taken as a true date, although there must be a slight margin of error. The first settlers acquired

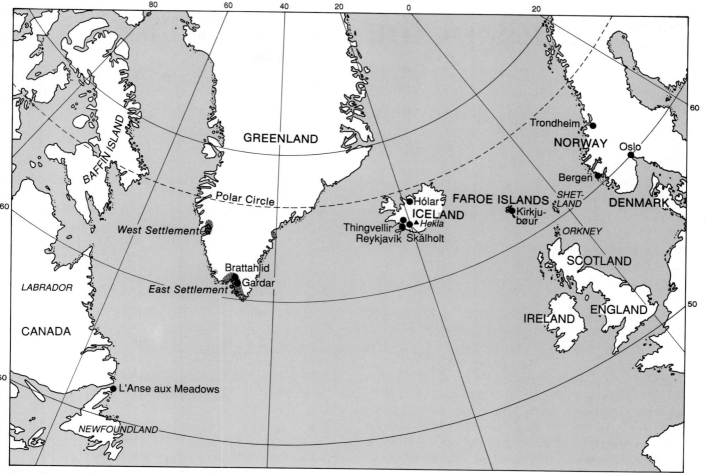

Fig. 1. The north Atlantic with the Faroe Islands, Iceland, Greenland and America.

extensive lands, considerably larger areas than those of a modern farm. Rivers, mountains or other natural boundaries often defined the land divisions. Written sources also record that the country was completely settled (or in other words the land had been claimed) before 930. By then all the earliest settlers had arrived, but later immigrants could often easily acquire land by gift or purchase.

Most of the settlers probably came from the east to that part of Iceland which was their first landfall after their journey from Europe. They would then mostly have sailed further west along the southern coast, for there are no good harbours until one reaches western Iceland. Reykjavík, which is said to be the site chosen by the first settler, Ingólfur Arnarson, is situated in the first ideal place, in the most southerly part of western Iceland with a good natural harbour well protected from the Atlantic rollers. Most of Iceland, even the farthest north, seems to have been

occupied early. Even though the soil in the north is less fertile than that in the south, it seems to have been a good agricultural region with other natural resources such as driftwood, fishing and opportunity for hunting for birds and seals to compensate for its poorer fertility.

The centre of Iceland has never been populated, although there were attempts to settle in a few places in the uplands to the south of the inland glaciers and, in one case, in the central highlands. All these settlements were, however, rapidly abandoned once it was realized that the grazing was poor and that the winters were long and appreciably colder than those of the lower-lying regions. Volcanic eruptions, particularly that of Mount Hekla in 1104, also destroyed some of the highland farms. The farmhouses and cultivated land were covered in volcanic ash. Erosion followed. Soil erosion began early in Iceland, becoming ever more pronounced in recent centuries.

Fig. 2. Thingvellir—the Thing *plain—east of Reykjavík. The Althing met here annually for 2 weeks at midsummer. It was founded c. 930 and became the assembly for, and the highest authority of, all Iceland. Cf. cat. no. 335.*

The first thing to be done in the new land was to establish a farmstead. The sites chosen seem to have been in the areas of greatest fertility; farms were built where there was a good outlook, near to water and cultivatable land. The first houses were modelled on the Norse longhouse or Viking hall, but temporary arrangements were made by digging small sunken-floored buildings which could be constructed quickly and with little effort. Such small structures have been discovered on early farmsteads such as Hvítárholt and Hjálmsstaðir in the south, Grélutóttir in the western fjords, and Granastaðir in the north. Usually about 4m long and 2.5–3m wide, they were dug into the ground and had low walls. Posts supported the roof, and most of them had a hearth, usually a type of oven. The entrance was either through the roof or in one corner. Later, permanent dwellings—the halls—began to be built.

Many of the halls have been excavated in various parts of Iceland, including, Klaufanes in the north, Skallakot and Hvítárholt in the south, and Grélutóttir in the west. They are of the same type as in western Norway, the Faroes and the Scottish islands. They were typically about 20 m long and 6 m across at the widest point in the middle, narrowing towards the gables. The long walls are consequently bowed when seen in plan. The floor extended along the middle of the house, and on each side of it were raised benches or surfaces on which people could sleep at night and sit during the day. There was an elongated hearth, for both cooking and heating, in the middle of the floor. The floor was bordered by two rows of posts against the benches, which supported low beams which held up the roof. The posts were originally earth-fast, but were soon replaced by posts supported on pad-stones to prevent rot. Shorter posts stood against the long walls to strengthen the walls on which the ends of the rafters rested.

The walls were built either of turf and stone or of turf alone, and in most cases their inner faces were panelled. The roof was also of turf, often with an inner lining of wood. The roof was supported on narrow rafters which rested on the purlins. The smoke hole was in the middle of the roof above the hearth; it also let in light, but there were other openings in the roof—in effect windows filled with translucent hides or animal foetal membranes, a method of admit-

Fig. 3. Reconstruction of the farm of Stöng, Thjórsárdalur, Iceland. Excavated in 1939. Cf. cat. no. 590.

ting daylight well known in Icelandic houses up to the present century. The light they gave supplemented that from the fire. The houses must, however, have been very murky, although there were naturally other sources of light. Lamps for train-oil, made of stone, were soon in use, but have not been found in the earliest houses.

Outbuildings had to be provided for livestock. These had stalls partitioned by large slabs of stone, with a barn at one end. We know less about the outbuildings than we do about the dwellings, but in most places the animals probably stayed indoors throughout winter, even though they must have been allowed outside as long as possible. Because timber was scarce, the turf construction of these large buildings, both the halls and the outbuildings, gave them the appearance of grassy hillocks. As the roofs and walls quickly became covered with grass the buildings merged into the landscape.

Other types of buildings must also have existed: storehouses for food, bath-houses, and privies. But soon, probably in the eleventh century, all these became incorporated with the hall which remained the largest and most important room in which everyone slept, ate, and worked on their household tasks. At an early stage a workroom for the women was added to one end of the hall. This contained the loom; the women wove and carried out other tasks there. The women's room also had a hearth, considerably smaller

than the one in the hall and probably intended only for heating. This room replaced the women's working huts which originally consisted of separate buildings. Other rooms were built onto the back of the hall. In the food storehouse, large milk churns for sour whey were sunk into the floor. Similar vessels were used for preserving food for the winter, whilst meat was probably hung from the roof and dried fish was kept in heaps.

In many places the inhabitants must have been forced to chop down or burn the woodland in order to develop land for growing fodder. Hay provided the winter fodder for the livestock. Undoubtedly animals often starved to death, as is recorded in the literature and indeed as happened in recent times. Most of the settlers were pagans, although some are mentioned as being Christians, and this is reflected in their burial customs. The dead were buried in the pagan manner; close to the farm, in a mound, on a dry slope, or near the shore. There was often a group of graves at each farm. The dead were buried with many of their personal possessions (cat. no. 324, 325). The men were interred with their weapons—knife, spear, axe, sword and shield—and often with a saddled horse or a dog; sometimes they were buried in a boat. The women had jewellery and various weaving tools or household equipment, occasionally a horse. The pagan belief was that people went to a new life after death and so needed the objects which they had used during their

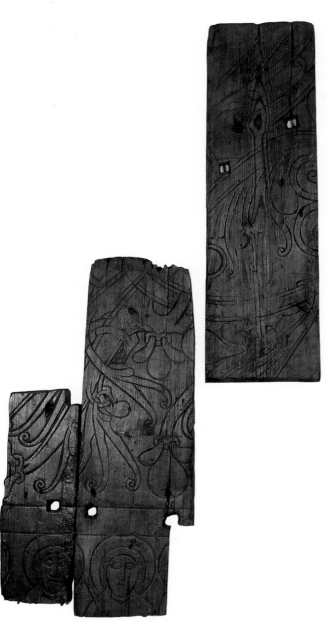

Fig. 4. Three of the four surviving panels from Flatatunga, Iceland. They date from the first half of the 11th cent. and are probably the earliest extant church decorations from Scandinavia. Cat. no. 454.

Fig. 5. Gold-embroidered vestments from the cathedral of Hólar, Iceland. Early 13th cent. Cat. no. 483.

lifetime. The burial customs are reminiscent of those in other places in Scandinavia at this time, but, with the coming of Christianity about 1000, the customs changed. People were now buried in churchyards, one to each parish, and the tradition of burying their worldly goods with them ceased.

The adoption of Christianity, by decree of the Althing, led to a radical change in Icelandic society. Churches were soon built on many of the farms, and priests with new learning were installed in several of them. A bishopric was inaugurated in Skálholt in the south of Iceland in 1056. Fifty years later, in 1106, another was founded at Hólar, for northern Iceland. These bishoprics survived until the nineteenth century when they were replaced by a single diocese based in Reykjavík, then a growing town. The greatest cultural contribution made by Christianity was probably the introduction of literacy. At first written texts were probably confined to the usages of the Church, but soon came the famous Icelandic literature which reached its high point in the High Middle Ages.

Christianity also brought with it new links with the Continent and Rome. Many priests and bishops were trained in foreign countries, and so developed strong connections with European culture. Icelandic ecclesiastical objects from the Middle Ages, both those which are mentioned in written sources and those which have survived, emphasize the importance of these connections. Despite its situation in the Atlantic, Iceland was far from isolated (cat. no. 326–37, 433, 454, 483, 510, 519–27, 588, 590).

TM

Fig. 6. Remains of the Viking Age settlement at Kvívík, Faroes. The buildings are good examples of Viking Age building tradition and also demonstrate the power of nature in that some of them have been washed away by the sea.

The Faroe Islands

The wave of emigrants which moved westwards from Scandinavia in the Viking Age also reached the Faroes. The islands' population mainly derives from west-Norwegian farmers who set out to find new lands in the North Atlantic. Their economic base was agriculture: the cultivation of crops and the raising of domesticated animals.

The emigrants who reached the British Isles had to fit in with the lifestyle of the local inhabitants. It has been suggested that the Faroes, also, were populated before the arrival of the Northmen by Irish monks or hermits. The archaeological evidence, however, gives us no reason to believe that the islands were inhabited before the arrival of the Norse.

Farms were founded along the coasts and fjords. The enclosed in-fields around the farms were used for growing grain and hay; the out-fields were used for pasture and turf-cutting. Turf was an important fuel, for the islands had no trees. Shielings for the transhumance of cattle were established in certain places in the out-fields. The traditions brought from the homeland were tested and adapted to the natural conditions of the islands.

Our knowledge of the early history of the Faroes is based largely on archaeology, for written sources are scarce. The classic example of a Faroese Viking Age farm is the site in the village of Kvívík on Streymoy. Excavations have revealed a dwelling, some 20 m long, with a central hearth and earth benches along the curved long-walls; the roof was carried on two rows of posts. Beside it there was a smaller building, a byre, with stalls along each side and a drain down the middle. As in other farmsteads known from this period, the buildings were basically constructed of wood, protected by wide outer walls of stone and earth. Even though building timber was scarce the tradition of building in wood—inspired from the homeland—continued, but was adapted to local conditions.

The household equipment and tools of the emigrants were both locally made and imported (cf. cat. no. 315–23). They include bowls and other objects of soapstone, slate and schist honestones, querns, and wooden bowls, buckets and spoons. Metal objects and iron slag have been found, but decorative objects such as combs, beads, brooches and other jewellery are rare; toys and a gaming piece give evidence of the leisure activities of both children and adults. The imports show that there were close contacts with the outside world, both with the Norwegian homeland and with other Norse communities south of the Faroes.

Local materials were also used; tufa was used for spindle-whorls and lamps, for example, and pottery was beginning

Fig. 7. View of Sandur, Faroes. In the background there is Skúvoy, where Sigmundr Brestisson is said to have lived. He was one of the main characters in Færeyinga saga (written early 13th cent.) and, according to the saga, he brought Christianity to the islands. Further to the left there are the islands of Stóra Dímun and Lítla Dímun, with Suðuroy farthest to the west. Many of the saga's dark activities took place here.

to be made, of which we have evidence from the eleventh century. Local resources were made the most of, and traditional customs from the homeland were modified or abandoned. Thus, transhumance and the milking of sheep were abandoned in the early Middle Ages in favour of extensive sheep-breeding. Some ancient field-systems demonstrate that the early method of cultivation was changed to one which could make use of the much larger and more easily worked wet areas.

We have only limited knowledge of the beliefs of the people before the introduction of Christianity. A pagan cemetery of twelve graves has been excavated at Tjørnuvík in northermost Streymoy. Eleven burials have recently been discovered south of the churchyard in Sandur on Sandoy but we still do not know whether they are pagan or Christian graves.

Both the king and the Church had interests in the Norse settlements in the Atlantic, and the Faroes were probably tributary to Norway in the eleventh century. Christianity came to the islands about 1000 and the first churches were built. A small stave church of Norwegian type has been excavated beneath the present church at Sandur. The Faroes

had their own bishopric in the early twelfth century, becoming subject to Trondheim in 1152/3, it was centred at Kirkjubøur on Streymoy, the cultural centre for the islands throughout the Middle Ages. Its historical remains illustrate the importance of outside influences and reflect little of the traditional medieval culture of the Faroes.

SVA

Fig. 8. Toy boat and horse from the Faroes. Viking Age. Cat. no. 315.

Fig. 9. Brattahlid, Greenland, where Erik the Red settled c. 985. Ruins from the Viking Age and Middle Ages can be seen; and the remains of Tjodhilde's church lie to the right of the gable of the modern church in the centre of the picture.

Greenland and America

In the thirteenth century there are exciting Icelandic descriptions of the settlement of Greenland and the subsequent journeys further west to Vinland, Markland and Helluland, these include *The Saga of Erik the Red* (cat. no. 337). The Icelandic narrators all agree in their descriptions of Erik the Red; at the end of the tenth century he went on a voyage of discovery to Greenland after being banished from Iceland for three years. Erik found Greenland so attractive that, after his three years in exile, he returned home to Iceland and persuaded others to follow him to Greenland. Many went and established a colony there.

The voyages to Vinland, Markland and Helluland took place shortly after the colonization of Greenland. The thirteenth century Icelanders do not agree as to who had the distinction of discovering the lands to the west. The Saga of Erik the Red says that it was Erik's son, Leif the Lucky. The second great Vinland saga, the *Saga of the Greenlanders*, attributes the discovery to Bjarne, son of the landowner Herjolf of Herjolfsnæs in Greenland. Both sagas agree that the settlement of Vinland was abandoned because of the natives, the 'skrællings', with whom the settlers came into conflict.

The Icelandic accounts attribute the colonization of Greenland to about 985 and the Vinland voyages to about 1000 and archaeological excavations confirm the date for Greenland. The discovery of Norse building-remains at L'Anse aux Meadows on the north point of Newfoundland in America suggests that it is in this region that the Vinland, Markland and Helluland of the Northmen should be sought (cat. no. 345–56).

The excavations at L'Anse aux Meadows do not show colonization in the traditional sense. The settlement consists of three main complexes, each with a dwelling and smaller outbuildings. There is also a smithy. The place was in use for only a short period around 1000 and the artifacts show that one of the main activities was ship-repairing. To-day, the site is interpreted as a base from which the Vikings set out to investigate the eastern seabord of America. There is still no convincing explanation of why there was no permanent Scandinavian colonization of America in the eleventh century. The Icelandic saga-writers may have been right in attributing its abandonment to the 'skrællings'. The Vikings may have met groups of Indians or Eskimos who were sufficiently well organized to prevent colonization; but it

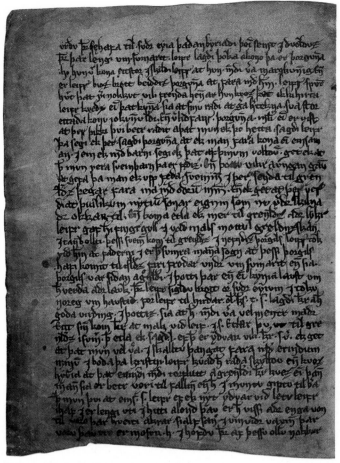

Fig. 10. Erik the Red's Saga (Hauksbók, fol. 96v). *This tells of Erik's son Leif being blown off course after a visit to the Norwegian king, and finding a new land, Vinland, with self-sown wheat and vines. Cat. no. 337.*

the fjords and at the heads of fjords and with access to deep valleys (cat. no. 338–44, 434, 565, 591). Not all sites were equally attractive, but it seems that all ecologically suitable niches were used for the initial settlement. From the very beginning, Viking society was hierarchically organized, both economically and socially. To a farmer's eyes the best places would have been the extensive and fertile moraine slopes at the heads of the fjords, with good potential for hay for winter fodder for the farm's cows, sheep and goats. These were the places where powerful men like Erik the Red set up their farms. The farming complex at Qassiarsuk in Tunulliarfik, in the East Settlement, has been identified as Erik the Red's farm, Brattahlid; whilst the biggest farm in the neighbouring Igaliku fjord is that of Gardar in the East Settlement, the seat of the bishop of Greenland.

Investigations of farm middens have provided an insight into the economy of individual farms. They have sketched a picture of the great farms with their predominence of cattle, and of the smaller farms of the more limited coastal and inland areas, where there was a predominance of sheep and goats. The smaller farms, even those inland, were greatly dependent on seal hunting and many of the small farms along the fjords must have been deliberately settled with this in mind; although the bones found in the middens show that the Greenland settlers hunted not only basking fjord-seals, but also caught migrating seals which they must have hunted from the coast. Reindeer were also very important to the Greenland economy.

The Vikings settled in Greenland at a time when Christianity was being adopted by the Nordic peoples. The first churches were founded soon after colonization; the earliest known church is Tjodhilde's church, probably built by Erik the Red's wife on his farm at Brattahlid in the eleventh century. All the churches in Greenland were built, as on Iceland, in relation to farms, and they probably belonged to the farm's owner who would also have control of the living. According to the Icelandic *History of Einar Sokkason*, the Greenlanders acquired their own bishop about 1124 after petitioning the Norwegian king; the bishop was granted the farm of Gardar. It is not known whether the bishop was appointed exactly as described in the saga, but the Greenlanders did get a bishop, and excavations in Gardar (now Igaliku) have revealed the remains of the medieval cathedral. A bishop's burial of about 1200 has been found in its north chapel (cat. no. 344).

Greenland was self-sufficient at a subsistence level, but if the inhabitants wanted to maintain a Scandinavian lifestyle —and the archaeological finds show that they did—imports from Scandinavia were necessary: primarily iron and timber, but also finer European luxury goods. The Greenlanders

could also be that Greenland fulfilled the needs of the Norse settlers for new land. Why should they go even further away from the limits of their known world?

The Scandinavian occupation of Greenland was concentrated in two main areas in south-western Greenland: the East Settlement in Nanortalik, Narsaq, Qaqortoq, Ivittuut and the south of Paamiut; and the West Settlement in modern Nuuk. When the Norse arrived the country was deserted, but remains of boats and stone implements showed that the area had been inhabited earlier, probably by Eskimos of the Dorset culture.

The coastline is characterized by archipelagos and fjords which penetrate deep inland, in some places right up to the ice cap. In contrast to the unsettled climate of the coast, that of the inner fjord areas is continental, providing luxuriant undergrowth, pasture and scrub. It was here that the Vikings established their farms; beside small watercourses along exported buckskins, cow hides, sealskins, polar-bear skins, ropes made from walrus hide, and, above all, walrus and narwhal tusks (cat. no. 591). Walrus and narwhal lived in the sea off north Greenland and the Greenlanders made hunting trips to Disko, Upernavik and perhaps even further north to Melville Bay in order to acquire the necessary material for trade with Europe. Iron objects of Scandinavian type found on Eskimo settlements in high-arctic Canada may indicate that the Greenlanders tried to trade their wares with the Inuit, either in Canada or Greenland.

A Norwegian description of Greenland of the second half of the fourteenth century mentions that the West Settlement was deserted and depopulated about 1360, and archaeological evidence supports this. The last written communication from the Norse Greenlanders dates from 1409 and mentions that an Icelandic couple were married the previous year in Hvalsfjord church in Greenland's East Settlement. After this is silence, although archaeological finds from the East Settlement indicate that it was still inhabited in the middle of the fifteenth century.

Many factors must have influenced the abandonment of the farms on the fjords of southern Greenland in the Middle Ages. Climatic deterioration, beginning in the twelfth and thirteenth centuries, and limited agricultural potential were two of them; but other problems were brought on by the settlers themselves, for example the over-exploitation of the natural vegetation. At the same time, the outside world was changing. Scandinavia was becoming more closely integrated into Europe and it was difficult for the Greenlanders to find a place in the new order. It was possible to survive in Greenland—the Eskimos show this—but that possibility diminished once the Norse Greenlanders decided that they wanted to continue their traditional life-style.

JA

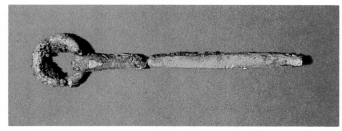

Fig. 11. Ring-headed pin c. 1000 found in L'Anse aux Meadows, Newfoundland, Canada. L'Anse aux Meadows is the only North American site to have produced remains of Viking Age settlement. Cat. no. 344.

Fig. 12. Bishop's crozier and ring from c. 1200, found at Gardar (Igaliku), Greenland. Cat. no. 344.

Finland

Pirkko-Liisa Lehtosalo-Hilander

Finland is the most easterly of the Nordic countries—a land of woods and women if we are to believe Adam of Bremen and some of his commentators. Finland was unknown to most Europeans during the Viking Age and, to those who did know about it, it was a land of mists and monsters. Swedes and Gotlanders were the only people who were more knowledgeable about the inhabitants of Finland. They were probably the only ones who realized that the Finns were not Saami, but people very similar to Scandinavians. Their language was different, but there were certainly some people along the coast of Finland who understood Swedish and traded with the Scandinavians.

Written records tell us very little about the Finns. If Scandinavian sagas and other written records were the only sources for Viking Age and medieval Finland, we would believe that there was a land called Finland, that it was periodically conquered by the Swedes, and that its kings had eligible daughters who could be married to Swedish kings—unhappily for them—and whose sons could become kings. We should also know that there were powerful witches and wizards, and also independent women who apparently liked men but who did not wish to marry (the dream, perhaps, of sailors and merchants!). When these women had children their daughters were very beautiful but their sons were monsters, with heads in the middle of their bodies.

In the far north, Finnish chieftains competed with Scandinavians for the furs of Lappland. Sometimes they were rivals, at other times they formed alliances against the Karelians. When a Norwegian king, St Olaf, tried to exact tribute, the Finns fled to the forests where they could defend themselves. Their witches and shamans conjured up a great storm and only the royal luck of St Olaf saved his ships from disaster. Later, the same Finns antagonized the Pope because they did not want to maintain the Christian faith once there were no armed bands to remind them of it.

Histories relate that St Erik, a Swedish king, conquered Finland in the middle of the twelfth century (cat. no. 536), and that his bishop, St Henry, baptized the Finns; but this is probably a much later story created to enhance the dignity of St Erik and his royal line. The Danes are also said to have conquered 'Finland' at the end of the twelfth century, but their dominance must have been short-lived.

The picture given by archaeology is different, and more diversified. It does not show us kings, shamans and witches, but a virtually egalitarian society with farmers and soldiers, hunters and traders, potters and weavers. Nor does it show signs of Swedish conquest—central-Swedish culture of a true Viking Age type only became dominant on the Åland islands.

Finns and Saami—permanent settlements and the wilderness

The Finns lived mainly in the southern part of the Finnish mainland, along the sea coast and on the shores of inland lakes. To the east and north lived hunters and fishers who may either have been ancestors of the Saami (Lapps) or of some other branch of the widespread Finno-Ugrians. Before the Slavs migrated to the north, vast areas of northern Europe formed the hunting and fishing territories of Finnish tribes, many of which, in contrast to the Finns in Finland, became extinct through assimilation with other peoples.

The Finns in Finland had begun to cultivate cereals long before the beginning of our era, and wheat, barley, rye and oats were grown during the Viking Age. Although they mainly practised slash-and-burn cultivation, there must also by then have been permanent fields. One of the areas with such fields was Eura, where most of the richest Viking-age remains are to be found.

Animals played a prominant part in burial ceremonies. From the material found in burial contexts we know that all the most important domestic animals were kept—cattle, horses, sheep/goats and pigs. Dogs were also buried with many of the men and some women, but no traces of cats have been found.

One animal, not domesticated but apparently very important to the Finns, was the bear. There are bears' teeth and claws among the bones from cremation cemeteries, and bears' teeth and bronze pendants modelled on them were attached to the breast-chains and clothes of the women. Strange clay artifacts, some of them resembling bears' paws, have been found on the Åland islands (cat. no. 234–7). Similar objects, rather more like beavers' paws, have been found frequently in cemeteries of the Finnic tribes of central Russia (cat. no. 298).

Finnish folklore and ethnology record that the killing of a bear was accompanied by special rites, including great feasts. The bear had many pet names, and it was believed that its paws, teeth and grease had healing properties. Such

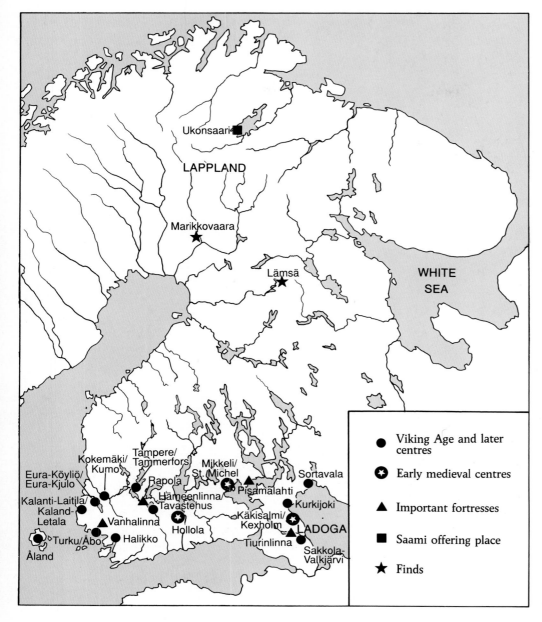

Fig. 1. *Finland.*

beliefs are probably reflected in the burial customs.

The Finns also hunted elk—the hides of which were often used to line the bottoms of graves—and other fur-bearing animals such as squirrel, sable, marten and fox. Their furs probably produced the surplus which enabled the Finns to acquire the fine west-European weapons which are found in their later Iron Age cemeteries (cat. no. 214, 220, 558).

Most of the Viking Age and early medieval objects discovered in Finland have been excavated in cemeteries. There are almost no hoards with Arabic coins, and, although there

are several eleventh-century silver hoards containing western coins and jewellery, these are small compared with those of Scandinavia.

Only a few Iron Age settlements are known; most of them are probably still occupied by modern dwellings. There are many hill-forts on steep, rocky hills beside bays and lakes, but few can have been permanently occupied and they were only resorted to in times of danger. Their most easily accessible slopes were protected by stone ramparts surmounted by timber walls and on their crests warning fires could be lit in times of danger.

Most of the hill-forts are unexcavated, and settlement sites also have mainly been dug on a small scale. Somewhat larger excavations, however, have recently been carried out on two settlements, both in the lake district of Tavastia. Varikkoniemi, in the present town of Hämeenlinna, has been equated with the town of Vanai mentioned in the Early Russian chronicles.

The settlement at Rapola in Valkeakoski (near to the largest hill-fort in Finland the ramparts of which are more than 1000 m long) must have been very large and had a long history. The earliest finds are from the fourth century, but its *floruit* must have been in the Viking Age and later. The hill-fort itself was probably the central fortress of the province of Tavastia.

The most important market centres must, however, have lain near the coast. A concentration of finds suggests that one of them was on the River Aura, in the present town of Turku (Åbo). Nearby is one of the most important hill-forts, known as the Old Castle of Lieto, which seems to have been permanently occupied at least for some time.

Another centre was near the small town of Uusikaupunki, in the Kalanti-Laitila area. This part of Finland seems to have had the closest contacts with the Swedes during the pre-Viking and Viking Ages, and many types of brooch and other ornaments originated there. New weapon types spread to the interior of Finland by way of the parishes of Kalanti, Laitila and Eura, and thence along the river Kokemäenjoki.

The importance of the Turku and Halikko regions increased in the eleventh century, when new centres also began to appear in the interior. One of these was on the site of the present town of Tampere; another lay at the southern end of Lake Päijänne near the town of Lahti; and a third on the north-west shore of Lake Saimaa where the town of Mikkeli now stands.

From the beginning of the Viking Age, permanent settlements were established on the north-west shore of Lake Ladoga, but they did not develop into really important centres until the twelfth and thirteenth centuries. A few very rich finds discovered at the end of the nineteenth century have enabled the Karelian culture of the Crusading period to be distinguished from that of western Finland. It has since been realized that many of the so-called Karelian forms had earlier prototypes in the Tavastian area, and that the contacts between the different centres of Finland were of a more permanent and peaceful nature than suggested by the scanty references in the Old Russian chronicles.

Fig. 2. The fortress at Pisamalahti, Sulkava, Savolax. In Finland fortresses usually lie beside waterways and on high outcrops with steep sides. The most exposed slopes were defended with stone walls and probably also with wooden palisades.

Fig. 3. Sword and spearhead with silver encrustation. 11th cent. Cat. no. 228, 229a.

Burial rites and personal property

Burial customs can be used to illustrate the close contacts between Karelia and western Finland. From the coast of the Gulf of Bothnia to the shores of Lake Ladoga the dead were buried in cairns, in cemeteries on level ground, or in flat graves. Both cremation and inhumation were practised, although cremation was predominant at first.

Cremation cemeteries on level ground were commonest; the remains of the pyre were covered either with thick layers of stone or with thinly scattered stones. Sometimes there are no stones and the cemeteries consist of large areas of ash and charcoal with broken and fire-damaged artifacts. The remains of a single burial pyre were generally scattered over the cemetery, but occasionally they were deposited in a specific grave.

In the coastal zone of south-west Finland, some people were cremated in boats—their remains being scattered over the cemeteries, a custom that was practised in Finland from at least the end of the sixth century. No inhumation burials in boats, nor boats under mounds (as found in Sweden and Norway) are known from Finland. In the interior of Finland, the custom of burying the dead in cairns of stone and earth continued until the twelfth century. Some of the cairns contain a single burial, others contain more burials, and both cremation and inhumation are known. In the Åland archipelago, cremations were covered by mounds; in this, as in other matters, the Åland islanders followed the customs of the Swedes.

Cremation cemeteries with their scattered remains are of little use for dating purposes but, fortunately, there is one part of Finland where inhumation was almost the sole rite. In the parishes of Eura and Köyliö, at the north end of Lake Pyhäjärvi in south-west Finland, the dead began to be inhumed from the end of the sixth century. An early Viking Age inhumation cemetery is also known from the south end of Lake Pyhäjärvi. Many of the most spectacular finds from the Finnish late Iron Age come from these cemeteries (cat. no. 200–3).

The appearance of inhumation graves in the middle of a country which originally had an almost exclusive custom of cremation has been the cause of much speculation. The similarity of the inhumations to the *Reihengräber* (literally: graves set in rows) of western Europe, and the new types of weapon which they contain, have been taken to indicate an influx of foreign soldiers with innovative customs and weapons. Nevertheless, Finland's culture soon became uniform and independent, and in the Viking Age similar artifacts were buried in both inhumation and cremation cemeteries.

From the beginning of the eleventh century inhumations were deposited in earlier cremation cemeteries; and some decades later the people of western Finland began to bury their dead in separate inhumation cemeteries. Belfries were erected in some of these, indicating the change to Christian practices. In some parts of Finland, however, the dead still continued to be buried clothed in their gala clothes, whilst in Karelia they were still provided with weapons and tools.

The long-lasting tradition of inhumation burial with grave-goods, and the fashion of decorating garments with small bronze spirals, has meant that we now know a good deal about Viking Age and early medieval dress. Although no complete garments are known, many early Finnish female dresses have been reconstructed (fig. 5).

A man may have been clothed in two smocks, with a belt and garters of colourful wool, decorated with spirals. His most handsome garment was his cloak: dyed blue, bordered with brighly-coloured braids, and decorated with small ornamental bronze spirals. It was fastened with a large

Fig. 4. Female grave from Luistari, Eura. Cat. no. 200. Excavation photo, cf. fig. 5.

penannular brooch, usually of bronze but sometimes plated with silver.

Some male cloaks were fastened with ringed pins decorated with Scandinavian type animal ornament (cat. no. 201). These pins were popular among the men who travelled to the East, and a fragment of a Finnish penannular brooch found on the island of Berezan in the Black Sea (cat. no. 312) suggests that there were Finns among the men who sailed along the great rivers of Russia. Finns had eastern contacts long before the Swedes appeared on the shores of Lake Ladoga.

Even before silver became popular in the eleventh century, the brooches used by men to fasten their cloaks had long been made of silver. But the fashion for cloaks was soon replaced by that for coats, open at the front and fastened by small buttons, often in the form of tinkling bells.

Male dress-fashion seems mostly to have reflected that

current around the Baltic Sea, but female fashion was more conservative. Throughout the Viking Age and later, women continued to wear the traditional mantle-dress resembling the Greek *peplos*, and only their jewellery and the amount of spiral decoration changed throughout that period (cat. no. 200, 220).

As in Scandinavia, Finnish women wore three brooches as dress fasteners, but they never adopted the Scandinavian oval brooches. Round brooches came into fashion in Finland at the end of the eighth century, and this continued to be the dominant shape throughout the Viking Age. The most popular purely ornamental objects were bead necklaces and finger-rings. The abundant use of ring ornaments and spiral decoration on clothing was a feature which the Finns had in common with their southern neighbours (cat. no. 249–50), and is a fashion which distinguishes them from the Scandinavians. Small bronze wire spirals were sewn onto garments almost everywhere where Finno-Ugrians lived, including Latvia.

This fashion came to Finland at the beginning of the Viking Age. At first the ornaments were small and rather simple, but in the tenth century men's cloaks, waistbands and garters were decorated with complicated interlaced ornaments, and at the beginning of the eleventh century the hems of women's aprons were decorated with large spiral appliqués. But it was not until the late eleventh century that women's cloaks with rich spiral decorations came into fashion in western Finland. These cloaks, with their spiral borders and applied roundels, stars, and crosses, seem to have been copied from the cloaks worn by the Madonna in Byzantine art. Perhaps some of the icons of the Eastern Church had fascinated Finnish travellers who then described them at home, their verbal images being skilfully transformed into ornament.

Traits indicative of contacts with continental fashion can also be seen. In the twelfth century the women wore a circular silver brooch, at the neck of their tunic, as depicted in contemporary manuscript illumination. The circular silver brooch became an essential part of female costume in eastern Finland, but it was often imported from Gotland or the Swedish mainland.

The abundant grave-goods also include many Iron Age tools (cat. no. 204–11). Knives and agricultural implements such as sickles, scythes and shears, are the commonest; but carpenters' and smiths' tools are also found, although not as frequently as in Norway.

Finns were not buried with their horses, but some graves contain bridle-bits, which might reflect a belief that there would be horses in the next world, and that they could then be mounted. Many men were buried with their dogs.

Fig. 5. Female clothing reconstructed on the basis of the finds from a grave in Luistari, Eura, Finland (cat. no. 200). It represents Finnish fashion at the beginning of the 11th cent. All the articles of clothing are of wool and the details are copied from the finds in one grave. The reconstructed dress is as similar as possible to the original; for example, the yarn was spun as the original and dyed with vegetable dyes. The basic design of the garment was the same throughout the Finnish area. The archaic dress, known as the Greek peplos, *was used in both west and east Finland. The chain-decorations with round brooches and spiral-ornamented apron are also important elements which distinguish the Viking Age Finnish female dress from the Scandinavian.*

Fig. 6. The island of Ukonsaari in Lake Enare, Lappland, Finland. On the island was a Saami cult-site in a cave containing antler, animal bones and animal teeth. A semi-circle of reindeer antlers was found outside the cave.

The other bones in graves do not represent complete animals, often just the skull is found, perhaps symbolic of a complete animal. Some bones may be the remains of food provided for the dead.

The containers found in graves were probably for food and drink. The carbonized remains found in some of them include crushed barley, hops, and raspberries; perhaps the components for a type of beer.

Fishermen, swordsmen, wealthy women

The Finnish table was apparently provided with many types of fish, not necessarily of types available locally. When salmon teemed in the rivers, men travelled miles to catch them. These men covered even greater distances on skis when they went out hunting, or they travelled by boat on the lakes and rivers of the Finnish wilderness (cat. no. 7, 21–2).

Some graves have been found in the vast wildernesses of the Finnish interior, and indicate that there must have been settlements there in the Viking Age. They probably represent buildings in which the hunters from southern Finland sheltered, either when hunting in the interior or when travelling to the more northerly regions in Lappland to collect furs which would be transported to the coast in favourable weather.

Many axes have been found far from permanent settlements. They indicate the routes followed by hunters and slash-and-burn cultivators. These finds are concentrated along the important waterways as far as northern Finland, where silver hoards and cemeteries of western Finnish type have also been found in Kuusamo, for instance (cat. no. 240), and Suomussalmi. An important meeting place for hunters and traders probably existed in this area.

The Finns' activities in Lappland may date from long before the Viking Age, but it was only then that the Finns began to exploit their wilderness to the full. About the beginning of the ninth century the trade routes to European markets opened up and the Finns could then exchange their furs for desirable commodities, especially swords. From the last decades of the eighth century Frankish pattern-welded swords had begun to arrive in Finland; and, later, swords inlaid with names such as *Ulfberht, Ingelrii, Inno, Beno*, and *Gicelin*, and also with Latin inscriptions, show their origins (cat. no. 214, 558). Some may have been provided with hilts in Scandinavia, others were hilted in Finland. Contrary to what has been claimed, the manufacture of weapons in Finland did not end at this time, but most spearheads and axes continued to be made in Finnish workshops following models current throughout Scandinavia (cat. no. 212–3).

The prevalence of these weapons in Finland has led to speculations about a foreign, probably Scandinavian, military caste living in Finland during the Viking Age. But, Scandinavian burial mounds are unknown in Finland, apart from on the Åland islands, and very few Scandinavian female ornaments have been found. Weapon graves were not new in the Viking Age; Finnish men had been buried with weapons from the beginning of the Iron Age.

It is true, however, that the genes of the western Finns are nearly (up to 75%) the same as the Swedes', the result of many various and close contacts. These contacts, however, have lasted for many thousands of years, and as Finns still speak Finnish today the Scandinavian influence must be seen as the result of a continuous infiltration of Scandinavian genes into Finnish blood rather than an overwhelming dominance of Scandinavian language and culture. Perhaps the sagas are correct in speaking of Finnish mothers and Swedish fathers. The language is the mother tongue, even though the fathers supply half the genes!

There is also archaeological support for the sagas when they describe the independent character of the Finnish women who were fatal to Swedish kings. Each of two women's graves found in the interior of Finland contained two swords. The swords are not commonplace ones, but richly ornamented and worthy of a chief (cat. no. 220, 230). All the other artifacts in these graves were normal Finnish female ornaments—but one contained a knife and a sickle, and the other a knife and shears. Both graves date from the second half of the eleventh century when there is also a female grave containing scales, weights, and a purse.

Fig. 7. *Jewellery from a female grave in Tuukkala, St Michel, Finland. C. 1200. The jewellery is characteristic of the dress of the Crusade period in east Finland. Cat. no. 221. Pointed-oval shoulder-brooches are typical in this region; in west Finland small penannular brooches were used.*

Women's graves became richer and richer during the Viking Age, not only in jewellery but also in tools and other furnishings. In the early Viking Age, for example, dogs, cattle and bridle-bits occur only in male graves; by the eleventh century a woman could be accompanied by a dog, her funeral could have been celebrated with roast beef, and she could have a bridle for her mount in the future world.

There were obviously wealthy and esteemed women in Finland at that time; but what of those men called 'kings' in the sagas? Were there really Finnish kings, or were the beautiful women whom the Swedish kings married simply the daughters of yeomen to whom the title of king was given as a status symbol? There are, as we have seen, no princely graves in Finland, but many weapon-graves contain fine swords. These are so common in Lower Satakunta, the

Fig. 8. Silver-inlaid weapons from 11th–12th cent. The sword was found in Eura and the axe in Masku, Finland. Cat. no. 231, 233.

Eura-Köyliö area, that it has been suggested that a royal *hird* (bodyguard) lived there.

There is further evidence for a concentration of power. When the Swedes consolidated their rule over Finland in the thirteenth century, an ancient system of taxation of Finnish, not Scandinavian, origin already existed. As we know from modern society, taxes will not be paid unless there is a strong central power to collect them.

The numerous hill forts also imply co-operation, and thus there must have been some centralized power; but we do not know whether this power was wielded by a king, as in other Northern countries, or by a council of elders. Archaeology suggests the latter.

Ancient magic and Christianity

According to folklore the most important people in Finland were magicians who could foretell the future, heal the sick, and announce the propitious times for the start of important enterprises. But they were not the only ones who could act as mediators between the people of this world and the spirits. Every tree, every bush, every beast, had its own spirit; and every person could, and had to, propitiate them with sacrifices and magical verses.

With all this magic and all these spirits, the Finns lived more or less happily with their neighbours. We do not know when they first heard of Christ; but Christian symbols began to spread in Finland much earlier than did the Christ-

Fig. 9. Reliquary containing St Erik's lower jaw, from Åbo (Turku) Cathedral, Finland. Cat. no. 536. St Erik was slain in Uppsala in 1160; according to legend he and Bishop Henrik together converted the Finns.

ian Eucharist. Cruciform decorations on brooches appear as early as about 800, and the earliest cruciform pendants have been found in eleventh-century graves (cat. no. 222, 224). These graves, however, are amply furnished with grave-goods, and both pagans and Christians probably existed alongside each other in Finland for a long time.

Archaeology shows that the people of northern Finland proper (Varsinais Suomi), the Kalanti-Laitila area, ceased to bury the dead with grave-goods as early as the eleventh century, and few furnished burials are known from the beginning of the twelfth century in Eura-Köyliö-Kokemäki. This part of Finland may have had such close connections with the Swedes that Christianity was adopted here earlier than anywhere else.

The southern part of Finland proper, around Turku, has been described as the centre of pagan belief, but crosses and pendant crucifixes have been found in graves there, and an early twelfth-century cemetery in Lieto is thought to be Christian. Christians and pagans probably lived side by side at first, but when the Church began to demand not only burial without grave-goods but also the payment of tithes, the Finns were not so accommodating. In both the Legend

of St Erik and the old folk poem on the murder of St Henry, the murderer Lalli is said to have been Christian. Lalli murdered the bishop because he had demanded board and lodging, by force, in Lalli's own house. This happened in Köyliö. In the neighbouring parish of Eura, people continued to be buried in the pagan cemetery of Luistari for at least two centuries after the transition to Christian burial customs. They wanted to rest alongside their ancestors, even if they had to relinquish the deposition of grave-goods.

In southern Finland proper and in Tavastia, furnished burials continued until the end of the twelfth century; and in eastern Finland and Karelia some graves contained grave-goods as late as the thirteenth and fourteenth centuries. The Finns were set in their ways, and it took a couple of centuries and many battles before the Christian Church and Swedish rule were established. For many hundreds of years after that, the growing of crops, the hunting of game, and the catching of fish still demanded the help of the old gods. In eastern Finland, the Eastern and Western Church fought over the souls of the people; in this region, in particular, the old beliefs and traditions maintained their power.

The Saami in Scandinavia

Inger Zachrisson

From time immemorial the Saami (Lapps), with their own culture and language, have lived in the North—in large areas of Sweden, Norway, Finland and also in a part of Russia. Their early history has been much discussed, but modern research has changed the traditional picture.

From the ninth to the thirteenth centuries the Saami region seems to have extended further south in Sweden and Norway than it does today—to nearly as far as the Oslo region. It also comprised large parts of Finland. In Russia the Saami reached as far south as the Ladoga and Onega regions. Archaeological discoveries from these areas show continuity back to the Stone Age, thus the ancestors of the Saami were not immigrants. As is sometimes stated, they 'have always been there' (from the last Ice Age).

The area occupied by the Saami was large and heterogeneous, consequently living conditions varied greatly—from the Atlantic coast, for instance, where fishing was predominant, to the great forests east of the mountains. Metal objects, including jewellery, from east and west indicate widespread contacts. Proximity to the Germanic/Scandinavian culture of Norway and Sweden involved the absorption of many cultural traditions. Increasing pressure from this culture led to some of the Saami on the Scandinavian peninsula becoming assimilated, and to their original homeland being diminished.

Hunting, gathering and fishing were of equal importance throughout the area. Sporadic cultivation of cereals and the raising of goats and sheep were also practised from the Stone Age onwards. Elk in the forests and reindeer in the mountains were hunted. The Saami were nomads, using areas of land according to the season. A few reindeer may have been kept as draught animals, for milk, and as decoys for hunting; but the intensive farming of reindeer is a fairly recent phenomenon.

Graves, settlements, sacrificial sites, and trapping pits are known from the period 800–1200 (cat. no. 238). The vast chains of trapping pits (cat. no. 241–2), sometimes with more than a hundred pits in a single row, indicate a well organized social system. The Saami were probably then, as later, organized in so-called *siida*-areas with the oldest man in the group as leader.

The two hundred or so prehistoric skis found in Fenno-Scandia all come from the early Saami area, and are not known further south. Thus, travel by skis may well have been learned from the Saami.

Archaeologists have investigated large Saami sacrificial sites in northern Sweden; these have produced quantities of animal bones, antlers, and metal objects. Bear-graves have also been excavated: the cult of the bear indeed was widespread. Saami pre-Christian religion influenced, and was influenced by, early Scandinavian religion; some Catholic traits were incorporated later.

In the ninth century the Norwegian Ottar described to King Alfred of Wessex the Saami who lived on the north coast of Norway: they traded skins and hides of marten, reindeer, bear and otter, as well as sacks of down from sea-birds, ships' ropes of walrus hide, and seal skins. In the winter they hunted, in the summer they fished in the sea. Ottar himself owned about six hundred domesticated reindeer, six of which were used as decoys to attract wild reindeer.

In the ninth and tenth centuries Norwegian chieftains travelled to the Saami of the interior, both to do trade and to exact taxes. By the end of the eleventh century the fur trade of the north was a Norwegian royal monopoly. Mutual respect seems to have characterized the intercourse between the Saami and the Scandinavians; the tax system may also have been of advantage to the Saami, who in this way could have an outlet for their wares. The Saami were particularly renowned for their precious furs, for their special bows, and for their skill as archers. One of their most important means of payment was miniver, the grey winter fur of the squirrel, which was brought south in enormous quantities, ultimately to trim the robes of bishops and nobles (cat. no. 239–40, 558).

The earliest Norwegian laws, written down before 1120 in south-east Norway, forbade Norwegians to travel to the Saami in order to have their fortunes told. The Scandinavians feared the supernatural skills of the Saami, and their shamanism. A seance with a drum is described in a late twelfth-century chronicle which deals with the same area. The Saami are there depicted as skilful hunters, and as nomads, living in tents made of birch bark. They ski over the packed snow, and with their wives and children drive their reindeer faster than a bird can fly.

Saami cult-site by Lake Rautasjaure in the far north of Sweden. The site is marked by a large boulder, glittering blue-green from its copper content. It stands 7m above the surface of the lake.

The way to the East

Ingmar Jansson with a contribution by Evgenij N. Nosov

The Baltic

In the Viking age, the peoples living around the North Sea (apart from Scotland north of the Firth of Forth), spoke Germanic languages. This linguistic community and its associated cultural unity made it easy for Scandinavians to travel overseas. On the other hand, the Baltic formed a marked linguistic and cultural boundary. In the south, between Kiel and the mouth of the Vistula, Slav languages were spoken; in the south-east, between the Vistula and the Daugava (western Dvina), the languages were Baltic; and north of the Daugava were Finno-Ugric languages. The Baltic is, however, a comparatively small sea, and in the middle of it Bornholm, Gotland and the Åland islands serve as bridgeheads for travellers to the East. During the centuries before the Viking Age these islands were populated by Scandinavians.

People have travelled across the Baltic Sea for thousands of years. For most of which time Finland, in particular, has had close connections with the Scandinavian peninsula. During the centuries immediately before the Viking Age, however, a trading site in Latvia provides the most obvious evidence of east-west contacts: Grobiņa (Grobin in German) on the west coast of Kurland. Here graves with male and female artifacts of mainland Scandinavian and Gotland type have been found in quantities sufficient to suggest that a Scandinavian population had been established on the site

(cat. no. 247). The Scandinavians established themselves at Grobiņa at some time in the seventh century, and maintained contacts with their homeland until the ninth century, when the site lost its importance.

Further south in the Baltic region two other trading centres must have had considerable Scandinavian elements in their population: Drużno (German: Drausenhof, ancient Truso) near Elbląg in modern Poland, which has produced eighth- and ninth-century objects of Gotland and mainland Scandinavian character; and Kaup near Višnevo (German: Wiskiauten) on the Samland peninsula in the modern Kaliningrad (German: Königsberg) area of Russia; this site has produced objects of mainland Scandinavian types of the ninth and particularly of the tenth century. Scandinavian artifacts are also numerous in other places, for example in south-west Finland and along the Daugava in Latvia, but their occurrence in these areas suggests a close relationship with Scandinavia rather than Scandinavian colonization.

Rus and Varangians

Contacts between the peoples around the Baltic Sea continued and intensified during the Viking Age. But a most striking feature of the Viking Age is that the Scandinavians penetrated further to the east and south-east. One thing which shrouds these easterly travellers in mystery is that the

Fig. 1. Istanbul-Constantinople-Byzantium. The Scandinavians called the city Miklagård, 'the great town'. The large dome to the right is the church of Hagia Sofia where runes were scratched by visiting Scandinavians.

The dome on the left is the Blue Mosque, built in the 17th cent. after the Turkish conquest.

Scandinavians were known by quite different names from those by which they were known in the west. Russian sources speak of *Rus* and *varjagi*; Byzantine sources mention *Rhos* and *varangoi*; and Islamic sources mention *Rus* and *Warank*. The terms are difficult to interpret, and only the second—*væringjar*—is also found in Scandinavian sources:

Rus/Rhos/Rus is the term which appears first; its earliest occurrence in a western source, the Frankish Annals of St Bertin, in the entry for 839: 'There came emissaries from the Greeks [Byzantium] sent out by Emperor Theophilus . . . The Emperor [Louis the Pious] met them in Ingelheim on 18 May . . . With the emissaries he [Theophilus] also sent men who called themselves the people of the Rhos. Their king, Chagan, had, they said, sent them in friendship. And he [Theophilus] desired . . . that through the goodwill of the emperor they might obtain leave and support to return home again through his empire, as their way to Constantinople led through the lands of barbaric and extremely wild people; he did not want them to use the same route on their homeward journey and thus expose themselves to danger. Close questioning about their journey led the emperor to conclude that they belonged to the people of the Svea and, as he thought that they were spies rather than peaceful emissaries to his and our kingdom, he decided to detain them until the true purpose of their journey could be discovered'.

Some years later, in the 840s, the Arabic scholar Ibn Khordadbeh wrote a geography of the world. At the end of his account he mentions Jewish merchants and continues, 'Concerning the trading routes which are used by the merchants among the Rus, who are a type of Saqaliba [best translated as 'northern people' or 'Europeans']; they trade in skins of beaver and black fox and swords, from the most distant tracts of the Saqlaba land to the Black Sea where the Byzantine emperor takes a tithe of them. And if they travel on the Don they pass Khamlidj, the town of the Khazars, where the prince takes a tithe of them. Then they sail out in the Caspian Sea and put in wherever they want on the coasts . . . They often take their wares on camel from Djordjan to Baghdad'.

An important later source is the ninth chapter of Constantine Porphyrogenetos's *De administrando imperio* which dates from about 950. In this he describes how the Slavo tribes each year build *monoxyla* (log-boats) and sail them to the Rhos in Kiev, who provide them with oars and other equipment so that in June they can set off down the Dnepr. The journey is perilous, both because the Dnepr rapids have to be navigated or circumvented by dragging or carrying the boats around them, and also because of the warlike nomads of the steppes who infest the banks. After many adventures

Fig. 2. Jewellery from a female grave in Kiev, Ukraine. 10th cent. The oval brooches are of Scandinavian type. Cat. no. 306.

on the river and the Black Sea, the Rhos reach Constantinople. Safe home again in the autumn the chieftains 'together with all the Rhos from Kiev' depart on 'poludia' (Slav: *poljud'e*, visiting, assembly of tribute and taxes) to their dependent Slav peoples where they stay over the winter and in spring they gather again in Kiev for a new voyage to Byzantium. Constantine Porphyrogenitos's description is very detailed. For instance, he gives the names of the Dnepr rapids in the language of the Rhos and of the Slavs; the Rhos names can be identified as Scandinavian, for example, 'Oulvorsi' (modern Swedish 'Holmforsen').

Thus, in the earliest times the term *Rus/Rhos/Rus* seems to describe Scandinavians who came from what is today Sweden to the regions of eastern Europe which in the tenth century grew into a state with its centre at Kiev—Rus/Rhosia/Rusiya, the early Russian state. Here they made up a specific class closely allied with the rulers. Judging by their names these rulers were often also Scandinavian. The Russian Primary (or Nestor) Chronicle indicates that the founder of the Kiev dynasty was Rurik (Scandinavian:

Rörik), a legendary figure whose historicity cannot be established; but his successors, his cousin Oleg (Helge), his son Igor (Ingvar) and wife Olga (Helga), are all known from reliable contemporary sources. Later generations of the dynasty have Slav names–Svjatoslav, Vladimir, Jaroslav—and from about this time, from the middle of the tenth century, Rus began to be used as the term for the Russian land and its ordinary inhabitants, where the Slav language and culture rapidly became dominant.

It is natural, therefore, to seek a Scandinavian origin for the name Rus; everything seems to support the interpretation, outlined as early as 1876 by the Danish philologist Vilhelm Thomsen, that the name derives from the Baltic Finnish *Ruotsi/Rootsi*, which in modern Finnish and Estonian means 'Swedish' but which itself derives from the Scandinavian *rodr* (modern Swedish *rodd*, rowing), a word which earlier also meant 'a crew of oarsmen'. With such a word the Scandinavians would have described themselves on their warlike and trading journeys across the Baltic Sea. Linguistic scholars think that the term was used in Baltic Finnish before the Viking Age. It is not known from Scandinavian historical sources but it does occur on two Uppland runestones of eleventh-century date. In one case it seems to mean rowing crew, 'He was the best farmer in Håkon's *rodr*'. In the other it seems to describe an area of land characterized by rowing, rowing crews and rowing routes. It tells of Toler, 'bailiff in the *rodr*' who erected the stone for the king. Uppland's coastal area was known as Roden in the middle ages, and the name lives on in today's Roslagen.

Varjagi, Varangians, is often used in Russian sources as a general term for Scandinavians. When the Nestor Chronicle, written in Kiev at the beginning of the twelfth century, decribes the appearance of the Rus in eastern Europe, the entry for 859 reads 'The Varangians from the other side of the sea' demanded tribute from various Finnish and Slav tribes. In 862 it is reported, 'The Varangians were driven over the sea and no tax was paid to them. People began to rule themselves, but there was neither law nor justice in the country. Tribe fought against tribe and civil war began. Then they said to each other, "Let us try to find a chief who can rule over us and administer the law among us" '. So they went over the sea to the Varangians, to the Rus. These Varangians are called Rus, just as others are called Svear. Some others are called Northmen, Angles or Gotlanders. The Čuds, Slavs, Krivičes and Ves said to the Rus, "Our land is great and fertile, but there is no rule in it. Come and rule us and lead us!" Three brothers and their retainers were chosen, and they took all the Rus with them, and came. The eldest brother, Rurik, settled in Novgorod; the second brother Sineus in Beloozero, and the third, Truvor, in Izborsk'.

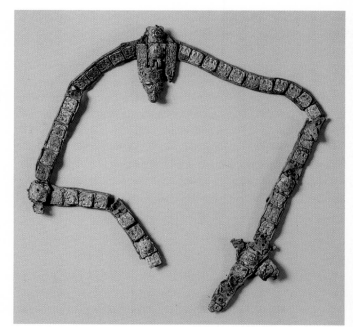

Fig. 3. Magnificent Scandinavian bridle from Gnezdovo, Russia. 10th cent. Cat. no. 301.

This broad sense of the word *varjag* cannot be original. In many citations in the Nestor Chronicle and other Russian texts, the Varangians appear both as Nordic warriors in the pay of the Russian chieftains, and also as merchants. Byzantine sources from the eleventh and twelfth centuries mention *Varangoi* as soldiers in a specific imperial guard which was made up of Scandinavians and, later, also Englishmen. It is in this sense that Varangians occur in Danish, Norwegian and Icelandic literature. The guard was called *vaering-jalid* (Varangian levy) and, if the sources are to be believed, was formed at the end of the tenth century. The most famous Varangian was Harald the Hard Ruler, descendant of St Olaf; after many years service in Byzantium and its colonies in Sicily, south Italy and Bulgaria, he returned to Norway to become its king (1047-66). Linguistic research has tried to derive the word *væringi* from a Nordic word *vár* (oath of allegiance) explaining that this would be a term relevant both to warriors and to merchants.

Warriors, merchants, colonists?

Written sources bear witness to the Scandinavians' activities in the east, both as soldiers and merchants, closely involved in the political developments which led to the rise of the early Russian state. Which of these activities were the more important for the travels in the east? Or was there possibly another factor, for example colonization, which played an important part in the expansion—as in the west?

We have a problem here. There are few written sources, and for the ninth and tenth centuries almost all the sources are from Byzantium or the Caliphate. These clearly do not give a complete picture of what was happening in eastern Europe. When the Nestor Chronicle mentions these centuries it relies mainly on oral tradition and it is not until the eleventh and twelfth centuries that we have good, more or less contemporary, written sources from Russia. It is the same in the North. The rich west Scandinavian sources date from the twelfth or thirteenth centuries or later. The information which they give about earlier times derives from oral tradition and is difficult to evaluate. Contemporary information is almost only provided by eleventh-century rune-stones. Thus archaeology is of the greatest importance —greater than in the west—in establishing the routes and the extent of easterly penetration. There is a great deal of archaeological evidence from the east—much more than from the west—and it is rapidly increasing through intensive Russian investigations on sites important in the origins of the Russian state. E. Nosov below (p. 82–3) outlines the new and remarkable finds from Staraja Ladoga and Novgorod. Here we will merely confine our discussion to general conclusions and pointers for the future.

The earliest Scandinavian finds from the area which was later to become the Russian state date from the 750s and come from Staraja Ladoga, the first trading centre on the route eastwards from the Gulf of Finland. By the second half of the eighth century, silver coins and other artifacts from the Islamic world were present here. The route mentioned by Ibn Khordadbeh must, then, have been in use at least half a century before he wrote his geography. At first, Scandinavian objects are few, but they increase in quantity towards the end of the ninth century, whilst in the tenth century there are many found in Pskov and the south-eastern Ladoga area in the north-west, Jaroslavl, Vladimir and Murom in the east, and at Kiev and Cernigov in the south (cat. no. 248, 268–312 and fig. 1). This distribution corresponds roughly to the extent of the Russian state, as described in the Nestor Chronicle. The most important sites are Gnezdovo outside Smolensk (cat. no. 300–4) and Bolšoe Timerevo near Jaroslavl (295–8).

The most numerous finds of undoubted Scandinavian origin are the oval brooches and other bronze jewellery characteristic of female dress (p. 192, fig. 1). These are often found in graves which are so similar to graves on the Scandinavian mainland that they must have belonged to Scandinavian immigrants. And, as there were so many

Fig. 4. Human representations in Scandinavian style from the Gnezdovo hoard, Russia. 10th cent. The filigree-decorated figure represents a woman. Cat. no. 304.

immigrant females keeping to their own fashions, we must assume whole families immigrated, men women and children.

Scholarly opinions differ; but I believe that the female jewellery, the amulets, and the other objects of mainland Scandinavian character (cat. no. 268, 278, 280–2, 300, 309) show that the Scandinavians came to Russia not only as traders and warriors, but also, for example, as farmers. The concentration of the finds along the waterways and in some important places, Gnezdovo on the Upper Dnepr for instance, suggests that Scandinavian colonization took place with the backing of northern chieftains and warriors who, according to the written sources, were active in the land.

Artifacts of Gotland, Finnish and East-Baltic origin are rare in Russia (cat. no. 274–5, 286) and we must assume that there were few emigrants from these regions during the Viking Age. Nevertheless, the rich finds from Gotland, Finland and the East Baltic countries, indicate intensive trading activities (cat. no. 143, 201, 249).

Scandinavian artifacts of ninth- and tenth-century date are rare outside the area of the Russian state, apart from some weapons found along the central and lower Volga, in the Crimea and in Romania. By contrast, objects of the nomadic people of the steppes and from the Caliphate are common in Scandinavia (cat. no. 27, 120–1, 132, 142–3, 314). Our thoughts may turn to the annals of St Bertin in which the king of the Rhos is called Chagan. This is not a Scandinavian name, but the royal title of the Khazars, a Turkish people who from the seventh to the middle of the

Fig. 5. Silver neck-rings from the Gnezdovo hoard, Russia's richest Viking Age hoard, which has many Scandinavian features. 10th cent. Cat. no. 304.

tenth centuries ruled a kingdom stretching from the Black Sea to the Caspian Sea, and from the Caucasus to the forests north of the steppes. There is much to suggest that the Khazars had a very strong political influence on the eastern Slavs before the consolidation of the early Russian state; and that the battles with the Khazars and later nomads, the Pecenegs and the Polovtsians, set a very pronounced stamp on the Rus warrior class and, through the Russian connections, on the warriors of Sweden. The dress of the wealthier classes in Birka and other places in Sweden was greatly influenced by the Orient, and belts, belt fittings,

axes and other objects in tenth-century graves not infrequently stem from the nomads of the steppes, or copy nomadic or even Islamic prototypes.

One of the reasons for the great influence from the steppe nomads was that the trade between the Caliphate and north and north-east Europe passed through their lands. Arabic

Fig. 6. The Vårby hoard, one of Sweden's most magnificent Viking Age hoards. 10th cent. The hoard contains objects from many countries; those from the East include belt-mounts and coins converted into pendants. Cat. no. 27.

Fig. 7. Axe of Parade, Russia. 11th cent. The motif with a snake pierced by a sword probably refers to the legend of the hero Sigurd, slayer of Fafnir. Cat. no. 299.

sources mention furs, slaves, falcons, honey and walrus ivory as being important products of the North. Ibn Khordadbeh also mentions swords, but they were probably not important in trade: it is not the European sword but the light, curved slashing sword of the nomads which became the symbol of the Caliphate's troops during this period. Silver, luxury clothing and silk flooded into the North from the Islamic world, and an impressive amount of silver and silk has been found in eastern and northern Europe. Many believe that the ninth- and tenth-century oriental trade along the rivers of eastern Europe was destined for western Europe, replacing trade along the classical routes through the Mediterranean which had been disrupted by the rise of Islam. Although this thesis is frequently discussed, it must be emphasized that what evidence we have for such long-distance trade through the Baltic to western Europe is difficult to interpret.

Byzantine objects are rare in Scandinavia during most of the Viking Age. This picture changes somewhat at the end of the tenth century when Byzantine Christianity became the official religion of the Russian state and Varangians formed part of the Byzantine army. Byzantine coins, however, do not rival in number the Islamic coins in Scandinavia—only some 600, compared with about 85,000 of the latter. In the eleventh century the Northmen left memorials of themselves in the Byzantine empire: runic scribbles in the church of Hagia Sophia, Constantinople, and a long runic inscription on a Classical marble lion which once stood in the harbour of Piraeus but which was taken as booty to Venice in the seventeenth century (p. 28, fig. 4). These inscriptions must have been carved by Varangians in the emperor's service. The route to the Byzantine empire is also marked by an eleventh-century runic memorial stone discovered on the island of Berezan at the mouth of the Dnepr in the Black Sea (cat. no. 312).

Epilogue

The political history of the tenth and beginning of the eleventh centuries contains many references to aristocratic connections between the Russian state and Scandinavia. The Norwegian king Olaf the Holy spent time at the court of Jaroslav the Wise in Novgorod during his exile before his return and death at the battle of Stiklestad in 1030. In fact these two kings were brothers-in-law, each married to a daughter of the Swedish king Olof Skötkonung. Jaroslav was married to Olof's legitimate daughter Ingegerd (in Russia called Irina and canonized), and Olof was married to the illegitimate daughter, Astrid. The fact that Jaroslav was given the legitimate daughter suggests that the Swedish king thought him the more powerful and important of the two.

There are few Scandinavian finds in Russia from the eleventh and twelfth centuries. By then the Nordic immigrants had probably been assimilated, and the new bands of Varangians who arrived were probably more strictly brought under the Byzantine rule which was established in the Russian state after its conversion to Orthodox Christianity. There are, however, a few examples of Scandinavian influence at this time (cat. no. 299, 311), and eastern influence on the North remained strong (cat. no. 239, 455, 486, 490–2, 495, 585). Many of the eleventh-century rune-stones

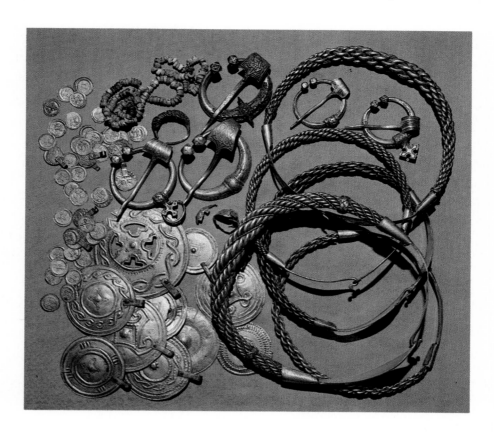

Fig. 8. Silver hoard from Kostivere, Estonia, deposited c. 1220–30 during the wars with the Danes and Germans. Cat. no. 253.

in Scandinavia tell of travels to *Gardar* and *Grekland* (Russia and Byzantium). *Serkland*, the Islamic world, is mentioned only in connection with a single journey—Ingvar the Widely-Travelled's disastrous voyage which was famous even on Iceland. One other eastern destination is mentioned: Jerusalem, which was the objective of many pilgrims during the earliest period of Christianity in Scandinavia (cat. no. 485).

During the twelfth century journeys to Byzantium and the interior of Russia became much more infrequent. There were fewer opportunities to serve in the imperial guard, and merchants ventured no further than Novgorod (cat. no. 290) and Smolensk, which became Russia's outlets to the west.

At the same time Scandinavian activities intensified in the Baltic countries. Trade, which largely seems to have emanated from Gotland, increased, particularly trade in magnificent swords and spearheads with silver decoration in the Urnes style (cat. no. 220, 228–30, 251–2). Warlike expeditions are mentioned in both directions across the Baltic Sea. Sigtuna in Sweden, for example, was attacked in 1187, and the Pope ordered the kings and bishops of Sweden and Denmark to mount a crusade against the heathens of Finland, Estonia and Kurland (cat. no. 253).

Christianity was fully imposed in the thirteenth century, bringing the Baltic countries into the sphere of the Roman Catholic church. Although parts of Estonia were under Danish rule for about a hundred years and Swedish farmers and fishermen settled along the coast of Estonia, the principal actors on the east Baltic stage were now no longer Scandinavians. Their place was taken by the Teutonic Knights and the Hanseatic merchants.

IJ

Fig. 9. The River Volkhov with Staraja Ladoga, the 'Aldeigjuborg' of the Scandinavians in the background on the right.

Staraja Ladoga, Gorodišče and Novgorod

Ladoga, Aldeigjuborg of the Nordic sagas, is the earliest trading and manufacturing centre of the northern part of eastern Europe (cat. no. 268–79). Founded in the middle of the eighth century near the mouth of the River Volchov, it has been known as Staraja (Old) Ladoga since the eighteenth century when Novaja (New) Ladoga was established closer to the mouth of the river. For the Vikings, Ladoga was the final objective of a sailing route through the Gulf of Finland, along the River Neva and the south coast of Lake Ladoga. Thence began the slow progress up-river, by long portages and dangerous rapids (particularly the Volkhov rapids, some 12 km to the south).

During the eighth and ninth centuries Ladoga was a large, unfortified settlement which concentrated on long-distance trade; it was an advanced manufacturing base with a multi-ethnic population; little importance was attached to

agriculture. In this way it may be compared with all the other early trading and manufacturing centres of the Baltic Sea.

Ladoga was not, as has sometimes been suggested, a fortified colony built by the Vikings, but there can be no doubt the Scandinavian presence there dates from the earliest periods of its history (cat. no. 268, 274). The earliest archaeological layer (E3) produced an oval brooch of seventh or eighth-century type, part of an iron neck-ring (probably a Thor's-hammer ring) of a type known in Sweden in the century before the Viking Age, a number of small wheel-shaped discs of Swedish type, and a small bronze handle with pre-Viking-age decoration. These objects of Scandinavian type were brought to Ladoga by the Vikings, some as personal belongings, others as trade goods: some were also made there.

Ladoga's multi-ethnic character is confirmed by the many different types of burials found in its neighbourhood. The Scandinavian cemetery of Plakun, of ninth- and tenth-century date, lay opposite Ladoga on the eastern bank of the Volchov. Nowadays only eighteen mounds are known, but some scholars believe that the cemetery may have covered an area some three times this size. Excavations have revealed cremations in boats, and an inhumation in a chamber-grave covered by a burnt boat. A striking feature of the burial rite was a sword thrust vertically into the ground near one of the graves. The grave-goods include sherds of two Tating-ware jugs with tinfoil decoration which come from Frisia. Both male and female burials are found: thus the graves represent a permanent, settled population in Ladoga, not simply warriors or merchants temporarily visiting the town.

Osteological examination of eighty-two Christian burials from the cemetery of the eleventh-century church of St Clement has demonstrated the presence of a Scandinavian anthropological type among Ladoga's population. The graves with these skeletons were confined to a specific area of the churchyard.

Trade and manufacture were highly developed in Ladoga and led to its becoming a great international port and trading centre for the Baltic region. But the absence of agricultural settlements around the town, and its position at the very edge of the Slav world prevented it from becoming a centre of the land of the Slovenes (the 'Novgorod Slavs').

The area of the upper Volchov was very different from that of the river downstream. At the end of the first millennium AD the sources of the Volkhov and the areas adjacent to Lake Ilmen in the north-west was the centre of a Slav population which had settled there. The main cause of development in this area was its fertile soils (which are suitable for agriculture) and its advantageous situation which enabled it to exact tribute from the people around Lake Ilmen. It was also placed at the crossing of important east-European trade routes (those between the Baltic Sea and the Volga, and the famous 'route from the Varangians to the Greeks', from the Baltic Sea to the Dnepr and the Black Sea).

Many Slav settlements lay on the low hills of the flood plain of the Volchov and Lake Ilmen. The most important of these was Gorodišče (the 'old town' or 'old fort'), which has often been called Ryurikovo Gorodišče by historians since the beginning of the nineteenth century. It is mentioned in Russian chronicles from 1103 onwards as the residence of the princes of Novgorod, having been one of the centres of Novgorod political life since the ninth century. Its topography determined its importance. Situated on an island where the Volchov river divides into two branches, Gorodišče formed a naturally defended focus for the surrounding land and the Lake Ilmen basin. The site was ideal for a trading and manufacturing settlement which could also control the abundant water traffic.

Gorodišče of the ninth and tenth centuries occupied an area of some four to seven hectares. Its centre, about one and a half hectares in extent, was surrounded by a ditch and, perhaps, a rampart. The objects discovered here indicate wide international trading connections and much manufacturing activity. The settlement was strongly influenced by northern Europe. In the ninth and tenth centuries it was inhabited by Slavs and Scandinavians (cat. no. 280–8), the Scandinavians being represented by two rune-inscribed amulets of sheet bronze, the figure of a Valkyrie, equal-armed and oval brooches, an iron Thor's hammer neck-ring and so on. Some brooches and mounts were made in the Scandinavian style in Gorodišče itself, according to the tastes of its inhabitants of Scandinavian origin—men and women, artisans and merchants, and warriors who served in the military guard of the Russian princes.

Novgorod (literally 'New town' or ' New fortress') was founded later than Gorodišče, about 2 km downstream from it. The first settlement on the site of future Novgorod appeared in the middle of the tenth century, and the 'New' fortress was built in 1044. Thus, Gorodišče (Old town) must have been its predecessor.

When the Scandinavians first reached Lake Ilmen, Novgorod was not in existence and the centre of the north Rus was called Holmgarðr. Place-name scholars have interpreted this name in several ways. Holmgarðr could mean 'the settlement on the island', or 'the settlements on the islands'. Whatever the explanation, Holmgarðr must be related to Gorodišče, which was the main site in the area.

Novgorod has produced some objects of Scandinavian type (cat. no. 289–90), but they are fewer than those from Gorodišče. It could be that Scandinavians lived only in defined areas of the town such as the market place and the royal court, in which there have been no major excavations.

Gorodišče—a trading, manufacturing, military and administrative centre on the confluence of the Volchov and Ilmen—seems to continue the functions of Ladoga, being a later variant of the same type of town. The difference between Gorodišče/Novgorod and Ladoga is that the geographical position of the former places enabled them to gather together all the strands of administration, and so become the capital of the northern Rus.

ENN

Fig. 1. The Slav temple-fortress of Arkona on the northern point of Rügen, Germany.

The West Slav lands and the North

Joachim Herrmann

For thousands of years contacts have existed between the peoples of the Scandinavian countries and those of the lands south of the Baltic Sea. In the Viking Age these ties reached new levels. These contacts led to the establishment of close relations on a number of levels between communities of different ethnic origins.

At the beginning of the Viking Age, Slav tribes and groups of tribes consolidated themselves politically to the east of the Elbe and the Bay of Kiel (that is to the east of the *Limes Saxoniae*, by which name this border of the Carolingian empire was known). The Obotrites were settled on the Bay of Wismar, to the east of the Saxons. The Wiltzi occupied the regions south of the mouth of the Warnow as far as Oderhaff. Some of the coastal areas beyond—particularly all the island of Rügen—were inhabited by the Rugieris. On both sides of the eastern mouth of the Oder (the Dziwna) lived the inhabitants of Wolin. They, like the Rugieris, were well-known to Arab geographers. East of the people of Wolin and as far as the mouth of the Vistula, groups of Slav tribes of different origin had settled and became known under the collective term 'Pomeranians' (literally, people of the sea). From the last decade of the tenth century, the Poles and their rulers sought with varying degrees of success to

incorporate into their confederation of states the Wolins and the Pomeranians and thus take over the coastal areas between the Oder and the Vistula.

These tribes were from time to time allies or enemies of the Franks, the Saxons, and the Scandinavians. Their commercial and cultural relations with the Scandinavian countries have left few traces in the written record. Archaeological discoveries, however, show that close cultural and commercial ties existed with Scandinavia from the eighth or ninth centuries.

From the end of the eighth century similar contacts existed with those parts of Saxony which belonged to the Frankish empire. These contacts were also related to the missionary zeal of the expanding Carolingian superpower. This missionary endeavour was aimed both at the Slav tribes of the southern Baltic and at the Scandinavians.

According to an eleventh-century source, monks from Corvey had reached the Slav coastal regions, and particularly Rügen, as early as the reign of Louis the Pious (814–40) in order to pursue their mission. A monk from Corvey, Ansgar, was sent by Louis to Denmark in 826 as a missionary. In 830 he travelled for the first time to Birka, in Sweden, and in 831 was appointed the first bishop and later (in 834)

Fig. 2. Gold hoard from the island of Hiddensee, Rügen. Second half of the 10th cent. Cat.
no. 265.

the first archbishop of Hamburg. He became papal legate to the Swedes, the Danes and the Slavs. The archdiocese of Hamburg was founded deliberately as a missionary diocese for both the Scandinavians and the Slavs, and thus became involved in the political, military and religious conflicts of the region.

Hamburg, situated on the border between the Frankish/ Saxon empire, Denmark and the Slav Obotrites, was exposed to all sorts of problems. As a result of Scandinavian assaults, as well as threats from the Obotrites, the seat of the archbishop was after 845 transferred to Bremen. The archdiocese of Hamburg-Bremen did, however, exercise considerable influence over Christian activities in Scandinavia, particularly in the tenth century, under the Saxon kings and the Ottonian emperors. As well as having an

important role in founding four Danish dioceses, it also established the diocese of Oldenburg just south of the Baltic coast in 968. Due to revolts among the Danes and the Slavs in 982–83, new alliances were formed which did not attain any lasting result until the beginning of the twelfth century. These reasonably well-documented military, political and missionary relations were established on the basis of lively mutual contacts between the peoples of the South Baltic and Scandinavia. These relations had reached a significant level as early as the eighth century, and Slav objects from the southern Baltic are found in archaeological contexts in Scandinavia. Likewise Scandinavian objects are found in the south Baltic regions. As well as such objects as single pieces of jewellery, weapons, and coins, hoards like those from Hiddensee and Ralswiek have been found—as has material

Fig. 3. Amber from workshops in the town of Wolin, Poland. Cat. no. 254.

from the merchant centre of Wolin and settlements and burial grounds in the region of the Pomeranians (cat. no. 255, 257–66).

There were many other types of contact which locked Scandinavian and Slav history together. Reasonably continuous trade and exchange primarily determined the relations between the coastal Slavs and the Scandinavians. As a result, merchant settlements were found in areas belonging to Slav tribes. These were to a great extent of markedly Scandinavian character, although the material culture was largely Slav. Similarly, artisans and merchants of Slav descent settled in or near Danish and Swedish markets.

War and raids nevertheless played a not inconsiderable part in the relations between the two groups of people. The first record of a Danish raid among the Obotrites occurs in 808. On that occasion Rerik (near Wismar/Mecklenburg), which was the Obotrite centre of commerce, was destroyed and the merchants were moved to Haithabu. A year later, the Danish king Godfred had the Obotrite king Dražko murdered, and so the bloody story continued. In 1168 or 1169 an end to this strife was achieved with the capture by the Danish king Waldemar and bishop Absalon of the Slav temple and fortification of Arkona (fig. 1), which brought large areas of the Slav coastal territory under Danish control.

The Danish conquests were partly carried out with—and partly in competition with and in spite of—the mighty Saxon duke Henry the Lion. As a result of these conquests Rügen became part of the diocese of Roskilde, which worked for Christian conversion. Mass baptisms took place

as early as 1168/9 and churches sprang up in Bergen and Altenkirchen to the south of Arkona. Monks from Denmark settled in the monasteries of Dargun near Demmin, Eldena near Greifswald and Kolbatz near Szczecin.

From the tenth century onwards Obotrite rulers and Polish dukes had been related by marriage to the ruling Danish families. The Danes exploited these connections in order to establish their supremacy on the southern coast of the Baltic, with help from Scandinavian settlers in Julin/Wolin (which is sometimes identified with Jómsburg). At the Obotrite-Wagrian fortification of Oldenburg in Holstein, archaeology has revealed numerous indications of close Scandinavian-Slav contacts in the tenth century.

Scandinavian influence was directed towards the coastal areas, and Danish campaigns did not go beyond the northern Slav regions, although occasionally they ventured into the areas of influence of the German empire (or rather that of the Saxons), but such happenings were rarely long lived.

Markets

From the second half of the eighth century trading places were established in the Slav areas west of the Oder, with substantial participation by Scandinavians. In the ninth century these achieved greater significance, whereas in the course of the tenth century such relations naturally receded as the Slav regions were conquered by the Germans. They are mentioned rarely in the historical record.

The following coastal market-places have been more or less comprehensively uncovered by archaeologists: Usedom

Fig. 4. Silver hoard from the trading site of
Ralswiek, Rügen. First half of the 9th cent.
Cat. no. 260.

by the western mouth of the Oder/Peene; Menzlin on the
lower Peene; Ralswiek and the temple castle of Arkona on
Rügen; and Rostock-Dierkow on the mouth of the Warnow.
Reric on the Bay of Wismar, not far from the main fortified
centre of the Obotrites at Mecklenburg, was a coastal market place until the beginning of the ninth century, although
the evidence for this is negligible. Similarly, there is no
archaeological evidence for commercial settlement at the
harbour that doubtless belonged to Oldenburg.

On the eastern mouth of the Oder stood Wolin—founded
probably in the ninth century it is also known in later
sources as Julin, Jumne, Jómsborg and finally Vineta. It was
to become the most powerful trading place in the West-Slav
coastal region. In the eleventh century, Wolin ranked 'as
one of the greatest of all cities of Europe; in it live Slavs and
other tribes, Greeks and barbarians. Also foreigners from
Saxony have the right of domicile. . . . The city is crammed
with goods of all the peoples of the North . . .', so wrote the
historian Adam of Bremen in purple prose. Decades of
excavations in Wolin have confirmed his account and in
particular proved the close ties between Wolin and the
Scandinavian regions (cat. no. 254–9). These relations have
found lively, if rather fictional, expression in *Jómsvíkinga saga*
(cat. no. 523).

East of Wolin, as early as the seventh or eighth century,
the coastal trading station of Kołobrzeg at the mouth of the
Parsetas was founded, based on the production of salt.
Further coastal trading points between the mouths of the
Oder and the Vistula were of more local significance. The
significance of a coastal trading point on the western mouth

of the Vistula near Puck north of Gdańsk is still not clear.
On the eastern mouth of the Vistula, almost in the country
of the Baltic Prussians, was situated in the ninth century the
coastal market-place of Truso (near the modern city of
Elbląg). Towards the end of the ninth century, an Anglo-
Saxon trader, Wulfstan, clearly described the sailing route
from Haithabu to Truso. Further to the west a Baltic trading-
place was evidently established to the south of the mouth of
the Njemen near Wiskiauten. Numerous finds of Scandinavian origin are known both from the region of Truso, as well
as from Wiskiauten. From the end of the tenth century, the
Polish state largely controlled the mouth of the Vistula. The
foundation of the fortress at Gdańsk, with its harbour and
settlements of artisans and tradesmen, gradually led to the
collapse of the old coastal markets of the region.

Excavations at Ralswiek on Rügen, have revealed details
of a typical Baltic trading-place. It was established in the last
quarter of the eighth century and had room for mooring
some fourteen or fifteen ships, there was a cult-place on the
beach and cemeteries in the neighbourhood. The settlement
was fundamentally organized around plots or groups of
houses to which belonged a main house and secondary
living- and working quarters. In these structures were
objects for domestic use and for trade.

Four ships—each of different function—were uncovered.
From the settlement and from the burial sites numerous
objects have been found—both of Scandinavian origin and
from other localities—brought to the site across the Baltic
(cat. no. 260–2). Among them was the fantastic treasure
fig. 4.

The Scandinavians and the Western European continent

Lucien Musset

The Vikings began to take an interest in the continent at about the same time as in the British Isles, that is during the closing years of the 8th century. The first known raid took place in 799 on the coast of what is now known as Vendée. It was undoubtedly the work of Norwegians. Very soon afterwards more raids followed: Charlemagne was anticipating them in 800, when he made a tour of inspection of the coastal regions between the Schelde and the Seine. The plundering expeditions continued, more or less regularly, until the middle of the 11th century. Altogether, the Viking period in this region lasted for the greater part of three centuries.

In the course of this long period there were many things that changed: the protagonists, their goals, our sources of information. Here, as in other regions, there was a clear break between "the first age of the Vikings", which came to an end about 930, and the second, much shorter, period of activity extending approximately from 990 to 1050. The Norwegians would seem to have been in the majority among the earlier raiders but the Danes soon usurped this position. From the first period we have hardly any other sources of information than Latin documents, while for the second phase there are some Scandinavian runic inscriptions, from which a few scraps of knowledge can be gleaned, and some illumination can be derived from Nordic literary sources. At all events, the pursuit of booty of every description would seem to have been the driving force behind the raids. Later, there was added to this the desire to seize exploitable territory and strategic positions.

Political motives also played a role on several occasions. At the beginning of the 9th century, there might have been a Danish desire to retaliate for the Frankish thrust into Saxony, then a wish to profit from the breaking up of the Frankish empire, and finally a desire to find a role to play in the dealings between England and her continental neighbours. There is no doubt, however, that it was to satisfy their appetite for riches, social status and glory that the Viking chiefs most often launched their assaults upon the West.

The social and economic context did not remain unchanged, particularly once the Scandinavian countries had recognised the value of coins as a means of exchange.

Hardly any trace has survived of the tremendous sums paid by the Carolingians in the 9th century. The metal that was handed over to the Vikings was almost always melted down immediately. The situation was completely different in the second Viking age. There was one thing that did not change, however, the capture of slaves remained a major motive from beginning to end (although this did not of course leave any archaeological traces behind). It is useless to ask whether the growth in wealth which can be traced in Scandinavia was first and foremost the result of an economy based on booty or of a positive balance of trade. There is no reliable way of determining this (cf. cat. no. 26, 122, 135). It is my own opinion that trade can hardly have become the most important element before the end of the 11th century.

In the beginning the Viking raids followed upon each other at irregular intervals, later they occurred more regularly. To begin with they were seasonal, taking place in the summer. Then they began to last longer, first for a whole year and soon even several years, with the Vikings taking up winter quarters on an island off the coast (e.g. Walcheren, Noirmoutier) or in a river, or in a fortified camp inland (such as Louvain in 884–892). One such 'army' might even continue in operation for six years, as happened in Gaul in 856–862. A number of the young men in Scandinavia were occupied in these ventures but there is no indication that the levies were really large. In fact it was neither an imaginary numerical superiority nor hatred of Christianity—as the West imagined—that was the cause of the long-lasting success of the Vikings, but rather the employment of new methods, the possession of excellent ships (the kingdoms on the continent had no fleets), a certain audacity, a remarkable ability to adapt to circumstances, possibly also a good intelligence network that enabled them to profit from the divisions between their opponents. It was all this that contributed to the widely held view that they employed diabolical stratagems. Their weaponry, on the other hand, could hardly be said to reflect radical innovations, although they did make greater use of the bow and the axe.

The Danes, more than the Norwegians, demonstrated an inclination to be law-abiding when the opportunity presented itself. They attempted to secure the property they had acquired by entering into legal agreements with their

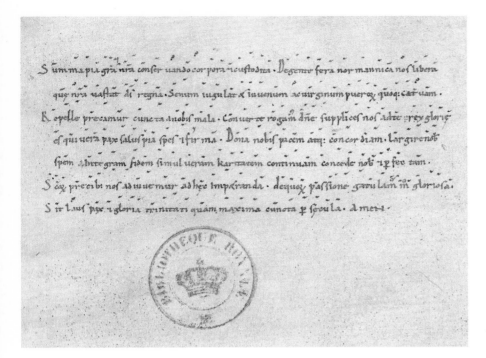

Fig. 1. Antiphonal from north France with a prayer for protection against Viking attacks. Second half of the 9th cent. Cat. no. 351.

victims and, as early as the 9th century, their lands were sometimes obtained by treaty and not merely by conquest.

Unfortunately, the direct contributions made by archaeology to our knowledge of Viking enterprises on the Continent are very slight. Even when the written documents or the linguistic evidence confirm that the influence of the

Fig. 2. Oval brooches from a female grave, Pîtres, Normandy. Around 900. Cat. no. 366. This is the only Scandinavian female grave known from the west continental mainland, although there are many in the British Isles and eastern Europe.

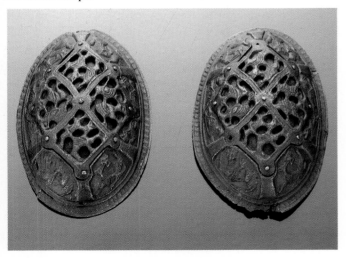

Vikings must have been considerable, as in Normandy, the results of archaeological research remain almost negligible. Paradoxically, it is on an island in Brittany (Groix) that the only boat-grave in the region has been found (cat. no. 360). Indications of resistance made by the natives are also very few: some fortresses along the cost of Flanders and Zeeland, a single small fort at Igoville, near Pont-de-l'Arche (Seine-Maritime) in Normandy, and perhaps Camp de Péran in Brittany (cat. no. 359). A few Scandinavian weapons have been found in rivers. There is only one grave on the continent which is certainly Scandinavian. This is the grave of a woman at Pîtres, on the Andelle, dating from the beginning of the 10th century (cat. no. 366).

The Viking attacks were comparatively isolated events to begin with. It was as though they were feeling their way by making some swift raids on the coasts in order to seize a few cattle, some slaves or movable goods, without penetrating into the interior. Later, they began to sail up the great rivers and explore their banks, and then set out from there to launch raids on the interior—often several hundred kilometres inland. Once the Carolingian kingdom had split up such ventures multiplied in the West Frankish kingdom and Lorraine. Saxony, which was in a position to make reprisals on Denmark, did not suffer so severely.

A new phase began when the resources of the lands under attack began to be exhausted. The Vikings then employed violence not only in direct pursuit of booty but also to

terrorise the people and persuade them to ransom themselves at a very high price. This was the era of the
'Danegelds', to employ a term borrowed from England.
Under an able leader, one and the same band of Vikings
would be able to double its profit by departing to intimidate
a second region while the first was gathering together the
amount of ransom demanded. At last, when the enfeebled
victims were no longer able to pay, one final method
remained: taking over the land—the source of all
wealth—and its direct exploitation.

The rhythm according to which these episodes follow one
upon the other varies from land to land. In western Gaul,
for example, the first expeditions up-river took place about
840, the first overwinterings of the armies were in 843 (on
the coast) and in 851 (inland), the first local ransoms were
paid about 841, the first full-scale regional 'Danegeld' in
845, and the conquest of Paris took place in the same year. It
was not until later that any territory was ceded to the
Vikings. The first lands seized by the Vikings yielded them
little profit and they soon abandoned their project (as in 826
in Rüstringen on the lower reaches of the Weser). Later,
however, profiting from their experiences in England, the
Vikings made a lasting success of their take-overs: the classical example is the colony established in 911 on the lower
Seine, the nucleus of the later duchy of Normandy.

One of the conditions in the treaties concluded with the
Frankish authorities was the acceptance of baptism by the
leader of the band in question. From 863, however, doubts
were expressed as to the efficacy of a sacrament administered under such conditions. The sending of Christian missions to Denmark and Sweden in the reign of Louis the
Pious (Ebo, archbishop of Rheims, and then Ansgar, a
monk from Corvey) can hardly be said to have met with
more lasting success. It was not until the 10th century that
things began to change.

The composition of the raiding bands varied greatly.
None of the bands, however, was a "national" army from
one of the Scandinavian countries. Recruited from among
volunteers or their personal followers by noble leaders, some
of royal rank, they contained men from many countries.
The army which settled in Normandy, for example, undoubtedly consisted mainly of Danes, even though the leader was
a Norwegian. Sometimes it even happened that exiles from
the continent enrolled in the bands. These "armies" would
keep together for several years, as long as they were successful, moving from place to place. Once they had exhausted
the resources in a region or after a defeat, however, the
troops would disperse, some to return home to the North,
others to take part in some other venture.

Such accounts of all these expeditions as are to be found

in the written sources tend to concentrate especially on their
negative aspects. Monotonous entries accumulate in the
chronicles: monasteries devastated (the monks, whose voca-
tion prohibited them from bearing weapons and whose
monasteries were often very wealthy, were an obvious target
for attack), towns sacked and burned (but not completely
destroyed, with such rare exceptions as fortresses like Bonn
or settlements built of wood such as Dorestad and Quen-
tovic), priests fleeing in every direction carrying their treasures and relics, the inability of the Frankish leaders to
organise any resistance (mobilisation was a slow process and
the Vikings tended to avoid pitched battles). In this way
Francia occidentalis was reduced to ruins and completely de-
stabilised.

When the Scandinavian raids began again after the relative calm of the years 930–980, it was in a less pulsating
rhythm as far as the continent was concerned. The ports of
Frisia, on the Weser and the lower Rhine, were sacked.
There were incursions of pirates on the coast of Aquitaine
and more important raids on Spain but there was nothing
comparable to the expeditions of the second half of the 9th
century. The last waves of Viking attacks ebbed away in the
1050s and, with the beginning of the conversion of Scandinavia, the general climate soon changed.

Now it is time to take stock in a more well-balanced
manner than is normal in traditional history-books. There is
no doubt that the damage inflicted by the Vikings was
considerable: aristocratic lineages were decimated, bishops
massacred—three in Gaul alone in a single year, 858–859,
monks killed, captured or held to ransom, bands of slaves
carried off to Scandinavia or resold, towns withered away
within their walls, while refugees and burial grounds
covered urban areas. The scope of our enquiry must be
expanded, however, so that less catastrophic effects can be
recorded. Firstly, there were tentative but intelligent
attempts at resistance (such as the idea of blocking the great
rivers by means of fortified bridges, initiated by Charles the
Bald in 862), other more spontaneous actions (such as the
restoration from about 860 or 870 of most of the town walls
originally constructed under the late Roman Empire, or the
building of protective walls around some suburban areas, as
in Arras). These actions did provide some form of protection, as shown by the checking of the Vikings in front of
Paris (in 885–886). No region was entirely depopulated.
Considerable quantities of precious metals that had been
lying idle in the treasuries of the churches were returned

*Fig. 3. Gold hoard from Hon, Norway. Second half of the 9th cent. The
large trefoil brooch is Frankish, and most of the hoard was probably
assembled in Francia. Cat. no. 26.*

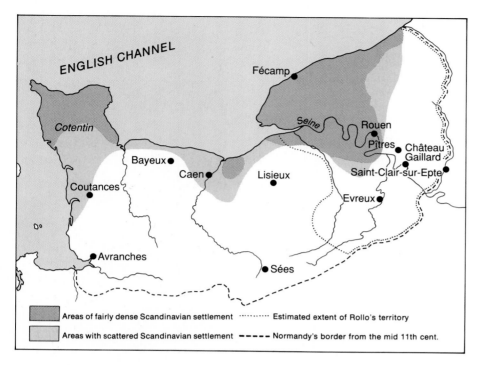

Fig. 4. Normandy.

into circulation, encouraging new economic currents to flow around the coasts of western Europe.

The first Viking expeditions were along the coasts of Gaul and Saxony; in 844 they reached Spain and in 859 they discovered the straits of Gibraltar. The northern coasts of the western Mediterranean were ravaged for some years: Muslim Spain, the South of France, Liguria and no doubt Tuscany. For a short time, the valley of the Rhône served as their axis of penetration. A few pirates even raided the coast of Morocco. No lasting gains were made in this area, which soon became the preserve of the Saracens (Muslims). The road to the Mediterranean was not forgotten, however. It served as an inspiration for the Norwegian crusades in the 12th century.

There were quite considerable settlements of Scandinavian colonists along the coast of Flanders and in neighbouring regions but these had no political significance. Normandy, on the other hand was a remarkable success. The Vikings had attempted to establish themselves along the lower reaches of two of the great rivers of France: on the Seine at Rouen in 911 and on the Loire at Nantes in 919. The second of these settlements collapsed after 937 but the first continued to expand and establish itself more securely. At the end of one generation, it was secure enough to withstand the great crisis which befell the Scandinavian colonies in the West in the middle of the 10th century (the Frankish king reoccupied Rouen in 943–945 but soon had to

beat a retreat from there). This was because the first leader to establish himself in Rouen, Rollo (Hrólfr), had been wise enough to base his realm (which was first known as a county and then—from the beginning of the 11th century—as a duchy) on close cooperation between Scandinavian immigrants (who continued to arrive until about 1020) and native Franks. He took upon himself the responsibility for preventing other bands of Vikings from sailing up the Seine—and kept his word. He recalled the archbishop to Rouen, while his son, William Longsword, gave endowments to the monks, reintroduced the striking of coinage (cat. no. 403) and married a Carolingian princess.

As the state of Normandy gradually expanded westwards (Central Normandy in 926, Western Normandy in 933), it would seem to have absorbed another army, of Anglo-Danish origin, which had settled in the Bessin, as well as some Celtic-Norwegians who had settled in the Cotentin. As was customary when treaties were made with Frankish kings, Rollo had agreed to be baptised. His companions followed his example and most of them married native women and began to speak the local French dialect. Well before the end of the 10th century, the Normans had almost unanimously elected to join forces with the Christian countries that surrounded them (cf. cat. no. 436).

The Scandinavian imprint on the area nevertheless remained obvious. Although there had not been immigration on a massive scale, many of the place-names are of

Some examples of Scandinavian personal names in Normandy

Scandinavian form	11th-century Latin form	Modern French form
Ásbjǫrn	Osbernus	Auber
Ásfriðr	Ansfridus	Anfray
Ásgautr	Ansgotus	Angot
Ásketill	Anschetillus	Anquetil
Ásmundr	Osmundus	Osmond
Thorgautr	Turgotus	Turgot
Thorgisl	Turgisus	Turgis
Thorsteinn	Turstinus	Toutain
Thorvaldr	Turoldus	Thouroude

Some examples of Scandinavian place-names in Normandy

Names in -*tot* Scandinavian *toft* "building-plot"

Old form	Date	Modern form	Meaning
Bramatot	1025	Brametot (Seine-Maritime)	Brami's building-plot
Coletot	1080	Colletot (Eure)	Koli's building-plot
Esculetot	1220	Écultot (Seine-Maritime)	Skúli's building-plot
Gonnetot	1206	Gonnetot (Seine-Maritime)	Gunni's building-plot
Herguetot	1232	Herquetot (Manche)	Helgi's building-plot
Ketetot	1200	Quettetot (Manche)	Ketill's building-plot

Some characteristic generics

bec 'stream', e.g. Carbec "Kári's stream"; Clarbec "the clear stream"
dalle 'valley', e.g. Oudalle "the valley of the wolves"
hom 'island, damp meadow', from Scandinavian *holmr*
hogue 'mound', from Scandinavian *haugr*
londe 'grove', from Scandinavian *lundr*
tourp 'hamlet', from Scandinavian *thorp*

Fig. 5. The Viking chieftain Rollo, founder of the Duchy of Normandy, was buried in Rouen cathedral, as were many of his descendants. His funerary monument dates from the 14th cent. and has been heavily restored.

Scandinavian origin (on the level of villages, not towns) in the Pays de Caux, the coastal area of the Bessin and the north of the Cotentin. A quite considerable number of Scandinavian personal names (mostly masculine but some few feminine ones) have survived (cat. no. 437). In the 11th century, a section of the upper nobility as well as people with maritime connections—for example whalers, who were quite numerous at that time—were very conscious of their Scandinavian origin. The peasant population, which was clearly in the minority, betrayed little trace of Scandinavian influence except for some agricultural terminology and a number of field-names in the west. The urban milieu was hardly affected by the Vikings and Norman art owes nothing to Scandinavian influence. Normandy nevertheless persisted for a long time as a mixed state with two faces—one Scandinavian, which was gradually fading, and the other Frankish, which little by little became the dominant one.

Fig. 6. Scene from the Bayeux tapestry, embroidered in the 1070s. William the Conqueror has crossed the Channel in specially built ships and made landfall in England. Soon afterwards he defeated the Anglo-Saxon king Harold Godwinson at the battle of Hastings and was crowned as king of England at Christmas 1066.

The only surviving traces of the Scandinavian dialect and Scandinavian law are to be found in matters concerned with the sea but it is certain that the local ducal dynasty remained aware and proud of its origin for centuries.

The originality of the Norman contribution to 11th-century France is open to discussion. There are those who consider that the "Norman myth" was created by the great Anglo-Norman historians of the 12th century. It is nevertheless certain that after the Norman population had been fully integrated into Frankish society, it retained certain characteristics which derived from the Scandinavian colonisation of the 10th century: an inextinguishable spirit of adventure, an ability to adapt to greatly varying conditions and to exploit these, a liking for effective political methods, a sense of solidarity uniting all emigrants from the Duchy.

Today it is clear that the conquests made by the Normans of Normandy in the 11th and 12th centuries can no longer be laid to the account of the Vikings. It can hardly have been before the 1030s that warfare in foreign parts became the most profitable industry of the Normans. Let us briefly mention the countries they visited: the southern third of Italy, which they approached by the overland route from about the 1020s; Sicily, conquered between 1060 and 1091; Antiochia and its principalities, about 1100; without taking account of the abortive settlements in Anatolia, Dalmatia, Catalonia (Tarragona), and, of course, England, acquired after the victory of William the Conqueror at the Battle of Hastings on 14th October 1066 (and the subsequent expansion into Ireland in the 12th century).

William was not a Viking but the ships which enabled him to disembark his forces in England owed much to Scandinavian traditions, as can be seen from the 'Bayeux Tapestry', and many of the military commanders who accompanied him were, like himself, of partially Scandinavian descent. The clerics who described the glorious exploits of William and his descendants rarely omitted to mention this. Nevertheless, in the period 1020–1030, a deep cleft had developed which separated Normandy from its links with Scandinavia. Although a few bonds can be seen to have been made between the Franks and the Scandinavians in the 12th and 13th centuries, these were not made because of Normandy. They simply reflect the prestige enjoyed by French civilisation under the Capetians and by French ecclesiastical schools.

This is, in fact, the route by which the first Norman author to write meaningfully about Denmark acquired his information. His name was Etienne de Rouen and he was active in the middle of the 12th century. Almost all the important men in the Danish church at the end of the 12th

Fig. 7. The Seine valley near Les Andelys (south-east of Rouen) with Richard the Lionheart's Château Gaillard. Richard was both king of England and duke of Normandy, and the castle was built 1196–8 to protect Normandy against the French king Philip August. In 1204 Château Gaillard was taken, and Normandy came under French control; for 300 years its lordship had been in the hands of the Vikings and their successors.

century and the beginning of the 13th had links with France: Archbishop Eskil (1137–1178) resided in Clairvaux on several occasions and died there; his successor, Absalon, the founder of Copenhagen (1178–1201), studied at Sainte-Geneviève in Paris, as did his nephew and successor, Anders Suneson (1201–1228). Under their patronage were written several Latin works of very high quality, owing much to their authors' education in France (cat. no. 528–30, cf. 466). The same contacts, however, were responsible for a political experiment which ended in disaster: the idea of forming an alliance between the Danish and French dynasties—by arranging for the marriage in 1193 of Philip II Augustus with the Danish princess Ingeborg, the sister of King Knud VI. It was only with great difficulty that the poor girl was rescued from the semi-captivity in which she was held by her husband, who had been filled with loathing for her immediately after their marriage (cat. no. 538).

Paris remained a great centre of attraction for Scandinavian students until the 14th century. It is merely to be looked upon as a rhetorical exercise, however, when Etienne de Tournai, the Abbot of Sainte-Geneviève, in about 1189 reminds Absalon and his king of the responsibility of their ancestors for the havoc wrought in the 9th century. Other points of contact have also been of significance but the famous episode in *Orkneyinga saga* in which the Orkney earl Rǫgnvald Kali composes love poems to Ermengarde, viscountess of Narbonne, seems undeniably most likely to be a literary embellishment (cat. no. 525).

Even if the Viking raids were one of the most important episodes in the history of the European continent in the medieval period, their significance should not be exaggerated: in the long run their consequences can hardly be said to have extended beyond the 9th century.

The Scandinavians in Britain and Ireland

David M. Wilson with a contribution by Richard Hall

The seas between Britain and Scandinavia have been at once a highway and a barrier throughout history. In the eighth century traders from Britain became a familiar element in the market-places of the continental North Sea coastline, whilst Scandinavians from the disparate kingdoms and polities of the North began to make their presence known in Britain. Merchants described as "Frisian" in Anglo-Saxon sources may well have been Danes and the fight in *c.* 789 at Portland on the south coast of England between a royal official's party and seamen from Hordaland in Norway was probably little more than a trading brawl which got out of hand and which was written up because of the murder of an important English official. The kingdoms of Britain in the eighth century lived in comparative peace and affluence; although politically divided, they were all Christian and united in doctrine and practice. This was a high period of British art and scholarship.

England had become politically and economically stable. The lands to the north of the Humber, to the west of Offa's Dyke, and across the Irish Sea were less organised, but they also seem to have been reasonably prosperous. Monasteries founded in remote spots round the coast of the British Isles had grown rich through patronage and hard work. Their large communities had become attractive as markets to both local and international traders; their wealth was obvious; they were ripe for pillage. Indeed, the monastic centres of Ireland were subject to plunder by native chiefs long before the Viking Age.

It was against one of these monasteries—Lindisfarne (on a tidal island off the coast of Northumbria)—that the first recorded Viking attack on England was made in 793, a date normally used to define the beginning of the Viking Age: *In this year dire portents appeared over Northumbria and sorely frightened the people. They consisted of immense whirlwinds and flashes of lightning, and fiery dragons were seen flying in the air. A great famine followed these signs and a little after that in the same year, on 8th June, the ravages of heathen men miserably destroyed God's church on Lindisfarne, with plunder and slaughter.*

Far to the west of Lindisfarne attacks on the Irish island monasteries of Inishboffin and Inishmurray were recorded in 795. The most holy place of all in the west—Iona, off the west coast of Scotland and the centre of the cult of St Columba—was plundered in the same year. These events established a pattern of raids which was to continue sporadically in Western Europe until the mid-830s. The isolation of the monasteries and the speed of the attacks usually allowed the raiders to retreat in safety after pillage. Occasionally, however, the Vikings were beaten off; as were those who attacked what was probably the monastery of Tynemouth in 794, as described by Simeon of Durham: *But St Cuthbert did not allow him to depart unpunished; for their chief was there put to death by the cruel Angles, and a short time afterwards a violent storm shattered, destroyed and broke up their vessels, and the sea swallowed up very many of them; some, however, were cast ashore and speedily slain without mercy.*

The raids of this initial phase carried out by both Danes and Norwegians were sporadic and uncoordinated, leaving traces casually in the historical documents. Archaeological evidence is minimal; burnt and broken book-mounts have been found at Whitby, together with moulds used to melt down the precious metals looted from the monastery. Traces of fire at Monkwearmouth and Jarrow have been associated—rather unconvincingly—with Viking attacks.

The raiders came to get rich quickly, seeking portable wealth. A few early treasures, most noticeably the rich treasures from Christian sites on St Ninian's Isle in Shetland or at Derrynaflan in Ireland, witness to the troubled times of the Viking raids when it was necessary to hide valuables in the ground. Objects found in Viking Age graves in Norway, allegedly torn from their original Christian contexts or looted from their original western home, may also reflect the raids (cat. no. 127–31).

Little of the real wealth of the British Isles of the early Viking Age has survived in Scandinavia. Much gold and silver must have been melted down; but not all portable loot, it must be emphasised, consisted of precious metals.

Fig. 1. Silver hoard from Cuerdale, England. It weighs about 40 kg and was buried by Vikings c. 905. Cat. no. 361.

Other things were also of value, most of which would leave no trace in the archaeological record—slaves, woollen goods and luxury foods. Until the 830s the only motive of the Scandinavian raiders seems to have been the attainment of wealth—initially there was no intention to settle the lands to the west.

The Scandinavian settlement

The first trace of any permanent Scandinavian settlement occurs in Ireland. In or about 841 they established defended harbours at Annagassan, Co. Louth, and at Dublin and used these centres as bases for raids elsewhere in Ireland. The Dublin settlement is perhaps represented by the rich, mixed cemetery at Islandbridge, Kilmainham, on the edge of medieval Dublin (cat. no. 243, 354–8). This cemetery included female graves, which would suggest permanent colonization by whole families in the second half of the ninth century.

No traces of settlement survive in the north and west of Scotland until well on into the ninth century—perhaps at the same period as the settlement of Dublin. Re-examination of old finds at various sites—Freswick Links in Caithness, Birsay in Orkney and Jarlshof in Shetland—has produced

no evidence of ninth-century settlement. Only finds at Tuquoy on Westray and in graves at Westness on Rousay might indicate a ninth-century settlement.

The English seem to have had a respite from Viking attack until the early 830s, when the raids resumed in a more potent and organized form. No longer did these consist of casual attacks on lonely monastic outposts, but rather of serious battles. In 851 the invading army wintered in England for the first time and later stormed London and Canterbury. This began the process which led to military conquest and the settlement of much of England. Wintering in England became the norm. Excavations at Repton, Derbyshire, have located what has been interpreted as a fortress of the Scandinavians who wintered there in 873-4. A mass coin-dated burial found here (fig. 2) presumably consists of some members of what is now popularly known as the Great Army who died of disease during that winter (cat. no. 352–3).

Then, in 876, the Vikings for the first time settled in England, under their leader Halfdan. In subsequent years they took over much of north and east England, so that to the north and east of a line drawn from London to Chester they had political control of the country. This region (the

Fig. 2. Bones from human skeletons, probably Vikings and their women. They were found in a burial-mound at Repton in England, where the Viking invaders had wintered 873–4. Cat. no. 353.

Danelaw) was never unified, though there appears to have been a kingdom based on York, another in East Anglia and some sort of hegemony in the Midlands (a curious unit known as the Five Boroughs, based on the fortified towns of Stamford, Leicester, Lincoln, Nottingham and Derby).

Danish settlement was founded firmly on agriculture. The Danes took over existing estates (particularly those of the Church), presumably breaking them up and distributing them among the settlers. Settlement was dense for, with the aid of the cheap labour available in the form of the conquered population, they were able also to take into production land that had previously been uncultivated and ungrazed. The whole process is traced today in the large number of place-names containing Scandinavian elements that survive in this region, names with such terminations as, for example, -by (e.g. Derby). Study of place-names in north-west England, an area probably settled after 900 mainly by Norwegians from the west and north, also shows that the Danes from north-eastern England crossed the Pennines to join them.

Practically no traces have been found of the settlers' farms, perhaps because they lie under present-day settlements. One site investigated near Ribblehead high in the Pennines may not be of Viking origin, but includes structures of a type that would have been lived in by Scandinavians of the late ninth or early tenth century.

Again there is no evidence of the form or pattern of rural settlement in the Danelaw. Considerable traces, however, of the incomers are to be seen in the memorial sculpture of Scandinavian taste which occurs frequently here. The Vikings with remarkable eclecticism copied and adapted the native sculptural tradition, embellishing it with elements derived from their own ornamental canon. These monuments—both the memorial crosses and the extraordinary "hogback" tombstones (cat. no. 368–72)—also hint at the quickness of the conversion of the incomers to Christianity; a speed which also explains the scarcity of burials of the pagan type (i.e. those with accompanying grave-goods) in England. Only a couple of cemeteries have been found in England (the great mass grave at Repton is one), but a large number of single graves found in existing churchyards might suggest that the incomers adapted the sanctified cemeteries of the existing Christian population.

Of urban settlement there is more to tell. They settled and changed existing towns, the most important of which was York, the seat of a king and an archbishop and a town of long mercantile tradition clearly documented in the historical sources of the pre-Viking period. At York and Lincoln, both Roman foundations, imported objects are found in profusion—silk from Byzantium, pottery from Syria and

from North Germany, quern-stones from the Rhineland, brooches from the Baltic and whetstones from Norway—all indicators of the long-distance trade which ended in towns controlled by the Scandinavians, (cf. cat. no. 371–85, 399–402). Much else must have been traded which has left no trace in the archaeological record: slaves, spices, oils, furs and so on.

Ideas also were introduced from outside England. Scandinavian art styles, for example, were adapted to objects of daily use. The Borre style being particularly popular, whilst the Jellinge style combined with the English art of the late ninth century to produce a remarkable—if rather coarse—amalgam of the art of two cultures.

The Scandinavian language was also introduced into England—the man who in the last years of the eleventh century scratched an inscription on a stone in Carlisle Cathedral in runes: *tolfin urait thasi runr a thisi stain* (Dolfinn carved these runes on this stone) was almost certainly a local Scandinavian-speaking man. Whether he was a survivor of a family which had settled there in the tenth century, or of one established in the time of Knut in the early eleventh century, or merely a recent incomer from the west or north, is not clear. The point is that the language was used.

Across the Irish Sea was another Scandinavian sphere of influence. Dublin, for example, one of four or five towns founded as Viking trading centres and fortifications in Ireland (fig. 3), was to receive new stimulus as a result of the settlement of the Scandinavians in England. Through it passed much of the north/south trade of the western Atlantic from Greenland to Bordeaux, controlled by the Scandinavian merchants of the city (whoever might have been in political control of the city at any one time) until the English conquest of Ireland in the late twelfth century (cat. no. 386–98, 404). Ireland was not settled in the same way as England; the Scandinavians here were not primarily interested in farming: although controlling a certain amount of agricultural land outside the cities, they were content to trade with all comers—including the Irish farmers who would feed them.

In Scotland there were no towns, but trading stations existed (probably as temporary or seasonal markets) established on beaches or in protected inlets. One such might have been Whithorn, which had a pre-Viking origin and was one of a group of such markets around the Irish Sea.

One type of find, however, is common to all three countries. In Ireland, Scotland and England, from the beginning of the Viking settlement, a large number of silver hoards have been found, containing bullion in the form of coins, ornaments and hacked up pieces of ornaments (cat. no. 361–64). The hoards appear most frequently in the first half

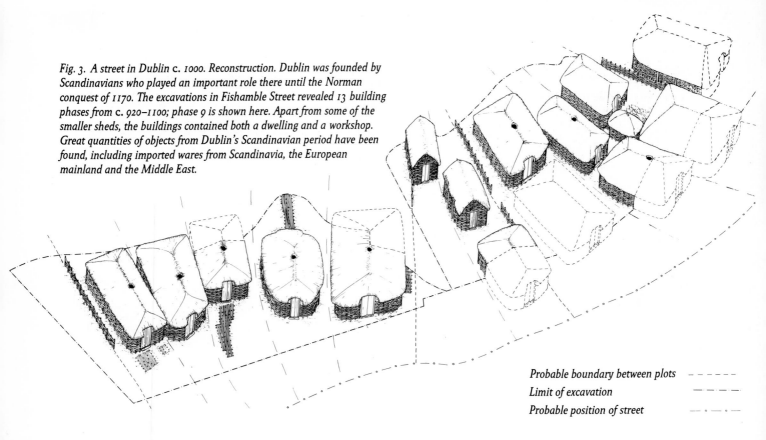

Fig. 3. A street in Dublin c. 1000. Reconstruction. Dublin was founded by Scandinavians who played an important role there until the Norman conquest of 1170. The excavations in Fishamble Street revealed 13 building phases from c. 920–1100; phase 9 is shown here. Apart from some of the smaller sheds, the buildings contained both a dwelling and a workshop. Great quantities of objects from Dublin's Scandinavian period have been found, including imported wares from Scandinavia, the European mainland and the Middle East.

Probable boundary between plots   – – – – –
Limit of excavation   – – – – –
Probable position of street   – – · – · –

of the tenth century, particularly in the west and north of the British Isles. They include the largest hoard from the western Viking world, from Cuerdale on the River Ribble in Lancashire (fig. 1). Hidden in a lead-lined chest in about 905, it contained some 7500 coins and about a thousand fragments of silver and ingots. The whole weighed well over forty kilos. In present-day values the hoard would be worth about £300,000—a lot of money to be carried around as cash—perhaps it was part of a Viking war chest.

The largest known gold hoard found in the Viking world came from Hare Island in the River Shannon. Melted down soon after it was found in 1802, it consisted of arm-rings which weighed nearly six kilos. The hoards reflect unsettled times. Buried and never reclaimed, we must assume that death (and probably violent death) supervened so that their location had been forgotten. Some English hoards reflect the wars of reconquest, others the internecine struggles between the dynasties of York and Dublin. They tell of a continuous state of political instability in the north and west of the British Isles in the first forty years of the tenth century, a period when the warring settlers and chieftains attempted to gain mastery of the region—or at least parts of it.

Almost as soon as the Vikings established themselves in the Danelaw, the English rulers began to challenge them. Alfred the Great, king of Wessex, began the campaign for the re-conquest with the re-taking of London in 886, at a period when the Danes were probably too involved in France to respond.

The reconquest of the north and east of England under Alfred's successors was not a smooth process, but by 954 the last Viking king of York, Erik Bloodaxe from Norway, had been expelled and the way was paved for the creation of a new kingdom of England under Edgar (959–75). Not all Scandinavians, however, were forced to leave the country, many had established themselves and stayed to be absorbed in the new country.

With the collapse of York, Dublin became increasingly important as an economic focus of the Scandinavians in the west and it was probably about this time that two great political entities were constructed in western and northern Britain. The Kingdom of Man and the Isles, based on the Isle of Man but extending up into the Hebrides; and the Earldom of Orkney, which controlled the northern Isles of Scotland, as well as Caithness and Sutherland (the nor- thernmost counties of mainland Scotland), which was to

Fig. 4. York, Coppergate 16–22. The illustration shows a partly sunken building, perhaps a dwelling with workshop, constructed of timber felled sometime between 970 and 1008. Similar buildings in the vicinity were erected c. 972–3.

York

York, almost as old as the millenium, had seen great days between AD 71–400 as a permanent Roman fortress and provincial capital, *Eboracum*. Roman defences, main roads and some of the major buildings remained a long lasting influence on the city's topography. In contrast little is known of York in the centuries after Roman military withdrawal, *c*. 400–600, but by the early 7th century it was a residence for the Anglo-Saxon kings of Northumbria. Layers datable to that era have hardly been found within the former Roman defences, but an excavation 1 kilometre downstream of the Roman walls, at the confluence of the rivers Ouse and Foss, has located a probable manufacturing and commercial centre. Datable to *c*. 700–850 it was perhaps the *wic* part of the famous town now called *Eoforwic*.

In the mid-ninth century the settlement was dramatically reversed. The *wic* site was abandoned, and this may be linked with the historically-attested arrival, victory and settlement of part of the Viking "great army", in 867. They enthroned their own candidates as kings, and then re-issued a York coinage to an improved standard, reached an accommodation with the church, and held power continuously until

927 and intermittently until 954, when York and its kingdom became part of the newly consolidated state of England—a political change which seems to have had little effect on the development of *Jorvík*, as it was now called.

In the late 9th and early 10th centuries the Roman defended areas on both sides of the river were linked by a new bridging point and re-fashioned with new churches, new streets, and a new lay-out of tenements which often ignored or cut across the earlier Roman plan. The town also expanded to cover the neck of land between the rivers, and it is in this vicinity that the timber houses and workshops are best preserved. Excavations in Coppergate showed how this Roman suburb had lain derelict for over four centuries until re-vitalised in the later 9th century. By the early 10th century new tenements had been carefully laid out, and this act defined the appearance of the area until our own time—tenements boundaries remained on the same lines, despite a rise in the ground level of up to 5 m. Buildings were focussed on the street frontage and this was a manufacturing quarter: metal-working in iron, copper-alloy, lead-alloy, silver and gold dominated the earlier period, and

was later supplemented by glass-working and wood-turning. Crafts such as jet- and amber-working, leather-working, bone- and antler-working, and textile-making were also practised, although not necessarily on a commercial scale. Altogether they show that York was now operating as a major production centre, and indeed it was probably the second largest and richest city in England. As a focus for trade it functioned both regionally, nationally and internationally—foreign goods arrived from Scandinavia, north-west Europe, the Mediterranean and the Near East. (cf. cat. no. 371–85, 399–402, 409, 432).

The Norman takeover, 1068–9, resulted in some deliberate razing of parts of *Jorvík* to make way for twin castles, and for water defences around one of them. A fire in 1069 destroyed the cathedral church, and the Normans built a new one on a different alignment; they also founded new religious houses, particularly St. Mary's Abbey. In essence, though, the framework of the Anglo-Scandinavian city underpinned other Norman rebuilding and is still the major influence on York today.

Richard Hall

Fig. 5. Tynwald Hill, Isle of Man. Every year the island's Parliament, Tynwald, takes its seat on the artificial mound together with representatives of the British Crown. The ceremony, as the word Tynwald itself, has roots in the island's Scandinavian period.

become one of the richest and most powerful elements in the Norwegian kingdom.

Excavation at Birsay, a small tidal island off mainland Orkney, has shown a major settlement, perhaps the chief seat of the earl himself. Two Orkney earls, Sigurd the Stout (c. 980–1014) and Thorfinn the Mighty (1014–1065), built the Orkney earldom up to its strongest pitch, controlling much of the north of Scotland and the Western Isles and turning the north into the mainstream of Christian culture. Thorfinn indeed established the bishopric and built a cathedral at Birsay. Although a powerful man, he acknowledged the overlordship of Harald Hardråda, king of Norway, and like his father, made continuous efforts to extend his earldom as far south as Man. Malcolm III of Scotland largely thwarted this ambition by claiming sovereignty over Thorfinn's Scottish earldoms and effectively cut him off from the south; certainly soon after his death Godred Sihtricson is described as king of Man. Godred seems to have emerged from Dublin and, after the battle of Stamford Bridge in 1066, came to Man with Godred Crovan, who ultimately established himself as king of Man (1079–95).

Sven and Knut—the conquest of England

In England from 980 onwards a new period of Scandinavian terror made itself felt as the old enemy pounced on a country wealthy and weakened after the death of the unifying king Edgar. At first the attacks were relatively insignificant. But their real purpose was revealed in 991 when the English agreed to pay £10,000 of silver coins so that the raiders would return to their own countries.

In 1003 Scandinavian Vikings were welded together under Sven Forkbeard. His assault on England was successful: he raised large sums of money over the years to finance his activities at home in Denmark. He paid off his Swedish followers who returned home to live it up in Sweden with the money that they had received at his hands and which is evidenced in the vast number of English coins found in the hoards of this period throughout Sweden. Having consolidated his power base in Denmark, however, Sven now had greater ambitions—nothing less than the conquest of England.

After a short campaign in the summer of 1013, Sven was recognised as king by all the English, but he died early in 1014. Every attempt of the deposed English king, Æthelred,

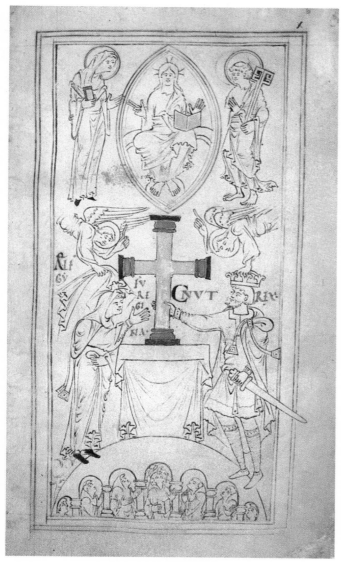

Fig. 6. King Knut and his queen Emma (Ælfgyfu) present an altar cross to the New Minster, Winchester, England. Drawing from the 1030s. Cat. no. 412.

to reconquer the country could not retrieve the situation and by 1017 Sven's son, Knut, was king and married Æthelred's widow Emma.

Archaeological evidence of this last Viking period, which lasted—in theory at least—until the death of Knut's son, Harthaknut, in 1042, is most spectacularly represented by the stone from the churchyard at St Paul's in London (cat. no. 416) and in the Liber Vitae of the New Minster at Winchester. By this time the Danes were Christian and Knut was accepted by the Christian kings of Europe as an equal. A tough administrator of his English kingdom, Knut

used his English wealth and his political skills to bolster his power in Denmark and (from 1028) Norway, so that he could style himself—with some justification—King of all England, of Denmark, of the Norwegians and of part of the Swedes.

Knut's empire was to collapse after his death in 1035. The English royal line finally regained control of the throne when Harthaknut died standing at his drink in 1042 and was succeeded by Edward the Confessor.

Post-Viking contacts

The Scandinavians did not, however, lose interest in their political claims to England until the end of the century. Magnus Haraldsson of Norway abortively attacked England in 1058, Sven Estridsson of Denmark also made feints towards England and Harald Hardråda of Norway invaded England in 1066. This latter was a major event. Harald was reinforced by men from the earldom of Orkney and also by the English king Harold Godwinsson's exiled brother, Tostig; his army may well have amounted to 9,000 men. They captured York, but withdrew to Stamford Bridge, where they were defeated by the English king, Harold Godwinsson. Harald Hardråda and Tostig were both killed in the battle and the Norwegians never again attempted to take the throne of England. Sven of Denmark made a feeble attempt to undermine William the Conqueror in 1070, but after his son's threatened invasion in 1085 the Scandinavians never again came back in a warlike fashion.

England, however, retained contact with Scandinavia whether through Dublin, the northern and western Isles or directly. A sufficient Scandinavian element in the population of the old Danelaw contributed at least some sympathy for the people of these lands and a welcome for their traders. The contact is clearly seen in the art of the post-Conquest period (cat. no. 428–9); in the Scandinavian-derived Ringerike and Urnes styles, as for example on the tympanum from Southwell Minster which bears ornament derived from these styles, dated by some to around 1120, but perhaps in reality forty years earlier. The Urnes style, so clearly seen on a large number of bronze objects (particularly brooches and book clasps), is also found in a rather derivative form in sculpture. It is quite possible that these two styles were introduced from the West, from Ireland where traces of a flourishing artistic industry based on the Ringerike and Urnes style has been recovered among the myriad of motif-pieces found in the Dublin excavations and in the art of the Irish church (cat. no. 397–8, 430–1).

Artistic contact directly eastwards with Scandinavia is to be seen in a school of ivory carving, typified by the Lewis

Fig. 7. Chessmen of walrus ivory, from the 12th cent., found on the island of Lewis in the Hebrides, Scotland. Cat. no. 615.

chessmen (fig. 7) and a number of other mid-12th-century ivory objects, which have a decorative vocabulary of distinct Scandinavian elements—a North Sea Romanesque (cat. no. 611–5).

Despite the formal supremacy of the archbishopric of Hamburg-Bremen, a continuing ecclesiastical influence from England expressed itself in Scandinavia in liturgical detail, gifts of relics and exchange of personnel, as well as in architecture. Olaf Tryggvason and Olaf Haraldsson recruited English missionaries and the Danes and the Swedes, wishing to minimize the influence of the German archdiocese, turned frequently to England for help. It is significant that an Englishman, Nicholas Breakspear, was sent to Norway in 1152 by the Pope to investigate the possibility of creating separate archdioceses in Norway and Sweden—succeeding only in Norway with the establishment of Nidaros (present-day Trondheim).

But the ecclesiastical influences were not all one way, as is demonstrated by the dedication of church-buildings in Britain to St Olaf and St Magnus. The cathedral of Orkney in Kirkwall, one of the most remarkable of northern European Romanesque buildings (fig. 8), is dedicated to the Orkney earl St Magnus, whilst churches of St Olaf in

London, York, Dublin and elsewhere tell of contact—commercial as well as ecclesiastical—between west and north.

One London church spells it out in more remarkable fashion: St Clement Danes. This church (which still stands in rebuilt form) is situated on the edge of the earlier commercial centre of the Anglo-Saxon capital—Aldwych. The trade symbolized by this church is reflected in a handful of early records and (in 1223) a formal commercial agreement between Norway and England. Fish was an increasingly important item of the English imports from Scandinavia, as the practice of eating fish on fast days increased demand, and it is almost certain that by the end of the twelfth century timber was also traded from the North, although evidence is thin.

The Scandinavians retained their mercantile contact with London, but in the early twelfth century gradually lost what must have been some sort of dominance when the Danish guildhall in London was sold to the Cologne merchants. The ports of the Wash, Lynn in particular, and Grimsby, were becoming more important to the Norwegians, who until the third quarter of the twelfth century at least were also reaching for Dublin by way of Orkney and the Western Isles.

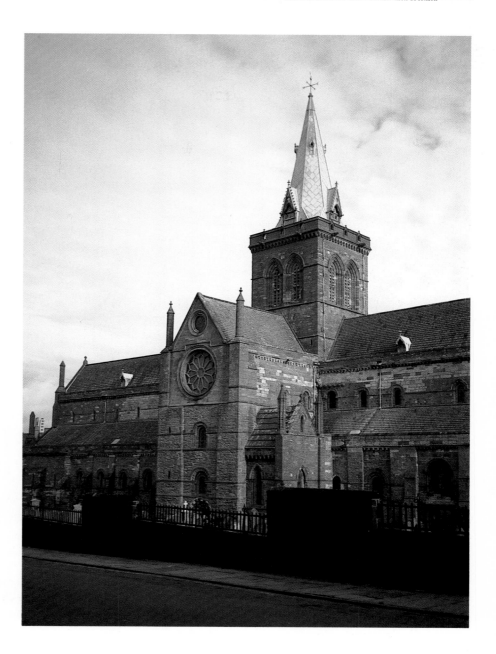

Fig. 8. The cathedral of Kirkwall, Orkney, begun 1137. It is dedicated to the islands' patron saint St Magnus, Earl of Orkney (killed in 1115).

From Dublin the merchants had access to the Continent and to the western seaboard of England, to the River Severn, whence they could reach the English heartland. From Ireland came, for example, leather goods and trans-shipped materials from the Continent; and from England, according to King Sverre in 1189, came "wheat, honey, flour and cloth".

The hostile pagan raiders of the late eighth century, had some four hundred years later become favoured traders with the kingdoms of the British Isles and full members of the Christian community of Europe.

Scandinavian names and words in Europe

Gillian Fellows-Jensen

The Vikings who set out from Denmark, Norway and Sweden to raid, trade and settle in eastern and western Europe left an indelible imprint on the host countries in the form of loanwords, personal names and, above all, place-names. Several factors worked together to determine the nature and extent of this imprint in the various countries. The most significant factor was the number of immigrants in relation to the size of the native population but the degree of mutual intelligibility between the host language and the Viking tongue also played an important role.

The Norwegian Vikings who made their homes in Shetland, Orkney, the Faroes and Iceland came to lands which were deserted or sparsely populated at the time. Iceland and the Faroes have survived to the present day as Scandinavian-speaking countries and in Orkney and Shetland a Scandinavian language continued to be spoken as late as the eighteenth century, although it was in losing competition with the Scots language from the fifteenth century. The Norwegian settlers in Ireland, the Hebrides, the Isle of Man and mainland Scotland, on the other hand, were minority groups surrounded by native Celtic-speaking people, while the Danes who settled in England and Normandy were hedged in by English-speakers and French-speakers respectively, and the Swedes who settled in Russia were surrounded by people speaking Slav languages.

The Scandinavian loanwords that have survived in Irish, Gaelic, French and Russian—all non-Germanic languages—are not very numerous. It would, of course, have been impossible for the Vikings to communicate at all fluently with their neighbours in Ireland, Scotland, Normandy and Russia without employing interpreters or becoming bilingual. In addition, in Ireland, Normandy and Russia, the Scandinavian colonies were comparatively short-lived and the Vikings who settled there were fairly quickly absorbed into the native populations. Norse domination of the Hebrides and Man, on the other hand, lasted for almost 500 years and the Scandinavian language probably did not drop finally out of use until the sixteenth century. The comparative rarity of Scandinavian loanwords in the Celtic languages, however, suggests that there could only have been a limited degree of linguistic contact between the Scandinavian and Celtic communities. In England, the Vik-

Fig. 1. Seal-matrix from York, England. It belonged to a 12th-cent. toll-collector with the Scandinavian name Snarri, which means 'the swift one'.

ings found a Germanic-speaking native population and although the Scandinavian and English languages had already differentiated themselves from each other to such an extent that linguistic contact would hardly have been possible without recourse to rude noises and uncouth gestures, there was nevertheless a basic shared vocabulary that must have made it easy for Scandinavian loanwords to be accepted in large numbers by the English.

There were some semantic fields in which Scandinavian loanwords were accepted by all the languages encountered by the Vikings. From the maritime world, for example, there is the term *biti* 'cross-plank in a boat', that was adopted into Russian as *bet'* and into French as *bitte*, while *thopta* 'rowing-bench' was adopted by the Irish as *tochta* and by the English as *thoft* (later developing to *thwart*). The field of legal and administrative terminology was also open to loanwords from Scandinavian. The old Scandinavian word for the law raiding parties, perhaps men in the service of the local ruler, perhaps farmers who had settled in the new countries under the protection of the armies, are recorded in written documents such as peace treaties, charters and land registers from the individual colonies. Unfortunately, the patriarchal nature of medieval society means that comparatively few female names are recorded in such documents. We would not expect to find female names among those of royal retainers whose services had been rewarded by grants of land, and women would normally only appear in lists of tenants if they were widows. The absence of Scandinavian female names from the records may in part, however, reflect an absence of Scandinavian women to act as name-models in the colonies.

There is some evidence to suggest that the Vikings married local women, as when a runic inscription on a Manx cross records that *Fiak* (Celtic *Fiacc*) was the son of *Thorleif hnakki* 'nape'. His Celtic name suggests that his unnamed mother was a Manx woman. On the other hand, a stone erected in memory of *ufaak sun krinais*, (Scandinavian) *Ofeig* son of (Celtic) *Crínan*), might point to a marriage between a Manx man and a Viking woman. In England it would seem to have been just as common for a man with an English name to give his son a Scandinavian name as for a father with a Scandinavian name to do so. This may sometimes have been because the mother was of Danish origin. The eleventh-century Earl Godwine of Wessex, for example, was married to *Gytha*, the sister of Jarl Ulf of Denmark. Of their eight children, five received Scandinavian names: *Svein, Harald, Tosti, Gyrth* and *Gunnhild*, while three were given English names: *Leofwine, Eadgyth* and *Ælfgifu*. In Normandy, some members of the ducal family took a Frankish name in addition to their Scandinavian one. *Rollo*, for example, called himself *Robert* in written documents and his daughter was referred to as both *Gerloc* and *Adelis*. Others followed their example. *Turstin* (*Thorstein*) was also known as *Richard* and *Stigand* as *Odo*. Soon, Frankish names had practically ousted names of Scandinavian origin from the nomenclature of Normandy.

In England Scandinavian personal names established themselves more securely and many new names developed on English soil, for example by-names such as *Bróklaus* 'trouser-less', *Serklaus* 'shirtless' and *Snarri* 'the swift one'. Many of the recorded names which end in -*ketil* such as *Brúnketil, Ormketil, Steinketil* and *Ulfketil* may also have arisen in England and been carried back from there to the Scandinavian homelands. In England, however, the Norman conquest in 1066 sounded the death-knell for Scandinavian personal names, and by 1200 practically everyone in England had a forename of Frankish or biblical origin. A few Scandinavian personal names have survived to the present day in the colonies where the Scandinavian language has dropped into disuse. *Olga* is

Fig. 2. Signpost in Normandy, France. The place-name La Houlgate occurs with varying spellings in many parts of Normandy. The name is of Scandinavian origin and originally meant 'hollow road'. The name of the commune Biéville-Quétiéville is the result of the amalgamation of two settlements with Frankish names, the second of which contains the Scandinavian personal name Ketil.

itself, *lagu*, is found in Celtic as *lagh*, in Old Norman as *lage* and in English as *law*. The term *rannsaka* 'to search a house for stolen goods' occurs in Celtic as *rannsachadh*, in Norman French as *rannsaquer* and in English as *ransack*. The Scandinavian word *embætti* 'office' was adopted into Russian as *jábeda* and, suggestively, acquired there the meaning 'back-biting'. It is only in English that Scandinavian loanwords are found in the vocabulary of all fields of daily life, often having displaced English words for the same concepts. Such common and necessary English words as *birth* and *die, fellow* and *husband, ill* and *ugly, leg* and *skin, kettle* and *steak, smile* and *mistake* were all introduced into the language by the Vikings, and hundreds of others besides.

In addition to their daily vocabulary, the Vikings took a range of personal names with them to their new homes. In the written sources we can read the names of the ruling Scandinavian dynasties in the colonies, for example *Oleb* (*Oleif*), *Olég* (*Helgi*), *Olga* (*Helga*) in Russia, *Amlaibh* (*Olaf*), *Gofraid* (*Guthrøth*), *Imar* (*Ivar*), *Ragnall* (*Ragnald*) in Ireland and Man, *Rolf* or *Rollo* (*Hrólf*), *Gerloc* (*Geirlaug*) and *Gunnor* (*Gunnvǫr*) in Normandy, *Anlaf* or *Olaf, Halfdan* and *Guthrum* (*Guththorm*) in England.

Names of humbler settlers, perhaps members of the Viking

Fig. 3. Signpost in Yorkshire, England. It points south to Slingsby, the Scandinavian name of which means 'Sleng's village', and to Malton, the Old English name of which means 'discussion village' (probably an administrative centre). To the north the signpost points to Nunnington, an Old English name which means 'Nunna's estate', and to Kirkby Moorside, the Scandinavian name of which—'church village'—is distinguished from many identical names by the addition of the English affix Moorside, originally 'moor's head', which refers to its situation on a ness or headland in the North Yorkshire Moors.

or 'the falls at the isthmus') to rapids on the River Dnieper between Kiev and the Black Sea, but these names have not survived in use.

The most significant place-names are those which reveal the areas in which the Vikings settled in significant numbers. In the early years the settlers used the pre-existing names and, where necessary, coined names descriptive of the local topography. A growing population, however, led to the splitting up of large estates into small independent units. The Norwegian settlers in the Northern and Western Isles of Scotland and the Isle of Man created names for these units in *-stathir*, for example *Grimista* 'Grim's place' and *Oddsta*, ('Odd's place') in Shetland, *Germiston* 'Grim's place' and *Tormiston* 'Thormóth's place' in Orkney, *Tolsta* 'Tholf's place' in Lewis, *Gretch*, probably 'Grettir's place', and *Leodest*, perhaps 'Ljótulf's place', in Man, or *-bólstathr*, for example *Isbister* 'eastern farm' in Shetland and Orkney, *Habost* ('high farm') in Lewis and Skye.

The Danes in England gave the smaller land-units names in *-by*, such as *Colby* 'Kóli's farmstead', *Grimsby* 'Grim's farmstead', and *Aislaby* 'Aslák's farmstead', or *-thorp*, such as *Sculthorpe* 'Skúli's outlying farm' and *Gunthorpe* 'Gunni's outlying farm', and still later, men moving out from the English Danelaw coined place-names in *-by* in southern Scotland, Man and south-eastern Wales. The element most frequently employed to coin place-names for small units in Normandy (cf. p. 93) was *toft*, as in *Colletot* 'Kóli's plot', *Écultot* 'Skúli's plot', *Étaintot* 'stone plot' and *Gonnetot* 'Gunni's plot'. The word *toft* originally meant 'building-plot' but it acquired the sense 'deserted settlement' and its popularity in Normandy may reflect the fact that much destruction was caused by the Vikings here before they settled down as farmers. Names in *-toft* are, however, also found in the Northern and Western Isles, the Isle of Man and England. In some cases the Vikings cleared new land for settlement. These areas are characterised by names in *-thveit* 'clearing'. Such names are particularly common in the high land in north-west England and south-west Scotland, for example four *Brackenthwaites* 'bracken clearing' in Cumberland and Dumfriesshire, but they occur throughout the Danelaw and are very common in woodland areas around the Seine in Normandy, for example *Thuit-Hébert, Le Thuit-Anger* and *Le Thuit-Signol* in Roumois, and are also found in Orkney and Shetland, for example as the simplex name *Twatt*.

Fig. 4. England, Wales, the Isle of Man and southern Scotland. The main areas of Scandinavian settlement are reflected in the place-names. After the Viking conquests in the second half of the 9th cent., the Scandinavian place-name suffix -by was often used to form place-names (e.g. Crosby) instead of English -tun, and -thorp instead of English -throp. There are also a number of hybrid names (e.g. Grimston) in which a Scandinavian personal name is compounded with the English element -tun.

still one of the most popular forenames in Russia, for example, and the forename *Somhairle* (*Sumarlithi*) and the surname *Macauley* (son of *Olaf*) are current in the Hebrides. In Normandy, *Angot* (*Asgaut*), *Anquetil* (*Asketil*), *Toutain* (*Thorstein*) and *Turquetil* (*Thorketil*) survive as surnames (cf. p. 93),while in England names such as *Harald* and *Eric* received a literary renaissance in the nineteenth century.

Many more Scandinavian personal names survive in the colonies as elements in place-names. As evidence for a Scandinavian presence in the various colonies, place-names have the advantage over loanwords and personal names in that they can be located exactly and hence used to demarcate the areas of Scandinavian settlement. Among the few names coined by the early raiders are those of small islands which they used for various purposes, for example *Dursey* 'Thor's island' and *Lambay* 'Lamb island' in Ireland, *Priestholm* in Wales, and *Torhulmus*, an eleventh-century name of a merely local currency for an island in the Seine. Viking traders in the east are known to have given Scandinavian names such as *Leanti* (*Hlæjandi* or 'the laughing one') and *Aeifor* (*Eithfors*

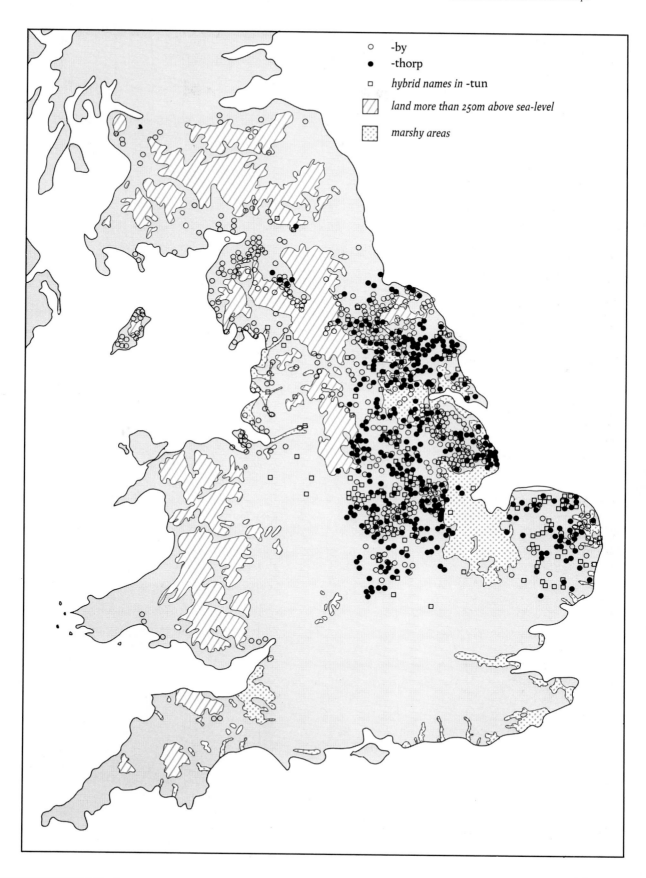

Pilgrimages and crusades

Niels-Knud Liebgott

When the Viking raids ceased in the middle of the eleventh century it did not put an end to the Scandinavian adventures abroad. Christian kings and chieftains still equipped ships for long journeys, but for totally different purposes. Their aims were no longer simply trade, plunder or conquest in foreign lands; they now wished to visit the great holy places of Christendom—particularly Rome and the Holy Land. Pilgrimages had begun.

When kings and chieftains—the people about whom we have the earliest knowledge—set out on journeys, they had many motives—penance or fulfilment of an oath, for example—but they often combined such motives with political aspirations. This is true of Knut the Great's journey to Rome in 1027, where he participated in the coronation of the Emperor Conrad II. It is also true of Erik Ejegod's first pilgrimage to Rome and Bari in 1098, during which he negotiated with the Pope for the establishment of the first Scandinavian ecclesiastical province.

Until about 1200 our sources tell almost exclusively of pilgrimages from Denmark and the west of Scandinavia. It seems probable that St Olaf visited the grave of St James at Santiago de Compostela as early as 1012–13 when he was travelling in France and Spain. Sighvat Thórdarson travelled from Iceland to Rome in 1030, and the Icelandic chieftain Gelli Thorkelsson also visited Rome about 1070. Erik Ejegod set out on a second pilgrimage for Jerusalem along the Russian rivers. He stayed with the Varangian guard at the Byzantine court, but never reached Palestine, for he died in Cyprus in 1103. The Norwegian king, Sigurd Jorsalfar (Sigurd the Jerusalem-traveller), journeyed to the Holy Land by another route. He travelled by way of England around the Iberian peninsula (stopping at Santiago), into the Mediterranean and arrived in Jerusalem in 1110. Rǫgnvald Kali, Earl of Orkney, and his companions took the same route to Jerusalem in the middle of the twelfth century and, as recorded in *Orkneyinga saga* (cat. no. 525), had a particularly eventful journey.

Even in the early years of the Christian period, however, pilgrimages were not confined to kings and chieftains. As early as the second half of the eleventh century there are reports of pilgrimages within Scandinavia—to the tomb of St Olaf in Trondheim, for example. It was not until the later Middle Ages, however, that pilgrimages were undertaken by large numbers of people, as a normal part of their spiritual life. A unique source, the fraternity book of the Benedictine

Fig. 1. Runic inscription on the small whetstone from Timans, Gotland, Sweden, mentioning both Jerusalem and Iceland. End of the 11th cent. Cat. no. 485.

monastery of Reichenau on Lake Constance, contains a list of the names of more than forty-thousand pilgrims who visited the monastery on their way to Rome in the eleventh and twelfth centuries. Almost seven hundred of these have names of Scandinavian origin; most are Danish, but there are a few Norwegians and thirteen Icelanders.

Both Erik Ejegod's second pilgrimage and Sigurd Jorsalfar's journey in 1108–10 are described as 'armed pilgrimages', and thus had more the character of Crusades. By taking part in a Crusade, people obtained the same absolution and indulgence as they would by making a pilgrimage.

Fig. 2. The Gundslevmagle cross was made in the Byzantine area and found in Denmark in a hoard from the second half of the 11th cent. Cat. no. 488.

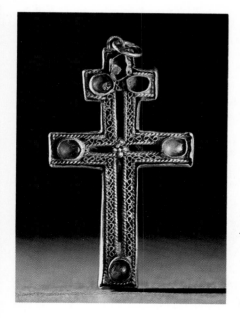

Fig. 4. Danish penny from the second half of the 12th cent. There is a ?palm frond on the obverse and a crusading flag on the reverse, the symbols of pilgrimage and crusade. The cross-emblazoned banner on the reverse is probably the earliest depiction of the Danish flag. Cat. no. 544b.

Fig. 3. Reliquary cross found at Tønsberg, Norway. It is probably 11th-cent. and contained a splinter of the True Cross. Cat. no. 489.

As early as the ninth century the Church offered pardons to those taking part in the struggles against the pagan Vikings and Muslims, but when Pope Urban II in 1095 called the Christian world to arms in order to recapture Jerusalem, the Vikings were among those who 'took up the cross'.

When Pope Eugenius III and Bernard of Clairvaux initiated the Second Crusade in 1147, the Danes, under the joint kings Sven and Knut, took up arms against their pagan Slav neighbours south of the Baltic. This war, which in ferocity and strength was basically a continuation of earlier Viking expeditions, carried formal papal approval as a Crusade, but was otherwise a total failure.

The full-scale attacks launched in the next few decades by the Scandinavians against their eastern neighbours were all carried out as Crusades. Valdemar the Great struck coins with a palm branch—the symbol of the Jerusalem pilgrims —on one face, and with a cross on the other (fig. 4). The capture of Arkona and the consequent conversion of Rügen in 1168/9 opened the way for the Danes to penetrate further east. But Knut VI's offensive against the Christian princes of Pomerania in the 1180s shows that the crusades were merely an excuse for ordinary piratical wars.

In 1171, Pope Alexander III encouraged the Scandinavian kings to stage a Crusade against heathen Estonia. The Estonian Crusade began in 1197 but met with little success until 1219, when the Danish king Valdemar Sejr was victorious at the battle of Lyndanise. Valdemar built a chain of forts to defend his newly conquered land, of which Tallinn ('The fortification of the Danes') was one. Through his conquest of Estonia, Valdemar brought almost all the Baltic lands, from Holstein in the west to the Gulf of Finland in

the east, under his control. That this short-lived Baltic Empire was formed in the name of Crusade is demonstrated by the fact that the king chose as his flag the arms of the Teutonic Knights, the Dannebrog—which is still the Danish national flag.

Although the motives for these wars were really little more than power politics, and although the methods were no different from those of the earlier Viking raids, this does not reduce their impact: partly because of these expeditions the Slav and Baltic peoples became absorbed into the western Church and culture. No other Crusade—apart from that which drove the Moors out of Spain—had such lasting effect.

Fig. 5. Crusader on a gravestone from Vejerslev, Mors, Denmark. C. 1200.

Scandinavia and Europe around 1200

Knut Helle

Around the year 1200 the Nordic world had become a part of Christian Europe. In the course of the twelfth century the churches of the North had been assimilated into the papal universal Church and had been organized into three ecclesiastical provinces. They had been deeply influenced by the Gregorian reform movement, and the first steps had been taken towards a compromise *libertas ecclesiae*. This happened basically in collaboration, but sometimes in contention and strife, with the royal authority.

Christianity under the authority of the Church formed at the same time the strongest link in the more comprehensively organised society which was beginning to evolve. Nevertheless, when it came to granting the Nordic countries an incipient 'national' identity, the unifying power of the king was just as significant. The pace of development towards state-like kingdoms in Denmark and Norway had accelerated from the middle of the twelfth century under organisational and ideological influence from Europe. There were similar tendencies in Sweden, but here the decisive break-through did not happen until the mid-thirteenth century. In Iceland political power was gathered in the hands of increasingly fewer local chieftains and this was in the process of undermining the balance in the social organisation of the Icelandic 'Free State'. Ultimately it meant that the ground would be ready for Iceland's subjection to the Norwegian crown, which in the thirteenth century established a 'Norwegian Empire' which included all the Norse island communitites from the Orkneys to Greenland.

Maintaining the contacts initiated by the Viking raids and later settlements, the Norwegian church and crown turned towards the west. In Denmark and Sweden, on the other hand, the crown, the church and the aristocracy focussed their attention on the old Viking routes to the east and took an active part in the eastwards expansion from western Europe in the twelfth and thirteenth centuries. The conversion of the Slavs, Balts and Finns was the ideological objective; but in practice territorial conquest, trade and colonization were equally important motives. Denmark was around 1200 in process of becoming the leading power to the south and east of the Baltic Sea. The Swedish church and crown, on the other hand, had established a bridgehead for further expansion in the south-west Finnish coastal region around Turku, the original Finland.

In time, however, German economic and political interests would dominate the countries around the Baltic. About 1200 Hanseatic merchants started to take the lead in the increasing east/west trade in north Europe, and were to play a decisive role in drawing Scandinavia into the 'commercial revolution' of the High Middle Ages. This accelerated the urbanization process. Established towns grew, new ones were founded, and an urban adminstration system on a European model began to take shape.

While Scandinavian expansion in northern Europe around 1200 was directed towards the east and west, the most significant cultural impulses came from the south—from continental Europe to southern and eastern Scandinavia: mainly by way of the British Isles to Norway and Iceland. Romanesque church architecture and art had spread throughout most of Scandinavia by the twelfth century and by the second half of the century the first Gothic elements began to appear. Foreign impulses met with local traditions and this encounter led to the flourishing of Scandinavian culture of the High Middle Ages.

The most original cultural product of this period, however, was in the field of vernacular literature; in the Norse chronicles and sagas, the North's greatest contribution to world literature. Here the Icelanders led the way by virtue of their narrative tradition and their special interest in literature. Already by about 1200 the foundations were laid for the sagas of the Norse kings, and the Icelandic sagas (the family sagas) were in embryo. At this time the Danish historian Saxo was writing his great work on the achievements of the Danes. This was written in Latin, for the vernacular tradition was not yet as strong in Denmark and Sweden as it was in the western Scandinavian area. In these areas the Scandinavian languages were first written down as the laws were codified, and they then advanced decisively throughout the whole of the Scandinavia. There were already differences of dialect which provided the starting point for the eventual development of the national languages of the Nordic countries.

Despite the fact that Scandinavia around 1200 must be regarded as part of Europe, we occasionally catch a glimpse of the distinctive cultural features of Scandinavian society, both collectively and individually. Not least among these was the freedom of the peasantry, the egalitarian aspects of which have left their mark to this day.

The east end of Trondheim cathedral, the archiepiscopal church of Norway. The building was strongly influenced by English architecture. The octagon east of the choir was built c. 1200 in early Gothic style and signals the advent of new architectural ideas.

Section of a painted memorial stone from Tjängvide, Gotland, Sweden. 8th–9th century. The scene shown is probably the arrival of the dead hero in Valhalla. Cat. no. 175.

Culture and society

People and language

Berit Jansen Sellevold
Jan Ragnar Hagland

The people of the Viking Age

There are many representations of people from Viking Age
Scandinavia, on stones and on textiles, in wood, metal and
other materials. They are also depicted in words. Yet, these
descriptions give only a vague impression of how the people
looked in real life. Visual and verbal descriptions are coloured by their situations and by the people who made them.
They are stylized (cat. no. 77–80).

Direct knowledge of people's physical appearance can,
however, be obtained from uncremated skeletal remains in
Viking Age graves. These do not tell of features such as the
colour of skin, hair and eyes, but they do tell of stature,
cranial and facial shape, the shapes of nasal cavities and eye
sockets, of teeth and of genetics. Diet, physical activity and
stress, diseases and injuries leave their marks on bones.
Skeletal remains give some idea of the standard of life
enjoyed by individuals in their formative years and also the
story of their later lives.

There are remains of some three hundred individuals
from Denmark and some sixty from Norway. Because of the
widespread practice of cremation very little material from
Sweden has been examined. In Denmark the skeletal material comes from burials and cemeteries from all over the
country, while in Norway most comes from the northern
districts. Such skeletal material is not representative of the
original population, neither as regards the number of individuals, their geographical distribution, nor their social
composition. In both countries it is mainly the upper social
classes which are represented. This is because it is mostly the
large, visible and rich graves which have been archaeologically examined and excavated.

The skeletal remains represent comparatively sturdy and
well developed individuals. In older adults there is extensive
evidence of osteo-arthritis, especially in the vertebrae. Such
evidence is found in most adult skeletons. Osteo-arthritis is
of course common today and is probably caused by physical
strain and ageing. In the Danish and Norwegian material
there are a few (male) skeletons with evidence of fatal
wounding (e.g. decapitation) (cat. no. 45), and also bones
with traces of healed wounds. But these are not common in
the surviving Viking Age material. The skeletons tell of
people who had a comparatively high standard of living and
who died as mature adults. There are very few skeletons of
children in the Scandinavian Viking Age material, this is
probably due to the fact that most dead children must have

*Fig. 1. The head of a Viking, carved in elk antler, from Sigtuna, Sweden.
Cat. no. 80.*

been buried in such a way that we do not find them today.

The upper class Viking Age Danes and Norwegians were
much alike: they were of medium height, almost medium-
headed (see below), had medium-broad faces, fairly narrow
noses and rectangular eye-sockets. They probably looked
very much like Danes and Norwegians do to-day, but they
were of somewhat smaller stature. Neither men nor women
were particularly tall: the average height of Danish men was
172.6 cm, while Norwegians were on average three cm taller,
i.e. 175.6 cm. There are no abnormally small or large individuals among the surviving skeletons: in Denmark the
shortest man was about 163 cm and the tallest about 185 cm
high. In the Norwegian material the shortest man was about
170 cm and the tallest about 181 cm. The average height of
Danish women was 158.1 cm and varied from about 150 cm

to about 167 cm. Norwegian women were a little taller than the Danish, averaging 159.6 cm (with a variation from *c.* 149 cm to *c.* 164 cm).

The average stature of both sexes was about 10 cm below today's averages in Denmark and Norway. Some 90% of a person's physical height is genetically determined, while 10% is thought to be decided by environmental factors such as diet and living conditions in formative years. The populations of the Viking Age and today probably have the same genetic potential as regards stature. The great average heights of the modern Scandinavian populations are probably due to very good living conditions.

Cranial shape is determined by the interaction of genetic and cultural factors. Most individuals in the Viking Age were long-headed (dolichocephalic), but the average breadth/length ratio is about 75.0, meaning that the breadth of the skull is 75% of its length; this is on the borderline between long-headed and medium-headed. Danish men and women had identical breadth-length ratios of 74.6, while Norwegian men were on average 73.6 and Norwegian women exactly on the borderline of long- and medium-headed, averaging 75.0.

Fig. 2 shows a grave from Haug at Melbu on Hadselya in Nordland, Norway. The cemetery lies close to a small turf-built church under a farm mound and dates from the period of transition from paganism to Christianity (it has been radiocarbon dated to between 900 and 1180 from the middle of the Viking Age until well into the Christian Middle Ages). Several of the dead had been buried with objects after the pagan fashion. They did not lie in the usual 'Christian' position, *i.e.* on the back with the head towards the west and the hands or arms crossed above chest or abdomen. The dead at Haug were buried in positions usually associated with pagan graves, for example as though sleeping on one side with the legs bent (crouched burial). Some lay face down.

The grave in fig. 2 (and those in the cemetery generally) is not like the large, rich graves which otherwise dominate the Norwegian grave and skeletal material from the Viking Age. But the skeletal remains are typical of Viking Age women of Norway. The skeleton, dated by radiocarbon methods to between 900 and 1030, is that of a young adult woman of some 20–25 years of age. Her skull has a breadth-length ratio of 75.7, almost exactly the average of Norwegian Viking Age women. Her face was of medium breadth and length, with a comparatively narrow nasal cavity and rectangular eye sockets. Her height is estimated at 160.7 cm, which is about 1 cm above average. Her bones were well developed and there were no traces of pathological changes. She had nice and even teeth, with no traces of caries or other dental diseases. She had been buried with a simple iron knife at her right hip. She was lying flat on her back, but her hands were not placed together on chest or abdomen. The grave was positioned west-east and her head was at the western end.

Throughout the first millenium AD the Danish population was very uniform in physical appearance and other genetically determined features. There seems to have been no intermingling with other population groups of a different genetic composition from the Danish. In Norway it has not been possible to analyze a similarly long time span, since there are long periods in Norwegian pre-history from which no unburnt skeletal material survives; either because of the burial custom (cremation) or because of circumstances of preservation, or other factors. While the Danish material appears very homogenous (nearly all the Danish skulls are long-headed), the Norwegian Viking Age material is more varied as it also includes several short-headed (brachycephalic) individuals. This probably represents a Saami element. Some Saami burials have been dated to the Viking Age, with Saami equipment and skeletons with 'Saami' features (i.e. short, broad, distinctly brachycephalic skulls with breadth-length ratios above 80.0). Skeletons with Saami features have also been found in typical Scandinavian Viking Age burials. Most Norwegian Viking Age graves, however, contain skeletons with Scandinavian features, i.e. long, narrow skulls of medium height.

B J S

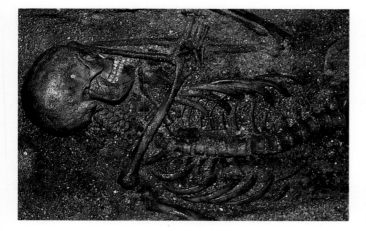

Fig. 2. Burial from the churchyard at Haug, Hadseløya in Nordland, Norway. The skeleton is of a young woman between 20 and 25 years of age, dated to the late Viking Age.

Language

What language did these people speak? The language in the greater part of what we today call Scandinavia was a variant of Germanic and was a northern branch of this group of languages. Then as now Lappish and Finnish were also spoken in this area. These latter are Finno-Ugrian languages and belong to a quite different family from the Germanic languages. Finno-Ugrian and Germanic were, and are, mutually incomprehensible, although there are some loan words in Finnish which show that there was very early contact with the Scandinavian languages. None of the non-Germanic languages in Scandinavia was written down as early as the period 800 to 1200.

By the sixth century the northern branch of Germanic had developed so many common features which are not found in the other Germanic languages that we can reasonably see it as a distinct Scandinavian language, usually called 'Common Scandinavian'. This language is chiefly documented in runic inscriptions. During the period 800–1200 it gradually develops geographically distinct features, so that we come to a clear division of dialect between East Norse and West Norse. The modern national languages, Danish and Swedish, have their linguistic roots in East Norse; while Icelandic, Faroese and Norwegian spring from West Norse.

Sources ranging from the eleventh into the thirteenth century name the Scandinavian languages spoken in the Viking Age *dǫnsk tunga* (Danish tongue). This indicates, if nothing more, that the differences within the Scandinavian language community in the Viking Age were not thought to be particularly great, even as late as the thirteenth century. An Icelandic saga text from the end of the thirteenth century even claims that there was a communal language in Norway, Denmark and England right up to the time of the Norman Conquest of 1066. The exact truth of such a statement need not concern us unduly, but it does help to demonstrate that there was a close connection between Scandinavian and the other Germanic languages up to and including the Viking Age.

Geographically, the Scandinavian language during the period 800–1200 extended over most of mainland Scandinavia, the Faroes, Iceland, Orkney and Shetland. At some times in this period the Scandinavian language must also have predominated in parts of northern France (Normandy), parts of England, Scotland, the Hebrides, the Isle of Man, Ireland and Greenland.

Across the whole of this area people whose mother tongue was Scandinavian would thus have understood, for example, the contents of a runic inscription which, irrespec-tive of spelling, could be *read* like this inscription on a cross from the Isle of Man: *Sandúlfr hinn svarti reisti kross þenna eptir Arinbjǫrgu konu sina* (Sandulf the black raised this cross in memory of Arinbjorg, his wife).

The language which was spoken, and to some extent also written, by Scandinavians in the Viking Age and the period immediately after was thus, as a linguistic system, rather different from the mainland Scandinavian languages of to-day (Danish, Norwegian and Swedish): they were more like modern Icelandic and, to a smaller extent, Faroese. Scandinavian languages in the period 800 to 1200 were inflected —grammatical categories, and to some extent sub-categories or classes within them, were expressed by inflexional endings. Nouns, for example, had forms which denoted gender, number and case; verbs had tense, number, mood and person; adjectives had gender, case, comparison, weak/strong form and so on. All these categories could also be divided into several inflexional classes, similar, for exam-ple, to that found in Latin grammar. From the point of view of modern mainland Scandinavia these languages seem to have a highly complex linguistic system, similar to the system of Old English as seen by the modern English. This rich inflexional system is very well preserved in modern Icelandic, and to some extent also in Faroese, even though these modern languages have not retained all the grammati-cal rules of the Viking Age and medieval language.

Viking Age and medieval West Norse are today together called *norrønt*, but no corresponding common term has been established for the East Norse languages. The Swedish language of this period is most often called Runic Swedish, while the Danish is ususually called Old Danish or Runic Danish, because runic inscriptions are the sources for our knowledge of the linguistic situation. Scandinavian was already a written language before the beginning of the Viking Age and was written in a particular Scandinavian variant of runic script. In the Viking Age, and up to the early twelfth century, the East Norse language in particular is well documented in a large corpus of runic inscriptions.

Latin script was introduced into Scandinavia in the sec-ond half of the eleventh century and was used, alongside runic script, for writing in the vernacular. West Norse, in particular, was developed as a written language in this medium at an early stage. With this process of literary development the need also arose for grammatical analysis and description of the linguistic system. From as early as in the mid-twelfth century, an Icelandic work survives which analyses the spoken language and the relationship between sounds (speech) and letters (writing). This, commonly called *The First Grammatical Treatise*, is unparalleled in the entire Germanic language area (cat. no. 521). It gives us a unique

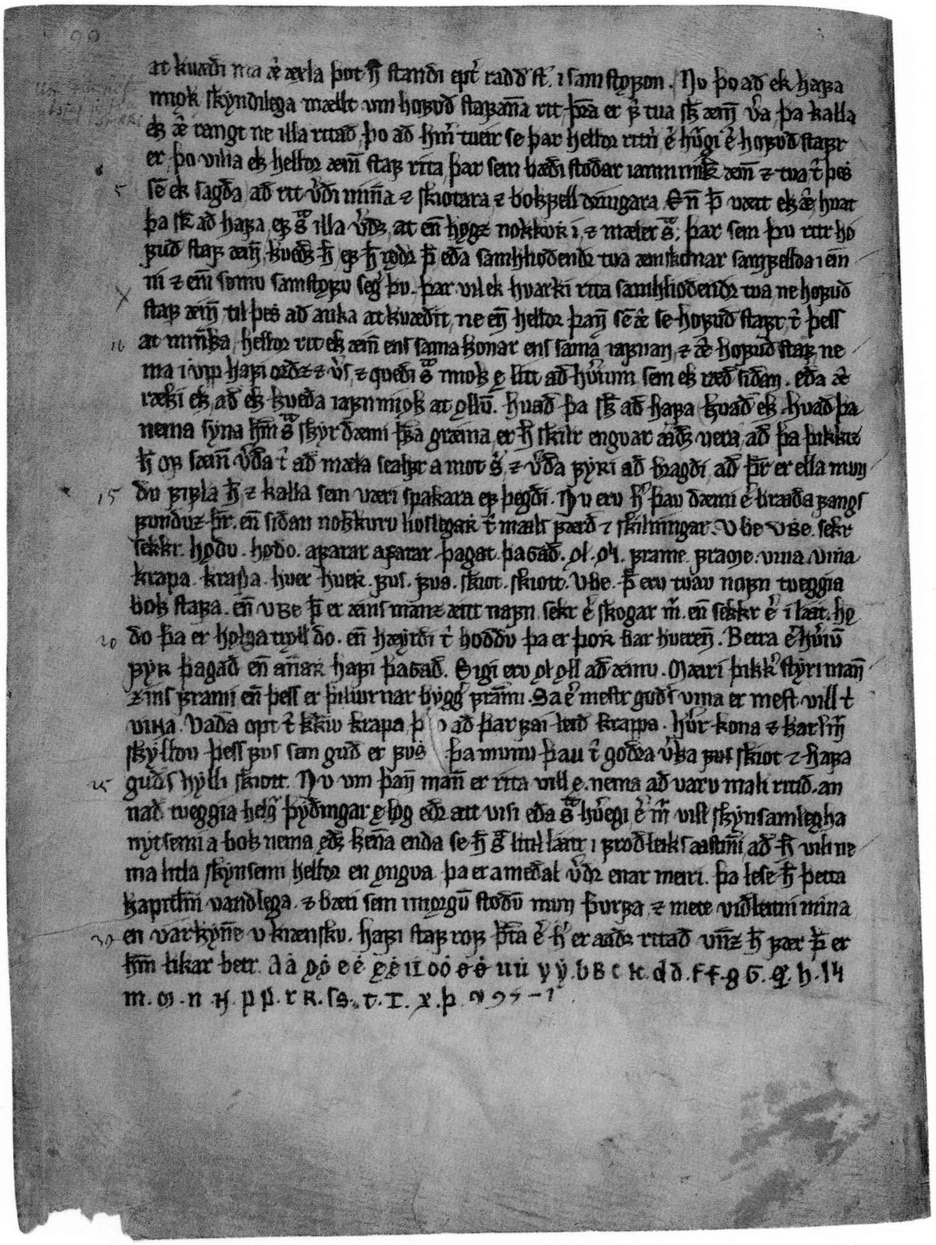

Fig. 3. Last page of the manuscript of the so-called First Grammatical Treatise (Codex Wormianus, p. 90). *This treatise, from c. 1150, contains a scientific argument for a reform of Icelandic orthography. It concludes with the proposal for an Icelandic alphabet. Cat. no. 521.*

insight into the Icelandic linguistic situation of its day and also, more generally, into West Norse. By the year 1200 West Norse was well established as a literary language and both religious and secular texts in various genres survive (cat. no. 336–7, 510, 518–27). By the same time Latin had also secured its position as a literary language across the whole of the Scandinavian area, perhaps especially in Church administration, but it was also used in learned works: history and hagiography (cat. no. 509, 515, 529–30, cf. 505–7).

J R H

Scandinavian society

Ole Fenger

The sources which tell of the social order of the period are archaeological and written. Archaeological sources comprise cemeteries, the dead themselves, the arrangement and equipment of the graves, the layout of settlements, farms, and houses, defensive works and forts; as well as tools, weapons, ornaments, coins, hoards and many other things. The written sources are both foreign and Scandinavian. The foreign sources tell not only of Viking raids, but also a little of events and society in Scandinavia, as in Frankish and Anglo-Saxon letters, in accounts of travel, and in chronicles. The oldest written sources in Scandinavia itself are runic inscriptions on stones or other objects. Although we know some thousands of inscriptions from Denmark, Norway, and especially Sweden, the majority dating from 950–1100, what they say is usually short and stereotyped, and (although some give information about occupation and function, and reveal differences of rank) the meaning of many words is obscure and our understanding of the societies referred to is very limited. It is significant that women play an important role in relation to the rune-stones, which are themselves monuments connected with the upper ranks of society.

After the Viking Age the Scandinavian countries enter the light of history as written native sources were produced which give new opportunities to understand the ordering of society.

In this respect the writing down of the law texts is of particular interest, since law regulated the social order of this period as it does of any other. The problem is that the earliest complete manuscripts date from the thirteenth century or later (cat. no. 518–9). Judging from the language used in these texts the contents must be older, but how old? Although the law texts record existing customs, it is difficult to say anything concerning the antiquity of such customs at a period when the kingdoms took shape—for this factor effected social ordinances; similarly the Church also wished to set its mark upon them.

However one central institution in the society represented by the laws cannot have been new—the *thing*, the settlement's assembly of free, adult, and able-bodied men. This institution must have performed in Scandinavia the functions basic to any society which had to make decisions in matters concerning common interest and at the same time dispel any conflicts that might arise.

The settlements were not isolated enclaves. Within a larger area, which we may call 'the land'—which would have its natural boundaries of sea, watercourses, mountains, and forests—there functioned a larger social entity with its own cult-place and its own thing-place—*landsting*—as a centre. In this common forum it was possible to treat conflicts at settlement level, so that peace could be restored and maintained to the common good of the land.

Top and bottom in society

The emergence of kingdoms did not change the inherited order of society at the level of the individual settlement or of the land. The *thing* continued to perform its ancient functions, which none of the organs of the kingdom could change or wished to change, since both Church and Monarchy gained from its pacifying functions. Despite the disturbances of the Viking Age in Europe, life in the villages from which the Vikings originated went on as before within the framework of an agrarian society. Although the population increased, new villages were founded, and new technology and new methods of cultivation were adopted, the order of society did not change at the local level.

Excavation of cemeteries and villages from the Iron Age and Viking Age show considerable social differentiation, represented by the size of houses, the tools, luxury goods, grave furnishings and so on. In some villages a single farm could be much bigger than the others, and this must be the farm of a potentate or chieftain—a seat of power whose owner may have been dominant at the *thing*, or had at least a larger say than others when decisions were to be made. This type of society has been described as 'chieftainship', but the power even of a chieftain or petty lord was circumscribed by law and custom, sanctioned by the society's religion and enforced by the *thing*.

Assuming the usual distinction between free men and thralls, it would even so be premature to suppose that freedom was in any way the same as equality. Freedom (or *frælse* as it was called) was based on property in its connotation of power or influence. Qualification for it came through property in the form of land. Land was the basis of society's existence, both as regards kinship groups and as individuals. The individuals, even if they themselves were warlords, were only seen as guardians of the kindred. Land

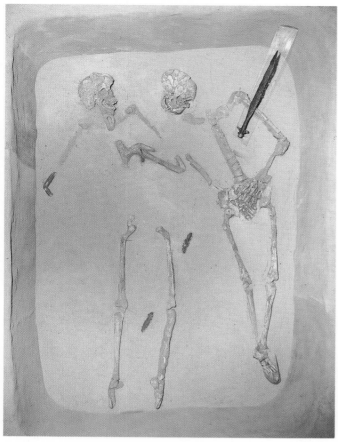

Fig. 1. Viking Age double grave at Stengade, Langeland, Denmark. The chief (to the left) was buried with a large spear; a bound and decapitated slave lies to the right. Cat. no. 45.

was the precondition for the survival of kindred and individual alike. The landless were either thralls or paupers, or were the merchants and craftsmen who became the citizens of the towns that originated and expanded between the years 800 and 1200.

Of the extent of slavery and the economic significance of thralls and their number, nothing definite is known. Their manumission or the purchase of their freedom is mentioned in several laws. Although the Church was in principle against slavery, even the Danish archbishop Absalon owned thralls, and liberated a number of them in his will of 1201. At that time slavery seems to have been disappearing throughout Scandinavia, but it was gradually being replaced by other forms of non-freedom and social dependency,

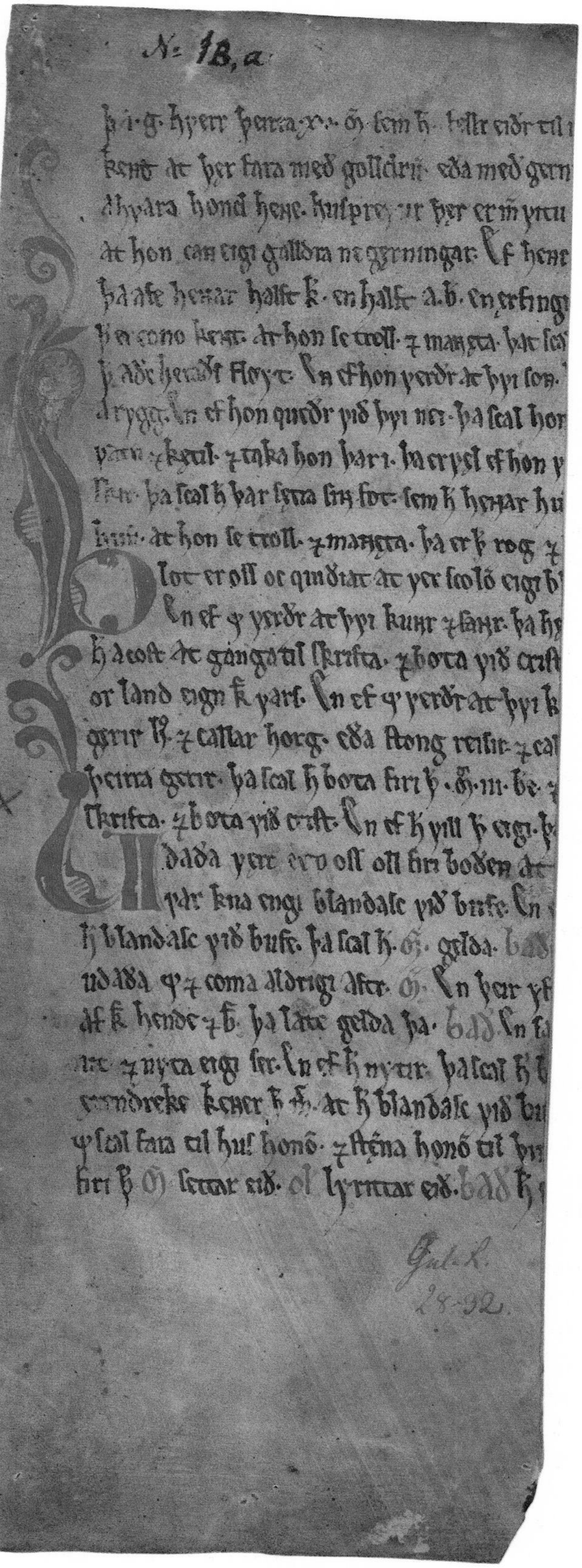

Fig. 2. Fragment of the Gulating law, Norway. Witchcraft, sacrifice and other misdeeds are forbidden. End of the 12th cent. Cat. no. 518.

typically by tying a man to his land. Thus the tenant acquired the protection of a person of power, but his legal independence was thereby limited and he was under obligation to pay dues and labour.

The lowest ranks of society also included farm-hands and domestic servants, who bound themselves for an agreed return. Throughout Scandinavia the word used for a household was *hjón*, a word which emphasized a partnership under the protection and guardianship of the householder, since the *hjón* included servants as well as wife and children.

Decline in social position could result from poverty, misfortune, illness, or old age. Then one could only hope for help from kindred. Selling of land is seen in the laws as a sign of extreme poverty, because possession of land was the acknowledged basis of existence. The kin had a duty to help and support its members in need. A survival of this in the Scandinavian laws is what was called *fledførelse*, by which a person (man or woman) surrendered all he possessed to his heirs in exchange for being supported by them in turn. This condition meant the total loss of legal rights; the heirs became responsible for the person supported, who could not go to the *thing*.

Family and kin

The regulation of questions of family and inheritance has a prominent place in the laws. Marriage cannot be dissolved, and legitimate children are favoured—in keeping with the wish of the Church. Only the Icelandic laws permitted divorce with the bishop's permission. Many rules show the great importance of the kinship group. Land had to remain with the kin, and therefore the spouse was excluded from a share in it. If anyone wished to sell his land, the kinsmen had prior right of purchase. In legal proceedings kinsmen supported each other, and after a homicide the culprit's kinsmen on the father's and mother's side were held collectively responsible for the man-price (*mandboden*) or the kin-fine (*ætteboden*, from the Nordic word for kin, *æt* or *ätt*). As this word is etymologically connected with *eiga*, to own, an ancient collective kin-ownership of land is implied.

With the coming of Christianity greater emphasis was laid on the individual and on personal guilt and personal responsibility, and this can be traced in the laws. For this reason the peasant farmer is the leading figure in the law texts. Some early descriptions represent the society behind the laws as a democracy, where all free peasants met at the *thing* and came to joint decisions on matters of common interest. It was once thought that everyone had the right to meet and vote, everyone was equal. But reality was different. Just as there were houses of different size in the villages and

Fig. 3. Seal-matrix of Radulf. Radulf was bishop of Ribe 1162–70 and chancellor to the Danish king. Cat. no. 514.

gifts of different quality were laid in the graves, the laws themselves show that some individuals had more weight at the meetings than others. Important decisions lay in the hands of a narrow upper class composed of families whose strength lay in solidarity and in landed possessions.

The Church preached that all were equal before God, and that it was harder for a rich man than a poor one to enter Heaven, but it could not take away the social differences between the rich and poor. The Church also taught that men and women were equal before God, and this also is reflected in the laws; but we cannot say how this effected daily life, still less do we know what the situation was before the laws were written down, for the position of women could have changed greatly between the 800s and the 1200s. We have seen that many women are mentioned in the runic inscriptions (cat. no. 497), and still more have been found in graves, but it is always the richest grave which tells us most.

The Church condemned polygamy, but we do not know whether it was ever common. A number of kings seem,

Fig. 4. Papal bull, 1196, from Pope Celestinus III to the cathedral chapter at Nidaros (Trondheim). The pope supports the cathedral chapter in the conflict between secular and ecclesiastical authority. Cat. no. 516.

however, to have had more than one wife, perhaps at one time, and in contemporary local histories it is said of the Scandinavian Counts of Normandy that they still had mistresses or multiple relationships, and that no distinction was made between legitimate and illegitimate offspring.

The law of marriage was part of ecclesiastical law, and in the thirteenth century marital suits began to be tried in the ecclesiastical courts. For this reason the Danish laws contain few rules on marital affairs, but the detailed rules about marriage in the Icelandic, Norwegian, and Swedish laws may bring us closer to earlier Scandinavian marriage law.

The basis of a marriage seems originally to have been a kind of purchase; if not a contract in the modern sense, at least an agreement whereby the person giving away the bride (usually her father), promised to transfer her to someone who was in return under an obligation to make him a payment determined by law, the *mundr* (or brideprice). Later this was given by him to the bride, and at a final stage it was paid directly by the groom to the bride. In the earliest Scandinavian law marriage was an agreement between the kin of the two parties, but under the influence of the Church the position of the woman became freer and her consent became necessary for the marriage to be valid; but the consent of her giver was still required. The earliest laws give no minimum age of marriage, but in due course those laid down by ecclesiastical law came to be applied—12 for females and 14 for males.

The marriage agreement included an agreement on the time of the wedding and on all its economic consequences, such as the extent of the wife's dowry and the shares of the parties in the joint assets. Here the Danish laws differ from the others in allowing joint ownership to come into force immediately without requiring a special decision. This so-called *fællig* included not only the husband and wife, but also their children and their spouses. On death, the *fællig* of a childless marriage was split equally between the survivor and the heirs of the deceased. If there were children a double share was calculated for the husband, wife, and each of the sons, and a single share for each daughter. A possible explanation of this is that upon marriage the daughters would obtain their dowry from the *fællig*.

The ecclesiastical prohibition of the exposure of infants to die has led to discussions as to whether the conditions of life in Scandinavia would compel parents to expose infants if it was felt that the survival of the family was at stake. This is mentioned once or twice in saga literature as a disgraceful act, whilst the Christian elements in the Norwegian laws condemned the exposure of infants unless they were deformed. If a child is born with its face at the back or its toes on its heels it shall be brought to church, baptized, and left in the church. According to Swedish and Danish law only healthy and normal new-born babies could be baptized. According to the Icelandic lawbook, *Grágás* (cat. no. 519), every newborn child must be brought to baptism as soon as possible 'of whatever creation it may be'.

The victory of Christianity in Scandinavia could not be marked more clearly than in the demand in the law for baptism as a condition for inheritance. 'Højmand that is a man buried in a mound cannot inherit', says a Danish law, and a *højmand* is a pagan, taking his designation from the old burial rite.

It is difficult to say anything in general from the surviving Scandinavian legal texts concerning rights of inheritance. There is no written material from Finland, and the earliest rules in the other countries differed widely from each other, except in so far as kinship was a condition for inheritance. The earlier Norwegian and Icelandic laws, however, state explicitly that a person without heirs could indicate at the *thing* or other assembly the person he wished to be his own heir. Originally it hardly mattered whether a child was born in or outside marriage, provided the father accepted it as his own. With the Church's condemnation of unmarried liaisons, there followed a diminution of the inheritance rights of children born outside marriage. Further, the partners in a marriage could not inherit directly from each other.

Is Scandinavian law special?

Just as the regulations concerning inheritance were very different in different countries and in different legal areas within them, many divergences can be pointed out which separate the earliest Scandinavian legal texts from each other. If, however, one looks for similarities instead of differences between institutions and laws, it is valid to speculate whether such similarities are little more than the core of Germanic law traditionally constructed as a counter to Roman law as practiced in the Roman provinces.

The answer seems to be that, if the common denominator is kept sufficiently low, a number of archaic traits can be found in Lombard, Frankish, and other legal texts from the period after the Migrations, which were foreign to Roman law even in its late and 'vulgarized' form. These traits recur in the earliest Scandinavian laws. But the situation is really more complicated. The fact is that in the legal sources that have been described as South-Germanic tribal laws, even the oldest written versions are profoundly influenced not only by Roman law in vulgarized form, but also by Christian ideology from a time when the legal system of the Church was still in its infancy. Thus it is an almost hopeless task to distinguish any indigenous and original laws of the Germanic tribes.

In Scandinavia of the eleventh and twelfth centuries the situation is quite different. Because influences from ecclesiastical law (and thereby also in part from Roman law) come into force at a time when canon law was already fully developed (having been established in a stable form by the Decree of Gratian of about 1140), we can observe in what respects the Scandinavian laws were similar to, and in what respects they differed from, the doctrine and legal sense of the Church in those areas of social and individual life which it saw as relevant. The Church might in due course demand the change of a local right that was unacceptable, but from long centuries of missionary experience it often chose to accept things as they were—even in important areas—and allowed the codification of legal rules which in principle were unacceptable. Scandinavia quickly became acquainted with the Decree of Gratian, perhaps through the papal

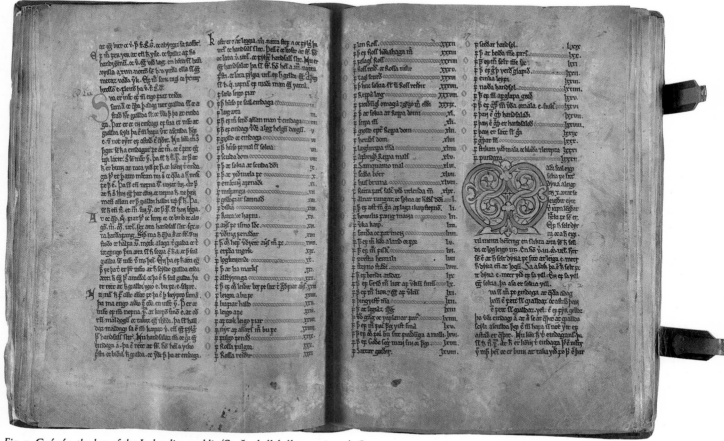

Fig. 5. Grágás, *the law of the Icelandic republic* (Staðarhólsbók, c. 1260–70). Cat. no. 519.

legate, the Englishman Nicholas Breakspeare (later Pope Hadrian IV), who in 1152 came to establish a Norwegian archbishopric and require that canon law be followed. Certainly the Decree of Gratian was known in Scandinavia in the 1160s.

Where the Nordic laws written down by clerics diverge from ecclesiastical doctrine and law, they are surely old laws, passed down from earlier times. This is particularly true of laws relating to guilt and responsibility, feuds and penalties. The Church denied the existence of responsibility without guilt, and of collective guilt and responsibility for negligent or accidental deeds; but these forms of responsibility remained in the laws. The same is true in legal processes, where the laws prescribe forms of proof which the Church resisted, but which could still be administered by the *things* without need of a genuine judiciary, of a system of resort, or of a central power with executive authority: for these did not exist. In the absence of executive authority law was enforced in a negative and passive way, in which defiance or contempt of the *thing* meant outlawry. The outlaw had no rights, he was unable to obtain the protection of the *thing*, and anybody could lawfully slay him. Judgement must be backed by power, otherwise it is not judgement. All law enforcement in Scandinavia was based at this period on passive duress in the form of outlawry and deprival of rights. This was a characteristic trait of Scandinavian law at a time when law enforcement elsewhere was in the hands of barons, feudatories, kings or emperors. For this reason laymen may have retained a role in Scandinavian legal practice which differed from that which pertained elsewhere on the continent.

Just as all Scandinavians, save the Finns and the Saami, were able to understand each other by virtue of a common language—the 'Danish tongue'—the earliest Scandinavian law texts contain so many basic similarities that it would be defensible to describe them in terms of being members of a Scandinavian legal family.

Resources and settlements

Peter Sawyer

Trade and towns

Commercial links between northern and western Europe were well established by the year 800. Ninth-century texts name several trading centres in Scandinavia; at Ribe and Hedeby in south Jutland, *Sciringesheal*—identified as Kaupang near Larvik south-west of Oslo, and Birka, in Lake Mälaren west of Stockholm. These have all been partly excavated and several other apparently similar, but unrecorded sites have been found, for example at Köpingsvik in Öland and, on a smaller scale, Paviken in Gotland and Skuldevig near the mouth of Roskilde Fjord. Anskar, the missionary archbishop of Hamburg-Bremen, who died in 865, established churches in three of these places, Birka, Ribe and Hedeby, and the account of his life by his successor, Rimbert, shows that merchants sailed not only between Birka and Hedeby, but also from these Baltic harbours to Dorestad, the great Frankish market near the mouth of the Rhine. According to Rimbert piracy was a serious problem, which suggests that the trade was regular and worth plundering. The fact that there are some 12,000 graves in the cemeteries of Hedeby, which lasted for less than three centuries, is one of several indications that it was a populous and important place. Rimbert reports that by the mid-ninth century there was a great abundance of goods both there and in Ribe, brought by merchants from Bremen and Dorestad, but he did not specify what they were, or what was offered in exchange.

There is no doubt that a great variety of Scandinavian produce reached western markets then, as later, but until the eleventh century furs were among the most important and valuable exports. Fur-bearing animals are found in all parts of Europe, but the best quality furs came from regions with the coldest winters and for western Europe Scandinavia and the lands east of the Baltic were an ideal source, for they could be reached by sea. Martens, sables, squirrels and other animals were hunted and trapped by the Saami as well as by Scandinavians and Finns. Some were forced to hand over part of their catch as tribute to rulers or chieftains or, less regularly, to armed raiders who undertook plundering expeditions. The exaction of tribute in Scandinavia is described in a ninth-century English text that includes some information provided by a Norwegian called Ohthere who visited the court of the English king Alfred. He lived in the far north of Norway and took tribute from the *Finnas*, that is the Saami:

'That tribute consists of the skins of beasts, the feathers of birds, whale-bone, and ship-ropes made from walrus-hide and sealskin. Each pays according to his rank. The highest in rank has to pay fifteen marten skins, five reindeer skins, one bear skin, and ten measures of feathers, and a jacket of bearskin or otterskin and two ship-ropes. Each of these must be sixty ells long, one made from walrus-hide, the other from seal.'

Tribute was similarly collected in many parts of Scandinavia, as well as in Finland and other lands round the Baltic. Scandinavians began to exploit the lands round Lake Ladoga in the eighth century, if not before, and soon after AD 750 they established a base at Staraja Ladoga, a short distance south of the lake. There must have been many places with a similar function, but on a smaller scale. The defended site recently discovered in Finland at Varikkoniemi, with a harbour and unusually large houses, has plausibly been interpreted as a base from which the Lake Region of Finland was exploited before Swedish invaders did the same from the fort called Tavastehus which they built nearby in the late thirteenth century.

The produce initially gathered by Scandinavians in Finland and north Russia was probably destined for western Europe, but by 780 some had discovered that they could as well sell it to Muslim merchants in the east. A tenth-century Muslim geographer listed goods that merchants bought in Russia, including many types of fur, skins, amber, wax, honey, falcons and 'fish-teeth', meaning walrus tusks. This list gives a good impression of what Scandinavians were then exporting to western Europe, and is a reminder that, although furs were a very important export, there were others. Walrus ivory was especially welcome in the ninth century because very little elephant ivory was then reaching western Europe. Walrus lived in arctic waters, and Ohthere described how he hunted them for their skins as well as tusks. Even in the twelfth century virtually all the ivory carved in England was from walruses that were then being hunted in the seas off Greenland as well as in north Norway (cat. no. 591–615).

Ohthere apparently took what he gathered, as tribute or by hunting, to sell in markets in south Scandinavia and perhaps in England. There were certainly other chieftains like him in North Norway. A house that was occupied from the eighth to the tenth century by chieftains or magnates like Ohthere has recently been excavated at Borg in the

Fig. 1. *Winter view of the Viking Age town of Birka, Sweden, seen from the north-east. In the foreground Hemlanden, a large cemetery with grave mounds. In the middle, the semicircular wall that surrounds the town itself,* the so-called 'Black Earth'. Above, to the left, the town's fortress stands on higher ground. In the background, Lake Mälar.

Lofoten islands. It was exceptionally long, 81 m., and the objects found in it, including exotic luxuries such as fine glass vessels and ornaments of gold and silver (cat. no. 154), were like those found in the major trading centres and rich graves of southern Scandinavia. Other remains nearby, including a large boat-house, confirm the impression that the men who lived in Borg had much the same status as Ohthere. Few had the opportunity to undertake such extensive voyages as he did. Most of them could, however, sell what they did not need in exchange for equipment or materials that were not available locally but could be obtained in seasonal fairs held in or near their home territory. Iron, whetstones and other things that have been found far away from possible places of origin show that there was an extensive exchange of produce between different regions of Scandinavia in the Viking Age.

Many of the seasonal fairs of medieval Scandinavia and Finland were held in the winter when ice, snow and frozen ground made it possible to travel long distances inland more easily and quickly than in warmer seasons; it was also the best time for furs. Such fairs were convenient for natives, but not for foreign merchants who came by sea. They could only sail in the summer months and did their business in coastal trading places under the protection of kings, who in return expected to benefit by sharing in the profits of trade, in the form of tolls and gifts from merchants.

So far as is known at present, the earliest of these centres for overseas trade was Ribe. In the early eighth century craftsmen periodically gathered there, apparently for quite short periods, and made bronze ornaments, bone combs, glass or amber beads, and various leather goods (fig. 3). Coins (cat. no. 152) and imports show that at that time Ribe traded with Frisia and the Rhine region, as it did throughout the Middle Ages. Ribe was probably founded by a king, it was certainly under royal authority in the ninth century when the king's consent was needed before a church could be built there. Some early houses and graves have recently been found. It is not yet possible to estimate the extent of

Fig. 2. Twelve imported half-finished axes, found at Gjerrild, Denmark. Viking Age. Cat. no. 93.

the original settlement but by the twelfth century a large timber-lined channel had been made west of the town, enclosing approximately 10 hectares. This area eventually declined in importance and became, in effect, a suburb of the medieval town which had as its centre the cathedral, built in the eleventh century on the other side of the Ribe river.

Hedeby was founded by the Danish king Godfred about a century after Ribe, but on a much larger scale. It was a good site, close to the main land-route that ran along the spine of Jutland and south into Saxony. A great variety of goods were imported not only from other parts of Scandinavia and the lands round the Baltic but also from western Europe. Hedeby flourished with a regular population of more than 1,000, and many more when markets were held. There are several indications that it was under royal control, including the fact that, as at Ribe, a church was established there only with royal permission. Coins were apparently struck there at various times in the ninth and tenth centuries (cat. no. 153), and remains of what appears to have been a tollhouse have been found in the harbour.

In the eleventh century Hedeby gradually declined and was replaced by Schleswig, on the north side of the fjord. Schleswig did not have such good access to the north-south route through Jutland but the larger ships that began to be used in the eleventh century were too deep to reach Hedeby's harbour. Being close to the frontier with Saxony, Schleswig was strategically important and it had both a royal residence and cathedral, but it did not long remain a major trading centre. New towns founded in the twelfth century, notably Lübeck, were better placed for the growing German trade with Scandinavia and the lands round the Baltic.

The other ninth-century trading centre visited by foreign merchants was Birka, founded at much the same time as Hedeby (fig. 1). It did not last as long as Hedeby, only about 150 years, and had a smaller permanent population; its cemeteries contain only about 3,000 graves. The material found in those graves suggests that many of Birka's inhabitants had close links with Russia and the lands beyond, Byzantine as well as Muslim (cat. no. 120-1, 132-4). Its main trade was, however, with western rather than eastern markets (cat. no. 125-7). It had little to offer Muslim merchants; there was little point in shipping slaves or furs from central Sweden to markets in Russia. The east was important for Birka as a source of goods that could be sold to merchants who traded in western Europe. By about 950 Scandinavians were finding it more difficult to exact tribute in the east and Birka then ceased to be a trading centre.

Its apparent successor, Sigtuna was founded towards the end of the tenth century. It had a regular plan, and by about 995 coins were being struck there for a Swedish king, Olof, implying that it was, like Hedeby and Ribe, under royal control (cat. no. 423, 552-3). Sigtuna seems to have been a Christian centre from the outset and by the early twelfth century had several churches, including a cathedral. Its economic function is, however, uncertain. Recent excavations have found little to indicate the presence of craftsmen or traders in the first hundred years of its existence (cat. no. 498, 505, 531, 576, 578, 582-4, 598). Sigtuna is thus very similar to both Lund and Trondheim, which were founded at much the same time, and soon became major royal and

Fig. 3. The trading place at Ribe, Denmark, in the 8th cent. Reconstruction. Soon after the year 700 an area by the river Ribe was divided into permanent plots on which many craftsmen worked when markets were held. Later Ribe developed into a town.

Fig. 4. ▲ *International trading-places in Scandinavia in the 9th cent.* ● *Towns in Scandinavia c. 1200. Finland, Iceland, the Faroes and Greenland had no towns at that time. Throughout the Middle Ages Trondheim was the northernmost town in Scandinavia.*

ecclesiastical centres; as in Sigtuna, few craftsmen were active in either place during the eleventh century.

The only urban development of any significance between the establishment of Hedeby and Birka, and that of Lund, Sigtuna and Trondheim, was at Århus in Jutland. A rampart was built there in the mid-tenth century enclosing an area of about 4 hectares in which craftsmen worked. Adam of Bremen, writing in the 1070s, described it as a city from which people sailed to other parts of Denmark and to Norway. That it had a similar range of contacts a century earlier is shown by the discovery there in tenth-century contexts of soap-stone and whetstones from Norway or Sweden, Baltic pottery and millstones from the Rhineland. By 948 Århus was considered, at least by the archbishop of Hamburg-Bremen, to have much the same status as Hedeby and Ribe; in that year he consecrated bishops for all three places, but it was a century before the see of Århus was permanently established.

Ribe and Århus, together with Schleswig, if that is considered a continuation of Hedeby, are the only medieval Scandinavian towns that existed much earlier than the year 1000, but many others were founded in Denmark and Norway at that time, including Odense, Oslo, Roskilde, Trondheim and Viborg. This urban expansion was encouraged by kings, indeed it was their power that made it possible. Kings could provide the protection traders and craftsmen needed and they could grant the privileges that enabled the embryo urban communities to flourish. In the eleventh century

Danish and Norwegian kings established episcopal sees in some of them, and endowed churches in others. In some there were royal residences and most of the mints in which coins were struck in the names of kings were located in these urban or proto-urban centres. The people who settled in these places were, in effect, royal tenants and paid rent to royal agents, who also collected tolls and other dues.

In Sweden, where royal power developed slowly, so too did urbanisation. By 1100 there were only four Swedish towns, and two of them, Lödöse and Skara, were in Göta-land, where royal authority was more effective earlier than in other parts of the medieval kingdom. In contrast, most of the medieval towns of Denmark and Norway were firmly established by the beginning of the twelfth century.

Rural settlement

The early development of rural settlement in Scandinavia is more obscure. Conjectures about it depend largely on the evidence of pagan cemeteries, place-names and the surviving traces of field systems, often interpreted in the light of dubious assumptions about social structure. Very few have been excavated and only in Denmark on a large-scale, but even there only a handful have been completely uncovered. There is, however, no doubt that there were regular villages as well as single farms in Denmark long before the ninth century, and one of them, Vorbasse in central Jutland, has been traced through successive stages back to the first century BC. (cat. no. 59, 81–3).

Most, perhaps all, Danish villages had some arable but until the eleventh century the economy was predominantly pastoral. Many farms had byres to shelter cows and oxen. They were much smaller than their modern successors, but there were surprisingly many of them. In the ninth century two of the houses at Vorbasse each had a byre with 22 stalls, and in the eleventh century several farms could house at least 50 animals. Few oxen were needed as draught animals —there was little arable—and the cows must have produced far more milk, cheese, butter, meat and skins than the farmers and their households needed. It therefore seems likely that some cattle produce was sold, even exported. The large heap of cattle dung, over 80 metres across that was accumulated at Ribe during the eighth century must have come from animals that were penned up, presumably awaiting slaughter or sale.

Excavations in many parts of Denmark have shown that most settlements were moved a few hundred metres at intervals varying from about one to three centuries. Such moves offered an opportunity to cultivate the fertilised ground where the cattle had been housed; traces of cultiva-

tion have been found on the site of one of the abandoned farms at Vorbasse. In the twelfth century Vorbasse was moved for the last time to a new site about a kilometre away, close to the best land for arable cultivation in the vicinity. Vorbasse seems to be typical in this respect; most Danish settlements were permanently established in the eleventh or twelfth centuries on sites that had not previously been occupied and that seem to have been chosen to be close to land suitable for arable farming. There was certainly a great increase in the area of ploughed ground and in the amount of cereal produced during the eleventh and twelfth centuries.

In eleventh-century Scandinavia, as in other parts of Europe, the population was increasing. This was made possible by an increase in the food supply which was in turn partly due to a general improvement in the climate that began then. The supply was also increased by the shift from pastoral to arable farming which yielded more food, but whether that was a cause or an effect of the population increase is uncertain. Two undoubted consequences were the expansion of many existing settlements, including the towns, and the creation of a very large number of new settlements. The name given to many of these new settlements in Denmark was *thorp*, now familiar in such place-names as Kastrup or Kirkerup. This expansion occurred mainly between AD 1000 and 1200, a period that also saw a rapid reduction in the extent of woodland. Most of the new settlements were, and remained, small with limited resources, and many were abandoned after the Black Death reduced the population by a third or more in the fourteenth century.

In other parts of Scandinavia the population increase of the eleventh and twelfth centuries had similar effects; existing settlements grew and thousands of new ones were created, many of them called *thorp* or *rud*, meaning 'clearing', for example Bolltorp, Konnerud or Fagered.

This medieval colonisation created many separate, isolated farms. That appears to have been the normal pattern of earlier settlement in Norway and in other regions that were predominantly forest and mountain. It was reproduced in Iceland by the Norwegian colonists who settled there in the ninth and tenth centuries. Thanks to volcanic activity, early farms can be studied more easily in Iceland than in Norway. Many in the vicinity of the volcano Hekla were abandoned after it erupted, probably around 1200, because they were smothered by volcanic ash. The disaster was not so sudden that the inhabitants could not remove their belongings and the most valuable building materials, including the main timbers, but enough was left, and has been preserved by the ash, to make it possible to study these

Fig. 5. Air photo of the Vorbasse area, seen from the north, Denmark. Red colouring marks the location of the village from the 8th to the 10th cent.

Blue indicates its location in the 11th cent. In the 12th cent. the village moved to its present site and can be seen in the background.

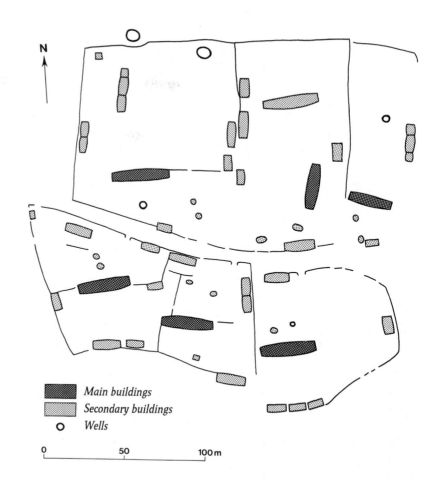

Fig. 6. The village of Vorbasse. C. 900. A preliminary plan of the excavated traces of buildings, fences and wells. There were six farms, three on each side of a central track. All were surrounded by fences with openings to the track. Each had a main building with byre at one end, as well as several smaller buildings, some simple with sunken floors. For a drawing of a possible reconstruction of the south-west farm, which had a smithy, see p. 137.

■ *Main buildings*
▨ *Secondary buildings*
○ *Wells*

0   50   100 m

settlements in some detail. The best known, called Stöng (cf. cat. no. 590), is illustrated p. 55, fig. 3.

In Sweden, especially where there were relatively large expanses of plain, there were many villages and hamlets in the thirteenth century. Their earlier history is uncertain. Some may have been formed by the subdivision of older farms. This happened even in Norway, especially in the west where subdivision into numerous holdings produced very compact, even congested, settlements in which the several buildings of the different farms were irregularly interspersed, with little space between them. In eastern Norway, where conditions were less cramped and sites for new settlements were more readily available, some farms were divided, but rarely into more than two. It is therefore unlikely that subdivision alone can account for the formation of the larger, regular villages of the Viking Age and earlier that have been uncovered by Danish archaeologists or are implied by the earliest Danish and Swedish laws.

The ability of village communities to regulate their own

affairs should not be underestimated, but it seems likely that lords had a significant role in shaping many villages. The fact that the number of farms in Vorbasse was almost the same from the eighth century to the twelfth suggests that its inhabitants were not free and independent landowners, whose property would be divided between heirs, but were tenants of a lord who, directly or indirectly through a steward, regulated the farms. That would also explain why, with one exception in the eleventh century, the farm enclosures were all much the same size, as were the dwelling houses. The regions where kings, magnates, bishops and major churches owned large amounts of land in the twelfth century tended to be those where large and regular villages were common. The general shift of Danish settlements to sites suitable for arable cultivation in the eleventh and twelfth centuries is more easily understood on the assumption that the initiative was often taken by important landowners who were eager to increase the yield of their own farms and to exact more as rent and tithe.

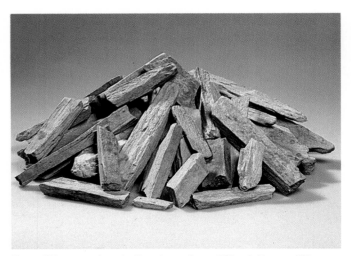

Fig. 7. *Whetstones for sale. Found in a ship at Klåstad, Norway. Viking Age. Cat. no. 89.*

Fig. 8. *Fish-hook, fishing spear and net-sinker from Norway. Viking Age. Cat. no. 85.*

Increasing trade

Most rural households depended for food on what they could grow, gather or catch, and obtained the fuel and building timber they needed in nearby woodland, but there were also needs that could not be satisfied locally. Some surplus was therefore required to be sold in town markets or seasonal fairs where such things as iron tools, weapons, and whetstones to sharpen them, could be obtained. Thanks to these exchanges Scandinavia was self-sufficient in most things; the needs of one region could be met by another. Inter-regional exchange, between mountain and coastal districts was particularly well developed in Norway (cat. no. 64, 89–92). There was, however, a demand for some imports. Cloth from England or Flanders was better quality than that produced in Scandinavia, and Norwegians supplemented their inadequate supply of cereals from England and Denmark. Churches were also furnished with such things as statues, panels to decorate altars, and crosses, which were obtained abroad in exchange for Scandinavian products that were in demand in other parts of Europe. In the twelfth century Scandinavians were still exporting furs as they had done three hundred years earlier, but furs became more fashionable in western Europe in the eleventh and twelfth centuries, and Scandinavia could not satisfy the rapidly growing demand. By the twelfth century most of the furs reaching western Europe came from Novgorod. Merchants from many parts of Scandinavia, including Gotland, obtained furs there. Some were sold in Slav trading places like Lübeck to German traders from Soest, Dortmund or other Westphalian towns, but others were taken to markets in England, Flanders and France. In 1158 Lübeck was refounded as a German town by Henry the Lion, who encouraged Norwegian, Danish, Swedish and Russian merchants to visit it. Germans then began to play a more active role in Baltic trade and in time established a major market in Gotland, at Visby. Baltic trade was, however, still largely in the hands of Scandinavians well into the thirteenth century and until 1227 Lübeck generally depended on the good will, even the protection, of Danish kings.

Scandinavia's share of the fur trade declined but there were some things, notably falcons and ivory, that it could supply better than anywhere else. There were also less exotic exports; the Danes were renowned horse breeders, Norwegian wood was used to line rooms in Windsor Castle, and Iceland could offer wool and a coarse cloth known as wadmal; and by the end of the twelfth century Scandinavia had begun to export what were later to be its most important products, dried cod and salt herring.

There was at that time, and long after, a general need for preserved food that could be eaten in the winter and spring. The need was most acute in the towns that were rapidly developing in many parts of western Europe in the eleventh and twelfth centuries. There were four main methods of preservation; smoking, fermentation, salting or drying. The simplest and cheapest was drying, which is best done in a cold climate; in warm weather food tends to rot before it is dry. Northern Norway was ideal; it had an arctic climate, strong winds, and fish, especially cod, were abundant in the coastal waters. By the fourteenth century dried cod, known as stockfish, accounted for 80% of the value of all Norwegian exports and there are indications that large quantities were already being produced early in the twelfth century.

The main production centre was in the Lofoten islands, and stockfish from the whole of north Norway was collected there to be shipped south in the spring, initially to Trondheim, which probably owed its rapid development in the eleventh century largely to this traffic. There was certainly a demand for this food at that time. Many towns in western Europe, especially in England and Flanders were already large in the eleventh century and stockfish would have been as welcome then as they were in 1200. By then Bergen had displaced Trondheim as the main market for the export of stockfish. It was founded in the late eleventh century, apparently by King Olaf Kyrre and flourished. It was more convenient for foreign merchants than distant Trondheim and certainly attracted many of them. A visitor at the end of the twelfth century reported that:

'There is dried fish (known as skrei) beyond telling. Ships and men arrive from every land: there are Icelanders, Greenlanders, Englishmen, Germans, Danes, Swedes, Gotlanders, and other nations too numerous to mention. Every nation can be found there if one only takes the trouble to look. There are also quantities of wine, honey, wheat, fine cloths, silver and other commodities, and a busy trade in all of them.'

A similar impression is given by a speech attributed to the Norwegian king Sverre, who died in 1202, that is quoted in his saga, written by a contemporary. The king thanked the English for bringing wheat and honey, flour and cloth, but complained that the Germans came 'in great numbers and impoverish the land by carrying away butter and dried fish, and encouraged drunkeness by importing wine'. A fuller list of Norwegian exports is given in the Norse translation of the Saga of Tristram, made in 1226. The translator elaborated on the original by describing a cargo taken to France by a Norwegian ship which included beaver, bear, sable and squirrel skins, walrus teeth, hawks and falcons, wax, hides, goatskins, stockfish, tar, oil, sulphur (from Iceland) 'and all sorts of northern wares'. The emphasis on luxuries is natural in a tale of chivalry, but it is likely that stockfish were already at that date Norway's most important and lucrative product. By then Scandinavia was also producing, and exporting, very large quantities of salt herring, but that came not from Norway but from southern Scandinavia, mainly from Öresund, where huge shoals of herring arrived in the late summer. Until the end of the twelfth century production was on a small scale, limited by the shortage of salt, but shortly before 1200 the salt deposits at Lüneburg began to be exploited, and that made large-scale salting possible. As a result merchants from many parts of Europe were attracted to Öresund, making the Skåne Market, held at the time of the fishery, one of the major fairs of thirteenth-century Europe. Lübeck's control of the salt supply gave it a great advantage in that fair. It had others, and in time dominated Scandinavia's trade, but in the year 1200 that still lay in the future.

Fig. 9. 'Sigmund owns this sack'. Runic inscription on a tally from Trondheim, Norway. Early 12th cent. Cat. no. 501.

House and home

Anders Ödman

Houses

The northern lands—from south Scandinavia to the Arctic Ocean and west to Iceland—comprise vastly different types of landscapes—marshland, plateaux, mountains, archipelagoes and great stretches of taiga with forests and bogs. The climate varies greatly, as do the conditions which support human and animal life. In the Viking Age and early Middle Ages almost all the Scandinavian population lived by agriculture, and this influenced building construction. People, animals and stores all had to be housed. The availability of building material also influenced structure.

The houses of south Scandinavia often had wattle walls plastered with clay based on a framework of oak posts. The roof was supported on purlins and covered with reeds or thatch. The timber framework was jointed and the roof tied together with withies. Houses with solid wooden walls and roof-shingles were not, however, uncommon, and in the Danish fortresses the walls and roofs of the great longhouses were of oak, and nails were used for fastening (p. 39, fig. 7).

In the extensively forested areas of the Scandinavian peninsula there was no shortage of wood—here the buildings were of blockhouse construction, built of straight-grown pine. Here also the roofs were usually made of birch-bark and turf, the underlying bark forming a watertight skin and the turf acting as insulation. All the timber used in Icelandic houses (apart from driftwood) had to be imported, so turf, earth and stone were mostly used for building. Here the roofs and walls were more than a metre thick (p. 55, fig. 3), the houses showing a clear relationship between climate and availability of building materials.

Just as there was a great diversity of building materials, so these were used in different ways. Wooden walls, for example, might be built of posts and wattle-and-daub: or constructed of timber-framing with horizontal planks between upright posts; other methods included 'stave-construction', where the walls consisted of a series of upright planks (cat. no. 82, 440); blockhouse construction of horizontal logs with lapped corners; or half-timbering with clay- or dung-clad panels. Different techniques might be combined in a single building.

As very few people lived in towns, by far the majority of houses from this period were built as farms. The Scandinavian longhouse consisted of a hall, in which the inhabitants lived, and under the same long roof a byre; there may also have been a store-room for agricultural produce and other goods. The longhouse, which often had curved walls, was a traditional Scandinavian building; but, towards the end of the Viking Age, larger farms tended to separate animal-houses and dwelling-quarters.

Another type of structure was the sunken-floored building, often only 3–4 m long and 2–3 m wide. The floor was dug into the ground to a depth of about a metre so that the walls were insulated by the earth against summer heat and winter cold. Such buildings were easily constructed and needed little building material. They often lay close to a longhouse, and were probably used for various economic purposes—weaving sheds, housing for small animals, servants' quarters, smithies and so on. Some settlements, however, consisted entirely of sunken-floored buildings, for example the trading site of Löddeköpinge in Skåne. These houses were probably used by a specialized population—probably merchants—who lived in them intermittently and did not need large, permanent dwellings. Sunken-floored buildings are rare after the Viking Age.

In the early Middle Ages new materials and building methods were introduced. The use of limestone revolutionized monumental building in the North, whilst in southern Scandinavia brick, a completely new building material, was introduced in the middle of the twelfth century. Bricks were expensive to produce and at this period these 'baked stones' were used only in royal, aristocratic or ecclesiastical buildings. Roof-trusses also appeared at this time, but post-borne roofs were normal until well on in the Middle Ages.

The earliest towns had buildings of standard size and building sites were divided up into equal plots. The earliest 'town houses' have been discovered in Hedeby and date from the ninth century. These had wattle-and-daub walls. In Sigtuna, about 1000, a combination of structural types—blockhouse and south Scandinavian daubed wattle walls—were used. On the Norwegian coast, houses in early towns such as Trondheim were built entirely of timber in blockhouse, framed, or stave techniques.

The traditional way of heating houses was with a long hearth in the middle of the room. The area around the hearth was warm, so the farmer and his family had their seats there; the lower ranks and servants occupied areas nearer to the gables.

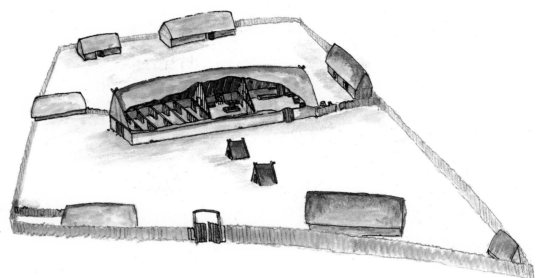

Fig. 1. *Farm in the village of Vorbasse, Denmark, c. 900. Reconstruction seen from the north (cf. plan p. 133). The farm is surrounded by a fence and subdivided by another fence. The gateway to the village street can be seen at the bottom. The main building has a byre with stalls at one end and dwelling-quarters at the other end. Six small buildings flank the fence and there is a smithy in the right-hand corner. Two small sunken-floored buildings are also shown.*

Fig. 2. *Well from the village of Vorbasse, Denmark. Cat. no. 81.*

The oven was an innovation in the Viking Age, perhaps brought in from the Slav regions, and is mainly found in the sunken-floored buildings of south Scandinavia (cat. no. 66). Apart from the unpleasant smoke which issued from the opening in its domed cover, the oven was a great advance in heating, also for cooking and baking bread. But the open, long hearth continued well on into the Middle Ages, as a status symbol, a source of light, and for the preparation of certain foodstuffs.

Brushwood from the surrounding countryside was most commonly used for firing ovens. Mature mixed woodland was felled, but regenerated in a few years. This coppiced woodland was an important source of fuel, building material, fencing and raw material for crafts.

Fire was made by striking a hardened steel against a piece of flint or quartz (cat. no. 61). The resultant sparks ignited tinder (bark of beech or birch which had been boiled in a lye of birch ashes and then dried). The embers from the tinder

Fig. 3. Full-scale reconstruction of a house from Hedeby, the greatest trading centre in Viking Age Scandinavia. The house was built in 870 and measured 5 × 12m. The walls were of wattle-and-daub in a timber framework and were supported by slanting, timber buttresses. The house contained three rooms: the main living room was in the middle and had wide wall-benches and a hearth.

were then applied to a ball of juniper bark or dried grass. They were then fanned into a flame which could be used to ignite the wood in the oven or hearth.

Most of the light in the house came from the hearth, but there were also small windows covered by finely-scraped skin or some other translucent material. The family worked by this light. If necessary the houses could also be lit by resin torches (made of moss roots) or by oil-lamps made of stone, pottery or metal (cat. no. 158, 590). Wax candles were introduced with the arrival of Christianity at the end of the tenth century, tallow being used when access to beeswax was limited. For many centuries the most important sources of light for both town and country dwellers were lamps using seal or herring oil, the latter produced in the great herring fisheries such as Skanör and Falsterbo.

The most common furnishings in houses were wall-benches with wooden supports and earth filling. The site of an upright loom is sometimes represented by a row of loom-weights, which had fallen to the floor when a house had burnt down. We have no evidence—nor is any likely to be found—which would show us the position of other furniture in a house; but some furniture—either complete or fragmentary—does survive, mostly stools and chests (cat. no. 70). Many keys and locks have been found. Chests may have been locked with bolts or with something comparable to modern padlocks. House doors were secured with lever locks of wood or iron (cat. no. 67–9, 432–5).

The best preserved furniture comes from the ninth- and tenth-century ship-burials of Oseberg and Gokstad (cat. no. 161–7). The queen buried at Oseberg had a bed with animal-head corner-posts, a chair with a woven seat, many chests, and a quantity of wooden tools and other objects of the highest quality.

In the eleventh and twelfth centuries furniture became more common, as there was a general increase in comfort. Finds from twelfth-century towns include a cradle and a child's chair (cat. no. 561–6).

We know little of the colours used in the houses. The furniture which has been preserved has almost all lost its paint, but some must have been coloured. A tapestry from

Fig. 4. Piece of carved furniture from Trondheim, Norway. C. 1100–50. Cat. no. 564.

Baldishol, Norway (p. 195, fig. 6), and an embroidery from Skog church in central Sweden preserve some colours, and some painted ecclesiastical objects survive (p. 213, fig. 4–6)); houses and furnishings must also have been painted.

Domestic utensils and food

The necessities for the preparation of food lay around the hearth. In the longhouse cooking was usually done on the central hearth, but in the late Viking Age the kitchen started to be separated from the living and sleeping quarters. Most of the cooking equipment excavated today consists of pottery. Native Viking Age pottery was usually a coarse, grey-brown ware, probably made on site. Pots are both flat- and round-based, perhaps reflecting the different types of

hearths used in various regions (cat. no. 65, 573). The import of luxury ceramics from the Rhineland began in the ninth century, and such items have been found in north Norway and central Sweden (as at Birka) (cat. no. 126, 154).

Contact between the Slav world and the Scandinavian Baltic is demonstrated by the characteristic grey-black pottery of the south coast of the Baltic. These pots are biconical, have a flat base, and are decorated with a wavy-line (cat. no. 573). Pottery of this type is found in eastern Denmark and as far north as Sigtuna, near Birka. The pottery was probably made by specialists, and the bases of the pots often carry a maker's mark. This 'black ware' was not fired in a kiln, but in a pit or clamp. The new type of pottery, which began to be made about 1200, demanded both wheels and kilns. This was lead glazed and was often decorated with pipe-clay or a slip of metal oxide. Modern

Fig. 5. Wooden key from Lund, Sweden. 1000–1050. Cat. no. 69.

Fig. 6. Bed from the Oseberg burial, Norway. Reconstruction. C. 800–850. Cf. cat. no. 162.

Fig 8. Hearth with brazier, cooking pots, food containers, ladles, spit and oven-rakes. Objects excavated in Lund, Sweden. 11th cent.

cookery began with the introduction of lead-glazed vessels (cat. no. 575), which appear in a variety of shapes—jugs, bowls, tripod pitchers, handled vessels, colanders, and mugs.

Although pottery was common in the coastal and inland towns, it was hardly used in the interior of Sweden, Norway and Finland, where the methods of food-preparation can be seen in excavated mounds of brittle-burnt stones which still survive along rivers and in the forests. These heaps of stones are all that remains of a method of cooking in which stones, heated in a fire, were placed in a pit with a vessel of bark or wood containing liquid or food. Meals may also have been prepared by placing joints of meat wrapped in leaves in such a pit. The pit would then be filled with hot stones and covered with turf. Such methods of preparing food are known from all over the world and were common in Scandinavia throughout the Viking Age, although food at this period was also prepared in cauldrons.

Not all cooking vessels were made of pottery. An important trading commodity in the Viking Age was the soapstone bowl from Norway or south-west Sweden (cat. no. 64,

90). They have been found complete or in fragments throughout the Scandinavian area, and were also exported. Cauldrons made of riveted iron-plates are also known (cat. no. 63), but they must have been expensive to produce.

A cauldron would have hung above the hearth of a Viking longhouse. Boiled pork was eaten at feasts, as it was eaten daily by the gods in Valhalla and would have been savoured by heroes killed in battle. Viking Age and medieval settlements have produced vast quantities of bone to demonstrate the kind of meat consumed—pig, cattle, sheep, goat, hens, ducks and geese (cat. no. 87). The most usual way of cooking meat would have been to boil it with water, herbs and root vegetables, but Viking Age spits have been found in archaeological contexts (cat. no. 62), demonstrating that some food was cooked over the fire on a skewer.

Many wooden objects were used in the kitchen—barrels, bowls, dishes, cups, spoons, ladles and so on. They were often very skillfully made—stave-built, carved or lathe-turned (cat. no. 59–61, 96, 159–60, 567–71).

Fig. 7. Metal-mounted chest from the Oseberg burial, Norway. C. 800–850. Cf. cat. no. 164.

Fig. 9. *Iron cauldron and frying pan, Norway. Viking Age. Cat. no. 63.*

The import of wine was also an innovation of the early Middle Ages. In the Viking Age the great landowners had wine and wine-glasses on their tables (cat. no. 125 and 154), but this was unusual. Wine only became a common drink with the beginning of the Christian mission, when it was needed for the celebration of the Mass, after which it was accepted by the aristocracy. Most of the Mass wine came from the Rhineland.

Diet and culinary equipment varied according to time and place, but they were also socially ordered. In aristocratic farms, royal castles and ecclesiastical residences the choicest cuts of meat were consumed, bread was made from wheat, and drinking vessels were made of glass and precious metals —archaeological finds from humbler settlements show a simpler lifestyle.

The contribution of game and fish to diet was dependent on the situation of the settlement. In south Scandinavia game was of little importance. Roots, beans and peas were important foods, as were the berries and fruit collected in the forest (cat. no. 86). Rose-hips, blueberries, red whortle-berries and nuts could have been mixed with rye, wheat or oats to make porridge. Cows' and goats' milk provided cheese. Little is known of the dishes which were actually eaten; the raw materials are found in archaeological contexts but the combinations in which they were used, the seasonings and presentation, are unknown.

The most common drink was probably ale, although there are many tales of the Vikings as mead-drinkers. There was also *beor*, a strong and sweet drink, probably a fruit wine, drunk from small beakers such as the Jelling cup (cat. no. 191).

A completely new diet came with the introduction of Christianity. Fish were needed for the fast-days, and the abundance of herring in Öresund was exploited by native and foreign merchants as early as 1200. Hundreds of thousands of tons of salted herring were exported. The towns of Skanör and Falsterbo in Skåne were founded in the early Middle Ages with an economy based on the herring fisheries, whilst along the Norwegian coast the export of stockfish to England became the staple trading commodity. In the Middle Ages herring and cod became the commonly exported material and also provided food for most Scandinavians.

Fig. 10. *Human head with mask on a wooden stick from Trondheim, Norway. C. 1200. Cat. no. 579a.*

Fig. 11. Coloured gaming-pieces from Gunnarshaug, Norway. C. 800. Cat. no. 123.

Everyday life

Archaeological evidence provides some idea of the activities carried on in a Viking Age house. Tools for the production of textiles are common—loom-weights; spindle-whorls made of clay, bone, glass, stone or amber; and pins. All of these are female implements and show that the women of the house made clothing from wool and linen (cat. no. 49–54, 576). Viking Age clothing was mainly made from local materials, most often from the wool produced on the farm, but sometimes decorated with braids of oriental silk. Cloth was often dyed (cat. no. 55–7, 174). In the Middle Ages cloth was imported into Scandinavia from the Continent and Iceland, and linen is common.

Male activities are also reflected in the objects found in the houses. Rakes, spades, wooden vessels, objects plaited from straw, birch-bark boxes and so on were made during the long winter evenings.

There were also other ways of passing the time. Gaming pieces of glass, amber, bone and walrus ivory demonstrate that *hneftafl* and other board-games were played (cat. no. 71, 123, 321, 342, 360, 572). Chess and its variants were introduced in the twelfth century (cat. no. 615). Bone dice are commonly found in early medieval towns. 'War games',

often mentioned in Icelandic sagas, were another way of passing the time. These had such names such as 'Glima wrestling' and were carried out on the house floors or in the yards. Music was made on the flute and the harp (cat. no. 72, 176), although Viking songs were described with little enthusiasm by an Arabic listener. In winter people travelled on skates and skis, both for communication and for sport (cat. no. 21–25).

Children's games are reflected in finds of toys: small wooden boats, horses and tiny pots. Miniature tools and weapons show that children's toys have been the same throughout the ages (cat. no. 13–14, 73, 279, 315, 378).

The people of the Viking Age and early Middle Ages are commonly thought to have been not very clean, but the archaeological evidence contradicts this view—the wash basin (cat. no. 46), for example, and the numerous excavated bath-houses. Every occupation site produces combs (cat. no. 47, 578) which were presumably used for catching lice but also for combing the hair. And one of the few 'portraits' which has been preserved (cat. no. 80), shows a Viking with neatly cropped and combed hair and beard.

Scandinavian paganism

Gro Steinsland

Religion, as a set of concepts about powers which rule over people's lives, together with rites and cult ceremonies which enable people to communicate with these powers, has existed in Scandinavia from earliest times. Traces of religious beliefs are found in burial customs and in rock carvings from as early as the Stone Age. But it is with the Viking Age that we first gain access to the religious concepts which determined people's actions and their social structures. We learn of Viking Age mythology and cults particularly through the written evidence of the Middle Ages, where runic inscriptions, eddaic and scaldic poetry, saga literature, legal material and histories give us an insight into the rich mythology and the distinctive view of the world which obtained in the pre-Christian community.

Despite local variations we can see that the Scandinavian peoples by and large worshipped the same deities. The Saami and Finns, on the other hand, who lived furthest north and east in Scandinavia, had their own mythological and cult traditions.

The Scandinavian religion was polytheistic and comprised a large number of gods and powers, both male and female. The best known gods are Odin, Thor, Frigg, Baldr, Heimdall, Gefion, Idun, Njörð, Frey and Freyja. Beside the gods there were many other mythological groups, a great many of which were female: *Völur*, giantesses, norns, *Fylgjur*, *Dísir*, valkyries.

Gods and powers were present throughout the cosmos, in heaven and on earth, in the sea and under the earth. Everywhere there were forces to which people had to relate, forces which helped and regulated, or which were hostile and dangerous. While the gods organized and ruled the world according to the primeval laws, their opposite numbers, giants (*Jötun*), represented the chaotic forces in life. The giants are primeval powers who want to destroy the order of the gods. But the gods were also dependent on the giants: in the language of myth it is said that the giants possess objects and wisdom which the gods need. Interaction is therefore the word which epitomizes the Scandinavian view of the world. Gods and giants enter alliances, for example marriage: in a sacred wedding of a deity and a giantess lies the origin of a new dynasty of kings or earls. Gods and giants are thus simultaneously opposites and allies in a dynamic process, the evolution of the world.

There are two groups of gods: *Æsir* and *Vanir*. The *Vanir* are the most typical powers of fertility and are represented by Njörð, Frey and Freyja. The *Æsir* are the other gods in the pantheon. *Dwarves* are clever craftsmen who live underground and who provide the gods with many of their attributes. *Elves* are a collective of fertility powers, associated with cultivated soil and departed ancestors. *Dísir* are female figures associated with objects and sovereignty; *valkyries* are female powers who select those who are to die in battle and accompany them to the after-life. The Valkyrie also greets the dead warrior on his arrival in Odin's realm, Valhalla. Such a scene of welcome is depicted on a Gotland picture stone (cat. no. 175). The slain warrior is carried to the realm of the dead on Odin's horse Sleipnir, the eight-legged horse of the dead. The *Völur* are particularly powerful female figures in Norse religion, they are wise and know the whole history of the world from beginning to end. Even Odin has to consult the *Völur* when he wants to know of matters unknown to others, living or dead. In the centre of the world sit female powers, the *norns*, who have power over destiny and who decide the fate and fortune of the individual. A colourful and vigorous cast of actors who step out to greet us from pre-Christian mythology.

The gods

Odin is one of the mightiest gods; he was praised by poets for he stole the mead of poetry from the giants and gave it to humans. Odin is an enigmatic god, he was above good and evil and was both feared and loved. It was Odin and his brothers who, in the primeval age of chaos, set the world in order and also created the human race when they gave Askr and Embla, the first human couple, breath and consciousness.

Odin is the god of wisdom. The deepest wisdom, the knowledge of runes, he found by crossing the threshold of death. The myth tells that he hung himself from the World Tree, *Yggdrasill*, for nine nights pierced by spears. The runes, and with them the mystery of writing, Odin later gave to man.

Fig. 1. Picture stone from Tjängvide, Gotland, Sweden. The scene at the top shows the reception of a dead hero in Valhalla. 8th–9th cent. Cat. no. 175.

Fig. 2. Piece of a human skull with incised runes including the god's name Odin. Ribe, Denmark. 8th cent. Cat. no. 178.

Fig. 3. Thor's struggle with the World Serpent. Part of a rune stone from Altuna, Uppland, Sweden. 11th cent. The scene shows the climax of the legend where Thor (together with the giant Hymir) are sailing over the sea to catch the monster. The bait is a bull's head; Thor stands with a hammer, ready to slay the serpent, which escapes at the last moment because the terrified giant cuts the fishing line.

Odin also has less attractive qualities. He is a sorcerer, a *seiðmaðr. Seið* is a particular Scandinavian form of shamanism. By means of ritual chanting and the observing of omens the practitioner of *seið* makes contact with powers to whom no-one else has access. By this means Odin gained power over life and death, he could deprive people of strength and wits, still the tempest and see all that was concealed. But the sorcerer enjoyed little respect in the community, for *seið* was originally a female practice. The Völur, therefore, practiced the art of *seið* with greater respect. That Odin taught himself *seið* shows that he breaks all barriers, including those which society placed between the sexes.

Odin was the god of the upper classes, he was worshipped by kings and rulers and by their scalds. He was thought to be the first ancestor of the Danish royal dynasty, the Skjoldungs, and, by the giant-woman Skaði, he was the ancestor of the powerful line of earls of Lade in Norway. He was also the god of the seafaring Vikings, who for long periods relinquished their ties with home.

To Odin's realm, Valhalla, came the dead warriors from the battlefield (cat. no. 1, 175). Those who died heroically in battle were chosen by Odin to join the warrior elite of the Other World, the *einherjar*, the dead warriors who held themselves ready for the last great battle, *Ragnarök*. When that takes place the dead heroes shall fight on the side of the gods.

Odin's wife was Frigg, clever and wise, the mother of Baldr. She is one of the Norse goddesses who were later derided by Christian poets because of her function as fertility goddess.

Thor was, in contrast to Odin, associated with the peasant population (cat. no. 179–81). Myths often make fun of this god, who is portrayed as a gluttonous giant, not unlike the Indian god Indra. Thor is the protector of the cosmos, in that he is continually trying to crush the tribe of giants. Many place names, such as Torslunda, Torshov, Torsker, demonstrate that Thor was a highly popular deity in the Viking Age. Several myths tell of his battles against cosmic opponents; once he even fished the World Serpent itself

Fig. 4. *Small male figure, probably the fertility god Frey, from Rällinge, Sweden. Early 11th cent. Cat. no. 182.*

between gods and giants. In the battle of Ragnarök he will lead all the forces which oppose the gods.

Frey is one of the great deities of the Viking Age. He is of the *Vanir* family, the son of Njörð and the brother of Freyja. Frey's character of fertility god is obvious and it is thought that he is represented in a phallic figure found in Sweden (fig. 4). Frey granted wealth, health and fertility. Together with the giant-woman Gerð he is the ancestor of the Swedish-Norwegian dynasty, the Ynglings.

Freyja is no less important than Frey. She was worshipped all over Scandinavia and was the great female deity of the Viking Age. Freyja gives luck in love, she represents sensuality and voluptuousness, but is not a typical mother goddess. She is a highly independent figure who, besides with fertility, is also associated with war—a double function which she has in common with the ancient Oriental goddesses. It is said that she and Odin share the dead warriors from the battlefield between them.

The world picture

The mythology shows that the Scandinavians had a comprehensive cosmology, i.e. concepts about the world process, about primeval times and about the creation and destruction of the world. In primeval times there was only a vast chaos, *Ginnungagap*—the immense void. From energies in this potent but unstructured chaos the world was created. The first generation of gods, Odin and his brothers, arranged the world. Sun and moon were set in their courses, the seasons were established, the earth was covered by green growth. In the centre of the world the gods built their homes in the place they called *Ásgarð*—the dwelling of the gods. People were placed between the gods and the giants in *Miðgarð*, i.e. in the dwelling in the middle. At the outer edges of the world lived the giants, this place was *Utgarð*—the dwelling at the outside.

The cosmic order which was established in primeval times was, however, vulnerable; it was threatened from all sides. Experience shows that the cosmos is a fragile balance which continually has to be maintained with the help of gods and people. The gods are constantly interacting with the forces in the cosmos; people's rites and cults, therefore, are of the utmost importance. It is this concept of the world as a vulnerable plurality which makes the Norse cosmology so dynamic and colourful. It is not dualistic, as is the Christian world picture, where good stands opposed to evil, rather Norse cosmology is characterized by interaction between all the various forces of existence.

from the sea and prepared to kill it (cat. no. 1 and fig. 3). Such an event would have had enormous consequences, for, although the Serpent is a giant-monster, it helps hold the world together by surrounding the earth and biting its own tail. This myth demonstrates that people in the Viking Age realized the limitations of brute force; at the same time it cunningly expresses the perception that the forces of chaos are indispensable elements in the greater cosmos.

Heimdall is a mysterious deity. The myth relates that he was born of nine giant-mothers. He is associated with the entire cosmos, he is its universal watchman and lives at the end of the rainbow. At the end of time he will raise the alarm when Ragnarök breaks out. Humans are called the children of Heimdall and one eddaic poem tells that the different social classes emanate from this god.

Loki is a peculiar figure in the Scandinavian pantheon (cat. no. 183). He is of giant stock and thus represents the opposite of the gods, but he is included in the circle of the *Æsir* because at the beginning of time he mixed blood with Odin and thereby became his foster-brother. Loki is treacherous, constantly fomenting strife and discord

In the centre of the world stands the World Tree, *Yggdrasill*. The name means 'Odin's horse' and refers to Odin hanging himself from its branches. The World Tree is a strong cosmic symbol, which is found in many other cultures. It symbolizes cosmic life itself, it nourishes the whole world, but it is, like the world, also under threat. All powers relate to the World Tree. Gods and goddesses gather there each day to hold assembly and to consult: under the tree sit the norns, the goddesses of Fate. The tree is also the target of the destructive forces which prey on the life of the cosmos.

Despite the efforts of the gods to uphold the world, destruction approaches. *Ragnarök*, 'the twilight of the Gods', implies a frightening knowledge of the future. Terrible natural castrophes herald the end. Three winters shall follow each other without any summers between; man and beast shall suffer in the dreaded Fimbul Winter. At the end a giant-monster shall extinguish the sun. Gods and giants will clash in an immense battle and destroy one another. The heavenly bodies will fall and the earth perish in a vast fire.

But there was also hope for a new life for future generations. In the eddaic poem *Völuspá* the *Völva* prophesizes that a new earth shall rise from the sea. There the fields will grow without being sown, new races of gods shall meet and man shall live in peace and harmony.

Cults

The pre-Christian religion was integrated into the life of the community, ritual acts formed a natural part of everyday life. Paganism was not a doctrinal religion, maxims were not moulded into dogma as in Christianity. The pivot of the religion lay in its rites, in cult and ritual. Through the cult, people maintained their contact with the higher powers and ensured their fortune, health and peace (cat. no. 177–90).

There were few religious specialists in the pre-Christian Scandinavian community. A separate priesthood or special sacral buildings were apparently not needed. Everyday rituals were taken care of by the male and female heads of each household. At the major social gatherings, for example the *thing*, the cult was led by the political and religious leader, the *goði*. Women could also be public leaders of cults, they were called *gyðjur*. We have seen that *seið*, the Scandinavian form of shamanism, was practiced by special people (*Völur*) and sorcerers (*seiðmenn*). *Seið* was, however, a religio-magic practice, which existed alongside the regular cults of the community.

This proximity of everyday life, community life and religion meant that the cult was not consigned to specific sacral buildings, although from the earliest times certain places in the landscape had, no doubt, suggested themselves as being holy. These could be characteristic mountain formations, holy mountains, rocks or groves. The great religious festivals, at which whole village communities gathered, took place in the hall of the main farm. During the festival the hall was decorated and sacrifices, *blót*, were made there. A large farm such as this, with a hall that was also used for religious ceremonies, was often called *hof*.

The major annual religious festivals were called *blót*. To *blóta* means to strengthen, and it was the gods who had to be given strength for their tasks by means of people's cult activities, of which sacrifice was the most important. Horses or pigs were slaughtered, people gathered round the sacred rites and the steaming cooking pots. The blood of sacrificed animals was especially sacred. The sacred drink, mead, was consecrated to the gods and they were toasted in it. The departed ancestors were also remembered with toasts. They drank too 'for a good year and peace', as the ancient formula says. Peace (*friðr*) was everything: peace in one's own community, peace with the higher powers, health and fertility for man and beast; peace also meant victory in foreign parts. In their sacred drunkenness people would have felt a strengthening of their own fellowship, as well as their fellowship with the higher powers. There was feasting in hall, and scalds recited myths and composed verses about the deeds of gods and heroes.

Fig. 5. Impressed gold foil with a 'loving couple', from Borg, Lofoten, Norway. 8th–9th cent. Perhaps a depiction of the holy marriage between a god and a queen of the giants. Cat. no. 154b.

Fig. 6. Animal-head post from the ship-burial at Oseberg, Norway. C. 800–850. Cf. cat. no. 166d.

Fig. 7. Two small male heads with horned head-dress. Left: Ribe, Denmark, cat. no. 184; right: Staraja Ladoga, Russia, cat. no. 268. 8th cent.

Saami mythology includes a number of gods and goddesses, who were closely associated with the natural forces of sun, moon, wind and thunder. Specific gods, male and female, performed their functions in the home, for example at the hearth, the door and with the reindeer herd.

The bear cult was a characteristic feature of the pre-Christian Saami religion and it is also known from Finnish religion (cat. no. 234–7). The bear was the supreme quarry in the hunt, and hunting of it was fraught with danger. It was therefore attended by an elaborate ritual apparatus. The *noaid* came with his drum: in ritual chant the dead bear was thanked for letting itself be caught and prayers were offered to its spirit so that it would not take revenge. The meat was cooked and shared in a solemn feast, while the bearskin and the bones were ritually buried. Men and women kept apart at this time, because it was thought that women could be harmed by that which had occurred at the slaying of the bear. Women, however, had their own specific tasks to perform during the three days of rites which surrounded the bear hunt, when the taboo was in force.

Saami

Our knowledge of the pre-Christian Saami (Lapp) religion derives from popular culture, the written evidence of Christian missionaries in the seventeenth and eighteenth centuries and archaeological finds.

The sacrificial sites lay out in the open air and the holy place was often a particular formation of mountain or rock, where a picture or symbol of a god was placed (cat. no. 242 and p. 68, fig. 6). The sacred site of the Saami was called *seite*. The shamanist cult was prevalent in the whole of the Arctic and sub-Arctic regions and the Saami and Finnish forms of the cult had obvious features in common.

The most important tool of the Saami shaman, the *noaid*, was his magic drum (cat. no. 241). The drum was made of reindeer skin, stretched over a frame and painted with figures representing the various gods and mythological powers. The shaman can prophesy by means of the drum. When a hammer is beaten rythmically against the drum a small bone 'pointer' moves around on the painted surface and gives answers. The rythmic drumming, together with the singing (*joik*) helped the shaman to achieve the level of ecstacy required to free his soul and allow it to travel in the cosmos. On his journeys the shaman could perform great deeds, free people from sickness and death, or avert evil. The Christian mission demanded that the shaman drums should be burnt, as they were the work of the Devil. Some shamans were executed.

The Conversion

In the Viking Age many Scandinavians learnt of the foreign religion practiced by people in Western and Southern Europe. Knowledge of Christianity reached Scandinavia partly through Christian missions from the West, South and East, and the Scandinavians also came into contact with the faith on trading and raiding expeditions abroad. The conversion, however, only gathered force when the kings and upper classes embraced the new faith. The large rune-stone at Jelling in Denmark relates that King Harald Bluetooth made the Danes Christian about 965. Denmark was finally converted to Christianity at the end of the tenth century. In Norway several kings attempted to convert the country, but lasting results were only achieved after the death of St. Olaf in 1030. In Iceland Christianity was introduced by a decision made at the Althing, the national assembly, in 1000. The group of pagans present at the Althing was no less numerous than the group of Christians, but the decision to adopt Christianity was based on the common conviction that the country should have only one law and only one religion.

Sweden remained pagan for longer. The pagan cult in Uppsala is thought to have continued until nearly 1100. Finland received early Christian impulses from the missionary activities in Sweden, but here the conversion also took a long time. The Saami peoples in the North retained their traditional form of religion for a long time and were conse-

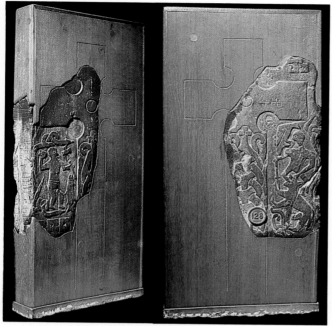

Fig. 8. Fragment of a cross-slab from Kirk Andreas, Isle of Man. This shows both pagan and Christian scenes, and has a runic inscription. 10th cent. Cat. no. 367.

Fig. 9. Altar cross from Veinge, Halland, Sweden. C. 1100. Cat. no. 473.

quently accused of being particularly skilled in magic. Christian missions among them gathered momentum in the seventeenth and eighteenth centuries.

With the transition to Christianity an immense—although gradual—change took place in Scandinavia. The process of conversion was from the outset closely connected with the strengthening royal power and it helped to increase the centralization of power. From a social system based on family and lineage, the Scandinavian countries gradually evolved into strong centralized powers with King and Church as their most important institutions.

Christianity is a didactic religion and it requires an educated clergy and its own sacred buildings. Christianity did not tolerate any other gods or cult activities than its own—the deities of the old religion were demonized and became 'instruments of the Devil'.

The new doctrines had a regularizing effect on people's everyday lives, as well as on their holy days. Eating habits and sexual mores were regulated according to the Church calendar, there were injunctions to observe the Sabbath and saints' days, fasting was introduced on holy days and in the period leading up to them. The Church introduced new rules for the contracting of marriage and union was prohib-

ited between people who were related closer than the sixth or seventh degree. New burial customs banned the burying of the dead on the farms, they had to be interred in consecrated ground round the church.

In all, Christianity brought to Scandinavia a completely new concept of the world and of people. Fundamental Christian ideas, such as sin and grace, were foreign to the Scandinavians. The teaching of the Church about the subordination of women to men was also new and was to alter the Scandinavian view of women radically. The perception of death was totally changed as doctrine freed the individual from his family relationships and gave him an individual choice between salvation and eternal damnation.

Culturally, the conversion resulted in the admission of the North into the fulness of European culture. The Scandinavians felt the need to define their own position within the Christian perspective of salvation and world history. This gave rise to a new consciousness of what was specifically Norse, a new horizon which appears in the learned writings of the Midddle Ages. The Latin art of writing, which had come to Scandinavia with Christianity, thus preserved the traditions of the pre-Christian faith and cult of the North.

Christianity and churches

Olaf Olsen

Christianity came late to the North. In Denmark, it became the religion of the king, and therefore also of the people, about 965. In Iceland the change to the new faith took place by decree of the Althing, traditionally exactly a thousand years after the birth of Christ. Norway and western Sweden were converted gradually in the years immediately before and, particularly after, AD 1000. In contrast, paganism continued to hold its own around Uppsala, in the heartland of the eastern Swedish state, until about 1100, whilst in Finland, only the south-western region showed traces of Christian influences.

A trustworthy written source, however, mentions a missionary journey to the North as early as about 700 when Willibrord, the Apostle of the Frisians, visited a Danish king, Angantyr. The words of Willibrord were lost on the pagan ruler, but he did give (or, rather, sold) 30 youths to the missionary who took them with him to teach them to become good Christians, no doubt with an eye to future missionary work. It is not known whether anything came of this initiative.

There is a great deal of archaeological evidence, however, which shows that just at the beginning of the eighth century Scandinavia was opening itself up to more extensive trade with Christian western Europe. Whilst the end of the century saw the beginning of the Viking raids, which were for hundreds of years to bring thousands of Danish, Norwegian and Swedish warriors and emigrants into close contact with the Christian peoples of western Europe, first in conflict but later also in peaceful co-existence and integration. These were the conditions which eventually gave rise to to the introduction of Christianity to Scandinavia. Followers of the new faith were encountered abroad, and were also met with as foreign merchants visiting the trading centres of the North.

Once Charlemagne had conquered Saxony and brutally crushed paganism there, the conquest and forced conversion of Denmark became a real possibility. The boundary of the Frankish empire extended as far as the southern border of Jutland. To legitimize the political and military campaign against the North, Archbishop Ebo of Rheims received, in 823, papal approval to evangelize in the northern part of the world, and Ebo himself went to the borders to prepare the mission.

At that time Denmark was ravaged by internal conflicts, with several members of the royal family claiming the Danish throne. One of them, Harald Klak, sought and obtained the support of the Frankish emperor. But as a dependent of the emperor he had to convert to Christianity. In 826, therefore, together with his immediate family and retainers

—some four hundred in all—he was baptized in Mainz, the Emperor acting as godfather.

Neither baptism nor Imperial support enabled Harald Klak to assume power in Denmark, rather they told against him. In the following year he was exiled in perpetuity. This first Scandinavian royal conversion is only noteworthy because, when Harald Klak returned to Denmark after his enforced baptism, he was involuntarily accompanied by Ansgar, a monk from the monastery of Corvey, who was to light the lamp of Christianity in the North. Ansgar stayed in Denmark for only a short while, probably because of his unfortunate association with Harald Klak, but in 829 he travelled to Birka in east central Sweden at the invitation of the local king. He stayed in Birka for more than a year and, on his return home, could report that although he had at first worked amongst the Christians in Birka, he had also baptized Swedes and built a church—the first in Scandinavia.

Encouraged by the successful outcome of the journey, the emperor Louis, established an archiepiscopate for Ansgar in Hamburg whence he could convert the Swedes, Danes and Slavs. When Hamburg was attacked and almost totally destroyed by the Vikings in 845 Ansgar fled to Bremen and took over the vacant bishopric which was soon elevated to become the archdiocese of Hamburg-Bremen. Ansgar resumed his Scandinavian journeys c. 850. In Denmark, where he acted as an emissary from the Emperor, he found favour with the king and quickly gained permission to build churches, first in Hedeby and then in Ribe. In Hedeby he was subsequently even allowed to furnish the church with a bell. Ansgar revisited Birka about 853 in order to install a new priest, as the previous one had been driven out by pagan pressure: in this he was successful and was able to reestablish the Christian congregation.

Birka, Hedeby and Ribe were the most important trading centres in Scandinavia at that time. It is clearly for this reason that the Christian mission used them as jumping-off points, for it was to these towns that the Christian merchants came. Foreign trade was vital to their prosperity and it was essential, therefore, for the local rulers to provide visiting merchants with protection and comfortable conditions. The merchants also demanded that they should be able to worship their God while they were in foreign lands. This gave the Christian mission a platform from which to operate. The priests in the trading centres could pursue their missionary activities under the guise of chaplains to

Fig. 1. *Bell found in the harbour at Hedeby, Germany. 10th cent. Cat. no. 199.*

seafarers, and they benefited from the protection accorded to visiting Christian merchants.

Ansgar died in 865. We know about his missions to the Scandinavian towns only because they were recorded by his successor Rimbert, who some years after Ansgar's death wrote his life, the *Vita Ansgarii*, which was to confirm Ansgar as a saint. There is no mention of any other missions from Hamburg-Bremen to the North for the next 70 years, and none of the three churches founded by Ansgar seems to have survived him for very many years. The end of the ninth century was one of the most turbulent phases of the Viking Age when great areas of north-west Europe were over-whelmed by increasingly more devastating Viking attacks. For the victorious Vikings there was little incentive to believe in the ineffectual God of those they had conquered, who was obviously in no position to ensure His followers victory, nor to protect them in peace.

This changed at the beginning of the tenth century. Western Europe learned how to protect itself against the piratical bands from the North and went on the offensive. In 934 a German army invaded Jutland to punish, 'the wild and unruly people of the Danes', and on the heels of the German soldiers came the Christian mission. This gave an opening for the archbishopric of Hamburg-Bremen. Archbishop Unni himself visited Denmark and then went on to Birka, where he died in 936.

There is no reliable account of the immediate outcome of Unni's journey, but the German mission now started again in earnest. In 948 the new archbishop, Adaldag, convened a German synod which was attended by three bishops of churches in Jutland: Ribe, Schleswig (Hedeby), and Århus. Whether the bishops actually presided in these towns is more questionable. An archbishop was ranked according to the number of his subordinate bishops and Adaldag had good reason to increase his staff when he met his colleagues from further south.

The real breakthrough of Christianity in Denmark came with the baptism of King Harald Bluetooth *c.* 965. This event was recorded immediately afterwards by the historian Widukind in his Saxon Chronicle, where it is connected with a miracle. During a religious dispute at the royal court, the priest Poppo carried red-hot iron in his hands, but remained unscathed. This convinced the king that there could be only one God, that of the Christians. King Harald himself proclaimed his new faith on an impressive rune-stone, which he erected to the memory of his parents

Fig. 2. *Harald Bluetooth's great rune-stone at Jelling. It was erected when Christianity was introduced to Denmark,* c. 965. *The text beneath Christ reads 'and made the Danes Christian'. Cf. cat. no. 193.*

Fig. 3. The Jelling monuments, Denmark. Aerial view from the north-west. The church stands between the two great mounds, with the two rune stones south of the porch. Harald Bluetooth's rune-stone stands in its original position, between the mounds.

between two great burial mounds at the royal centre of Jelling in Jutland (fig. 2–3). The decoration of the stone is dominated by an image in relief of Christ crucified. Between the mounds Harald also built a great wooden church with a burial chamber under the floor. To here Harald translated a body, probably that of his father Gorm, who (leaving his pagan burial-mound) was thus brought posthumously to Christianity (fig. 3).

The stone has an inscription which records in runes that King Harald, 'made the Danes Christian'. As in the pagan period the king had important cult functions—it would have been unthinkable for the king to have one faith and his people another. The king could hardly have preserved his throne after baptism had not the great men of the kingdom

been disposed to adopt the new religion. In Denmark, the conversion to Christianity happened so rapidly and so peacefully that it could not have been the result of the German mission alone, for this had been active for only a few decades. There may have been Christian influence at the same time from the descendants of the Danish farmers, who in the wake of the Viking raids, had been living in England and Normandy since the 870s. Many of them had quickly converted to Christianity.

English influence becomes evident in the following phase when the new Church had to be organized and the country provided with priests. Soon after the conquest of England in 1013, Sven Forkbeard and Knut the Great sent English bishops to Denmark. By doing this, they violated the rights of the Archbishop of Hamburg, who consequently captured a newly-appointed English bishop on his way to his Danish see and forced him to accept the archiepiscopal authority of Hamburg-Bremen.

In Norway, King Håkon Adelstenfostre, who had been brought up in the English court and was therefore a Christian, tried to convert Norway to Christianity about 950. He was probably met with some sympathy in west Norway where there were close contacts with England, but in Trøndelag (the most densely populated part of central Norway) his plans met so much resistance that he had to give up all idea of conversion. In western Norway, however, priests began to appear and in the 970s an English bishop is recorded. In the most southerly parts of Norway, which were under the rule of the Danish king, conversion to Christianity probably continued at much the same rate as in Denmark.

The heathen opposition in Trøndelag was first overcome *c.* 995 by another Christian king, Olaf Tryggvason; but he reigned for only a few years before being slain in battle in about 1000 against the kings of Denmark and Sweden. This gave a short breathing-space to paganism in Norway until, some 15 years later, King Olaf Haraldsson introduced a new wave of Christian missionary activity based more on the sword than on the word. Pagan resistance to Christianity remained strongest in Trøndelag. This finally led to conflict, and in 1030 Olaf was slain at the battle of Stiklestad, fighting against the people of Trøndelag. This was an internal conflict, not simply a religious war. Pagans and Christians fought on both sides. Despite the defeat and death of the Christian king Olaf, however, the battle of Stiklestad marks the true end of paganism in Norway. Stories grew concerning miracles at the murdered king's tomb, and his reputation as a saint finally overwhelmed any lingering pagan opposition.

The German Church was only modestly influential in the conversion of Norway. The most important religious influences came from England, which was the most obvious source in west Norway for the reception of European ideas. Both Olaf Tryggvason and Olaf Haraldsson brought bishops from England to Norway. Nevertheless, the main figure in the early Norwegian church, Bishop Grimkel, formalized his position by visiting Bremen and accepting the authority of the archbishop there.

The conversion of Iceland must be seen in the light of events in Norway—the motherland of the Icelandic republic. The Althing's decision to adopt the Christian faith *c.* 1000 was almost certainly influenced by Olaf Tryggvason's struggle against paganism in Norway—although mission-

aries to Iceland seem also to have been sent from Hamburg-Bremen. Iceland acquired its first bishopric—Skálholt—in 1056.

The situation in Sweden is, if possible, even more obscure since written sources are almost entirely absent. Both English and German missionaries were active in western Sweden and about 1000 a strong Christian king, Olof Skötkonung, was on the throne. (A bishop in Skara, in Västergötland, from the 1020s came from Bremen.) Olof Skötkonung tried to extend his power into Svealand, the eastern and still predominantly pagan part of Sweden, but without permanent success. Opposition to the Christian king was strong, and the capture and slaughter of missionaries is recorded. Nevertheless, Christianity made progress in the Mälar valley—quite reasonably, as it was there that international trade was centred. Sigtuna became the seat of a bishop about 1060, but a little further to the north the population was still predominantly heathen. This was due to the proximity of the last strong bastion of the pagans—the central shrine of the Svear, Gamla Uppsala, where great annual sacrifices were still flourishing when Adam of Bremen described Scandinavia about 1070. The pagan cult at Uppsala did not lose its grip until about 1100, but by then paganism had also died out. Christianity had finally triumphed throughout Scandinavia. Only the Saami in the extreme north clung to their old religion.

In Finland, the start of a change in burial customs suggests Christian influence as early as the middle of the eleventh century, but it is doubtful if this reflects a change of belief in the pagan population. The account of a Finnish Crusade, said to have been led by the Swedish king, Erik the Holy, about 1150 is more myth than history. There was very little Christianity in Finland until well on in the thirteenth century.

Fig. 4. Bronze head of a tau-crozier. Found at Thingvellir, Iceland, where the Althing met. C. 1100. Cat. no. 335.

Fig. 5. *The great mounds and holy site of Gamla Uppsala, Sweden. The church stands in the background. Lithograph 1857–9.*

Churches

In contrast to the pre-Christian sanctuaries of the North, the Christian Church demanded that specific buildings should be erected, dedicated only to religious worship. Thus, hundreds of churches appeared throughout Scandinavia. Parochial divisions were not established at the same time; they were first formed in the twelfth century when the Church demanded fixed contributions from the congregations in the form of tithes. The first churches were founded by individuals—kings, noblemen or great landowners —who in the pagan period had been responsible for the communal worship of the pagan gods and who would have summoned the people of the region to sacrificial festivals on their estates. The churches were thus usually founded within the largest estates in the village or region.

The first churches were built in wood, for stone buildings were unknown in Scandinavia in the Viking Age. Most of them were quite small, rectangular in shape and often provided with a narrower choir at the east end of the nave. In slightly larger churches, the roof of the nave was carried on two rows of free-standing posts inside the church. This form did not necessarily follow that of the aisled basilicas favoured in the Christian kingdoms to the south and west, but rather they followed the form of roof-support found in the large secular buildings of contemporary Scandinavia.

None of these earliest churches survive, but evidence for them has been found in Denmark, Norway and Sweden in excavations beneath the Romanesque churches which replaced them in the twelfth and thirteenth centuries. Sometimes there are traces of two or even three wooden churches beneath a stone church. As they were usually constructed of upright earth-fast posts, the early wooden churches had only a limited life. And quite often the first church was destroyed by fire. Although many of the churches were small they were by no means plain. There are many surviving remains of carved and painted wood from early churches (cat. no. 440), the most spectacular example being that of Urnes in west Norway where a portal with rich and elegant animal ornament from *c.* 1070 (p. 181, fig. 6) was re-used in the succeeding twelfth-century church.

The Catholic Church demanded that its churches should be built of stone. The early wooden churches were, there-

Fig. 6. Borgund stave-church, Sogn, Norway. Second half of the 12th cent.

fore, gradually replaced by masonry buildings—in Denmark and Sweden few wooden churches survived after the first two centuries of Christianity. It was different in Norway, where the church's wishes were disregarded and the tradition of building in wood continued. The twelfth century saw the development of Scandinavia's most original contribution to ecclesiastical architecture—the unique Norwegian stave-churches. The church was, as it were, lifted off the ground by replacing the earth-fast wall-posts by walls supported by a sturdy framework of sill-timbers resting on boulders. On this frame was built an elaborate, tall structure which, at its core, had a small nave and chancel, sometimes with a semi-circular apse: this was surrounded by a verandah which had a pentice roof, portal and upper storey; above this the high roof-ridge was capped with a turret and often a spire. The points of the gables were decorated with carved dragon-heads, and over the portals were crosses. The interior appeared as a forest of high, sturdy posts with carved capitals connected by carved cross-timbers and round-vaulted aisles; there was an overwhelming profusion of carving around the portals and on the partitions. This matchless luxuriance is already to be seen in the twelfth-century church of Urnes, and is fully developed at Borgund, which dates to shortly after 1150 (fig. 6). Although the carvings show stylistic traces of European art—which spread to Scandinavia partly through the agency of the twelfth-century cathedral-builders—the substance of the art of stave churches was original and indigenous. There were once hundreds of stave-churches in Norway; but only some thirty survive, many in a greatly modified form. This is a breath-taking architecture, one without parallel in Europe.

Whereas the wooden churches grew out of the highly developed timber-building tradition of Scandinavia, specialists had to be brought in from outside when churches were to be built of stone. The stone churches thus illustrate both ecclesiastical and secular contacts between Scandinavia and the rest of Europe.

The first certainly documented stone church in the North was built in Roskilde about 1027. Its patron was Estrid, sister of Knut the Great. Some ambiguous remains under Roskilde cathedral are all that remain of this church. Immigrant masons were clearly active in Denmark for some years, for under St Jørgensbjerg church, by the harbour of Roskilde, traces of the foundations of a small stone church have been excavated and dated by a coin hoard (cat. no. 539) to the years before 1040. A portal from this church (re-used in the present building) has prototypes in eastern English ecclesiastical architecture, indicating the origin of the masons. As in all Danish eleventh-century churches, the building material was tufa (a porous light-weight calcareous stone formed around springs) which can be easily quarried in blocks while damp.

About 1060, Denmark acquired a stable ecclesiastical organization with a diocesan system, which had been negotiated by the Danish king with the archbishopric of Hamburg-Bremen. In Skåne there was a problem for the Bishop of Lund had been appointed from England: this the archbishop of Hamburg-Bremen could not tolerate. A rival Scanian bishopric was set up for the archbishop's appointee, in Dalby some 10 km from Lund. The problem of the two bishops was sorted out a few years later after the bishop in Lund died. The surviving bishop moved from Dalby to Lund, and Skåne again became a unified diocese. This episode influenced church architecture. In Lund a stone church with English features was built, whilst in Dalby the church had German prototypes. The basilica at Dalby is still largely preserved—the oldest extant church in Scandinavia.

In the second half of the eleventh century about a dozen basilicas were built throughout Denmark, including four cathedrals. They are all rather different but their ground plans and architectural details look predominantly to the South—to the Rhineland and Westphalia. But even at the turn of the century the Danish Church still had some connection with England. In 1086 King Knut the Holy was murdered in St Alban's church in Odense. As with Norway earlier, Denmark now had its royal saint; and, when a monastic organisation was grafted on to the new cathedral in Odense, where Knut was to be buried, the monks were brought in from an English Benedictine house. The monks arrived while St Knut's church was still being built, in time to model the west front of the church on an English prototype. The slightly later church of Venge Abbey in Jutland, the plan and decoration of which are reminiscent of English architecture, may have been colonized by English monks from Odense.

The eleventh-century churches in Denmark were usually of high technical and architectural quality. The immigrant craftsmen did their work well. But the Danes soon mastered the craft sufficiently so that they no longer needed foreign assistance. The basilica at Tamdrup, Jutland (built in the early twelfth century) shows, however, that the specialists were sometimes sent home too early. There is actually

nothing wrong with the masonry, but as architecture this church in its earliest form was an abortion—low, squat, and badly proportioned.

In Norway, so far as we can judge, no eleventh-century stone churches survive, but it is known that King Olaf Kyrre (died 1093) built a great stone church in Trondheim to house the tomb of St Olaf, and also founded a church in Bergen. Both have completely disappeared in later rebuilding. A small basilica, later incorporated into the monastic buildings of Selje on the Atlantic coast, was possibly built as a bishop's church in the 1070s.

Nor do many eleventh-century stone buildings still survive in Sweden. There could have been early churches in Västergötland where Christianity was first established. In this province, at Skara (Sweden's oldest bishopric), a stone cathedral was indeed built towards the end of the 11th century (remains of its crypt have been excavated under the present cathedral). The only existing masonry building in western Sweden which could have been erected before 1100 is the impressive church tower of Husaby; the royal manor where, traditionally, Olof Skötkonung was baptized. The tower, in which English influence has been postulated, was possibly built against the west front of a stave church. In east Sweden only two stone churches could date from the eleventh century: St Per and St Olof in Sigtuna. Both are now ruinous, a fact which may make them appear older than they truly are. Their masonry is strangely cyclopean, with both English and Continental features. Each has transepts and a crossing tower, features which have been put down to Byzantine influence, perhaps channelled through Russia. But Russian ecclesiastical architecture is quite different, and the mixture of architectural impulses which Scandinavia acquired at that time from central Europe also had Byzantine features. Similarly, English stylistic traits may have arrived by way of Germany.

In Denmark, the twelfth century was the great period of church building. The Church had become sufficiently established for the modest eleventh-century bishops' churches to be replaced by Romanesque cathedrals of European standard. An economic basis was now in place which facilitated the foundation of the first monasteries; but only a few of these houses had the means to indulge in large-scale building. In the villages, however, the introduction of tithes and the establishment of a parochial system led to replacement of the aristocrats' proprietary wooden churches by parish churches of stone.

In 1103, Lund, in face of bitter opposition from Hamburg-Bremen, was elevated to become the archiepiscopate of the whole of Scandinavia and the Atlantic Isles. The recently completed cathedral was, however, inadequate for

Fig. 7. The east end of Lund cathedral, Sweden (then Denmark). This part of the church was completed by the mid-12th cent. when Lund was still the archiepiscopal seat for the whole of the North.

such a status and was soon replaced by a magnificent cathedral of Scanian sandstone. This church took some sixty years to build and must have been finished about 1180—it has a tall, blind-arcaded apse (fig. 7), with a large crypt, a choir and transepts, a long aisled nave and twin towers in the west. No single prototype can be cited. Whilst the ground plan most closely suggests a southern German prototype, much of the architectural detail points to the English Channel region, and much of the architectural sculpture reflects Italian masons. All these traits were united in a magnificent whole, to provide a cathedral which was to be a source of inspiration of church builders throughout Scandinavia.

Among the other large masonry churches of Denmark prominence must be given to the cathedral of Ribe. This grand building was constructed of tufa from the Rhineland and sandstone from the Weser, brought to the west Jutland town as ballast in merchant ships. The prototypes for the church also lie in the Rhineland. In Viborg, the cathedral was built of finely cut granite ashlar, a material which became the trade-mark of church building in Jutland. In

many ways Viborg cathedral is a miniature version of Lund, although it also adopted features from Ribe.

Good building stone is rare in Denmark west of Öresund, and from about 1160 locally-made bricks began to be used. The first brick-makers were probably brought from Lombardy, but Danish masons and builders quickly learned to take advantage of the special characteristics of the new material and were able to develop its decorative potential. The first great brick churches were the monastic churches of Ringsted and Sorø, whilst the end of the twelfth century saw the beginning of the construction of the greatest of all ecclesiastical monuments in brick—Roskilde cathedral. This building was much influenced by French architecture, but, as it was not completed until well on in the next century, it will not be discussed here.

Almost all of Denmark's two thousand medieval parish churches are Romanesque, most of them probably built before 1200. They are remarkable not only because of their date, but also because most of them still exist in good condition. Commonly they have later additions—west towers, chancel extensions, porches, sacristies and so

*Fig. 8. Bishops' seats in Scandinavia c.
1200. Finland had none. Lund, Trondheim
(Nidaros), and Uppsala were archiepiscopal seats. The archdiocese of Trondheim
encompassed Norway, the Atlantic Islands
of Greenland, Iceland and the Faroe Islands, the Shetlands, the Orkneys, the
Hebrides and the Isle of Man.*

on—but such features have not obscured their Romanesque
character. The churches are small, and in their earliest phase
usually consisted of a rectangular nave with a narrower—
sometimes apsidal—chancel at the east end. Some of them
have a western Romanesque tower, perhaps with special
accommodation for the church's patron.

Despite general similarities, all the churches are different.
The many variations depend on building material, on size
and on details of footings, portals, windows and so on. In
part these differences result from the age of each church and
partly on particular local traditions. Thus, for example, the
twelfth-century churches of Jutland are characterized by the
widespread use of granite ashlar (fig. 9), a wealth of decorated portals and other sculptural details.

The earliest of these parish churches were influenced
stylistically from England or Germany. Later, the great
native churches began to provide the exemplars, and in
many cases the craftsmen. There are some departures from
the norm. Round churches, for example, occur occasionally
in all parts of the country—particularly on Bornholm. The
prototype for these churches was the Church of the Holy
Sepulchre in Jerusalem, but their immediate origin was
most probably in central Europe.

In southern Norway many small basilicas were erected in
the first half of the twelfth century, and are very similar to
those built in Denmark about 1080. The most important of
these was the cathedral of St Halvard in Oslo, now known
only from excavation. The earliest surviving great church in
Norway is the cathedral in Stavanger which became the seat
of a bishop about 1125. The first bishop, who came from
England, found a substantial Romanesque church; its nave
is still standing and shows distinct English stylistic traits.
Bergen had a cathedral and a dozen other Romanesque
churches, now destroyed and almost unknown; most of
them were partly or entirely built in the twelfth century.
The church of St Mary, however, still stands; it is a great
aisled basilica which was built in its present form in the
decades after 1150, probably with the help of masons from
Lund. English influence can be seen in its later phases,
undoubtedly coming by way of Lyse Abbey, south of
Bergen, which was founded in 1146 by Cistercian monks
from Fountains in Yorkshire.

A number of monasteries were founded in Norway in the
twelfth century. Munkeliv in Bergen is of particular
architectural interest; as early as the 1130s it had a church
with crypt, modelled on Lund. St Olaf's monastery in Tøns-

berg—with Norway's only round church—was built about 1200.

The most notable church-building of the twelfth-century took place in Trondheim. The cathedral here was the centre of the cult of St Olaf and the bishopric was, in 1152, elevated to an archdiocese comprising the five Norwegian sees and those of the Atlantic Isles—the Faroes, Iceland, Greenland, Orkney, Shetland, the Hebrides and Man (the last being taken over from the archiepiscopate of York). Even before the elevation of the see, the planning and possibly the building of what was to become the greatest cathedral of the North was in hand. It was profusely decorated with sculptural features appropriate to the building material; the local soapstone was easily carved. The only parts of the new church to be completed in the twelfth century were the vast transepts (clearly inspired by Lincoln Cathedral), and a magnificent free-standing chapter-house on the north side of the choir, known as the House of Vestments. The cathedral became even more splendid when the great octagonal chapel was added to the east end shortly after 1200 to cater for pilgrims to the shrine of St Olaf (illustrated p. 113).

The parochial system was also adopted in Norway in the twelfth century. Although most of the new parish churches were still built of wood, some stone churches were erected in the Romanesque style in the countryside (p. 27, fig. 3); these are influenced by English architecture, although such influence has usually come through a great Norwegian church. Particularly fine examples are to be seen in Trøndelag.

In Sweden, Christianity was sufficiently widespread by 1100 for the country to be divided into dioceses with resident bishops. There were unusually many dioceses around Lake Mälar, perhaps because the Church needed to make a particular mark in a region where pagan opposition had been strongest. After the final victory of Christianity over paganism, the bishopric of Sigtuna was transferred to Gamla Uppsala about 1140. An aisled church was built on the site of the earlier pagan cult-centre, and this in turn became the seat of the archbishop of the Swedish kingdom when, in 1164, Sweden was detached from the Lund archiepiscopate and set itself up as an independent ecclesiastical province. The new archbishopric finally acquired a cathedral suited to its dignity as late as 1270, when its site was moved some 5 km down the Fyris river to the village of Östra Aros which, under its new name of Uppsala, became a cathedral city.

The five other Swedish dioceses also had cathedrals in the eleventh century, but their early stone churches have been obscured through extension or rebuilding. And, although Sweden also acquired some monastic houses at this time,

Fig. 9. *Sædding church, W. Jutland, Denmark, is a typical Jutland rural parish church, built of squared granite blocks, in the 12th cent.*

their original stone churches have disappeared with later rebuilding. The best preserved monument is the spectacular but ruined church of the Cistercian monastery at Roma on Gotland, built before 1200. It is a noble building, but austere in style in the spirit decreed for their daughter houses by the Cistercians.

Parish churches in Västergötland are largely similar to those found in Denmark. Many stone churches were built here in the early twelfth century. Västergötland, however, shows stronger evidence of English influence in architectural detail, and there are more early west towers than there are in Denmark. A considerable number of stone churches were built in eastern Sweden, where a specific type, with a tower over the chancel, developed—perhaps to provide a refuge for the populace in times of trouble. These towers acquired a particularly elaborate form on Öland. In contrast, the neighbouring island of Gotland (which because of its high-quality limestone was already an exporter of church sculpture), has few traces of Romanesque architecture, as almost without exception the churches on the island were totally rebuilt during the following centuries.

In distinction to the wooden churches, the Romanesque stone churches of Scandinavia contributed no new element to contemporary European architecture. They are, however, remarkable for their variety and for their considerable number. Further, unlike most of the Romanesque churches of Europe, they have been less modified by later rebuilding. We must, therefore, be grateful for their survival; they are an incomparable part of the heritage of the Scandinavian people.

Runes and rune-stones

Raymond Page

It is often said that the Vikings were illiterate, but this is not so. True they were not literate in the Christian and modern sense of the word, for they had no books. But they had an alphabetic script, runic, each letter of which was known as a rune. This they used for a variety of purposes. How far they employed it on practical day-to-day affairs—for messages, records, marks of ownership and things of that sort—is a matter of some dispute. Certainly there is little direct evidence for the commercial use of the script in Viking times; though much survives from rather later medieval times in finds from such urban sites as Trondheim and Bergen (cf. cat. no. 501–2).

Runes were designed as characters to be inscribed, and in Viking times they were cut in wood, bone, metal and stone. But runes were not a Viking invention. The script had been used in the north for many centuries before the Viking Age, for the earliest surviving inscriptions date from a couple of centuries after the birth of Christ. Nor were runes specifically Scandinavian. Several Germanic peoples wrote in them: Continental Germans, Goths, Frisians, Anglo-Saxons as well as the North Germanic peoples from whom the Vikings sprang. Nor was there a single type of runic script: details of letter forms vary from region to region and century to century. By the Viking Age the runic alphabet used in the north had sixteen characters, set in the distinctive order called the *futhark* after the phonetic values of its first six letters (cat. no. 498). Even then there was no standard form of the script. There were two main variant forms (fig. 1): the short-twig runes (also known as the Swedo-Norwegian runes, though they are not confined to those countries) and the long-branch runes (sometimes called the Common or Danish runes). There were individual and local variants as well, and the two principal rune-rows were not kept discrete but could intermingle with each other, as happened with the runes used by the Viking settlers of the Isle of Man.

A glance at the two principal Viking rune-rows suggests they were not particularly well developed for representing the sounds of early Scandinavian. There was an inadequate range of vowel runes, for while there are letters for *i*, *a* and *u*, there is none for the common vowel *e* nor, for much of the Viking Age, is there a distinctive *o*-rune. Moreover, though there are symbols for the consonants *k* and *t*, there are none for their voiced parallels *g* and *d*. Conversely while there is a rune for the voiced consonant *b*, there is no voiceless equivalent *p*. This presents problems for the runemaster trying to write some Norse words. For example, whoever inscribed the two great memorial stones at Jelling, Jutland, had to refer to the king known later as Gorm. The nearest he could get to it was *kurmR*, for his alphabet had no letters for *g* and *o*. King Harald Bluetooth had to be called *haraltr* because there was no letter *d*. Moreover, the runemasters had curious spelling habits: *n* and *m* could be missed out before certain consonants. The result is that the word 'king', *konungr* in classical Old Norse, is spelled on the two Jelling memorials *kunukR*. The word *kumbl*, 'monument', appears as *kubl*. When you add to this the facts that some common words were abbreviated, and that word division and punctuation were not consistent, it is clear that interpreting runic texts is a matter for experts, and even among them there is likely to be dispute as to the proper way of taking a group of letters or words.

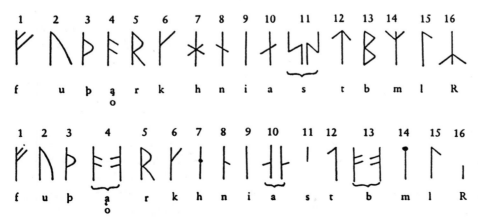

Fig. 1. The two main variants of Viking Age runes. Above, long-twig runes. Below, short-twig runes.

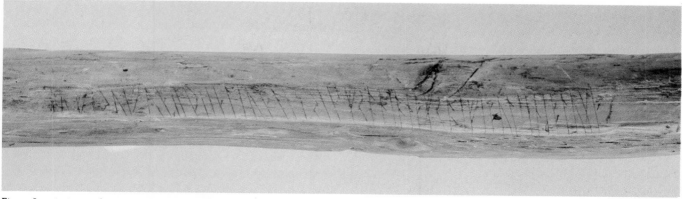

Fig. 2. Inscription in short-twig runes on a stick from Staraja Ladoga, Russia. It is a verse which has been interpreted by scholars in widely differing ways. Cat. no. 278.

The geographical spread of Viking runes is odd. Of course they are found in Denmark, Norway and Sweden, though unevenly, with much larger numbers in Sweden (especially after 1000 AD.) than in the other countries. But there are no Viking Age runes known from the settlements in Iceland. The Vikings took runes with them to many of their overseas colonies, for they can be found in the Orkneys, Shetlands, the Western Isles and mainland of Scotland. There is a sparse scatter in England and Ireland, and a surprisingly large number on the Isle of Man (cat. no. 367, 405–7, 416). Yet there are none in Normandy. The Vikings also left runes in some south Baltic trading centres (cat. no. 258, 261) and in some of their eastern territories: in parts of Russia (cat. no. 278, 282, 312) and indeed as far afield as Byzantium (Istambul) and Piraeus, Greece (p. 28, fig. 4). Far across the Atlantic runic texts have been discovered in the Greenland settlements (cat. no. 339, 565). They are quite often found in North America too, but no serious scholar has yet accepted any of these as genuine. Such varied distribution patterns may simply indicate differences in population density, with runes absent where people are few. But it is more likely that it represents differences in social structure, with runes used by particular social groups or within certain legal and political systems, more dominating in some areas than others.

The most remarkable surviving runic monuments, and certainly the ones that tell most about the nature of the Vikings, are those on stone, either cut on free-standing worked stones or in the living rock, on cliff faces or standing boulders (cat. no. 175, 193, 449, 497, 560). These are very common in parts of Sweden, in Uppland, Södermanland, Öster- and Västergötland and Småland, with numbers too on Öland and Gotland. They are fairly plentiful in Den-

mark, including the coastal regions of southern Sweden which were part of medieval Denmark; and there are a few also in Norway. Such stones often record public pronouncements, and so are placed in prominent places where all could see them: put up by the road-side for wayfarers to read, set at river crossings, erected at legal moot-places. They may form parts of more ambitious monuments, as at Glavendrup, Fyn, where the rune-stone stood as part of a ship-setting. They may be put in groups, like those at Täby, Uppland, which the local squire Jarlabanki set up at each end of a causeway to immortalise his fame, his ownership of the whole of Täby, and the fact that he made the "bridge" (p. 49, fig. 8). Or they may be elaborate carvings on rock faces, like the one at Hillersjö, Uppland, whose text begins with a stern instruction to the passer-by, 'Read this!' and then goes on to expound an elaborate chain of inheritance whereby a woman, Geirlaug, came into property that had once been the family estate of her son-in-law.

Most famous of all rune-stones are those at Jelling, Jutland, where they form part of a complex of monuments by which a royal dynasty publicly proclaimed its importance (cf. p. 37, fig. 5, pp. 153–4, figs. 2–3). The earlier rune-stone, small and not very distinguished, records a queen: 'King Gorm made this monument (the word is technically plural) in memory of his wife Thyre, Denmark's glory'. The second, raised by their son King Harald, is rightly thought the greatest of rune-stones, with decorative carving and an assertive inscription (cat. no. 193). Harald's was no empty boast. Other written sources agree that he had some claim to rule all Denmark, to the overlordship of parts of Norway, and that during his reign in the later tenth century the Danes were converted to Christianity. Thus the Jelling

Fig. 3. Rune-stone from Morby, Uppland, Sweden. This was raised and a 'bridge' built there for the soul of the woman Gillög. 11th cent. Cat. no. 497.

In this the runic inscriptions show aspects of the Viking Age inadequately recorded by other sources: something of the nature of social organisation and loyalties, a confirmation of the wide range of action; a suggestion of the values men lived by. When, on the small island of Berezan at the mouth of the River Dnieper in Russia, a Viking buried his comrade, he put up an inscription for his trading partner (*félagi*, literally 'someone who puts down money in a venture') (cat. no. 312). He was not only commemorating the man, he was in part proclaiming that he had taken control of the joint business and was responsible to Karl's family for their share in the profits. When King Svein's army besieged the fortified town of Hedeby, South Jutland, probably towards the end of the tenth century, one of the attackers, Skardi, was killed. He had been a *hemthægi* of Svein's, literally 'one who received a home from him', presumably a member of the kings's household. Svein put up a memorial celebrating this man 'who had travelled in the west, and now met his death at Hedeby'. In part he was publicly declaring his responsibility for a man killed in his service.

Commonly described are the more familiar Viking activities, raiding and trading abroad. Yet even here the rune-stones act as a corrective to our other sources. It is well known that the Danes ravaged England under Sven and Knut in the late tenth/early eleventh century. The rune-stones reveal that Knut's armies were not exclusively Danish. At Väsby, Uppland, Sweden, is a stone raised by one Ali to his own glory. 'He took Knut's payment in England.' From Galteland, Austagder, Norway, is a stone, now in fragments, which Arnstein put up for his son Bior. 'He met death in the army when Knut attacked England.'

Something of the immense outgoing vigour of the Viking Age is reflected in these rune-stones. They commemorate Rognvald who 'was leader of a troop of men in Greece', probably a captain in the Emperor's Varangian guard (Ed, Uppland); Spialbodi who 'met his death in Novgorod, in Olaf's church', presumably indicating that there was a colony of Vikings with their own church, St Olaf's, in this Russian town (Sjusta, Uppland); Sven who 'often sailed in his splendid ship round Domesnes to Semgallen' (Mervalla, Södermanland); Gudver who 'was west in England, he took his share of *danegeld*, manfully he attacked townships in Saxland' (Grinda, Södermanland). We also learn something of what the Vikings did with the profits from their expeditions. At Veda, Uppland, is a stone to Arnmund who 'bought this estate, and he made his money in the Russian towns.' At Ulunda, Uppland, a man is celebrated for the wealth he brought into the family in a stanza of alliterative verse: 'he travelled boldly, he made money abroad among the Greeks for his heir'.

monuments, as well as being pious memorials to a royal couple, are political and dynastic propaganda.

At a lower level this is a characteristic of many Scandinavian rune-stones. They are often memorials to the dead but serve a public purpose as well. In an illiterate age there had to be some method of registering a death openly, particularly if it were the death of a rich or influential person since matters of inheritance, allegiance and debt needed to be sorted out. Rune-stones served this semi-legal purpose. It was specially important to record a death far from home, hence the number of runic inscriptions that tell of journeys abroad and battle in distant lands. The heirs were deeply concerned, so the names of those who put up the rune-stone, often relatives in different degrees, are prominently stated. The distinction of the dead must be stressed, hence the emphasis many rune-stones place on his exploits or her achievements.

But not all adventures ended prosperously. From several parts of Sweden, mainly in the Lake Mälar region, men went on a disastrous expedition to the East. They were led by one Ingvar, later known in Icelandic legend as 'the Far-travelled'. These were men of some consequence, owners of ships, leaders of crews. Many did not return. Their memorials remain as evidence (cf. fig. 4): to Gunnlaif who 'fell in the East with Ingvar'; to Banki who 'owned the whole of a ship and steered it east in Ingvar's host'; to Skardi who 'left here for the East with Ingvar and lies in Serkland' (Arab-held territory). Nor were all Vikings noble. There were villains among them. At Söderby, Uppland, is a stone put up in memory of Helgi. 'And Sassur killed him. He did a deed of shame, betrayed his comrade.' At Braddan, Isle of Man, is the fragment of a cross. The name of the man it commemorated is lost, but the rogue who destroyed him is immortalised: 'and Hrosketil betrayed under trust the man bound to him by oaths.'

This is but a small sample of the immense richness of the Viking rune-stones. They tell too of the peaceful activities at home, of running a farm, of hospitality at the big house, of building causeways and maintaining hostels for wayfarers. They tell too of the rights and activities of women (cat. no. 497). Indeed, the most splendid of the Norwegian ones is a tall, decorative stone from Dynna, Oppland. A mother erected it for her daughter Astrid: 'and she was the handiest girl in Hadeland.'

How many people could read these runic texts we do not know. Presumably a good number or there would be no point in putting them up. We do not know how readers were taught, nor even how rune-masters got their training. Certainly some lay-people could write runes, for we find them scratched, more or less casually, on all sorts of objects (cat. no. 19, 76, 348). For example: from an unknown Norwegian site comes a reliquary, Celtic work, apparently brought to Scandinavia as plunder in Viking times. On its base is scratched the owner's mark: 'Rannvaik owns this box' (cat. no. 131). Whether people who could write this could write much more it is impossible to say. A number of casual inscriptions of this sort contain errors or are hard to interpret, and this may point to a very limited literacy. We

Fig. 4. The Gripsholm stone c. 1050 in Södermanland. The runes tell of the hero Harald, brother of Ingvar, who was slain in a renowned expedition to the East. The inscription ends with a verse which praises the courage of those who took part.

must be aware, then, that the rich runic material from the Viking Age may represent a limited social and educational class, and not draw too general conclusions from what we read in inscriptions.

Runes survived the Vikings, continuing in use through the Middle Ages and even later. They occur side by side with Roman lettering on Christian memorial stones (cat. no. 450), and form a commercial script, for merchants' labels, personal letters and casual graffiti in the great towns of medieval Scandinavia (cat. no. 498–507, 531).

Fig. 5. Runic inscription on a silver neck-ring from the island of Senja, north Norway. It is a verse about a successful raid on Friesland resulting in rich booty. 11th cent. Cat. no. 348.

From oral poetry to literature

Preben Meulengracht Sørensen

Early narratives and pictures

At Rök, Östergötland, Sweden, at the beginning of the ninth century a chieftain raised a rune-stone in memory of his dead son. Many similar memorial stones carved with Scandinavia's earliest script are known from the succeeding centuries, but the Rök stone is rather special. Not only does it carry the longest and one of the oldest northern runic inscriptions, it is also the first attempt in Scandinavia to transform oral narrative into script.

The text consists of extracts from heroic tales and myths. One of them is a verse about Thjodrek, a verse in the same style and metre as the heroic poems which, 400 years later, were written down on parchment. Thjodrek has been identified with thee famous Ostrogothic king Theodoric the Great (died 526) who was the subject of many poems in the Germanic lands, and also in the North. We do not know why he was mentioned on the Rök stone; perhaps the dead could be honoured by giving them a relationship with heroes of earlier times.

Today the meaning of much of the inscription is obscure and this must also have been true at the time at which it was carved. Knowledge of runes was the preserve of a few and, furthermore, part of the Rök inscription is carved in secret runes which could only have been understood by the initiated. Thus the script was apparently not used as a means of communication, but rather as decoration. The whole of the tall, narrow stone is covered with large beautifully–formed runic letters—even on the top where only the gods could read them. Here indeed the god Thor himself is invoked.

The closest parallels to the Rök stone are the roughly contemporaray Gotland picture-stones which illustrate myths, sagas and possibly also rites (cat. no. 1, 175). The Rök inscription attempts to do in writing what is done in pictures on the other stones: namely, to preserve and perpetuate something essential in oral narratives and poems.

From the Viking Age and right up to the high Middle Ages we find traces of oral poems and narratives in the pictures which were carved in stone or wood, or woven in cloth. Incised into an ice-smoothed rock at Ramsund in Sweden, the story of Sigurd the dragon-slayer (*Siegfried* of the later German *Nibelungenlied*) is depicted in a series of pictures. Three other Sigurd pictures are known from Sweden and four have been preserved on the Isle of Man, on the

Fig. 1. The Rök stone, Östergötland, Sweden. The front face with part of a verse about Tjodrek, 'Tjodrek the bold/ king of sea-warriors ruled over Reid-sea shores; now he sits armed on his Gothic horse/ shield strapped, prince of Märings'.

western fringes of the Viking world. In Norway, the Sigurd legend is carved on portals of stave churches dating from about 1200, including that from Hylestad (cat. no. 442). The Norwegian pictures show that the old tales could be absorbed unchanged by Christian culture, but that paganism had to keep outside the church itself—as at the entrance to it.

Fig. 2. The Sigurd engraving on the Ramsund rock, Södermanland, Sweden. 11th cent. The runic band which frames the picture is the dragon Fafnir, guardian of the gold, pierced by Sigurd's sword. The other scenes from the legend show Sigurd roasting the dragon's heart; then burning his thumb, which he sucks, so that he tastes the dragon's blood: he was thus able to understand the language of the birds. The birds tell him that his foster-father, Regin the smith, wants to kill him for the dragon's gold. Sigurd then kills Regin. Regin is depicted with the severed head and smiths' tools beside him. Sigurd's horse Grane is tethered to the birds' tree, the gold on its back. Cf. fig. 4.

Just as widespread as the legend of Sigurd and the dragon was the myth of Thor and the World Serpent, the mighty sea-monster which in the Scandinavian picture of the world lay beneath the ocean and embraced all lands. The story in which Thor goes fishing and tries to drag the monster out of the sea is described in the scaldic poetry of the Viking Age and depicted on a Gotland picture-stone of about 800 (cat. no. 1); it is found a couple of centuries later at Hørdum in Jutland, at Altuna in Sweden, and on a stone from Gosforth in northern England.

These pictures presuppose a knowledge of the story, without which they cannot be understood. We find their content again in the poems of gods and heroes which were written down in Iceland in the thirteenth century, and from the pictures we may conclude that such poems were known throughout Scandinavia in the Viking Age in oral form.

Writing and the Scandinavian renaissance

Scandinavia's ancient script, runes, was in everyday use in the Viking Age both for practical purposes and for litera-

ture. Short poems in Old Norse or Latin, pagan incantations and Christian prayers were carved in runes on wood and other materials. Longer texts, however, used the new Latin language on parchment and at first Latin was confined to ecclesiastical and royal documents and books. An early example is the Dalby Gospels (cat. no. 509), a gospel-book written about the middle of the 11th century in what was then Danish Skåne. About 1120 Ælnoth—an Anglo-Saxon who lived in Odense for most of his life—wrote, in Augustinian mode, a chronicle of Knut the Great. There must also have been an early life of Norway's holy king St Olaf who was slain in 1030, but the earliest surviving record is the *Passio Olavi*, which dates from the end of the twelfth century and was written in England to the order of the exiled Norwegian archbishop Øystein.

During the course of the twelfth century, secular works concerning Norwegian and Danish kings were also composed; and, towards 1200, traditions from the Viking Age and early Middle Ages really began to be absorbed into the new literary culture. In Denmark this coincided with the high point of Scandinavian Latin literature, Saxo's *Gesta*

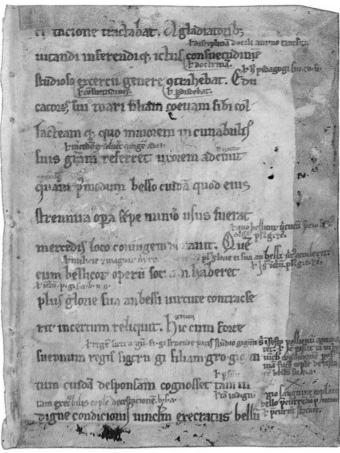

Fig. 3. The Angers fragment of Saxo's Gesta Danorum, *c. 1200. The width between the lines allowed space for corrections and additions, and the fragment is possibly from Saxo's own working copy. It comprises part of the first of sixteen books. This page (fol. 2r) contains the beginning of the history of King Gram and the Swedish princess Gro. Cat. no. 529.*

Danorum of c. 1200, which records the actions of the Danish kings from the earliest times to Saxo's period (cat. no. 529, 530). The aim of this great work was to glorify the fatherland by describing its splendid early history, and one of Saxo's ambitions was to demonstrate to the learned world that Denmark had had ancient poetry which could be compared in quality with the Classics. He did this by recreating Danish heroic poetry in a classical Roman style. Saxo based his stories of the earliest times on oral tradition—on legends, myths and poems.

In his prologue Saxo writes that the Icelanders' 'treasury of evidence of ancient happenings' was one of his sources. The Icelanders themselves converted this treasury into literature on a much greater scale than that of the other Nordic peoples. The western Scandinavian countries—Norway,

Iceland, the Orkneys, Faroes and Greenland—formed a specific cultural area. The Scandinavian languages were of course closely related, but, whereas the Danes had their closest contacts with the Continent and the Swedes' connections were directed predominantly towards the east, west Scandinavia had its closest contacts with the British Isles. The use of the vernacular in Britain encouraged the west Scandinavians to write in their own language—Old Norse—and not in Latin which was general elsewhere. As early as about 1125 the Icelander Ari Thorgilsson wrote a short history of Iceland, *Islendingabók* (cat. no. 520), in the vernacular, and the earliest version of *Landnámabók* (cat. no. 336) (a genealogical-topographical work about the colonization of Iceland c. 870–930) probably dates from the same time.

About 1150, an Icelandic scholar wrote a short philological treatise (cat. no. 521), which set out to adapt the Latin alphabet to the Icelandic phonetic system, 'so that it will be easier to write and read, as now is the habit in this country, laws and genealogies or exegeses of holy scripture or the learned historical works which Ari Thorgilsson has written in books with such outstanding wisdom'. The quotation gives us an idea of the kind of Icelandic literature which existed in the middle of the twelfth century and, apart from the genealogical works, exactly the same type of written studies were familiar in Norway and Denmark. Everywhere laws were written down in the vernacular: in Norway before 1100, in Iceland in 1117, in Denmark by 1170 at the latest, and in Sweden a few years later (cat. no. 518–9).

In the western Scandinavian countries the use of the vernacular displaced Latin as the main written language (cat. no. 520–5). The dominant position of written Old Norse was the single most important precondition for recording of the old oral tradition on parchment, produced in splendid redactions in Iceland and the other western Nordic countries. Another prerequisite for its success was the new European interest in history and poetry, and a third was that this interest began in Norway, Iceland and Denmark so soon after the conversion to Christianity, at a time when the pre-Christian tradition was still alive. It is significant that the same is not true of Sweden, where the fact that Christianity and the Latin script were adopted later (about 1100) precluded the Swedes from the early European renaissance.

It was not until the beginning of the nineteenth century that ancient Finnish traditions were written down. In Karelia, a medical doctor, Elias Lönnrot, collected heroic poems and brought them together into the great national epic *Kalevala*, which in its longest version (published in 1849) comprises 22,795 lines.

At the end of the twelfth century and in the course of the thirteenth century the culture of the North experienced its own early, intense renaissance. The combination of a number of factors—written culture, a fascination with the ancient world, and a rich oral tradition—produced (almost explosively), particularly in Norway and Iceland, a literature unique in medieval Europe. The sagas of Saint Olaf and Olaf Tryggvason had been written down in Iceland before 1200; and, about 1200, the history of the Norwegian King Sverri was written in Old Norse. Danish events are recounted in the Icelandic *Skjǫldunga saga* which tells of Danish kings and in *Jómsvíkinga saga* (cat. no. 523). Oral traditions, and probably also written stories, gathered in the rich culture of the Orkneys led to the production of the early *Orkneyinga saga* (cat. no. 525)—the story of the earls of Orkney. In the west *the sagas*, long prose narratives, became the form in which old tradition and new literature could be melded together: the history of kings (the *Kings' sagas*—cat. no. 526–7) and of the Icelanders themselves in old times (the *Saga of the Icelanders*) or stories of contemporary events (*Sturlunga saga* and the *bishops' sagas*), saints' lives, ancient legends (*fornaldarsögur*) and translated romances (*riddarasögur*) were all modified into sagas. It was not only oral narratives that were translated, scaldic poetry was of particular relevance because of the new interest in ancient times (see p. 172). Some of the earliest sagas, for example *Egils Saga Skallagrímssonar* (cat. no. 524), deal with the scalds of the Viking age; and the royal sagas and most of the some thirty-five sagas of the Icelanders contain scaldic verses. A total of some six thousand scaldic verses are preserved.

Poems of gods and heroes

The second great poetic genre of the Viking age, *the Eddas*, were written down independently. One of the reasons why these poems were remembered was that they related pre-Christian myths and heroic sagas with a wealth of subtle circumlocutions known as *kennings*. In the high Middle Ages the eddas became fashionable as poetic sources for pagan times and they were written down as a part of the interest in the ancient past. They are preserved in the famous manuscript *Codex Regius*, which now contains ten poems concerning gods and nineteen poems about heroes. The collection, which is usually called *The Poetic Edda*, is the most important basis for our knowledge of the heroic poetry of the Viking Age, as well as of Scandinavian (and Germanic) mythology. Single poems of the same type were written down in other manuscripts. Heroic poetry is also known from England and Germany, but there it has a different form and spirit from the poetry of the North. Poems about pre-Christian gods are preserved only in the North.

The Poetic Edda begins with *Voluspá*, in which the ancient seeress tells Odin, in a great vision, about the cosmic course from the creation of the world to its destruction at Ragnarǫk. This is followed by three more Odin poems, *Hávamál*, *Vafþprúnismál* and *Grímnismál*, which tell of the lives of gods and men. The poem *Skírnismál* deals with Frey and his love for the beautiful giant's daughter Gerd. The servant Skírnir is sent away to Jötunheim (the world of the giants) to win her, but only after terrible threats and curses does she yield to him. Five poems relate to Thor; one of these is the *Hymiskviða*, which tells the story of Thor's attempt to kill the World Serpent.

The heroic poems in the collection mainly concentrate on the saga cycle of Sigurd and his wife Gudrun. After Sigurd's death Gudrun becomes the dominating figure. Two poems describe her grief and her anger against the brothers who killed her husband. In *Atlakviða* she marries Atli (the historic Attila, died 453), who dupes the same two brothers and slays them. The poem ends with Gudrun's frightful revenge in which she slaughters her two sons by Atli and serves them to their father at dinner. She then kills Atli, sets fire to the royal hall and burns all the retainers. In the cycle Gudrun lives on to experience yet another tragedy. In the last poem, *Hamðismál*, she encourages the sons of her third marriage to revenge their half-sister Svanhild who, unprotected by King Jǫrmunrekk, had been trampled to death by a horse. The poem describes their heroic battle and death.

While the scaldic poems are art at the highest level, the eddaic poems of the Viking Age were a functional medium for knowledge which had to be remembered. Their verse form is simple. As in other early Germanic poetry, alliteration is the dominant principle but the Scandinavian poems differ from the Germanic ones in that they are divided into stanzas. The two main types of verse are *fornyrðislag* ('metre of ancient words') and *ljóðaháttr* ('metre of chants'), with eight and six lines to each stanza. An example of the first type is verse 3 of *Voluspá* with its picture of the world before the gods created the cosmos:

> Of old was the age
> when Ymir lived;
> Sea nor cool waves
> nor sand there were;
> Earth had not been,
> nor heaven above,
> But a yawning gap,
> and grass nowhere.

An example of *ljóðaháttr* is verse 139 of *Hávamál*. For nine days Odin has been hanging on Yggdrasil (the World Tree), and thus learns the secret of the runes:

> I had no bread,
> no drinking horn;
> I looked down,
> I took up the runes,
> shrieking I took them,
> And so fell back.

There is no agreement about the age and origin of the Edda poems. It is certain that the preserved poems were written down in Iceland in the thirteenth century and that Saxo knew the same types of poems about 1200. We also know that heroic poems and myths of gods occur on the Rök stone (about 800). But it is impossible to date the oral poems before they were written down. We can only say that the poems perpetuate a tradition which had an ancient, pre-Christian content, and that in the Viking Age they were current throughout Scandinavia. Some of the poems seem to have survived reasonably unchanged, while others are recreations of old poems.

In the 1220s the Icelandic chieftain Snorri Sturluson wrote a work which was both an introduction to scaldic art and an account of pagan mythology (cat. no. 521). The book came to be called the *Edda*—a word which can be interpreted both as 'great-grandmother' and as 'poetics'—which later gave the name to the eddaic poems because Snorri cited them as his sources. His book has no counterpart in foreign literature, but is an expression of the pursuit of the ancient past in contemporary Europe, and is perhaps the finest example of what has here been called the renaissance of the North. Snorri wished to improve knowledge of scaldic poetry and in his prologue he gives this, and pre-Christian belief, a place in the Chistian cosmos. Using prevalent European medieval ideas with originality, he carried the Scandinavian royal lines back to the Classical world. He thought that the pagan gods, the Æsir, came to Scandinavia from Troy and that they spread their families and language through the North. In this way Snorri devised a direct continuity between Scandinavia and the areas which were in the Middle Ages considered to be the centre of the world and the origin of culture. And, equally important, the language and poetry of Scandinavia were explained as being as old and as venerable as Latin.

The North and Europe

Snorri's scholarly interpretation expressed a Scandinavian self-confidence, a belief in an independent cultural identity, which was both inspired by contemporary European fashions and was in contrast to them. The Nordic peoples picked up everything that was new in Europe—religion, writing, Classical and modern literature and learning—but they also made it clear that they themselves had an early history and a poetry which was on a level with those of the Continent.

In *Orkneyinga saga* (cat. no. 525), the meeting between troubadour poetry and scaldic poetry is described. About the middle of the twelfth century the earl and scald, Rǫgnvald, sailed from Orkney on a pilgrimage to the Holy Land and on the way he and his retinue, which included two Icelandic scalds, visited the countess Ermengarde at Narbonne—the focus of homage by troubadours. According to the saga the Scandinavian scalds entertained the countess with their poetry and in one of the preserved stanzas the troubadours' simpler style is imitated. Ermengarde could hardly have understood anything of the Old Norse poetry, but for the scalds the meeting was an opportunity to display a poetry which—created for kings—was just as ancient and fashionable as that of southern France.

Linguistic differences prevented Nordic literature from becoming known in Europe in the Viking Age and Middle Ages. The North was, on the other hand, open to many inspirations and influences from outside; but they were adopted on the North's own cultural terms. When in the twelfth century the Norwegians became interested in Anglo-Norman romances such as Thomas's *Tristan et Iseult*, Chrétien de Troyes' *Yvain*, and the German ballads and stories of Didrik of Bern, they did not read them in French or German but had them translated into the prose of the sagas. A vast amount of foreign literature of widely differing character, both religious and secular, was translated into Old Norse in the course of a few decades; but most of all it was the North's own early history which was used as a subject for its literature. With writing as a tool and oral tradition as their material, the Scandinavians of the high Middle Ages re-created the Viking Age as an exceptional epoch, the quintessence of the Northern character.

Fig. 4. Portal of the stave church at Hylestad, Norway, with scenes from the Sigurd legend. C. 1200. Cf. fig. 2. Cat. no. 442.

Scaldic poetry

Jónas Kristjánsson

Around the year 100 AD Tacitus wrote in his *Germania* that songs were the only form of recorded history or annals of the Germanic peoples—by songs he meant narrative poems which were performed, or rather chanted, aloud. Tacitus based his account on contemporary knowledge of the Germanic tribes who lived in the areas bordering the Roman Empire, north of the Rhine and the Danube, but what he wrote of the Germanic annals in all probability also applied to the people in Scandinavia and indeed to most Germanic tribes of ancient times. Before the introduction of Christianity they had no written literature in our sense of the term. The unique Germanic runic script was almost exclusively used for short inscriptions on loose objects and, later, on memorial stones to the dead. But poetry was common to all Germanic peoples and its form and content survived well into the Christian era. All the Germanic peoples spoke closely related languages or dialects and, because the poems were composed in very free metre, they could travel from country to country, from people to people and adapt to new linguistic forms. The old Germanic metre was not at all like the Latin metres which became the basis for all poetry in the Christian world, even up to modern times. This metre has no fixed number of syllables to each line, no regular rhythm and no rhyme in the usual meaning of this term. Its characteristic feature is that great emphasis is laid on the words which the poet considers to be the most important and that these words are stressed by alliteration, so that two or three words in two consecutive lines (also called a 'long line') begin with the same sound (vowel or consonant). This ancient Germanic metre is found in the eddaic poems and in Old German and Old English poems, such as *The Hildebrandslied* and *Beowulf*. The following stanza from *Atlakviða* may serve as an example. This is one of the oldest poems in the collection known as *The elder Edda* and is probably from the ninth century:

Rín skal ráða   rógmálmi skatna
svinn, áskunna   arfi Niflunga;
í veltanda vatni   lýsask valbaugar,
heldr en á hǫndum gull   skíni Húna bǫrnum.

The Rhine shall be master   of the metal of man's strife,
the god-sprung river rule   the inheritance of the Niflungar;
in rolling waters rather   shall the foreign rings glint
than that gold should shine   on the Huns' children's hands.
(Transl. Ursula Dronke)

Fig. 1. The rune-stone from Karlevi, Öland, Sweden. Raised c. 1000 in memory of the chieftain Sibbe, son of Foldar. On this stone is the only surviving scaldic verse which was written down in the Viking Age. It is in the dróttkvætt *metre.*

But the Scandinavians also composed in other metres and some of these are highly sophisticated. The noblest of all was the so-called *dróttkvætt* (i.e. the metre suitable for the retainers of a lord). The order of words and sentence structure display deep convolutions and ingenuity. There is both alliteration and rhyme within each line, as well as a rich use of circumlocutary tricks, the most important of which are known as *heiti* and *kenninger*. A *heiti* uses a circumlocution in the form of a synonym, preferably an unusual or poetic word. A *kenning* consists of a picturesque description of an important word (thus 'blood' becomes 'ocean of the wound'; a 'ship', the 'waves' horse'; or a woman 'the field of gold ring'). There are thousands such, and they take for granted a knowledge of myth and heroic legend. It was an important element in the skald's art that he could vary and polish his often subtle painting of pictures.

Whilst this poetry was by implication accessible only with difficulty, it had at the same time through hundreds of years fascinated and tested patience and insight. An example of such poetic speech is a half-verse of dróttkvætt composed by Egill Skallagrímsson during a stormy passage. The alliteration is here printed in bold type and rhyme in italic (The kennings are as follows: the 'prow's bull-calf' is the ship: the 'ship's road' is the sea and the 'mast's giant' is the storm).

> Þél hǫggr stórt fyrir stáli
> stafnkvígs á veg jafnan
> út með éla meitli
> andærr jǫtunn vandar.

> With the shock of hail's chisel
> the mast's giant hews
> The prow's bull-calf's smooth way
> into a coarse file.
>
> (Transl. D.M. Wilson)

Old Scandinavian poetry is traditionally divided into two main groups, eddaic and scaldic. These two terms were, however, introduced in later times and the distinction between them is sometimes unclear; many poems straddle both groups. To the eddaic poems are assigned poems about pagan gods and ancient Germanic heroes; scaldic poems praised kings and other great men, and also comprised individual stanzas or short poems composed on specific occasions. Many scaldic poems were created in *dróttkvætt* or other similarly elaborate metres, but some of the most famous were composed in the old Germanic metre or in other free metres. The oldest scaldic poems were created by Norwegian scalds, but many of the most famous were produced by Icelanders.

The sagas describe, with romantic elaboration, how Icelanders travelling to foreign countries, went before the king and, having created poems eulogizing his achievements, were rewarded with gold and gifts. But the scalds also composed on other occasions: whilst travelling on land or at sea or at happy or sad events (cat. no. 524–5). Fighting and killing were the favourite subjects, but the scald could naturally also sing of beautiful women and the trials of love.

Poems which were preserved in oral tradition were probably often accompanied by explanatory legends, and (when the sagas began to be written down in the twelfth and thirteenth centuries) the writers used such legends along with the poetry as source material for history. In order to support the veracity of the written sagas the authors quoted liberally from poetry—from praise-poems in the sagas of Norwegian kings and from the occasional poems in the sagas of the Icelanders—consequently much of this poetry survives as components of the sagas. One reason that so much poetry by Icelandic scalds survives may be that the sagas were written in Iceland and therefore build mainly on the Icelandic corpus of legends and poems.

The old authors of the Icelandic sagas were quite convinced that the scaldic poems were their most reliable sources—so far as they went. The great Icelandic saga writer Snorri Sturluson (1179–1241) used them to their best advantage. In his work on the history of the kings of Norway *Heimskringla* (cat. no. 526–7) he quotes liberally from the ancient poetry in support of his account and, in his prologue, he has some wise words to say about the value of this source. He traces them back to Harald Fairhair, who was the first to become king of large parts of Norway in the late ninth century: 'There were scalds in Harald's court whose poems the people know by heart even at the present day, together with all the songs about kings who have ruled in Norway since his time, and we rest the foundations of our story principally upon the songs which were sung in the presence of the chiefs themselves or of their sons, and take all to be true that is found in such poems about their feats and battles: for although it be the fashion with scalds to praise most those in whose presence they are standing, yet no one would dare to relate to a chief what he, and all those who heard it, knew to be false and imaginary, not a true account of his deeds; because that would be mockery, not praise.'

Then Snorri goes on to tell of the historian Ari the Wise Thorgilsson, for whom he with good sense had a high regard, and at the end of the prologue he returns to the source value of the scaldic poetry: 'But the poems seem to me least corrupt, if the metrical rules are observed in them and if they are sensibly interpreted.' (Transl. S. Laing and P.G. Foote)

King Harald Fairhair's most famous scalds were Þorbjörn hornklofi and Þjóðólfr of Hvin. Þorbjörn composed the so-called *Haraldskvæði* about Harald's victories and about life at court. Here we catch a glimpse of a king's hall eleven centuries ago, we see the warriors and scalds, berserks and jesters in the service of the king. The contents are richer than is usual in scaldic poetry, since the poem is composed in the old free Germanic metre. Generally speaking, it is very like the heroic poems of the Edda:

> One sees from their gear   and from their gold bracelets
> that they are on close terms with the king;
> they dispose of cloaks red   and beautifully striped,
> of swords wound with silver,   ring-woven corselets,
> gilded baldrics   and chased helmets,
> bracelets worth wearing   which Harald picked out for them.
>
> (Transl. P.G. Foote)

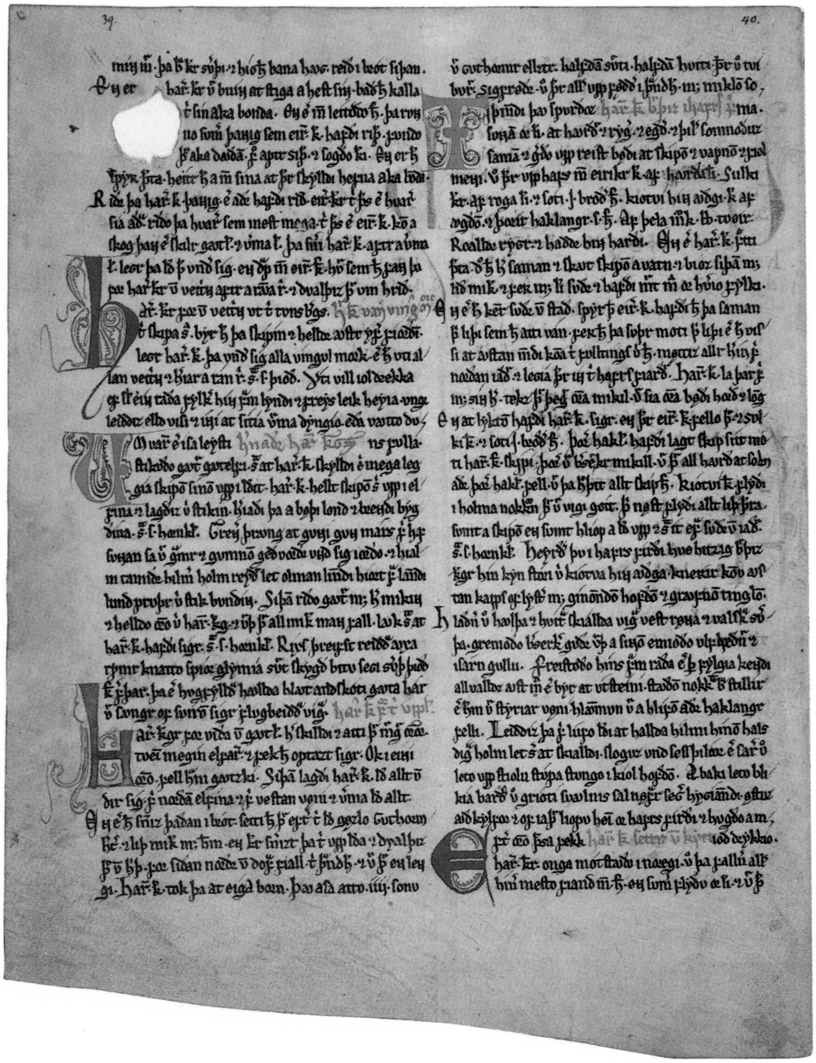

Fig. 2. A page from Harald Fairhair's saga from Snorri Sturluson's Heimskringla, *Codex Frisianus (fol. 10v). Cat. no. 527. In the chapter beginning with initial H is a stanza from* Haraldskvæði: Uti vill jól drekke … *In English translation: If he has his own way/ the valiant warrior/ he will feast and fight/ away from home./ When young he hated fire-heat/ and sitting around inside/ he hated heated women's rooms/ and down-lined mittens.*

One of Norway's most eminent scalds was Eyvindr Finnsson whose nickname was *Skáldaspillir*, (spoiler of scalds). His most famous poem is *Hákonarmál*, a memorial poem to King Hakon the Good who was killed in 960. Hakon was Christian and had been fostered by King Athelstan in England, but Eyvindr was pagan like most Norwegians of his day, and in the poem he has the king go to Valhalla and thanks him for having taken good care of the pagans' sacrificial sites. The light eddaic metre enables the scald to soar and allow us to hear the din of battle as the king falls:

> Wound-fires burnt in bloody gashes,
> swords leaned towards men's vitals,
> wound-sea surged on the headland of swords,
> flood of javelins fell on the foreshore of Stord.
> (Transl. P.G. Foote)

The greatest of all the ancient scalds was Egil Skallagrímsson, who lived in the tenth century. He was a son of one of Iceland's mightiest settlers and was himself the most powerful man in his district. A whole saga is written about his life, an outstanding work of literature—whatever one may think of it as a historical source. As a child Egil longingly composed poems about the great days to come, when he would be allowed to go abroad with Vikings and "hack down man after man". His dreams came true. He sailed to foreign countries, went on Viking expeditions and composed verses about mighty kings. He composed a large number of occasional verses replete with powerful poetic imagery. He came into conflict with the Norwegian Viking king, Erik Bloodaxe, who at that time ruled over York in England and, when the king wanted to have him killed, he saved his own life by composing, during a single night a twenty

Fig. 3. Egils Saga *(fol. 3v). This damaged fragment of the saga (3 leaves) contains the poem* Hǫfuðlausn *(Head-ransom) almost complete. The beginning of each stanza is marked by an initial and a* v *(for* vísa, *verse) in the margin. Cat. no. 524.*

stanza poem of praise to the king set to a melodic metre modelled on an English form. When the king had heard the poem he reprieved Egil and the poem has since been known as *Hǫfuðlausn*, 'head-ransom' (cat. no. 524).

But Egil's greatest renown as a scald came from two poems in simple metre, one about his friend who stood by him in York, the other about the two sons he lost under tragic circumstances.

The poem about Arinbjörn, *Arinbjarnarkviða*, is only preserved in the famous manuscript containing sagas of the Icelanders, *Möðruvallabók*, where it is written separately on a page following Egil's saga. This page is, however, partly illegible and the end of the poem was on the following leaf, which is now lost. *Sonatorrek*, "sad loss of sons", is just as

badly preserved, but for a different reason. Although it survives in its entirety, it is known only in late paper manuscripts where it is somewhat corrupt. Enough of these poems survive, however, to demonstrate the magnificent qualities of this poet, the first in Scandinavia to emerge as a personality. The poems radiate strongly-felt emotions and are honed with vigour and word-craft. We are not offended, even when he views his work with Horatian self-satisfaction in the last stanza of *Arinbjarnarkviða*, which by a stroke of good fortune survives in a single manuscript redaction of Snorri's *Edda*:

> I was early wakeful,   I gathered words together
> with the morning labours   of the speech-servant [tongue];
> I built a stack of praise   which will long stand,
> not hasty to collapse,   in the courtyard of poetry.
>
> (Transl. P.G. Foote)

The saga relates that when Egil learnt of the death by drowning of his son Böðvarr, he at first decided to starve himself to death. His daughter persuaded him to postpone this until he had composed a memorial poem. Another of his sons had died from disease a short time before and the scald recalls them both. The poem is an implacable indictment of Odin and Ran (goddess of the sea), who had robbed him of his sons. Earlier he had had a good relationship with Odin, god of war and poetry. Now the friend has failed him. But Egil gathers strength as he composes, and at the end he has won a victory over his grief and reconciled himself with the gods through his poetry:

> The enemy of the wolf Odin,   used to battle,
> gave me a skill   removed from blemish
> and such a cast   of mind that I made
> open enemies   of wily plotters.
>
> Yet glad   in good heart
> and not cast down   shall I wait for death.
>
> (Transl. P.G. Foote)

One of the best known of the later scalds was Sighvatr Þórðarson. He was scald to King Olaf Haraldsson, who was canonized after his death at the battle of Stiklestad in 1030. When the battle took place Sighvatr was on pilgrimage to Rome, a journey which in effect saved his life. When he heard of the death of his king he expressed his grief symbolically:

> The high, leaning cliffs round all Norway   seemed to me to smile
> when Olaf was alive   —I used to be known on ships.
> Now afterwards, the slopes seeem to me   much less friendly
> —such is my grief.   I had the king's complete favour.
>
> (Transl. P.G. Foote)

Art

Signe Horn Fuglesang

Since ornament is that aspect of Viking art which is best preserved, it has provided the basis of art-historical surveys of the period. Animal motifs are the most important element within it, and because of the continuity of their use they provide the best sources for the study of the development of style in Scandinavia in the period *c.* 750–1200. The types and the style features of the animals changed, however, in the course of time; partly through influence from western Europe, partly by development and innovation at home. But animals did not totally dominate the ornamental repertoire—both ribbon and plant motifs were important in the tenth and eleventh centuries and, again, in the Romanesque art of the twelfth century.

In so far as religious ideas were transmitted through art—in Viking Scandinavia as in the rest of Europe—they came through the use of representational art. This happened with the appearance of Romanesque art in the twelfth century. At this period the symbolic interpretation of animals and other ornamental motifs became very popular in Europe, and artists turned for inspiration to Physiologus (cat. no. 522) and similar allegorical zoological books of the Late Antique. Romanesque animals in Scandinavia are a part of this world in as much as they can be interpreted symbolically; but the animals of Viking Age art cannot be interpreted in this manner.

Artistic convention was also strong outside the area of ornament. Even the sketchy drawings of animals and ships, which may appear naturalistic when considered alone, conform to pictorial categories which were repeated unchanged throughout the centuries: ships, horses and dogs form the chief motifs on the planks of the Oseberg ship (cat. no. 10) as well as in the chancels of the stave-churches.

Scandinavian and European in the Viking Age

The relationship between Scandinavian and European art in the Viking Age provides a remarkable supplement to the historical sources. It is noteworthy, for example, that the mounts which came from the British Isles and are found in ninth-century graves in Norway (cat. no. 128–9, 157) were never copied in Scandinavian workshops, nor did they influence the development of style in Scandinavia. Either such work was no longer fashionable when it arrived in Norway, or it did not find its way to the workshops which set the fashion. On the other hand, contemporary English animals and, somewhat later, Carolingian motifs were, for example, copied in Danish workshops (as at Ribe and Haithabu), and both groups of motifs were developed independently and adapted to the Scandinavian repertoire.

All this is relevant to historical problems concerning the early development of towns in Scandinavia and the status of craftsmen. Geography, then as later, dictated the different contacts between the Scandinavian countries and Europe; thus the import of eastern material was mainly confined to Sweden (cat. no. 27, 119–21, 132–4). It is, however, remarkable, that very little eastern ornament was copied in Scandinavia, and in no case can it be demonstrated that Russian, Byzantine or Slav art had any impact on Scandinavia in the Viking Age.

It is also noteworthy that the influence which Scandinavian art exerted abroad during the Viking Age was so limited in time and space. A separate Anglo-Scandinavian art, for example, was created in England in the tenth century, centred on the Scandinavian settlements; but there is nothing to indicate any Scandinavian influence in the art of Normandy, which was settled by Scandinavians at the same time. Such differences would appear to reflect the varying composition and objectives of the immigrant groups in the two areas. When the Irish workshops developed their own version of the Urnes style around the year 1100, there was no ethnic connection and the use of Scandinavian models must be due to other reasons, such as a desire to revitalize the domestic Irish tradition.

The archaeological sources

Our knowledge of Viking art derives primarily from archaeological finds. The nature of the find circumstances, however, does not remain the same throughout the period. From *c.* 800 it became increasingly popular in some parts of Scandinavia to bury the dead in their finery—women with jewellery and men with weapons. This custom peaked in the first half of the tenth century and then gradually declined in the second half of the century.

After about 975/1000 graves are no longer an important archaeological or art-historical source—hoards become more important. The earliest hoard which can be dated by means of the associated coins was deposited about 925; after this hoards increase in number until the eleventh century. There are clearly fewer hoards than grave finds, but on the other hand coin-hoards can normally be dated with some precision.

Decorated rune-stones also belong to the late Viking Age. A small number of rune-stones have survived from the second half of the tenth century in Denmark and from the first half of the eleventh century in Norway, but the greatest number of decorated memorial stones are found in Sweden, where they date from about 1025/1050. They are mostly executed in the Urnes style (cf. cat. no. 193, 497, 560).

Archaeological excavation in medieval towns in the last few decades has produced a large amount of new material which throws light both on everyday life and on art; this is particularly true of the eleventh and twelfth centuries. Otherwise church art is the most important source for an understanding of the development of Romanesque art in the twelfth century.

Ornamental styles

Viking Age ornament is normally divided into stylistic groups. There is often an exclusive connection between motifs and style, but this is not necessarily so. 'Gripping beasts', for example, are used in various forms in three style groups for some one and a half centuries between c. 775/800 and c. 925/950 (the 'Broa-phase', the Oseberg style and the Borre style), whereas the characteristic geometric interlace of Borre seems to be confined to that style and lasted for about 50–75 years. The different styles are briefly summarized here.

The 'Broa phase', of the second half of the eighth century, consists of a mixture of motifs and styles which are all represented on a series of bridle-mounts from Broa on Gotland (cat. no. 176.) The ribbon-like animals (of Salin style III:E) take the form of elongated S shapes, often with the body split into wide loops and balloon-like openings at the hips (fig. 1a) (cf. cat. no. 29). Long, thin tendrils create a network of open loops around the main animals. These ribbon-like creatures are a late manifestation of the Scandinavian animal ornament which emerged in the sixth century. At the same time, however, the Broa workshop used motifs introduced from western Europe; semi-naturalistic animals and birds of a form known in Frankish manuscripts and metalwork (fig. 1b). The third main Broa motif is the 'gripping beast', a compact cat-like creature with feet which grip its frame and neighbouring animals (fig. 1c) (cf. cat. no. 30); it is never split or woven into looped patterns. The gripping beast is probably of Anglo-Saxon origin—the squirrel-like creatures of the English inhabited vine-scroll are closely related.

These three genetically different groups of motif were used throughout Scandinavia in the second half of the eighth century and the borrowed elements must reflect increased trade with western Europe at this period.

The Broa motifs are still found in the ninth-century Oseberg style; but by then the European loans have taken an indigenous form. The Oseberg style derives its name from the famous woman's ship grave from Oseberg in Vestfold, Norway, with its fantastic collection of high quality carved wooden objects. The new developments of the Oseberg style are most clearly seen in the work of the so-called 'Baroque master' (cat. no. 166a). Compact animals are set side by side in carpet-like patterns covering the whole surface, and fewer loops occur. The relief is plastic and graded into many planes to give the effect of light and shade. These new features were probably a Scandinavian

Fig. 1. Three of the gilt-bronze mounts from Broa, Gotland, Sweden, cf. cat. no. 176. a: Animals in style III/E. b: Semi-naturalistic animals. c: Gripping-beasts. Second half of the 8th cent.

creation, perhaps influenced by contemporary 'renaissance tendencies' in England and France. Nevertheless, all the animal motifs were developed from types which were first used in the 'Broa phase'. The Oseberg style is normally dated to the first three quarters of the ninth century.

The Borre style takes its name from a grave at Borre in Vestfold, Norway, (fig. 2) which produced a set of harness mounts consisting, like those from Broa, of groups of motifs of various origins and period: debased successors of Style III:E animals; a remodelling of the gripping beast; a new western European version of semi-naturalistic animals, and —most importantly—a Scandinavian, and highly original variant, of European ribbon motifs (cf. cat. no. 31).

The artists who created the Borre style had a liking for taut, equilateral geometric motifs, especially circles and squares, as inter alia in the ribbons of the characteristic ring-chains and pretzel-like knots. Plant motifs such as acanthus and vine-leaves were copied from Carolingian trefoil and tongue-shaped mounts from baldrics of the period c. 900. In Scandinavia, however, these forms were adapted as brooches for women's clothing (cat. no. 135–7). The Borre

Fig. 2. Six of the gilt-bronze mounts from Borre, Vestfold, Norway, cf. cat. no. 169. Their decoration has given the name to the Borre style. C. 900.

The Mammen style is the important innovative art phase which signals the beginning of the Late Viking Age. It is named after the silver-inlaid axe-head from a grave at Mammen in Denmark (fig. 4), which is dated by dendrochronology to 970–971 (cf. cat. no. 35). On one side is a bird with wings and tail feathers formed like tendrils, on the other a plant ornament. The use of single motifs is new, but the style is in a direct descent from the pretzel knots of the Borre style and from the linear elements of the Jellinge style.

The great memorial stone which King Harald Gormson raised at Jelling in the 960s to commemorate his parents and his own achievements is a unique monument (cat. no. 193). Above that part of the inscription which tells of Harald's military victories there is a lion entwined by a snake—the earliest example of such a motif in Scandinavia. The forerunners of the motif are found in contemporary European art and its successors in the series of snakes and lions which occur in the eleventh-century Ringerike and Urnes styles. Above the text "and made the Danes Christian" is a crucifixion scene in which Christ is bound by a plant. This is also a European image reproduced in the Scandinavian ornamental tradition.

Closer to European art are the caskets from Bamberg and Cammin (cat. no. 266–7). Semi-naturalistic lions, birds and snakes are entwined in lush scrolls, and both the motifs and the style are close to contemporary German and English art. This phase probably lies nearer the year 1000, but the Mammen style proper flourished in the second half of the tenth century.

Most Mammen motifs continued in use in the Ringerike style, although there were stylistic changes. The ornament of the memorial stone at Vang in Oppland, Norway, is typical. An axial double scroll is surrounded by short asymmetrically placed tendril shoots and terminates in a rosette cross, the four arms of which consist of a broad leaf flanked by narrow ones (fig. 5). Both types of composition are imported. The groups of narrow vine shoots are of Ottonian origin, whilst the alternation between wide and narrow leaves is an Anglo-Saxon trait. The Ringerike style was probably created in Denmark c. 1000, in close contact with the newly established Church in Scandinavia.

Its subsequent distribution in Scandinavia partly followed the traditional paths of rulers, craftsmen and trade, and partly the establishment of the Church (cf. cat. no. 36–7). The Ringerike style is used, for example, as decoration above the saints on the wall planks from Flatatunga, Iceland (cat. no. 454), which is probably the earliest surviving church decoration in the North. In contrast to the other stylistic groups, the Ringerike style does not take its name from a single important find. It got its misleading name from the reddish Ringerike sandstone of the Oslo area which was used for some of the memorial stones. In fact there is not a

style is the earliest Scandinavian style to be used in the Viking settlements in Iceland, England and Russia. It is normally dated to the period 850/875–925/950.

The Jellinge style is the only group which is based solely on one motif which comprises ribbon-like and S-shaped animals (cat. no. 33). Chronologically it overlaps both the earlier Borre style and the succeeding Mammen. The style takes its name from the animals on the small silver stemmed cup from the royal grave at Jelling, in Jutland. On this object two elongated S-shaped animals drawn in profile are intertwined in diagonal symmetry (fig.3). When the Jellinge animal is found together with Borre style ornament, late Borre stylistic elements are used—as, for example, on a mount from the silver hoard from Vårby in Sweden (deposited c. 940 (cat. no. 27). The Jellinge style flourished in the first half of the tenth century and is without doubt a Scandinavian—possibly a Danish—invention, but it was perhaps inspired by contemporary S-shaped animals in England.

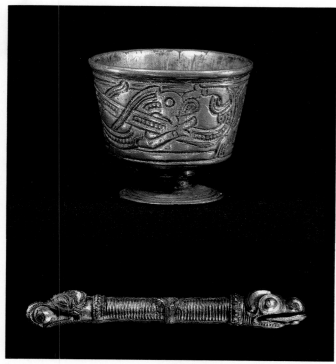

single object in the Ringerike style from Ringerike.

The Urnes style is the last 'Nordic' phase. The name is taken from one of the finest surviving examples of medieval Scandinavian art, which appears on the carved timbers of the earliest church at Urnes in Sogn, Norway. (The timbers were subsequently re-used in the surviving twelfth-century church (fig. 6)). In contrast to the Mammen and Ringerike styles, animals make up the most important group of motifs in this style—extremely stylized quadrupeds (including lions), as well as ribbon-like animals and snakes. The winged dragon appears for the first time in Scandinavia, possibly drawn from England. The cross is often used—65% of the eleven hundred or more memorial stones in Uppland have crosses and 25% have Christian inscriptions. Behind the patterns of the Urnes style lies a principle of homogeneity— open loops form figures-of-eight or sinuous, interpenetrating, multi-looped patterns. Only two line widths are used, and heads and feet are fined down to become elongated terminals (cat. no. 38, 497, 560). The Urnes style is also closely tied to the Church and was used to decorate the early stave-churches in all Scandinavian countries. Created in the second quarter of the eleventh century it continued in use into the twelfth century.

Fig. 3. Silver cup (cat. no. 191) and silver mount (cat. no. 192) from Jelling, Jutland, Denmark. The cup is from the king's burial in the North mound. The mount is from the burial in the church. The ornamentation on the cup has given the name to the Jellinge style. Second quarter of the 10th cent.

Fig. 4. The decoration on the silver-inlaid axe from Mammen, Jutland, Denmark, has given its name to the Mammen style. Third quarter of the 10th cent. Cat. no. 173.

Fig. 5. Memorial stone at Vang, Oppland, Norway, with decoration in the Ringerike style. First half of the 11th cent.

The Urnes-Romanesque transition took various forms in different Scandinavian workshops (cf. cat. no. 39–40). Most of the Romanesque motifs were developed in the Mediterranean area in the course of the eleventh century; a few, such as the winged dragon, were created in northern Europe. In the twelfth century this new decorative art was introduced into Scandinavia. In some workshops it was combined with the traditional Urnes style, but when this happens the Urnes elements are limited to the ribbon-like animals and snakes, to the multi-looped patterns and to figures-of-eight. The workshop which produced the fine altar frontal from Lisbjerg in Denmark used both types of decoration and demonstrated the interesting effects which could be produced. The iconography and figural style of the altar are purely Romanesque, some borders have Romanesque decoration, others reflect the Urnes style (cat. no. 467).

The prototype for the Norwegian stave-church doorways of the "Sogn-Valdres type" was also created at the junction between Urnes and Romanesque: the jambs have Romanesque spriral scrolls interlaced with Romanesque winged dragons whose bodies have retained the multi-looped figures of the Urnes style. Traces of the Urnes style have almost completely disappeared from the doorways which date from the last quarter of the twelfth century; they are, however, still present on that from Ål (cat. no. 441), which is somewhat earlier. In Ireland a similar mixture of styles was produced on twelfth-century metal reliquaries and in stone sculpture.

Romanesque decoration can be divided into a number of local styles which reflect the various cathedral workshops and schools of immigrant craftsmen. Most Romanesque motifs had been developed in the Mediterranean region during the eleventh century and were derived from various places and media: some innovations were based on Classical motifs or the designs found on oriental textiles. Romanesque ornament introduced a great number of new animal forms to Scandinavia, it also brought in Romanesque spiral scrolls and the single scrolls; and at the same time geometric motifs became fashionable. Occasionally, it is possible to identify the area from which the motifs were imported. The decoration of the cathedral at Lund in Skåne, for example, can be compared to that of the Rhineland, a comparison born out by documentary evidence. Elsewhere we must rely on comparative stylistic analysis—the Norwegian winged dragons and spiral scrolls, for example, are paralleled in eastern England. Romanesque ornament was also used in secular contexts, as for example on objects excavated from twelfth-century levels in the medieval towns. By about 1200 the Romanesque style had definitely become outmoded, as had the popular taste for decoration which characterized the two preceding centuries. It is hardly a coincidence that it was the Romanesque motifs which provided the starting point for the archaising forms which characterize much of Scandinavian folk-art as late as the seventeenth century.

Pictorial art

Pictorial art must have been much more important than can be inferred from accidentally surviving examples. Poems describing representational art were written down around 1200 and have survived. They tell of pictures painted on shields and in the halls of chieftains. Otherwise the decorated memorial stones are our most important source for pictorial art, but the decoration of runic stones followed local fashion which sometimes lasted only a short time. Most of the stones which are of significance for pre-Christian iconography were erected on Gotland in the late eighth

Fig. 6. Portal from the stave-church at Urnes, Sogn, Norway. The carvings from the church which was built here in the second half of the 11th cent. were reused. They have given the name to the Urnes style.

or early ninth centuries and in Britain in the tenth century. The motifs of a ship and a horseman dominate the Gotland stones, pictures which are usually thought to symbolize the journey of the deceased to Valhalla and at the same time to mark his social status (cat. no. 1, 175).

The fragment of tapestry from Tune in Østfold, Norway, depicting men and women beside a ship, suggests that such iconography was not limited to the memorial stones. The famous fragments of a tapestry from Oseberg (p. 47, fig. 5) include men, warriors, horsemen and carts forming a scene which has been tentatively interpreted as a religious procession, but which might as easily be a narrative scene based, for example, on a migration period saga.

Otherwise the Gotland stones display a large number of scenes presumably taken from myths and heroic sagas which can only occasionally be identified—few written versions have survived and, like the pictures, what remains is accidental. Nevertheless, these Gotland monuments are important since they show that a representational art, distinct from ornament, existed, and had an iconography which must have been clearly understood by the contemporary educated Scandinavian.

No picture from the middle of the ninth to the mid-tenth century has survived in Scandinavia. This lacuna can partly be filled by using the material from north-west England and the Isle of Man, where a small number of Anglo-Scandinavian and Norse stones have survived which are decorated with scenes known from eleventh-century Scandinavia, scenes to do with hunting or the Sigurd saga.

The great Jelling stone from the 960s marks the beginning of both a new use of pictorial stones and a new, Christian iconography. The memorial stone from Dynna, Norway, from c. 1025/1050, shows that the Adoration of the Magi was known as a motif, whilst the row of saints on the panels from Flatatunga, Iceland, indicates that church decoration was based on European models (cat. no. 454). The Swedish memorial stones of the eleventh century are normally decorated with animals and crosses (cat. no. 560); those that had pictures display hunting scenes and episodes from the Sigurd and Völsunga saga (p. 167, fig. 2). Only one Swedish stone has an expressly pagan iconography, the picture of the god Thor fishing for the Midgard serpent on a stone from Altuna Church, Uppland (p. 146, fig. 3). Otherwise few figural scenes have survived and the eleventh century seems to be a typical transitional phase in the use of pictures: the pagan gods and the journey to Valhalla were no longer current themes; at the same time, however, few Christian images were available for the artists to use as models.

Representations of Christian images do not occur in great numbers until the twelfth century and then survive chiefly in ecclesiatical art: as reliefs on stone churches and fonts, on altar frontals, in wall paintings and as devotional statues.

There are three main regions for stone sculpture (p. 210) —Jutland, Lund and Gotland—and it is interesting to note that each separate workshop specialized in different groups of motifs, some of which were theologically quite advanced. Stone sculpture elsewhere in Sweden (and in Norway) was much more primitive and emphasised the decorative. The earliest representations of saints in Scandinavia survive on reliefs on fonts from Gotland and on the Lisbjerg altar frontal (cat. no. 467). At Lisbjerg the saints are grouped on either side of the important theological axis—the Madonna and Child (the Incarnation), the Crucifixion, and the Second Coming (the Day of Judgment). Normally, however, the minor arts display a more complicated iconographic programme; as on the Gunhild Cross (cat. no. 607).

Wooden figures—representing the Crucifixion, the Virgin and a number of saints—only appear in any quantity with the Gothic art of the thirteenth century (cf. cat. no. 466). Twelfth-century devotional sculpture has survived best in Sweden (p. 208). Here both style and iconography show Germany to have been the most important area of influence; the group of Madonnas, for example, to which that from Viklau belongs is closely paralleled in the Rhineland (cat. no. 461). Saints as devotional statues seldom occurred in the twelfth century, and devotional statues of Scandinavian saints, such as the kings Olaf, Knut and Erik, belong without exception to the Gothic period.

On the whole it seems that the transition from Viking to Romanesque art was less of a break than is usually assumed. Within the decorative arts a workshop tradition combined Urnes style elements with Romanesque motifs until well on into the second half of the twelfth century. The ornamental motifs were changed. The Romanesque animal world was richer than that of the Vikings, and some of the animals were probably interpreted symbolically.

Within pictorial art the differences were naturally more sophisticated. Pictures with a religious content must have been a fundamentally new element in Scandinavian culture, as also were the presence and function of Christian statues. That Christian images as such were known in an earlier period is demonstrated by the Crucifixion on the Jelling stone. Secular pictures which had been used in the Late Viking Age were happily incorporated in the decoration of churches; as in the Sigurd scenes on the Norwegian stave-church doorways from c. 1200 (cat. no. 442). As Romanesque art was gradually introduced into Scandinavia —mainly from Germany and England, in the course of the first half of the twelfth century—it enriched Scandinavian culture, but it was not essentially alien to it.

Fig. 7. Virgin and child, detail from the Lisbjerg altar, Denmark. Mid-12th cent. Cat. no. 467.

Artifacts and manuscripts

Burial customs in Scandinavia during the Viking Age

Anne-Sofie Gräslund, Michael Müller-Wille

The graves and grave-goods of the pagan Viking Age are a rich source of information for the economic, social and religious structure of this pre-literate, early medieval society. They can also be used as an indication of settlement and as a basis to estimate the size of the population (cat. no. 43–5, 176, 324–5). The burial customs were variable in both regional and social terms and both cremation and inhumation were practised.

Cremations, which were predominant in the North during most of the Iron Age, took a number of forms in the Viking Age: urn burials, where the cremated bones were contained within a pottery vessel; bone layers, where the cremated bones were scattered within the grave (in both these types of burial the bones were deposited after being separated from the charcoal and soot of the funeral pyre); cremation pits, where all the remains of the pyre (bones, charcoal, grave-goods and so on) were put in the same hole in the ground; and cremation layers, where the remains

from the pyre (burnt bone, objects, charcoal, soot and ashes) were scattered on the ground surface. Large quantities of bone of horse, dog, cattle, pig, sheep/goat, cat and fowl (representative of all the domestic animals found in Viking-age settlements) are often found among the cremated remains. The funeral pyre was built either immediately on the place of burial or somewhat separated from it in a cremation area, from which the bones would have been carried to the burial place. Cremation burials were normally marked by a stone-setting or a mound.

Inhumations also vary in form: the most common are chamber-graves, pit-graves—sometimes with and without coffins—and boat burials. The chamber-graves consist of large, wide and deep pits which often reveal traces of a solid wooden structure—corner posts, wall-panelling, floor and roof. Both men and women were buried in chamber-graves, often with rich grave-goods. A few graves were double. Some chamber-graves contain horse skele-

tons; in Birka, for example, the horses lie on a ledge outside the burial chambers themselves. We do not know whether chamber-graves were of native origin or whether the idea was an innovation imported from elsewhere—the evidence would suggest the latter. Precursors of this type of burial can be seen in north-western Europe, particularly in Friesland, Lower Saxony and Westphalia.

A coffin-grave consists of a burial pit in which traces of a wooden coffin may be found in the form of wood and/or iron nails. An inhumation found with no traces

Fig. 1. Burial mounds in one of the cemeteries (south of the fortress) at Birka, Sweden. Some 1100 of the c. 3000 graves around this great Viking Age town (see p. 127, fig. 1) were excavated by Hjalmar Stolpe from 1871 to 1895. The unprecedentedly rich finds from these graves led to a changed view of the Viking Age and are still central to all Viking Age research. Stolpe also excavated a part of the 'Black Earth' (the occupation area of the town); 1990 saw the beginning of renewed excavations there.

of a coffin does not necessarily mean that it was uncoffined, for the remains of the coffin may have disappeared completely: on the other hand it might have been a shroud burial in which the textiles, birch-bark or hides which wrapped the body have decayed.

Viking Age boat-burials could be either inhumations or cremations. A large number of rivets among the remains of a pyre may constitute a cremated boat-burial. The custom of cremation in a boat and the subsequent raising of a mound over the cremated remains is described in the 920s by the Arab traveller Ibn Fadlan, who tells of the ceremony surrounding the burial of a Viking chieftain in the land of the Bulgars, near the River Volga.

Boat inhumation, already known from the pre-Viking Vendel period, continues into the Viking Age; as is demonstrated in the cemeteries of Vendel, Valsgärde and Tuna in Alsike in Uppland, and at Tuna in Badelunda in Västmanland (cat. no. 43, 44). Burial in full-sized sea-going vessels is known from Norway (Borre, Tune, Gokstad and Oseberg p. 25, fig. 1 and p. 44, fig. 2) and Denmark (Ladby).

In Denmark, as in large parts of Norway, south Sweden, and on Gotland, cremation and inhumation were in use simultaneously, although inhumation was the more common. The graves display great variation of shape—circular, square and triangular stone-settings or lines of stones, boat-shaped outlines of stones, stone circles (*domarringar*), upright stones and mounds. The burials within these features are normally cremation layers, cremation pits, or simple inhumations. Elsewhere in Sweden cremation predominated up to the late Viking Age, when it was superseded by inhumation, probably under the influence of Christianity.

In the ninth and tenth centuries the most common form of burial in eastern Sweden was cremation; the cremation layers were covered by low mounds or surrounded by circular stone-settings. They lie together in small groups; the smallest indicating a farmstead, fairly large groups indicating a village, and even larger groups, as at Birka, indicating a 'town'. The cemeteries often consist of a large number of clearly visible burial mounds, which are to this day a characteristic feature of the Swedish landscape. In the late Viking Age the burial mounds were replaced by rectangular lines of stones which defined simple coffined or uncoffined inhumations, oriented E-W, and without grave-goods.

In Denmark, Norway and Sweden great mounds with a diameter of more than 20 m, often standing on a spectacular site, are known. Only a few have been excavated, but they have been built at all periods, from the Bronze Age to the Viking Age. The north mound at Jelling (p. 154, fig. 3) and the mounds at the Norwegian sites of Borre (p. 36, fig. 4), Oseberg and Gokstad are remarkable examples from the Viking Age.

These great mounds, like the chamber-graves and rich grave-goods, have been interpreted as evidence for a differentiated social stratification in the Viking Age. Thus, equestrian burials from the old Danish area have been attributed to the *thegns* and *drengs* named on rune-stones who were probably in the service of the king, who probably worshipped Odin and hoped to reach Valhalla. The female equivalent of these great burials were the richly furnished graves in which the woman was buried in a waggon, sometimes accompanied by a horse; such women certainly belonged to leading families. The rich chamber-graves from the trading centres of Hedeby and Birka reflect the international connections of these sites, and probably represent the families of prominent foreign and native merchants.

Conversion to Christianity was a long and slow process in Scandinavia and was not completed until the end of the Viking Age. The progress of Christianity through the Viking Age can be followed by studying such features of the burial ritual as the steady trend towards a practice of east-west oriented inhumation graves, which is clearly of religious significance.

Fig. 2. Male grave from Birka (Chamber grave 581). Mid 10th cent. The burial was richly furnished and contained silver decorations from a conical cap (cat. no. 133) a sword, axe, spear, shield, bronze dish, stirrups, and horse-harness. Two horses were interred in the eastern part, on a ledge about 60cm high. Wood-cut (1889) after a drawing by Stolpe.

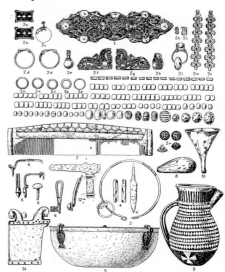

Fig. 3. Grave-goods from a rich female grave from Birka (Chamber grave 854). 9th cent. The furnishings include jewellery, a ring with Thor's hammer amulets, a comb, casket-mounts and a key, a bronze dish, glass beakers, a pottery vessel with cruciform decoration, a 'smoothing board' and smoothing stone, a knife and whetstone (also 2 iron-mounted wooden buckets, not illustrated here). Drawing from the great 1943 Birka publication.

Christian graves and funerary monuments

Göran Tegnér

The earliest Christian graves, which are certainly present in Viking Age cemeteries, are difficult to find. Inhumations without grave-goods in graves which are aligned east-west should, in theory, be Christian, but they may also be burials of the poor or of slaves.

As the Church became more established during the eleventh century, many churches were built and Christians were buried in enclosed churchyards where there might be social distinctions. The sites nearest the church, particularly those under the eaves, were the most sought after; but priests and aristocrats were buried inside the churches. In some early medieval churchyards the men were buried to the south of the church and women to the north. Burials were usually in simple wooden coffins of varying types but burials without coffins also occur. The graves were probably marked above ground. The dead were usually buried with their arms at their sides, and in

shrouds; less frequently they were dressed in everyday clothes. Many graves excavated in the churchyards in Lund, Sweden, contained branches of deciduous trees, a feature encountered elsewhere in early-medieval graves in Sweden and Denmark. We do not know the beliefs which lay behind this practice.

Charon's pennies occur in Denmark and Sweden, reflecting the ancient Greek custom of placing a coin in the mouth of the dead as payment to the ferryman Charon for the journey across the Styx.

Burials inside the churches were usually stone-lined, generally built of slabs, but in some cases carved out of a single block of stone, trapezoidal or rectangular in shape and often with a carved niche for the head. When bricks began to be used in south Scandinavia at the end of the twelfth century, cists were also built of brick.

A large number of eleventh- and twelfth-century funerary monuments are preserved in the Nordic countries, but they are somewhat unevenly distributed. They are very common in Denmark and Sweden (particularly in Västergötland), extremely rare in Norway, whilst only a few fragments survive in Iceland and Finland. Those in Denmark were usually carved out of granite, but limestone and sandstone were used in Sweden and Skåne. In addition to these stone monuments there would also have been wooden ones.

Upright memorial stones are uncommon, the most usual types of grave-stone being a rectangular or trapezoidal slab, which might be either flat or convex (p. III, fig. 5). The earlier slabs probably acted as lids to the coffins themselves, but the later ones merely marked the burial above ground. The slabs sometimes have separate stones as gables, which may be rounded at the top or of cruciform shape. The Swedish rune-stone found farthest from Sweden, at Berezan in the Ukraine (cat. no. 312), is probably a gable stone.

Coffin-shaped or house-shaped funerary monuments include both true coffins made of slabs, and massive stone monu-

Fig. 2. Eskiltuna sarcophagus from Vreta Monastery, Östergötland, Sweden. Second half of the 11th cent.

ments of coffin-like form; these are sometimes almost house-shaped with architectural decoration on their long sides. In Denmark one type of monument has a saddle- or hipped-roof, usually decorated at the gable ends. These coffin- or house-shaped monuments occur both with and without separate gable stones. The shape of some of them is reminiscent of the English 'hogback' stones of the tenth century (cat. no. 368, 369).

A type of memorial specific to Sweden is the 'Eskiltuna cist', a limestone or sandstone monument made up of lateral slabs, a lid and tall, pointed slabs as the gables. The decoration—animals and interlace deriving from rune-stone ornament—is usually carved in low relief and is of very high quality. The 'Eskiltuna cists' usually carry runic inscriptions in Old Swedish and date from the second half of the eleventh and the beginning of the twelfth century: almost all are now only preserved as fragments. They occur mainly in the plains of Västergötland and Östergötland, and are presumably the graves of great landowners.

Fig. 1. Bishop Adalward's funerary chalice, Skara cathedral, Sweden. C. 1064. Cat. no. 477.

Gotland has a unique type of burial monument. It is made of four upright slabs standing above ground each with a pictorial illustration. They are mostly pre-Christian but the latest, the famous coffin from Ardre (cat. no. 449) with its long runic inscription and pictorial decoration, is from the Christian period.

The cross, in many forms, is the most common decoration on grave stones. It is sometimes combined with figural representations or other motifs. Crosses on eleventh-century rune-stones are often highly decorative (cat. no. 560), but later examples seem to reflect actual altar or processional crosses. A cross with a long stem, which is the commonest form of this motif, is sometimes transformed into a tree of life by the addition of plant ornament.

Figural motifs include Christ, the Lamb of God, apostles, saints and other figures of Christian significance; the battle between good and evil is depicted in various ways. Sometimes the dead are shown waiting for the resurrection, or represented simply by a symbol such as a sword or crozier.

Although the Scandinavian funerary monuments were made in native workshops they were strongly influenced by Continental and English models. These foreign influences arrived in various ways; masons employed in building the cathedrals must have been of crucial importance in their introduction. The English connection can be seen, for example, in the magnificent monument from Botkyrka, Södermanland, Sweden (cat. no. 450), dating from the 1130s.

The inscriptions on the grave-stones vary in length and content. The Swedish material is by far the richest. Latin or the early Scandinavian languages (carved in the Latin or the runic alphabet), record the person buried in the grave, as well as the person responsible for erecting the monument, and sometimes the name of the man who carved the monument or the runes.

Fig. 3. Stone coffin from Ardre, Gotland, Sweden. 11th cent. Cat. no. 449.

Fig. 4. Burial monument from Botkyrka church, Södermanland, Sweden. C. 1130. Cat. no. 450.

Thor's hammers, pendant crosses and other amulets

Anne-Sofie Gräslund

In all periods and cultures people have worn amulets as good-luck charms or as protection against danger—the Scandinavians of the Viking age were no exception.

The Thor's hammer is a form of pendant of distinct amuletic character; that it really is the symbol of the god Thor is supported by statements in the *Edda*, as well as by contemporary iconographic evidence (p. 146, fig. 3). Small, iron Thor's hammers threaded onto neck-rings made of iron rods are found in ninth- and tenth-century graves (almost always cremations and nearly all from the east Mälar area). They are also found on Åland, in Finland and in Russia (cat. no. 179, 280, 300). About fifty silver Thor's hammers are known from hoards, graves and settlements. They have a wide distribution, mostly being found in south and central Scandinavia, but there are some in Trøndelag and Iceland. They can be dated to the tenth and early eleventh centuries, whilst on Gotland they continue through the eleventh century. A few are known from Poland and England. They may also be of bronze or amber (cat. no. 142, 180–1, 255, 333, 352).

The silver hammer-shaped pendants are usually cast, but they may also be cut from sheet metal, formed from a hammered rod, or soldered together from chased sheet-silver. They are all different, although some main types can be distinguished—undecorated, with punched or filigree embellishment

They vary in shape and size. The hammer head may be boat-shaped, rectangular, or with a central point. It may be small and neat, or sturdy and solid. The shaft may be of even width or, frequently, taper towards the top. The punched or stamped decoration may be present on one or both sides, most usually around the edge but sometimes over the whole surface. It is sometimes cruciform. On those with filigree decoration the top of the shaft and the loop form the head of a bird of prey (cat. no. 181). On other hammers there are filigree spirals and loops, together with granulation.

Fig. 1. Silver Thor's-hammer, Skåne, Sweden. C. 1000. Cat. no. 181.

It is impossible to say whether the Thor's hammers were used in cult ceremonies, although the frequent deposition of Thor's-hammer rings in the top of an urn in a cremation layer suggests a role in burial rites. A similar custom may be represented by axe-shaped amber pendants from graves in Gotland which have been shown, by examination under the microscope, to have been made specifically for burial as they display no traces of wear. On Åland, Finland and in Russia, bears' claws may have had a magical and ceremonial significance, as did perforated animal teeth (cat. no. 234–5, 298).

Pagan amulets also include pendants in the form of strike-a-lights, signifying life-giving and purifying fire, and pendants in the form of shields decorated with a whorl pattern (a sun symbol)—both are associated with fertility cults. The same is true of pendants in the shape of miniature tools, for example shears (cat. no. 190).

Staff-shaped pendants have been interpreted as shaman staves, a symbol dedicated to Odin. Chair-shaped pendants may also be associated with the Asa gods, the chair symbolizing an enthroned god; both Odin and Thor have been suggested as the god represented (cat. no. 187). Rings may also have been status symbols. Female figures, sometimes with a drinking horn (cat. no. 186, 281), are interpreted as

Valkyries; on the Gotland picture-stones they welcome warriors to Valhalla (cat. no. 175).

During their travels abroad many Scandinavians came into contact with Christianity before the Viking Age. When this new religion gained a foothold in Scandinavia it was reflected, for instance, by pendant crosses buried in graves, in hoards and in settlements. Other Christian amulets occur—reliquary pendants, *bullae*, and pendants with images of saints. Pendant crosses are primarily found in graves in Sweden and Finland, whereas those from hoards occur in all Scandinavian countries. In Denmark in particular there is a clear distinction between hoards with Thor's hammers and hoards with crosses. The former date from the tenth and the beginning of the eleventh century, the latter from the time after about 1025.

Pendant crosses occur in varying forms—simple cast or cut crosses; undecorated, with stamped and punched decoration or with filigree; palmette crosses; crosses with three roundels at the end of each arm; crucifixes; reliquary crosses (*encolpia*) and so on (cat. no. 37, 196–8, 222, 224, 488–96).

At Birka, simple pendant crosses with punched decoration, probably of native manufacture, occur in female graves of the

Fig. 2. Two iron amulet-rings from Torvalla, Uppland, Sweden. 9th–10th cent. Cat. no. 190.

Fig. 5. Gold cross from Orø, Denmark, c. 1100. Cat. no. 493.

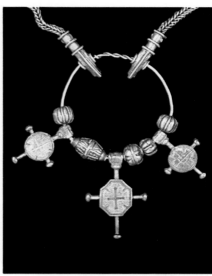

Fig. 6. Chain with Byzantine-inspired crosses, Suotniemi, Käkisalmi (Kexholm), Ladoga-Karelia. C. 1200. Cat. no. 495.

Fig. 3. Mould from Trendgården, Jutland, Denmark, shows that craftsmen worked for both Christian and pagan masters. Second half of the 10th cent. Cat. no. 195.

Fig. 4. Silver crucifix, Birka, Sweden. C. 900. This is the earliest surviving representation of Christ in Scandinavia. Cat. no. 196.

tenth century. Similar examples have also been found in Danish and Norwegian hoards, and in female graves on Gotland where one has also been found in a male grave (unique in Sweden). In Finland pendant crosses occur in eleventh-century male graves and in Karelia as late as the thirteenth century. As men did not normally wear neck ornaments, this indicates the great symbolic value of the cross—these men had probably come across Christianity when they were abroad. The technical simplicity of even the early crosses indicates that their symbolic value was greater than their decorative worth.

Palmette crosses are found in eleventh-century hoards but also in thirteenth-century graves in Karelia. Their bungled Ringerike style suggests a Scandinavian origin. Crosses with roundels are concentrated in the Baltic area and have a long life—from the eleventh to the fourteenth centuries. Their place of manufacture is disputed—Novgorod and the eastern Baltic have both been suggested.

The earliest Scandinavian crucifix is the filigree example from a tenth-century grave at Birka (cat. no. 196). There are

many eleventh-century types. A group of double-sided crucifixes come from Finnish graves and Swedish, Danish and Norwegian hoards; similar ones are known from Russia and the Baltic States. Christ is sometimes tied rather than nailed to the cross. Many of the crucifixes have stylistic traits; interlace and spirals, for example, which clearly indicate Scandinavian manufacture. The Halikko crucifix (cat. no. 496) is an example of a non-Scandinavian cross; it was probably made in the Rhineland in the first half of the eleventh century.

Encolpia (reliquary crosses) were originally a Byzantine type. The Dagmar cross and the Gundslevmagle encolpion (cat. no. 488), are examples of Byzantine imports. Reliquary crosses of indisputable Scandinavian manufacture also occur, some modelled on eastern originals, as for example one from Old Uppsala (cat. no. 532), and some being independent Scandinavian versions of the eastern model—as, for example, that from Gåtebo (cat. no. 492). Here the artist has elegantly translated the eastern form into a Scandinavian one, using native Urnes ornament.

Dress

Sigrid H. H. Kaland

The archaeological finds which provide the basis for reconstructing Viking Age dress have come both from graves and from large settlement sites such as Birka, Hedeby and Kaupang. We have detailed information on clothing, as well as patterns, the quality of the material used, and the use of items of adornment. The surviving remains of dress are primarily from clothes which have belonged to the middle and upper classes. The finds allow for several interpretations concerning details of clothing, which was otherwise apparently uniform; there are, however, national, local and social differences.

Of the clothes themselves, only fragments of cloth have survived (cf. cat. no. 55–7, 174). The reconstruction of Nordic costume is therefore based on several sources: brooches, contemporary illustrations on the Swedish pictorial stones, the Oseberg tapestry from Norway (p. 47, fig. 5), miniature human figures, and documentary evidence (cf. cat. no. 1, 44, 175, 186, 200–1, 221). The position in the graves of the fragments of cloth and brooches, together with their analysis and other evidence, has provided the basis for the reconstruction of male and female dress.

The women's costume consisted of a long, loose-fitting shift or sark, with or without sleeves and with a split-opening at the neck which could be fastened with a small brooch. Over this she wore a garment rather like a pinafore dress (or spencer) which was fastened below the shoulders with a pair of brooches (fig. 1, centre). This garment could either be sewn as a tube or be open at the sides. The shoulder brooches were usually oval, but in Finland they were round (cat. no. 200) and on Gotland they were shaped like animal heads (cat. no. 274). The distribution pattern of oval brooches shows that this was a Nordic fashion which emigrant women took with them and they are found from Dublin to the Volga (cat. no. 101, 245–6, 355, 365–6). In Finland (p. 67, fig. 5) an apron edged with bronze spirals could also be worn.

The outer garment usually took the form of a rectangular or semicircular cape folded into a triangle and worn as a shawl or draped across the shoulders. It could be decorated with woven bands (and with bronze spirals in Finland) or trimmed with fur. It was fastened in front with a brooch which took various forms at various times: equal-armed, disc, trefoil, zoomorphic, etc. Outer garments of leather were also worn.

The finds, however, show that costume could vary. At Hedeby there is evidence that the woman's gown in the tenth century was tailored at the waist to emphasize the form of the body. The undergarment could even be lined and have applied decoration, while both at Birka and Hedeby the remains of sleeves from a jacket or cape have been recorded.

The head was usually covered with a scarf knotted like a kerchief; otherwise, a woven, patterned headband was worn. In Sweden and Finland a band was worn

■ *Gotland woman's dress with animal-head brooches*

■ *Scandinavian woman's dress with oval brooches*

■ *Finnish woman's dress with circular brooches*

●●● *Sporadic finds of all these types of brooches*

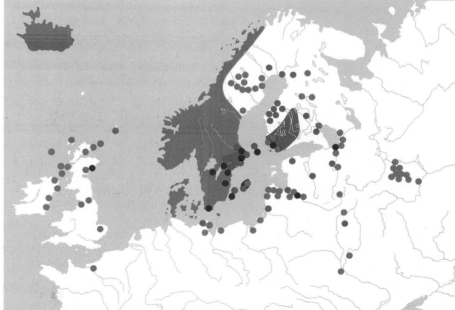

Fig. 1. 10th-cent. Scandinavian female clothing and its geographical distribution, based on finds of shoulder brooches.

Fig. 2. *Fragments of embroidered clothing (watercolour 1869) from a male grave at Mammen, Denmark. C. 970. Cat. no. 174a.*

Fig. 3. *Reconstruction of male clothing from Mammen, Denmark. Cf. cat. no. 174.*

simple garment, while the overshirt had a split neck fastened with a small brooch. Shirts were of medium length and relatively straight, but a wide, belted type is also known, and both types occur in pictorial representations. High status graves, as at Mammen and Birka, show that shirts could be decorated with tablet-woven braids embellished with gold and silver thread, or with embroidered figures. Some had rows of buttons and some were even made of silk (cat. no. 132, 134, 174, 201).

The man's outer garment was a wide cloak fastened with a brooch on the right shoulder or under the arm, often using a ring brooch (cat. no. 140, 364). The cloak could be decorated with bands, trimmed with fur or edged with another textile. In Finland it was often decorated with bronze spirals. To make it warm and weather-proof, it was sometimes lined with wool or even filled with down. Thick leather capes were also probably worn. Various head-coverings are known, including simple woollen caps and hats. Different kinds of hats can be seen on the picture stones and fine mounts are known, for example, from Birka (cat. no. 133).

Shoes were of two main types, either cut in one piece and sewn up over the instep, or made from a sole and separate upper stitched together (cat. no. 48). Boots and ankle boots are also recorded. Fine shoes could also be decorated (cat. no. 507).

Jewellery may be divided into two groups: functional objects which depended for their form on their use with garments; and items worn purely for decoration. Functional objects of adornment for women include in particular the small round brooches and the larger oval, trefoil and equal-armed brooches, which are found over a wide area. Regular accessories for special wear were the pair of shoulder brooches worn at the top of the tunic. Functional items of adornment on the man's costume included ring-headed pins

and ring brooches, which were used for fastening the cloak at the shoulder. Most types of jewellery are common throughout the Nordic countries, but some are typical of particular areas, as in Gotland and Finland. Ornaments for purely decorative use include armrings, neckrings and finger-rings of gold, silver and bronze, as well as necklaces.

While men's dress in the eleventh and twelfth centuries was on the whole similar to that of the Viking Age, women's dress changed in the second half of the tenth century throughout most of the Nordic world. The tunic with its typical shoulder straps fastened with brooches disappeared and was replaced by clothes cut in a more European way, but such dress is only known from pictorial representation.

across the forehead, which in Finland was elaborately finished with bronze spirals.

Little male dress survives, the best examples being from Birka, Hedeby, Viborg and from high status burials. The most important garments were trousers, undershirt, shirt and cloak, as elsewhere in Europe. There is also evidence for jackets, and for stockings or foot cloths wound around the feet and legs. Shoes are also found. The trousers were long and narrow or wide and loose-fitting, and they could be gartered below the knee. The wide trousers needed stockings or some similar garment which could be held up by hooks or straps. This type of trousers was probably for special wear: remains of wide pleated trousers are known from Hedeby (cat. no. 55). The linen undershirt was a

Weapons and their use

Pirkko-Liisa Lehtosalo-Hilander

Horned helmets and broad-bladed battle-axes characterize the fearsome Vikings of popular imagination. But the helmets of the Viking Age were not horned, and this type of battle-axe did not become popular until the end of the period. Earlier, the axes were of a different type, and other forms of weapons were favoured.

The sword was the predominant weapon in west and southern Scandinavia, with the spear apparently being more common in the east. In Norway, some two thousand swords have been found and only some thousand spearheads; these proportions are reversed in Sweden and Finland. Battle-axes were also more common in western than in eastern Scandinavia, and it is these axes on a long handle, sometimes decorated, wielded with two hands by Danish and Norwegian Vikings, which are best remembered in western Europe (cat. no. 111–4).

Further east, the Arabic writer Ibn Miskawayh (d. 1030) described Scandinavian warriors who captured the trading town of Berda'a, south of the Caucasus, in 943/4; according to him, every Northman carried a sword and, he writes, 'They fight with spear and shield, they gird themselves with a sword and carry a battle-axe and a dagger-like weapon. And they fight as foot-soldiers, particularly those who come by ship'. The 'dagger-like weapon' of his description may be the long, narrow fighting knife commonly found in male graves around the Baltic Sea. Fully equipped weapon-graves in Sweden and Finland contain both sword and fighting knife—often in a scabbard with bronze mounts—and also one or two spearheads (cat. no. 43, 201). The sword was obviously a slashing weapon, swung with one hand, while the other hand thrust the knife.

Swords were studied and classified by the Norwegian archaeologist Jan Petersen at the beginning of this century. He found that all the letters of the alphabet were insufficient to classify the different types of hilts distinguishable in the abundant Norwegian examples. Some of those which he then designated as Norwegian

Fig. 1. Helmet from the chieftain's grave, Gjermundbu, Norway. 10th cent. Cat. no. 108.

have later been discovered to be of general or specific European type.

The magnificent swords which are most often displayed and illustrated make up only a part of all the swords which were used in Scandinavia. By far the greater proportion were simple swords without

Fig. 3. Swords with Rhenish blades, discovered in Finland. 9th–12th cent. Cat. no. 214.

Fig. 2. Chain mail from the Gjermundbu burial, Norway. 10th cent. Cat. no. 108.

silver inlay or any special treatment of the hilt. For the true warrior, the qualities of the blade were much more important (cat. no. 108–10, 171, 214, 220, 228, 230–1, 557–8). The blades were usually 5–6 cm wide and some 70–80 cm long, the total length of the sword being less than a

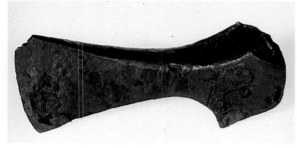

Fig. 4. Battle axe from the Viking fortress of Fyrkat, Denmark. 10th cent. Cat. no. 111.

metre; but, particularly at the end of the Viking Age, some swords could have blades which were more than a metre in length. The heaviest swords weighed more than 2 kg and in the best examples the hilt was heavy enough to balance the blade.

Sword blades were usually double-edged, although single-edged long swords were used, particularly in Norway, during the early Viking Age. At the beginning of the period many blades were pattern-welded, but later they were more usually inlaid with signs, symbols or letters (cat. no. 214). Some dozens of swords, particularly in Finland and Norway, carry the name Ulfberht and others have Latin inscriptions. They show that the blades were manufactured in west-European smithies and distributed thence, despite all the attempts made by Frankish kings to prevent their export to their barbarian neighbours. Scabbards were usually made of wood, lined with fleece and covered with leather (cat. no. 352). Some scabbards had metal mounts at their openings, and metal chapes to protect their points (cat. no. 217, 324).

Viking-Age spears were 2–3 m long, the socketed iron head making up between 20–60 cm of this (cat. no. 115-7, 212-3). The shaft was usually of ash and no more than 3 cm thick. The earliest Viking-Age spearheads in Scandinavia include those with wings on their sockets, which seem to have been of continental origin. Their blades are often pattern-welded and their sockets decorated with forged, pointed

Fig. 5. Two warriors. Representations of the months on the tapestry from Baldishol, Norway. C. 1200.

arches. Similar pointed arches are also present on a number of other spearheads which differ from the winged type by their long, narrow and elegant shape. They became the commonest type of spearhead in Scandinavia in the early Viking Age.

The spearheads which became popular in the tenth century had long sockets and ridged blades: their sockets were slight and some were inlaid with silver. In the eleventh century the heads became heavier and the shafts thicker. These later blades were triangular or rhomboid, often beautifully pattern-welded; the sockets were either faceted or decorated in silver with interlaced animals in the Urnes style (cat. no. 229, 251, 252). Discoveries in Finland show that, although heavier spears were used in the twelfth century, the development towards the true lance had begun (cat. no. 232).

As with spears, bows-and-arrows were used both for hunting and warfare (cat.

no. 88, 118). Up to the end of the twelfth century simple bows were used, but then the cross-bow came into use. The earliest of these are found in Denmark, and initially seem to have been weapons for the leading warrior-class.

The shields of the Viking Age were circular, up to a metre in diameter, and made of wood. Some were painted, others covered in leather. Many had an iron boss in the centre; a narrow iron binding sometimes encircled the edge. The grip lay behind the boss. There are well preserved tenth-century circular shields from the Gokstad ship-burial in Norway, whilst elongated, tapering ('kite-shaped') shields are depicted in the twelfth-century illustrations. Some Scandinavians used metal-mounted helmets and chain mail, but these are only rarely preserved in graves (cat. no. 108). Leather jerkins and caps were probably also in common use, and the 'berserks' of the sagas, with their frenzied inhuman strength, may have been named after the bearskin shirts which they wore in battle.

Written sources tell us that the Scandinavians fought mainly on foot, but many equestrian graves, particularly in Denmark and Sweden, show that horses were also used for riding and as pack animals. True cavalry did not appear in the North before the twelfth century when new weapons such as lances and cross-bows came into use.

Iron

Gert Magnusson

Iron and its production has held a crucial economic position in most human societies. In many cases access to iron was decisive for a society's technological development in building, agriculture, shipbuilding, military power and many other technical activities.

In Scandinavia in the Iron Age and Viking period, iron was extracted from bog ore by direct iron-production in small bloomery furnaces. In this method the temperature is just high enough to produce molten slag, with the residual iron being removed from the furnace in the form of a bloom which, in theory, is ready for smithing. At a higher temperature the iron acquires a high carbon content and forms pig iron, which could not be used in this early period. The advantage of direct iron-production was that it needed only fairly simple structures which could be built quite easily by members of a farming community. Each firing of the furnaces lasted from six to eight hours and produced a bloom of between 5 and 20 kg in weight.

In the early Iron Age, most iron-production sites must have been near permanent settlements. The amount of slag found shows that production was very limited and mainly designed to fulfill the needs of a farm or village. From the Roman Iron Age onwards there was an increasing demand for iron in Scandinavia. The limited local resources were incapable of increasing production unless the ironworkers became colonizers and exploiters of wastelands, such as the mountain valleys and plateaus of south Norway (cat. no. 91) or the forests of Dalarna, Hälsingland, Gästrikland and Småland in Sweden. In some cases iron production was the basis for a permanent settlement, but elsewhere resources were inadequate and the settlement was soon abandoned. The amount of slag found on iron-production sites enables us to calculate that some areas of Småland and Gästrikland produced 10,000 tonnes or more of iron in the Viking Age and early medieval period.

The relationship between those who produced the iron and the smiths who fashioned it is difficult to understand, but production probably lay in the hands of ironworkers and not of the smiths. Smiths' graves are never found in iron-producing areas.

The quality and characteristics of the iron, resulting from the composition of the ore and the process of production, were very important. We must assume that the ironworkers could estimate the quality of the ore. By converting the bloom into raw iron (bars), the ironworker could, before it reached the smith, reveal some of its qualities; such as its suitability for smithing, its tensile strength and so on. There were regional types of iron bars in Scandinavia: scythe-shaped, spade-shaped, axe-shaped and so on (cat. no. 92–3, 95). By checking the iron bars, their suitability and general usefulness could be ascertained. The smith then had to rely on his tools (cat. no. 94, 268) and his own skill. A skilful smith must have been of the greatest importance to his master. Even though a smith's work was largely heavy manual labour, he could hold a high social posi-

tion. Some smiths were legendary and figure in sagas and stories—Regin, for example.

The end of the twelfth century saw one of the most important innovations in the history of iron and iron production—one that made the mass production of iron possible. This innovation was the blast-furnace, examples of which have been found by excavation. The blast-furnace resulted in indirect iron-production and the production of pig iron, and became the most common method of extracting iron from rock ore throughout the Middle Ages down to modern times. The new technique demanded that the blast-furnaces should be taller than those used before, further they had to be fired continuously for many weeks; this caused the introduction of water power to drive the bellows. Continuous work made further demands on the labour force and shift-working was introduced, each shift being made up of four to six men.

Most of the ore for these huge furnaces was quarried or mined, and it is significant that the earliest blast furnaces have been

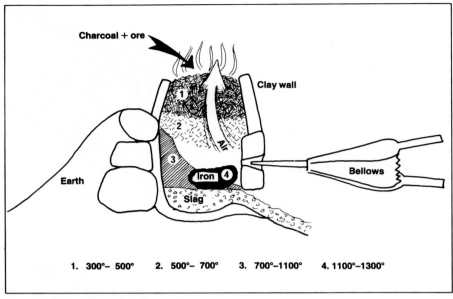

Fig. 1. Production of iron from bog ore in a smelting furnace.

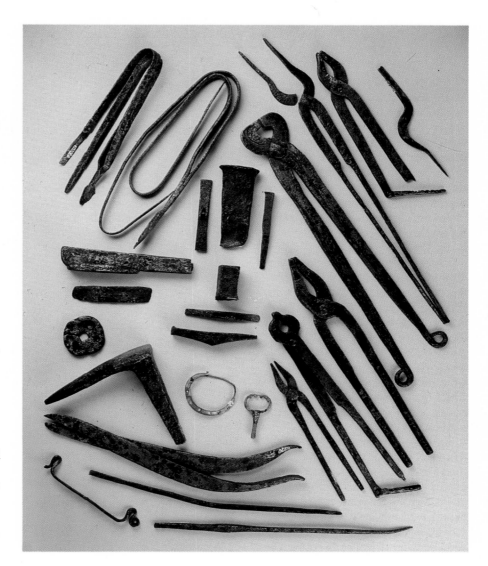

Fig. 2. *A hoard of smith's tools from Staraja Ladoga, Russia. Mid 8th cent. Cat. no. 268.*

discovered in the areas around iron mines where particularly suitable ore is found, at Norberg in Västmanland, Sweden, for example, where two iron-mining areas, the Klackberg and Risberg fields, were in use as early as the twelfth century.

At the beginning of the 1980s archaeologists excavated a complete blast-furnace complex dated to between the end of the twelfth and the mid-fourteenth centuries. The place had long been known as Lapphyttan (the second element in the name meaning "smelting house"). The excavations revealed an entire early-medieval industrial complex, with a blast furnace, eight finery hearths, slag heaps, dams, dwellings, a stable, and a shed. Lapphyttan is the earliest complex of this type known outside China and it is probable that the origins of the blast furnace in Europe are to be found in Germany or Sweden. They later became common in Europe and throughout the world.

Iron is mankind's most important metal because it is hard, can be shaped, and is cheap to produce in large quantities. Most iron was made into everyday objects such as nails, rivets, and mounts, or into more complicated things such as cauldrons and locks (cat. no. 263, 467). It has also been used for ornamental purposes (cat. no. 41, 172, 458, 616) and elaborate weapons such as swords and axes (cat. no. 108–16, 173, 228–33), in which iron of differing qualities were pattern-welded. These objects tested the skill of the smith to his limits.

Fig. 3. *Excavation of the blast-furnace complex at Lapphyttan, Sweden. The introduction of the blast-furnace technique at the end of the 12th cent. enabled iron to be mass produced.*

Mass production in the Viking Age

Signe Horn Fuglesang

Many mounts and objects of personal adornment in the Viking Age were mass-produced. Investigations into the techniques used in their manufacture are interesting in themselves, but they may also be used for information about the economy and for the history of crafts. Since almost all secular material from the rest of Europe is lost, Scandinavian investigations can contribute uniquely to an understanding of common European techniques and manufacturing processes.

The best evidence for technical agreement between Europe and Scandinavia is provided by the gold and silver filigree work (p. 200), but continental finds also produce occasional parallels for casting. The commonest type of Scandinavian jewellery comprises the the oval brooches which were used to fasten the shoulder straps of the woman's dress (p. 192, fig. 1). Simply stated such brooches were made by casting one shell between positive and negative clay moulds.

The original could either be a freshly made wax model or an older brooch. The model was covered with layers of thin clay to produce a master cast of one or more pieces. This master cast was the most important link in the process as it could be used again and again. A number of moulds were then made by pouring molten wax into the master. The decoration was retouched and details added if necessary. The final mould was made by covering the wax cast with clay, and it is this clay mould which had to be broken in order to retrieve the finished brooch. Fragments of such moulds show the presence of a brooch maker in, for example, Ribe, Denmark (cat. no. 101–2).

Characteristic of this casting technique is the impression of textile on the back of the finished article. Textiles were used to reinforce the wax master cast. The earliest known examples of such impressions occur on seventh-century Avar silver work from eastern Europe. Textile is not always used, however: for example, not all the twenty-two mounts from Broa (cat. no. 176)

Fig. 1. The manufacture of oval brooches.

Making the mould

a 'Casting models' in solid wax are formed in a master bearing the impression of either a ready-made brooch or a newly-designed model. Each wax model is retouched and details may be added.

b A mould is made by covering the wax model with many thin layers of tempered clay.

c The wax having been melted, runs away (known as cire perdue*). Wax pegs are inserted for the hinge plates and catch-plate.*

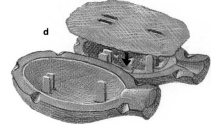

d A small piece of cloth is dipped in melted wax, and while still warm and flexible is pressed into the mould. This determines the shape and thickness of the resultant brooch.

e The lower piece of the mould is built up over the cloth with tempered clay. The complete mould is heated and the melted wax runs out.

f The two pieces of the mould are separated and the cloth removed. The mould is reassembled and the edges sealed.

Casting the brooch

g The mould is heated and bronze melted in a crucible. The molten metal is poured into the mould while it stands in the hearth.

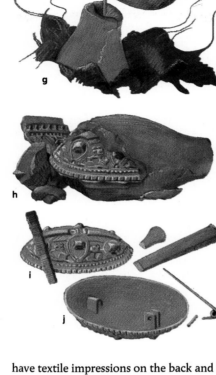

h The mould gradually cools down. It is broken and the brooch removed.

i The upper surface of the brooch is reworked.

j The catch-plate is bent, holes are bored in the hinge plates and the pin attached. The brooch is ready.

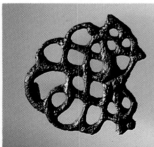

Fig. 2. Mass-produced oval brooch of the most common 9th-cent. type. From Meløy, Norway. Cat. no. 101b.

Fig. 3. Mould and Urnes-style brooches c. 1100–1150, from Lund, Sweden. Cat. no. 589.

have textile impressions on the back and it is likely that the wax cast could have been reinforced with other material. The same technique was used to produce oval brooches, mounts and sword hilts in the ninth century—it occurs in the manufacture of both bronze and silver objects.

The Scandinavian jewellers were artists and worked for the higher levels of society; they made their original model by hand, probably in wax. Trimming marks made with iron edged tools on the finished product show that less gifted smiths also worked in this way, but most brooches appear to have been made by making casts of finished objects, only small details being

changed by retouching or adding to the master cast. It is possible to gain some idea of the extent of the production from the quantity of objects which have survived —some six hundred examples of the commonest ninth-century oval brooch survive and some fifteen hundred of the commonest tenth-century type. A single type of object can vary widely in quality, in all shades of competence from the finest to the completely misunderstood (cf. cat. no. 101). Generally, however, the normal casts lie within a fairly narrow field of reasonably competent craftsmanship and it is such products which are ascribed to a professional body of smiths.

C. 900 a new manufacturing technique was introduced which was used, *inter alia* for copying trefoil brooches. This new technique has not yet been sufficiently studied, but it would make chronological sense if it had been derived from Carolingian workshops (cat. no. 136–7). It is possibly that same technique which was again used in the eleventh century for the serial production of Urnes style zoomorphic brooches (cat. no. 38, 589).

There was apparently a reaction in the tenth century against mass-produced, cast bronze jewellery. Fine filigree work became fashionable instead—splendidly crafted in gold and silver (cat. no. 32, 105–7, 142, 265)—and for the less wealthy, cast copies of filigree jewellery (cat. no. 31). Fashions in mounts and weapons also changed—mass-produced relief-castings were replaced by engraved and inlaid decoration, each item presumably being individually worked by hand. How this change in fashion should be interpreted with regard to society, the economy and to crafts is a fascinating—and as yet unanswered—question.

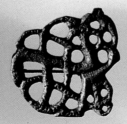

Gold- and silver-smithing

Wladyslaw Duczko

Objects of gold and silver form an important and interesting group of artifacts from the Viking Age. The large quantity and the multiplicity of types bear witness to the high status of goldsmiths in a society which had easy access to metals, and outside contacts which served as a source of inspiration and innovation.

The levels of society with which the goldsmiths were involved were those of kings, chieftains and noblemen. The connection was traditional and inevitable, for these classes had special needs (the distribution of valuable gifts for example) and the necessary economic background. They also had contacts with similar classes in Scandinavia, in the rest of Europe, and in the Orient. These contacts were responsible for the relative homogeneity of Scandinavian fine metalworking, in which native traditions were merged with foreign influences. All the precious metals had to be imported, from the Caliphate, Germany, France and England. Silver was predominant, but gold had a higher value and unrivalled prestige, as is shown by the presence of gilding on most bronze and much of the silver jewellery.

The goldsmiths' products—dress accessories, jewellery, drinking vessels, horse equipment—were important to many social classes. They were primarily decorative, but also demonstrated the social status, religion and ethnic origin of the owner. They were also of economic significance. In Viking Age Scandinavia there was no developed monetary system, so silver and gold were weighed. Because of this, jewellery was chopped up (to become *hacksilver*) or was of a standard weight, as were neck-rings and arm-rings which could double as ornaments and as a means of payment (cat. no. 141–53).

The Scandinavian goldsmiths had a multiplicity of manufacturing and decorative techniques at their disposal: casting, forging, filigree and granulation, chasing, niello, gilding, plating and inlaying with precious stones and glass. The only technique absent from their repertoire was enamelling.

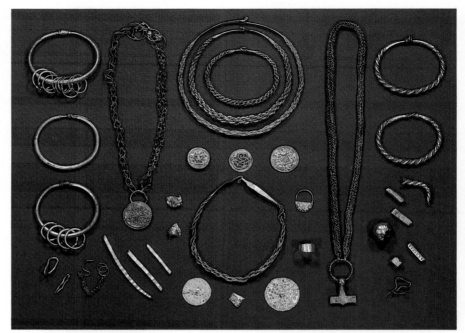

Fig. 1. Selection from the Sejrø hoard, Denmark, including twisted arm-rings, plaited neck-rings, chain, and brooch with filigree ornament. Right: a simple Thor's hammer on chain, second half of the 10th cent. Cat. no. 142.

A substantial part of the goldsmiths' work was devoted to the manufacture of high-status objects such as neck-rings and arm-rings made of a flat band, a single rod, or up to 12 twisted rods. The twisted rings were quite new to Scandinavia and have oriental prototypes. From Byzantium came the skill of making fine, elastic, chains in a crochet-like technique or of small linked rings (cat. no. 142).

Some techniques were very popular and were used throughout the Viking Age: punching with repeated triangular stamps (cat. no. 143), niello, inlaying of silver (using black silver sulphide (cat. no. 103)), and filigree and granulation, which were introduced into Scandinavia from western Europe and developed into high art.

Denmark has a special position in the Viking Age goldsmith tradition, for its proximity to the Continent encouraged political and artistic development. The Danish smiths were probably responsible for the introduction into Scandinavia of jewellery such as the trefoil brooch (cat. no. 135–7), and they also began to make bowls to replace drinking horns (cat. no. 36, 124, 532). In tenth-century Denmark there was both high-quality casting (p. 198, fig. 99) and filigree, characterized by the consistent use of interlace and animal motifs (cat. no. 32, 142). The art of filigree came to maturity at the court of Harald Bluetooth; workshop finds at the fortresses of Fyrkat and Trelleborg suggest that power-centres were also important artistic centres. But the most important of the Jutland sites was Hedeby where, for example, forty-two bronze patrices for embossing sheet metal for filigree jewellery have been found (cat. no. 105). The jewellery from the hoard from Hiddensee (cat. no. 265), a Thor's hammer pendant from Skåne (cat. no. 181), and a gold spur from Værne Kloster, Rød, Norway, are some of the most magnificent examples of filigree art. This technique reached its apogee in the eleventh century when the Jutland

Fig. 2. *Oval brooch; bronze with gilding, silver and niello. From Birka, Sweden. 9th cent. Cat. no. 103.*

Fig. 4. *Filigree-decorated gold brooches from Hornelund, Jutland, Denmark. C. 1000. Cat. no. 107.*

smiths made splendid objects such as the gold brooch from Hornelund (cat. no. 106, 107). These royal filigree jewels were of the highest status and they, or imitations of them, are found throughout Scandinavia —in Russia, England and Iceland.

Local specialities were also developed, penannular brooches, for example, of Irish type, which were designed to fasten men's cloaks; magnificent objects of silver, with niello and gold filigree. They were introduced to Scandinavia by way of Norway and were also made in Sweden and Russia (cat. no. 138–40, 219, 364). Another local type was the large and heavy cast brooches from eastern Sweden and Russia (cat. no. 305).

The goldsmith's art was particularly lively and original on Gotland, where the smiths were expert in most techniques and were willing to absorb foreign influences. Their outstanding tenth-century products were drum-shaped brooches (cat. no. 104), and bracteates. Both types of object display filigree motifs borrowed from north-German enamelled brooches, which in their turn were inspired from Byzantium. In the eleventh century the smiths of Gotland developed an art which was a combination of earlier Gotlandic forms, copies of eastern Slav jewellery, and variants of Danish brooches. This Gotland jewellery had a wide distribution outside the island

and can easily be recognized in finds from Estonia, Finland, Öland and the Swedish mainland.

The products of the Scandinavian goldsmith in the Viking Age show a wealth of forms and techniques without parallel in the earlier periods. The goldsmith created an eclectic art which, nevertheless, is very lively, thanks to his skill and his ability to combine native traditions with the cultural heritage of Europe.

Fig. 3. *Equal-armed brooch; silver with gilding and niello. From Elec, Russia. 10th cent. Cat. no. 305.*

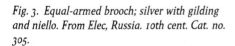

Fig. 5. *Drum-shaped brooch; bronze with gilding, silver, gold and niello. From Mårtens, Gotland, Sweden. 11th cent. Cat. no. 104.*

Bone, antler, amber and walrus ivory

Niels-Knud Liebgott

The archaeological deposits of the Viking Age and early Middle Ages—apart from much more eye-catching metal objects such as weapons and jewellery—are characterized by a large number of decorative and utilitarian objects, such as tools, made of bone and antler. As a rule ordinary bone was used for slightly coarser objects such as knife handles, whilst polished metatarsal bones of cattle and horses were used as skates (cat. no. 24). Long bones from other animals and birds were used to make flutes (cat. no. 72), and bone was also of importance in the manufacture of the pins and combs which have been discovered in many Scandinavian towns. Not until about 1200 were the single-sided combs of earlier times replaced by technically more complicated double-sided combs; but in the course of the Viking Age comb-making developed into a craft in its own right (cf. cat. no. 47, 97, 271, 376).

In the Viking Age, combs were usually made from antler and were often finely shaped and decorated, sometimes with an openwork back-plate with a metal-foil inlay (cat. no. 578). Later, bone became the more common raw material. Antler mostly came from native deer (red deer, elk or reindeer where they occur), but there are examples of comb-makers in south Scandinavia importing elk antler. The splendidly carved plates on the now lost Cammin casket (fig. 2) were probably of elk, since elk antler provides large flat surfaces and its structure is much less coarse than bone. The only available bone of large dimensions is the very coarse whalebone which, particularly in north Scandinavia, was used for making many objects, weaving swords and linen-smoothing boards (for example cat. no. 50, 54), and even in the manufacture of small items of furniture.

Amber was not as common in the Viking Age and early Middle Ages as it had been in some earlier periods. It occurs in abundance along the North Sea coast of Denmark and even more commonly along the southern coast of the Baltic Sea. Dur-

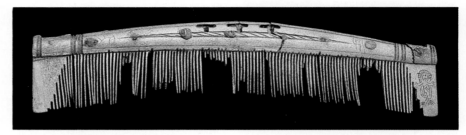

Fig. 1. Comb of elk antler from Sigtuna, Sweden. Right: grafitto of the Christ Child. 11th cent. Cat. no. 578.

ing the Viking Age it was particularly popular for beads and small pendants, as can be seen from discoveries at Wolin, Hedeby, Ribe, Birka, York and Dublin (cat. 189, 254, 375, 385). Comparatively easy to work, amber was also used to carve small figures, for example the gaming piece from Roholte in Denmark (cat. no. 77), for anthropomorphic amulets such as those from Oysund and Borg in north Norway (cat. no. 74, 154d), for Thor's hammers (cat. no. 255), and for other small objects such as spindle-whorls (cat. no. 49, 576).

When the Scandinavian craftsman of the period of about 1000 chose elk antler to decorate the Cammin casket, he probably used it as a substitute for the very rare

Fig. 2. Cammin casket. Scandinavian shrine from the cathedral treasury, Kamień, Poland. C. 1000. The large ornamental plates are of elk antler. Photo of the shrine, now lost. Cf. cat. no. 266.

elephant ivory which was extremely scarce in Scandinavia before 1200. Nevertheless, some ivory combs, probably for liturgical use, have been found in the episcopal towns of Lund and Sigtuna (cat. no. 597–8). Other objects made of elephant ivory include a Byzantine book-cover depicting the crucifixion, which dates from the beginning of the eleventh century (cat. no. 481).

Scandinavia was not the only place to have had little access to elephant ivory, for it was rare throughout north-west Europe including the British Isles. A substitute for 'real' ivory was walrus ivory (cat. no. 592). As early as about 890 a north Norwegian chieftain called Ottar described the hunting of walrus along the coasts of northern

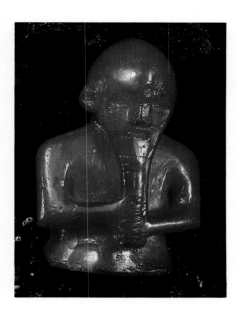

Fig. 3. Amber gaming-piece from Roholte, Denmark. Viking Age. Cat. no. 77.

Fig. 5. The Gunhild Cross, Denmark. Carved c. 1150 in walrus ivory. Cat. no. 607.

Norway and the White Sea for their tusks and hides (the latter used for ships' ropes) and presented two tusks to the English king Alfred the Great. The hunting of walrus in these northerly regions, and from about 1000 in Greenland, provided the carvers' workshops of north and western Europe with ivory for more than three-hundred years (see p. 204). It is facinating to think that some of the most magnificent works of art produced in workshops throughout western Europe at this time relied on a material acquired on hunting expeditions to the Arctic Ocean around north-west Greenland. The occurrence of walrus ivory in western Europe illustrates regular contacts with the most northerly parts of Scandinavia and with Greenland. Walrus skulls found in Greenland, Dublin and many other places (cat. no. 591, 593), show that this huge mammal also fascinated people for its own sake.

Fig. 4. Small bird of amber from Borg, Lofoten, Norway. Cat. no. 154d.

The earliest west-European works in walrus ivory date from the second half of the ninth century, the time of Ottar (cat. no. 599). Such early examples have not been preserved in Scandinavia but an Anglo-Saxon piece of about 1000, probably from a book-cover, is known (cat. no. 601). The plates which encase the famous shrine which came from Bamberg (cat. no. 267), and which dates to about 1000, are probably of walrus ivory and if so, are the earliest examples of outstanding Nordic craftsmanship in this material (cf. the casket in San Isodore, León, Spain, p. 204). In the North, walrus ivory was fairly common and was thus used for simple objects such as pins and gaming pieces (cat. no. 71, 342, 360, 572) and was carved in many places.

A number of splendid Scandinavian works in walrus ivory survive from the twelfth century. The Gunhild cross (fig. 5) seems to have been carved in Denmark in the middle of the twelfth century,

although probably by a German artist; but the seal from Roskilde (cat. no. 604) is probably a local piece. The gaming pieces from Lewis in the Hebrides (cat. no 615), the mount from Munkholm near Trondheim (cat. no. 612), and the great unprovenanced reliquary in the British Museum (cat. no. 611), are products of a west-Norwegian workshop, probably the archiepiscopal town of Trondheim. The crozier from Gardar, Greenland (cat. no. 344), was probably carved in Trondheim, but may have originated in Iceland.

Walrus ivory in Western Europe

Danielle Gaborit-Chopin

Fig. 1. Reliquary carved from a whole walrus tusk. Carved in Norway, second half of the 12th cent. Cat. no. 611.

Ever since remote antiquity, elephant ivory has been prized as a precious material; because of its whiteness, its smooth surface and its rarity. It was used exclusively for precious articles, and especially for royal and sacred liturgical objects. This tradition lasted throughout the period of the Byzantine Empire and the early Middle Ages in Western Europe. The ivory came from Asia and Africa, by way of the Mediterranean, but it gradually became extremely rare and even completely unobtainable in some areas. An appropriate substitute therefore had to be found, and walrus ivory, which was much better for such purposes than bones of large land- or sea-mammals, became the favourite material.

Ivory from walrus-tusks, which was used in Northern Europe during the Romanesque period, in reality looks rather similar to that of elephant-tusks; its surface is white, with a yellowish tint, smooth and shiny, without the speckles characteristic of mammal-bone. Walrus-ivory, however, differs in certain respects from elephant-tusk ivory, and this gives rise to some of the distinctive features of Romanesque ivory-carving. Walrus-tusk is oval in section and smaller in scale; it is therefore not possible to fashion sizeable figures from it, and only narrow plaques can be cut from it. With its fine surface-layer the slightly soapy-textured walrus-ivory cannot be carved in great depth without revealing the large-grained osteodentine matter in the pulp-cavity. Apart from exceptional pieces such as the reliquary from the British Museum (cat. no. 611), walrus-ivory objects are therefore often of small dimensions or built up of several pieces assembled together, and the carving is in low relief. It should be noted, however, that ordinary items were made of bone, whereas walrus-ivory, like elephant-ivory, was reserved for more refined pieces.

During the Romanesque period walrus-ivory was not used everywhere or at all times. For obvious reasons only Scandinavian craftsmen continued working with it

and used it for carving all sorts of objects, including some great masterpieces such as the Gunhild Cross (cat. no. 607).

In Italy, on the other hand, elephant-ivory could still be obtained, and walrus-tusk was not used there; nor was it used by the Spaniards, although they did use whale-bone. The only object made of walrus which remains in a Spanish treasury, the small open-work box from San Isidoro de León, is an imported Scandinavian piece.

Because of their constant contacts with Scandinavians, the English became familiar with the use of this material. From as early as the tenth century they used it for fine carving in the Winchester style (cat. no. 600). From the eleventh and twelfth centuries boxes, caskets, small plaques, tau-crosses, bas-reliefs, appliqué relief-figures and even fully-rounded figures bear witness to the skills deployed in this activity, of which the great Bury St. Edmunds Cross (New York, The Cloisters) undoubtedly represents the highest achievement.

In Dublin, which was under strong Scandinavian influence, carving in walrus-ivory also took place (cat. no. 593–5). Some of the finest medieval sculptures carved in this material, however, are of Scandinavian origin: the extraordinary chessmen (cat. no. 615) were found in the Isle of Lewis, but are probably of Norwegian origin, perhaps from Trondheim, as is the remarkable unprovenanced reliquary in the British Museum (cat. no. 611). Through its relations with Scandinavia and England, the Meuse region from an early date became acquainted with walrus-ivory. Here it was carved into objects for even the highest-ranking personages during the eleventh and twelfth centuries, as is demonstrated by the Cross of Countess Sibylle (cat. no. 608). Walrus-ivory was never exclusively used in the other Germanic countries, where elephant-ivory did not become really rare until the twelfth century. In Cologne, the ivory workshops of that time used it in a distinctive fashion, placing small plaques of ivory side by side, each held by a frame, to make up large carved reliefs representing scenes of the Childhood of Christ and the Passion.

The economic conditions of northern Europe were also experienced in France. Recourse was only made to walrus-ivory in the north-western and western regions however. The tau-cross from Moutiers-en-Tarantaise (twelfth century) in the Alps is an English or Norwegian piece. Scarcity of elephant-ivory began to be experienced in this region from the second half of the ninth century onwards: it is from the court of Charles the Bald that the first examples of walrus-carvings can be observed—the appliqué figures, for example, carved in the 'Liuthard style' on the Missal of Saint-Denis (c. 870, Paris, Bibliothèque Nationale), and mounts with representations of the Apostles from a portable altar (cat. no. 599). Later, under the influence of the major English abbeys, the monks of Saint-Omer in Artois used walrus-ivory, first adopting the delicacy of the Winchester style of around the year 1000 (Virgin and St. John; Saint-Omer, musée Sandelin), and then, about 1100, turning to the vigorous Romanesque geometric forms (found, for example, in the famous series of the Elders of the Apocalypse in Museums in Saint-Omer, Lille, London and New York). It was perhaps in a workshop linked with the Abbey of Saint-Denis that the openwork plaques of a portable altar (cat. no. 609) were carved; the extremely elaborate nature of this piece sets it on a par with the finest elephant-ivory carvings of this period. On the other hand, in spite of their links with England, the craftsmen from Normandy (cat. no. 603) and Anjou made only limited use of walrus-ivory as a raw material (Ulger's cross, Angers, Cathedral Treasury).

But in the second quarter of the thirteenth century the reappearance of elephant-ivory is evident everywhere: imported in large quantities from Africa by way of the Norman and Flemish ports, it was carved in the workshops of Paris and sent out throughout all of Europe; it soon became the basic material for Gothic

Fig. 2. Two walrus-ivory panels from a casket or portable altar. Carved in Francia c. 870–80. Cat. no. 599.

ivories. It is worth noting that while the great Norwegian oliphant from the Sainte-Chapelle in Paris (Florence, Bargello), probably a gift from King Magnus of Norway to King Philippe III of France, is actually a huge carved walrus-tusk, the body of the magnificent Christ of Herlufsholm in Denmark, dating to the first third of the thirteenth century, is carved from an enormous block of elephant-ivory, and only the arms are made of walrus-ivory.

Fig. 3. Walrus-ivory panel showing the Baptism of Christ. Carved in England in the second half of the 10th cent. Cat. no. 600.

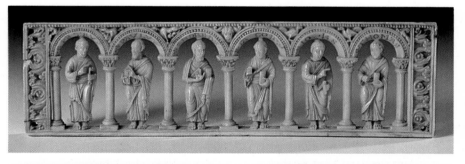

Fig. 4. Two walrus-ivory panels from a portable altar. Carved in France in the mid-12th cent. Cat. no. 609.

Wood-carving

Erla B. Hohler

This is one of the areas in which Scandinavia apparently differs from the rest of Europe in that so much decorative wood-carving has survived. This is probably because objects happen incidentally to be better preserved. Our impression of the rich wood-carving art of the Viking Age is based on one fortuitous discovery, the Oseberg ship burial, which contained a full set of magnificent fittings and furnishings in almost perfect condition from a royal hall. Similarly, the rich material from the post-Viking Middle Ages really comes almost exclusively from the Norwegian stave-churches, the survival of which is due partly to a dry climate, and partly to an impoverished Norwegian society which could not afford to replace the wooden churches with stone buildings. Some examples of wood-carving have also survived in Iceland, Sweden and Denmark, and there must have been decorated wooden objects in countries further south. Furniture and other fittings are documented in lands of the people whom the Vikings encountered as they travelled southwards through Europe. France, Germany and England all had wooden churches—and they were presumably decorated—but everything has vanished.

Another reason for the survival of wooden objects is that in the rest of Europe professional artists traditionally had other media in which to express themselves—art forms such as stone sculpture and illuminated texts, which were more prestigious—and above all more permanent. In the northern world, however, the art of building in stone and the art of writing did not arrive until the introduction of Christianity. It was, therefore, wooden architecture and its ornament that attracted the best talents; thus a tradition grew up in which the art of wood-carving assumed a respected place.

Both pine and oak were used, and worked with tools which were not very different from those still used today: knife, chisel, gouge and file—everything except the v-shaped gouge, which is of more recent date. There are many kinds of relief

Fig. 1. Detail from the Romanesque portal of the stave-church at Ulvik, Norway. C. 1130. The open, rounded relief and the interlace composition are stylistic descendants of Viking Age art.

Fig. 2. Detail of work from Oseberg, Norway: the second 'Baroque' animal-head post, cf. cat. no. 166a. First half of the 9th cent. The complicated composition represents a high point in the art of wood carving.

and many effects are achieved. Most pieces have a simple pattern in relief on two horizontal planes, but the relief can be deep or shallow, dense or open (cat. no. 40, 441). The incisions may be straight-sided and the edges sharp, or they may be gently sloping and rounded, all producing different effects (fig. 1). Many medieval crafts seem to be modelled on European models, particularly the products of the ivory carver and the goldsmith. On the other hand the very complex carving from Oseberg, which is executed on several horizontal planes with the deepest motifs only visible through gaps in the outermost patterns (cat. no. 166 and fig. 2), appears to have no surviving parallels in contemporary European art. Relief on several planes in the round, which is known in stone carving, is only rarely adopted (cat. no. 451); whilst chip-carving, which became so important in all countries in the late Middle Ages, is totally absent.

The treatment of the surface is of paramount importance for the final result: smooth and polished, or rich with many small details. The surface detail of the Oseberg objects has been so worked upon that the motifs themselves are often almost obscured (cat. no. 166 and fig. 3). On some of the pieces traces of paint have been found—black, white, red and yellow; painting would naturally have made the motifs more understandable.

All manner of objects were decorated. At Oseberg (p. 44, fig. 2; p. 50, fig. 10), the decoration on the boat is limited to the stem and stern posts, but the cart and sledges are covered with decoration of great complexity, often enriched with small studs of silver or pewter (cat. no. 166a). These were hardly objects for everyday use: such objects would by contrast have had simple decoration, often merely incised with the point of a knife (cat. no. 567–70).

The Oseberg objects have a courtly background and provide evidence for the work of several, very accomplished carvers. The other major class of surviving examples of the wood-carver's art, the decora-

Fig. 3. Detail from the Oseberg find: the largest draw-bar from the sledge, one of the finest works of the 'Baroque master' with details picked out in silver/pewter. First half of the 9th cent.

tion on the Norwegian stave-churches, must also be regarded as specialist work. Here master carvers or the professional workshops involved in the construction can be identified. Seventy-six great ornamental doorways have survived in Norway (cat. no. 441–2), as well as several smaller doorways, a large number of wooden capitals, chancel screens and other decoration (cat. no. 42, 443, 459). A large quantity of ecclesiastical wooden material has also survived in Sweden and Iceland (cat. no. 453–4), and decorated wood from churches as well as secular contexts continues to be found in archaeological excavations (cat. no. 563–5).

The designs are generally ornamental. There is, extraordinarily, little narrative carving. The sagas tell of pictorial representations, but such pictures are in other media, such as textiles and painting; what do survive are the great pictorial stones

from Gotland, carved with scenes from mythology. The splendid cart from Oseberg has amongst its purely decorative ornament a couple of figural scenes (fig. 4), the meaning of which is unknown, otherwise all the Oseberg objects are decorated with animal ornament. A few of the stave-church doorways illustrate heroic stories (cat. no. 442), but most are decorated with inhabited vine-scrolls. After the introduction of Romanesque art to the North, vine-scrolls, lions and dragons are preferred above everything else, even in ecclesiastical art.

Wood-carving styles follow European stylistic developments, but retain strong local characteristics. It has been argued that the wood-carver's art should be particularly traditional and conservative —but this is hardly correct in respect of the work of the professional craftsmen. Here new ideas were quickly adopted. On

Fig. 5. Font from Alnö church, Medelpad, Sweden. C. 1200. The motifs and technique are derived from Romanesque stone sculpture but the sense of style is Scandinavian.

the other hand, there is clear evidence in the simpler and more vernacular work of a tendency to stick to the earlier ideas of animal ornament. In this context the font from Alnö (fig. 5) provides a good example: in form it is Romanesque, the inspiration for the four lions around the base comes from European fonts, as do the figures of Christ and his angels which decorate the basin. But these figures are caught up in a world of intertwined serpents which can only have Scandinavian prototypes. As new impulses were gradually adopted, the towns became the centres for crafts, and in the course of the thirteenth century the conservatism of the Nordic wood-carver's art disappears. The interaction between distinctive Nordic characteristics and the strong impulses from abroad must be discussed later in relation to other art forms.

Fig. 4. Figural scene from the Oseberg waggon. First half of the 9th cent. Its significance is unknown.

Twelfth-century wooden sculpture

Göran Tegnér

Large parts of Scandinavia have escaped the devastation of modern wars. But the Reformation and the attitudes of more recent times are responsible for what survives of wooden medieval sculpture. Although they form only a small proportion of what there once was, a considerable number of sculptures have survived. In Sweden, Iceland and Norway the earliest preserved sculpture dates from the first half of the twelfth century; in Denmark it is from the second half of the same century; and in Finland, the last Scandinavian country to be converted, the earliest wooden sculptures date from the thirteenth century.

Even in the eleventh century there must have been a good number of churches in Scandinavia. These first-generation churches were, with a few exceptions, built of wood. During the twelfth century the building of stone churches began in earnest in Denmark and Sweden, and most of the surviving wooden sculptures were intended for them: crucifixes and calvary groups above the chancel arch, and the figures of the Virgin and saints from the two side altars were normal in country churches. In contrast to the purely decorative art, these wooden sculptures did not derive from pre-Christian artistic traditions, but took continental and English art as their models.

Some sculpture was probably imported, but there must have been Scandinavian workshops in which immigrant and native craftsmen worked together. Many factors must have been instrumental in the development of this church art—geographical situation, missions (from England and Germany) and ecclesiastical and trading contacts. The dioceses must also have been influential; foreign masons and artists were usually active in the mason's workshops of the cathedrals and much of the provision of furnishings for the churches must have been controlled centrally.

The early twelfth-century crucifix from Åby, Denmark, is made of gilded copper on a wooden core (cat. no. 460). The figure of Christ is crowned, stands upright, and has staring eyes: here we see Christ as judge and victor over death. Some wooden crucifixion figures from Sweden and Norway are comparable. They are, or were, crowned and have the same frontality and the same stylization of the body. This group includes the twelfth-century crucifix from Ufsir, in northern Iceland, which is carved in birch and is definitely a local product. The shape of the beard and moustache shows a relationship with, for example, details of decoration in the stave churches of Norway and the Lewis chessmen; the high-Romanesque crucifix from Tryde, Skåne (cat. no. 463), is also executed in the same style. This figure is one of the finest from the old Danish area and is dated to about 1160. The body, in the round, is modelled with powerful realism.

Another group of crucifixes is related to the well-known late tenth-century Gero crucifix in Cologne cathedral, showing the dead Christ with drooping head and bent legs, hanging by his arms. This group includes the twelfth-century crucifix from Horg, N. Trøndelag, Norway, and some well preserved Gotland examples from the end of the twelfth century. The most famous product of the Gotland workshop, which was probably based in Visby, is the exquisite Madonna from Viklau (cat. no. 461). The output of this workshop displays the style which developed in north France in the twelfth century, but which must have reached Gotland by way of Cologne.

Some of the earliest sculpture in Sweden comes from Västergötland; such, for example, is a monumental figure of Christ from Svenneby (c. 1130). Christ is depicted in tunic and stole, standing on a console, with outstretched arms and with no nails in hands and feet. Total frontality is broken only by a slight turn of the head. The type is unusual and has oriental origins; there are, however, parallels in Ottonian manuscript art.

The fragmentarily preserved, mid-twelfth-century, life-size Christ from Danderyd in Uppland (cat. no. 464), is one of a group of Uppland and Norwegian crucifix-

Fig. 1. Crucifix from Tryde church, Skåne, Sweden. C. 1160. Cat. no. 463.

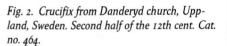

Fig. 2. Crucifix from Danderyd church, Uppland, Sweden. Second half of the 12th cent. Cat. no. 464.

Fig. 3. Madonna from Viklau church, Gotland, Sweden. Mid 12th cent. Cat. no. 461.

Fig. 4. Saint's head from Urnes church, west Norway. End of the 12th cent. Cat. no. 465.

es. It is carved in a species of lime tree which is not found in Sweden, and so must be an import. Its style suggests that it came from western Germany.

The twelfth-century sculptures of the Virgin show a crowned and enthroned Madonna with the Christ child on her knee, at the visitation of the Magi. The earliest surviving example of this group is probably the Virgin from Mosjö (Närke, Sweden) which dates from the middle of the twelfth century (cat. no. 462). She has no crown but her hair is beautifully braided and her eyes are large and sad. The origin of this figure is disputed. Her clothing falls in folds, after the English manner, a feature it has in common with the late twelfth-century Madonna from Urnes (cat. no. 617).

At the end of the twelfth century a western German, but French inspired, style influenced depictions of the Virgin in the North and this can be seen in Sweden, Norway and Iceland. One characteristic is that the seated Christ child has crossed legs. The earliest Scandinavian example comes from Appuna, Östergötland, Sweden.

From about 1200 French influence was strong in Denmark. Influences mainly travelled through the port of Roskilde, where a fragmentary crucifix has been preserved (cat. no. 466).

Statues of saints were also common in the twelfth century. Most of them followed the model of the Virgin: enthroned and flanked by elaborate pillars. Many of them depict totally unknown bishops, who may have been local saints, but they may represent bishop-saints such as Thomas à Becket or Nicholas of Myra. At the beginning of the thirteenth century we begin to see the earliest depictions of St Olaf, the Norwegian king who died in the battle of Stiklestad in 1030 and was to become one of the most popular Scandinavian saints. He carries his attributes: the axe and the tools of his martyrdom. Later in the century a carved figure of this royal saint from Dädesjö, Småland, Sweden, was placed in a cabinet above a prostrate warrior, his assassin: the symbol of vanquished paganism.

Fig. 5. Madonna from Urnes church, west Norway. Second half of the 12th cent. Cat. no. 617.

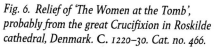

Fig. 6. Relief of 'The Women at the Tomb', probably from the great Crucifixion in Roskilde cathedral, Denmark. C. 1220–30. Cat. no. 466.

Stone sculpture

Jan Svanberg

In Scandinavia, three-dimensional sculpture in the form of reliefs and occasionally free-standing figures was an innovation resulting from the Church's introduction of the art of building in stone. Foreigners were called in to build cathedrals—as early as in the beginning of the twelfth century in Lund—and they taught the new technique to local masons. The new methods were adopted in country churches, many of which were built in stone during the twelfth century; their external walls were often decorated with reliefs and they sometimes had reliefs above their chancel arches. The churches also had stone fonts, many of which were richly decorated with figural sculpture. Few countries have as many fonts of this type as Sweden and Denmark.

More than fifty signatures, representing about forty masons, are known from the Romanesque period in Scandinavia; they occur mostly in Denmark and south and central Sweden, and there are a few in Norway. Most of them are written in runes in the Scandinavian languages but about twenty are written in the Latin alphabet and in Latin, but, even in these the masons mostly have Scandinavian names. Nevertheless, most of the masons remain anonymous and are known in modern terminology under designations such as 'Byzantios'. Their carving technique, Christian motifs, and Romanesque style were derived directly or indirectly from Europe and the international Romanesque, and yet the Scandinavian inheritance from the Viking Age is still sometimes apparent. This may appear in stylized dragons, plaited hair or flowing loops, whilst motifs from the bloody *Völsunga saga* occur in Norway; they include Sigurd's slaughter of Fáfnir, on a relief from a doorway at Nes and on a capital from the demolished church at Lunde, and Gunnar playing his harp in the snake-pit, on a font signed by *Sven* at Norum, now in the Museum of National Antiquities, Stockholm.

When Lund became the centre of an archbishopric in 1104, a gang of foreign masons led by the Italian *Donatus* was brought in to build a great metropolitan church richly decorated with stone reliefs. The carvings show Lombardic influence with loops, interlace and stylized animals; a Byzantine-influenced style with elegant lions, fabulous beasts and foliage; and Germanic features as well, including characteristics of Westphalian masons. All three styles spread into the Scanian countryside, where they can be seen in carvings and on fonts; five of the fonts are signed by *Mårten*, one by *Tove*, and a portal by *Carl*. One of the finest artists is 'Mäster Majestatis' whose lively narrative style and elongated figures with thoughtful faces can be seen on six fonts in south Skåne.

'Mäster Majestatis' also initiated a workshop on Gotland which produced a portal and a number of fonts; 'Hegvald', so called after the person who commissioned one of his ten fonts, was clearly inspired by 'Mäster Majestatis'. These fonts swarm with figures and narrative scenes in a rustic and very expressive style, and perpetu-

Fig. 1. Sandstone font from Tingstad church, Östergötland, Sweden. It was carved by the Gotland master Sighraf. End of the 12th cent. Cat. no. 452.

Fig. 2. Granite font from Nørre Snede church, Jutland, Denmark. C. 1150. Cat. no. 451.

ate Viking Age taste in the plaited manes and nostrils of the terrifying lions which crouch around their bases. The Byzantine-derived style of Lund resulted in about fifteen fonts and a long frieze on Vänge church being carved by 'Byzantios' on Gotland. His figures, animals and fabulous beasts, in precise low relief, process under round-headed arches. 'Mäster Majestatis', 'Hegvald' and 'Byzantios' worked in the third quarter of the twelfth century. These three masters were succeeded by *Sigraf*, who was the leading mason on Gotland until the market for fonts on the island was exhausted. Only five of his fonts are known from Gotland, but about twenty are known as exports to Germany, Denmark and the Swedish mainland (for example the Tingstad font, cat. no. 452). He delighted in depicting the birth of Christ in a clear and graceful style; the Viking Age style was abandoned and he replaced the monsters on the earlier font bases with sacred figures. But the motifs of his two great facade friezes on the churches of Grötlingbo and Väte derive from the early Germanic heroic saga of Theodoric the Great.

As in Skåne and on Gotland, the masons of the Swedish mainland worked in limestone. The sculptures are at their richest in Västergötland, where the figural style is coarser and heavier than in the other two regions. This is demonstrated by the sculptor who decorated the cathedral of Skara and the church of Forshem with reliefs in a coarse but very expressive form. The *Othelric* reliefs on the tympana and fonts have a more rounded and polished style (the mason probably came from Germany). 'Bestiarius' worked in Småland and Östergötland; he decorated his fonts with animals and fabulous beasts in arcades. In Uppland some fonts are decorated with animals within English-inspired foliate roundels.

The stone sculpture of Norway is mainly of soapstone, and is influenced from England. A great number of reliefs and fragments from the first half of the twelfth century come from the many unknown churches in Trondheim. They show how the masonic workshop at the cathedral acted as a crucible for art styles: Anglo-

Fig. 3. Four capitals of soapstone from churches in Trondheim, Norway. First half of the 12th cent. Cat. no. 444–7.

Saxon and early Norman impulses merged with native wood-carving traditions to form an imaginative and finely detailed style (cat. no. 444–7). Later in the twelfth century the fully developed Norman style from England came to brand the figures on the corbels in the transepts of the present cathedral at Trondheim and the capitals in Stavanger cathedral. Influences spread thence to country churches, where

Fig. 4. Portal relief in limestone from Sønder Kirkeby church, Denmark. C. 1200. It shows the two men responsible for the programme on the portal, and its financing: the priest Conrad and the nobleman Toste. Cat. no. 448.

reliefs (such as those signed by *Botolf* in Skjeberg) occur occasionally.

In Denmark, stone sculpture is rare on the islands, where limestone is sometimes used, as in the reliefs from Sønder Kirkeby on Falster (cat. no. 448). But the numerous sculptures of Jutland are carved in hard granite; the shapes are coarser and the details fewer than elsewhere in Scandinavia where softer stones were used. In the granite carving of the three Jutland cathedrals of Schleswig, Ribe and Viborg, lions are frequently depicted. They fight with each other or with other animals, they attack men, or stand guard. All over Jutland, lions are found on the doorways, walls, and fonts of country churches (even when these are made of granite); double lions are common, as on the font at Nørre Snede (cat. no. 3, 451). Strength and monumentality characterize the reliefs from the church of Øster Starup where a lion is seen eating a man and St Michael fights the dragon. Prolific named masons in Jutland include *Horder* (in Djursland) and *Gøti* (in the Ålborg region).

Church treasures and wall decoration

Ebbe Nyborg

Contemporary written sources tell of how kings, bishops and great magnates furnished Scandinavia's churches with great opulence. Thus, one saga tells that the Norwegian Crusader king, Sigurd Jórsalafari (1089–1130) erected an altar frontal in the church of the Holy Cross at Kungahälla, which he had ordered from Greece: made of copper and silver, it was splendidly gilded and decorated with enamel and precious stones. Great bronze chandeliers, shaped like the City of Jerusalem, are recorded at Dalby and Roskilde. Whilst in Lund Cathedral the crucifix group under the chancel arch was of gilt copper, the figure of Christ probably being fashioned in pure silver. In front of this group precious reliquaries were hung which held remains of Denmark's royal saint, Knut.

Very little of this wealth survives in the cathedrals and monasteries today—although in Odense Cathedral a pair of almost life-size shrines dating from about 1100 still survive. One contains the bones of the same St Knut, wrapped in a silken cloth, woven with a pattern of eagles. The metal casing with its ornament executed in bronze relief has largely disappeared, but fragments survive—as do impressions of it in the underlying wood. From the enigmatic basilica at Tamdrup all that survives is a series of bronze plates decorated in relief, presumably from a large shrine which held the remains of St Poppo (fig. 1). Small shrines of this type only survive complete now from such minor sanctuaries as Jäla and Eriksberg in west Sweden (fig. 2) and Filefjeld and Vatnås in Norway. The continuous arcading of the Vatnås reliquary probably reflects that which, according to literature, decorated St Olaf's magnificent shrine in Trondheim Cathedral.

Scandinavia's oldest ecclesiastical treasures are remarkable in that they come almost exclusively from country parish churches. Some spectacular objects preserved in small churches may well have been transferred from more important places, but time and again one is struck by

Fig. 1. Gilt-copper relief from Tamdrup church, Jutland, Denmark. C. 1150. The scene shows Poppo, who converted the Danish king to Christianity, and is probably from Poppo's shrine. Cat. no. 468.

Fig. 2. Reliquary of gilt-copper from Eriksberg church, Västergötland, Sweden. Second half of the 12th cent. Cat. no. 469.

the rich furnishings which, from the very beginning belonged to what were apparently quite ordinary parish churches. Such treasures are among the most impressive evidence of the Europeanization of the Viking kingdoms, and at the same time emphasize Scandinavian prosperity and the widespread cultural connections of the North in the pre-Hanseatic period (cat. no. 467–82).

Of liturgical vessels in precious metals, all that survives, however, are a few chalices (cat. no. 478). Much more impressive is the survival of a large number of base metal objects for use in the liturgy—altar- and processional crosses, censers and aquamaniles, some of which may date from as early as the 11th century—the engraved cross from Veinge in Skåne, for example (cat. no. 473). Of much greater sophistication is the gilt-bronze crucifix from Lundø, which may relate back to late Anglo-Saxon art (cat. no. 475). Native production of church metalwork really started in the 12th century. Most extraordinary is a group of twenty-two almost identical, cast and engraved bronze crosses of Byzantine character (cat. no. 474), the distribution of which clearly points to their having been made in the archiepiscopal town of Lund. The extensive building of parish churches at this time sparked a considerable demand for specialized church furniture.

The Romanesque parish churches have indicated through excavation an arrangement which seems to have conformed to a fairly fixed plan. The high altar in the chancel was supplemented by side altars in the nave on either side of the chancel arch, often with an altar in front of the chancel bearing a crucifix, relating to the Rood under the chancel arch. The font was situated in the middle of the nave, the long walls of which were often lined with low benches of stone or wood.

Wall paintings were present in some of the early wooden churches and became common in the twelfth century, particularly in the rich lowlands of south Scandinavia. Since the middle of the last century paintings have been uncovered in more than a hundred-and-fifty churches, often, however, they are merely damaged, faded remains cut by later Gothic vaulting (cat. no. 456).

Not only the chancel and the chancel arch, but also the walls of the nave were frequently completely covered with figural friezes, mostly set against a deep-blue (lapis lazuli) background. Their framed ornament displays the complete canon of the antique, richly varied acanthus foliage and meanders, sometimes with small medallions which contain icons, fabulous animals, pictures representing the months or battle between virtue and vice. Best preserved are paintings on the soffits of the chancel arches, in altar niches and in the half-domes of apses where, above the high altar, there is almost always a grand depiction of Christ, *Majestas Domini*, enthroned in apocalyptic majesty. Christ is also frequently placed above the chancel arch, often as the centre point of an immense representation of the Last Judgement or of a series of scenes from the Passion. In these schema the sacramental aspect is dominant and often specially emphasized. This is also the case on the area round the chancel arch. The painted decoration here framed the Rood—the main image of Christ's presence at the Eucharist. Patrons and founders are normally depicted at the bottom of the east wall of the nave but they sometimes intrude themselves into the chancel arch.

The paintings in Måløv (fig. 4) are typical of the dominant schools in the old East Danish area (Sjælland-Skåne). The technique of fresco is here seen at its best and one can only marvel that a refined, Byzantine court art came to be so directly reflected in, for example, the pure *hodegetria* pose of the Måløv Madonna. This is a highly developed art certainly, one which established itself fully formed in Scandinavia and probably came by way of Italy and western Germany.

The paintings on the rich Baltic island of Gotland also show a pronounced Byzantine character, but here the influences clearly came from the East (cat. no. 455). Russian painters seem to have decorated both the first generation of wooden

Fig. 3. Interior of a typical Romanesque parish church in south Scandinavia. Reconstruction based on excavation.

churches on the island and a couple of the early stone churches as well. There is a fairy-tale air about Garde Church where painted in the tower arch are two magnificent eastern saints who could just as well have been produced in Novgorod or Pskov (fig. 5).

The paintings in Jutland are of a different character. They are strikingly varied

Fig. 4. Madonna. Wall painting in a niche for a side altar in Måløv church, Sjælland, Denmark. C. 1200.

and raise a thousand iconographical and stylistic question. The earliest surviving Scandinavian frescoes occur in the royal church of Jelling and the church at Tamdrup. Here the drapery is expressed as a series of stiff lines which belong to the period about 1100. The most outstanding of all Scandinavian Romanesque wall paintings, however, are to be seen in the tiny church at Råsted. Here is the most completely preserved scheme of Romanesque painting, in a style which seems to be related to English manuscript art of the early twelfth century. Above the side altars are Mary and St Michael, whilst over the chancel arch, Christ is enthroned between Peter, Paul and the Apostles (*traditio legis*). The walls of the chancel display a sophisticated rendering of the life of Christ, which culminates above the high altar in the east. To the north of the window is the Massacre of the Innocents and to the south a strange Crucifixion (fig. 6). The design stresses the sacramental; telling of the juxtaposition of divine and human sacrifice as seen in the Mass represented by the sacrificial deaths of Christ and the Innocents (the first martyrs). The Jutlandic paintings of a slightly later

Fig. 5. Eastern saint. Wall-painting in Garde church, Gotland, Sweden. C. 1175–1200.

period include representations of the legends of Saints, and other more secular themes—which speak of the courtly romances of the period of the Crusades. This is particularly true of the many battle and equestrian scenes which are best paralleled in England (at Claverley in Shropshire) and France (at Cressac, Poncé and Sainte-Marie-aux-Anglais). Their Christian message is often difficult to see. Tournament scenes, as at Lyngby, must be seen as reflections of the aristocracy's delight in warfare, although the motifs may well have been thought of as allegories of the battle between good and evil.

The pictures of horsemen call to mind the Bayeux tapestry. Indeed, the painted battle friezes so often found on the walls of naves of churches may be seen to some extent as counterparts to, and substitutes for, tapestries. Churches did not only contain specifically ecclesiastical textiles; they sometimes also owned embroidered and woven hangings for the chancel or for the walls above the benches of the nave, as in the secular houses of the aristocracy. In the church of Hvammr in Iceland, for example, a hanging depicting the life of Charlemagne is mentioned.

Fragments only of this most perishable medium have survived. The woven tapestry from the church at Skog in Sweden clearly demonstrates a continuity of tradition from the pre-Christian Oseberg textiles. The embroidered hanging from Høylandet (cat. no. 484) and the woven fragment from Baldishol (p. 195, fig. 5) in Norway, are clearly influenced from the Continent.

In the major churches of Scandinavia the altar furnishing and crucifixes, as we have seen, were made of glittering gold, silver and precious stones—after the ancient tradition of sumptuous decoration of the most holy objects which still survive in a few great European treasuries. Objects from the small Scandinavian churches show that similar pieces had also been common in the parish churches of the time. Altar frontals would normally have been of painted and gilded wood, as also were the Roods in the chancel arches, and the carved figures which became popular on side altars. But metal casings were far

Fig. 6. Massacre of the Innocents and Christ being nailed to the Cross, painted c. 1150 around the east window of Råsted church, Jut-

from unusual—not perhaps of precious metal, but made of thin copper plates, carefully embossed in relief, firegilded and adorned with glittering crystals. Of the seventeen metal-covered surviving altar frontals from the Christian world in this time, eleven are Scandinavian. To these may be added (even rarer) five retables,

Fig. 7. Knights in quest of the Holy Grail. Detail from the painted frieze of knights, c. 1200, in Skibet church, Jutland, Denmark.

land, Denmark. In the foreground is the original high altar, which supported a golden retable. Cf. cat. no. 482b.

erected at the backs of high altars, and six crucifixes, probably all intended to hang in chancel arches.

The crucifix from Åby (cat. no. 460) is probably the earliest. It portrays a stylized, full frontal Christ in Majesty wearing a royal crown and a strange, collar-like necklet. It must date from about 1100, as

does a similar crucifix from Lisbjerg which, in a cut-down form, was used on the slightly later altar of the church (cat. no. 467). Among other crucifixes, special mention must be made of the late twelfth-century image from Tirstrup, a moving portrait of a more human, dying Saviour. Traces of paint on the wooden core behind the copper suggest that this was originally a carved crucifix which was later given a gilded covering.

The copper casing of the Tirstrup crucifix must be attributed to the same east Jutland craftsmen who, in the middle of the twelfth century, created the most magnificent of the Scandinavian golden altars, that from Lisbjerg (cat. no. 467). Characteristic of the workshop is the lavish ornament which skilfully combines Viking Age interlaced animals with the newly-acquired Classical repertoire of richly variegated foliage, birds, lions, centaurs and so on. This decoration almost swamps the fluttering figures with their undulating dress-hems—probably influenced from England. There is, however, a certain monumentality in the altar's central figure, an attenuated Virgin and Child, enthroned as a *sedes sapientiae* (throne of wisdom) in the heavenly Jerusalem. An inscription on the distinctive arched retable refers to a (now lost) crucifixion group in the middle and reads: 'In the sign of this Cross, healing is given at the tree. Here Man is healed who received his wounds from the apple. Behold, Man what pain I bear for you. Believe and doubt not: My death is your life. Without knowledge of his Creator, Man is but a dumb beast'.

Two of the Jutland golden altars have similar arched retables but only that at Sahl is completely preserved with the original crucifix in the middle. Here Christ's wound is the center of an arched structure which with gates, towers and angelic guards, represents the new Jerusalem, as sent down by God to earth (Revelations, chapter 21).

As no direct European parallels to these metal-clad arched retables survive, it has been suggested that they might be a specific Scandinavian (or Jutland) form of early retable. It is important in this context

Fig. 8. Golden altar with arched retable in Sahl church, Jutland, Denmark. The altar shows Rhenish influence and was probably made in Ribe c. 1200.

that carved wooden examples of Scandinavian arched retables are also known (without metal cladding). These are designed both for high altars and for altars before the chancel arch. The form of these latter was clearly dictated by a wish to have an architectural arch as as frame to the crucifix. As well as being aesthetically pleasing, this composition would also emphasize all the symbolic connotations of the arch as cosmic symbol, triumphal arch, gateway to paradise and vault of Heaven. There is much to indicate that the arched retable was developed for the altar in the chancel arch, and was only later transferred to the high altar within the chancel. When it was used on a high altar the retable arch would also relate to the architecture by enclosing the east window. This was probably the case at Råsted, where behind the original altar, fragments

of a golden altar have been found which must have carried a metal-clad retable (fig. 6). All indications are that this too was shaped as a cosmic arch around the east window, through which came the divine light.

Such a sophisticated correlation between architecture, wall painting and furnishing—as an accompaniment to the liturgy—cannot have been confined to the small churches in Scandinavia. It must reflect much wider developments in the chancel arch and altar arrangements once to be seen in the great Romanesque churches throughout Scandinavia and Europe. The treasures miraculously preserved in the small churches of Scandinavia are major sources for our knowledge of high medieval ecclesiastical stage-setting, both in the North and in core areas of western culture.

Manuscripts and Latin literary culture

Erik Petersen

Scandinavia was late in becoming part of the Latin literary culture of Western Europe, a culture so inseparably bound up with the Christian Church that before the arrival of the Church, books, with their distinctive contents and purpose, were incomprehensible, written in a language no-one had mastered and containing texts no-one could understand.

The sources for early books in Scandinavia are sparse. Only a few manuscripts written before the year 1200 have survived and the knowledge that can be gathered concerning them from other sources is mostly uncertain and imperfect. It must be assumed that many more manuscripts originally existed than those which survive. Some losses can be attributed to harsh treatment of books of the old Church during and after the Reformation (cat. no. 508). Another catastrophe occurred with the burning of Copenhagen in 1728, when the University Library's rich collections of medieval Scandinavian source material were lost, although the collection of Icelandic manuscripts, which was also kept in Copenhagen, was saved. It is for this reason that the source material for the study of Icelandic literature, culture and history is, radically different from that which pertains for the other Scandinavian countries.

European manuscript culture had a long history and established traditions behind it when it first came to Scandinavia. The outer form of books, and the materials on which they were written, were not altered in Scandinavia: the characteristic features of the Western European book, the codex, were retained. The script was Latin and, until well after the year 1200, Carolingian. The manuscript texts which survive from this period were mostly written in Latin and were, as in the rest of Europe, written for use in churches or monasteries. The earliest extant manuscript which can be associated with Scandinavia is, typically, a Gospel Book—the Dalby Gospels (cat. no. 509). The common features of European literary culture, as regards form, contents and language, are more conspicuous in Scandinavia than

any divergences attributable to the North. Scandinavia's contribution to literary culture in this period lay primarily in its ability to be receptive, by importing manuscripts and receiving stylistic and liturgical influences from abroad—from England, Germany and France.

Scandinavia had a script of its own before the arrival of Latin, but it was not connected with books. There are only two known examples of the use of runes in Scandinavian books; both are late and do not reflect any real tradition. One is a fragment, the other a manuscript miscellany *Codex runicus* dating to about 1300.

The first contact with European literary culture was established in connection with the missionary activities of Ansgar, 'the Apostle of the North'. Ansgar came from the Benedictine monastery of Corbie in Picardy. He was the head of the monastic school there, an office he later held in the daughter house at Corvey in Saxony, which was founded in 822. With such a background Ansgar might well have become the connecting link between Scandinavia and Carolingian literary culture, but no such contact was made. A hundred years were to pass before Scandinavia became Christian and another couple of hundred years before the literary culture finally won through in Scandinavia.

The Dalby Gospels (cat. no. 509) is thought to be the earliest book produced in the North. Its value as a source for the study of books in eleventh-century Scandinavia is, however, somewhat limited because of uncertainty about its origins. The Dalby Book seems to display international uniformity rather than anything clearly and specifically Scandinavian. In form and contents it links Scandinavia with the rest of Europe. *The Skara Missal* (cat. no. 511), which dates from the first half of the twelfth century, has also been in Scandinavia since the early Middle Ages and this was possibly also produced here.

The Rules of the Canons in Lund, dated to about 1123, are the oldest to survive from any religious community in Scandinavia. They yield little information about literary culture, but in the section

about the office of Cantor state: 'The Library shall be in the care of the Cantor. He must therefore know the names of the books and shall write down which of them are not in the Library, so that no book shall be lost through negligence'. We cannot draw any extensive conclusions about the interest in, and the care of, books in Lund; there may not even have been a large library; but that an office relating to books is mentioned at all is a clear indication that the book at this time was finally consolidated within Scandinavian culture.

The extent of book production inside Scandinavia is unknown. Lund, which was an archbishopric and the home of many monasteries, has left us the richest material. Liturgical books, annals and a capitulary are among manuscripts which survive. Some were made locally, while others were imported—as for example a splendid Gospel Book written for St. Lawrence's Church in Lund and produced in Helmarshausen, Germany, in the 1140s (cat. no. 512). Richly illuminated twelfth-century manuscripts were in private ownership in the Middle Ages; the *Folkunge Psalter* (cat. no. 513), for example, may indicate the growing importance of books as sacred treasures and as material wealth in Scandinavia as elsewhere.

An entry in the donations register from the church in Lund states that Archbishop Absalon gave the Cathedral, 'various books'. Absalon's will (1201) makes no mention of this gift, but it does enjoin Absalon's clerk, the historian Saxo, 'to return to the Monastery of Sorø the two books the Archbishop had lent to him'. One of these books was a Justinus, copied in France (cat. no. 528). This mention of a 'secular' text indicates the breadth of literary culture that had been achieved in Scandinavia by this time; and this impression is confirmed by Saxo's own chronicle, which was written in a highly stylistic, learned and imitative Latin (cat. no. 520).

By about 1200 there was no longer a sharp intellectual divide between Scandinavia and the rest of Europe. The book, which for a couple of centuries had contributed to great changes within Scandinavia, had now made this region a part of a wider world.

Fig. 1. *The Dalby book, fol. 26v. 11th cent. The Evangelist Matthew is seen decorating the initials of the Gospel. Above, an angel, the symbol of the Evangelist. Possibly produced in Skåne (then Denmark). Cat. no. 509.*

Fig. 2. *Crucifixion scene from the Skara missal. From Skara cathedral, Västergötland, Sweden. Mid 12th cent. Possibly made in Skara following a French prototype. Cat. no. 511.*

Fig. 3. *Dedicatory page of Gospels from Lund cathedral, Skåne. C. 1140. Above, St Lawrence, the patron saint of the cathedral. Probably produced in Helmarshausen, Hesse, Germany. Cat. no. 512.*

Fig. 4. *The Folkunge Psalter, fol. 12r. The illustration is from a series of scenes from the Life of Christ and shows the Flight into Egypt. 12th cent. English. Cat. no. 513.*

Icelandic manuscripts

Jónas Kristjánsson

Christianity was adopted as law at the Icelandic *Althing* (parliament) in the year 1000, after an arrangement had been reached with the pagans. At first Christian theology came to Iceland mostly from England, partly directly, partly by way of Norway. Later, ecclesiastical and literary influences also came from Germany, Denmark and France. In the eleventh century the faith took root; churches were built and local priests took over from the foreign missionaries. A bishopric was established at Skálholt in southern Iceland in 1056 and another in Hólar in northern Iceland in 1106; these two bishoprics were the most important cultural centres in the country until a capital was established in Reykjavík at the end of the eighteenth century. At the seats of the bishoprics were schools where, almost continuously, aspiring priests could be educated. Monasteries were also important cultural centres. At least eleven monastic houses were established in Iceland in the Middle Ages, nine for men and two for women, many of which continued to function right up to the Reformation in the sixteenth century.

The social structure in Iceland was in many respects unique, and the organization of the Church was also different from that which prevailed in most European countries. The leading men in the country wanted to ensure that they did not lose power to the new institution and it became quite common for the *goði* and other large farmers to build churches on their farms and have their sons ordained. Consequently the Icelandic Church was for a long time completely dependent on secular power. It was a national Church.

Literary pursuits were, however, not confined to monasteries and bishops' seats, for many large farms with churches became centres for spiritual employment. At the same time the monasteries were of a more secular character than those in other countries, for the monks were often older, major farmers who had been ordained at an early age and later sought peace after an eventful life. In most other countries the literate were to a large extent an isolated class, living behind the walls of churches and monasteries, their written language was normally Latin and their literary output almost entirely religious or strongly Christian. In Iceland, however, the learned had both feet in the secular world and they cultivated the country's cultural heritage. Nearly all learned Icelanders wrote in the vernacular, not in Latin (cat. no. 521). Religious works were translated or rendered into the vernacular, several foreign branches of learning were also treated in Icelandic (cf. cat. no. 510, 522) and a unique medieval literature developed which was extensive, varied and of high stylistic quality. The best known works are the two *Eddas*: the poetic *Edda* (or elder Edda) and Snorri's *Edda* (or younger Edda) (cat. no. 521). To them can be added the sagas—a literary genre highly varied in form as well as content (cat. no. 337, 523–7). The great majority of these, however, only survive in later copies (see also cat. no. 336, 519–20).

At this time the skins of animals were, by and large, the only material available for making books in Europe. In Iceland vellum was probably always made from calf's skin. There are no written accounts of how the skins were prepared in Norway or Iceland, but something can be deduced from the surviving books themselves and

Fig. 1. The earliest surviving Icelandic manuscript is this fragment, from c. 1150, of a collection of sermons (Homilia). This leaf (fol. 2r) shows part of a sermon for St Michael's day. Cat. no. 510.

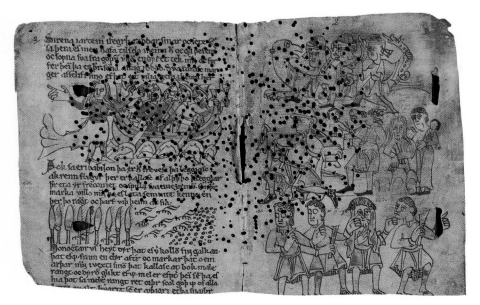

Fig. 2. The text on natural history, Physiologus, was translated into Icelandic in the 12th cent. This fragmentary manuscript is from c. 1200. Cat. no. 522.

from practices in more southerly countries. It is clear from the Icelandic manuscripts that the art of tanning was mastered on the island: the parchment is thin and supple and originally it was almost as white as modern book paper.

When the vellum was ready, it was cut into rectangular pieces of varying size, according to the format required for the book. For the largest books one skin folded in half formed two sheets of folio size. Smaller sizes were produced by folding several times. The folded sheets were arranged in gatherings, usually eight sheets to each gathering. The columns then had to be positioned correctly and the lines marked out: traces of this formatting survive in some manuscripts. In large format books the text was usually written in two columns, as in the later large, printed books. A quill pen was used for writing, often taken from a goose or a swan. The ink was the same dye as used for colouring cloth black; fortunately it was very durable, for the books have seen considerable wear during the centuries.

When the writing was finished, the gatherings were sewn together with twine onto thick straps and then bound between wooden boards. Holes were made in the boards and the straps were fastened to them with wedges. There is no evidence that the boards were covered or decorated, but some must have been. Although the

binding was plain, it was good for the vellum: the boards are strong, the leaves are not clamped at the spine and consequently the leaves lie quite flat and the books open easily.

Many Icelandic manuscripts are decorated and the illuminations reveal the independent development of the Icelandic manuscript tradition. A comparison, however, between Icelandic vellum manuscripts and foreign medieval manuscripts reveals great differences. The foreign books have light-coloured and even vellum, their initials are often embellished with gold and they stand out as magnificent examples of the art of book production. Icelandic vellum, on the other hand, has darkened because the books were read and used for centuries, handled by hands often none too clean, and kept in poor dwellings. By contrast to the almost mechanical accuracy of the foreign craftsmen, the writing and illumination of the Icelandic manuscripts have a character which is akin to the fresh original of the literature itself. If modern eyes may find some manuscripts primitive in execution, this view may also chime with the scribe of an Icelandic book who wrote:

> Gold does not gleam in me,
> nor glittering staves on lines.
> All my beauty here I show
> in literary elegance.

The sixteenth and seventeenth centuries saw a growth of interest in the ancient Icelandic literature. The leading Scandinavian countries, Denmark and Sweden, vied with each other to collect manuscripts, to have them printed in the original or in translation, or to use them as material for new historical works. As a result, most Icelandic vellum books and many paper copies left the country. Some ended up in the royal libraries in Copenhagen and Stockholm, but the majority was collected by the Icelandic bibliophile Árni Magnússon. A professor at Copenhagen University, he spent many years travelling round Iceland as an emissary of the Danish government. He was thus able to form an outstanding collection. On his deathbed in 1730 he bequeathed all his books to the University of Copenhagen—at that time also the university of Iceland.

For centuries Copenhagen was the centre for the study of Icelandic manuscripts. But after Iceland's independence in 1918 a movement arose for the return of the manuscripts. At first the idea met with strong resistance from Denmark, but in 1961—and again in 1965—the Danish Parliament decided to present most of the manuscripts to Iceland. Two manuscript institutes were founded, one in Copenhagen and one in Reykjavík, both named after Árni Magnússon, and the handing over of the manuscripts still continues. Today the study of Icelandic manuscripts flourishes in both places.

Scandinavian coins

Lars O. Lagerqvist

←Fig. 1. Two sceattas of Frisian type, discovered in Ribe, Denmark. 8th cent. Obverse and reverse. Scale 2:1. Cat. no. 152.

Fig. 2. Silver coin with cocks and boat, from Hedeby. C. 825. The coin has been converted into a pendant and was found in a grave at Birka, Sweden. Obverse and reverse. Scale 1:1. Cat. no. 153a. ➤

In the Middle Ages west European coinage was mainly struck in silver. Between the fall of the Western Roman Empire in 476 and the rise of the Frankish Empire about 800 both gold and silver coins were minted, but silver coins became ever more common from the beginning of the seventh century, and gold coins ceased almost completely from the middle of the eighth century. The expansion of the Caliphate and Islam cut off the import of this precious metal.

From the end of the eighth century to the mid-thirteenth century the silver *denarius* was the basis of west European coinage. Apart from its name, it had nothing in common with the Roman denarius, and it appears under different names in France, England, Germany and Scandinavia. It formed the basis of a system of weights of precious metal (mark, pound, etc.). This period corresponds to the Viking Age and early Middle Ages in Scandinavia. Up to the twelfth century there was a distinct abundance of silver as new mines were opened up and worked in Europe and the East.

One of the many mints used by Charlemagne (768–814) was Dorestad in Frisia, where the coins were most commonly struck without pictorial representations, having only legends on each face. The first coins struck in Scandinavia were imitations of these.

Imported coins were, however, long dominant in the Viking Age. Until shortly after the middle of the tenth century, Arabic silver dirhems were pre-eminent. Then the number of Arabic coins declined and they cease to appear in the hoards at the beginning of the eleventh century.

The great silver mines of the East seem to have been worked out, the Russian state had emerged and made both trade and looting more difficult; the dirhems deteriorated. From the end of the tenth century German *pfennige* and Anglo-Saxon pennies (Danegeld and loot) predominate in finds of coins. Byzantine coins also occur.

Denmark (cat. no. 142, 152–3, 423–5, 539–44)

Independent minting began with imitations of popular, well-known types. This stage was followed by the development of local coin types. In Scandinavia, Carolingian coins were the first to be imitated, more specifically Charlemagne's denarii from Dorestad. The imitations either copied both faces of the originals or coupled the obverse with different, largely Scandinavian, motifs on the reverse—animals, for example, deer, cocks, Viking ships and so on. There are also types which eschew imitations of Carolingian originals on either face. A later group comprises the so-called half-bracteates, that is coins which are so thin that each face shows signs of the striking on the other. They include low-weight coins which perpetuate the Dorestad motif, and some types where the motif consists of more or less pure decoration.

The more 'degenerate' Dorestad imitations and pennies with Scandinavian motifs seem to have been struck at Hedeby (Haithabu) in Denmark (now in Germany), probably about 825–860. The later, thin coins (*c.* 900–985) were also issued from Hedeby, but at the end of the period

were also struck further north. Their source is not known.

Minting of coins with a legend, copying Anglo-Saxon originals, began about 995 in Denmark, Norway and Sweden. The first Danish coin is signed by the moneyer Godwine from England—the name is also known from contemporary Norwegian and Swedish mints—and carries on the obverse Sven Forkbeard's name and title together with a stylized portrait. This type is very rare. Coining became more common during the reign of Knut the Great (1018–1035). The dominant mint was Lund but others, such as Roskilde, are known. Most of the pennies are very similar to contemporary English coins.

Under the influence of silver coins imported from Byzantium at the end of the tenth century until shortly before the middle of the eleventh century (the motifs of which differ greatly from the more common Arabic, German and English coins). Byzantine-derived motifs appear on many Danish coins of the period 1050–1100: such images include the monarch and Christ, or Christ alone with a Gospel-book. Runic inscriptions are common on coins of Sven Estridsen (1047–1074).

In the eleventh century Denmark acquired a more strictly controlled national coinage. As in Norway and Sweden, this was adapted to the Scandinavian weight system based on 1 mark = 8 öre = 24 örtugar, but the different countries varied the numbers of pennies to a mark.

The twelfth century is characterized by a progressive devaluation of the coinage. Pennies were increasingly alloyed with copper. At the beginning of the thirteenth century the ratio of the mark in silver to the mark in pennies was 1:2–1:3; this meant that two or three marks in coin had to be given for 1 mark of pure silver. There were many coin types in the twelfth and thirteenth centuries. As the bishops minted coins in these centuries some issues have a king's portrait on one face and a bishop on the other. Bracteates were also struck in the twelfth century.

Norway (cat. no. 423, 545–51)

The first Norwegian coin was struck about 995, by the English moneyer Godwine, in Anglo-Saxon style. It is smaller than the contemporary Danish and Swedish coins. Only three examples are known. The symbolic royal portrait on the obverse shows that the coins were struck for a king Olav of Norway, presumably Olav Tryggvason (995–1000).

The later Norwegian issues of Olav Haraldson the Holy (1015–1030) also show strong English influence but they were rapidly barbarized. The reign of Harald Hardråde (1047–1066) produced coins with runic inscriptions. During his reign the king's name disappeared from the coins and the first devaluation of the coinage also took place. These light-weight coins were known as *Haraldsslatta*. Under Magnus Barefoot (1093–1103) the silver content was restored but the weight was reduced to about half.

In the twelfth century small bracteates were minted with varying motifs (crosses, croziers, spirals, kings' profiles and so on), these are difficult to date. Sverre (1184–1202) also struck double-sided coins with (following English prototypes) the king's name and a crowned, bearded head on the obverse.

Sweden (cat. no. 143, 423–4, 426, 552–5)

More coins (mainly Arabic dirhems) were imported into Sweden than into the other Scandinavian countries. More than half of them have been found on Gotland. There is no evidence of native minting until the 990s, when, in the reign of Olof Skötkonung (c. 995–1022) a national coinage, based on Anglo-Saxon prototypes, developed in Denmark, Norway and Sweden.

Many Viking-age imitations of these coins—with confused legends—show that they were very popular. Some, or perhaps most, of the imitations must have been struck in Scandinavia.

Minting probably began in Sigtuna about 995 and continued, with some interruptions, until 1030/35. The issues of Olof and his successor Anund Jakob (died about 1050)—those which date from about 995–1030/35—are mostly imitations of Æthelred II's and Knut's coins. Most obverses show stylized busts and legends giving name and title. The reverse, with a cross in the centre, refers to the name of the English moneyer and the name of the mint. A large number of barbarized coins can by die-linking be related to strikings with readable legends. The find in 1990 of a lead trial-piece of an obverse and reverse of a barbarized penny strengthens the localization of many of these anonymous groups to Sigtuna. Other groups derive from Denmark (possibly Lund).

Coin import and circulation characteristic of the Viking Age continued until about 1125, but for the next seventy-five years there seems to have been no minting in Sweden. A silver hoard weighing some 10 kg, from Lummelunda, Gotland, deposited after 1143, is the last find of typically Viking Age composition.

When coins began to be minted throughout Sweden in the mid-twelfth century the standard was not the same throughout the country. From this standpoint the country was divided into three.

Fig. 4. Lead trial-piece of a coin-die from Sigtuna, Sweden, cat. no. 553, and a coin minted under Olof Skötkonung with almost the same legend and picture.

In Svealand there were 192 pennies to the mark, in Götaland there were 384. In an imprecisely defined area comprising parts of south-east Sweden (Gotland and probably Öland and the neighbouring mainland) a mark corresponded to 288 pennies. The weight had been reduced but not the silver content.

The earliest medieval Swedish coins were minted about 1140: they were double-sided pennies on the almost independent island of Gotland; also minted were anonymous bracteates from Lödöse, the Swedish harbour on the Göta älv near the Norwegian border.

Minting in Svealand began under Knut Eriksson (1167–1196), probably about 1180, with some ten types of bracteate. The Archbishop in Uppsala also controlled a mint at the end of the twelfth century (cf. Denmark).

Fig. 3. The earliest Scandinavian coins bearing a king's name were all struck c. 995 and

imitate the Anglo-Saxon 'crux' type. a Sven Forkbeard of Denmark. b Olaf Tryggvason of

Norway. c Olof Skötkonung of Sweden. Obverses and reverses. Scale 1:1. Cf. cat. no. 423.

Detail from the Hylestad portal, Norway. C. 1200. The picture shows the hero Sigurd, slayer of the dragon Fafnir (right) and the evil blacksmith Regin (left) in the process of forging the sword called Gram. Cat. no. 442.

Catalogue

Catalogue

The **numbering** in the catalogue corresponds in most cases to the order of the exhibits. The 617 entries are divided into four main sections. The running head at the top of the pages indicates the main section and the sub-section. A comprehensive and slightly more detailed summary of the themes of the exhibition and the contents of the catalogue can be found immediately below.

Illustrations: All the objects, with only a few exceptions, are illustrated. All the illustrations are accompanied by the catalogue number. When an illustration is not included on the same pages as the catalogue number, its page number is indicated in the heading of the entry. In most cases these are references to colour-illustrations included in the introductory chapters of the catalogue.

The texts of the **catalogue-entries** have usually been supplied by the lending institutions. Names of the authors of these entries are indicated by their initials. The full names of the authors and their institutions are given in the appended list.

Authors of catalogue entries

AC   Axel Christophersen, Riksantikvaren, Utgravningskontoret for Trondheim

AM   Arnold Muhl, Museum für Vor- und Frühgeschichte, Berlin

ASG   Anne-Sofie Gräslund, Uppsala universitet

AZ   Anna Zariņa, Vēstures Institūts, Riga

BKB   Birthe Kjølbye-Biddle, Repton Excavation Project

BLW   Birgitta Linderoth Wallace, Canadian Parks Service, Halifax

BP   Björn Petterson, Sigtuna museer

CD   C. Donnellier, Archives nationales, Paris

CH   Claude Hohl, Archives départementales de la Seine-Maritime, Rouen

CN   Clara Nevéus, Riksarkivet, Stockholm

CW   Claes Wahlöö, Kulturen, Lund

DC   Debbie Caulfield, National Museum of Ireland, Dublin

DG   Denis Grisel, Archives départementales de Saône-et-Loire, Macon

DGC   Danielle Gaborit-Chopin, Musée du Louvre

DLM   Ditlev L. D. Mahler, Føroya Fornminnissavn, Tórshavn

DMW   David M. Wilson, The British Museum

DT   Dominic Tweddle, York Archaeological Trust, York

EBH   Erla B. Hohler, Universitetets Oldsaksamling, Oslo

EEG   Elsa E. Guðjónsson, Islands Nationalmuseum, Reykjavík

EJ   Erik Jondell, Riksantikvaren, Utgravningskontoret for Trondheim

EJEP   Elizabeth J. E. Pirie, Leeds City Museum

EKK   Emma K. Kublo, Novgorodskij Gosudarstvennyj Muzej

EL   Elsa Lindberger, Kungliga Myntkabinettet, Stockholm

ENN   Evgenij N. Nosov, Institut Istorii Materialnoj Kultury, St. Petersburg

EP   Erik Petersen, Det kongelige Bibliotek, Copenhagen

ER   Else Roesdahl, Aarhus Universitet

ES   Ernst Stidsing, Kulturhistorisk Museum, Randers

FA   François Avril, Bibliothèque nationale, Paris

FG   Finnbogi Guðmundsson, Landsbókasafn Íslands, Reykjavík

FL   Fritze Lindahl, Danmarks Nationalmuseum, Copenhagen

FV   Françoise Vallet, Musée des Antiquités Nationales, St.-Germain-en-Laye

GSM   Gerd Stamsø Munch, Tromsø Museum

GT   Göran Tegnér, Statens historiska museum, Stockholm

GW   Gun Westholm, Gotlands fornsal, Visby

GZ   Guntis Zemītis, Latvijas Vēstures Muzejs, Riga

HC   Hampus Cinthio, Lunds Universitets Historiska Museum

HJM   Hans Jørgen Madsen, Forhistorisk Museum Moesgård, Århus

HK   Helge Kongsrud, Riksarkivet, Oslo

HL   Henriette Lyngstrøm, Danmarks Nationalmuseum, Copenhagen

HLü   Hartwig Lüdtke, Archäologisches Landesmuseum, Schleswig

HMJ   Henrik M. Jansen, Svendborg og Omegns Museum

HVA   Henrik von Achen, Historisk Museum, Bergen

IH   Inga Hägg, Archäologisches Landesmuseum, Schleswig

IJ   Ingmar Jansson, Stockholms universitet

IM   Irmelin Martens, Universitetets Oldsaksamling, Oslo

IU   Ingrid Ulbricht, Archäologisches Landesmuseum, Schleswig

IZ   Inger Zachrisson, Statens Historiska Museum, Stockholm

JA   Jette Arneborg, Danmarks Nationalmuseum, Copenhagen

JB   Janet Backhouse, The British Library, London

JBr   Jan Brunius, Riksarkivet, Stockholm

JEK   James E. Knirk, Universitetets Oldsaksamling, Oslo

JES   Jan Eric Sjöberg, Göteborgs arkeologiska museum, Gothenburg

JGC   James Graham-Campbell, University College London

JH   Joachim Herrmann, Berlin

JK   Jónas Kristjánsson, Stofnun Árna Magnússonar, Reykjavík

JL   James Lang, English Heritage, Newcastle upon Tyne

JPN   Jean-Pierre Nicolardot, Directeur des fouilles du Camp de Péran, URA 880 de CNRS

JR   Jonas Ros, Sigtuna museer

JS   Jørgen Skaarup, Langelands Museum, Rudkøbing

JSa   Jacques Santrot, Musées départementaux de Loire-Atlantique, Nantes

JSJ   Jørgen Steen Jensen, Danmarks Nationalmuseum, Copenhagen

JSM   Jan Skamby Madsen, Vikingeskibshallen i Roskilde

KB   Karin Berg, Skimuseet, Oslo

KJ   Kenneth Jonsson, Kungliga Myntkabinettet, Stockholm

KS   Kolbjørn Skaare, Universitetets Myntkabinett, Oslo

KSo   Kalle Sognnes, Vitenskapsmuseet, Universitetet i Trondheim

LF   Laurence Flavigny, Musées départementaux de Seine-Maritime, Rouen

LFS   Lars F. Stenvik, Vitenskapsmuseet, Universitetet i Trondheim

LTB   Lena Thålin-Bergman, Statens historiska museum, Stockholm

LW   Leslie Webster, The British Museum

MÅ   Marit Åhlén, Runverket, Stockholm

MB   Martin Biddle, Hertford College, Oxford.

MD   Michel Dhénin, Bibliothèque nationale, Paris

MDG   Martine Dalas-Garrigues, Archives nationales, Paris

MDOH   Michael D. O'Hara, London

MH   Marta Hoffmann, Oslo

MK   Marita Karlsson, Ålands museum, Mariehamn

MMA   Marion M. Archibald, The British Museum

MP   Michel Petit, Direction des Antiquités d'Ile-de-France

MR   Mats Roslund, Sigtuna museer

MS   Marie Stoklund, Danmarks Nationalmuseum, Copenhagen

NS   Neil Stratford, The British Museum

OID   Olga I. Davidan, Gosudarstvennyj Ermitaž, St. Petersburg

OVB   O.V. Bondarec, Gosudarstvennyj Istoričeskij Muzej, Kiev

PGH   Poul Grinder-Hansen, Danmarks Nationalmuseum, Copenhagen

PLLH   Pirkko-Liisa Lehtosalo-Hilander, Helsinki universitet

PM   Petter B. Molaug, Universitetets Oldsaksamling, Oslo

PP   Patrick Périn, Musées départementaux de Seine-Maritime, Rouen

PS   Peter Springborg, Københavns Universitet, Copenhagen

RÓF   Raghnall Ó Floinn, National Museum of Ireland, Dublin

SH   Steen Hvass, Vejle Museum

SJ   Stig Jensen, Den Antikvariske Samling, Ribe

SK   Sigrid H. H. Kaland, Historisk Museum, Bergen

SSH   Steffen Stummann Hansen, Hørsholm Egns Museum

ST   Sten Tesch, Sigtuna museer

SVA   Símun V. Arge, Føroya Fornminnissavn, Tórshavn

SY   Susan Youngs, The British Museum

TC   Tom Christensen, Roskilde Museum

TE   Torsten Edgren, Museiverket, Helsinki

TM   Thór Magnússon, Islands Nationalmuseum, Reykjavík

TS   Thorgunn Snædal, Runverket, Stockholm

UN   Ulf Näsman, Aarhus Universitet

ÜT   Ülle Tamla, Ajaloo Instituut, Tallinn

VN   Valérie Neveu, Bibliothèque municipale de Rouen

VÖV   Vilhjálmur Ö. Vilhjálmsson, Islands Nationalmuseum, Reykjavík

VPV   V. P. Vancugov, Odesskij Archeologičeskij Muzej, Odessa

VV   Volker Vogel, Archäologisches Landesmuseum, Schleswig

VVM   V.V. Muraseva, Gosudarstvennyj Istoričeskij Muzej, Moscow

WF   Wladyslaw Filipowiak, Muzeum Narodowe, Szczecin

WH   Wendy M. M. Horn, The Manx Museum, Douglas

The Exhibition
Order of catalogue entries

Models and reconstructions

The Gokstad Ship
 (Det Nationalhistoriske Museum på Frederiksborg,
 Denmark)

The Skuldelev Ship, no. 3
 (Vikingeskibshallen, Roskilde)

The Mekrijärvi Boat
 (Finlands sjöhistoriska museum, Helsinki)

Scandinavian female garment
 (Norsk Kulturråd/Åse Folkvord)

Scandinavian male garment from Mammen
 (Danmarks Nationalmuseum, Copenhagen)

Finnish female garment from Luistari
 (Kauttuan museo, Finland)

Hedeby house constructed in 870
 (Archäologisches Landesmuseum, Schleswig)

Trondheim house constructed in 1003
 (Vitenskapsmuseet, University of Trondheim)

Hemse Church
 (Hamburger Museum für Archäologie)

Borgund Church
 (Universitetets Oldsaksamling, Oslo)

Scandinavia 800–1200

2

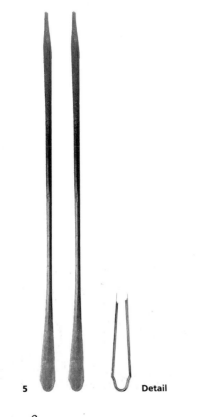

5   Detail

1

Limestone (paint modern).
H. from bottom line 210cm.
Ardre church, Gotland, Sweden.
700–800. Gotland.
Statens Historiska Museum, Stockholm
11118:VIII

Picture stone *(Illustrated p. 2)*

Easy accessibility to limestone enabled the Gotland sculptors to carve 'picture stones' (burial and memorial stones) from the 5th cent. onwards. They are richly illustrated with scenes from myths and sagas, some of which can be found in later west-Scandinavian literature. In the 6th and 7th centuries the stones were normally phallic in shape, with the representation of a sailing ship in the lowest field. Cists made of four low stones and a curved cap-stone are also known. Cat. no. 1 and 175 are the most important monuments from the beginning of the Viking Age. Dating depends on the winged spearheads which point up from the stern of the ship on cat. no. 1 and the bearded axes carried by the men on the upper pictorial field of cat. no. 175. The stones seem to be a jumble of disconnected scenes.

The Ardre stone was used as flooring in a church and its figures are badly worn and difficult to distinguish. The upper field seems to show Valhalla and a hero arriving in the warriors' paradise (better seen in cat. no. 175). The lowest pictorial field shows, among other things, Wayland the Smith as captive of king Nidud. As vengeance he cuts off the heads of Nidud's two sons and makes their skulls into drinking vessels from which the health of the king will be drunk. After raping the king's daughter, Wayland turns himself into a bird and, having told the king what he has done, escapes from the court. The centre of the illustration on the picture stone is taken up by the cross-section of a forge, with hammer and tongs; to the right of the smithy are the beheaded sons of the king and to the left Wayland as a three-headed bird, together with a woman—presumably the king's daughter. To the right there is a snake pit, and lower down and to the left is a scene which perhaps represents Thor as fisherman. In the middle Thor cuts off the head of one of the giant Hyme's oxen to use as bait. The

scene to the left under the sailing ship shows Thor and Hyme, in a small boat fishing for Midgardsorm (The World Serpent). The ship is unusually unobtrusive here. The ship's master sits in the stern by the steering oar, with a shield and spear behind him. A man with an anchor stands aft and controls the sail.   IJ

Bibl.: Lindqvist 1941–2, I *passim*, figs. 139–40, II 22ff., fig. 311; Davidson 1967, 124f.; Buisson 1976, *passim*, Taf. 1–9; Nylén 1978, 70f.; Meulengracht Sørensen 1986, 269, fig. 3

2

Oak.
376cm × 55cm × 20cm.
Skuldelev, Roskilde Fjord, Denmark.
Beginning of 11th cent. Scandinavian.
Vikingeskibshallen, Roskilde, M.285.

Ship's prow

Prow of the small merchantman Skuldelev 3. The prow is cut from a single piece of wood and allows for 7 strakes on each side; these would have been fastened to it by iron nails. Its strongly curved tip draws together the flexible lines of the whole ship. The ship was 14m long and 3.30m wide, and could have carried some 5 tons of freight stowed amidships. It was propelled by a large square sail.

This and 4 other ships were excavated from the bed of Roskilde Fjord in 1964. They were sunk here in the middle or at the end of the 11th cent. to obstruct one of the fairways to the important town of Roskilde.   JSM

Bibl.: Olsen and Crumlin-Pedersen 1967; Olsen and Crumlin-Pedersen 1969; Graham-Campbell 1980, no. 278

3

Gilt copper.
L. 29cm.
Tingelstad church, Gran, Oppland, Norway.
1100–1150. Scandinavian
Universitetets Oldsaksamling, Oslo, C36648

Weather vane

Pierced gilt-copper plate with profiled frame riveted along the edges. Along the vertical edge is an old repair and a more modern method of attachment, a wedge-shaped piece is missing. The dragon crest is of brass, cast in 5 pieces and riveted to the frame. There is a hole with signs of wear in the curved frame and through the dragon's jaw. The decorative lines are punched and the cuts made,

3

rather inaccurately, with a chisel. There are a number of later inscriptions. The motif represents David rescuing the sheep from the lion's mouth, the whole surrounded by tendrils.

Used probably as cat. no. 417 (cf. cat. no. 616). The figural style and type of tendrils suggest first half of 12th cent. The long hair of the figure shows the merging of the David motif with that of Samson.　　**EBH**

Bibl.: Bugge 1925; Swarzenski 1954; Blindheim 1982a; Blindheim 1982b; Blindheim 1983

4　　　　　　　　　　　　　　　　Oak
Cross-section 420cm.
Äskekärr, Starrkärr, Västergötland, Sweden.
10th cent. Scandinavian.
Göteborgs arkeologiska museum, GAM 46456

Cross-section of the Äskekärr ship　(Not illustrated)

Reconstructed cross-section of the ship amidships; many original parts, all of oak.

The ship, excavated in 1933, was a merchantman. It has been dated by dendrochronology to *c.* 930, but was still in use *c.* 1000. The hull is well preserved but most of the upper port side is missing, as are stem and stern which were of the same type as cat. no. 2. It was 16 m long, and 4.5 m amidships, 2 m high from the bottom of the keel to the gunwale. The 12 very thin strakes on each side are fastened with iron rivets (cf. cat. no. 6). The seventh strake above the keel is considerably thicker and strengthens the hull; it was known as *meginhúfr* (the strongest strake). A heavy mast-step amidships shows that the ship was built for sail. In contrast to contemporary warships, which were designed so that they could be rowed at great speed, the Äskekärr ship had only a single pair of oars for manoeuvering.　　**JES**

Bibl.: Humbla 1934

5　　　　　　　　　　　　　　　　Pine.
L. 370–400cm.
Oseberg, Sem, Vestfold, Norway.
c. 800–850. Scandinavian.
Universitetets Oldsaksamling, Oslo, no number

Two oars

The blades of the oars have a moulded edge and curve towards the points. The grip tapers to an outer diameter of 5cm. Some oars from the ship (cf. cat. no. 155), had traces of painted decoration at mid length.

The Oseberg ship had 15 pairs of oars, one to a man. Their lengths varied in relation to their position in the ship. The longest were used fore and aft, where the height above the waterline was greatest. When excavated the oars were found to be in different parts of the ship, some were still in the rowlocks aft.

IM

Bibl.: Osebergfundet I (Schetelig) 1917

6　　　　　　　　　　　　　　　Iron, oak.
L. *c.* 113cm.
Fribrødre River, Falster, Denmark.
2nd half of 11th cent. Scandinavian-Wendish.
Vikingeskibshallen, Roskilde, D203/82; 6980, 6995A, D313/83, D543/83, D554/83, D567/83

Two ship's planks with trenails, six iron nails　(Not illustrated)

Two quarter-hewn strakes held together clinker-fashion by willow trenails and caulked with moss and sheep's wool. Nails for fastening the strakes and roves of iron.

At end 10th cent. the Fribrødre river was a place where old ships were broken up and repaired and new ships were built. Falster's situation in the area of mixed Danish and Slav culture is reflected in the finds from this shipyard. The use of trenails for the clinkering of strakes is a specifically Slav trait; iron nails were used in Scandinavia. Iron nails were, however, also used on the ships from the Fribrødre river, particularly on the prows and in repairs.　　**JSM**

Skamby Madsen 1984; 1987; 1991

7　　　　　　　　Aspen (Populus tremulus).
L. 92cm.
Mekrijärvi, North Karelia, Finland.
Finnish.
Finlands sjöhistoriska museum, Helsinki, 0880

Fragment of sewn boat

The boat discovered at Mekrijärvi consisted of more than 400 fragments which made up 30% of a whole boat which had an estimated length of at least 8.5m. The stem, stern and ribs are of spruce, the rest of aspen. It is of a type known by Scandinavian scholars as a 'five-part boat'; i.e. it consists of a hewn (often concave) keel, stem and stern; and 2–3 strakes, and is sewn together. This boat has been dated by radiocarbon to the early 16th cent., but many of the 20 or so sewn boats found in Finland (e.g. Keuruu and Rääkkylä) date from end of the 12th or early 13th cent.

The technique of sewing boats together is known from the late Iron Age, but continues to the present day in parts of N Scandinavia and N Eurasia. Sewn boats are also mentioned in Snorre's *Magnúss saga blinda ok Haralds gilla*, according to which Sigurd Slemme, when wintering in N Norway in the 1130s, had the Saami build him 2 boats which were held together with animal sinews, they had no nails, and had 'knees' of osier.　　**TE**

Bibl.: Forsell 1983; 1985

7

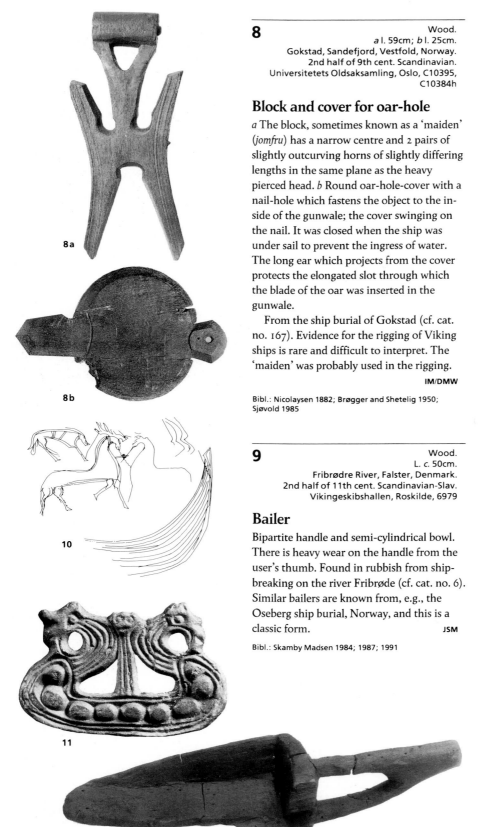

8a

8b

10

11

9

8

Wood.
a l. 59cm; *b* l. 25cm.
Gokstad, Sandefjord, Vestfold, Norway.
2nd half of 9th cent. Scandinavian.
Universitetets Oldsaksamling, Oslo, C10395,
C10384h

Block and cover for oar-hole

a The block, sometimes known as a 'maiden' (*jomfru*) has a narrow centre and 2 pairs of slightly outcurving horns of slightly differing lengths in the same plane as the heavy pierced head. *b* Round oar-hole-cover with a nail-hole which fastens the object to the inside of the gunwale; the cover swinging on the nail. It was closed when the ship was under sail to prevent the ingress of water. The long ear which projects from the cover protects the elongated slot through which the blade of the oar was inserted in the gunwale.

From the ship burial of Gokstad (cf. cat. no. 167). Evidence for the rigging of Viking ships is rare and difficult to interpret. The 'maiden' was probably used in the rigging. **IM/DMW**

Bibl.: Nicolaysen 1882; Brøgger and Shetelig 1950; Sjøvold 1985

9

Wood.
L. *c*. 50cm.
Fribrødre River, Falster, Denmark.
2nd half of 11th cent. Scandinavian-Slav.
Vikingeskibshallen, Roskilde, 6979

Bailer

Bipartite handle and semi-cylindrical bowl. There is heavy wear on the handle from the user's thumb. Found in rubbish from ship-breaking on the river Fribrøde (cf. cat. no. 6). Similar bailers are known from, e.g., the Oseberg ship burial, Norway, and this is a classic form. **JSM**

Bibl.: Skamby Madsen 1984; 1987; 1991

10

Pine.
L. 95cm.
Oseberg, Sem, Vestfold, Norway.
c. 800–850. Scandinavian.
Universitetets Oldsaksamling, Oslo, Oseberg 340

Graffiti on floor board

Floor board from the Oseberg ship (cf. cat. no. 155). The under-side has incised sketches of a ship's prow and animals, including 2 opposed horses or deer, one unfinished. The complete one has an arrow in its chest and above it is a quadruped, probably a dog. The prow is carved with a sure hand, whereas the animals are less well executed. **IM**

Bibl.: Schetelig 1917, fig. 116; Wilson and Klindt-Jensen 1966, 27f.; Fuglesang 1980b

11

Gilt copper-alloy.
L. 5.9cm.
Lillevang, Bornholm, Denmark.
Mid-9th cent. Scandinavian.
Danmarks Nationalmuseum, Copenhagen, C2894

Boat-shaped brooch

Shaped like a Viking ship with dragon heads fore and aft, pronounced strakes, shields along the rail, and a face at the masthead. From a female grave. The brooch is unique, demonstrating the great and acknowledged importance of ships at that time. **HL/UN**

Bibl.: Vedel 1878, 237, Pl. VII:2; Vedel 1886, 182f., fig. 375, appendix XB1–B2; Brøndsted 1936, no. 121:10; Glob 1977; *The Vikings in England*, 1981, 66, D24

12

?Limestone.
L. 88.1cm.
Birka (Black earth), Uppland, Sweden.
9th–10th cent. Scandinavian.
Statens Historiska Museum, Stockholm, 8139:7

Mould

One half of a mould for the head of a small beast of prey used to decorate a dress pin or something similar. Prototypes, on a larger scale, must be sought in ships' figureheads, furniture, buildings, etc. Some small iron coils similar to the mane on this object are known from the prows of pre-Viking-age boats buried at Valsgärde, Sweden, and from Ladby, Denmark (cat. no. 360). Also in the mould is the hollowed form for a pin with a flat head. **IJ**

Bibl.: Holmqvist 1956, 39, 51f., fig. 26; Oldeberg 1966, 81, fig. 136; Arwidsson 1977, 98; Graham-Campbell 1980, no. 443

13
Wood.
L. 18cm.
Trondheim, Norway.
c. 1100–1125. Norwegian.
Vitenskapsmuseet Trondheim, N30997/FA448

Stem of toy boat

Part of the starboard side of a miniature boat is damaged. Incised lines indicate the two upper strakes and the stem. The flat base and hole for a peg show that it was made up of many parts. Found during excavations on the Public Library Site.

This is thought to have been a toy, possibly carved by a skilled craftsman. It is a model of a Nordic merchantman (*knarr*), a roomy and sturdy boat which carried freight to England, Iceland and Greenland. Note the curved stem, the oar-holes in the gunwale and the marking of the strakes (cf. cat. no. 2). **AC/EJ**

Bibl.: Christophersen 1987, 56f.; Edgren 1988

14
Wood.
L. 12.7cm.
Trondheim, Norway.
c. 1075–1125. Norwegian.
Vitenskapsmuseet Trondheim, N97259/FU450

Toy horse

Stallion carved from a flat piece of wood; the head with mane, the sexual organ and tail are given special attention. Parts of the head and forelegs damaged.

From the excavations on the Public Library Site where other objects thought to have been toys were found (cf. cat. no. 13). Most of the toys were horses, carved in a more or less amateur fashion (cf. cat. no. 315). **AC/EJ**

Bibl.: Christophersen 1987, 62f.

15
Iron.
Gjermundbu, Norderhov, Buskerud, Norway.
10th cent. Scandinavian.
Universitetets Oldsaksamling, Oslo, C27317 p, q, s.

Stirrups, spurs, bridle

Pair of stirrups with high, pointed hoop, broad foot-plate and wide strap-holder in same plane as the bow; there are 2 knops at the bottom of hoop, above the foot plate; the arms of the hoop extend below the foot-plate. H. 22.9cm. Pair of spurs with undecorated arms and squared neck, thickest at outer end; pronounced offset at transition to prick. One spur preserves its strap mounts with square double-plates and rivets. L. 16.8cm. Bridle with rings of rectangular cross-section and a tripartite bit with short, figure-of-eight central link. L. 21.1cm.

Harness and other horse equipment is common in Viking-age graves over large areas of Scandinavia, horses themselves are often buried in graves. Stirrups and spurs are far less usual and, although they occur throughout the period, they mostly belong to the later phase. They also have an uneven geographical distribution. Spurs and stirrups indicate status and it has been suggested that their presence in graves means that the owners had special functions in the emergent political structure. **IM**

Bibl.: Grieg 1947. For horse equipment see Petersen 1951; Forsåker 1986; Braathen 1989

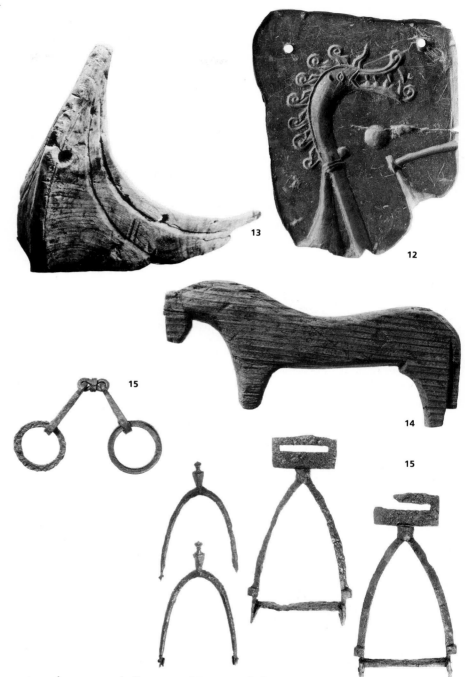

13

12

15

14

15

16

16

17

18

19

Detail

16
Iron.
Width of bow 10.5cm.
Rangá eystri, S Iceland.
10th cent. Scandinavian.
Islands Nationalmuseum, Reykjavík, 2452

Horse hobble, fragment

Bow from horse hobble. Hobbles of this type normally consist of two bows with two loops through which pass hasps; the hasps are here missing. A short chain joins the bows to prevent a horse from bolting. This type, known from Trelleborg, Denmark, and from Norwegian Viking-age graves, was probably in use in Iceland up to 20th cent. This example was found by the river Rangá, and is probably from a Viking-age cemetery.   **VÖV**

Bibl.: Nørlund 1948, 134, pl. XXXII:1; Petersen 1951, 66; Eldjárn 1956, 260–62

17
Gilt copper alloy, silver, niello.
L. 41cm and 42cm.
Mammen, Jutland, Denmark.
Mid-10th cent. Danish.
Danmarks Nationalmuseum, Copenhagen,
C1063

Mounts from two harness bows

Two almost identical sets of mounts from harness bows, mounted on modern wood. Richly decorated in the Jellinge style with interlace, animal ornament, and a few human figures. The terminals are formed as apotropaic animal heads (cf. cat. no. 34), each holding a small gripping beast in its mouth. The central ridge-mount of one of them shows a man being swallowed by a monster, the other mount shows a woman carrying a plant. These motifs must have a pagan meaning but their meaning is now obscure.

Harness bows were used to secure the reins on the backs of horses. These richly ornamented examples were probably used on ceremonial occasions. Such objects are found only in Denmark. The mounts were found in the refuse from a bronze-smith's workshop in a Viking-age settlement near Mammen church, probably the site of a chieftain's farm.   **HL/UN**

Bibl.: Brøndsted 1936, no. 34; Wilson and Klindt-Jensen 1966, 97ff., Pl. XXXVf.; Graham-Campbell 1980, no. 491; Roesdahl 1980, 49f.; *The Vikings in England* 1981, 152; Schmidt-Lornsen 1986; Schmidt-Lornsen 1990, no. 76; Näsman 1991a

18
Wood (yew).
L. 101.2cm.
Lund (Kv Färgaren 22), Sweden.
1000–1050. Scandinavian.
Kulturen, Lund, KM 53.436:483

Walking stick

The handle of the walking stick is roughly carved into the form of an animal head. Few walking sticks have been found but the simple, almost accidental, shape of this example and of cat. no. 19 suggests that, at least in 11th cent, that they were in common use.**CW**

Bibl.: Blomqvist and Mårtensson 1963, 222–4

19
Wood (maple).
L. 98.5cm.
Lund (Kv Glambeck 4), Sweden.
c. 1050. Scandinavian.
Kulturen, Lund KM 59.126:795

Walking stick

The handle is shaped like a dragon's head, its mane embellished with interlaced plant decoration. The name of the owner—Ulfkil—is carved in runes. The decoration is related both to the English Winchester style and to the Scandinavian Ringerike style; both of which are typified by rich plant ornament. The name Ulfkil can be associated with a moneyer and goldsmith working in Lund in 11th cent. Two silver brooches, one from Lund and one from Vejleby, Lolland, Denmark, carry the inscription ULFKILILU-DAN (Ulfkil in Lund Denmark).   **CW**

Bibl.: Mårtensson 1968; Cinthio 1990

20
Oak.
H. 175–260cm; cross-section 27 × 27cm.
Ravning Enge near Jelling, Jutland, Denmark.
c. 979–80. Danish.
Vejle Museum, VKH533

Framework of bridge with four piles *(Illustrated p. 48)*

The 4 piles formed one section of the bridge. Each pile is of squared oak, trimmed with an axe, and pointed. The length of the piles varies according to the contour of the river-bed. The bridge's superstructure is not preserved.

The bridge, which has been dated by dendrochronology, was more than 700m long and at least 5m wide. Each section consisted of 4 supporting piles, buttressed by a sloping post on either side; the sections were 2.4m apart. The bridge could carry some 5 tons. It is one of many great construction works works from the reign of Harald Bluetooth, and is contemporaneous with the fortresses of Trelleborg type.   **SH**

Bibl.: Ramskou 1980; Schou Jørgensen 1988; Roesdahl 1990a

21
Wood.
L. 60.5cm; 54.9cm.
Junnila, Kauttua, Eura, Satakunta, Finland.
11th cent. Finnish.
Satakunnan museo, Pori (Björneborg),
16962:1–2

Two skis

Fragmentary points of two skis decorated with interlace and longitudinal grooves on the upper face, with grooves on the lower face. They were found in a small marsh 2km from the cemetery of Luistari, Eura. Radiocarbon dated to end of the Viking Age.

The skis from Eura and from Laitila (cat. no. 22) belong to a type with high foot-support and narrow runner which seems to be west Finnish. Skis of this type are often decorated. In the Viking Age this usually consists of interlaced ribbons.   **PLLH**

Bibl.: Valonen 1972; 1980, 41–44, 106; Naskali 1989, 15–17

22
Pine.
L. 93.0cm.
Valko, Laitila (Letala), Varsinais-Suomi, Finland.
Viking Age–Crusade Period. Finnish.
Finlands Nationalmuseum, Helsinki, 13783

Ski *(Illustrated p. 51)*

Fragment of ski decorated with horizontal lines, wavy lines, interlace and an unusual ring-chain decoration; on the sides and skiing surface are longitudinal grooves, the runner is unusually wide. Discovered in ditch-digging. It has been dated on stylistic and geological grounds to the Viking Age and by radiocarbon to the Middle Ages (cf. cat. no. 21).   **PLLH**

Bibl.: Hirviluoto 1956; Jungner 1979, 30; Valonen 1980, 41–44, 106; Naskali 1989, 15–17

23
Pine.
L. 205cm; 194cm.
Vosseskavlen, Hordaland, Norway.
1170 ±70 (C^{14}). Norwegian.
Ski Museum, Oslo, SK201 a–b

Pair of skis

Norway's oldest pair of skis, one ski is well preserved, has a profiled tip, rounded back and horizontal attachment hole. The second ski is broken at tip and curved upwards at front and back. Found in a valley on N side of Vosseskavlen, 1500m above sea level, when the glacier withdrew.

In early times skis were used primarily for hunting, trapping, transport and communication. Most have been found in bogs, the earliest being dated by C^{14} as *c.* 5,200 years old (the Kalvträsk ski, Sweden). N Norwegian rock carvings illustrate skiing about 2000 BC. Skis have usually been grouped according to their means of attachment, but varying types in different areas suggest that they must be classified according to different use, availability of material, traditions of craftsmanship, terrain and climate. The word *ski* is Norwegian, both the word and the skis themselves being taken up outside Scandinavia (cf. cat. no. 21–22).   **KB**

Bibl.: Lid 1930, 161f; Bø 1966, 16; Vaage 1960, 9; Vaage 1981, 54–56

24
Bone.
L. *c.* 20cm.
Lund, Sweden.
1000–1100. Scandinavian.
Kulturen, Lund, KM 66.166:1444, 1511

Ice skates

Skates were made from the metatarsals of cattle or horses and were fastened to the foot by leather straps. At the front the strap is threaded through a hole and at the back it is hooked round a wooden plug fitted into a hole. When travelling the skater pushed himself along with a stick which may have had an iron tip. Skating as known today was not possible as this type of skate did not cut the ice. Skates are common finds and were also toys. Skating is depicted in *Carta Marina* by Olaus Magnus in 1539.   **CW**

Bibl.: Cinthio 1976, 383ff.

21

23

24

25

25   Iron.
H. 4.3cm; 3.8cm.
Holter, Nes, Akershus, Norway.
9th cent. Scandinavian.
Universitetets Oldsaksamling, Oslo, C10271

Two crampons

Iron rods, with turned up ends, the central part is hammered flat and the underside produces a short spike. Found in a male grave which also contained horse equipment. Crampons (sometimes known as calkins) were used by men and horses when travelling over ice and snow.   **IM**

Bibl.: Petersen 1951, 62–66

26   Gold, silver, semi-precious stones, glass.
Total weight of metal 2.548kg.
Hon, Øvre Eiker, Buskerud, Norway.
2nd half of 9th cent.
Universitetets Oldsaksamling, Oslo, C719–51,
12210–11, 13451–54, 14473–4, 14616–17,
30259

The Hon hoard   *(Illustrated p. 91)*

a Trefoil brooch, originally a mount, with squared arms. It consists of a convex gold plate covered with gold foliate decoration, in the centre is a trefoil. The arms are divided into 3 fields by filigree wires. Each central field has 3 leaves seen from above; the outer fields have S-shaped tendrils. The borders of the central field are nielloed and the other borders are of filigree. L. 11cm. *b* Neck- and arm-rings. Large neck-ring twisted from 3 rods expanding into 5 knops decorated with punched circles; diam. 31cm. Neck-ring plaited from 6 thin rods, diam. 24.5cm. Arm-ring of 3 bulky rods, diam. 8cm. Arm-ring of 5 plaited rods, diam. 9cm. Arm-ring of a single gold rod, diam. 7cm. All the rings are closed with knots. *c* 2 finger-rings with geometric decoration and glass inlay in the centre; one of twisted double gold rod. *d* 6 gold beads, 5 with filigree decoration, one

smooth and faceted. *e* 25 gold pendants: 8 flat with filigree of varying patterns; the largest has 4 inward facing masks at the edges joined by curved bands which define four fields—all in filigree: diam. 4.2–2.3cm. 8 are circular, decorated with filigree (7 with geometric patterns, 1 with animal ornament); the 3 smallest had stone or glass inlays in the centre; only one survives; diam. 1.4cm. 2 oval with back plate, bordered with filigree spirals; one set with an antique carnelian engraved with a male figure; l. 2–4cm. 3 circular with high rim; plate pierced with 9 holes in form of cross; diam. 1.5cm. Pendant in the shape of a coiled snake, diam. 2.5cm. Circular, domed jewel with cloisonné garnets; diam. 2cm. Cruciform filigree-decorated pendant, l. 2.5cm. Circular jewel with double-beaded rim, inlay now missing; 2 loops on each side; Greek inscription on the back; diam. 2.2cm. Square fragment with filigree, 1.2cm. *f* Silver pendants: 2 trapezoidal with animal figures, l. 1.9cm. 7 cut from strips; edged with interlace, with animal ornament in central field. *g* 2 gold tubes: one, with filigree and 2 loops, is open at the ends, l. 4.2cm. The other closed at one end, l. 4.2cm. *h* 120 beads, mostly glass but 7 with gold foil. Most of single colours. Some of hardstone; some threaded on small rings of gold or silver wire. *i* 20 gold and silver coins, all with loops for suspension. Many of the silver coins are gilded: 1 E Roman, 2 Byzantine, 1 Merovingian, 10 Arabic, 5 Carolingian, 1 Anglo-Saxon. The earliest coin is that from the Eastern Roman Empire, 354/7; the latest are Byzantine, Arabic, and Frankish from *c.* 850.

The Hon hoard was discovered in a bog, appearing in several parcels in the 19th cent. It is the largest Viking-age gold hoard to have been found in Scandinavia and illustrates the far-flung activities of the Vikings. All the objects in this hoard are of the highest quality. The brooch (*a*) is of the highest quality of Carolingian gold work. Only a few of the objects are of Scandinavian workmanship. They include the Borre-style mounts (*f*). The large neck-rings (*b*) were probably made in Russia. The neck-ring (*e*) is probably Anglo-Saxon. The small gold tubes (*g*) probably come from the same context as the gems shown in *e*. The coins show similar widespread connections and the composition of the hoard supports the possibility that it

was part of the ransom exacted by the Vikings in 858 from the abbey of St Denis near Paris.   **IM**

Bibl.: Grieg 1929; Arbman 1937, 151, 183–89, Taf. 48, 60; Skaare 1976, no. 33; Graham-Campbell 1980, no. 486; Heyerdahl-Larsen 1981; Skaare 1988

27   Silver, gold, gilt silver, niello.
Weight 1.4kg.
Vårby, Huddinge, Södermanland, Sweden.
10th cent. Scandinavian, E European, Islamic.
Statens Historiska Museum, Stockholm, 4516

Vårby hoard   *(Illustrated p. 79)*

a 2 rings from ring-headed pins, cast and worked silver with filigree decoration on gold foil inlays, and niello on the knops, diam. 13.5cm, 11.4cm. *b* 19 square belt-mounts with plant decoration in relief, cast silver gilt, l. 4.2cm. *c* circular brooch with openwork animal ornament, gilt, silver gilt, diam. 9.0cm. *d* 41 beads of foil, filigree and granulation, silver. *e* 9 pendants with openwork animal ornament, cast, silver gilt, 3.6–4.5cm. *f* 4 onion-shaped belt mounts converted into pendants, secondarily riveted loops, cast silver, with gilded relief decoration and niello, l. (without loop) 2.8–2.9cm. *g* 1 tongue-shaped belt-mount converted into pendant with secondarily riveted loop, cast silver with traces of gilding, l. (without loop) 5.0cm. *h* 6 Islamic and pseudo-Islamic coins, silver, secondarily gilded.

The Vårby hoard, which was concealed in a wood near the sailing route to Birka, must have belonged to a family with far reaching contacts. The ring-headed pins (*a*) were made in Scandinavia modelled on British prototypes and were used for fastening a man's cloak. The mounts from his belt are oriental (cf. cat. no. 132). The woman's outer garment must have been held together by a Scandinavian brooch (*c*) decorated in Borre style. On her neck or breast she wore Slav and western-inspired Scandinavian beads (*d*), Scandinavian pendants with Borre style decoration (*e*) (cf. cat. no. 304), and oriental belt mounts and coins converted into pendants (*f–h*). All the coins are of oriental character but four have crosses, showing that they were not minted in the Caliphate, but somewhere in E Europe. Some of the belt mounts were made within the Caliphate—some outside it.   **IJ**

Bibl.: B.E. & H. Hildebrand 1878, 3ff., pl. 1–2; Wilson and Klindt-Jensen 1966, 93, 118, pl. 32 a–b, d; Graham-Campbell 1980 no. 163, 352; Rispling 1987, 75ff., fig. 1

28

Whale bone.
L. 33cm.
Bleik, Andøy, Nordland, Norway.
Prob. 8th cent. Norwegian.
Tromsø Museum, Ts3538a

Graffito of a ship

Roughly cut piece of whale bone. A ship is scratched on the naturally curved upper face. The stem and stern are steep and high and the strakes run up to them. Wavy lines and possibly a stem are scratched above the ship. The piece is cut and damaged, and there are the beginnings of a bored hole in the centre.

Found during ditch-digging, with a bead and 17 (mostly larger) pieces of whale bone which are probably raw material for tools.

GSM

Bibl.: Christensen 1988, 15f.

28

29

Bronze.
L. 7.8cm.
Lamøya, Kaupang, Tjølling, Vestfold, Norway.
9th cent. Scandinavian.
Universitetets Oldsaksamling, Oslo, C27220n

Animal-shaped brooch in Oseberg style

Animal-shaped brooch in Oseberg style. Animal in profile, with long neck, head bent forward. Long lappet and tongue. Foreleg with pear-shaped hip; the hindquarters expand into a pattern of interlaced ribbons. Broken and repaired in Viking Age. From a female inhumation.

IM

Bibl.: Wilson and Klindt-Jensen 1966, 78, pl. XXIIId; Graham-Campbell 1980, no. 149; Blindheim, Heyerdahl-Larsen, Tollnes 1981, 216, Pl. 64

29

30

Copper alloy.
L. 9.1cm.
Lisbjerg (near Århus), Jutland, Denmark.
9th cent. Danish.
Danmarks Nationalmuseum, Copenhagen,
C11331

Oval brooch with gripping beasts

One of two almost identical brooches from Lisbjerg. The upper surface is divided into 12 fields, the 8 largest decorated with gripping beasts, characteristic of 9th-cent. art. Viking-age oval brooches were usually of standard design and stereotyped decoration (cf. cat. no. 101). The brooches from Lisbjerg are exceptions and unique.

HL

Bibl.: Wilson and Klindt-Jensen 1966, Pl. XXIVa *et passim*; Graham-Campbell 1980, no. 487; *The Vikings in England*, 1981, 33f.

31

Nielloed silver-gilt.
L. 20.4cm.
Birka, grave 561, Uppland, Sweden.
10th cent. Scandinavian.
Statens Historiska Museum, Stockholm, Bj 561

Ring-headed pin in Borre style

Ring-headed pins were used to fasten men's cloaks. This splendid example is of east Scandinavian type with cast, perforated animal ornament on the head and the ring. The decoration is a good example of the Borre style, characterized by coarse interlace and many animal masks seen from above, with protruding eyes, stubby snouts, and small usually rounded ears. The top of the pin is formed as an upturned animal head biting the back of an openwork animal, which has a ribbon-like body and neck, three-dimensional head and fore- and hind-legs, two of which cross in front of the curved body and two grip the animal behind the ears. Two animal heads in profile protrude from the interlace inside the ring.

IJ

Bibl.: Arbman 1940–43, 180f, Taf. 42:2; Wilson and Klindt-Jensen 1966, 92, pl. 31b; Graham-Campbell 1980, no. 205

30

31

32

33

34

35

36

32   Silver. Diam. 6.2cm.
Hunderup (Nonnebakken), Odense,
Fyn, Denmark.
Second half of 10th cent. Danish.
Danmarks Nationalmuseum, Copenhagen,
C6271

Disc brooch in Borre style

Made of 2 dished plates, the upper one in pressed relief (cf. cat. no. 106), with 4 gripping-beasts in Borre style set off by filigree and granulation; the heads meet in centre. Pin and catch-plate on back, with suspension ring. From Nonnebakken—a ring-fort of Trelleborg type probably built *c.* 980.

The brooch is a fine example of 10th-cent. Danish jewellery. The decoration is a late version of the Borre style (cf. cat. no. 169), which flourished for 100 years from *c.* 875. The brooch shows one of the most important motifs of the style: the gripping beast with long, curved neck and a long, thin body twisting back in a loop under the head. **HL/ER**

Bibl.: Skovmand 1942, 83f., no. 28; Wilson and Klindt-Jensen 1966, 87ff., Pl. XXXIVb; Roesdahl 1977, 167f.; Graham-Campbell 1980, no. 137

33   Bronze. L. 11.3cm.
Morberg, Røyken, Buskerud, Norway.
10th cent. Scandinavian.
Universitetets Oldsaksamling, Oslo, C21438a

Oval brooch in Jellinge style

Double shelled oval brooch; the upper openwork decorated in Jellinge style (Petersen type 57) with 3 ribbon-shaped animals with heads in profile. The animal bodies form separate fields; each animal has 2 legs with pronounced hip spirals; the bodies are hatched. A double, hatched, band encircles the base. Probably from a grave; found with an identical brooch. A rare type.   **IM/DMW**

Bibl.: Petersen 1928; Petersen 1955, no. 29; Graham-Campbell 1980, no. 124

34   Bronze. L. 6cm.
No provenance.
Mid-10th cent. Danish.
Danmarks Nationalmuseum, Copenhagen, 5254

Mount from harness bow

The mount is from the decorated end of a harness bow of specifically Danish type (cf. cat. no. 17). Its shape as an animal head with bared teeth presumably has an apotropaic significance. The decoration, in high relief, is of interlaced parts of animal bodies. Stylisti-

cally it falls between the Jellinge and Mammen styles.   **HL/UN**

Bibl.: *Nordisk Tidsskrift for Oldkyndighed*, 1832, 192ff., pl. 1:3; Worsaae 1859, fig. 484; Rygh 1885, no. 596; Fuglesang 1991

35   Red-deer antler. L. 28cm.
Køge beach, Sjælland, Denmark.
Late10th cent. Scandinavian.
Danmarks Nationalmuseum, Copenhagen,
C18000

Handle of a walking stick in Mammen style

The handle follows the natural shape of the antler. One side of the socket is decorated with a Mammen-style mask, the other with an animal. The point is shaped like an animal head. Stray find, 1920.

The Mammen style developed out of the Jellinge style in mid-10th cent. and continued until the early 11th cent. The animals in this style are large and full-bodied, in contrast to the earlier ribbon-shaped animals (cf. cat. no. 33, 191); plant ornament is also popular. The silver-inlaid axe from Mammen (cat. no. 173); gave its name to this style, of which the most important monument is the Jelling stone (cat. no. 193).   **HL/ER**

Bibl.: Brøndsted 1920, 253–55; Wilson and Klindt-Jensen 1966, 119–33; Fuglesang 1980a, no. 98, Pl. 59–60; *The Vikings in England*, 1981, 28, 34

36   Bronze originally gilt.
Rim mount: diam. *c.* 8cm. Side mount:
h. 5.5cm.
Århus, Jutland, Denmark.
c. 1000–1050. Scandinavian.
Danmarks Nationalmuseum, Copenhagen,
C9487

Drinking-horn mounts, Ringerike style

The rim mount has a scalloped lower edge and remains of small rivets. The mount from the body of the horn is slightly curved, with 4 lobes and a boss. Decorated in Ringerike style: on the rim mount are 7 strutting birds, their legs, wings, necks and heads ending in tendrils; the neck of each bird interlaces with the wings and tail of the bird in front.

The Ringerike style was partly influenced by the contemporary English Winchester style, characterized by abundant tendrils (cf. cat. no. 418, 600). The most flourishing period of the Ringerike style, first half of the 11th cent., coincides with Danish rule in England (cf. cat. no. 416–7).   **HL/ER**

Bibl.: Müller 1900; Fuglesang 1980a, no. 36, Pl. 20; *The Vikings in England*, 1981, 173, 179

37
Silver.
H. 4.7cm. Chain: l. 76.0cm.
Bonderup, Sjælland, Denmark.
c. 1050. Scandinavian.
Danmarks Nationalmuseum, Copenhagen,
14190

The Bonderup cross, Ringerike style

Flat pendant cross of silver with openwork palmette ornaments in Ringerike style. The contours are emphasized by engraving with niello. The chain is attached to the cross's suspension ring by animal heads in the later Urnes style. Found with two silver neck-rings, a potsherd and 240 coins; the hoard was deposited *c.* 1060–70. While the cross is unique, several chains with animal heads in Scandinavian styles are known from which Thor's hammers and crosses are suspended (cf. cat. no. 493). **FL**

Bibl.: Kielland 1927, 53; Skovmand 1942, 155ff.; Holmqvist 1963, 9f.; Fuglesang 1980, 102, no. 31; *Danmarks middelalderlige skattefund*, 1991

38
Bronze.
L. 5.3cm.
Roskilde, Sjælland, Denmark.
2nd half of 11th cent. Scandinavian.
Danmarks Nationalmuseum, Copenhagen,
D4698

Brooch in Urnes style

The brooch is an openwork cast represent-ation of a large, slender animal caught up in plant fronds. The animal has an elongated head, pointed-oval eye, long neck-lappet and pronounced spiral at the hip. The brooch is a typical example of the Urnes style, the last of the Viking-age art styles, which flourished in 2nd half of the 11th cent.; it is named after the wooden sculptures at Urnes, Norway. It is also a good example of the so-called Urnes brooches which are found throughout Scan-dinavia (cf. cat. no. 588–589). **FL/ER**

Bibl.: Wilson and Klindt-Jensen 1966, chapter VII; Fug-lesang 1981a; Fuglesang 1981b; Lindahl 1982

39
Silver.
Diam. 15.1cm.
Tuukkala, Mikkeli (St Michel), Savo, Finland.
c. 1200. Finnish.
Finlands Nationalmuseum, Helsinki, 2481:90

Penannular brooch

The brooch is of sheet silver with flat ring and longitudinal ridge; it is decorated with stylized acanthus, interlace, straight lines and zig-zags in rocked-line technique.

The decoration on the brooch is typical of 12th-cent. finds from east Finland including pointed-oval and penannular brooches in bronze, finger-rings, ear-rings, belt mounts, knife scabbards and handles (cf. cat. no. 221), and objects of bone, birch-bark, and wood. Only a few objects with acanthus decoration are known from west Finland but the reason for this may be that furnished graves were uncommon there as early as the mid-12th cent. **PLLH**

Bibl.: Strandberg 1938; Nordman 1945, 228–32; Lehtosalo-Hilander 1988, 27–30

40
Pine.
H. 154cm.
Torpo church, Hallingdal, Norway.
c. 1100. Norwegian.
Universitetets Oldsaksamling, Oslo, C.10814

Fragment of stave-church portal

This cut-down fragment is an edge-mould-ing originally set against the flat frame of the doorway. The plank is in flat relief, without detail or modelling. The decoration consists of slender winged dragons with Urnes-style heads, the bodies in open loops.

Discovered when the stave-church was demolished in 1880. It presumably belonged to an earlier church. Stylistically it belongs to the transition between Urnes and Romanesque. **EBH**

Bibl.: Blindheim 1965; Hauglid 1973; *Norges Kirker, Buskerud* I, 1981, 118

37

38

39

40

41

41

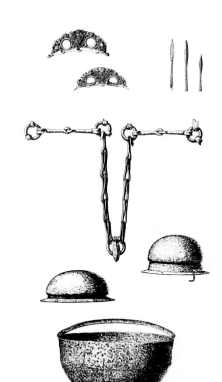

41

Iron and copper.
H. 49cm.
Arnafjord church, Hafslo, Sogn og Fjordane, Norway.
c. 1150? Norwegian.
Historisk Museum, Bergen, MA281A

Lock plate

Perforated iron plates riveted to a copper base. In the centre a 3-stepped, raised key-hole plate surrounded by perforated iron sheets decorated with dragons, lions and geometric ornament. A copper plate shows a contrasting colour through the perforations. From the main plate a series of spurs take the form of dragons' heads, crosses and C-shaped curls; all with punched decoration.

The mount is one of a pair, the other carries a door-ring and is made in the same way. Many similar sets are known from east and west Norway, whereas elaborate hinge-straps are unusual. The perforated iron ornament over a copper plate seems to indicate a 12th-cent. date, and is repeated on many stave-church doors; the spurs are similar—but the motifs vary.   **HVA/EBH**

Bibl.: *Kulturhistorisk Leksikon for nordisk middelalder* III 1958, *s.v.* Dørbeslag; Karlsson 1988, I, 136

43

42

Pine.
H. 140cm.
Torpo church, Hallingdal, Buskerud, Norway.
13th cent. Norwegian.
Universitetets Oldsaksamling, Oslo, C.10602

Bench-end in the Romanesque style

Cut-down bench-end, with various holes and scratches on inner face. The decoration consists of a dragon's head with a man between its jaws, a snake, and simple interlaced spirali-form tendrils. The man wears a short tunic, narrow trousers, and has a pointed beard and fringe. The animal head has a wrinkled nose, teeth and drop-shaped eye. The tendrils have composite flowers. The carving is low and dense. This object was secondarily used as a bench-end but indications suggest it originally functioned as one side of a lectern.

The dragon's head is related to the Hemsedal head (cat. no. 459) and Norwegian 12th–13th cent. stave-church art in general—as is the foliage.   **EBH**

Bibl.: Blindheim 1965; *Norges Kirker, Buskerud* I, 1981, 137

42

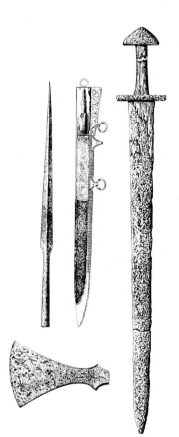

43

Scandinavia in the Viking Age

43   Iron, gilt bronze, antler, stone. Boat Grave IX, Vendel parish, Uppland, Sweden. 10th cent. Swedish. Statens Historiska Museum, Stockholm, 7250

Boat-burial from Vendel *(Only partly illustrated)*

In the cemetery near Vendel church leading men of one family were (from the late 6th to the 11th centuries) inhumed in boats with full equipment for the future life: magnificent weapons, horses, dogs, hawks, households goods and food for the journey in the form of entire animals, joints of meat, hams, etc. The grave-goods are particularly rich, especially in the pre-Viking-age burials (the years 550–800 are consequently known in Sweden as the Vendel period). The status of the people buried here has been much discussed—great landowners or chieftains with an important role in iron production have been suggested—contacts with western Europe have been pointed out. The man buried in Grave IX was an adult. He had two horses and three dogs as well as the following artifacts:

Weapons Double-edged sword, dagger, spearhead, axe, 2 shield bosses and shield mounts, 20 arrowheads, a whetstone. *Horse equipment* 2 crests from harness bows, bridles for two horses, a bit, a halter, 2 rings, 4 calkins. *Personal equipment* Penannular brooch, bronze belt-fittings, comb and case, 2 knives, 2 shoe nails, pendant whetstone, flint, 3 bone gaming-pieces, arabic silver coin. *Other objects* iron cauldron with handle, handle of bucket, flesh hook, nails, double hook, saw-toothed iron tool, iron hook with loop and iron ring, iron ring with strap mount, bronze strap mount, various pieces of iron. *The boat* had 382 iron rivets (10 exhibited). Fragmentary sandstone 'burial globe'.   **GT**

Bibl.: Stolpe and Arne 1912; *Vendeltid* 1980; *Vendel Period Studies* 1983

44   Boat Grave VI, Tuna, Alsike parish, Uppland, Sweden. 10th cent. Swedish. Statens Historiska Museum, Stockholm, 10289

Boat-burial from Tuna in Alsike *(Only partly illustrated)*

The place-name Tuna is evenly distributed as a farm name throughout central Sweden and indicates a farm of particular importance, it often produces rich burials. This is true of Tuna in Alsike where there is a group of rich Viking-age chamber-graves and boat-burials. Grave VI contains a wealthy female burial with a gilt-bronze trefoil brooch, 2 gilt-bronze oval brooches, a bronze dress-pin, a necklace of carnelian and rock-crystal beads and 12 pendant silver rings (each with single beads of different types), tweezers, comb, pottery vesels, crest of a harness bow, curry comb. Some of the objects could have come from an earlier male grave. They include 2 shield bosses, and part of a shield grip, the saddle bow and the curry comb. It is also unclear whether the horse belonged to the female burial (rich horse equipment is recorded from female graves). There are also small fragments of horse equipment such as horseshoe nails and mounts, remains of shears, a fragment of an Arabic coin, part of a key and two pottery vessels.   **LTB**

Bibl.: Arne 1934; Müller-Wille 1970; Ambrosiani 1980; Schönbeck 1980

44

45   Skeletons in reconstructed grave; iron. Stengade, Langeland, Denmark. 10th cent. Danish. Langelands Museum, LMR Stengade 2 gr. F2; 8277:549

Double grave *(Illustrated p. 121)*

Reconstructed burial pit which once contained a wooden coffin, about 2.1 × 1.4m. In it lay the skeletons of 2 men, about 25 and 35 years old, the older decapitated and with bound feet—undoubtedly a slave. The younger man, the main subject of the burial, was dressed in a silk shirt and had a silver- and copper-inlaid spear.

The Stengade grave is, like the contemporary grave from Lejre, Sjælland, one of the few definite archaeological proofs of human sacrifices associated with burial of high-status Vikings. The Arab, Ibn Fadlan, wrote an eye-witness account of human sacrifice at a Viking chieftain's burial on the Volga in the 920s.   **JS**

Bibl.: Skaarup 1976

46

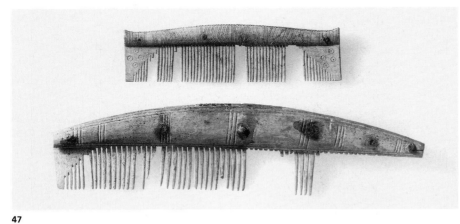

47

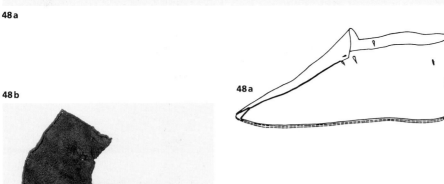

48 a

48 b

48 a

48 b

46
Bronze.
Diam. 21.5cm.
Hørning, N Jutland, Denmark.
Mid-10th cent. West European.
Danmarks Nationalmuseum, Copenhagen,
C31306

Wash basin

Basin of thin, bronze sheet with incised Scandinavian decoration on base. From a rich female grave where it stood on a small table. Archaeological discoveries of wash basins, decorated combs, tweezers and ear-scrapers show that personal hygiene was regarded as important.   **HL/UN**

Bibl.: Krogh and Voss 1961; Müller-Wille 1987, 65ff., catalogue 62ff.; Voss 1991

47
Horn (possibly of elk), iron rivets.
L. 19.7cm.
Birka (Black earth), Uppland, Sweden.
9th–10th cent. Scandinavian.
Statens Historiska Museum, Stockholm,
5208:676, 763

Two combs

In the Viking Age combs were made from whatever antler was most accessible: red deer, elk, reindeer. In Birka elk was most commonly used. Before *c.* 1000 almost all combs were single-sided; double-sided combs only became common later. Long, single-sided combs with broad, slightly-curved connecting-plates and double-contour decoration are particularly characteristic of the 9th century; shorter combs with narrower but more curved connecting-plates, without contour decoration, characterize the 10th century types. Both types were, however, made at the same time and had a wide distribution outside Scandinavia from the British Isles to Russia (cf. cat. no. 97, 271, 376, 578).   **IJ**

Bibl.: Unpublished. On combs from Birka, see Ambrosiani 1981

48
Leather.
a 55 × 12cm; *b* 19 × 17cm.
Haithabu (settlement excavation), Germany.
9th/10th cent. Local.
Archäologisches Landesmuseum, Schleswig

Two shoes

a half-shoe for adult, with seam on front and side (type 4 GvW); *b* half-shoe for child, laced (type 2 GvW), with 6 lace holes.

Goatskin was used for most of the shoes at Haithabu, and variations in the 117 shoes studied there show differences in fashion and social status.

IU

Bibl.: Groenman van-Waateringe 1984

---

49   *a* Clay, *b* soapstone, *c* amber.
Diam. *a* 3.1cm; 3.9cm; 4.4cm.
Birka (Black earth), Uppland, Sweden.
9th–10th cent. Scandinavian and SE Baltic.
Statens Historiska Museum, Stockholm, 1865, 1922, 1949

Three spindle-whorls

a Biconical; *b* discoid, decorated with simple loops around perforation; *c* hemispherical with encircling lines; red amber, shaped by trimming and turning. Spindle-whorls were mounted on iron or wooden spindles and are basically weights which facilitate the spinning motion when making thread; varying weights were used for different materials. They were widely distributed. Generally soapstone examples are from Norway and west Sweden, amber from the southern Baltic. Spindle whorls *b* and *c* may have been made in Birka itself from imported material. Biconical spindle-whorls mainly came from the west Baltic Slav area.

IJ

Bibl.: Unpublished. On spindle-whorls, see Gabriel 1988, 209ff., 245ff., 255ff., Abb. 42–45, 56, 60–63

---

50   Whale bone.
L. 91.5cm.
Grytøy, Trondenes, Troms, Norway.
9th cent. Norwegian.
Historisk Museum, Bergen, B274

Weaving batten

Double-edged, with marked transition from blade to handle. Weaving battens (or 'swords') were used to push the weft together when weaving on upright looms. They are mostly of iron but whale bone was used in Norway; some have a simple decoration at the transition between blade and handle, or on the blade itself.

SK

Bibl.: Petersen 1951; Sjøvold 1974

---

51   Horn, probably elk.
L. 4.1cm.
Birka (Black earth), Uppland, Sweden.
9th-10th cent. Scandinavian.
Statens Historiska Museum, Stockholm,
5208: 1644

Weaving tablet

Weaving tablets were used to produce braids for decorating Migration-period and later dress. In the Viking Age these braids were often embellished with gold or silver thread, and many were imported from the East (cf. cat. no. 174).

IJ

Bibl.: Unpublished. On weaving tablets from Birka, cf. Geijer 1938, 76ff.

---

52   Bronze, iron.
Needle case: l. 5.7cm. Shears: l. 14cm.
Meløy, Rødøy, Nordland; Kvåle, Slidre, Oppland. Norway.
9th cent. Needle case: ?Norwegian; shears: Norwegian.
Historisk Museum, Bergen, B5393, B3275

Needle-case and shears

a Cylindrical needle-case of sheet bronze. Open at both ends and with small bronze ring in middle. Needle cases were made of bronze, iron or bone and have been found in rich female graves, and in settlements. *b* Shears with circular bow with nicks and engraved lines on arms above blades. Shears occur in many sizes, from small cloth shears some 10cm long, to sheep-shearing shears 38cm long. Most are made in one piece but some have welded bows. Some fine shears have decorative details or may be encased in a box. Shears were deposited in both male and female graves, the small ones being found only in the latter.

SK

Bibl.: Petersen 1951; cf. Roesdahl 1977, 97, 100, 136

51

49

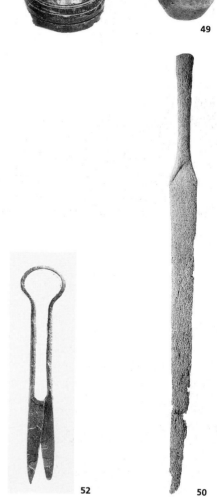

52

52

50

53 Whale bone. L. 34.5cm.
Grytøy, Trondenes, Troms, Norway.
8th-9th cent. Norwegian.
Historisk Museum, Bergen, B272

Smoothing board

Square plate with openwork facing pair of animal heads in profile. The heads touch at the eyes, which are circular with a nicked socket. Open jaws with 3 large upper and lower teeth and 4 back teeth. Plate with edging line and meander border at bottom. Back undecorated. Found with weaving batten (cf. cat. no. 50).

More than 40 similar plaques have been found in Norway, mostly along the coast. Occasional examples occur in Sweden, Orkney and Ireland—all probably of Norwegian origin. They are mainly found in rich female graves, often with imported objects. The Irish example is similar to the Grytøy plaque. They were probably used as plaques for smoothing linen but only one, from Birka grave 854, has been found with a glass linen smoother. SK

Bibl.: Petersen 1951, 334; Sjøvold 1974, 139,254, pl. 60; Graham-Campbell 1980, no. 90

53–54

54 Glass. Diam. 7.6cm.
Granvin, Hordaland, Norway.
Viking Age. Continental.
Historisk Museum, Bergen, B6657

Linen smoother

Upper surface smooth, back slightly concave with marks of shaping. Similar glass balls are usually 6.5–8.5cm diam. They were probably imported from the Continent with other glass products and have been found in female graves or as stray finds in Scandinavia and the Viking west. Probably used to smooth textiles before sewing. One (from Birka) was found with a whale-bone plaque (cf. cat. no. 53). Similar smoothers were used until the 19th cent. SK

Bibl.: Petersen 1951; Haevernick and Haberey 1963

56

55 55 55

55 Wool. H. *c.* 38cm; w. *c.* 15cm.
Haithabu (harbour excavation), Germany.
10th cent. Scandinavian.
Archäologisches Landesmuseum, Schleswig,
Hb72A–B; Hb91A

Clothing: knee-breeches

Badly worn fragments from front gore and crotch of a pair of very fully-cut knee-breeches (sometimes called 'knickerbockers') made of combed wool in plain weave. Except for the front gore of densely woven rep, the trousers consist of two layers of very fine (almost transparent) tabby, sewn together. The fabric, which is woven in a crepe technique, still retains a ribbed texture. Originally the front was dyed red and the back yellowish-green.

The fragmentary pair of breeches are unparalleled, but contemporary illustrations from all parts of Scandinavia show that this garment was a basic element of clothing in the Viking Age. The Haithabu find provides basic information about fabric, texture, weaving and sewing. The technical details indicate that breeches were produced in a local tradition common to the Scandinavian peoples, and were not, as previously assumed, an innovation from the Orient. IH

Bibl.: Hägg 1984; Hägg 1985, 28–38, 163–8 *et passim*

56 Wool. L. *c.* 20cm and 25cm.
Haithabu (harbour excavation), Germany.
10th cent. Scandinavian.
Archäologisches Landesmuseum, Schleswig
Hb56A; Hb77

Coarse woollen cloth, 'loden'

Two fragments of loden twill from different outer garments. The texture is similar to that

56

57

of a modern coat fabric. The woollen material has been fulled and given a hairy nap which gives protection even against wind and rain.

Loden fabrics start to appear at Haithabu in 9th and 10th cent. They reflect a local change in technology, the impetus for which probably came from the West. Loden cloth,

so important in a cold and wet climate, was
soon a dominant feature of clothing at
Haithabu. **IH**

Bibl.: Hägg 1984; Hägg 1985, 73–89 *et passim*; Hägg 1991

57   Wool. L. *c.* 16.5cm.
Haithabu (harbour excavation),
Germany.
10th cent. Scandinavian.
Archäologisches Landesmuseum, Schleswig
Hb19

Clothing with imitation fur

Imitation of fur trimming—a piece of
woollen cloth with an unusually heavy nap—
sewn to a piece of fabric. Probably from an
outer garment.

Such fabrics had many functional advan-
tages, but this was not the only reason why
they became popular. This type of material,
dyed in different colours, was also used as a
substitute for fur by the less wealthy for
various garments, and as trimmings around
the hem or neck. The 'fur' is often of a
different colour from the rest of the garment.
     IH

Bibl.: Hägg 1984; Hägg 1985, 73–89 *et passim*

58   Mayen basalt.
Diam. 45.3cm; wt. 10.5kg.
Trelleborg, Sjælland, Denmark.
End of 10th cent. Rhenish.
Danmarks Nationalmuseum, Copenhagen,
Q237

Quern stone

Almost circular upper stone of rotary quern.
Many Viking-age households possessed rotary querns, either of local stone or, like this,
of imported basalt. The import of Rhenish
quern stones to Denmark, which began in
the 8th cent., is one of the first signs of the
economic expansion which characterized the
Viking Age. They must have been imported
in quantity as they occur on virtually all
Viking-age settlements.   **HL/UN**

Bibl.: Nørlund 1948, 125; Graham-Campbell 1980, no.
49–50; Roesdahl 1980, 140, fig. 37; Näsman 1984, 94f.,
fig. 11; Müller-Wille 1985, 91f., Abb. 12; L.C. Nielsen 1986,
194ff.

59   Wood.
Bucket: h. 21cm. Bowl: diam. 29cm.
Dough trough: l. 65cm.
Vorbasse, Jutland, Denmark.
Viking Age (after 734). Danish.
Vejle Museum, VT:GN83,24; 130,3; 83,16

Bucket, bowl and dough trough

The bucket is stave-built of ash; the osier
hoops are joined with a willow catch. The

59

60

58

bowl is of elm, cut in one piece and with
pierced handle. The dough trough is cut
from a block of ash. Containers such as these
must have been in daily use in Viking-age
villages (cf. cat. no. 159, 160) and their forms
continued for a long time. The bowl was
found in the well (cat. no. 81), the bucket
and trough are from another well dated by
dendrochronology to 949.   **SH**

Bibl.: Hvass 1979; 1984; 1986. For the bucket cf. Graham-
Campbell 1980, no. 35

60   Wood.
L. 36.5cm.
Haithabu (settlement excavation), Germany.
9th–10th cent. Scandinavian.
Archäologisches Landesmuseum, Schleswig

Bowl with animal head

Shallow bowl of lentoid form, with a flat,
swallow-tail grip at the rounder end; the
other end tapers to a head of a bird of prey.
The remains of a carved fish can be seen on
the handle; on the base the stand is marked
with concentric ellipses.

The bowl is carved from deciduous wood.
It is made in the shape of a bird's body with
its typically Scandinavian bird's head in the
round; its grip is in the form of the bird's tail.
An object of high quality.   **IU**

Unpublished

61

a iron; *b* iron and wood; *c* birch.
a L. 9.5cm; *b* l. 19cm; *c* l. 23.5cm.
Lund (Kv S:t Clemens 8, Kv Färgaren 22),
Sweden.
1000–1050 (strike-a-light and ladle);
c. 1200 (knife). Scandinavian.
Kulturen, Lund, KM 66.166:1559, 156, KM
53.436:1089

Strike-a-light, knife and ladle

Strike-a-lights were personal equipment. They could be carried hanging from a belt or in a pouch with other fire-lighting equipment (tinder and flint). Knives too were personal and essential all-purpose tools. They were carried suspended at the waist by everyone. Ladles and spoons were made of wood and used in cooking and at mealtimes.   **CW/DMW**

Bibl.: Blomqvist and Mårtensson 1963; Nilsson 1976, 233ff.

62

Iron. L. 111cm.
Lund (Kv S:t Clemens 8), Sweden.
1000–1050. Scandinavian.
Kulturen, Lund, KM 66. 166:2007

Spit

At one end a suspension ring, a point at the other: the prongs being cut from the shaft and bent forward. The shaft has been twisted. The spit could have been used in a long-house of Viking-age type where cooking over an open fire was the only form of roasting. Many spits have been found in Scandinavia, including one from the fortress at Fyrkat, Denmark. Boiling was the commonest way to cook meat, partly because the meat was seldom fresh—spits may have been a kitchen tool of the upper classes. **CW**

Bibl.: Nilsson 1976, 233ff.; Roesdahl 1977, 133, 191f.; Graham-Campbell 1980, no.46

63

Iron.
Pan: l. 85cm; w. 25. Cauldron: 18.5cm.
Velo, Jevnaker, Oppland; Kopsland, Notodden,
Telemark, Norway.
Viking Age. Scandinavian.
Universitetets Oldsaksamling, Oslo, C16512,
C24121

Frying pan and cauldron

(illustration p. 142)

The frying pan is round and slightly concave; the handle riveted to its centre. The cauldron is made of 3 iron plates riveted together: from top to bottom the straight rim has 2 loops and the handle consists of a flat, square iron rod with upcurved ends.

The frying pan is from a burial mound. The cauldron was found inverted; probably over a cremation. Cauldrons, frying pans and other cooking equipment are found in both male and female graves. Such male graves are often well furnished. Viking-age society is thought to have been rigidly sex-specific, and cooking was a female activity. Kitchen equipment in male graves is probably to be associated with providing food in the after life. **IM**

Bibl.: Petersen 1951, 369–80, 419–21

64

Soapstone. Diam. 33.5cm.
Fitje, Gloppen, Sogn og Fjordane,
Norway.
9th cent. Norwegian.
Historisk Museum, Bergen, B3246

Bowl

Soapstone bowls were common as cooking-vessels in Viking-age Scandinavia. They were usually 35–40cm diam. (cf. cat. no. 90), and undecorated, but with rims of many different shapes. An iron handle was often attached through lugs. Soapstone vessels provided an even and long-lasting heat. Soapstone quarries are known from Sweden and Shetland, but mainly from Norway whence there was considerable export in the Viking Age (cat. no. 257, 262, 381). Soapstone vessels seem to have gone out of general use in 11th cent., but in Norway they were used until 15th cent. when they were replaced by pottery. **SK**

Bibl.: Petersen 1951; Skjølsvold 1961; Resi 1979

65

H. 23.3cm.
Næssund, Mors, Jutland, Denmark.
9th–10th cent. Jutland.
Danmarks Nationalmuseum, Copenhagen,
C6829

Pottery vessel

Hemispherical vessel with inverted rim and 4 repair holes. From a grave.

Pottery in the Viking Age was often of poor quality: the clay was frequently coarsely tempered and the vessels were hand made and fired at low temperatures, their shapes often being sloppy. In Jutland round-bottomed vessels were made even before the Viking Age; Norwegian soapstone vessels copied their shape. In east Denmark and Sweden flat-bottomed vessels were favoured, as they were in the Slav area (cf. cat. no. 573). Pottery vessels were used, alongside vessels of wood, soapstone, iron, etc., for the storage and serving of food (cf. cat. no. 59, 63, 64). **HL**

Bibl.: Brøndsted 1936, 87–88, no. 6; Roesdahl 1980, 137–38

61

62

64

65

66
Oak. The largest l. 15cm.
Haithabu (settlement excavation),
Germany.
9th-11th cent. Local.
Archäologisches Landesmuseum, Schleswig

Heads of two oven-rakes

In Haithabu such oven-rakes were always made of oak and were used for raking embers and remains of burnt wood out of baking ovens once they were sufficiently warmed for the bread to be put in. The rakes became carbonized through use and were finally so small that they were thrown away. Many oven-rakes are known, all diminished in size through use, and always without a handle.

Oven-rakes were only necessary for the dome-shaped baking ovens used for making leavened bread of rye or wheat. If barley or oats were the staple cereal then bread was unleavened and cooked over an open fire. The type of loaf we know today was introduced into Scandinavia after rye had been introduced into NW Europe.   IU

Unpublished

67
Iron.
Lock: l. 10.1cm. Key: l. 4.5cm.
Sdr. Onsild, N Jutland, Denmark.
10th cent. Scandinavian.
Danmarks Nationalmuseum, Copenhagen, no
number (1009/72)

Lock and key for box

Lock with well preserved mechanism, rectangular lock-plate, curved hasp and fragmentary key *(not illustrated)*. Found with hinges and handle of a box in a female grave; the preserved wood was maple. Excavations of well-furnished female graves of 10th cent. have frequently revealed iron fittings from boxes in which Viking women kept their valuables (cf. cat. no. 68).   HL

Bibl.: Roesdahl 1976

68
Bronze. L. 7.1cm.
No provenance.
9th cent. Scandinavian.
Danmarks Nationalmuseum, Copenhagen,
22246

Key

Cast key; handle decorated with 4 gripping beasts in defined fields. Probably for a box. Locks and keys for boxes, chests and doors are common in the Viking Age (cf. cat. no. 67, 69). They indicate ownership, and are

often of simple construction. The housewife was the guardian of the keys and responsible for those objects which were locked up. As early as the Viking Age theft from locked areas was probably regarded as more reprehensible than general theft, and punished accordingly.   HL

Bibl.: Almgren 1955, 66 *et passim*, Pl. 22a; Brøndsted 1960, 368; *Kulturhistorisk leksikon for nordisk middelalder* XII, 1967, *s.v.* Nyckelbärare

69
Wood (beech).
L. 17.5cm.
Lund (Kv Färgaren 22), Sweden.
1000-1050. Scandinavian.
Kulturen, Lund, KM 53.436:745

Key   *(Illustrated p. 139)*

The key belonged to part of a wooden dead-lock for a door. This type of lock is of great antiquity and is still to be found today, particularly on simple outhouses. Such locks are always on the outside of doors. Their origin lies in the Classical world.   CW

Bibl.: Blomqvist and Mårtensson 1963, 123f.

70
Wood (birch).
L. 40cm.
Lund (Kv Färgaren 22), Sweden.
11th cent. Scandinavian.
Kulturen, Lund, KM 53.436

Stool

The three-legged stool was common in a period otherwise devoid of furniture and was used in home and workshop. The shape has persisted up to the present day as a milking stool (cf. cat. no. 389).   CW

Bibl.: Blomqvist and Mårtensson 1963, 137f.

66

70

67

68

71

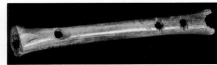

72

73

74

75

Bibl.: Moeck 1954; Brade 1975; *Fornnordiska klanger* (recording)

struments (cf. cat. no. 176b). All are made from the long bones (tibia) of animals or birds, sheep's tibia being the most common; they are very similar to modern recorders. They were blown from one end and the quality of the music can be altered by pressure on a sharp cut in the shaft on the upper side. The Birka flute has three holes, one such air-hole and two finger-holes. Its musical potential has been displayed in a modern recording.   **GT**

71	Walrus ivory, bone. H. ('king') 3.9cm. Baldursheimur, N Iceland. 10th cent. Scandinavian. Islands Nationalmuseum, Reykjavík, 1 and 6

Gaming-pieces and die

Twenty-four turned pieces of walrus ivory, a 'king' of whale bone and a bone die, probably used in the game of *hneftafl* which is often mentioned in medieval Icelandic literature. The small man's figure may be a miniature representation of a god (cf. cat. no. 77). The set comes from a rich male grave discovered in 1860. Gaming-pieces, including whole sets in glass (cf. cat. no. 123), are known from many other Scandinavian graves. In Iceland turned or carved gaming-pieces have been found in 3 Viking-age graves and in ruins from the Viking Age and early Middle Ages.   **VÖV**

Bibl.: Kålund 1882, 70–1; Eldjárn 1956, 95–161, 357–61; Eldjárn 1973, no.1; Graham-Campbell 1980, nos. 92–101

72	Bone (sheep metatarsal). L. 14.3cm. Birka (Black earth), Uppland, Sweden. 10th cent. Swedish. Statens Historiska Museum, Stockholm, 5208:1635

End-blown flute

Musical instruments are very rare among archaeological finds from the Viking Age and early Middle Ages, primarily because of the perishable material from which they were made. Among those which have survived are simple end-blown flutes although there must have been more sophisticated in-

73	Wood. L. 22.8cm. Haithabu, Germany. 9th–11th cent. Archäologisches Landesmuseum, Schleswig

Toy boat

A toy open boat—presumably a rowing boat—carved in hard wood. It fits the ship-building tradition of the period, but lacks the detail which might be expected of a model, which supports its interpretation as a toy. Toy ships occur as objects in harbour sites in a milieu where ship-building had a major influence (cf. cat. no. 13, 315).   **IU**

Bibl.: Graham-Campbell 1980, no. 104

74	Amber. H. 4.7cm. Øysund, Meløy, Nordland, Norway. 9th cent. Scandinavian. Tromsø Museum, Ts7587

Figure of a bear

Shaped like a ring; the foreleg grips the inner side of the hind haunches, the back leg grips the neck, the head curves towards the hind-quarters. The ears point forward, the eyes are represented as sockets, the snout is oblique with 2 nostrils.

Found during excavation of a damaged burial mound with human bones, beads, and fragmentary iron objects. It belongs to the small group of figures in amber and jet found in Scandinavia (cf. cat. no. 75, 410). Apart from the bird figure (cat. no. 154d) it is the only such figure from north Norway. **GSM**

Unpublished

75   Jet. 5.2cm.
Nedre Voll, Tønjum, Lærdal, Sogn og
Fjordane, Norway.
9th cent. Scandinavian (raw material English).
Historisk Museum, Bergen, B6275

Gripping beast

The body of the animal is curved round so
that the back feet grip the nape of the neck;
the forelegs pass between the back legs with
a paw between chin and neck. Seen from the
side the face has round eyes, protruding
snout, and large jaws with tusks. The snout
is slightly damaged. From a male grave in a
mound, the other grave-goods being weapons
and beads (cf. cat. no. 30, 74).   **SK**

Bibl.: Shetelig 1944

76   Gilt bronze. L. 8.3cm.
Viborg, Jutland, Denmark.
Early 10th cent. Scandinavian.
Danmarks Nationalmuseum, Copenhagen,
C7429

Brooch with runic inscription

Cast brooch with plant ornament on front;
flat back with white metal and partly preserved pin and catch plate; beneath the pin a
runic inscription: LUKISLIUA. Viking-age
runic inscriptions are not only associated
with monumental rune-stones. Many everyday objects such as combs, tools and
jewellery have short inscriptions which are
often difficult to decipher. There are at least
four widely differing interpretations of the
few runes on this brooch; it may be a short
ownership-formula.   **HL**

Bibl.: Brøndsted 1936, 108, no. 37; Moltke 1976, 295–97;
Wamers 1984, 77ff., 118, no. 7, Abb. 9.2

77   Amber. H. 4.7cm.
Roholte, Sjælland, Denmark.
10th or 11th cent. Scandinavian.
Danmarks Nationalmuseum, Copenhagen,
C24292

Gaming-piece *(Illustrated p. 203)*

Small half-length male figure. Bald pate;
ears, eyes, nose and mouth shown; both
hands grip the long beard. Two small drilled
holes in back of head.

Similar small figures, each holding his
beard, are known from other Scandinavian
finds in other materials (whale-bone, walrus
ivory, bronze, cf. cat. no. 71, 182, 309, 602);
cat. no. 71 is one of a set of gaming-pieces,
this must have had a similar function.   **HL**

Bibl.: Roesdahl 1990, no. 75; Graham-Campbell 1980, no.
99–101, 513

76

78   Gilt and tinned bronze.
Pin l. 12.0cm.
Høm, Sjælland, Denmark.
10th cent. Scandinavian.
Danmarks Nationalmuseum, Copenhagen,
C6605

Men's heads

Penannular brooch. The terminals of the
ring and the top of the pin are decorated
with male heads. Ring and pin are tinned;
the heads are gilt. Stray find.

The heads are versions of Scandinavian
masks of the period, with grooved ears and
staring eyes. The typical beard of the period,
with moustache, is well illustrated. This type
of penannular brooch is an elaborate Scandinavian version of the penannular brooches
made by Vikings in the British Isles under
the inspiration of Hiberno-Saxon forms (cf.
cat. no. 140). The brooch is a good example
of how the Scandinavians were influenced by
foreign fashions, but changed them to suit
northern taste.   **HL**

Bibl.: *The Vikings in England*, 1981, 29; Graham-Campbell
1987b, 238f.; Roesdahl 1990c, no. 69

79   Gilt copper-alloy.
L. 9.9cm.
Ågerup, Sjælland, Denmark.
10th cent. Scandinavian.
Danmarks Nationalmuseum, Copenhagen,
11869

Women's heads

Oval brooch with 9 knobs; 4 shaped like
female heads. This is one of a pair of almost
identical brooches found in the same field in
the 19th cent.; they are probably from the
same grave. The brooches are noteworthy for
the small female heads; although oval
brooches were the most characteristic Viking-age female jewellery, this is the only example of female features being included in
the design.   **HL**

Bibl.: Schou Jørgensen 1975, 95, no. 71; Fuglesang 1990,
no. 68

78

79

80   Horn (?elk).
L. 22.4cm.
Sigtuna (Kv Trädgårdmästaren), Uppland,
Sweden.
11th–12th cent. Scandinavian.
Statens Historiska Museum, Stockholm, 22044

Tine terminating in a warrior's head *(Illustrated p. 116)*

This cheerful 'Viking' from the occupation
layers of Sigtuna is a rare example of a naturalistic human portrait from the transition
from the Viking Age to the Middle Ages. It
decorates the end of a long, antler tine which
had been set at an angle in an object of
unknown type. The warrior has a short
beard, a fairly long moustache, and hair in a
roll at the back of the neck. He wears a
conical helmet decorated with ring-and-dot
around the edge, along the nose guard and
in four rows up to the top of the helmet. The
same decoration also runs in three rows
along the faceted crest. The end is roughly
carved. Some suggestion of what might be
clothing is carved on the shoulder.   **IJ**

Bibl.: Cinthio 1948, 108ff., fig. 1; Holmqvist 1955, 78, fig.
135; Graham-Campbell 1980, no. 482

82

81

Oak.
Depth 240cm; max. width 35cm; width
at bottom 60cm. Ladder l. 198cm.
Vorbasse, Jutland, Denmark.
734 (dendrochronological dating).
Vejle Museum, VT:GN130, VT:GN130,78

Well and ladder   *(Illustrated p. 137)*

Conical well, built of split oak (associated
with the re-used wall planks cat. no. 82). The
oak ladder with open treads stood in it. The
spade and pitchfork (cat. no. 83) and the
bowl (cat. no. 59) lay at the bottom of the
well. This well is one of seven from the fully
excavated Viking-age village of Vorbasse,
which had seven farms. Five farms had a well
inside their fence; this one lay outside. Five
wells have been dated dendrochronologically, dates range from the 720s to 951 (probably the date range of the village).   SH

Bibl.: Hvass 1979; 1984; 1986

82

Oak.
H. 206cm; 210cm; 204cm.
Vorbasse, Jutland, Denmark.
Early 8th cent.
Vejle Museum, VT:GN130,47; 130,68; 130,76

Three wall planks

The planks are made from radially cleft oak
and all have a 21cm long tenon at the top;
they have been smoothed by an axe. The
tenon was probably set in the wall plate, and
the planks indicate the height of the house
walls. They were reused in a well (cat. no.
81).   SH

Bibl.: Hvass 1979; 1984; 1986

83

83

Oak.
Spade: l. 97cm. Pitchfork: l. without
handle 66cm.
Vorbasse, Jutland, Denmark.
Viking Age (after 734). Danish.
Vejle Museum, VT:GN130,2; 130,4

Spade and pitchfork

The well-preserved spade has a flat, worn
blade. Three prongs and a little of the handle
of the fork remain. Both tools were common
in Viking-age villages, but only a few are
preserved. These were found in a well (cat.
no. 81). The form continued into historic
times.   SH

Bibl.: Hvass 1979; 1984; 1986

83

84

Iron.
Halstad, Ringebu, Oppland; Flakstad,
Vang, Hedmark; Koll, Gjøvik, Oppland; field
under Loftsgarden, Seljord, Telemark, Norway.
Viking Age. Norwegian.
Universitetets Oldsaksamling, Oslo, C21098d,
C24466g, C9039, C24443

Leaf knife, sickle, scythe, plough share

a Leaf knife, broad blade with strongly
curved back; l. 33.3cm. *b* Sickle with saw-
tooth cutting-edge, backward-bent tang and
double rivet; l. 22.7cm; *c* Sickle blade; l.
58cm; *d* Plough share. Pointed, the back with
flanges for gripping the stock of the plough;
l. 13.4cm.

From graves. Sickles are common, and are
found in both male and female graves, but
the other objects chiefly appear as male
equipment. All the scythes are designed for
angular shafts to give the correct balance.
Although the harvesting of leaves for winter
fodder must have been important, leaf knives
are seldom found in graves.   IM

Bibl.: Petersen 1951, 123ff.; Hagen 1953

85

Iron, stone.
a l. (fish-hook) 7.6cm, *b* l. (spear)
19.8cm, *c* l. 10.6cm.
Koltjønn, Tokke, Telemark; Fossesholm, Øvre
Eiker, Buskerud; Uggestad, Hurum, Buskerud,
Norway.
Viking Age. Scandinavian.
Universitetets Oldsaksamling, Oslo, C19724c,
C1272, C7201

Fish-hook, fish spear, sinker

(illustrated p. 134)

a Fish hook; *b* Fish spear with round cross-
section and 2 barbs. *c* Sinker made of a
pebble with 2 grooves for a line lengthwise
and crosswise.

Found in male graves, the hook and spear
inland; the sinker by the coast. The spear was
found near a waterfall in low-lying country
and was probably used for salmon fishing.
Sinkers were used on both lines and nets.
They are almost always found singly and
were used for line fishing, particularly in
deep water. Fishing equipment is uncommon in graves and does little justice to the
importance of fishing. Nets and other tools
of organic material are almost never preserved, but are recorded in medieval written
sources.   IM

Bibl.: Petersen 1951, 263ff.

86
Haithabu, Germany.
10th–12th cent. Imported; local.
Archäologisches Landesmuseum, Schleswig

Plum stones and sloe stones

The waterlogged soil at Haithabu has pre-served the remains of uncarbonized fruit stones and kernels. Many hundreds of thousands of plum and sloe stones (Prunus domestica L. ssp. institia C.K. Schneider, and Prunus spinosa L.) were preserved, and have been investigated botanically.

Both types were important for their vitamin C. Sloes were collected as a native wild fruit, their cultivation had not then be-gun. In the Viking Age plums had reached as far as Skåne, but the dimensions of these stones suggest that all but three were from plums imported as whole fruit (they are all of the same variety, with a fruit length of *c.* 3cm). They were probably blue plums. Knowledge of grafting, plant breeding and diversification only became widespread with the foundation of monasteries. IU

Bibl.: Behre 1983

87
Haithabu (harbour excavation),
Germany.
9th–11th cent. Local.
Archäologisches Landesmuseum, Schleswig

Animal bones

Most of the bones found in the harbour were refuse from meals, although both domestic and wild species were found. At Haithabu, pigs and cattle were the most common food-animals, followed by sheep/goat, and domes-ticated fowl, such as hens, ducks and geese. Fish, particularly herring, were also con-sumed. Goats were most important for their skins. Sea eagles were also represented, prized for their plumage. Dogs, horses and cattle were the most common domesticated animals. Cats are represented, as are rats which here make their first appearance in Scandinavia.

It is impossible to draw any conclusions about the proportion of consumption of animal products in relation to agricultural production, but it may be assumed to be equivalent to that in the later Middle Ages. IU

Bibl.: Becker 1980; Johannsson 1982; Hüster 1990

84

86

87

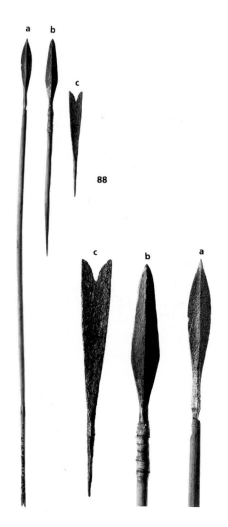

88
Iron, wood, resin, birch bark, tendons.
a Snøhetta, Oppdal; *b* Brattfonna, Opp-dal; *c* Rundhøgda, Femund, Sør-Trøndelag, Norway.
c. 800–1000. Scandinavian.
Vitenskapsmuseet, Trondheim, T11190, T17696, T16477

Three hunting-arrows

a Lanceolate iron point with square tang and sharp curve towards the spike. Birch shaft with notch for bowstring and remains of resin to hold flights which were lashed with cord; l. 69.0cm. *b* Iron point in part of birch shaft; l. 37.5; the shaft was first lashed and then covered with birch bark. *c* Iron point with notched blade; l. 18.1.

a–b were used in hunting reindeer, the bones of slaughtered reindeer were found with *a*. *c* was for hunting birds; the find spot suggests that large woodcock or grouse were the prey. The notched blade prevented the arrow from glancing off the feathers when the bird was hit. LFS

Bibl.: Farbregd 1972; Sognnes 1988

89
Schist.
L. 5–0.8cm.
Klåstad, Tjølling, Vestfold, Norway.
9th cent. Scandinavian.
Universitetets Oldsaksamling, Oslo, C33768b

26 rough-outs for whetstones
(illustrated p. 134)

Raw material for whetstones in different shapes and sizes, mostly of square cross-section. None shows signs of use. Found in a Viking-age wreck near Kaupang, forming part of the cargo. The stone comes from a quarry in Eidsborg, Telemark. Unused whet-stones have been found in early medieval deposits in Skien. Eidsborg hones are known from many sites in N Europe (cf. cat. no. 383). IM

Bibl.: Christensen and Leiro 1976; Resi 1991, 52f.

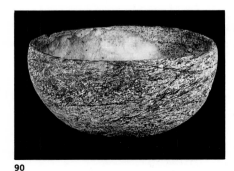

90

Soapstone.
Diam. 57.5cm.
Kollsøyo, Fjellberg, Hordaland, Norway.
Viking Age. Norwegian.
Historisk Museum, Bergen, B11495

Bowl

Hemispherical bowl with slightly incurved rim, the largest example of a common Viking-age type apart from that later adapted as a font in Orslev church, Fyn, Denmark. In the Viking Age soapstone bowls were important exports from Norway and SW Sweden (cat. no. 64). **SK**

Bibl.: Graham-Campbell 1980, no. 40; cf. Roesdahl 1980, 138f.

91

Iron.
Dokkfløyvann, Gausdal, Oppland, Norway.
Viking Age—early Middle Ages. Scandinavian.
Universitetets Oldsaksamling, Oslo, C37463, C37467, C37459

Three lumps of slag

Bottom slag formed in furnace hearths, 25.2 × 22 × 6cm. 2 pieces of slag tapped horizontally out of a furnace, 16.5 × 16 × 7cm and 11.2 × 10 × 3.5cm.

Found on various iron-production sites. The most common type of furnace was one heated with bellows and tapped horizontally. Diam. of hearth 30–50cm. The furnaces vary in shape. The Norwegian ones often have upright slabs or boulders as support or insulation. The hearths stand on earth, or sometimes on stone slabs. The slag was frequently tapped off during smelting, but some slag was always left in the furnace. **IM**

Bibl.: Magnusson 1986; Martens 1988

92

Iron.
L. 23.5–33cm.
Hverven, Norderhov, Buskerud, Norway.
Viking Age—Middle Ages. Scandinavian.
Universitetets Oldsaksamling, Oslo, C37551

Twelve iron bars

Thin bars with blade, stem, and perforated heads. Casually smithed, with fractures in the welding seams. The shape is modelled on large, heavy axes and the bars were shaped thus for ease of transport.

The bars were found in a river terrace and are part of a hoard of 137 bars of variable size and weight. Hoards of iron are common in the inland areas of east Norway, many of them found beside routes of communication. The hoards seldom contain datable objects. The bars are first encountered in 6th cent. and are the *teint jern* of medieval written sources. They are evidence of major iron production in Norway (cf. cat. no. 91).
IM

Bibl.: Martens 1979

93

Iron, spruce.
L. (stick) 73cm. Axes: l. 18–19cm.
Gjerrild beach, Djursland, Jutland, Denmark.
Viking Age. Scandinavian.
Danmarks Nationalmuseum, Copenhagen, C24854

Twelve axes on a stick *(Illustrated p. 128)*

Twelve unfinished, iron, axe heads on a spruce stick. A knob at one end of the stick, a notch at the other. The axes give an insight into Denmark's import of iron objects in the Viking Age. These must have been brought from Norway or Sweden, as spruce did not grow in Denmark. They were probably washed ashore from a wrecked Viking ship. **HL**

Bibl.: Thorvildsen 1950; Graham-Campbell 1980, no. 419

94

Iron, baked clay.
Bygland, Kviteseid, Telemark, Norway.
Mid-10th cent. Scandinavian.
Universitetets Oldsaksamling, Oslo, C27454

Smith's tools

Large smithing-tongs with straight ends; l. 62.1cm.
Plate shears with curved grips; l. 25.6cm. Sledge hammer with rounded-square cross-section; l. 14.7; w. 6.6; t. 5.5. Double-pein hammer with slightly curved long-section, grooves around socketing hole; l. 12cm. Tack hammer with with rectangular cross-section; l. 7.9cm. Chisels l. 12.7cm. File with rectangular cross-section, one pointed and one transverse end; l. 27.2cm. Elongated oval draw-plate with 24 holes of varying diameters l. 14.8cm. Sledgehammer with small hammering surface; l. 14.5cm. Pein hammer; l. 8.2cm. Anvil with rectangular surface, slightly tapering towards foot; l. 9.8cm. Nail-iron with 6 deep holes in groove; l. 25 cm. Auger (for making shafting holes in axes etc.) of rounded rectangular cross-section; l. 25.6cm. Casting ladle with square bowl and narrow sloping handle; bowl 10.3 × 5.4cm. Mould of baked, asbestos-rich

clay; depression on upper and lower side; l. 12.2cm.

This is a selection of tools from Norway's richest smith's grave. The grave-goods also included 4 swords, 4 spears, 7 axes, 2 shield bosses and 13 arrowheads, plus a few other objects. The weapons were probably made by the smith. 3 spearheads have decoratively inlaid blades and silver-encrusted sockets; they show that a smith in a small inland valley was master of the most elaborate techniques. **IM**

Bibl.: Blindheim 1963; cf. Petersen 1951, 71ff.

95
Oak, iron.
Mästermyr, Sproge parish, Gotland, Sweden.
c. 1000. Swedish.
Statens Historiska Museum, Stockholm, 21592

Tool chest with tools

Chest (oak, l. 89cm), currency bars, saws (large saw with wooden handle, l. 61.4cm, saw blade, l. 34.5cm; hack-saw, l. 24cm), 5 spoon bits (l. 44.2–24.4cm), 2 adzes and 2 axes (adzes, l. 19.8cm, 15.5cm; 1 narrow axe, l. 22.0cm; 1 fragmentary axe, l. 15.0cm); draw-plate (6.7 × 7.8cm), lead punch-pad (5.9 × 5.0cm), 4 hammers (striking hammer, l. 14.8cm; pein hammer l. 24.5–19.7cm), smithing tongs (l. 56.0cm), plate-shears (l. 46.7cm), bell of sheet iron (h. 22.5cm), 2 traction rings for wagons (1 in figure-of-eight form, the other with one small and one big ring connected by a spiral; l. 13.6, 23.4cm). The find also includes files and rasps, knives, cold chisels and chisels, a fire basket, and several fragmentary metal vessels and locks.

The chest was discovered in 1936 when ploughing what was, in the Viking Age, a lake; the chest was encircled by an iron chain. It contained the largest collection of tools of this date so far found: iron-working and carpenters' tools, raw material, unfinished and finished products.

The owner of the chest was a smith who could make tools, rivets and nails, and could also work in sheet metal to produce iron cauldrons, bells, locks, etc. He could also cast, weld and decorate bronze. He was also a carpenter, perhaps even a shipbuilder, wheelwright, and joiner. **LTB**

Bibl.: Oldeberg 1966; Graham-Campbell 1980, no. 415–16; Arwidsson and Berg 1983; Thålin-Bergman 1983

94

95

96
Maple, ash. H. 11cm.
Haithabu (settlement excavation), Germany.
10th cent. Local.
Archäologisches Landesmuseum, Schleswig

Bowl and lathe-turning cores

Thin-walled, lathe-turned bowl with flat base and delicate out-turned rim, narrow decorative ridge beneath. Two lathe-turning cores of maple (Acer), one of ash (Fraxinus).

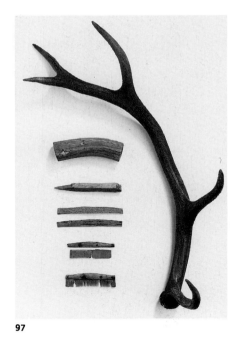

97

99

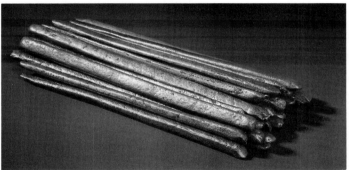

100

98

Turning-rings are visible on the conical upper side almost as far as the apex; a 2cm wide stem survives at the bottom of two of the examples. The third is turned on both sides.

Most of the wooden domestic vessels used at Haithabu were turned, maple being the preferred wood. A pole lathe was used. The blank, roughly shaped, was revolved between a bed of two uprights. A resilient pole—the branch of a tree—was fixed above the bed—perhaps to the roof—and a rope, attached to its end, was looped round the work and secured to a hinged board which functioned as a treadle. Reciprocating motion was achieved by alternately releasing and tightening the bough by means of the treadle. When the rope kicked back the work could be cleared of shavings.   **IU/DMW**

Bibl.: Schietzel 1970

97   Red-deer antler.
Complete comb l. 11cm.
Haithabu (settlement and harbour
excavations), Germany.
9th–11th cent. Local.
Archäologisches Landesmuseum, Schleswig

Raw material, refuse, half-finished, and finished combs

These objects illustrate the making of a comb from a single red-deer antler; shed antlers collected in the forests and antlers from deer killed by hunters were cut up using saws and other tools. The different parts of antlers were used for the varying components of the combs.

Hundreds of thousands of fragments of antler, and (from 11th cent.) of bone, show that combs became more and more common after the beginning of the 10th cent. Increasing demands for hygiene and more craft specialization meant that combs were made at many places using what was virtually mass-production (cf. cat. no. 47).   IU

Bibl.: Ulbricht 1978

98   Brass.
L. 24.5cm.
Haithabu (harbour excavation), Germany.
Unknown date. Rhenish.
Archäologisches Landesmuseum, Schleswig

Bars

25 bars of high-quality brass with 19–22% zinc, all cast in same open mould. The slight variations in weight and size are the result of the method of casting. 12 bars exhibited.

This metal was used occasionally at Haithabu. As the bars were found together in one place in the harbour they must be regarded as raw material brought in as merchandise.

IU

Bibl.: Drescher in preparation (information pers. comm. H. Drescher)

99   Bronze.
L. 13.6cm.
Austnes, Bjarkøy, Troms, Norway.
Early 9th cent. Norwegian.
Tromsø Museum, Ts907

Equal-armed brooch

The middle is slightly narrowed and raised. The brooch is densely decorated with masks and animal ornament in geometric patterns, originally with 14 loose knobs (Troms type).

Found with human bones, 2 bronze oval brooches, an amber bead, axe and iron tools. Probably from a double flat-grave.   **GSM**

Bibl.: Sjøvold 1974, 143f., 205, 208

100   Gilt-bronze.
L. 6.5cm.
Lejre, Sjælland, Denmark.
c. 850–950. Scandinavian.
Roskilde Museum, LEOP11

Mount

This originally triangular or trapezoidal mount is decorated with ribbon-shaped animals in relief. Upper part missing; 2 rivet holes for attachment, possibly to a casket, remain.

Found during excavation of an extensive settlement complex which included a bow-sided building some 500 m² in area. The building and the rich finds, together with the monuments and finds in the neighbourhood (e.g. ship-settings), show that Lejre was an important centre from the 7th to 10th cent. The place played a central role in the cycle of legends about the earliest Danish royal

dynasty, the *Skjoldungs*; both Danish chronicles and Icelandic sagas from 12th and 13th
cent. place the royal court at Lejre. A scaldic
poem of the 11th cent. also associates Lejre
with the king. Thietmar of Merseburg's
chronicle of 1016 says that Lejre had been a a
central pagan sacrifical site.   **TC/ER**

Bibl.: Christensen 1987a; 1987b (with references). Cf.
Skovgaard-Petersen 1977, 36–39, 43f.

101 Bronze, gilt, silver, tin/lead; iron pin.
L. *a* 10.9cm; *b* 10.6cm; *c* 9.9cm; *d* 9.8cm.
Birka grave 556, Uppland, Sweden; Meløy, Hed-
rum, Vestfold, Norway; Nord-Fron, Oppland,
Norway; Tibble parish, Uppland, Sweden.
9th–10th cent. Scandinavian.
Statens Historiska Museum, Stockholm, Bj 556
(*a*), 7571:383 (*d*), Universitetets Oldsaksamling,
Oslo, C 11878 (*b*), C 4585a (*c*)

Oval brooches of type P 37

(b illustrated also p. 199)

'Mass production' was characteristic of the
Viking Age. Cast-bronze jewellery was
usually showy, of little aesthetic worth, and
usually made by copying earlier brooches.
Good examples of this can be seen in the
9th-cent. brooches of type P 37, known from
Ireland to the Volga. The original variant (*a*)
has detailed, three-dimensional, animal ornament. Wax models must have been used
when copying these (cf. cat. no. 102). There
was sometimes hardly any retouching of the
casts made from these models and relief is
reduced to incised and misunderstood lines.
Ribs and masks were often added to the
ornamental fields. Animal ornament is
changed into incomprehensible whorls.
Brooches *b–d* are examples of such simplifi-
cation. Brooch *a* is gilded and decorated with
sheet silver on the borders and had tin/lead
knops (not preserved): *b–d* have no such embellishment. The smallest brooch, *d*, has a
superficial resemblance to the 9th-cent.
brooches but must have been made at least a
century after the first brooches of Petersen
type 37.   **IM/IJ**

Bibl.: Paulsen 1933, 60, Taf 20:4; Arbman 1940–43, 176;
Sjøvold 1941–42, 30f., fig. 5a; Jansson 1985, 46ff., fig. 37,
39, 40. For general information on Viking-age jewellery
see Petersen 1928

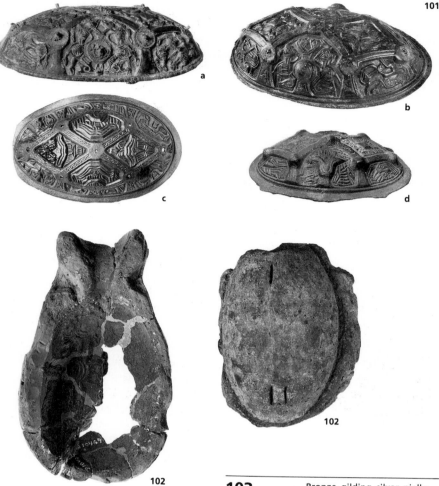

101

a

b

c

d

102

102 Clay. L. 8.0cm; 6.4cm.
Ribe, Denmark.
c. 800. Danish.
Den Antikvariske Samling, Ribe, ASR9, ASRdiv

Moulds for oval brooches

An upper and lower mould for oval brooches
(cf. cat. no. 101). The impression on the
upper mould, which includes gripping
beasts, shows that it is for brooches of 'Berdal type' (cf. cat. no. 103). The lower mould
shows impressions of the textile which was
used in its production (cf. p. 198, fig. 1).

Many hundreds of fragments of moulds
have been found in the market centre of
earliest Ribe, illustrating the process of
bronze casting during the decades around
800. Excavations of workshops show that the
craftsman often concentrated on a single
brooch type; in the interim he probably also
made other products.   **SJ**

Bibl.: Bencard 1979; Brinch Madsen 1976; Brinch Madsen
1984

102

103 Bronze, gilding, silver, niello.
L. 9.8cm.
Birka, grave 550, Uppland, Sweden.
9th cent. Scandinavian.
Statens Historiska Museum, Stockholm, Bj 550

Oval brooch of Berdal type

(Illustrated p. 201)

The brooch is of cast bronze, partially gilded
and partially decorated with nielloed silver
foil, a thick silver cord, and cast-silver crown-
like knobs and quadrupeds. Oval brooches of
the Viking Age are usually simple. This
brooch is an exception; it has original and
skillfully carved relief decoration in the 'gripping beast' style, and silver decoration in a
multiplicity of techniques. It belongs to the
'Berdal group', which is characterized by elements reminiscent of a large crouching
animal. In this example there are four large
paws along the edge. Many 8th-cent. oval
brooches were in the form of crouched quadrupeds.   **IJ**

Bibl.: Arbman 1940–43, Taf. 59:3; Jansson 1985, 31f., fig.
17–18

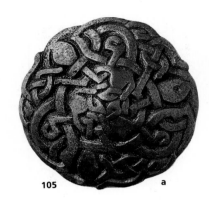

104 Bronze, partially gilt, silver, gold, niello.
Diam. 7.6cm.
Mårtens, Grötlingbo parish, Gotland, Sweden.
11th cent. Gotland.
Statens Historiska Museum, Stockholm, 12151:9

Drum-shaped brooch *(Illustrated p. 201)*

Gotlandic drum-shaped brooches were used to fasten women's outer garments centrally on their breast. This is a magnificent example which was buried as a treasure. It was cast in bronze in 12 parts and almost totally covered with gold and silver worked in varying techniques. The gold plates on the top and sides carry embossed decoration with their edges outlined in filigree and their surfaces filled with granulation. This is typical of Scandinavian filigree work of the Viking Age. The brooch comprises the whole of Viking-age stylistic history from the 9th- and 10th-cent: 'gripping beasts' are present on the sides and the top; Ringerike style (introduced to Scandinavia *c.* 1000) on the 'buttresses', and 11th-cent. Urnes style on the base. This traditionalism is characteristic of Gotland.　　　　IJ

Bibl.: Stenberger 1947–58, vol. I, 50 f., vol. II, 84 f., 170–74, Abb. 141; Wilson and Klindt-Jensen 1966, 89, pl. 30 f–h; Thunmark-Nylén 1983, 77 f, fig. 53 b

105 Bronze.
a Diam. 5.4cm. *b* l. 4.3cm.
Haithabu (harbour excavation), Germany.
End of 9th cent. Scandinavian.
Archäologisches Landesmuseum, Schleswig

Two patrices

Circular dished patrice (*a*) for the manufacture of disc brooches in Borre style, and patrice (*b*) for the manufacture of cruciform pendants with birds' heads.

Excavations in the harbour of Haithabu produced a complete set of goldsmith's patrices—42 in all. They were used to make the basic shape of pendants and disc brooches from thin gold or silver sheet, such as those known from Hiddensee (cat. no. 265) and

elsewhere (cat. no. 32, 107). The resultant relief was emphasized by filigree and granulation. Such dies made it possible to manufacture jewellery of the same basic shape in an efficient and economical manner.　　IU

Bibl.: Schietzel and Crumlin-Pedersen 1980; Roesdahl 1981a; Drescher 1989

106 Lead alloy.
Diam. 6.5cm.
Viborg, Jutland, Denmark.
Early 11th cent. Danish.
Danmarks Nationalmuseum, Copenhagen,
C30697

Patrice

Circular, dished patrice with flat back. From a settlement excavation. Patrices were used in the manufacture of mass-produced jewellery of precious metal. The sheet metal was placed on a yielding base and the die hammered or pressed into it. A pattern in relief was produced which was then embellished with filigree and granulation (cf. cat. no. 32, 105). The pattern on this patrice is very similar to one of the Hornelund brooches (cat. no. 107).　　HL

Bibl.: Krongaard Kristensen 1988, 194, fig. 5; Krongaard Kristensen 1988–89

107 Gold.
Diam. 8.5cm, 8.6cm; wt. 75.7g, 62.5g.
Hornelund (near Ribe), Jutland, Denmark.
c. 1000. Danish.
Danmarks Nationalmuseum, Copenhagen,
C7144, C7145

The Hornelund brooches

(Illustrated p. 201)

Both brooches are made from 2 dished plates, the upper one with impressed relief decoration embellished with filigree and granulation mostly in the form of plant ornament.

a Ornament on the face dominated by 3 loops around the middle with heart-shaped patterns around rim. *b* Ornament in main field in 4 openwork roundels separated by animal heads; there is an empty setting in the centre and in the middle of each field; scrolled tendrils around rim. Stray find (1892), with a gold arm-ring.

The plant ornament shows influence from W Europe, but the technique is Scandinavian and one brooch (*a*) was made on a patrice such as cat. no. 106. The other brooch is unique.　　HL

Bibl.: Skovmand 1942, 67–71, no. 14; Wilson and Klindt-Jensen 1966, 140, Pl. LXII:f; Graham-Campbell 1980, no. 142

108
Iron, silver, copper.
Gjermundbu, Norderhov, Buskerud,
Norway.
10th cent. Scandinavian.
Universitetets Oldsaksamling, Oslo, C27317

Chain mail, helmet and sword
(Mail-coat and helmet illustrated p. 194)
Chain mail: some 85 fragments, most from a mail-coat but some may be from the neck-guard of a helmet. The form of the mail-coat cannot be reconstructed; h. *c.* 55cm; about 4 rings per cm².

Helmet: reconstructed from fragments. Crest with short spike, a binding strip and 4 iron plates. Base of cap encircled by rim *c.* 6cm wide; nose- and cheekbone-guard originally decorated with diagonal incrustation. Chain mail at neck. Max. diam. 23.2cm.

Sword (Petersen type S), in 3 pieces. Only upper part preserved; l. 50cm. Hilt inlaid with silver and copper.

From a male cremation, richly furnished with weapons, riding gear (cf. cat. no. 15), cooking equipment etc. The mail coat and helmet are the best preserved from Viking-age Scandinavia; others are known only from small fragments. There are many depictions of helmets, mostly of conical shape (cf. cat. no. 80). Helmet, chain mail and sword were the weapons of a chieftain. **IM**

Bibl.: Grieg 1947; Graham-Campbell 1980, no. 271; Wilson 1985, 222f.

109
Iron, brass, silver.
L. 89.5cm.
Bjørnsholm Søndersø, N Jutland, Denmark.
9th cent. Hilt Scandinavian.
Danmarks Nationalmuseum, Copenhagen,
C1572

Double-edged sword
Double-edged sword with pattern-welded blade in 3 pieces; point missing. Guard and pommel-guard straight, tripartite pommel. The cast hilt is decorated with silver and brass in geometric patterns. A stray find.

The Vikings' most prestigious weapon was the sword, usually a double-edged slashing sword. Their hilts were of variable shape, material and technique. The blades had a fuller along the blade to reduce the weight and increase the flexibility (which could be further increased by pattern-welding). Scandinavian smiths clearly made blades, but some were imported from W Europe (cf. cat.

no. 214. Hilts (like this one) were usually Scandinavian. **HL/ER**

Bibl.: Roesdahl 1980, 152f.; *The Vikings in England* 1981, 45, 65, no. D12:2. For swords see Petersen 1919; *Kulturhistorisk leksikon for nordisk middelalder* XVII, 1972, *s.v.* 'Sverd'

110
Iron, silver, copper alloy.
L. 87.5cm.
Svere, Lier, Buskerud, Norway.
First half of 10th cent. Scandinavian.
Universitetets Oldsaksamling, Oslo, C4397

Sword
Double-edged sword (Petersen type P). Hilt slightly curved, widest at the ends; slightly pointed pommel. Hilt inlaid with silver, herring-bone encrustation on a copper-alloy base. Found in a male grave with other weapons, tools and horse equipment. **IM**

Bibl.: Petersen 1919, 134f.

111
Iron.
L. 14.5cm.
Fyrkat, near Hobro, Jutland, Denmark.
10th cent. Scandinavian.
Danmarks Nationalmuseum, Copenhagen,
D150-1966 (on loan to Sydhimmerlands
Museum, Hobro)

Axe *(Illustrated p. 195)*
This sturdy axe (top of cutting-edge missing) belongs to Petersen's type H and is from a grave in the Viking-age fort of Fyrkat, built by the king *c.* 980 (cf. cat. no. 117). The grave also contained a knife, a whetstone and four weights. Axes were common weapons and are often found in male graves (cf. cat. no. 43, 112–4, 173, 194). **PGH/ER**

Bibl.: Roesdahl 1977, 80–82, 136; Graham-Campbell 1980, no. 263

112
Iron.
L. 21.5.
Kjølvejen. Over Hornbæk near Randers,
Jutland, Denmark.
c. 975–100. Scandinavian.
Kulturhistorisk Museum, Randers,
KHM 332/82-BÆT

Axe
Broad-bladed axe-head with shafting flanges and remains of wooden haft; traces of textile on one face. It lay along the right side of the body in a grave which also contained an iron knife. The cemetery of about 110 excavated graves is one of the largest Viking-age cemeteries in Denmark. The axe is a common late Viking-age weapon. **ES**

Bibl.: For axes see Petersen 1919

109   110

112

113

Iron, silver.
L. 16.5cm; w. cutting-edge 31.5cm.
Trelleborg, Sjælland, Denmark.
End of 10th cent. Danish-west Slav/Baltic.
Danmarks Nationalmuseum, Copenhagen,
Q1613

Axehead

Large T-shaped axe with silver inlay; notch in socket. Geometric decoration damaged. From a grave in the Viking-age fortress of Trelleborg.

Broad axes like this were normally used for smoothing timber but such a magnificent example as this must have been a weapon and symbol of power (cf. cat. no. 173). An unusual type of axe found in Danish and W Slav areas around the S Baltic. **HL/UN**

Bibl.: Nørlund 1948, 136, Pl. XXXVIf.; Paulsen 1956, 164ff., fig. 86a–b; B.H. Nielsen 1991

114

Iron and gold. L. 14.1cm.
Botnhamn, Lenvik, Troms, Norway.
First half of 11th cent. Scandinavian.
Tromsø Museum, Ts1982/56

Inlaid axe

Axe of Petersen 1919 type fig. 45, but with symmetrical blade. The area around the shaft-hole inlaid with gold and decorated in Ringerike style on the broad sides. Remains of gilding show that the narrow sides were gilt, and slight traces in the corrosion before conservation indicated that the faces had also been gilded.

Found in early 20th cent., in a field in Bothamn on the island of Senja, about 2km from the scree where the silver hoard, cat. no. 348, was found. The two finds belong to the same generation. **GSM**

Bibl.: Unpublished. On axes in general see Petersen 1919

115

Iron. L. 40.3cm.
Prestegården, Østre Toten, Oppland,
Norway.
9th cent. ?Continental.
Universitetets Oldsaksamling, Oslo, C20909

Spearhead

Heavy spearhead with wings on the socket which are inlaid with geometric decoration. A stray find; signs of charring suggest a cremation grave. Recent investigations in Norway and Sweden show that a high percentage of such spearheads were inlaid and that there is a correspondence between the inlaid blades and the decoration on the socket. Thought to have been made in a specialized workshop on the Continent. **IM**

Bibl.: For spearheads see Petersen 1919, 22–26; Thålin-Bergman 1986

116

Iron, copper, silver.
L. 46.5cm.
Rønnebæksholm, Sjælland, Denmark.
10th cent. Scandinavian.
Danmarks Nationalmuseum, Copenhagen,
C9488

Spearhead

Socket decorated with geometric pattern and interlace in encrusted copper and silver. Grave-find.

Spears, swords and axes were the Vikings' most important weapons. Many long spearheads are known as stray finds and from graves. The sockets may be decorated with inlaid patterns, as here, and the blades may be pattern-welded. Short throwing spears are also known (cf. cat. no. 117) but they are uncommon and play no part in traditional grave furniture. **HL**

Bibl.: Nørlund 1948, 137; Ramskou 1950, no. 23; Roesdahl 1980, 155f. For spears see Petersen 1919

117

Iron.
L. 26.5cm.
Fyrkat fortress near Hobro, Jutland, Denmark.
10th cent. Scandinavian.
Danmarks Nationalmuseum, Copenhagen,
D1651/1966 (on loan to Sydhimmerlands
Museum, Hobro)

Spearhead

The short, light and simply made spearhead (Petersen type K) must be from a throwing spear. It was found in the guard-house at the west entrance to the fortress (cf. cat. no. 111). In graves of the period heavy thrusting spears are more common than throwing spears (cf. cat. no. 116). **PGH/ER**

Bibl.: Roesdahl 1977, 38f.; Graham-Campbell 1980, no. 260

118

Iron.
L. 16.8cm, 15.1cm, 12.5cm.
Kjølstad, Sør-Odal, Hedmark, Norway.
10th cent. Scandinavian.
Universitetets Oldsaksamling, Oslo, C37550f,g,h

Three arrowheads

Two arrowheads of normal Viking-age type. A long, slender arrowhead with short barbs below and at right angles to the main blade. From a richly furnished male cremation.

Arrowheads are much rarer in burials in agricultural areas than in the valleys. They were mainly for hunting and are seldom found in warrior graves. **IM**

Bibl.: Farbregd 1972; Wegraeus 1986

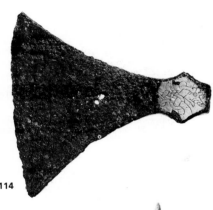

113

114

115 116

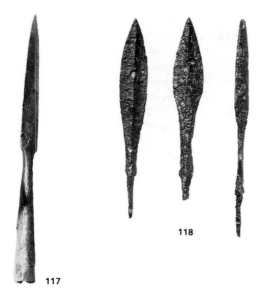

118

117

119

119

Bronze.
H. 8.4cm.
Helgö, Ekerö, Uppland, Sweden.
6th–7th cent. North Indian.
Statens Historiska Museum, Stockholm,
25514:2200

Buddha figure

Helgö was a trading centre from the migration period to the Viking Age and many objects indicative of long-distance trade have been found there. This Buddha, unique in Europe, is the most exotic object to have been found there. It probably arrived during the Viking Age by way of the east European rivers. We do not know if the inhabitants of Helgö held it in any particular regard. When it was found a leather strap encircled its neck and left arm. IJ

Bibl.: Holmqvist 1961, 112, Abb. 18–20, Pl. A; Ahrens 1964, 50ff.

120

Silver (possibly bronze with high tin content), gilding.
L. 5.0cm.
Birka, grave 838, Uppland, Sweden.
8th–9th cent. Khazar or ?Volga-Bulgarian.
Statens Historiska Museum, Stockholm, Bj 838

Strap-end converted to brooch

The mount is cast and decorated with a bird of prey and an owl, surrounded by formalized interlace. It was originally a mount for a belt of 'oriental' type, probably made within the Khazar or Volga-Bulgarian area (cf. cat. no. 132). As with most other early oriental belt-mounts found in Sweden, it has been converted into a woman's brooch. It was found in a 10th-cent. female grave, fastening the burial garments. A pin was attached to its back, and a silver ring for a chain or ribbon passes through one of the rivet-holes of the original mount. IJ

Bibl.: Arbman 1940–43, 310ff., Taf. 95:4; Jansson 1986, 80ff.

121

Silver, bronze, gilt.
L. 8.2cm.
Birka grave 464, Uppland, Sweden.
9th cent. ?Volga-Bulgarian.
Statens Historiska Museum, Stockholm, Bj 464

'Locket'

The 'locket' (previously interpreted as a needle case) consists of two bell-shaped silver sheets and a narrow rim of bronze welded onto the edge of the silver to form a capsule some 0.8cm thick. At the top is a hole and a narrow bronze housing in which are the remains of a silk ribbon by which the locket hung. The mount originally enclosed some sort of textile bag (no longer present). The object may have been some form of amulet, or may have contained some aromatic substance. It is decorated with an oriental 'tree of life'. Parallels are known from the Volga-Bulgarian state and this object must derive from that area, from the Eurasian steppes, or from the Caliphate. Similar items in the East are found as pendants on one side of the breast in female graves. IJ

Bibl.: Arbman 1940–43, 132f., Taf. 167:1; Arwidsson 1984; Jansson 1988, 579f., Abb. 7

120

121

122

122

124

125a

125b

122
Silver, gilt, niello.
L. 12.7cm.
Als, Denmark.
Early 9th cent. Frankish.
Danmarks Nationalmuseum, Copenhagen,
14201

Strap-end reused as brooch

Fragmentary; plant ornament and gilt on front; on back, acanthus tendril and Latin inscription inlaid with niello: EGO IN D. NOMINE + ERMADU(S) ME FECIT (I, in God's name, Ermadus made me). 4 original rivet-holes show that it was reused as a brooch. Stray find.

The Vikings returned from their raids with fine silver mounts from shrines, sword belts, etc.; many were converted into female jewellery or were the inspiration of new jewellery forms. **HL/UN**

Bibl.: Arbman 1937, 151f., no. 19, Taf. 50:2a–b; Roesdahl 1980, 237f., fig. 98; Wamers 1985, 73–79, Taf. 44:1

123
Glass.
H. 1.7–2.0cm.
Gunnarshaug, Torvastad, Karmøy, Rogaland, Norway.
c. 800. Imported.
Historisk Museum, Bergen B4438

Sixteen gaming-pieces (Illustrated p. 143)

11 gaming-pieces of light-blue glass, 1 of dark-blue with brown top and yellow point, 4 of yellow glass with brown top. From a grave.

Gaming-pieces are found in graves (cf. cat. no. 71, 360) and settlements. The number of pieces in each find varies but they are of the same form, apart from one which diverges in colour or shape. They occur in many materials, glass examples being imports from Europe. Similar pieces are known from rich graves in Norway, Sweden, the Ukraine and Kiev. **SK**

Bibl.: On gaming-pieces in general see Murray 1952; Graham-Campbell 1980, no. 92–101

124
Silver, gilt, niello.
Large cup: h. 9.7cm. Small cups:
h. 3.9–2.4cm.
Fejø, (N of Lolland), Denmark.
Late 8th cent. and ?10th cent.
Continental; Danish.
Danmarks Nationalmuseum, Copenhagen,
C1458, C1459

Cups

One large and 4 small silver cups. The large one (repaired in antiquity) is decorated with chip-carving and engraving, gilt and niello. There are 3 decorative zones, all divided into fields; the two uppermost have arcades with animals or stylized plants surrounded by animal ornament in Anglo-Carolingian style; the lowest zone is narrow and has rectangular fields with alternating stylized trees and animal ornament. The smaller cups vary in size. They are wide, with round bottoms; 3 have an incised zig-zag band beneath the rim. Found 1872; 5 small cups lay inside the large one, 1 was damaged.

The cups made up a drinking set. The large cup was presumably the holder for the drink, perhaps the strong fruit wine *beor*. Three similar sets are known from Denmark, from Ribe, Terslev and Lejre. The small cups are probably Danish; the large one an import or loot from W Europe. It is one of the finest examples of Anglo-Carolingian art, which developed in Germany in late 8th cent. under strong Anglo-Saxon influence. The cup is thought by Wamers to have been for liturgical use. **HL/ER**

Bibl.: Skovmand 1942, 93, no. 35; Wilson 1960; Fell 1975; Graham-Campbell 1980, no. 325; Roesdahl 1980, 135f., 141; Wamers 1991

125
Glass.
H. 8.9cm; 10.2cm.
Birka, graves 542, 649, Uppland, Sweden.
a 9th cent. *b* 8th–9th cent. Islamic, Frankish.
Statens Historiska Museum, Stockholm, Bj 542, Bj 649

Drinking cups

Glass drinking vessels were used by chieftains in Scandinavia from the Roman Iron Age. *a*, found in a male grave, is one of a few vessels from the Caliphate which probably came from what is today Iran or Iraq. It is decorated with enamelled birds flanking the 'tree of life'. Vessel *b* is pale-green in colour, its rim decorated with yellow-white *reticella* trails and simple yellow trails around the neck and body. Similar vessels with *reticella* decoration and and polychrome trails are characteristic of glass imports from western Europe, particularly the Rhineland, in 8th and 9th cent. (cf. cat. no. 154*e–g*). **IJ**

Bibl.: *a*: Arbman 1940–43, 167, Taf. 1941; Lamm 1941, 11f., pl. 3. *b*: Arbman 1937, 52; Arbman 1940–43, 228f., Taf. 189:2; Baumgartner & Krueger 1988, no. 15

126   Pottery with tinfoil.
H. 24.3cm.
Birka grave 551, Uppland, Sweden.
9th cent. Frankish.
Statens Historiska Museum, Stockholm, Bj 551

Jug

The jug is dark grey, with geometric decoration in tinfoil, an equal-armed cross at the bottom. Such jugs are known as Tating ware (called 'Frisian jugs' in early references) and are characteristic finds in early Viking-age trading sites from Southampton to Staraja Ladoga. The production site of the pottery is unknown but is thought to be in the Rhineland. Recent discoveries at St-Denis outside Paris have suggested that the pottery was made more towards the centre of the Frankish kingdom. This jug was found in a female grave with a Frankish glass beaker (cf. cat. no.154*h*).   IJ

Bibl.: Arbman 1940–43, 173f., Taf. 220:2; Selling 1955, 44ff., Taf. 2:1. For general comments on Tating ware see Hodges 1981, 16–18, 61–68, 86–94

127   Birch, bronze (fittings mounted on modern wood).
H. 18.5cm; diam. of rim 19.5cm.
Birka, grave 507, Uppland, Sweden.
8th cent. Hiberno-Saxon.
Statens Historiska Museum, Stockholm, Bj 507

Bronze-mounted bucket

The bucket was found in a female grave from *c.* 900 and was probably used for serving drink. The birch body consisted of a lathe-turned cylinder flaring out towards the top, the bottom sealed by a disc attached by a seam. The walls are completely covered by bronze: two broad bands with rich engraving, u-shaped rim and binding base. The handle escutcheons are cast in openwork. The handle is also made of u-shaped sheet bronze, with a wooden lining. The decoration consists of two horizontal zones of birds entangled in foliage, and a lower zone of spirals. It is thought to be either N English or Pictish.   IJ/DMW

Bibl.: Arbman 1940–43, Taf. 203–4; Bakka 1963, 27ff., fig. 23; Wilson 1970, 8–9; Graham-Campbell 1980, no. 318; Wamers 1985, 34

128   Copper alloy, enamel, millefiori.
H. 7.7cm.
Myklebostad, Eid, Sogn og Fjordane, Norway.
8th–9th cent. Hiberno-Saxon.
Historisk Museum, Bergen, B2978

Hanging-bowl escutcheon

(Illustrated p. 19)

3-dimensional male figure with large head, pronounced eyebrows and large eyes. Drooping mouth suggestive of moustache and beard. Body consists of a rectangular plate inlaid with enamel and millefiori.

The escutcheon is one of 3 on a hanging-bowl which was also decorated with enamel and millefiori on its bottom. The male figure is of Insular type. The decorated body is comparable with St Matthew in the Book of Durrow and equivalent use of millefiori is known from the 8th-cent. Manton Common hanging-bowl. Stylized male figures with enamel and millefiori are also known from a handle in the Oseberg ship. This escutcheon is from a male boat-burial.   SK

Bibl.: Shetelig (ed.) 1940, V, 100–2; Henry 1954, pl. 33; Henry 1956; *The Work of Angels*, 1989, no. 51 (S.Youngs)

129   Gilt bronze, amber, glass.
L. 8.8cm.
Romfohjellen, Sunndal, Møre og Romsdal, Norway.
Early 9th cent. Insular.
Universitetets Oldsaksamling, Oslo, C6185

Mount

Rectangular mount with raised edges, one end is severed. The base plate is decorated with animals in profile and interlace. The decoration is dominated by 3 whole and 1 now damaged three-dimensional animal figures in high relief, with large heads biting the bodies, eyes of blue glass, curled tails and vestigial limbs. Between the animals is an amber stud.

Probably from a male grave. Designed for ecclesiastical use, probably a book mount of W Scottish or Irish origin.   IM/DMW

Bibl.: Shetelig (ed.) 1940, V, 61f.; Graham-Campbell 1980, no. 313; Wamers 1985, no. 37, Taf. 17:4 et passim; *The Work of Angels*, 1989, no. 139 (L. Webster)

126

127

129

130 — Tinned copper.
Diam. 12cm.
Vinjum, Aurland, Sogn og Fjordane, Norway.
8th cent. Hiberno-Saxon.
Historisk Museum, Bergen, B7731

Water sprinkler

Spherical sprinkler with handle, from a woman's grave, consisting of 2 hemispheres forming base and lid. 7 holes in base, surrounded by incised spirals; oblique grooving under the junction, triple zig-zag lines above. Towards the top animal ornament, interlace and tendrils. The handle or neck is cast, grooved, and ends in a stylized animal head.

Originally thought to be a censer but a comparable vessel from Swallowcliffe Down, Wilts., England, has shown it to be a water sprinkler for either ecclesiastic or domestic use. Neither object carries Christian symbols, nor are they formed like censers. The function has been tested by a copy.   **SK**

Bibl.: Shetelig (ed.) 1940, V, 58–9; Bakka 1963, 33; Wamers 1985, no. 67; Speake 1989; *The Work of Angels*, 1989, no. 121 (L. Webster), cf. no. 42

131 — Copper alloy, tin, enamel on yew (taxus).
H. 10.0cm.
Unknown Norwegian provenance. (Mentioned in inventory of Det kongelige Kunstkammer, 1737).
End 8th cent. with later additions. Irish or Scottish.
Danmarks Nationalmuseum, Copenhagen, 9084

Ranvaik's shrine

House-shaped reliquary. Base and lid are of hollowed-out wooden blocks covered with riveted tinned plates of copper alloy and solid mounts of copper alloy. Some details emphasized with red enamel. On the front are three rectangular fields with settings missing, surrounded by cast key-patterned mounts. The back has three circular enamelled mounts surrounded by engraved interlace. On the base there are grafitti with the bows of Viking ships and interlace, and an inscription in Nordic runes *c.* 1000: RANVAIK A KISTU THASA (Ranvaik owns this casket).

Nine house-shaped reliquaries of this type are known. The closest parallel is a contemporary shrine from Monymusk, Scotland, with its suspension loops partly preserved. The decoration on the Ranvaik shrine suggests that it was made in the Scottish-Pictish

area. The runic inscription shows that by *c.* 1000 it was in Norse ownership. The relics it contains demonstrate that in the Middle Ages the shrine served its original function as a reliquary. Nothing suggests that it was ever buried.   **PGH/ER**

Bibl.: Graham-Campbell 1980, no. 314; Blindheim 1984; Wamers 1985, 106; O'Meadhra 1988; *The Work of Angels*, 1989, no. 131 (S. Youngs)

132 — Bronze (leather modern).
L. (buttons) 1.3–1.5cm;
(mounts) 1.9–2.0cm.
Birka grave 716, Uppland, Sweden.
10th cent. Steppe nomad or Kiev-Russian.
Statens Historiska Museum, Stockholm, Bj 716

Buttons and belt from oriental male clothing

a Eight cast buttons. *b* Belt (reconstructed) with buckle and about 50 mounts with plant decoration. The man in this grave had been clothed in a kaftan with buttons and a belt with many mounts of oriental type. This is characterized by long, decorative mounts hanging beside one leg and many mounts with loops designed to hold objects such as a knife, a whetstone, etc. Other details show that the belt was already damaged when deposited, and that the mounts probably come from three belts.

Belts of this type were worn by the warrior class in the eastern parts of the Caliphate, and by the nomadic tribes of the Eurasian steppes. In the 10th cent. the type was introduced into the Russian state, and thence into east Scandinavia. Kaftans of oriental style, fastened with bronze buttons, were also adopted by Russian and east Scandinavian leaders. Moulds for mounts of oriental type, including one identical to the mounts here, have been found in Kiev; one carries an Arabic inscription. These mounts may have been made in the neighbourhood of Kiev.   **IJ**

Bibl.: Arbman 1940–43, 249f., Taf. 89; Jansson 1986, 98ff., Abb. 14–15

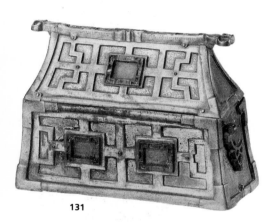

130

131

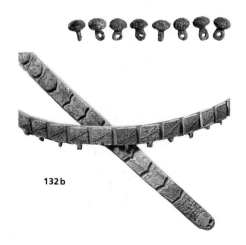

132b

133

Silver.
L. *a* 6.6cm; *b* max l. 4.3cm.
Birka, grave 581, Uppland, Sweden.
10th cent. Kiev—Russian.
Statens Historiska Museum, Stockholm, Bj 581

Cap mounts

a Pointed mount of silver foil with granulation, remains of silk inside. *b* Four plum-shaped 'tassels' of silver-thread embroidery and braids with edgings of silver foil and (?)mica, now lost.

Found in a male grave, beside the head. The conical mount had been fastened to the point of a cap, and the four tassels (originally filled with organic material) had hung from ribbons attached to the top. The cap was at least partly of silk. One other cap with a silver mount is known, also from a Birka grave, but it had gold-embroidered braids rather than tassels (cat. no. 134*b*). The geometric granulation on the mounts is characteristic of the Dnepr region and the caps must have been made for leading members of society in Kiev or its region.   IJ

Bibl.: Arbman 1940–43, 188ff., Taf. 94:1–2; Geijer 1938, 119, 146f.:, Abb. 42, Taf. 34:1–2; Graham-Campbell 1980, no. 336; Duczcko 1985, 98f., fig. 136; Hägg 1986, 66, 70

134

Gold thread.
a L. 27cm. *b* L. 26cm. *c* L. 23cm.
Birka grave 542 (a), 644 (b), 736 (c), Uppland, Sweden.
10th cent. Eastern or Scandinavian.
Statens Historiska Museum, Stockholm, Bj 54, 644, 736

Braids

Some male and female graves in Birka and in some other places in east Scandinavia contain dress ornaments of gold or silver thread. They are woven, embroidered or plaited. The decorations can sometimes be shown to have been attached to clothing of oriental character, but no more definite identification has been made. Parallels to these braids are found in the Russian state and Byzantium but some may have been made in Scandinavia following foreign models.

These three braids trimmed the edges of male caps. In grave 644 the cap was pointed with a conical silver mount of Kiev-Russian type at the point, cf. cat. no. 133. The cap and probably the kaftan in the same grave were perhaps rewards for serving in the Russian royal guard.   IJ

Bibl.: Arbman 1940–43; Geijer 1938, 101f., Taf. 27:1,3,4; Hägg 1986, 70, tab. 7. For surveys see Hägg 1983; Jansson 1988, 592ff.

135

Silver, gilt, niello.
Max. measurements: trefoil mount l. 9.8cm; oval mounts 6.3cm; strap end 13.6cm.
Östra Påboda, Söderåkra, Småland, Sweden.
9th cent. Frankish.
Statens Historiska Museum, Stockholm, 1296

Sword mounts

Frankish sword mounts are depicted in Carolingian illuminated manuscripts. This is the most complete set so far found. The buckle is represented by a fragment, and the tongue-shaped mount is damaged. The broken nature of the objects indicate that they had been acquired as payment. They were concealed in the ground with part of a twisted arm-ring. The cast mounts are decorated with acanthus-leaf ornament characteristic of Carolingian art. Many similar trefoil or tongue-shaped mounts have been found in Scandinavia, usually associated with female brooches (cat. no. 122, 136). They gave rise to later copies which are usually decorated with Scandinavian animal ornament (cat. no. 137).   IJ

Bibl.: Arbman 1937, 147ff., Taf. 45; Fraenkel-Schoorl 1978, 378f., fig. 20 a–c; Graham-Campbell 1980, no. 327; Wamers 1981, 102ff., 125, Abb. 4–5

133

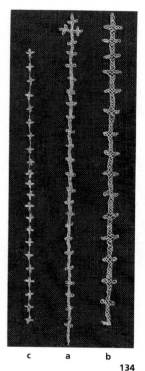

c   a   b

134

135

136

137

138

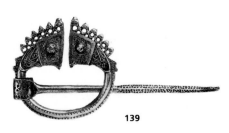

139

136
Silver.
H. 5.8cm.
Huseby, Skaun, Sør-Trøndelag, Norway.
9th cent. Frankish.
Vitenskapsmuseet, Trondheim, T8526

Trefoil mount

Cast mount with plant decoration. Each lobe had 3 small rings of sheet silver below the rivets, one now survives. Similar rivets are in the junction between the lobes. A secondary perforation occurs near the tip of one of the lobes.

Found in a female grave of early 9th cent., with a pair of oval brooches and a silver chain. The mount was probably secondarily used as a pendant but was originally part of a Frankish baldric (cf. cat. no. 135). This form inspired Norwegian trefoil brooches (cf. cat. no. 137). **KS**

Bibl.: Shetelig 1917, 266, fig. 272; Graham-Campbell 1980, no. 328; Wamers 1981, passim, 466, 2.2

137
Bronze.
L. 8.8cm.
Blaker, Lom, Oppland, Norway.
10th cent.
Universitetets Oldsaksamling, Oslo, C6743

Trefoil brooch

Cast brooch in Borre style. Each lobe has an animal figure with a broad mask at the outer edge and a twisted body with beaded decoration and 2 legs towards the raised central field. The rim has a close-set 'nn' pattern.

Found in a female grave. Trefoil brooches were used by women to fasten their shawls or cloaks. The type goes back to 9th cent. and has its origins in Frankish trefoil sword-mounts (cf. cat. no. 135–6). **IM**

Bibl.: Petersen 1928; Petersen 1955, 10, no. 40

138
Gilt silver, amber, glass.
Diam. 9–9.4cm.
Snåsa, Nord-Trøndelag, Norway.
8th–9th cent. Irish.
Universitetets Oldsaksamling, Oslo, C758

Pseudo-penannular brooch

The brooch has a closed ring with cast interlace decoration. The upper part of the hoop has 2 settings for inlay. The terminals are divided into small fields. A large circular setting surrounded by 3 segmental fields is in the middle of each half; there are circular settings with remains of blue glass at the end of the terminals, where they join the loop. 4 small double spirals protrude from the edge;

2 decorated circular fields on the back. The head of the pin is an expanding triangle with interlace and 4 settings, 2 of amber, surrounded by interlace. L. of pin 9cm (broken).

The brooch is probably from a 10th cent. female grave. It belongs to a group of magnificent late 8th–9th cent. Irish brooches. **IM/DMW**

Bibl.: Shetelig (ed.) 1940, V, 66f.; Wamers 1985, 111, Taf. 33:1. For the type see Ó Floinn 1989

139
Silver, gold.
L. of pin 21cm; diam. of ring 9.8cm.
Hatteberg, Kvinnherad, Hordaland, Norway.
9th cent. Norwegian.
Historisk Museum, Bergen, B8377

Penannular brooch

Silver penannular brooch with cast and punched decoration. Animal heads with open jaws and tongues at joint of ring and terminals. Gold filigree plates with domed rivets are fixed in centre of terminals, the edges of which are embellished with 6 animal masks. Pin bent round ring decorated with punch marks. Back of ring plain. From a hoard containing silver neck-ring and gold arm-ring.

A comparable example is known from Hedeby and a fragment is in the Cuerdale hoard (cat. no. 361). The Hatteberg brooch is the product of a Norse craftsman working in an Insular tradition. **SK**

Bibl.: Bøe 1934; Johansen 1973; Graham-Campbell 1975, 152f.; Graham-Campbell 1980, no. 194; Graham-Campbell 1987b, 234ff.

140
Silver, gold, niello.
Diam. (ring) 11cm; l. pin 31.3cm; wt. 356g.
Møllerløkken, Odense, Fyn, Denmark.
10th cent. Scandinavian.
Danmarks Nationalmuseum, Copenhagen, 16370

Penannular brooch

Silver penannular brooch with spherical terminals and long pin. On the flat sides of the end of pin and terminals are gold mounts with animal motifs in gold filigree and granulation; the remaining surfaces have animal-ornament set-off by niello. Stray find 1857.

This brooch is a fine example of the ball-type penannular brooch which developed in Scandinavia under the inspiration of the large penannular brooches (thistle brooches) which were popular with the Vikings in the west (cf. cat. no. 219, 364). These brooches were influenced by Irish and Scottish dress-pins (cf. cat. no. 138–9). Penannular brooches were used by men to fasten their cloaks on their right shoulders. **HL/ER**

Bibl.: Skovmand 1942, 85–86; Graham-Campbell 1980, no. 198

140

---

141   Gold, silver.
Total wt. of gold 291g; silver 2115g.
Slemmedal, Grimstad, Aust-Agder, Norway.
Deposited 915–20. Scandinavian, imported.
Universitetets Oldsaksamling, Oslo, C36000

The Slemmedal hoard

Gold: 1 twisted, 1 plaited and 2 simple arm-rings; 1 simple finger-ring. 1 cruciform pendant with stamped decoration and central boss. Oval pendant with filigree ornament. Ring-shaped rod and small bar. Silver: 7 twisted arm-rings. 1 fragmentary neck/arm-ring of thin wire twisted around a rod. 9 arm-rings and fragments of various shapes. 4 oval, silver-gilt mounts with foliage decoration (3 with loops); 2 mounts have runic inscriptions on the back which read 'SLUTHI' (a man's name, Slodi) and 'THUFRITHR THURA' (women's names Turid and Tora). Rectangular gilt mount with geometric decoration. 3 large spherical terminals of ringed pins, 2 from the ends of the ring, 1 from the head of the pin.

Found in a crack in a rock near a lake. The hoard consists of a mixture of native and foreign objects. The silver-gilt mounts are definitely imported and the oval ones were probably made on the boundaries of the Empire, perhaps in Hedeby. The origin of the rectangular mount cannot be determined. The ringed pin is from the British Isles. **IM**

Bibl.: Blindheim 1981; Liestøl 1981; Skaare 1981

141

---

142   Silver.
Wt. about 1880g.
Sejrø, W Sjælland, Denmark.
Second half of 10th cent. Hoard of
S Scandinavian type.
Danmarks Nationalmuseum, Copenhagen,
17270, 18112-119, 18192-205, 18583, C4810,
KM&MS: FP187, 191, 195, 203. SCB1 4, 694, 757

The Sejrø hoard *(Illustrated in part p. 200)*

Silver hoard found 1858. It consists of complete, chopped up, clipped and unfinished jewellery, bars and coins. Almost all the jewellery is of Scandinavian type. The 146 coins are of Danish, Arabic, English, German and Bohemian origin; most are Arabic, minted by the rulers of the Samanid dynasty in central Asia. The composition of the hoard is typical of S Scandinavian hoards deposited in mid-second half of the 10th cent. Silver was used for payment by weight, and the many small fragments show that even small transactions were paid for in silver (cf. cat. no. 148). The jewellery gives an insight into the many techniques mastered by the craftsmen of the period.

The jewellery includes: a smooth Thor's hammer on a plaited chain; 3 circular brooches with filigree and granulation (1 with 3 pendant chains); 3 plaited neck-rings; 2 smooth arm-rings (1 with smaller rings attached); 1 arm-ring with profiled lower face and small rings; 2 twisted arm-rings; 1 plaited arm-ring; 1 band-shaped finger-ring; 1 crescent-shaped Slav ear-ring. Coins on exhibition: 5 Danish, minted early 10th cent., probably in Hedeby; 2 contemporary Anglo-Saxon coins, Æthelstan or Eadred; 1 German, Archbishop Bruno of Cologne (953–65), the hoard's latest datable coin; 10 Arabic dirhems, some of which are certainly contemporary imitations from the huge area between central Asia and Denmark, as is a big unminted blank twice the weight of a normal dirhem. **HL/JSJ**

Bibl.: Skovmand 1942, 103–7, no. 41; Galster 1964; Schou Jørgensen 1975, 68f.; *The Vikings in England*, 1981, 128, 151–54, no. H2, H10, H11

143

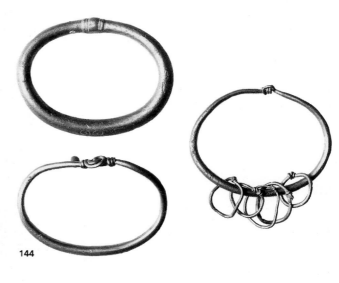

144

143   Silver, gold.
Total wt. 3783g, of which 26g gold.
Fölhagen, Björke parish, Gotland, Sweden.
End of 10th cent. Gotland, Scandinavian,
Eastern and Western.
Statens Historiska Museum/Kungliga Mynt-
kabinettet, Stockholm, 3547

The Fölhagen hoard *(Illustrated in part)*

1 bow-shaped filigree ornament of unknown use; 49 beads, most with filigree and granulation; 19 pendants, most with filigree; 8 complete bracelets with stamped decoration; 2 deformed arm-rings; fragments of filigree brooch, neck- and arm-rings, bracelets etc.; 1 silver bar; 1 gold bar; whole and fragmentary Islamic, German, Bohemian, Byzantine and English coins (originally 1241, mainly Islamic and German; latest minted 991–1040). Most of the coins have been dispersed. In order to give a true impression of the original coin content, 20 of the original Islamic and German coins have been supplemented by coins from other Swedish coin hoards (Statens Historiska Museum, Stockholm, 16217, 18744, without number).

One of Gotland's most magnificent silver hoards, concealed in an oriental copper bottle of the same type as cat. no. 314. Deposi-

tion must have been shortly after 991, before English coins were common in the hoards of the Baltic region. The pendants include two miniature stools, probably symbolic thrones (cf. cat. no. 187) and 13 face masks. The masks are all made of sheet silver, a flat lower sheet and an embossed upper one with the main pattern in relief, detailed in filigree and granulation. Face masks and face-mask pendants have a long history in Scandinavia, but the granulation on the Fölhagen pendants is of eastern type. The geometric granulation on the unique small face-mask pendant has close parallels in Kiev-Russian jewellery (cf. cat. no. 133a). Western and eastern traditions are combined in the filigree spirals and geometric granulation patterns on the other 12 pendants. Parallels are known from Estonia and Ingermanland. The pendants were probably made on Gotland, where the craftsmen often adopted and developed elements from West and East (cf. cat. no. 585).   IJ/EL

Bibl.: Stenberger 1947–58, vol. 1, 196ff., vol. 2, 21ff., Abb. 170–173; *Corpus nummorum saeculorum IX–XI qui in Suecia reperti sunt*, vol. 1:2, 1977, 65ff.; Graham-Campbell 1980, no. 165, 332, 521; Duczko 1983, 343, 347ff., fig. 16, 19–20

144   Gold.
L. 8.7cm, 8.1cm, 8.5cm; wt. 247.7g,
72.5g, 64.5g.
Kragerupgård, Sjælland, Denmark.
10th cent. Scandinavian.
Danmarks Nationalmuseum, Copenhagen, Dnf.
9/30, 10/30, 11/30.

Three arm-rings

a Cast in one piece with a skeumorphic clasp; engraved spirals on thickest part of ring. *b* Circular-sectioned rod with twisted clasp; 5 small rings with twisted clasps attached to it. *c* Ring of circular-sectioned rod with pointed ends twisted into spiral clasp. Found close together in a lump of black earth, all that remained of the bag or the container in which they were originally concealed.

Such objects were obviously used as jewellery but their function as wealth was equally important; the small rings represent additional wealth. Gold was used to gild silver or bronze objects; the actual number of gold objects is small and their value accordingly high. Hacked gold is very rare in hoards or deposits, but these arm-rings, like the silver arm-rings, seem to be related to a weight system.   HL

Bibl.: Skovmand 1942, 110–11, no. 43; Schou Jørgensen 1975, 95, no. 70. See also Munksgaard 1962; 1978

145

Gold.
L. 7.7cm; wt. 24.2g.
Råbylille, Sjælland, Denmark.
9th–early 10th cent. Scandinavian.
Danmarks Nationalmuseum, Copenhagen,
MMCLV

Arm-ring

Band-shaped arm-ring, wide and pointed at the front with twisted clasp; decorated with bosses and stamped ornament—triangles, trees, crosses and small animal heads within heart-shaped frames. Stray find. This bracelet is a splendid example of a type characteristic of the early Viking Age (cf. cat. no. 147).   HL

Bibl.: Skovmand 1942, 36, 41, no. 11; *The Vikings in England*, 1981, 31, 33, no. B35

146

Gold.
L. 8.2cm; wt. 71.2g.
Aggersborg, N Jutland, Denmark.
10th cent. Scandinavian.
Danmarks Nationalmuseum, Copenhagen, Dnf.
130/71

Arm-ring

Twisted from 2 profiled rods with 2 twisted gold threads between them; the plain terminals are twisted together. When found it was buckled, it has now been straightened.

Found in post-hole of a 41m-long building which was pulled down immediately before the great fortress was built *c.* 980.   HL

Bibl.: Roesdahl 1981b, 113, fig. 6; Roesdahl 1986, 65–67, 73–75, fig. 13f.

147

Silver.
Neck-ring: diam. 23.0cm. Arm-rings:
diam. 5.5cm, 7.2cm, 6.5cm.
Illebølle, Langeland, Denmark.
9th cent. S Scandinavian, Eastern.
Danmarks Nationalmuseum, Copenhagen,
11248, 15603, 16429, 19443

Neck-ring and 3 arm-rings

a Neck-ring formed of a narrow band with simple, close-set, stamped decoration and hooked clasp. *b* Spiral arm-ring of partly twisted and partly stamped rod; the ends terminating in S-loop. *c* Band shaped arm-ring with pointed expansions in centre; stamped decoration along edges and in middle. *d* Band shaped, spiral arm-ring with close-set simple stamped decoration corresponding to that of the neck-ring; half of the hooked terminal is missing. Probably from a hoard.

Spiral arm-rings such as *b* are known only from Denmark and Gotland; they were

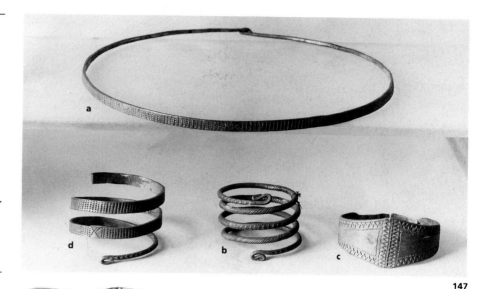

147

145

146

148a

148b

probably imported from the Bulgar state on the central Volga. The band-shaped rings are probably S Scandinavian.   HL/UN

Bibl.: Skovmand 1942, 33f., no. 7; Munksgaard 1962, 97

148

Silver.
L. 7.0cm, 6.0cm; wt. 130 g.
Hørdum, N Jutland, Denmark.
9th cent. Scandinavian.
Danmarks Nationalmuseum, Copenhagen,
16055, 16056

Two arm-rings

a Massive band-shaped ring decorated with striations and a cross in centre (cf. cat. no.

363). *b* Band-shaped ring with geometric ornament in longitudinal strips. Found with another silver ring like cat. no. 145, 147c. Like cat. no. 147 this is a good examples of a S Scandinavian hoard of the early Viking Age in which the jewellery and bars were often deposited whole, whereas those from mid-10th cent. include numerous small fragments (cf. cat. no. 142).   HL

Bibl.: Skovmand 1942, 29f., no. 2

149

Silver.
L. 8.6cm.
Orupgård (Brahesminde), Falster, Denmark.
Viking Age. Scandinavian.
Danmarks Nationalmuseum, Copenhagen, Dnf.
14/48

Arm-ring

Massive cast ring with decoration in high relief; outer face convex, inner face slightly concave. Stray find. This ring is a particularly fine example of this well-known type of Scandinavian arm-ring. **HL**

Bibl.: Skovmand 1942, 177, no. 18; Graham-Campbell 1980, no. 227

150

150

Bronze, lead, linen.
L. (balance arms) 18.5cm.
Jåtten, Hetland, Rogaland, Norway.
9th cent. Hiberno-Saxon.
Historisk Museum, Bergen, B4772

Scales, weights and bag

Bronze scales with tinned pans and folding balance arms with trefoil ends, from each of which hangs a 4-link chain ending in a bird. These each support 3 chains carrying the pans which are decorated with segmented circles. 8 small lead weights of differing shapes: cuboid, cylindrical, square, discoid; 2–43g weights. Linen bag of 2 pieces sewn together hemmed at the top: h. 6.5.

The scales, the weights and the bag were discovered in 1891, buried beside a stone and enclosed in a bronze container with Insular decoration, together with a bronze ring-headed pin. Scales of this type are thought to be W European, particularly Irish, imports into Scandinavia. The chains on these scales are paralleled by chains on Hiberno-Saxon reliquaries. The weight system is discussed by Brøgger and Kyhlberg (cf. cat. no. 151, 356, 357). **SK**

Bibl.: Brøgger 1921; Shetelig (ed.) 1940, V, 155–66; Jondell 1974; Kyhlberg 980; Graham-Campbell 1980, no. 306

151

Iron with thin, sheet-brass overlay.
Diam. 1.1–2.2cm. Wt. when found
3.99g; 8.22g; 22.92g; 31.37g; 39.32g.
Hemlingby (Norelund), Valbo, Gästrikland,
Sweden.
10th cent. Scandinavian.
Statens Historiska Museum, Stockholm, 19802

Five weights

These weights, found with rivets, weapons etc., in a male cremation, seem to form a fairly complete set of weights of the standardized form common in Viking-age Scandinavia. They are formed as flattened spheres, the flat areas, on all but the lightest, carry weight marks: 1,3,4 and 5 circles. The fifth weight is damaged.

Spherical and smaller polyhedral weights of Viking-age N Europe probably had oriental prototypes, and thus follow the oriental system of weights. The weights were also associated with the later medieval Scandinavian system in which 1 mark = 8 öre = 24 örtugar. The Hemlingby weights may represent half an öre and 1, 3, 4 and 5 örtugar, respectively (cf. cat. no. 150). It is difficult,

151

however, to draw positive conclusions about this as the weights have been distorted by corrosion and damage. **IJ**

Bibl.: Arbman 1933, 11f., fig. 21; Hatz 1974, 110, 119f.; Kyhlberg 1980, 245f.

152

Silver.
Wt 0.86g, 0.81g.
Ribe, Denmark.
8th cent. ?Frisian.
Danmarks Nationalmuseum, Copenhagen,
KM&MS, FP 3727.2; 3727.4

Two sceattas *(Illustrated p. 220)*

Wodan/monster type. Archaeological excavations in the past 25 years have uncovered a steadily increasing number of Frisian sceattas, minted after c. 720; most have been found in Ribe and its neighbourhood. A particularly large number of the Wodan/monster type have been discovered (more than 135 in Ribe alone) and it has been suggested that they were minted there. This has not yet been proved, but numerous finds demonstrate a widely accepted monetary economy in this part of S Jutland. **JSJ**

Bibl.: Bendixen 1981; Metcalf 1985; Malmer and Jonsson 1986

153

Silver.
Wt. 0.85g, 1.06g, 0.34g, 0.30g.
Birka grave 526, Uppland, Sweden (1877); no
provenance; Nonnebakken, Odense, Denmark
(1909); Grønnerup, Denmark (1842).
Kungl. Myntkabinettet, Stockholm, KMK
101752. Danmarks Nationalmuseum, Copenhagen, KM&MS, Thomsen 1303; FP565; FP15

Four Danish coins c. 825–c. 980
(a illustrated also p. 220)

a Obverse and reverse show 2 opposed cocks and ships with sail. There are no known numismatic antecedents for the birds, but many Carolingian coins have representations of ships. Type Malmer KG4, Tuppar/Båt A2. Probably struck in Hedeby c. 825. One of the earliest Danish coins (cf. cat. no. 152). *b–c* Obverses and reverses with Charlemagne and the name of the Frisian town Dorestad. The coins show the development of Danish copies of Charlemagne's coins struck in Dorestad in late 8th cent.; they became thinner and lighter, and the motifs were less intelligible, as with all coin imitation throughout the ages. The series started in the early 9th cent. and ended c. 975/80. Type Malmer KG2, KG9b. Minted early 9th cent., probably in Hedeby, and c. 975/80. *d* Coin

154 h

153

with a the cross motif, showing Christian influence. Type Malmer KG10a. Struck *c.* 975/80, reign of Harald Bluetooth. **JSJ**

Bibl.: Malmer 1966; Bendixen 1976; Bendixen 1981

---

154   Gold, jet, amber, glass, pottery, iron. Borg, Vestvågøy, Nordland, Norway. 8–9th cent. Scandinavian, imported. Tromsø Museum, Ts8334a,b; 8335w,ah; 8336el,m,dp,div.; 8337div.; 8338cw,dw

Finds from a chieftain's house,
Lofoten   *(b and d illustrated also p. 148, 203)*

From the excavation of a chieftain's house (p. 35, fig. 3). After an 8th-cent. rebuild the house was 83m long and most finds were within it. Farming and fishing were the most important means of livelihood and most artifacts reflect daily life. But some things are unusual, rarely found in Norwegian contexts, and reflect the high social standing of the site, with long-range contacts to south and west (e.g. the sherds of glass and pottery vessels from the Continent, and simple gold objects). The most obvious sign of status can be seen in the size of the central room, 112m, which has been interpreted as a chieftain's hall.

a Jewel of sheet gold, pear-shaped and hollow; the narrow, undecorated upper part is curved as though to form a socket; the rest decorated with filigree; 2 pinholes at 'bottom'. L. 2.45 cm. *b* Amulet, figured gold plaque, of thin gold sheet depicting a man and woman embracing; found in a post-hole from the foundation of the building; 8th cent. *c* Fragment of jet ring; prob. 9th cent., raw material, English. *d* Bird figure (?swan), amber; the hole between the neck/head and body of the bird is balanced so that the figure might have been a pendant; prob. 9th cent.; raw material from south Scandinavia or the Baltic. *e* 2 joining sherds of a *reticella*-glass

bowl of type Valsgärde 6, blue with applied yellow and blue trails; *c.* 700–50; imported. *f* Glass sherd probably early funnel-beaker type, light green with gold-foil, the decoration of which includes parallel lines, rhomboids and crosses; *c.* 800; imported. *g* Connecting sherds of a glass palm cup; light green; thickened and everted rim; a fault in the glass in one place; a ridge beneath the rim on each side and an irregularly curved ridge above; end 8th cent.; imported. *h* Connecting sherds of the upper part of a 'Tating ware' jug; traces of tin foil; early 9th cent.; Rhenish. *i* Iron guard of sword; pointed-oval cross-section; remains of brass inlay; early Viking-age. *j* Iron sword-pommel; triangular; inlaid with brass in vertical stripes; early Viking-age.   **GSM**

Bibl.: Stamsø Munch, Johansen, Larssen 1987; Stamsø Munch and Johansen 1988

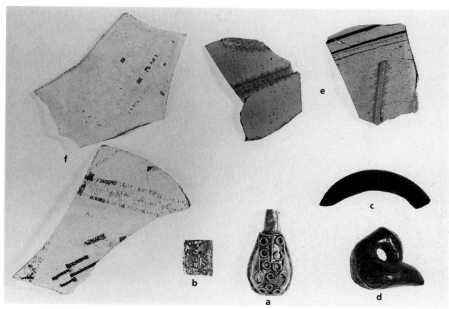

154a–f

154g

154

155

156

157

158

155　　　　　　　　　　　Leather (probably goat).
L. 25.3cm.
Oseberg, Sem, Vestfold, Norway.
c. 800–850. Scandinavian.
Universitetets Oldsaksamling, Oslo, Oseberg
304

Shoe from Oseberg

Right shoe of a pair. Restored. The sole rises
to a point at the back. The upper consists of
a main piece joined over the instep, with a
triangular piece added at the ankle. Found
with a slightly longer and wider left shoe in a
box in the prow, another pair of shoes and
some fragments were also found. The shoes
have many similarities with others from the
early Middle Ages but nevertheless have
their own specific characteristics.

The Oseberg ship burial was in a large
mound (see p. 44). It is the most richly
furnished grave known in Scandinavia with
an enormous number of wooden objects.
The wooden carvings alone have an area of
12–15m², and show great stylistic and artistic
variation. The burial of two females—probably a queen and a slave—is dated *c.* 800–
850. The identity of the supposed queen is
unknown.

The ship was 21.5m long, with mast, oars
and other equipment. Behind the mast was a
wooden burial chamber which contained
many objects. The dead queen was placed on
the bed. The chamber had been robbed of
most of the 'queen's' bones and jewellery.

Many grave-goods lay outside the burial
chamber, with most of the large objects—
the waggon, sledges and the 12–15 horses—
in the prow. The Oseberg burial also contained furniture, cooking utensils, textile
equipment, transport and riding equipment,
and farming tools. There was also personal
equipment, a tent and other objects which
are difficult to identify. The mound was excavated in 1904. All finds (apart from the
textiles) have been published in detail. The
grave is central to Viking-age research (cf.
cat. 156–66).　　　　　　　　　　　　　IM

Bibl.: Grieg 1928; Blindheim 1959. For Oseberg see Brøgger, Falk, Shetelig (eds.) 1917–28; Brøgger and Shetelig
1950; Sjøvold 1985

156　　　　　　　　　　　　　　Antler.
L. 22cm.
Oseberg, Sem, Vestfold, Norway.
c. 800–850. Scandinavian.
Universitetets Oldsaksamling, Oslo, Oseberg
156

Comb

Single-sided comb, the curved back plates
being attached to the composite central part
by small rivets. The decoration is the same
on each side, has a central field with interlace, side fields with simple two-strip interlace, and small, 2-dimensional, animal heads
at the ends. The ornament was inlaid with
organic material, probably resin. Found in
chest 156 at Oseberg (cf cat. no. 155).

IM/DMW

Bibl.: Grieg 1928; Ambrosiani 1981

157　　　　　　　　　Gilt-bronze, enamel.
L. 4.2cm.
Oseberg, Sem, Vestfold, Norway.
8th–9th cent. Hiberno-Saxon.
Universitetets Oldsaksamling, Oslo, Oseberg
157

Enamelled mount

Mount in the shape of a truncated pyramid,
inlaid with red, yellow and blue cloisonné
enamel in cells between cast frames. Simple
geometric patterns. Broad borders define the
top and the trapezoidal sides; subdivided by
narrower borders.

From the Oseberg burial (cf. cat. no. 155).
Position in the ship unknown. Original use
unknown, possibly a belt mount. Made in
the British Isles in 8th cent.　　　　　　IM

Bibl.: Grieg 1928; Wamers 1985, 20, no. 116, Taf. 15:5;
The Work of Angels, 1989, no. 52 with colour plate

158　　　　　　　　　　　　　　　Iron.
H. 86cm.
Oseberg, Sem, Vestfold, Norway.
c. 800–850. Scandinavian.
Universitetets Oldsaksamling, Oslo, Oseberg
151a

Lamp

The lamp is made up of a stem and a bowl.
The stem is a twisted wrought-iron, pointed,
rod. At the top are 3 brackets supporting a
hemispherical bowl with a narrow out-
turned rim. The lamp was in chest no. 149 in
east of burial chamber (cf. cat. no. 155).

Lamps of the same type are known from a few Norwegian Viking-age graves. The fuel would have been fish, seal or whale oil. **IM**

Bibl.: Grieg 1928

159

Yew, brass.
H. 17.5cm.
Oseberg, Sem, Vestfold, Norway.
c. 800–850. Imported.
Universitetets Oldsaksamling, Oslo, Oseberg
303

Bucket

Bucket made of 17 staves, the base of 2 pieces. Held together by brass hoops at top and bottom and 3 intermediate hoops. Suspension loops for the handle are part of the rim mount. The handle is a square brass rod with flattened centre flanked by simple animal heads. Found in bucket 302 (see cat. no. 160) which lay in a barrel in the prow (cf. cat. no. 155) with another bucket—upturned.

Buckets of this type were imported, probably from England. The finest example is the so-called Buddha bucket from Oseberg with enamelled escutcheons of human figures. **IM**

Bibl.: Grieg 1928

160

Pine, iron.
H. 30.5cm.
Oseberg, Sem, Vestfold, Norway.
c. 800–850. Scandinavian.
Universitetets Oldsaksamling, Oslo, Oseberg
302

Bucket

Bucket made of 10 staves, widest at the bottom. The hoops were originally of beech, fastened with 3 vertical rows of iron tacks with flat heads. The bottom is in one piece and caulked with resin. The handle, attached by simple bent iron loops, is of twisted iron rod with an elongated plate in the middle. A runic inscription on the outside: *asikrir*, 'Sigrid owns' (the bucket).

Found in a barrel in the prow (cf. cat. no. 159). (For the Oseberg grave see cat. no. 155). Stave-built vessels for holding liquid were common in the Viking Age (cf. cat. no. 59) **IM**

Bibl.: Grieg 1928

161

Oak, iron.
L. 66.5cm.
Oseberg, Sem, Vestfold, Norway.
c. 800–850. Scandinavian.
Universitetets Oldsaksamling, Oslo, Oseberg
178

Chest

Simple chest with flat lid, made of 6 planks. Front and back are trapezoidal, narrowing towards top. The base jointed into a groove in the side planks which also had rebates for the bottom plank and rebates in the side edges for the front and back which were secured by nails. The chest stood on the side planks which extended 6cm below the base. The lid was attached by 2 simple iron hinges. Rectangular lock-mount on the front; an iron hasp in the lid fitted into the lock.

One of 3 chests in the burial chamber at Oseberg (cf. cat. no. 155, 164). There were also fragments of at least 3 others. This one contained either crab apples or grain. Chests are common in both male and female graves in the Viking Age, but usually only the metal fittings are preserved. **IM**

Bibl.: Grieg 1928

159

160

161

165

163

164

162

Beech.
L. 220cm.
Oseberg, Sem, Vestfold, Norway.
c. 800–850. Scandinavian.
Universitetets Oldsaksamling, Oslo, K.69

Bed (copy) *(Illustrated p. 140)*

There were 3 magnificent beds in the Oseberg burial (see cat. no. 155) all of the same construction. Fragments of one or two were found in the burial chamber and its entrance. The third, in the prow, is the basis of this copy. It was also fragmentary and some of the details are uncertain. Two simpler beds were also found.

The frame consisted of two decorated head-planks, two broad side planks, two foot posts and six base planks. A head-board was dovetailed through the head planks and secured by wedges. The side boards were fastened by trenails to the head planks and dovetailed and wedged through the foot posts. The six bottom planks were mortised into the side planks. The head-planks are decorated with openwork animal heads which have incised inner contours. The head-planks are painted, partly to accentuate the carved ornament, partly with simple geometrical figures. **IM/DMW**

Bibl.: Osebergfundet I, 1917; Schetelig 1920; Grieg 1928

163

Beech.
H. 67cm.
Oseberg, Sem, Vestfold, Norway.
c. 800–850. Scandinavian.
Universitetets Oldsaksamling, Oslo, K.70

Chair (copy)

Box-shaped base of 4 rectangular boards jointed into corner posts. The back posts, slightly slanting, continue above the seat and frame the chair-back which is also a wooden

plank. The boards of the base have recessed central fields within a narrow border with carved parallel grooves. The inner fields were painted with polychrome animal ornament bounded by geometric borders. The holes near the upper edges of the boards show that the seat consisted of cord or bast plaitwork (not preserved).

Found low in the Oseberg ship, near the mast-fish (cf. cat. no. 155). No other box-shaped chairs are known from the Viking Age, but there are several medieval examples. **IM**

Bibl.: Schetelig 1920; Grieg 1928

164

Oak, iron.
L. 108–113cm.
Oseberg, Sem, Vestfold, Norway.
c. 800–850. Scandinavian.
Universitetets Oldsaksamling, Oslo, K.68

Chest (copy) *(Illustration of original also p. 140)*

The same construction as cat. no. 161, but with curved lid. The chest is decorated with iron bands 6–6.5cm wide, each with 3 rows of tinned nail-heads. The front and back have 11 vertical bands with corresponding bands on the lid—horizontal bands clasp each corner. The lock consists of a long horizontal mount on the front, 3 hasps and 3 rods terminating in animal-head ends. The lid has 9 hinges made of simple cramps.

Found in the burial chamber of the Oseberg ship (cf. cat. no. 155). The chest contained tools and shows no sign of having been robbed. Another highly decorated chest (no. 156 in the find) had been robbed and destroyed in antiquity. **IM**

Bibl.: Grieg 1928

165

Beech.
H. 119cm.
Oseberg, Sem, Vestfold, Norway.
c. 800–850. Scandinavian.
Universitetets Oldsaksamling, Oslo, K.73

Weaving frame (copy)

Simple upright frame. The uprights are jointed into the foot plank which has broad, rounded ends with a wooden transverse beam above. The weft support was about 33cm long, of round cross-section, and was attached to the transverse beam with cords. The lower ends of the uprights have holes with pegs for adjusting the height of the beam.

Found in the burial chamber of the Oseberg ship (cf. cat. no. 155). The chamber also contained remains of many other looms and textile equipment. This is a special weaving frame of unknown function. One possibility is that tapestry (which is made up of narrow strips of cloth) may have been woven on such a frame. The original interpretation as a frame for making knotted lacework cannot be correct.   IM

Bibl.: Grieg 1928; Geijer 1979

---

166   Hardwood, probably lime.
Max. h. 59cm.
Oseberg, Sem, Vestfold, Norway.
c. 800–850. Scandinavian.
Universitetets Oldsaksamling, Oslo,
K.51,66,50,49

Four animal-head posts (copies)

(Illustrations are of originals, d see p. 149)
Plastic, strongly modelled and decorated animal heads with large eyes, perforated nostrils, and jaws with large teeth. The posts, which form the necks, are slightly curved, the lower parts plain or with simple motifs. The posts have flat bases with horizontal shafts, square tapering to round cross-sections, mortised into them. The heads are named after the various masters to whom Shetelig (1920) gave names.

a 1st Baroque post. Carved in high relief on many planes. The artist combined traits from older styles with gripping beasts to form a new and original unity and, in spite of the wealth of detail, he produced a fine homogeneity. The original is decorated with many small tinned nails. Found in the burial chamber as a pair with the '2nd Baroque post' (not exhibited).

b Animal-head post no. 174. Carved in flat relief. A single gripping beast on the top of the head; birds on the back of the head, the cheeks and the neck are in the same style as on the 'Academician's post' (*d*), but without its certainty of composition and fine carving. Found in the burial chamber as a pair to 'the Carolingian post' (*c*). Shetelig attributed the two to the same master because of technical similarities in the carving.

c 'Carolingian post'. Carved in low plastic relief. The back of the head and the 2x3 oval fields on the neck are decorated with a multitude of small, four-legged gripping-beasts. Found in a pair with (*b*).

166a

166b

166c

d 'Academician's post'. Carved in flat relief. On each side of the mid axis lie two opposed and elegantly interlaced animals. Found in the prow.

Four of the 5 posts were found in the burial chamber (cf. cat. no. 155). Their function is uncertain but they are assumed to have been cult objects. They cannot have been fastened to other objects or to parts of buildings. One of the posts had a pair of tongs through the jaws when found.   IM

Bibl.: Schetelig 1920; Wilson and Klindt-Jensen 1966; Fuglesang 1982; Fuglesang, forthcoming.

167

167

168

167
Oak.
H. 140cm.
Gokstad, Sandefjord, Vestfold, Norway.
Second half of 9th cent. Scandinavian.
Universitetets Oldsaksamling, Oslo, C10408

Two bed-planks *(Illustrated also on cover)*

Broad backward-leaning planks which served as the head-posts of a bed of the same construction as that from Oseberg (cat. no. 162). The tops are formed as forward bending animal heads with pointed snouts and gaping jaws with teeth and ornamental tongues. They have upright pointed ears and large round eyes with pronounced eyebrows. Incised inner contour lines and decoration on the flat surfaces, but without detail. One is double-sided, the other single.

From the ship burial in a great mound, buried *c*. 900; excavated 1880 (illustrated p. 25). The bed-posts were found in the prow. The man buried here belonged to the highest social class, but his identity is unknown. The burial chamber was astern of the mast but had been robbed, as at Oseberg (cf. cat. no. 155). All the weapons had been removed and although the wealth of the preserved grave-goods cannot compete with those of Oseberg, the objects were numerous, various, and of very high quality. The most important metal objects were the harness and belt mounts (cat. no. 168). Most of the grave-goods were found in the prow. Wooden objects include 3 boats, many beds, tent frames, a sledge, and ship's equipment (see cat. no. 8). **IM**

Bibl.: Nicolaysen 1882; Schetelig 1920; Brøgger and Shetelig 1950; Sjøvold 1985

168
Gilt bronze.
L. (strap-end) 7.3cm.
Gokstad, Sandefjord, Vestfold, Norway.
Second half of 9th cent. Scandinavian.
Universitetets Oldsaksamling, Oslo, C10437,
C10439, C10441b

Buckle, belt-slide and strap-end

Cast openwork strap-mounts. Decorated with ornamental ribbons which have up to 3 raised lines with transverse nicks and small smooth fields at the junctions.

a Tongue-shaped strap-end with plain, gilt bronze back plate.; the border alternates beading with smooth fields containing incised triquetras; the central area is filled with interlace; the strap was made fast between the back and the underlying bronze plate; *b* Belt-runner with curved sides and slightly convex surface with interlace; *c* Buckle with cast decoration on the broad, curved hoop and sides; interlace with profile head towards the centre of loop; engraved geometric patterns on the edges of the loop.

From the Gokstad ship burial (cf. cat. no. 167). Found in a corner of the burial chamber. **IM**

Bibl.: Nicolaysen 1882; Fuglesang 1982; Fuglesang forthcoming

169
Gilt bronze, leather.
Borre, Vestfold, Norway.
c. 900. Scandinavian.
Universitetets Oldsaksamling, Oslo, C1804

Harness mounts *(Illustrated in part, see also p. 178)*

Most of the mounts are from the bridle. Parts of the original straps are preserved, but the original shape cannot be reconstructed (cf. cat. no. 301). These mounts give the name to the Borre style in which interlace plays an important part. The two-stranded interlace bands are often cut by marked nicks, which contrast to the flat fields on the animal heads and limbs, corners and extensions.

a 43 rectangular mounts, each with an animal with face as mask, ribbon-shaped interlaced body, and accentuated fore- and back leg; *b* 3 rectangular mounts with highly curved surface; they have a jumbled animal with mask, surrounded by a beaded border; *c* bit formed of 2 long-necked animals in profile, forward bent heads, and wavy mane; small animal figure in central field; *d* openwork strap-ends with symmetrically interlaced animals with masks under the loop and small feet at the narrow ends, surrounded by double bands with smooth corner fields; *e* 2 buckles with beaded ends on the side bows and 2 profile heads on the central bow, and 2 strap-distributors with interlace; *f* 2 single strap-ends with ring-chain. The other mounts belong to other parts of the harness; *g* 2 square mounts, each with a quadruped in profile with backward looking head, marked hip-spirals and legs towards the beaded border; *h* 2 trapezoidal mounts with interlaced animal with profile head towards the pointed

169

170

corner; edging bands with smooth corners. *i* 2 double strap-mounts, decorated as *f*.

The Borre find represents the remains of a ship-burial of the same character as Oseberg and Gokstad (cf. cat. no. 155, 167). The ship was 17m long. Most of the mound was destroyed in the 1850s by a gravel pit and only some grave-goods were recovered, some in fragments. The harness mounts represent the most important finds. The burial mound was one of originally 9 mounds in the Borre cemetery which also contained 2 large cairns and some smaller mounds. They form the largest group of monumental mounds in the North (illustrated p. 36). New excavations of 2 of the large mounds have given C[14] dates of 7th cent. Thus Borre must have been a power centre for some centuries both before and during the Viking age. **IM**

Bibl.: Brøgger 1916; Wilson and Klindt-Jensen 1966; Graham-Campbell 1980, no. 489; Fuglesang 1981a; Fuglesang 1982

170
Gold.
Diam. 30–32cm. Wt. 1830g.
Kalmargården, Tissø, Sjælland, Denmark.
10th cent. Scandinavian.
Danmarks Nationalmuseum, Copenhagen,
Dnf. 1/77

Neck-ring

The neck ring is plaited from 4 double-twisted gold rods, joined together by a link decorated with stylized plant ornament. About half of one of the 4 double-twisted rods was cut off in antiquity; original weight *c.* 2kg. Stray find, 1977. Similar neck-rings are known but they are usually of silver and not nearly so large. **HL**

Bibl.: Munksgaard 1977; Graham-Campbell 1980, no. 215; Vebæk 1980, no. 81

171
Iron with silver and gilt bronze.
L. 96.7cm.
Boat chamber-grave, Haithabu, Germany.
Mid-9th cent. S & W Scandinavian; sword-chape
Frankish.
Archäologisches Landesmuseum, Schleswig
KS12302Bb

Sword

Two-edged sword with five-lobed pommel. Pommel and upper hilt in one piece, encrusted with silver, as is the guard. The silver has niello decoration and is divided into fields with silver wire. The grip, of wood, is almost totally decayed. It was defined by a decorated lower hilt of gilt bronze. The scabbard of wood, covered with leather, remains preserved on the blade. The sword is the most magnificent of three found in the boat chamber-grave. A nobleman, perhaps the King Olaf mentioned by Adam of Bremen, was buried here in a boat *c.* 20m long, with two men of his retinue and complete weaponry, including three horses and all their trappings. He also had a complete service for the table. The shape and decoration of the sword relate it to the Carolingian Empire. For this reason it could have been made in either south or west Scandinavia, or in its find-place, Hedeby. **IU**

Bibl.: Müller-Wille 1976a; Graham-Campbell 1980, no. 249

172
Iron, silver, copper.
Stirrups: h. 35.0cm. Spurs: l. 22.0cm.
Nørre Longelse, Langeland, Denmark.
10th cent. Danish.
Langelands Museum, C488, C489

Stirrups and spurs

Well-preserved set of stirrups and spurs with unusually fine inlay of silver and copper wire in interlace patterns. The spurs end in flat animal-masks. The grave also included a Hiberno-Saxon dish of 8th–9th cent; it is one of the most magnificently furnished of the many 10th-cent. equestrian burials in Denmark. Related riding equipment is found in other graves, including a grave from Stengade, also on Langeland. **JS**

Bibl.: Brøndsted 1936, 167ff., Pl. IV–IX; Graham-Campbell 1980, no. 291. Cf. Brøndsted 1936, 150ff., Pl.II–III

171

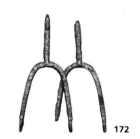

172

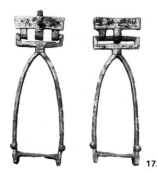

172

174d

174e

173

173   Iron, gold, silver.
L. 17.5cm.
Mammen (Bjerringshøj), central Jutland,
Denmark.
Second half of 10th cent. Danish.
Danmarks Nationalmuseum, Copenhagen,
C133

The Mammen axe   *(Illustrated also p. 179)*

Iron axe with gold inlay in the groove between neck and blade, and inlay of silver wire and silver pins on all flat surfaces. From a richly furnished male grave; other grave-goods include textiles (cat. no. 174), a bronze cauldron and a large wax candle. The burial chamber has been dendrochronologically dated 970/1.

The decoration on the axe is exceptionally fine and has given its name to the Viking-age Mammen style. Triquetras, tetrograms, a mask and a spiral are present on the neck. On one side of the blade there is foliate ornament, a bird on the other. Silver-inlaid axes were status symbols for the most prominent men in the Viking Age (cf. cat. no. 113). The man buried in Bjerringshøj no doubt belonged to the court of Harald Bluetooth (see cat. no. 174).   **HL/UN**

Bibl.: Worsaae 1869; Brøndsted 1936, no. 35; Paulsen 1956, 101ff., fig. 40–41; Wilson and Klindt-Jensen 1966, 119ff., Pl. LIIf; Graham-Campbell 1980, no. 493; Fuglesang 1991; Iversen, Näsman, Vellev (eds.) 1991

174b

174c

174   Wool, silk, silver, gold.
Mammen (Bjerringhøj), central Jutland,
Denmark.
Second half of 10th cent. Danish.
Danmarks Nationalmuseum, Copenhagen,
C135-C138

Fragments of man's dress

(a illustrated p. 193)

a Fragment of brown woollen cloth; embroidered border with human faces; l. 41.5cm. *b* Fragment of brown woollen cloth; embroidered with animals and masks; l. 20cm. *c* Three tablet-woven and plaited woollen braids; 10 × 1cm; 9.5 × 1.5cm;

11 × 1.5cm. *d* Two brown silk decorative braids with gold embroidery; l. 22cm. *e* Two padded armlets of silk; diam. 8.5cm.

These textiles from the rich male burial of Bjerringhøj are unique. Unfortunately they suffered heavy damage when being retrieved in 19th cent. Clothing from the corpse and remains of pillows and blankets existed. The clothing can be reconstructed (p. 193, fig. 3) by comparison with manuscript illustrations, e.g. the picture of Knut the Great (cf. cat. no. 412). The armlets (*e*) and neck border may have been part of a shirt embroidered with animal figures and masks. (*b*) The long braids (*d*) may have been used for fastening the cloak which was probably decorated with the embroidered border (*a*). These textiles, together with the silver-inlaid axe (cat. no. 173), show the high status of the dead. The burial has been dendrochronologically dated 970/71.   **HL/UN**

Bibl.: Worsaae 1869; Brøndsted 1936; Graham-Campbell 1980, no. 356; Hald 1980. 102–118, no. 76; Munksgaard 1984; Bender Jørgensen 1986, 226; Munksgaard 1988; Iversen, Näsman, Vellev (eds.) 1991

175   Limestone (paint modern).
Present h. 175cm.
Tjängvide, Alskog, Gotland, Sweden.
8th–9th cent. Gotlandic.
Statens Historiska Museum, Stockholm, 4171

Picture stone   *(Illustrated p. 145)*

Fragmentary picture-stone very similar to the Ardre stone (cat. no. 1). On the left edge of the upper pictorial field are two vertical rows of partly legible runes: '... FUÞR ...' and 'FUÞORKHN ...'; the second part is the beginning of the runic alphabet (the *futhark*). A longer runic inscription runs along the right edge of the lower pictorial field. Only a part of it is legible: '... raised the stone for Hjoruv, his brother ...'

The lower field is filled by a magnificent ship, and in the upper field is a well-preserved scene usually interpreted as Valhalla. On the top right there is a spear, a falling and a fallen man, with a bird in flight to the left—all probably illustrative of a battle. Below that a hero on an eight-legged horse (?Odin's Sleipner) rides to Valhalla, carrying a drinking horn in his upraised hand. He is welcomed by a Valkyrie with hair in a long pony-tail, clad in cloak, apron and trailing skirt. She offers some indeterminate object (on another stone it is a drinking horn) (cf. cat. no. 186). Behind her stands a dog, above which there is another Valkyrie offering a drinking horn to a man carrying an axe, probably one of the warrior inhabitants of Valhalla. Above is Valhalla itself, the great hall with many doors, where the heroes feasted every evening after the day's fierce battles.   IJ

Bibl.: Lindqvist 1941–42, vol. I, *passim*, fig. 137–8, vol. II, 15ff., fig. 305–6; *Sveriges runinskrifter* XI 1962, 190ff., pl. 55–57; Buisson 1976, passim, Taf. 14–15; Nylén 1978, 69

---

176 Iron, bronze, gilt bronze, amber.
Broa, Halla, Gotland, Sweden.
c. 800. Gotland.
Statens Historiska Museum, Stockholm,
10796:1, 11106:1

The burial from Broa (Illustrated also p. 177)

Iron sword with cast-bronze hilt; gilt pommel and grip, decorated with animal ornament; blade broken. Amber bridge of stringed instrument. Bridle, two-part bit of iron, the ends finishing in perforated spheres threaded with iron rings and traces of further rings. 2 bronze buckles with buckle-plate of sheet metal; 1 cast-bronze strap-distributor with central face-mask, in one of the four strap-holders an almost complete iron and bronze-covered mount; 22 highly-decorated strap mounts of gilt bronze, with attachment loops at their backs. The straps would have had a width of 2.8–3.6cm.

The gilt-bronze sword hilt is richly decorated in a Gotland variant of Style III/D–E. The amber bridge is from a six-stringed instrument, perhaps a lyre. The burial also contained a horse and a dog. The horse's bridle with its gilt fittings is one of the foremost monuments to Scandinavian stylistic history. Each mount is decorated in cast decoration of the greatest skill, with stylised quadrupeds and birds in Vendel style III/E.

Gripping-beasts are also depicted on two mounts; they are forerunners of the more robust gripping beasts of the Viking Age. Because of the Broa harness mounts, the Scandinavian art style at the transition to the Viking Age is often called the 'Broa style'. IJ

Bibl.: Salin 1922; Almgren 1955, 88–95, pl. 46–56; Wilson and Klindt-Jensen 1966, 70ff., figs. 31–38, pls. 21–22 g,i; Nerman 1969–75, vol. I:1, 142f. + figs.

---

177 Iron.
Gudingsåkrarna, Vallstena, Gotland,
Sweden.
9th–11th cent.
Statens Historiska Museum, Stockholm, 19639,
etc

Weapons from an offering

Bent sword; tongs; spur; key; axe; 13 spear-heads.

Since the turn of the century, many weapons (mainly spearheads but also axes and swords) have been found in the half kilometre of marshy land separating the farms of Stora and Lilla Gudings, Vallstena parish; they are of early and middle Viking-age date. Other objects such as currency bars and smithing tongs indicate ironworking. Migration-period bronze neck-rings and Vendel-period bracteates have been found nearby; together they suggest an ancient tradition of offerings. Such cult offerings are known in Scandinavia from the Bronze Age; in the Viking Age they are mainly found on Gotland. GT

Bibl.: Thålin-Bergman 1983; Müller-Wille 1984

---

178 Human bone.
L. 8.5cm.
Ribe, Denmark.
8th cent. Danish.
Den Antikvariske Samling, Ribe, ASR 5M73

Skull fragment with Odin's name
(Illustrated p. 146)

Part of a human skull with 61 incised runes. The reading is uncertain but the text shows the name of Odin and other names. It was probably a protective formula or an amulet against illness. The piece is dated before 800 by the letter forms, and this fits well with the archaeological evidence. SJ

Bibl.: Moltke 1976, 285–88; Graham-Campbell 1980, no. 511; Moltke 1985, 151–53, 346–49

---

179 Iron. Diam. 16.9cm.
Ullna, Östra Ryd, Uppland, Sweden.
8th–9th cent. E Swedish.
Statens Historiska Museum, Stockholm,
25848:94

Thor's-hammer ring (Illustrated p. 276)

The most common type of amulet ring in eastern central Sweden and on Åland is the so-called Thor's-hammer ring; about the size of a neck-ring made of narrow, partly twisted iron rod with iron pendants in the shape of small Thor's hammers (rather more like clubs or spades), or sometimes rings or spirals. The hammer was the attribute of the god Thor and the rings must therefore be connected with his cult. They are otherwise only common in the area of the Russian state (cf. cat. no. 280, 300). IJ

Unpublished. See Ström 1984 for general information

176

177

179

180

183

180 Silver.
H. with ring: 4.8cm.
Rømersdal, Bornholm, Denmark.
Second half of 10th cent. Danish.
Danmarks Nationalmuseum, Copenhagen, 597

Thor's hammer

The front is decorated with impressed circles and rouletting. The wedge-shaped upper arm is perforated to carry a simple ring. From a hoard with complete and well preserved jewellery, including another Thor's hammer and many neck- and arm-rings. Thor's hammers were the symbol of the god Thor and occur in many materials. In Denmark they were replaced by crosses *c.* 1000 if not before.   HL

Bibl.: Skovmand 1942, 130ff., no. 63; Müller-Wille 1976b, 57f., Catalogue 4; Graham-Campbell 1980, no. 522

181 Silver.
L. 5.1cm.
Skåne (unprovenanced), Sweden.
c. 1000. S Scandinavian.
Statens Historiska Museum, Stockholm, 9822;810

Thor's hammer *(Illustrated p. 190)*

Made of two sheets of silver, the back plain, the front embossed with decoration in relief. Details of the pattern are outlined in filigree and the surfaces between the filigree are filled with granulation or bits of filigree. The decoration of the hammer is foliate. The suspension loop is shaped like a broad animal mask. Loops of this type are characteristic of the filigree art of Denmark under Harald Bluetooth and Sven Forkbeard. This example shows the continuation of paganism even in wealthy circles during the reigns of the first Christian kings of Denmark.   IJ

Bibl.: Strömberg 1961, vol. 1, 162; vol. 2, 162, Taf. 74:12

182 Bronze.
H. 6.9cm.
Rällinge, Lunda, Södermanland, Sweden.
c. 1000 or 11th cent. Scandinavian.
Statens Historiska Museum, Stockholm, 14232

Figure of the god Frey *(Illustrated p. 147)*

In his history of the archbishopric of Hamburg-Bremen (*c.* 1070), Adam of Bremen records that in the pagan temple in Uppsala, the major cult site of the Svear, statues of three enthroned gods were worshipped: Thor the god of thunder, Odin the god of war, and Frey the god of fertility who 'brings peace and enjoyment to the dead. His statue also has an immense male organ'. This figure of Frey, one of the few fairly definite representations of a god known from the North, gives an idea of the appearance of the Uppsala statue. He wears a conical cap and holds his beard, a symbol of growth. The shape of the moustaches and decoration on the back shows that the figure is from the late Viking Age, the missionary period in the Svea kingdom when most of the kings and nobles were already Christian. Similar figures seem to have been used as gaming pieces (cf. cat. no. 77).   IJ

Bibl.: Salin 1913, 406ff., fig. 1; Gjærder 1964, 95ff., fig. 1; Davidson 1967, 123, pl. 59; Graham-Campbell 1980, no. 513

183 Soapstone.
H. 20cm.
Snaptun, near Horsens, Jutland, Denmark.
c. 1000. Scandinavian.
Forhistorisk Museum, Moesgård, 72 A

Bellows-shield

Almost semi-circular piece of soapstone with flat base, a transverse perforation at the bottom. At the top an incised male head with hair, eyebrows, twirled moustache, eyes, nose and mouth. The stone was found accidentally on the beach in 1950. It is a bellows-shield from Norway or perhaps SW Sweden. The man's head is convincingly interpreted as a representation of the god Loke who had his mouth sewn up after losing a bet.   HJM

Bibl.: Glob 1959; Gestsson 1961; Graham-Campbell 1980, no.421; Madsen 1990

184 Lead alloy, clay.
L. 4.2cm. L. 5.6cm.
Ribe, Denmark.
8th cent. Danish.
Den Antikvariske Samling, Ribe, ASR540x1, ASR7

Man's mask and mould *(The mask is illustrated p. 150)*

The mask has a horned head-dress representing 2 birds. Similar masks were produced in the mould. They are thought to depict Odin with the ravens Hugin and Munin. Similar motifs are known from E England, Sweden and Russia (cat. no. 185, 268).   SJ

Bibl.: Jensen 1986; Jensen and Fransen 1987; Jensen 1990, no. 71

185

Bronze.
H. 2.8cm.
Ekhammar, Kungsängen (Stockholms-Näs),
Uppland, Sweden.
c. 800. Scandinavian.
Statens Historiska Museum, Stockholm, 30245:6

Figure of 'dancing god'

This cast figure, with a loop at the back, shows a man wearing a head dress crowned by two horns ending in birds' heads, and holding a sword in one hand and crossed staves (probably spears) in the other. The same cremation grave also contained a figure of a man in profile, dressed as an animal and holding a (?)coiled snake which he is biting. Many similar figures and depictions are known, the earliest from the Migration Period, the latest from the Viking Age. They seem to portray people, perhaps mythical, performing various rites (cf. cat. no. 184, 186).

IJ

Bibl.: Rindquist 1969, 287ff., fig. 1

186

Silver.
L. (lower) 3.2cm.
Birka grave 825, Uppland; Klinta, Köping,
Öland. Sweden.
10th cent. Scandinavian.
Statens Historiska Museum, Stockholm, Bj 825;
128

Figures of horseman and woman

Both figures are cast. One shows a warrior on horseback, a sword at his side; the other a woman with a drinking horn in her outstretched hand. The warrior was found with other figures in a female grave (a horseman, a woman and a miniature strike-a-light). The woman's figure was found in a silver hoard with many pendants. Women's jewellery also includes occasional figures of silver or bronze with one or two attachment loops at the back. These two are reminiscent of the scenes of Valhalla on the Gotland picture stones where the hero is met by a Valkyrie with a drinking horn (cf. cat. no. 1, 175). These small dress ornaments probably also had a symbolic or magical significance (cf. cat. no. 185, 281).

IJ

Bibl.: Arbman 1940–43, 298ff., Taf. 92:11; Geijer 1938, 151f., Taf. 38:4; Stenberger 1947–58, I, Abb. 41; Davidson 1967, 130, pl. 62f.; Graham-Campbell 1980, no. 518; Arwidsson 1989, 56f. For general information about amulets see Arrhenius 1961; Fuglesang 1989

187

Silver alloy.
H. 1.52cm.
Haithabu (south cemetery), Germany.
c. 900. Scandinavian.
Archäologisches Landesmuseum, Schleswig, KS
Hb W394

Throne-shaped amulet

Grave-goods from a coin-dated grave (Haithabu 188) included a pendant shaped like a rectangular throne with square seat, vertical tripartite back with a bird's head on each side of a central knob and arms in the shape of three-dimensional lions. Three holes at the back of the seat and in the back itself indicate that a figure (perhaps a god) had originally been placed there (cf. cat. no. 188).

This pendant amulet is related to other finds associated with the gods Odin and Thor. Details of the throne, such as the lions and the central knob, show similarities with medieval Imperial thrones and their forerunners. The amulet was probably associated with Odin.

IU

Bibl.: Arrhenius 1961; Drescher and Hauck 1972

188

Gilt bronze.
H. 2.9cm.
Gudme, Fyn, Denmark.
10th cent. Scandinavian.
Danmarks Nationalmuseum, Copenhagen,
J/4620/82

Male figure

Three-dimensional, cast figure in Borre style, partly gilt, with outstretched arms and slightly splayed legs; the extremities of arms and legs missing. Stray find 1987.

This small figure is one of the latest of many finds from the power-centre recently recognized at Gudme. The figure is unique and has been interpreted as Christ. If this is so, it joins the Jelling Christ (cat. no. 193) as the earliest representation of Christ in Denmark. As it has no specifically Christ-like attributes, and as Christ is normally depicted with his legs together, this figure could well be a pagan amulet.

HL/ER

Bibl.: Munksgaard 1987

184

185

186

186

187

188

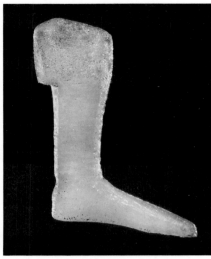

189

189

190

193

194

189
Amber.
H. 3.4cm.
Haithabu (settlement excavation), Germany.
9th–11th cent. Local.
Archäologisches Landesmuseum, Schleswig

Leg-shaped amulet

Amulet in the form of a human leg or boot. Carved with a knife and then polished. Unworked at upper end where the natural surface of the amber is visible. In the Viking Age amber was usually made into beads although there are also gaming-pieces and a small group of objects (e.g. axes) thought to be amulets. The unworked upper part of this piece suggests that it may have been mounted, as were other such objects. The find of a similar unfinished amber amulet suggests that they were made locally. Amber today is said to bring good health, this may have been so in the past.   IU

Bibl.: Graham-Campbell 1980, no. 461; Ulbricht 1984; Ulbricht 1990

190
Iron.
Diam.: 13.3cm; 3.3cm.
Torvalla, Skederid, Uppland, Sweden.
9th–10th cent. E Swedish.
Statens Historiska Museum 6263

Amulet rings   *(Illustrated p. 190)*

Iron rings of various sizes with attached miniature objects are common forms of amulets, particularly in Södermanland, Uppland and on Åland (cf. cat. no. 179). They are usually found in graves, above or around the burial urn, indicative of their magical intent. Sometimes, as here, many amulet rings are present in the same grave. The amulet *a* with its pointed expansion symbolizes a strike-a-light. The miniature objects represent a spear, a sickle or scythe, and a spade or club. The last has been interpreted as a hammer and it has been suggested that the three objects are the attributes of Odin, Frey and Thor. The small, simple ring (*b*) has three miniature scythes suspended by their perforated blades.   IJ

Bibl.: Jungner 1930, 70ff., fig. 18–19; Arrhenius 1961, 143ff., 152f., fig. 5

191
Silver, niello, gilding. H. 4.3cm.
Jelling, Jutland, Denmark.
Mid-10th cent. Danish.
Danmarks Nationalmuseum, Copenhagen,
CCCLXXII

Jelling cup   *(Illustrated p. 179)*

Cast, stemmed cup, with slightly splayed bowl, short stem expanding in middle, and almost flat, circular foot. Gilding on the interior, and traces of gilding and niello in the grooves of the external decoration. Decorated with 2 entwined ribbon-like animals in classic Jellinge style and, opposite them, a scaly motif. Found 1820 in the burial chamber of the north mound at Jelling, dendrochronologically dated 958/9. The cup was repaired at an unknown time.

The Jellinge style is named from this cup which is one of the few extant objects from the pagan chamber-grave in Denmark's biggest burial mound. King Gorm was probably buried there before his remains were removed to a new grave in the church once Christianity had been introduced (cf. cat. no. 192–3). The cup has, for little reason, been called a chalice (Schultz) but it was more probably a secular drinking vessel.   HL/ER

Bibl.: Kornerup 1875; Schultz 1952; Wilson and Klindt-Jensen 1966, 95f., pl. XXXIVa; Roesdahl 1974, 212–14, fig. 3a–c; Roesdahl 1980, 141; Krogh 1982; Christensen and Krogh 1987

192
Silver with niello, partly gilded.
L. 7.5cm.
Jelling Church, Jutland, Denmark.
10th cent. Scandinavian.
Danmarks Nationalmuseum, Copenhagen, no number

Strap-end mount from Jelling
(Illustrated p. 179)

The strap-end has an animal head in Jellinge style at each end. One head, with round snout and round eye, has a riveted plate between its jaws which attached it to a leather strap. The other head with oval eye grasps a ball. The mount probably swung free. The finely chased and engraved work is decorated with niello and gilding.

It was found in 1979, with a similar but smaller mount and remnants of gold thread, in the grave of a middle-aged man. The skeletal remains suggest that this was a reburial and that the body was that of King Gorm, whose son Harald Bluetooth in the 960s transferred his remains from the pagan grave under the north mound at Jelling to a Christian grave in the church (cf. cat. no. 191, 193). **FL**

Bibl.: Krogh 1980; Krogh 1982, 202–3

193

Original of granite.
H. above ground 243cm.
Jelling, Jutland, Denmark.
c. 965. Danish.
Danmarks Nationalmuseum, Copenhagen

Jelling stone (cast) *(Original illustrated also p. 37, 153)*

The Jelling stone stands in its original position, between two great mounds (cf. p. 154, fig. 3). It was raised by King Harald Bluetooth (d. c. 987) who introduced Christianity to Denmark. The stone is a 3-sided boulder with an inscription in horizontal lines on one face and pictures on the other two, carved in relief above a single row of runes. The inscription reads, 'King Harald had these memorials made to Gorm his father and to Thyre his mother. That Harald who won for himself all Denmark and Norway and made the Danes Christian'. One pictorial face shows Christ, the other the 'great beast' entwined with a snake.

The Jelling stone is a dynastic monument. It glorifies Harald and his exploits and is a master work of the Mammen style. It probably inspired the many rune-stones which thereafter were decorated with pictures, and also the 'great beast' which was to become one of the most powerful motifs of Scandinavian art for the next hundred years (cf. cat. no. 38, 264, 416–7). **ER**

Bibl.: Jacobsen and Moltke 1941–42, no. 42; Wilson and Klindt-Jensen 1966, 119ff.; Fuglesang 1981c; Krogh 1982; Moltke 1985, 202–23; Roesdahl 1989

194

Iron.
L. 21.9cm.
Ludvigshave, Lolland, Denmark.
End 10th cent. Scandinavian.
Danmarks Nationalmuseum, Copenhagen,
C9115

Axehead

Broad-bladed axe with cross in the perforated blade. From a grave.

Reconstructions show that although such axes were strong enough for practical use, they probably also had a ceremonial function similar to the gold and silver inlaid axes (cat. no. 113–4, 173). Perforated axe blades are unusual in the Scandinavian Viking Age. The cross does not necessarily mean that the owner was Christian but it indicates the strong Christian influence on Scandinavian culture in the late Viking Age. During the period of the Christian mission weapons were seldom deposited in graves, but even at end of 10th cent. the axe could be a symbol of the warrior class. **HL/UN**

Bibl.: Brøndsted 1936, no. 92; Paulsen 1956, 66ff., fig. 25c; Schiørring 1978; Näsman 1991b

195

Soapstone.
L. 9.2cm.
Trendgården, N Jutland, Denmark.
Second half of 10th cent. Danish.
Danmarks Nationalmuseum, Copenhagen,
C24451

Mould for cross and Thor's hammer *(Illustrated p. 191)*

Rectangular mould for a Thor's hammer and 2 crosses, and for oblong bars on the other 3 sides. Possibly reused as a weight. Stray find. In Denmark the transition to Christianity took place fairly peacefully. This mould may be regarded as an illustration of this: the craftsman could accommodate orders from people of both religions. **HL**

Bibl.: Roesdahl 1977, 48f.; Graham-Campbell 1980, no. 429. Cf. Resi 1979, 64ff.

196

Silver gilt.
L. 3.4cm.
Birka grave 660, Uppland, Sweden.
c. 900. Scandinavian.
Statens Historiska Museum, Stockholm, Bj 660

Pendant crucifix *(Illustrated p. 191)*

The crucifix is made of two sheets of silver welded together: one plain which forms the back and loop, and one embossed, showing the figure of Christ on the front. The details are outlined in filigree and granulation, with filigree also on the loop. This is the earliest crucifix known from Scandinavia. The filigree technique being typical of Viking-age Scandinavia, the object was presumably made here. **IJ**

Bibl.: Arbman 1940–43, 231ff., Taf. 102:2; Graham-Campbell 1980, no. 527; Gräslund 1984; Duczko 1985, 55ff., fig. 61–4

197

Silver.
H. 7.0cm.
Trondheim (Dronningensgate), Norway.
c. 1040. Scandinavian.
Vitenskapsmuseet, Trondheim, T16978a

Pendant crucifix

Cross with Christ on both faces. Body and head in sheet silver; hair, moustache/beard, hands and feet in filigree, as also the figure outline and the edge of the cross. A triangular pendant on a plaited silver chain was associated with the crucifix.

From a hoard deposited c. 1040 containing a similar crucifix and more than 930 coins, mostly English, Danish and German, but also some Arabic. **KS**

Bibl.: Marstrander 1950, 143–49; Graham-Campbell and Kidd 1980, pl. 112; Graham-Campbell 1980, no. 530; Fuglesang 1981c

198

Silver, glass.
Cross: h. 3.6cm.
From an unknown site in Norway. Mentioned in the inventory of Det kongelige Kunstkammer 1737.
11th cent. Scandinavian.
Danmarks Nationalmuseum, Copenhagen, 9090

Pendant cross with two beads

A primitive depiction of Christ engraved on each side. As on early Byzantine figures, Christ is clad in a long-sleeved colobium. A loop with suspension ring is riveted to the cross. Two glass beads are fastened to the ring.

Similar flat crosses with engraved figures of Christ or with other decoration are known throughout Scandinavia—e.g. from Hågerup, Selsø and Bjerre Banke. **FL**

Bibl.: Kielland 1927, 61; Blindheim (ed.) 1972, no. 76; *Danmarks middelalderlige skattefund*, 1991

198

197

199
Bell metal.
H. 51.5cm; wt. 24.3kg.
Haithabu (harbour excavation 1978), Germany.
Late 10th cent.
Archäologisches Landesmuseum, Schleswig

Bell (Illustrated p. 153)

Its shape places this among the earliest bells of the 11th and 12th cent. Its profile and thin walls makes its closest parallel the 8th-cent. bell from Canino, Viterbo, Italy. Recent investigations have shown that the bell (and a cymbal from Hedeby) was made of copper from Rammelsberg, Herzen (pers. comm. Drescher). (Composition: copper 75.33%, zinc 17.37%, lead 6.56%).

The bell, together with other fragments of bells and cymbals, is perhaps the most important evidence of the Christian missions to northern Europe, which began in 9th cent. In addition to *Vita Anskarii* and a letter from Hrabanus Maurus of Fulda to Bishop Gautbert in Birka telling of the despatch of a bell and cymbals, there are also numerous stray finds (parts of croziers, portable altars, brooches with Christian motifs) indicative of the Christian mission and liturgy. This bell enables us to reconstruct in detail the methods of casting, and to understand the rules of construction which are known from later periods.   IU

Bibl.: Drescher 1984; Drescher and Rinker 1986; Drescher 1991

Finland

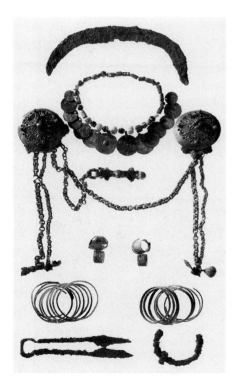

200

200

200
Iron, bronze, silver, glass, clay.
Luistari (grave 56), Eura, Satakunta, Finland (scabbard from Osmanmäki, Eura).
c. 1020–1050. Finnish (coins and beads imported).
Finlands Nationalmuseum, Helsinki,
18000:1624-1770, 2700:58

Objects from a woman's grave
(Illustrated in part)

A flat-based pottery vessel with cord decoration, knife, sickle, shears, and fragmentary iron bridle, plus a complete assemblage of jewellery with 2 disc brooches and an equal-armed brooch, 2 iron chain-holders with spiral terminals, bronze chains with small pendant bells and other pendants, 2 spiral arm-rings and 4 bronze finger-rings, necklace with 36 glass beads, 10 Arabic and 2 Western coins, and 2 circular silver pendants. (The bronze-mounted knife-scabbard from grave 56 is fragmentary so a similar one from the cemetery of Osmanmäki is exhibited).

The objects are typical of female graves of SW Finland during the last phase of the Viking Age. The necklace includes the largest number of coins so far found in a Finnish grave. They show that the grave dates from after 1018. Fashions changed in the mid-11th cent. The bronze jewellery and a spiral-decorated apron in this grave resulted in the preservation of textiles through metal oxidation; thus it has been possible to reconstruct the Eura dress (p. 67 fig. 5). PLLH

Bibl.: Lehtosalo-Hilander 1982a, 89–94; 1982b, 187; 1984 45–48

201
Iron, bronze, silver, gilt bronze, stone, clay.
Luistari (grave 348), Eura, Satakunta, Finland.
c. 930–950. Finnish, Scandinavian, Kufic.
Finlands Nationalmuseum, Helsinki,
18000:3874-3945

Objects from a man's grave
(Illustrated in part)

Sword, 2 spears, seax, 2 smaller knives, wool-shears and scythe blade, 2 purses (one with bronze mounts for flints, the other of leather for a set of weights, Arabic coins and coin fragments), bronze-handled strike-a-light with 2 horsemen, padlock, pendant whetstone, cloak-pin, bronze rings, silver braids and other dress details, 2 pottery vessels, etc. The man lay in a wooden chamber 320 × 130cm, a dog at his feet and 2 pottery containers for food at his head. He was wrapped in a dark blue cloak with spiral ornaments, and around his neck there were narrow silver braids sewn onto gold-yellow silk. Silk fibres were found elsewhere in the grave suggesting he wore a silk tunic. The cloak-pin is decorated in Borre style. Its ring is of gilt and silvered bronze, but the pin is of iron. Similar pins were popular with the Scandinavians who sailed along the Russian rivers; they have been found e.g. at Birka (cf. cat. no. 31). The coins indicate that the burial dates from after 927 and the weapons show that it is at latest c. 950.   PLLH

Bibl.: Lehtosalo-Hilander 1982a, 237–40; 1982b, 186; 1990

202
Bronze, glass.
Luistari (grave 118), Eura, Satakunta, Finland.
900–950. Bronze jewellery Finnish.
Finlands Nationalmuseum, Helsinki, 18000:2282-2297

Jewellery from a girl's grave

Necklace of 65 glass beads, a circular brooch, 2 spiral arm-rings, finger- and toe-rings and 2 small bells, all of bronze. The child, who also had 2 pottery vessels with food, was 3-4 years old. 4 very similar girls' graves with spiral arm-rings and toe-rings have been found in Luistari, all probably from 10th cent. 2 also contained Arabic coins. The small bells, probably souvenirs from the East, have been found in Viking-age childrens' graves in Sweden and Finland. **PLLH**

Bibl.: Lehtosalo-Hilander 1982a, 25–26, 122–24; 1982b, 116, 185

203
Bronze, iron.
Luistari (grave 273), Eura, Satakunta, Finland.
Early 9th cent. Finnish.
Finlands Nationalmuseum, Helsinki, 18000:3107-3109

Objects from a boy's grave

A penannular brooch with faceted terminals, a tanged spearhead (l. 18.9cm) and an iron knife found with a very slender boy, only 70 cm tall. The brooch is a miniature version of similar items common in men's graves in the Viking Age; the spearhead copies the slender tanged spearheads popular in Finland in the early 9th cent. (cf. cat. no. 212).

Weapons designed for children have been found in half a dozen graves in the Luistari cemetery. The earliest is from 8th cent., the latest from 11th cent. **PLLH**

Bibl.: Lehtosalo-Hilander 1982a, 26, 183; 1982b, 184–85

204
Iron. L. 14.8cm.
Pahosaari, Jaala, Häme, Finland.
1000–1200. Finnish.
Finlands Nationalmuseum, Helsinki, 18115

Axe

Finnish axe with concave sides and sturdy shaft-flanges, decorated on the neck with zig-zags between straight lines, with short transverse incisions from the line towards the edge. Axes of this type are uncommon in graves, mostly being found as stray finds. They are indicators of the hunting and slash-and-burn cultivation in the Finnish forests. **PLLH**

Bibl.: Vuolijoki 1972, 23–25

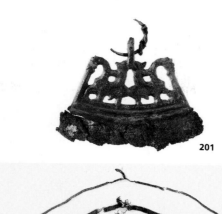

201

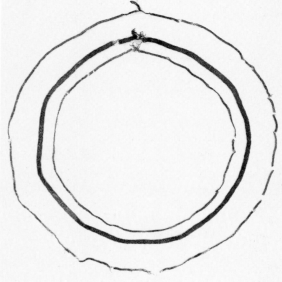

201

201

202

203

204

206

205

Iron.
L. 19.0cm; 13.6cm.
Nautela, Lieto, Varsinais-Suomi, Finland;
Hovinsaari, Räisälä, Ladoga-Karelia.
1000–1200. Finnish.
Finlands Nationalmuseum, Helsinki, 14320:2;
2592:267

Ploughshare and hoe

Ploughshare with rounded point and flanged socket. Broad-bladed hoe with rounded edge. Only 4 objects thought to be ploughshares have been found in Finland, 2 on Åland. Some dozen hoes have been found, most from Ladoga-Karelia. They were probably used for digging up the roots of bedstraw (*Galium mollugo* or *Galium boreale*) which were used as a dye for textiles.　　　**PLLH**

Bibl.: Schvindt 1893, 175; Kivikoski 1973, 127, 148

205

207

206

Iron.
L. 45.0cm; 11.8cm.
Vilusenharju, Tampere (Tammerfors); Luistari,
Eura, Satakunta, Finland.
11th cent. Finnish.
Finlands Nationalmuseum, Helsinki, 17208:408;
23183:67

Scythe blade and leaf knife

Scythes are common in Viking-age male graves in Finland. In Karelia agricultural tools were not placed in graves until the 12th cent. but in west Finland only a few graves later than the late 11th cent. contain scythes and sickles. It is often difficult to distinguish sickles from leaf knives, but this small iron artifact from Luistari is probably the blade of a leaf knife, used by women to gather winter fodder.　　　**PLLH**

Bibl.: Lehtosalo-Hilander 1982b, 54–57

207

Iron, resin.
L. 16.6cm; diam. 2.0cm.
Hovinsaari, Räisälä; Herramäki, Pyhäjärvi.
Ladoga-Karelia.
12th cent. Finnish.
Finlands Nationalmuseum, Helsinki, 2592:46;
2493:2

'Chewing gum scraper' and resin

Chewing gum is perhaps the world's oldest stimulant; Finnish finds show that it was used as early as the Stone Age. Late Iron-age cemeteries have revealed chisel-like artifacts with a curve below the tang, interpreted as scrapers for pine and spruce resin.

When a lump of resin was accumulated it was put into an ant-hill. When the ants had impregnated the resin with their acid it could be chewed until it was a plastic and malleable lump. It was then ready for use and could, for example, be given as a present.　　　**PLLH**

Bibl.: Vilkuna 1964, 302–3

208

Iron.
a–d Vilusenharju, Tampere (Tammerfors), Satakunta; *e* Viibusfjället, Inari (Enare), Lappland; *f* Leikkimäki, Kokemäki (Kumo), Satakunta; *g* Moisio, Mikkeli (St Michel), Savo (*g*). Finland.
1000–1200. Finnish.
Finlands Nationalmuseum, Helsinki, 18556:581, 588, 589, 583; 13767; 1174:11; 11070:13

Arrowheads

a-d: 1 fork-shaped and 2 transverse-edged tanged arrowheads and 1 spearhead with triangular blade and tang. L. 13.0cm; 10.2cm; 22.7cm; 12.2cm. *e*: arrowhead with notched blade and tang l. 22.4cm. *f*: arrowhead with rhomboid faceted blade and tang l. 18.9. *g*: tanged arrowhead with barbed blade and transverse barbs on shaft, l. 11.3cm.

Arrowhead *g* is unique in Finland, the others represent fairly common forms. Arrowheads are rare in Viking-age graves in Finland but their numbers increase in the Crusade period. Hunting arrows with transverse and fork-shaped points have been found in wildernesses as far as Lappland.　**PLLH**

Bibl.: Kivikoski 1973, 116–17, 145; Lehtosalo-Hilander 1982b, 40–41

209

Iron. L. 19.0cm.
Vilusenharju, Tampere, Satakunta,
Finland. Viking age. Finnish.
Finlands Nationalmuseum, Helsinki, 18556:565

Snaffle-bit

Snaffle-bit with two-part mouthpiece and spiral-ended bars. Snaffle-bits are not as common as bridoons in Finnish finds, but some dozen are known from the Viking age. The bit from Vilusenharju has unusual cheek-bars but is generally similar to Viking-age bits. The cemetery of Vilusenharju has produced objects of both Viking-age and Crusade-period date.　　　**PLLH**

Bibl.: Kivikoski 1973, 128

210

Stone. L. 24.0cm; 8.6cm.
Luistari, Eura, Satakunta, Finland.
?Viking Age. Finnish.
Finlands Nationalmuseum, Helsinki, 22346:165, 1038

Hand quern

A fragmentary quern with grinding stone, probably a primitive hand quern. Many grinding stones have been found at Luistari, but only one other quern-stone fragment. These primitive querns were probably in use until the Viking Age.　　　**PLLH**

Bibl.: Kivikoski 1973, 127, 150

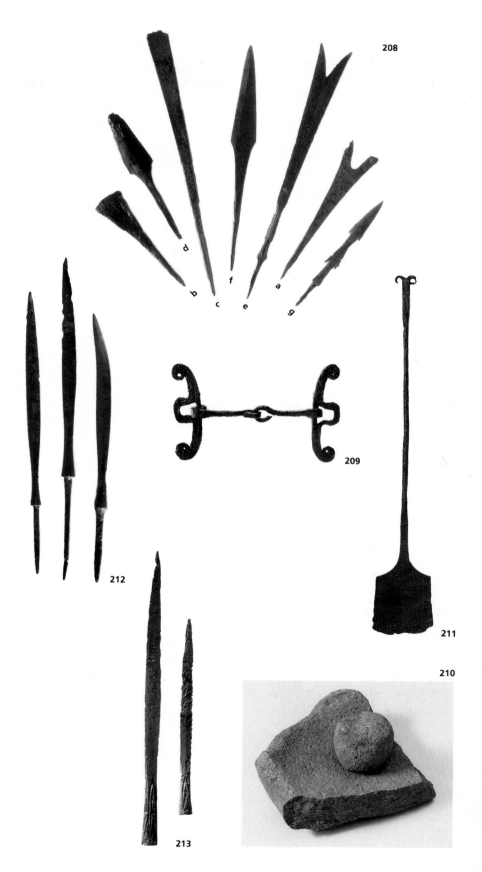

211

Iron. L. 95.0cm.
Osmanmäki, Eura, Satakunta, Finland.
10th cent. ?Finnish.
Finlands Nationalmuseum, Helsinki, 1913:2

Fire shovel

Shovel with square blade and long handle
with two loops. It was given to the museum
with some 10th-cent. female jewellery; an
identical shovel has been found in a female
grave from the same cemetery. They clearly
had some connection with the position of a
woman as the keeper of the hearth.

Fire shovels occur in Finland in various
periods but Viking-age examples have been
found only in Eura. Parallels are known from
burial mounds in SE Ladoga region (cf. cat.
no. 292). Other objects underline the contacts between the two areas.   **PLLH**

Bibl.: Kivikoski 1973, 129–30; Lehtosalo-Hilander 1982c, 77

212

Iron.
L. 44.0cm; 50.0cm; 40.4cm.
Ristimäki, Turku (Åbo), Varsinais-Suomi,
Finland.
9th cent. Finnish.
Finlands Nationalmuseum, Helsinki, 6913:348,
355, 356

Three tanged spearheads

Long-bladed spearheads, from a flat-grave
cremation cemetery. Finnish variants of the
early Viking-age type of flat and slender
spearhead. When hafted they looked like
socketed spearheads.   **PLLH**

Bibl.: Salmo 1938, 252–53; Lehtosalo-Hilander 1982b,
30–31

213

Iron. L. 45.5cm; 30.8cm.
Uosukkala, Valkjärvi, Ladoga-Karelia.
9th cent. Scandinavian.
Finlands Nationalmuseum, Helsinki, 3870:2,3

Two spearheads

These spearheads, with pattern-welded
blades and sockets with forged ogival ornaments, were discovered in a cremation grave,
together with a sword and an axe.

Slender, flat spearheads with decorated or
plain sockets were very popular in Finland in
the early Viking Age. More than 500 spearheads of this type have been discovered, but
only some 70 are decorated with ornamental
grooves, and only about 40 of these have
pattern-welded blades. Spearheads of this
type must have been made in many different
workshops throughout Scandinavia.   **PLLH**

Bibl.: Lehtosalo-Hilander 1982b, 25–30, 39; Lehtosalo-Hilander 1990; Thålin-Bergman 1986, 16–17

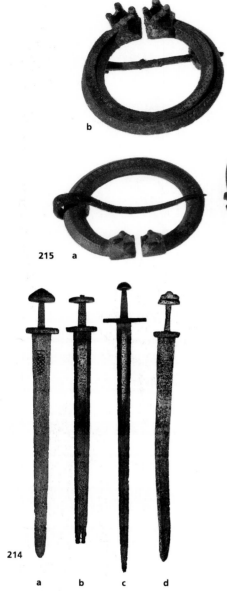

215 a

214

a   b   c   d

214　　　　Iron, bronze, copper, silver.
L. 92.0cm; 85.0cm; 98.5cm; 90.0cm.
a Peltorinne, Hämeenlinna (Tavastehus), Häme;
b Jussila, Tiihala in Kangasala, Häme; *c* Tyrvää,
Satakunta; *d* Vilusenharju, Tampere (Tammerfors), Satakunta. Finland.
a, b: 800–950; *d*: 11th cent.; Rhenish with Scandinavian hilts; *c*: 12th cent. Rhenish.
Finlands Nationalmuseum, Helsinki, 18402:1;
6245A:1; 11840; 17208:588

Four swords with inscriptions

(Illustrated also p. 194)
a Double-edged sword with triangular
pommel and straight, broad guard (Petersen
type H); bronze wire on pommel and guard;
ULFBERHT on blade.

b Double-edged sword with straight guard
and pommel bar; knop and point of blade
missing; on guards remains of silver and copper wire; on one face of blade the name
INGELRII, cross and diagonal lines on other
face,
c Double-edged sword with lenticular one-
part pommel, and long, straight guard. One
side of blade inscribed IISO ME FECIT;
INNOMNEDHI on other side.
d Double-edged sword with trilobe pommel,
straight guard and iron casing on grip; remains of silver on all parts of hilt. One side
of blade inscribed BENO ME FECIT;
INNOMIEDMI on the other side.
　　Sword blades with inscriptions are quite
common in Finland. Some 30–40 examples
with the name ULFBERHT are known,
about 7 with INGELRII; the names IISO,
INNO and BENO are rare. In addition to
these names—those of west-European
smiths—the blades also carry Christian inscriptions such as IN NOMINE DOMINE
(at least 12 examples), DEUS MEUS or
AMEN, showing that they were not made in
the pagan North. The name ULFBERHT,
however, is written in many different ways
and occurs on sword blades from several
centuries, so these sword blades may also
have been made outside their original
centres of production.　　　　　**PLLH**

Bibl.: Leppäaho 1964, 14–16, 34–47; Tomanterä 1978,
31–38, 67–68; Thålin-Bergman 1983, 269–72

215　　　　　　Bronze, iron, silver.
a Papinsaari, Kuhmoinen, Häme; *b* Luistari, Eura, Satakunta; *c* Ehtamo, Köyliö (Kjulö),
Satakunta; *d* Kilokari, Laitila, Varsinais-Suomi,
Finland.
a 9th cent.; *b–d* 10th cent. Finnish.
Finlands Nationalmuseum, Helsinki, 16864;
23607:481; 11580; 25039

Four penannular brooches with 'pegs'

a Bronze brooch with iron pin, faceted terminals with 4 'pegs', ring with stamped
decoration. Diam 6.8cm; *b* Bronze brooch
with faceted terminals and separate silver
disc on ring's top facet, pin under ring. The
punching was done after the disc was
attached because the stamps are visible on
the upper facet of the ring. Diam. 7.6cm; *c*
Bronze brooch with 'pegs' on the terminals
and 2 quadrupeds on the ring, pin under
ring. Diam 8.5cm; *d* Bronze brooch with
animal-head ends, the animals' ears as pegs,
pin under ring. Diam 7.1cm.
　　a is 9th cent. and represents the earliest
and simplest variant of these brooches. *b* is
an unusual variant but 2 identical ones have
been found in the cemetery at Luistari, both
from graves with swords of Petersen type H.
The unusual brooch, *c*, with quadrupeds has
a parallel from the neighbouring parish of
Huittinen. *d* also has parallels, one from
Kangasala in eastern Satakunta, one from
Eura, the neighbouring parish to Laitila, one
from Gotland and one from Norway. But all
four lack 'pegs' and differ in detail.
　　The custom of decorating bronze artifacts
with small lugs was general in west Finland
throughout the Viking Age. The earliest
artifacts with 'pegs' were deposited in graves
in early 9th cent., and the latest round
brooches with high 'pegs' are from the mid-
11th cent. Penannular brooches with 'pegs'
date mainly 800–950. Finnish men used
them as cloak fasteners and their distribution from Norway to the island of Berezan in
the Black Sea illustrates the Finns' contacts
with the Viking world.　　　　**PLLH**

Bibl.: Petersen 1928, 189; Salmo 1956, 42–45; Lehtosalo-
Hilander 1982b, 102–3; Carlsson 1988, 33, 72, 249;
Lehtosalo-Hilander 1990

216
Bronze with gilding and silver.
L. 25.6cm.
Syllöda, Saltvik, Åland, Finland.
10th cent. ?Scandinavian.
Ålands museum, Mariehamn, 292

Decorative pin

Decorative pin in bronze with undecorated shaft covered in white metal and gilt head with silver plating. The upper end of the pin is decorated with a lion's head, an eliptical capital with 4 longitudinal ribs and a small cube with trimmed-off corners. A tang continues from the cube, surmounted by a hollow sphere with 8 round (2 missing) and 4 square (3 missing) silver plates with filigree ornament. Between the plates are 12 knobs with silver plates at the ends. The head of a lion with open mouth is riveted to the top of the pin head. Both lion-heads are pierced behind the teeth to take a ring.

This pin has an almost exact parallel in grave 832 in Birka. Some have suggested that they were made in Ireland or England, others in northern France, both these ideas no longer find favour: they were probaby made in Scandinavia under influence from the British Isles. **MK/PLLH/DMW**

Bibl.: Dreijer 1956, 17–25; Holmqvist 1959, 34–37, 62–63; cf. Graham-Campbell 1980, no. 206

217
Bronze.
L. 7.0cm.
Astala, Kokemäki, Satakunta, Finland.
10th cent. Scandinavian.
Finlands Nationalmuseum, Helsinki, 8338:39

Scabbard-chape

The chape is decorated with openwork Jellinge-style ornament. An interlace band runs around the edge; 2 entwined quadrupeds in centre. The ornament is the same on both sides.

Bronze chapes with Scandinavian ornament are rare in Finland, only 7 being known; 2 are decorated with birds and must be Swedish imports (cf. cat. no. 310, 374). Later chapes with palmette, cross or interlace motifs are rather more common; about 15 have been discovered in late Viking-age or Crusade-period cemeteries. **PLLH**

Bibl.: Paulsen 1953, 46–47; Kivikoski 1973, 114, 143–44

218
Bronze.
L. 14.5cm.
Vilusenharju, Tampere (Tammerfors),
Satakunta, Finland.
11th cent. Finno-Ugrian.
Finlands Nationalmuseum, Helsinki, 18556:821

Pendant with webbed feet

Pendant with spiral-decorated disc, from the lower edge hang 5 chains, 4 terminating in a charm in the shape of a webbed foot (the fifth missing).

Pendants with charms are not common in Finland, most come from the East. Such ornaments were popular with the Finno-Ugrians of Russia. They sewed them on their clothes; in Finland and the SE Ladoga region they were probably fastened to breast-chains. **PLLH**

Bibl.: Meinander 1973, 146–51; Nallinmaa-Luoto 1978, 110, 274; cf. Graham-Campbell 1980, no. 109:25

219
Silver.
L. 37.0cm.
Untamala, Laitila, Varsinais-Suomi, Finland.
10th cent. ?Scandinavian.
Finlands Nationalmuseum, Helsinki, 11243

Thistle brooch

Penannular brooch with spherical pin-head and terminals. The surfaces of the hollow knobs have brambled fronts and ring-stamped marigold patterns on the back. The long pin has an almost round cross-section near the head, but in the middle and towards the point it is sharp-edged and decorated with stamped triangles, ring-and-dots and broken lines.

This is the only brooch of this type in Finland and was imported: it is probably a Norse variant of a well-known British type; in the British Isles massive examples were particularly fashionable among the Norwegian Vikings (cf. cat. no. 140, 364). Sometimes the pins were long enough to be dangerous. **PLLH/DMW**

Bibl.: Cleve 1941, 12–22; Kivikoski 1973, 99, fig. 726; Graham-Campbell 1980, no. 196

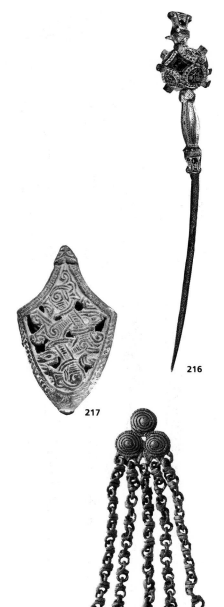

216

217

218

219

220

220

222

223

220   Iron, bronze, silver.
Suontaka, Tyrväntö, Häme, Finland.
11th cent. Finnish, W. European, Scandinavian.
Finlands Nationalmuseum, Helsinki, 17777:1–8

Female grave with weapons

(a also illustrated p. 185)

a Sword with bronze hilt with Urnes-style decoration. L. 92.0cm. *b* Sword blade without hilt, decorated with figures infilled with silver wire. L. 93.8cm. *c* Knife and scabbard with bronze mount. L. 16.1cm. *d-e* 2 small pointed-oval brooches decorated with quatrefoil and palmettes. L. 5.7cm, 5.6cm. *f* Chain holder with double spirals. L. 3.9cm. *g* Penannular brooch with small, flat terminals. Diam. 3.4cm. *h* Iron sickle. L. 23.2cm.

The grave is exceptional as, according to the excavator, it contained 2 swords which probably belonged to a woman. Sword *a* has a unique hilt, its decoration most closely paralleled on Gotland, but it has been suggested that it could have been made in Finland. Sword *b*, without hilt, has one face decorated with 3 groups of 3 billets, 2 wheel-crosses, simple Latin crosses, a hand and a sun—all probably Christian symbols. Its other face shows spirals, a double rhomboid, birds' head, crescent moon, and a bouquet of 3 trefoils. The bird and the hand are present on a sword from Leikkimäki (cat. no. 228), and hand and bouquet on 3 swords with discoid pommel from Halikko, SW Finland.

The female jewellery in the Suontaka grave represents fairly common types found in other graves, dated 11th cent. Another grave with the same combination of female jewellery and 2 swords was found in a cemetery some 13km from Suontaka (cat. no. 230).   **PLLH**

Bibl.: Leppäaho 1964, 76–77; Keskitalo 1969, 83–98; Nylén 1973, 161–67; Tomanterä 1978, 40–43

221   Silver, bronze, iron.
Tuukkala, Mikkeli (St Michel), Savo, Finland.
c. 1200. Finnish; the circular brooch ?Swedish.
Finlands Nationalmuseum, Helsinki, 2481:188–190, 192–195

Female jewellery from Savo

(Illustrated p. 69)

a Brooch of sheet silver, circular and domed, decorated with a cross on an engraved base, palmette leaves between the arms of the cross. Diam. 6.1cm. *b–c* Pointed-oval brooches of bronze, with palmettes. L. 8.0cm, 8.2cm. *d–e* 2 cruciform, pierced, chain-holders of bronze. L. 6.5cm. *f* Penannular brooch of thin silver sheet decorated with stylized acanthus, crosses and straight and zig-zag lines. Diam. 15.1cm. *g* Knife with bronze handle, in a scabbard with bronze mounts with plant decoration. L. 18.0cm.

This assemblage of jewellery is characteristic of east Finnish female graves of the Crusade Period although the penannular brooch and scabbard are unusually richly decorated. The circular brooch is probably Swedish, but similar brooches are so common in east Finnish contexts that they may have formed part of traditional female dress.   **PLLH**

Bibl.: Kivikoski 1973, 134; Lehtosalo-Hilander 1984, 10–16, 28–39

222   Bronze, iron.
Ristimäki, Turku (Åbo), Varsinais-Suomi, Finland.
11th cent. Finnish, cross ?Eastern.
Finlands Nationalmuseum, Helsinki, 14349:77, 78, 88–90

Child's grave with cross

a Cross of tinned bronze with three roundels at each terminal, l. 5.3cm, and bronze chain of double rings. *b* Iron knife. L. 8.9cm. *c* Small bearded axe. L. 9.6cm. *d* Penannular brooch with small flat terminals, l. 2.9cm, fragment of chain-mail.

The artifacts were found in a grave: the coffin was only 120cm long. Probably a small boy whose axe and knife were playthings. The fragment of chain-mail on his chest may have been of magical significance, as may have been the cross which was found in the grave-fill. Such crosses were current in 11th–13th cent. and were probably made in many places, including Finland.   **PLLH**

Bibl.: Kivikoski 1973, 140; Purhonen 1987, 41–45

223
Bronze.
Diam. 25.1cm.
Rantala, Kuhmoinen (Kuhmois), Häme, Finland.
12th cent. German.
Finlands Nationalmuseum, Helsinki, 1232:1

Dish

The dish is engraved with 4 winged figures, probably symbolizing the vices—pride, idolatry, hate and envy. It was found with a silver-encrusted axe, a battle axe and a working axe, a spearhead and 11th-cent. female jewellery. These artifacts may have come from several graves. Such so-called 'Hanseatic' dishes are common in Scandinavia; the closest parallels to this example are, however, from Poland. The dish from Kuhmoinen was probably made in a 12th-cent. workshop on the Elbe. **PLLH**

Bibl.: Edgren 1987, 86–93; Ruonavaara 1989, 153–65

224
Silver.
L. 5.7cm.
Taskula, Turku (Åbo), Varsinais-Suomi, Finland.
11th cent. ?Scandinavian.
Finlands Nationalmuseum, Helsinki, 11275:29

Cross

Double-sided, cast, silver-gilt, cross; on the front Christ in low relief, on the reverse a figure probably the Virgin. The terminals of the braided silver chain end in animal heads.

The cross, probably made in Scandinavia, was found in a late 11th-cent. male grave which also contained a bronze bowl, 2 silver penannular brooches, a spearhead with silver-inlayed socket, shears, scythe, pieces of silver, remains of a belt, etc. The burial is dated after 1036 by a German coin (Conrad II, 1024–1039; Herman II, 1036–1056, Cologne). **PLLH**

Bibl.: Kivikoski 1973, 141; Purhonen 1987, 37–39, 43–45; Tomanterä 1984, 74–75

225
Bronze, leather.
L. 80–85cm.
Mikkola, Ylöjärvi, Satakunta, Finland.
11th cent. Scandinavian.
Finlands Nationalmuseum, Helsinki, 14622:88

Belt

This belt with strap separators and square and animal-head bronze mounts was found in a male grave, in a position showing that the strap with small mounts had been loose.

Another strap, but without mounts, was attached to the separator on the right side and passed through the belt buckle. The loose strap may have been used to attach a sword or axe to the belt; or, in the Hungarian manner, as a decoration over the stomach. **PLLH**

Bibl.: Kivikoski 1973, 119, 121–22; Jansson 1986, fig. 10:1, 10:9

226
Silver.
L. 51.0cm.
Linnaniemi, Hämeenlinna (Tavastehus), Häme, Finland.
11th cent. ?Finnish. ?Eastern.
Finlands Nationalmuseum, Helsinki, 3090:1

Chain with coins

The chain consists of 16 rings linked by pairs of braided chains. 5 Kufic and 4 Western coins, and 4 silver pendants hang from the rings and chains. Originally, 7 more Kufic coins may have been fastened to the rings. The Western coins and pendants are probably later additions. The chain was found in a silver hoard deposited *c.* 1090. Fragmentary chains of the same type are known from other 11th-cent. hoards, and an almost identical necklace was found as a stray find in Hauho, some 25km from Hämeenlinna.**PLLH**

Bibl.: Appelgren 1905, 3–26; Bäcksbacka 1975, 16–17, 100–7; Graham-Campbell 1980, no. 155; Tomanterä 1984, 70–73

224

226

225

227   a   b   a   b

229b

230

227   Silver.
a Luistari, Eura, Satakunta; *b* Saramäki,
Turku (Åbo), Varsinais-Suomi. Finland.
Finlands Nationalmuseum, Helsinki, 18000:991;
15189:121

Two Finnish coin-imitations

a Bracteate, imitation of the obverse of a
Samanid dirhem (Nasr b. Ahmad, Tashkent,
932/3), about 1000. Diam. 3.2cm. *b* Imitation
of a Byzantine coin of Constantine IX
(1042–1055), probably 1040s. Diam. 3.1.

The bracteate was found in a partially
destroyed female grave, no doubt from a
necklace with other coins. The imitation is
from a male grave which also contained a
spearhead, a purse containing weights and a
piece of silver, a scythe blade, and an Arabic
coin (Mansur b. Nuh, Buchara 971/2). Both
coins lay close to the neck.

Some 30 imitations of Byzantine and
Arabic coins are known from Finland, all
have loops for suspension. They are thought
to have been made in Finland as pendants.

                                     PLLH

Bibl.: Sarvas 1966, 5–13; Talvio 1978, 26–38

228   Iron, silver, gold.
L. 105.0cm.
Leikkimäki, Kokemäki (Kumo), Satakunta,
Finland.
11th cent. Blade W European, hilt
Scandinavian.
Finlands Nationalmuseum, Helsinki, 1174:1

Sword   *(Illustrated p. 65)*

Sword with silver-plated hilt, decorated with
Urnes-style animals, spirals and palmettes:
birds and an open hand on one side of blade,
letters and a crozier on the other side—all
inlaid with gold wire.

The sword was discovered in a cemetery
before 1870. It belongs to a group of magnificent swords very similar to Viking-age
Scandinavian examples, mostly found to the
east of the Baltic. 17 whole or partial swords
of this type are known from Finland, some of
them found with silver-decorated spearheads
(cf. cat. no. 229), in 11th-cent. graves.   PLLH

Bibl.: Leppäaho 1964, 70–77; Tomanterä 1978, 62–77;
Lehtosalo-Hilander 1985a, 5–36

229   Iron, silver.
a Hulkkunanmäki, Lieto (Lundo),
Varsinais-Suomi; *b* Vilusenharju, Tampere
(Tammerfors), Satakunta. Finland.
11th cent. Scandinavian.
Finlands Nationalmuseum, Helsinki, 9562:2;
17208:691

Two spearheads   *(a illustrated p. 65)*

a Spearhead with triangular blade and silver-
encrusted socket, decorated in Urnes style. L.
38.7cm. *b* Spearhead as above. L. 33.5cm.

Spearheads with silver encrustation are
fairly common in 11th-cent. Finnish finds;
some 70 examples have been discovered in
SW Finland. A number of spears have been
found with silver decorated swords, some in
pairs. The decoration on the sockets is in the
Swedish rune-stone style so they are
assumed to have been made in Sweden (particularly Gotland), but probably in various
places as some blades are pattern-welded,
others not. Some of the animal ornament on
the sockets is normal, that on others is
unique; similar spearheads with plant decoration occur in the Baltic States.   PLLH

Bibl.: Lehtosalo-Hilander 1985a, 12–36; 1985b, 237–50

230 Iron, bronze.
L. 82.0cm.
Pahnainmäki, Kalvola, Häme, Finland.
11th cent. Blade W European, hilt ?Finnish.
Finlands Nationalmuseum, Helsinki, 5960:1

Sword

Sword with bronze hilt decorated with palmettes, acanthus fronds, interlace, etc.; the blade with indistinct figures in pattern-welding. The hilt has the same shape as the silver-plated sword hilts fairly common in Finland in 11th cent. The cast-bronze motifs include some which occur on the commonest type of Finnish pointed-oval brooches (cf. cat. no. 221). They are found mainly in Ladoga-Karelia and E Finland, but about 10 have been discovered in Häme, as this one.

The sword was placed at the foot of a female grave, together with another fragmentary sword with semi-circular iron pommel (cf. cat. no. 220). The grave is dated mid-11th cent. by an Otto-Adelheid coin (990/1000–1050). **PLLH**

Bibl.: Hällström 1947–1948, 53–55; Lehtosalo-Hilander 1966, 22–39; Sarvas 1972, 41–42; Tomanterä 1980, 157

---

231 Iron, silver.
L. 113.0cm.
Pappilanmäki, Eura, Satakunta, Finland.
12th cent. ?Scandinavian.
Finlands Nationalmuseum, Helsinki, 65

Sword *(Illustrated also p. 70)*

Double-edged sword with circular pommel and long guard with expanded ends and three equally-spaced discs. Pommel and guard decorated with silver wire hammered into the iron in spirals, zig-zags, acanthus, palmettes and crosses. The sword was discovered mid-19th cent. with 3 spearheads, wool-shears and at least 3 bits, but it was not a closed find. Later excavations on this cemetery revealed graves of Vendel-period and Viking-age date. This sword can be attributed to 12th cent. It is unusually long.

In Finland 6 swords, 1 fragmentary guard, 5 spearheads and at least 7 axes are known, all decorated in the same technique of silver wire. Finnish manufacture has been assumed, but the decorative motifs on these weapons are much the same as those in Carolingian manuscript illumination. This method of decoration was used on many different artifacts, from Ireland in the west to Russia in the east, and was no doubt carried

out in many workshops. The weapons were, however, made in forges with Scandinavian traditions. **PLLH**

Bibl.: Leppäaho 1964, 84–91; Tomanterä 1980, 157–61

---

232 Iron, silver.
L. 31.7cm.
Suomela, Vesilahti (Vesilax), Satakunta, Finland.
11th cent. Scandinavian.
Finlands Nationalmuseum, Helsinki, 3010:21

Spearhead

Spearhead with silver-inlayed socket and down-turned wings terminating in animal heads; pattern-welding on the blade. It was found with 5 sword fragments, an axe, and a stirrup, probably from a horseman's grave. Other Viking-age weapons have been found on the same site, but there have been no excavations. **PLLH**

Bibl.: Leppäaho 1964, 118–19; Tomanterä 1978, 90; Lehtosalo-Hilander 1985a, 15–18, 32

---

233 Iron, silver.
L. 15.3cm.
Humikkala, Masku, Varsinais-Suomi, Finland.
End 11th/early 12th cent. Scandinavian.
Finlands Nationalmuseum, Helsinki, 8656:47:5

Axe *(Illustrated p. 70)*

Broad-bladed axe with flanges on each side of socket, a distinct offset between the blade and cutting-edge. The butt and upper blade inlaid with silver.

This magnificent axe was found in a grave together with a penannular brooch, a Byzantine silver coin (Basilios II–Constantine XI, 976–102), a knife in a bronze-mounted scabbard, and a pendant whetstone. The coin lay on the neck of the dead man and the burial was probably some decades later than the coin. **PLLH**

Bibl.: Leppäaho 1964, 126–27; Tomanterä 1978, 78–92

---

234 *a* Kylämäki, Laitila (Letala), Varsinais-Suomi, Finland; *b* Osmanmäki, Eura, Satakunta, Finland; *c* Suotniemi, Käkisalmi, Ladoga-Karelia.
a c. 800; *b* 10th cent.; *c c.* 1200. Finnish.
Finlands Nationalmuseum, Helsinki, 16165:412, 426, 463; 1913:9; 2487:7

Bear's claws and teeth—used as pendants

a 10 bear's claws (*not illustrated*). *b* Bronze pendant with 2 bear's teeth. *c* Bear's tooth with supension hole. L. 7.3cm.

Bears' claws, teeth, paws and other parts of the body played an important part in folk-magic and medicine in Finland. These claws and teeth from the Viking Age and Crusade period were probably also associated with similar practices. **PLLH**

Bibl.: Kivikoski 1965, 24–27

232

231

234

c

b

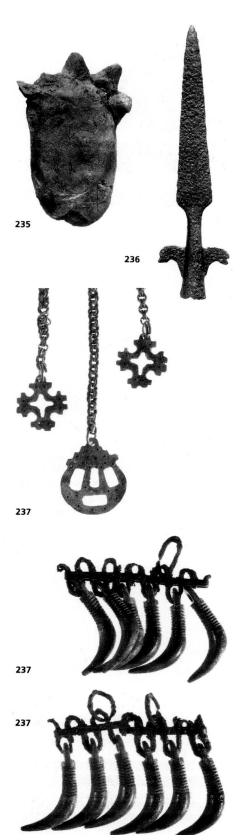

235

235

236

237

237

237

235

Clay.
L. 9.4cm.
Västergårdsbacken, Hjortö, Saltvik, Åland,
Finland.
Viking Age. Local.
Finlands Nationalmuseum, Helsinki, 4627:278
(on loan to Ålands Museum, Mariehamn)

Bear's paw

Objects of baked clay which are sometimes likened to a bear's (more often a beaver's) paw, are found in Vendel-period and Viking-age graves on Åland. In central Russia, where they also occur in graves, they have been associated with the beaver cult (cf. cat. no. 298). Since the clay paws are earlier on Åland, the Russian finds have been taken as evidence of journeys eastwards by Åland Islanders but Russian scholars believe that the beaver cult originated in central Russia in the Stone Age. **PLLH**

Bibl.: Kivikoski 1934, 384, fig. 3; Kivikoski 1965, 27–31

236

Iron.
L. 38.0cm.
Myllymäki, Moisio, Nousiainen (Nousis),
Varsinais-Suomi, Finland.
12th cent. ?Scandinavian.
Finlands Nationalmuseum, Helsinki, 9142:1

Spearhead

Socketed spearhead with flat triangular blade and 2 wings ending in animal heads; narrow pattern-welded strip on blade.

2 spearheads, and perhaps one other badly damaged example, with animal-head wings, have been found in Finland; all from end of 11th cent. or 12th cent. The animals have been interpreted as lions, but they may well be bears. Only the spears which were used in later times to hunt bears had wings—in contrast to the lances normal at that period. **PLLH**

Bibl.: Nordman 1931, 198–99; Leppäaho 1964, 124–25

237

Bronze, iron.
Lehtimäki, Kalanti, Varsinais-Suomi,
Finland.
Early 11th cent. Finnish.
Finlands Nationalmuseum, Helsinki, 15131:1–3

Female jewellery of magical significance

3 bronze chains, double-linked ending in pierced pendants, 2 cruciform and 1 tear-shaped, all decorated with stamps; 2 suspen-sion-bars of bronze and iron with six pendants like bears' teeth.

A stray find, it could be from a grave or a hoard. All objects probably belong to an early 11th-cent. female dress. The chains with pendants hung from shoulder-brooches, the bears' teeth pendants decorated pieces of cloth which hung down from a belt on the woman's hips (Finnish: *kaatterit*). **PLLH**

Bibl.: Kivikoski 1965, 22–26; Kivikoski 1973, 109–10; Vahter 1932, 183–94

238

Bone, reindeer antler, bronze, soapstone.
Vestvatn, Skjerstad, Nordland, Norway.
11th/12th cent. Saami.
Tromsø Museum, Ts6251a,g,h,u,å,bå

Saami settlement-finds

a Bone hoop of unknown use; fragmentary; 6.2 × 7.0cm; upper face with cross-hatched decoration, back undecorated; the only known parallel (from Eiterjord, Beiarn) is a bronze mount. *b* 2 arrowheads of reindeer antler of rhomboid cross-section; l. 13.3cm; 12.9cm. *c* Tool of reindeer-antler; the edges lie along the grain of the antler for maximum strength; l. 29cm. *d* Penannular brooch, bronze, rhomboid cross-section; tapering towards the terminals which were originally faceted; decoration on the surface; diam. 5cm. *e* Handled ladle of soapstone, 4 fragments; flat bottom to ladle, curved upper surfaces; handle decorated with longitudinal grooves; total l. 18cm.

These artifacts come from a building some 200m above sea level, 4km from the bottom of Misværfjoden where early Saami settlements have been found. Some of the artifacts are Norwegian but many have parallels in Saami contexts, e.g. the hoop and arrowheads. The striated decoration on the handled ladle is known only from this area and from the Arjeplog/Piteå district of north Sweden, one end of a cultural route. The artifacts and antler objects show that farming, hunting and fishing were important. The settlement in Vestvatn was first thought to be Norwegian with Saami influences, but it is now thought to be entirely Saami. **GSM**

Bibl.: Stamsø Munch 1967

239

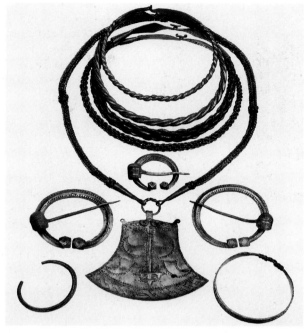

240

239 · Silver.
Pendant: total l. 50cm. Neck-rings:
diam. 19cm; 19cm; 16.5cm.
Eidet indre, Skjervøy, Troms, Norway.
Late 11th cent. Eastern (Finnish-Saami),
Scandinavian.
Tromsø Museum, Ts4400a–d

Pendant and neck-rings

a Axe-shaped pendant of hammered silver
plate, decorated with stamped triangles, a
cross, and many S-shaped figures in low relief. 5 small, almost rhomboid 'clatter pendants' hang from rings on the lower edge,
the back of each being decorated with an
arrow or 3-toed bird foot. The whole pendant is attached to a ring with a knot and 4
spirals, this is connected to a chain of plaited
silver wires (cf. cat. no. 240).

3 neck-rings: *b* twisted from 4 rods and 2
thin wires; *c* twisted from 3 pairs of rods; *d*
twisted from 7 thin rods. Found in 1949 in a
disused stone quarry. **GSM**

Bibl.: Sjøvold 1974, 172, 331; Graham-Campbell 1980, no.
330

240 · Lämsä, Kuusamo, Finland.
11th cent. N and E Scandinavian.
Finlands Nationalmuseum, Helsinki,
13350:1–10

Silver hoard

a Braided chain, l. 70.5cm, with an axe-
shaped pendant decorated with chasing and
punching, l. 10.2cm. *b* Neck-ring of 6 plaited
tapering rods and 6 cord-like thin rods; at
each end a socket ending in a stamped plate
and hook. Diam. 16.1cm. *c* Neck-ring plaited
from 8 tapering rods, undecorated ends.
Diam. 17.6cm. *d* Neck-ring plaited from 3
single and 3 cord-like double rods, end
sockets stamped. Diam. 14.8cm. *e* Neck-ring
plaited from 2 single and 2 double rods, ends
hammered flat, one with a slot, the other
with a hook. Outer faces decorated with engraving and punching. Diam. 12.9cm. *f* Arm-
ring of a rod hammered flat, the ends round
and intertwined. Diam. 7.8cm. *g* Arm-ring
with open tapering ends , square cross-section, punched decoration. Diam. 6.3cm. *h-i* 2
penannular silver brooches with flat square
terminals and central ridge, decorated with
stamps; the heads of the pins kidney shaped.
Diam. 8.0 and 7.9 cm. *j* Penannular brooch
of silver with 5-sided ring and faceted end
knobs, trapezoid pin head, rich stamped
decoration. Diam. 5.0cm.

The hoard, probably concealed at end of
11th cent., contains objects from different
sources. The best parallels to the brooches
and arm-rings are found in W Finland and
on Gotland; the neck-rings are paralleled in
N Norway, Karelia, Häme and Estonia. The
axe-shaped pendants and plaited neck-rings
are typical of silver hoards from areas in
Norway and Finland populated by Saami (cf.
cat. no. 239). They may have been acquired
by the Saami as payment for furs. **PLLH**

Bibl.: Björkman 1957; Kivikoski 1970; Lehtosalo 1973,
105–13; Zachrisson 1984, 98–104

238

241

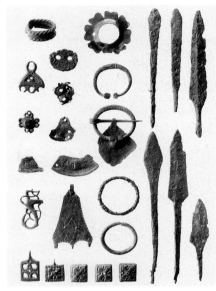

242

The Vikings and Europe

243 Iron, gilt copper-alloy, silver, niello.
L. 92.0cm.
Kilmainham-Islandbridge, Dublin, Ireland.
9th cent. Scandinavian.
National Museum of Ireland, Dublin, Wk 33

Sword

Iron double-edged sword with incomplete blade. Traces of a scabbard occur along the sides of the blade. The hilt and guard are elaborate castings of gilt copper-alloy. The decoration on both is the same: vertical or horizontal rows of geometric shapes cast in chip-carved technique. The hollow geometric shapes are inlaid with three ring-and-dot devices of silver and niello. The horizontal bands of the hilt and guard are bordered by inlaid twisted silver and copper wires. The crest of the pommel has beaded and twisted silver wires. The grip is provided with a scalloped mount decorated with stylized plant motifs.

This is the most elaborate of the 40 or so swords from the Kilmainham-Islandbridge cemetery. It belongs to Petersen type D which is of Norwegian origin, as are most of the Scandinavian imports from the site. **RÓF**

Bibl.: Bøe 1940, 21–22

241 Antler, iron.
H. 18.3cm.
Nordset, Rendal, Hedmark, Norway.
11th cent. Saami.
Universitetets Oldsaksamling, Oslo, C26831a

Drum stick

T-shaped drum-stick with slightly curved hammer-head. Plain grip, head with incised decoration including double interlace and Ringerike-style interlace. At the top a flat iron mount with small lugs at each end. Found in a mound of burnt stones with other objects of medieval type.

The drum was a shaman instrument used to induce trances. **IM**

Bibl.: Manker 1938; Manker 1950; Fuglesang 1980a, no. 95, Pl. 57

242 Silver, pewter/lead alloy, copper alloy,
iron, glass, mica, flint, quarzite.
Vindelgransele, Lappland, Sweden.
11th cent.–c. mid-14th cent.
Statens Historiska Museum, Stockholm, 22815

Saami sacrificial deposit

The site where the deposit was discovered was excavated on the banks of the Vindel älven, south Lappland, in 1941. A number of small *seitar* (cult objects, usually in the form of naturally shaped stones or carved wood), bone and antler (mostly reindeer), and other artifacts, had been laid on a close-packed paving of rounded stones, at least 7m². These objects had been used by Lapps, many of them as pendants, dress accessories, on drums, etc. Some seem to have been amulets. Many are of north-east European (mostly Finno-Ugrian) origin, some are of north-west European or local manufacture. Fur trading was probably the prime reason for these contacts. One north-west European brooch is of silver, another of pewter/lead alloy. 16 artifacts of eastern type, 5 of north-west European type, and 10 pendants (some of Lappish type) are of copper-alloy. 8 arrow-heads (many of Lappish type), and parts of keys, locks and rivets are of iron. Glass beads are also present. **IZ**

Bibl.: Serning 1956; Zachrisson 1984

243

244

245

246

244   Silver.
Total wt. 1001g.
Skavsta, St Nikolai, Södermanland, Sweden.
c. 1000. Scandinavian.
Statens Historiska Museum, Stockholm, 14916

Skavsta hoard

Hoard of 32 objects, some with stamped decoration: 4 complete ring-pins, the ring of another, 3 complete and 2 fragments of twisted neck-rings, 6 twisted arm-rings, 11 arm-rings of simple, round-section rods, 3 band-shaped arm-rings, 2 smaller rings.

This mass of characteristic Scandinavian silver jewellery was held together by 2 neck rings and forms the greater part of a silver hoard which also contains 1 whole and 2 half rings from ring-pins, a piece of pointed-oval foil, a fragment of a chain and 37 whole or fragmentary coins, mainly Islamic and German, a few English. The latest coins are Otto-Adelheid pennies minted c. 991–1004. Thus the hoard must have been concealed c. 1000.   IJ

Bibl.: Tillväxten 1913, 264f., fig. 53–64; Arne 1915, 37, fig. 78; Hatz 1974, 214, Fundkartei no. 55

245   Gilt bronze, iron pin.
L. 11.4cm.
'Moscow region' (probably Vladimir area), Russia.
10th cent. Scandinavian.
Statens Historiska Musem, Stockholm, 18918

Oval brooch, Russia

This brooch belongs to the general type P 52, but differs from other examples as the central and side fields of the perforated upper shell are filled with interlace. It was bought

in an antique shop in Moscow and is provenanced 'Moscow region', it probably, however, comes from the burial mounds near Vladimir where many Scandinavian objects have been found. A hole in the edge by the catch-plate, repaired with a riveted bronze sheet, was for the attachment of a jewellery chain.   IJ

Bibl.: Graham-Campbell 1980, no. 121

246   Bronze.
L. 11.5cm.
Hrísar, N Iceland.
10th cent. Nordic.
Islands Nationalmuseum, Reykjavík, 7346

Oval brooch, Iceland

Double-shelled oval brooch with remains of gilding; the most common type found in Iceland (Petersen type 51c). The brooch is from the grave of a middle-aged woman; it also contained a ring-headed pin and a lead spindle-whorl.   VÖV

Bibl.: Petersen 1928, 62–67, fig. 51c; Eldjárn 1956, 114, 300; Jansson 1985 67–83

247   Bronze, glass.
Box-brooch diam. 5.5cm.
Smukumi, grave XI, Grobiņa, Latvia.
9th cent. Scandinavian and Baltic.
Latvijas Vēstures Muzejs, Riga, V7145:1,5–7, 9–10, 12–17, V 7138:7

Grave of a ?Gotland woman

(Illustrated in part)
Box-shaped brooch; equal-armed brooch; 2 twisted neck-rings in fragments, 3 bangles; spiral arm-ring in fragments; spiral finger-

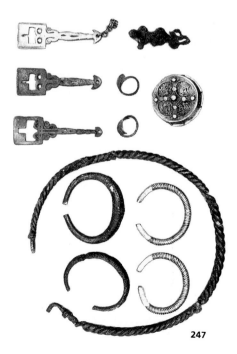

247

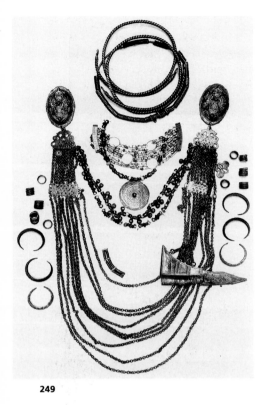

249

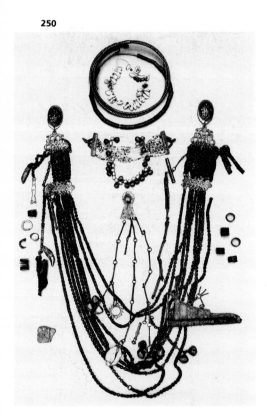

250

ring with expanded centre; 3 keys; necklace with glass and bronze beads.

The flat cemetery of Smukumi is part of the large archaeological complex of Grobiņa which is characterized by burial customs and artifacts of Scandinavian (probably Gotland) origin. 100 graves excavated by B. Nerman, P. Stepins and V. Petrenko, produced ashes, burned bones and fire-damaged grave-goods which were buried, after cremation, in pits 10–15cm deep.

The complex also includes burial mounds with similar grave-goods (the Grobiņas Priedulāji cemetery) which are believed to have been built by settlers from central Sweden. The Scandinavian settlement of Grobiņa was occupied *c.* 650–800 and had a large proportion of traders. Some Scandinavian graves contained neck-rings, breast chains and other jewellery more characteristic of the indigenous local Balts than of Scandinavians, indicating cross-cultural influences.

GZ

Bibl.: Nerman 1958, 18f., fig. 81–99; Latvijas PSR arheoloģija 1974, fig. 77

248　　　　　　　　　　　　Bronze.
　　　　　　　　　　　　　　　H. 3.6cm.
　　　　　　　　　　　　　Daugmale, Latvia.
　　　　　　　　　　11th cent. ?Scandinavian.
Latvijas Vēstures Muzejs, Riga, A 9964:1585

Warrior figure holding ring

A small, flat figure with plain back of a bearded man holding a wreath or ring in one hand. Discovered during excavations in the prehistoric fortress of Daugmale which, during the 10th–12th cent. was an important political and economic centre on the lower Dyna (Daugava), some 25km above its mouth in the bay of Riga. The costume and shape of the sword-hilt indicate that the figure is Scandinavian. According to Oxenstierna it is a depiction of the dwarf Andvare in the Sigurd legend, with his magic ring. Ginters and Ozols have compared it to the Gotland picture-stones and linked it with beliefs about the after-life, suggesting that the figure may represent a travelling companion for the deceased. A similar figure, probably cast in the same mould, is known from Lučič on the upper Dnepr in Byelorussia. It was discovered in a grave, wrapped in bark next to the skeleton's hand.

GZ

Bibl.: Balodis 1934, 399ff.; Ginters 1944, 6; Oxenstierna 1959, 205; inters 1981, 12ff., Abb. 4

249　Bronze, iron, silver, glass, cowrie shells.
　　　　Diam. of neck rings: 19.2–21.0cm.
　　　Salaspils Laukskola, grave 120, Latvia.
　　11th cent. Livonian, Baltic, Scandinavian,
　　　　　　　　　　　　　　　Eastern.
　Vēstures Institūts, Riga, VI 128:1198–1201,
　　　　　　　　　　　　　1203–1223

A Livonian woman's jewellery

3 neck-rings, 2 twisted and 1 with coiled bronze wires; 2 necklaces, 1 with glass beads, 10 small bells and 17 cowrie shells—the other with glass beads, a circular pendant and 4 silver coins adapted as pendants; a multi-strand necklace held together by 2 bead spacers; a breast ornament consisting of 2 double-shelled oval brooches with animal ornament, chains in 9 rows, 2 pendants and a knife in a scabbard; 6 arm-rings; 10 spiral finger-rings.

The large Livonian (Baltic Finnish) flat cemetery from 10th–13th cent. at Salaspils Laukskola lies on the N bank of the river Dyna (Daugava), opposite the fortress of Daugmale (cf. cat. no. 248). 610 graves have been excavated, two-thirds of which are inhumations and one third cremations. This woman was buried in a wooden coffin with head to NW. She wore a Livonian dress with an extravagantly rich profusion of mainly bronze jewellery. She also had an axe, a pair of scissors, and a bronze-decorated cloak spread to cover her. Most of the objects are native Livonian, but some show contacts with Baltic tribes (the neck-rings), Scandinavians (the oval brooches, cf. cat. no. 250), and eastern countries (cowrie shells from the Indian Ocean, coins from the eastern Caliphate (struck 904–930), beads). **AZ**

Bibl.: Latvijas PSR arheoloģija 1974, fig. 118; Ginters 1981, 33, Abb. 29

250　Bronze, iron, silver, glass, cowrie shells,
　　　　　　　　　　　　　bone, amber.
　　　Diam. of neck rings: 20.4cm–21.2cm.
　　　Salaspils Laukskola, grave 94, Latvia.
　　11th cent. Livonian, Baltic, Scandinavian,
　　　　　　　　　　　　　　　Eastern.
　Vēstures Institūts, Riga VI, 128:923–929,
　　932–936, 940, 942–943, 945–946, 948

A Livonian woman's jewellery

3 neck-rings, 2 twisted, looped together —one with attached coils; an annular brooch with various pendants hanging on chains; 2 necklaces, one of glass beads and 19 small bells, the other of small bronze rings and 30 cowrie shells; multi-strand bead neck-

lace held together with 2 bead spacers; 7 spiral finger-rings; 2 finger-rings; a breast ornament consisting of 2 small single-shell oval brooches with plant decoration, 8 rows of chains and pendants (1 amber, 2 animal teeth, 1 needle case, 1 knife in scabbard, 1 fragment of key).

This inhumation, in the same cemetery as cat. no. 249, contained a woman in a similar Livonian dress, with a pottery vessel at her feet and a bronze-decorated cloak over her. There are similar proportions of Baltic, Scandinavian and eastern objects. The annular brooch and bead spacers are Scandinavian (?Gotland). The oval brooches are, as shown by their size, decoration, and casting, indigenous—but copying a Scandinavian model which was out of fashion in Scandinavia at this time. Oval brooches were adopted for Livonian dress because Livonian women wore a dress similar to that used in Scandinavia. In the 11th and 12th cent. Scandinavian oval brooches were also copied in eastern Finland and Karelia (cf. cat. no. 221), and in the SE Ladoga region. **AZ**

Bibl.: Zariņa 1988, Abb. 31

---

251   Iron, silver.
L. 42.3cm.
Viltina, Saaremaa (Ösel), Estonia.
11th cent. Scandinavian.
Ajaloo Instituut, Tallinn, 3884:3905

Spearhead

The most obvious Scandinavian influence in 11th-cent. Finland, Estonia and Latvia is seen in the weapons, particularly the spearheads, with inlaid-silver decoration in Scandinavian style (cf. cat. no. 229, 252). This spearhead has a pattern-welded blade and socket decorated with silver inlay of interlace and spiral decoration in Ringerike style.**ÜT/IJ**

Bibl.: Selirand and Tõnisson 1984, pl. 26. For silver-inlaid spearheads in the eastern Baltic see Nerman 1929, 103f.; for Scandinavia see Fuglesang 1980a, 29ff.

---

252   Iron, silver.
L. 48.0cm.
Krimuldas Tāleni (Cremon), Latvia.
11th cent. Scandinavian.
Latvijas Vēstures Muzejs, Riga, A 65121

Spearhead

The spearhead is splendidly pattern-welded along the midrib, and the socket is inlaid in silver with Urnes-style animal ornament. It is

one of a group of silver-decorated Scandinavian spearheads found in Finland, Estonia and Latvia, probably made on Gotland (cf. cat. no. 251).   **GZ**

Bibl.: Riga-Katalog 1986, 76f., Taf. 23:8; Nerman 1929, 108, Fig. 102; *Latvijas PSR arheoloģija* 1974, pl. 77:10

---

253   Silver, bronze, glass.
Neck-rings diam.: 15.7cm–17.0cm.
Kostivere, Rävala (17km E of Tallinn), Estonia.
12th cent. (deposited after 1208), Baltic, Scandinavian and German.
Ajaloo Instituut, Tallinn, 3797:1–31, 42–46,48

Kostivere hoard *(Illustrated p. 81)*

5 plaited neck-rings with welded-on hooked end-plates, weight 370–380g; 5 penannular brooches with faceted terminals, 2 with Urnes style decoration on the ring and pinhead, 2 with cruciform projections; 18 circular pendants of decorated sheet silver and riveted bronze loops, one of the pendants possibly decorated in Urnes style; twisted finger-ring; convex (?)rivet with animal ornament; 100 yellow, green, white, brown and blue glass beads (total beads in hoard 113); 6 coins converted to pendants (total coins in hoard 121 Danish and German including bracteates, date of latest coins 1208).

This splendid hoard was concealed in a settlement at the beginning of 13th cent., during the wars against the Germans and Danes. It is characteristic of late hoards that the jewellery is mainly indigenous; earlier hoards contain objects only from other countries. The two annular brooches with animal ornament in Urnes style are definitely Scandinavian, more specifically from Gotland.   **ÜT/IJ**

Bibl.: Tõnisson 1962, 190, no. 18, pl. 19:1–2, 20–22; Selirand and Tõnisson 1984, 136, pl. 25

---

254   Wolin (*Altstadt* and *Silberberg*), Poland. 9th–11th cent. Slav.
IHKMPAN-Warsawa, Wolin

Amber. Raw material and products *(Illustrated p. 86)*

From various workshops in Wolin. Amber is found in large quantities along the south Baltic coast (cf. cat. no. 385, 395). From 9th to 12th cent. there was intensive amber working in trading centres such as Truso, Gdańsk, Kołobrzeg, Szczecin, Kamień and, particularly, Wolin where it was an important element in the economy. Its *floruit* was

in the 10th cent. when the specialized workshops in the *Hauptviertel* of the town dominated production. Most common products were spherical, faceted, cuboid and conical beads, figures, amulets and pendants including 3 horses' heads, half moons, and Thor's hammers (cat. no. 255). The round beads were probably for Islamic rosaries. The amber came from the region of Kamień. **WF**

Bibl.: Wojtasik 1957; Filipowiak 1985; Filipowiak 1991, 19

248

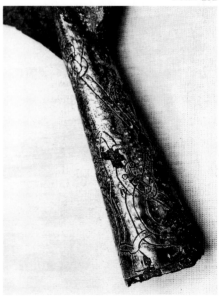

251

Detail 252

255

256

257

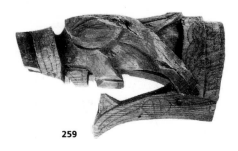

259

255
H. 2.3cm.
Wolin (*Altstadt*), Poland.
Second half of 10th cent.
IHKMPAN-Warsawa, Wolin 1842/75

Thor's hammer of amber

From 9th to early 11th cent. amber was
worked by craftsmen in many workshops in
Wolin. Beads, jewellery, gaming-pieces and
pendant amulets were made in large quantities for export and the home market (cf.
cat. no. 189, 254). Products also included
Thor's hammers.   WF

Bibl.: Wojtasik 1957, 99–152, 152–54; Filipowiak 1985,
127 f.

256
H. 21.0cm.
Wolin (*Vorstadt*), Poland.
9th cent. Slav.
IHKMPAN-Warsawa, Wolin 113/52

Pottery vessel

Wheel-thrown, grey, heavily restored. Large
quantities of pottery have been found in
Wolin, of which this 8th–10th-cent. type W_I
(K.A. Wilde) or Fresendorf (E. Schuldt) is
particularly interesting. The vessels are
wheel-thrown, tall, decorated on the shoulders with horizontal wavy lines and oblique
impressions. Because of its good quality and
handsome appearance this pottery, like the
Feldberg type, was exported to Scandinavia.
                                             WF

Bibl.: Wilde 1953, II, 25ff., pl. 1–III; Schuldt 1956; Callmer
1988a

257
H. 13.5cm.
Wolin (*Silberberg*), Poland.
10th–11th cent. Scandinavian.
IHKMPAN-Warsawa, Wolin 1511/66

Sherd of a soapstone bowl

The sherd was found in the craftsmen's
quarter, the *Silberberg*. It is one of many
10th–11th-cent. soapstone sherds found
throughout Wolin. Usually from large vessels, they have often been reused, e.g. as
ingot moulds. Soapstone shows close contacts with Scandinavia.   WF

Bibl.: Filipowiak 1985, 132–3; Filipowiak 1988

258
Yew (*taxus sp.*).
L. 14.7cm.
Wolin (harbour), Poland.
Early 11th cent. Scandinavian.
IHKMPAN-Warsawa, Wolin 695/79

Rune stick

Rune stick, fragmentary: the text is incomplete and difficult to read. It was found with
other Scandinavian objects, a dragon's head
(cat. no. 259) and a sherd of a soapstone
vessel, inside a building by the harbour. The
house was probably occupied by a Scandinavian merchant.   WF

Bibl.: Filipowiak 1985, 133; Filipowiak 1986, 23;
Filipowiak 1988; Filipowiak 1991, 29

259
Yew (*taxus sp.*).
L. 5.0cm.
Wolin (harbour), Poland.
Early 11th cent. Scandinavian.
IHKMPAN-Warsawa, Wolin 694/79

Dragon's head

The dragon's head was found with other
Scandinavian objects in a building by the
harbour (cf. cat. no. 258). The size and shape
is reminiscent of the animals' heads on the
Cammin casket (cat. no. 266). In the flat
neck there is a hole for attachment, suggesting that the head was intended as a decoration for a box or similar object.   WF

Bibl.: Filipowiak 1985, 133; Filipowiak 1986, 23;
Filipowiak 1991, 28f.

260
Silver.
Total wt. (coins) 2750g.
Ralswiek, Kr. Rügen, Germany.
First half of 9th cent.
Münzkabinett der Staatlichen Museen, Berlin

Hoard from Ralswiek *(Illustrated p. 87)*

The hoard was found in the main settlement
area at Ralswiek in 1973, beneath the remains of house 157/16. It was deposited in a
a large willow basket buried in front of the
hearth and covered with ashes. The building
belonged to settlement B and was burnt
down, along with most of the rest of the
settlement, in mid 9th cent. The person who
hid the hoard probably died or went away
because of the fire. The container held 2211
whole or fragmentary silver coins, and part
of a Permian arm-ring. The latest coin is
from the time of Caliph Al-Watik (842–847)

and was probably struck in 842. Most of the coins, some 1700, are from the Abbasid caliphate of end of the 8th cent. and the first four decades of 9th cent. Most of the coins were minted in the Middle and Near East. 12% come from Islamic mints in Africa.

This find from Ralswiek is the largest hoard of Arabic silver coins known in Europe before the middle of the 9th cent. Many of the coins are mint-fresh and had not been in circulation when hoarded. They probably arrived in Europe along the caravan route to Bulgar, then *via* Staraja Ladoga to the Baltic—a well-known Viking-age trading route.　　JH

Bibl.: Herrmann 1978, 168–71

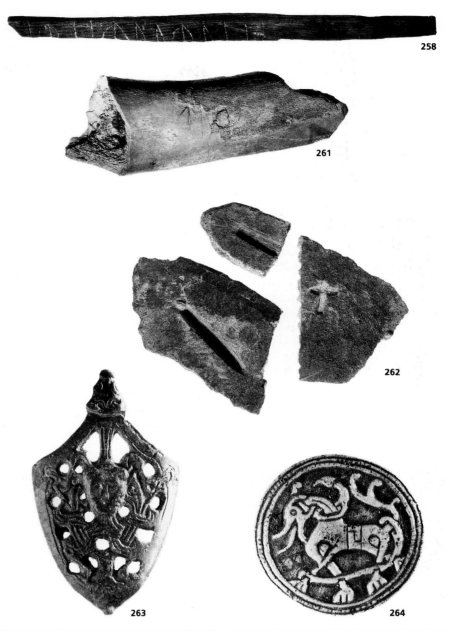

258

261

262

263

264

261　　Animal bone.
L. 8.1cm.
Ralswiek, Kr. Rügen, Germany.
Viking Age. Scandinavian.
Kulturhistorisches Museum, Stralsund, Hd 648

Bone with runes

Animal bone with carved runic inscription which can be read as TU ... The bone lay beside boats 1–3, immediately beside a cult site of 8th–9th cent. date which was discovered in later excavations.　　JH

Bibl.: Herfert 1973, 13f., Abb. 4i

262　　Soapstone.
L. 14.5cm; 10cm; 6cm.
Ralswiek, Kr. Rügen, Germany.
Viking Age. Scandinavian.
Kulturhistorisches Museum, Stralsund,
Schulg. 14.5.66, Hd5043ab, Hd4849b

Three moulds

Sherds of many Scandinavian soapstone bowls are found on Viking-age settlement sites (cf. cat. no. 64, 90), including Ralswiek. Some sherds are perforated and some preserve the iron rivets which attached the handles. Some fragments were secondarily used as moulds.

There are also large quantities of hones of Scandinavian schist; a few of the smaller ones being perforated as a whetstone for suspension from a belt, beside the knife.　JH

Bibl.: Herfert 1973, 10, pl. 5f.; publication in preparation

263　　Bronze. L. 6.6cm.
Nimschütz, Kr. Bautzen, Germany.
10th cent. Scandinavian type.
Landesmuseum für Vorgeschichte, Dresden,
D252/83

Scabbard chape

Chape of a sword scabbard, decorated with animal heads, interlace and centrally placed human masks. Similar chapes are known from Scandinavia and Russia (cf. cat. no. 330). The place where it was found, a Slav settlement, lies by the *Via Regia* which went from Kiev to Erfurt, and then by way of Mainz to Spain.　　JH

Bibl.: Coblenz 1975; Coblenz 1978, 142–43

264　　Bronze.
Diam. 4.8cm.
Carwitz, Kr. Neustrelitz, Germany.
11th cent. ?Scandinavian.
Museum für Ur- und Frühgeschichte, Schwerin,
E2487

Decorative plaque

Decorative plaque with animal ornament in Ringerike style (cf. cat. no. 416–7); found in 1837 on an island in Lake Carwitz. It must have come from a Slav settlement-site on the island, of 11th–12th cent., which has subsequently been found through excavation.　JH

Bibl.: *Corpus archäologischer Quellen* ... 1979, no. 56/33

265
Gold.
Total wt. 598.2g.
Hiddensee, Kr. Rügen, Germany.
End 10th cent. ?Danish.
Kulturhistorisches Museum, Stralsund, 1873:
a–d, f–g, i, 450. 1877: 39a–b, 91–92, 162, 176

Hoard from Hiddensee (*Illustrated p. 85*)

Hoard of gold jewellery, mostly found in 1872, other objects being found up to 1874. The circumstances of the find are unexplained. Neither Hiddensee nor Rügen lay under Piasten rule. The hoard was probably made in Denmark at end of the 10th cent. Patrices for similar jewellery have been found at Haithabu (cat. no. 105).

The extant objects are: a neck-ring of 3 plaited wires with stamp decoration, 153g; circular decorative plaque, diam. 8.0cm, originally with a pin, decorated in filigree and granulation, 114g; 4 small and 6 larger (6.4 × 6.4cm) cruciform pendants with combinations of stylized birds of prey and cross motifs, embellished with interlace, (cf. cat. no. 181), total 309.4 g; 4 spacers in the shape of elongated filigree beads, total 21.8g. The hoard is probably the greater part of a princely necklace but some of the smaller spacers are now missing. **JH**

Bibl.: Paulsen 1936; *Corpus archäologischer Quellen...* 1979, no. 44/221

266
Horn, wood, gilt bronze.
L. 63cm.
The cathedral treasury of Kamień (Pomorski),
Poland. Lost at end of Second World War.
c. 1000 with later alterations (base and parts of
lock-plate). Scandinavian.
Danmarks Nationalmuseum, Copenhagen

Cammin casket (cast) (*Illustration of original, p. 202*)

Shaped as an inverted boat with truncated ends, or as a house. The wooden core was covered with ?elk-antler plates—22 in all —clasped by riveted, engraved, gilt-bronze mounts which terminate on the roof with separately cast three-dimensional animal and bird heads. The plaques were decorated with animals and masks caught up in interlace. The bronze binding-strips are engraved with vegetal scrolls and the larger bronze mounts have zoomorphic motifs. The base and the lock-plate have been modified.

The shrine is said to have contained relics of St Cordula (a follower of St Ursula), but the means by which it came to Kamień are unknown. It is of unique shape but is distantly related to the English hogback tombs (cf. cat. no. 368–9), and has been compared to houses of Trelleborg type (p. 39, fig. 7).

The classic Mammen-style ornament foreshadows the looser tendril ornament of the Ringerike style. In detail it is ornamentally close to the Bamberg Casket (cat. no. 267, cf. cat. no. 259). **DMW**

Bibl.: Goldschmidt 1918, II, 59, no. 192; Wilson and Klindt-Jensen 1966, 126, pl. LV–LVI; Fuglesang 1980a, passim

267
Ivory (probably walrus), gilt copper,
wood.
About 26 × 26cm.
Bamberg, Germany.
Second half of 10th cent. Scandinavian.
Bayerisches Nationalmuseum München MA 286
(original), Danmarks Nationalmuseum,
Copenhagen, 835 (cast)

Bamberg casket (cast) (*Illustration of original, p. 21*)

The core of the casket consists of small oak plates on top of which there are 16 ivory plates in low relief attached to the wood by gilt-copper strips and small rivets. The middle of the lid, which may once have been removable, is decorated with a spherical rock crystal. The original lock- mechanism was in the lid. The lock in the side wall and the suspension mechanism are later. The incised decoration and plastic modelling on the ivory reliefs and metal mounts are in the Mammen style. This typical Scandinavian decoration, dated 2nd half of 10th cent., shows birds, quadrupeds, anthropomorphic masks and plant patterns. Such magnificent caskets were always luxurious products (cf. cat. no. 266), presumably used for keeping personal possessions. This masterpiece of Scandinavian decorative art is also traditionally known as 'Kunigunde's jewel-box' because of confusion with a casket from Bamberg Cathedral treasury which no longer exists. Written sources indicate that this casket was in the collegiate church of St Stephan in Bamberg at the beginning of 17th cent. when it was used as a reliquary. **AM**

Bibl.: Goldschmidt 1918, II, 58, no. 189; Schetelig 1918; Wilson and Klindt-Jensen 1966, 124–26, Pl. LIV; Fuglesang 1980a, passim; Muhl 1988

268
Iron, bronze.
Staraja Ladoga (horizon E3),
obl. St Petersburg, Russia.
Mid-8th cent. Scandinavian and east European.
Gosudarstvennyj Ermitaž, St Petersburg, 2551/
1–22

Hoard of smith's tools (*Illustrated p. 150 and 197*)

Anvil, 12.5cm; 7 tongs (1 a fragment), l. 19.2–41.8cm; 3 goldsmith's hammers; 2 spoon borers, bent together; plate-shears, l. 31.2cm; cold chisel; square piece of iron; nail-iron; pointed iron rod for piercing holes; disc with central hole (?a type of anvil); ?handle of chest with scrolled ends. 2 finished bronze objects: a temple-ring of Baltic type, diam. 6.0cm, and the handle of an unknown object (l. 5.4cm) depicting a pre-Viking Scandinavian figure of a male head crowned by 2 horns terminating in opposed birds' heads.

This collection of tools was discovered in the earliest occupation level of Staraja Ladoga and clearly had belonged to a smith with many skills, rather like the one from Mästermyr (cat. no. 95). He had worked with both coarse and fine blacksmithing and in the production of jewellery. The bronze handle (cf. no. 184), and other details, indicate that this craftsman from Staraja Ladoga's earliest period was of Scandinavian origin. Scandinavian influence is traceable in many crafts in Ladoga up to 10th cent. (cf. cat. no. 269, 271–2). **OID/IJ**

Bibl.: Rjabinin 1980, 161ff., fig. 2–3; Vierck 1983, 9ff., Abb.2, 3:2; Kirpičnikov 1988, 319f., Abb. 12

269
Iron, wood.
L. 13cm; 16cm; 12cm.
Staraja Ladoga (horizon E–D),
obl. St Petersburg, Russia.
8th–10th cent. North European type.
Gosudarstvennyj Ermitaž, St Petersburg, 2698/
250, LS–1975, SL831

Knives

3 knives (2 with wooden handles preserved) of north European type with straight backs and offsets at transition to tang. The type is characterized by a manufacturing technique in which the blade is made of 3 welded layers: a central layer of steel, which forms the cutting-edge, and 2 enclosing layers of iron.

In the Viking Age this north European type spread to N parts of Rus, demonstrating

Scandinavian influence in various parts of early Russian culture.   OID/IJ

Bibl.: Minasjan 1980, 72ff., fig.4. For the method of manufacture in Scandinavia, Arrhenius 1989

270

Leather.
L. 23cm; 10cm.
Staraja Ladoga (horizon E3), obl. St Petersburg,
Russia.
8th cent.
Gosudarstvennyj Ermitaž, St Petersburg,
LDG–329, LDG–342

Two shoes

The woman's shoe is sewn together from 2 parts: upper (with a small piece inserted over the instep) and sole (with triangular reinforcement at the heel). The upper is decorated with spirals. Shoes of similar design are known in Scandinavia, e.g. in the Norwegian Oseberg burial (cat. no. 155). The child's shoe is made of a single piece of leather fastened by laces on the front and at the heel.

OID

Bibl.: Ojateva 1965, 43ff., fig. 1 below right, 2:3; *Duisburg und die Wikinger* 1983, 73, Abb. 3, 78

271

Antler.
L. 19.0, 10.5.
Staraja Ladoga (horizon E3, D),
obl. St Petersburg, Russia.
8th cent., 10th cent.
Gosudarstvennyj Ermitaž, St Petersburg,
LS–1984, LD–719

Two combs

Composite, single-sided combs with eliptical backs of Frisian-Scandinavian type were characteristic of Staraja Ladoga in the 8th—10th cent. Manufacturing refuse shows that they were also made there. The comb with 2 contour-grooves and groups of ring-and-dots is 8th cent.; the other with raised ends on the back and geometric ornament of parallel and crossed lines is 10th cent. (cf. cat. no. 47).   OID

Bibl.: Davidan 1962, 95ff., fig. 1:4, 3:9; Davidan 1982, 171ff., fig. 1:16

272

Burr-like wood.
Diam. 13.5cm.
Staraja Ladoga (horizon E3), obl. St Petersburg,
Russia.
8th cent.
Gosudarstvennyj Ermitaž, St Petersburg,
LDG–437

Bowl

The bowl is lathe-turned with flat base and encircling groove near the base. Many lathe-

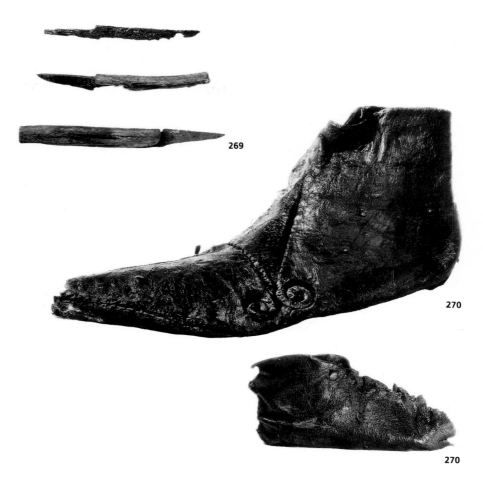

269

270

270

271

271

272

turned objects from Staraja Ladoga's lowest levels show that this technique was already practised during the earliest phases of the town (cf. cat. no. 96, 268).   OID

Bibl.: Davidan 1970b, 82, fig. 1:11, 2:3274

273

274a

274b

274c

275

273
Pottery. H. 10cm; 11cm.
Staraja Ladoga (horizon E),
obl. St Petersburg, Russia.
8th–9th cent.
Gosudarstvennyj Ermitaž, St Petersburg,
LDG–129, LDG–134

Two vessels

The pots are hand-made of clay, with large-grained tempering; they have horizontal rims and marked shoulders. They are typical of the lowest layers at Staraja Ladoga where other forms are also found, e.g. large bi-conical vessels with cuts in the upper part. Wheel-turned vessels first appear in 10th cent. OID/IJ

Bibl.: For general information of pottery in Staraja Ladoga, see Davidan 1970a, 80, fig. 1–2; Rjabinin 1985, 36f., 64, fig. 9, 25–26

274
Bronze. L.5.5cm, 8.7cm; 5.5cm.
Staraja Ladoga (a horizon E3, b–c horizon D), obl. St Petersburg, Russia.
a 8th cent.; b, c 10th cent. Scandinavian.
Gosudarstvennyj Ermitaž, St Petersburg,
LDG–403, LG–653, LD–921

Scandinavian woman's brooches

The small, plain, oval brooch *a* with a groove around the edge as its only decoration is from mainland Scandinavia and the only pre-Viking Scandinavian brooch to have been found in the Rus area. It was discovered in Staraja Ladoga's earliest occupation deposit. The equal-armed brooch (*b*) with highly stylized animal ornament is from mainland Scandinavia and the animal-head brooch (*c*) with interlace is from Gotland. Equal-armed brooches were used to fasten female outer garments while animal-headed brooches had the same function as oval brooches in other parts of Scandinavia: to fasten the dress below the shoulders. Bronze jewellery of Gotland manufacture is seldom found outside that island. OID/IJ

Bibl.: Raudonikas and Lauškin 1959, 27ff., fig. 5, 7, 9; Davidan 1970a, fig. 5:6; *Duisburg und die Wikinger*, 1983, 75

275
Iron, bronze.
Diam. 5.6cm; 4.5cm.
Staraja Ladoga (horizon E3, E2),
obl. St Petersburg, Russia.
8th cent., 9th cent.
Gosudarstvennyj Ermitaž, St Petersburg,
L–1978, LDG–346

Two penannular brooches

Both brooches have rolled terminals. One of iron with square cross-section, the other of bronze with hexagonal cross-section and fine incised lines around the edges of the terminals. They are of types (sometimes called 'horseshoe-shaped', brooches) which in the Viking Age were widely distributed from Sweden to the region between the Volga and Oka. They were particularly popular with the Balts and are, therefore, thought to be Baltic, but could be from Ladoga with its strong Scandinavian and Finnish elements. OID

Bibl.: Davidan 1986, 102, fig. 2:11–12. For general information about penannular brooches of eastern type see Salmo 1956; Malm 1966; Ginters 1984

276
Antler. L. 10cm.
Staraja Ladoga (horizon D),
obl. St Petersburg, Russia.
10th cent. Scandinavian.
Gosudarstvennyj Ermitaž, St Petersburg,
LD–678

Animal head

The head, with its flat lower end, has been fastened to an object of unknown type. It has eyes in a bulging forehead, powerful teeth in its gaping mouth, and a ring around the neck. There is a large oval hole in the crown. The neck and body are decorated on one side with geometric ornament. The head is stylistically close to wooden carvings in the Norwegian ship-burial at Oseberg (cf. cat. no. 166). OID/IJ

Bibl.: *The Dawn of Art*, 1974, no. 105; *Duisburg und die Wikinger*, 1983, 74, fig. 5

277
Wood. H. 27cm.
Staraja Ladoga (horizon D),
obl. St Petersburg, Russia.
10th cent. Slav.
Gosudarstvennyj Ermitaž. St Petersburg,
LD–117

Pagan idol

Wooden figures of this type, obviously manifestations of pagan religious belief, are often discovered on W and E Slav settlements. The identity of the god is unknown. This bearded, armless male figure has a cap (?helmet) pulled low over his forehead, a belt around his waist and short pleated skirt. OID

Bibl.: *The Dawn of Art*, 1974, no. 104; *Duisburg und die Wikinger*, 1983, 77, fig. 9

278

278

Spruce.
L. 42cm.
Staraja Ladoga (horizon E2), obl. St Petersburg, Russia.
9th cent. Scandinavian.
Gosudarstvennyj Ermitaž, St Petersburg, LS–1969

Rune stick *(Illustrated also p. 163)*

On one side of the stick is a runic inscription consisting of 52 incised symbols and 3 symbols on the other side. The runes belong to the late 16-rune *futhark*, closely related to the so-called short-twig runes or Swedish-Norwegian runes which were prevalent in Sweden and Norway in the 9th and 10th cent. The interpretation is disputed. According to Kiil the inscription is an invocation of luck in hunting and the stick was the shaft of an arrow which acted as a shot in a trap: 'The tail [= the back part of the arrow] is covered with owl [= something bushy, e.g. feathers]; the lustre [or sharpness, i.e. the arrowhead] attracts the prey in large numbers'. **OID/IJ**

Bibl.: Admoni and Silman 1957; Kiil 1964; Liestøl 1970, 122f.; Melnikova 1977, 158ff., fig. 86

279

Wood.
L. 13.9cm; 20.0cm; 13.0cm.
Staraja Ladoga (horizon E3, E2, D), obl. St Petersburg, Russia.
8th–9th cent.
Gosudarstvennyj Ermitaž, St Petersburg, LDG–442, SL–1540, LD–244

Two toy swords and a toy horse

These toy swords copy contemporary swords of Frankish type which in the second half of the 8th cent. began to spread over Europe. The sword with straight hilt and triangular pommel (horizon E2) is a faithful copy, close to Petersen type H. For wooden toys cf. cat. no. 315. **OID**

Bibl.: Davidan 1976, 115, fig. 7:7, 8:13

280

Iron.
Diam. 5.4cm.
Gorodišče, near Novgorod, Russia.
Second half of 9th cent. Scandinavian.
IIMK, St Petersburg, NOE-82/RG-359

Amulet ring with Thor's hammer

Gorodišče, or Rjurikovo Gorodišče, grew up as a nodal point by Lake Ilmen in the mid-9th cent. Scandinavians made up an impor-

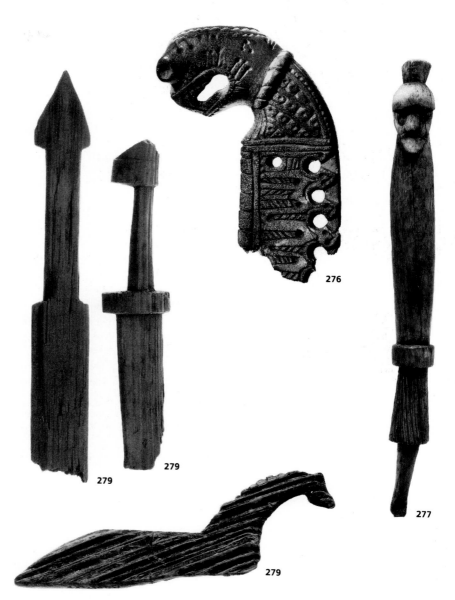

276

279

279

277

279

tant part of the population, as shown by finds of jewellery and amulets of Scandinavian type. This is a miniature version of the Thor's hammer rings (normally of the size of neck-rings), characteristic of eastern central Sweden and Åland and discovered within the Early Russian area (cf. cat. no. 300). Like the large rings, it is made of a square-section, partially twisted iron rod. **ENN**

Bibl.: Nosov 1984, 147f., fig. 1:3; Nosov 1988, 163, fig.1

280

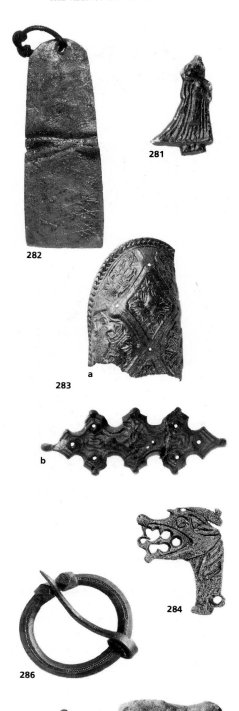

281
Silver.
H. 2.7.
Gorodišče, near Novgorod, Russia.
9th–10th cent. Scandinavian.
IIMK, St Petersburg, NOE-83/RG-195

Female figure

A woman, possibly a Valkyrie, with a long plait at the back of the neck and trailing dress. A loop on the reverse would have enabled the figure to be worn on a necklace like similar figures found in Scandinavia, cf. cat. no. 186. This is the only object of its type from the Early Russian area.   ENN

Bibl.: Nosov 1987, 82, fig. 3:3

282
Bronze.
L. 5.8cm.
Gorodišče, near Novgorod, Russia.
c. 1000. Scandinavian.
IIMK, St Petersburg, NOE-83/RG-355

Amulet with runes

One of 2 identical amulets from Gorodišče, consisting of an elongated bronze sheet with a small suspension ring of bronze wire in a hole at one end. 12 runes on one face have been deciphered as 'May you not lack manhood'. Other symbols are present on the other face. Amulets of the same form are known, e.g. from Staraja Ladoga, Roskilde, Denmark, and Sigtuna, Sweden.   ENN/IJ

Bibl.: Melnikova 1986, 210ff,; Melnikova 1987, 163ff., fig. 1–2

283
Bronze.
L. 7.0cm; 9.1 cm.
Gorodišče, near Novgorod, Russia.
9th cent. Scandinavian.
IIMK, St Petersburg, NOE-83/RG375, NOE-82/RG 185

Two brooches

Female dress of the early Viking Age usually had 3 brooches: 2 oval brooches fastening the tunic on each shoulder, and another (often equal-armed) brooch in the middle of the chest, holding together the outer garment. The fragmentary single-shell oval brooch (a) and the equal-armed brooch (b) belong to the commonest 9th-cent. types in Scandinavia (P37 and P58 respectively) (cf. cat. no. 101), but such early types are rare in Russia. The rivet holes at the intersections of the strapwork of the oval brooch and in the lobes of the equal-armed brooch were for attaching silver-covered bosses of pewter/lead.   ENN/IJ

Bibl.: Nosov 1987, 81, fig. 3:5–6; Nosov 1988, 163, fig. 2–3

284
Lead.
H. 4.2cm.
Gorodišče, near Novgorod, Russia.
10th cent. Scandinavian.
Novgorodskij Gosudarstvennyj Muzej, KP 25402/D 26–442

Dragon's head

The dragon's head is flat but decorated on both sides, the neck formed as a socket with a loop at the back. Probably the head of a dress pin. Parallels are known from Birka and Hedeby. A mould of a dragon's head of different appearance but similar function is seen in cat no. 12.   ENN/IJ

Bibl.: Polubojarinova 1972, 222f., fig. 4:2; Nosov 1990, 157, fig. 62:5

285
Bronze.
L. 4.4cm.
Gorodišče, near Novgorod, Russia.
10th cent. Scandinavian.
IIMK, St Petersburg, NOE-82/RG-185

Bridle mount

The mount is in openwork, decorated with interlace and an animal mask in the Borre style. Parallels in Scandinavia, e.g. from the ship burial at Borre, Norway, show that the mount was from a bridle (cf. cat. no. 301).   ENN

Bibl.: Nosov 1984, 147, fig. 1:2; Nosov 1987, 82, fig. 3:2

286
Bronze.
Diam. 6.0cm.
Gorodišče, near Novgorod, Russia.
10th cent. Finnish.
IIMK, St Petersburg, NOE-83/RG-270

Penannular brooch

The brooch indicates relationships between Finnish culture and the Ladoga area. It has faceted terminals with beading on the upper surfaces, a characteristic decoration on much Finnish Viking-age jewellery.   ENN/IJ

Bibl.: Nosov 1990, 123, fig. 45:3

287
Sandstone.
L. 7.1cm.
Gorodišče, near Novgorod, Russia.
9th–10th cent. Slav.
IIMK, St Petersburg, NOE-82/RG-158

Mould

Mould for casting small spiral ornaments and small rings or balls, probably used as beads.   ENN/IJ

Bibl.: Nosov 1990, 131, fig. 51:4

289

288

290

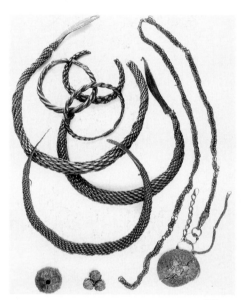

291

288

Iron.
L. 6.8cm–7.5cm.
Gorodišče, near Novgorod, Russia.
9th–10th cent. *a* Slav, *b* Scandinavian.
Novgorodskij Gosudarstvennyj Muzej, K 36157/
6, 117, 124, 177

Four arrowheads

Numerous arrowheads are characteristic of
finds from Gorodišče, indicating that the site
housed a considerable number of warriors.
The arrowheads also give an idea of the
origin of the warriors. 3 (*a*) are barbed and
socketed, a type characteristic of the Slavs.
About a third of the arrowheads found are of
this type so Slavs must have been fairly
numerous. Arrowhead *b*, with a narrow lanceolate blade and offset tang, is Scandinavian. **ENN**

Bibl.: Nosov 1987, 79, fig. 4; Nosov 1990, 164f., fig. 40, 42

289

Wood.
L. 45.5cm.
Novgorod (Nerev quarter), Russia.
Mid-11th cent. Early Russian.
Novgorodskij Gosudarstvennyj Muzej, KP
32435/A 73/7

Fragment of ?chair or sledge

Written sources often mention Scandinavians in Novgorod, but there are few definite
objects of Northern origin. The decoration
on this piece of wood is probably influenced
by Scandinavian animal ornament. It shows
4 animals in a row, the back of each body
being knotted around the neck of the animal
behind. The tongues and lappets are drawn
out into interlace. **ENN/IJ**

Bibl.: Kolchin 1989, vol. 1, 177, no. 139; vol. 2, 421, pl. 175

290

L. 33cm.
Novgorod, Russia.
Second half of 11th cent.
Novgorodskij Gosudarstvennyj Muzej, HIM
33014-194

Birch bark letter

Novgorod is famous for the many letters and
other documents written in the Cyrillic alphabet on birch bark which have been discovered
by excavation in the town's occupation layers. The documents are written in Old Russian and give an unusually many-sided picture of life in this trading metropolis. This
document (No. 526) contains a list of debtors
and their debts. Various places within the
Novgorod principality are mentioned—the
Luga region, the town of Russa, lake Seliger,
etc. One of the people it mentions had the
Scandinavian name *Asgut* (Asgautr). **EKK/IJ**

Bibl.: Arcichovskij and Janin 1978, no. 526

291

Silver, gilding, niello.
Diam. 5.6cm (brooch), 36–46cm (neck-
rings).
Sobači Gorby near Novgorod, Russia.
11th cent. Early Russian with Scandinavian and
eastern elements.
Gosudarstvennyj Ermitaž, St Petersburg, 1006/
1–10

Hoard from Sobači Gorby

Circular brooch with granulation and filigree, 3 chains attached, one with animal-head
terminal; 3 twisted or plaited neck-rings with
terminal plates partly broken; 3 twisted or
plaited arm-rings, one with twisted terminals, one with nielloed terminals, one with
broken terminals; 3 beads with geometric
granulation; hemispherical, cast, gilt mount
with plant ornament in relief.

The hoard was discovered by the River
Volchov, about 10km N of Novgorod, and
also contained 336 Islamic, Byzantine and W
European coins struck 898–107. The
jewellery is characteristic of early Russian
culture at the end of the Viking Age with its
amalgam of Slav, Scandinavian and Eastern
elements. The brooch is of the Scandinavian
Terslev type but no Scandinavian brooches
have such granulation of triangles and
rhomboids. This decoration is Slav (see, e.g.,
the beads), the brooch thus is a hybrid Scan-
dinavian-Russian type, probably made in
Novgorod (cf. cat. no. 143, 585). **OID/IJ**

Bibl.: Otčet Archeologičeskoj komissii 1906, fig. 159–160;
Korzuchina 1954, 100f.

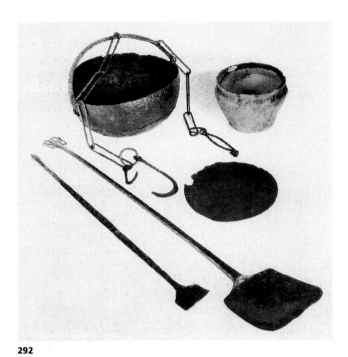

292

Iron, clay.
Zaozere, mound 6, complex VII, SE
Ladoga region, obl. St Petersburg, Russia.
10th cent.
Gosudarstvennyj Ermitaž, St Petersburg, 700/
76–80, 82

Ritual hearth

Iron cauldron with handle; iron chain from which the cauldron was suspended over the fire; frying pan made of a circular, slightly concave, iron plate; 2 iron shovels (for baking or ?frying, cf. cat. no. 211); handmade pottery vessel.

Particular to the Ladoga region is the presence of a ritual hearth with its cooking equipment on the site of a burial mound. The mound was built over it with burials at different times and different levels within it.

OID/IJ

Bibl.: Raudonikas 1930, 44–45, fig. 27, 29, 38, 46; Arbman 1955, 40ff., pl. 3–4

294

293

293

293

293

297

293

Bronze, iron, bone, textile.
Zaozere, mound 6, complex VIII, SE
Ladoga region, obl. St Petersburg, Russia.
10th cent. Scandinavian, Finnish, Slav.
Gosudarstvennyj Ermitaž, St Petersburg, 700/
84–87, 90–93

Female grave *(Illustrated in part)*

Oval brooch, bronze, Scandinavian (one of two from the grave); temple-ring of bronze wire with twisted ends and orange glass bead, Slav; 2 clattering pendants of bronze, decorated with animal heads and a human head, Finnish; finger-ring of decorated sheet bronze: bronze bells; knife with bone handle; fragment of wool textile.

The first person buried in mound 6 at Zaozere was probably this woman dressed in clothing decorated with Scandinavian, Finnish and Slav jewellery. This mixture is characteristic of the SE Ladoga area and makes it difficult to determine ethnic origins, Scandinavian and Finnish elements were probably present in the population.   OID/IJ

Bibl.: Raudonikas 1930, 45–46, 48–49, fig. 27, 29, 47–51; Arbman 1955, 40ff., pl. 3–4

294

Iron, bronze, stone.
L. sword 93.2cm.
Zaozere, mound 6, complex V, SE Ladoga
region, obl. St Petersburg, Russia.
10th–11th cent. East, west and north European.
Gosudarstvennyj Ermitaž, St Petersburg, 700/
48–50, 52–55, 57–59, 61, 456

Male grave

Sword, blade inlaid with the word CEROLT; spearhead; axe; 3 rod-shaped and 1 transverse arrowheads; 16 cast bronze belt-mounts with plant ornament, 13 circular, 2 rhomboid, 1 tongue-shaped, w. 1.4cm; whetstone of banded schist perforated at one end and with remains of iron suspension loop; padlock key with pierced rectangular bit.

The later burials in mound 6 at Zaozere included this cremation with cremated bones and artifacts at a level halfway up the mound. The equipment is characteristic of male graves throughout north and eastern Europe, thus his ethnic origin is difficult to determine. The inscription on the sword shows it to be west European, probably a product of Rhenish workshops. The axe is of Scandinavian type. The transverse arrowheads are characteristic elements of the hunting equipment of the forests of north Eurasia (cf. cat. no. 208). The belt is of an Oriental type which in 10th and particularly 11th–12th cent. was widespread in eastern Europe and the Baltic area (cf. cat. no. 132).

OID/IJ

Bibl.: Raudonikas 1930, 44, fig. 28, 32, 38–41; Kirpičnikov 1966-1971, vol. 1, 29f., pl. 2:3, 17:2, vol. 2, pl. 14:2

295

Bronze, gilding, silver, iron, glass, semi-precious stone, antler.
L. (oval brooches) 10.6cm; 10.7cm.
Bolšoe Timerevo, obl. Jaroslavl, Russia.
First half of 10th cent. Scandinavian, Islamic, English.
Gosudarstvennyj Istoričeskij Muzej, Moscow,
103949, inv. 2366/ 62, 64–71

Female grave *(Illustrated in part)*

2 bronze, double-shelled, oval brooches with animal ornament; circular bronze brooch with interlace, diam. 3.5cm; antler comb with bronze mounts with interlace; necklace with 6 blue and yellow glass beads and 7 faceted rock-crystal beads; silver finger-ring with inset carnelian with Arabic inscription; iron knife with handle bound with silver wire; pendant made of Arabic coin (Baghdad 803–804); pendant made of English coin (Edmund c. 900).

The archaeological complex of Timerevo lies in the Upper Volga region and consists of a settlement and cemetery of 485 graves. They were of a population of mixed ethnic origin—Finns, Scandinavians and Slavs—in which the Finno-Ugrian element was dominant. Some graves belonged to members of a chieftains' guard. Imports from the Orient and Mediterranean countries show that the population took part in international trade.

This grave (no. 348) consisted of a pit 2.9 × 1.9m, 0.6m deep, dug through a cremation layer. The woman had been buried seated, with head to W, a burial custom known from both Early Russia and Scandinavia. The burial rite and the grave-goods show that she was of Scandinavian origin.

VVM

Bibl.: Fechner and Nedošivina 1987, 85, fig. 9

296

Wax.
H. 10.0cm.
Bolšoe Timerevo, obl. Jaroslavl, Russia.
Late 10th cent.
Gosudarstvennyj Istoričeskij Muzej, Moscow,
103390, inv. 2129/162

Candle

Wax candle, shaped by hand, discovered on the wooden roof of a large chamber in one of the richest warrior burial-mounds in Timerevo (grave 100). The reason for its presence was no doubt protective magic. Candles have been found in a similar position in the contemporary burial mounds of Mammen and Jelling, Denmark.

VVM

Bibl.: Fechner and Nedošivina 1987, 84, fig. 5:4

297

Bronze.
L. 4.5cm; 4.6cm.
Bolšoe Timerevo, obl. Jaroslavl, Russia.
Second half of 10th cent. Scandinavian.
Gosudarstvennyj Istoričeskij Muzej, Moscow,
98561, inv. 1946/583–584

Bird-shaped hooks

The hooks are made in the shape of birds' heads with 3 attachment loops. The interlace decoration is in Borre style. Similar hooks are known from Scandinavia and Gnezdovo, and are usually (as in Birka grave 905) interpreted as garter tags. They may, however, have been used for fastening a box for scales (cf. cat. no. 302).

VVM/IJ

Bibl.: Jaroslavskoe Povolže 1963, 17, fig. 7

295

296

298

298

Clay tempered with much organic
material.
L. a–b 13.5cm; diam. c 16.8cm.
Bolšoe Timerevo (a–b); Michajlovskoe (c),
obl. Jaroslavl, Russia.
10th cent.
Gosudarstvennyj Istoričeskij Muzej, Moscow,
103949, inv. 2366/146; 98561, inv. 1945/552;
44730, inv. 290/155

Two clay paws and a clay ring

a–b Paws from graves 120 and 401; *c* the ring from grave 46. Ritual clay paws (beaver paws) and clay rings of this type are common

300

300

302

in 10th-cent. cremations in the Volga region around Jaroslavl and in the regions around Vladimir and Suzdal in NE Russia. Similar paws also occur in many 7th–10th-cent. graves on Åland (cat. no. 235) and one has been found in a 6th/7th cent. cremation in Södermanland, Sweden. Much current debate on their relationship centres on the direction of distribution: from the Finno-Ugrian area of NE Russia to Åland's Scandinavian milieu with Finno-Ugrian influences, or *vice versa*. **VVM/IJ**

Bibl.: Jaroslavskoe Povolže 1963, 87, fig. 50. The most recent debates (with references to earlier works) can be found in Jansson 1987, 782f.; Callmer 1988b.

299 Iron, gold, silver, niello. L. 6.0cm. Kazan region, Russia. First half of 11th cent. Early Russian. Gosudarstvennyj Istoričeskij Muzej, Moscow, 34213, 1959/1

Axe of parade *(Illustrated p. 80)*
This small axe, probably discovered in the central Volga area, is richly inlaid with gold and silver. One face shows a tree of life flanked by 2 birds, the other face has a ribbon-shaped dragon transfixed by a sword; on the roundel on both sides of the shaft-hole is the letter A. The axe type is Steppe Nomadic in origin, the decoration probably being mainly inspired by Scandinavia and Byzantium. A dragon pierced by a sword is a common motif in Scandinavian art (e.g. on runestones) and represents Fafnir being killed by Gram, the sword belonging to the hero Sigurd. **VVM/IJ**

Bibl.: Sizov 1897; Paulsen 1956, 122ff., Abb. 56; Kirpičnikov 1966–71, vol. 2, 35, pl. 19; *Slavjane i skandinavy*, 1986, 248, fig. 82

300 Iron, bronze. L. of sword 98.5cm, spearhead 51.7cm; Thor's hammer ring diam. 15.0cm. Gnezdovo, obl. Smolensk, Russia. 10th cent. West European; Scandinavian. Gosudarstvennyj Istoričeskij Muzej, Moscow, 80135, 1798/66, 1071/5, 7, 65–9

Male grave from Gnezdovo
Iron sword with pitted decoration on hilt and ULFBERH+T inlaid on blade (*not illustrated*); iron spearhead with pattern-welded blade and socket decorated with deeply incised grooves; iron Thor's hammer ring with 2 hammers and 2 circular amulets; iron

shears with suspension loop; iron tweezers with suspension loop; iron knife; 2 iron crampons.

Gnezdovo is an archaeological complex at the middle of the route 'from the Varangians to the Greeks'. It has a fortress, an undefended settlement, and more than 3000 burial mounds which make it Europe's largest medieval cemetery. Gnezdovo had a mixed Slav-Baltic-Scandinavian population and grew up as a result of international trade. Many of the graves are of warriors. The artifacts exhibited come from Kuscinskij's excavations in 1874 and apparently all derive from the same grave although this cannot be proved. The sword and spearhead are early, probably of 9th-cent. Frankish workmanship. Swords with the name of the Frankish master Ulfberht are known from most of Europe. The Thor's hammer ring is of a type of amulet rings deriving from central Sweden and Åland (cf. cat. no. 179, 280) and it is assumed that the buried man was Scandinavian. **VVM/IJ**

Bibl.: Sizov 1902, pl.4:13, 7:17; Fechner 1967, 62ff., fig.7; Kirpičnikov 1966–1971, vol. 1, 30f., pl. 1:1, 16:1, vol. 2, 9, pl. 1; Kirpičnikov 1970, 56f., 70f.

301 Leather, gilt bronze. Gnezdovo, obl. Smolensk, Russia. 10th cent. Scandinavian. Gosudarstvennyj Istoričeskij Muzej, Moscow, 42536, 1537/1538

Bridle *(Illustrated p. 76)*
Parts of the forehead and cheek straps (width 1.5cm) of the bridle, decorated with 46 cast and gilt-bronze mounts with animal ornament in Borre style; the large mount in the middle of the forehead strap has a hinge and animal-head pendant. Many similar bridles are known from Scandinavia, including one from the ship burial at Borre, Norway (cat. no. 169), after which the Borre style is named.

The Gnezdovo bridle was found in a mound with a cremation burial but outside the cremation layer, thus it was not destroyed by fire. **VVM/IJ**

Bibl.: Sizov 1902, pl. 12:1; Kirpičnikov 1973, 25f., pl.7

304

303

302

Bronze.
L. of balance arm 10.8cm.
Gnezdovo, obl. Smolensk, Russia.
10th cent.
Gosudarstvennyj Istoričeskij Muzej, Moscow,
42536, inv. 1537/1631

Folding scales

Each pan is decorated internally with a finely engraved rosette; circles decorate the exteriors and the balance arm. Folding scales for weighing precious metals—generally thought to be an Oriental invention—are common from Russia to the British Isles in the Viking Age (cf. cat. no. 150, 356, 500).

VVM/IJ

303

Iron, silver.
L. 43.5cm.
Gnezdovo, obl. Smolensk, Russia.
10th cent.
Gosudarstvennyj Istoričeskij Muzej, Moscow,
42536, inv. 11537/77

?Knife

This two-edged 'knife' is unique. A mask in cast silver at the transition between blade and hilt suggests that the object is Scandinavian, perhaps made by Scandinavians in Russia since no similar object is known in Scandinavia. The knife was found lying on top of a cauldron in which there was the horned skull of a ram, and some wool. This, and the blunt cutting-edges, have led to much discussion concerning the function of the object—dagger, offering, ritual knife, weaving sword, linen beater?

VVM/IJ

Bibl.: Sizov 1902, 91, fig. 58–60; Spicyn 1905, 63; Rybakov 1949, 41, fig. 14; Fechner 1965; Petruchin 1975, note 41

304

Silver, gold, gilding, niello, bronze,
iron, glass.
Gnezdovo, near Smolensk, Russia.
10th cent. Scandinavian, Slav, Oriental.
Gosudarstvennyj Ermitaž, St Petersburg, 994/
1–7, 9–18, 20–51, 53–56, 58–67, 69–72, 74–82,
85–87, 89–104

The Gnezdovo hoard *(Illustrated also p. 20, 77–8)*

2 Slav temple-rings of silver wire with glass beads; 6 neck-rings, 1 tubular, diam. 35cm, with melon-shaped knobs decorated with gold foil and filigree; 2 east Scandinavian circular brooches, cast, with plastic animals, 1 with 3 clattering pendants on chains; 46 beads of sheet silver, most with granulation of Slav character, others with filigree, some plain; 21 cast pendants (18 Scandinavian with openwork animal ornament or, in one case, a face-mask, 3 of Oriental or Steppe-Nomad character—2 converted from belt mounts); 21 pendants of sheet silver (1 large capsule, 7 lunulae of east Slav type with geometric granulation, 1 shaped like a female figure of Scandinavian character, the remaining 12 round—2 have Slav granulation, the remainder filigree of west European/Scandinavian type); 8 coins, most converted to pendants, 2 Sassanian, 1 Indian, the rest Islamic (the hoard contains 20 coins in all, the latest 953–4); 2 Scandinavian oval brooches of bronze; 1 iron sword, fragmentary.

This great silver hoard, discovered in 1868, is Russia's most famous Viking-age hoard. It consists almost entirely of jewellery, mostly of Scandinavian or Slav character but some objects are of Oriental/Steppe-Nomad type. The most prominent Slav decorations are the lunulae pendants, characteristic of the Dnepr region; the most interesting Scandinavian objects are the circular brooches with plastic animals (cf. cat. no. 305), and the many cast pendants with close parallels in the Swedish Vårby hoard (cat. no. 27). The filigree decoration on the unique tubular neck-ring (was it designed to adorn a statue of a god?) is of Scandinavian/Western character.

The bronze oval-brooches and the iron sword are unusual components of a hoard; perhaps they belonged to graves discovered at the same time as the hoard. **OID/IJ**

Bibl.: Arne 1914a, 42ff., fig. 21–24; Guščin 1936, 53ff., pl. 1–4; Korzuchina 1954, 87f.; Wilson and Klindt-Jensen 1966, 93; Duczko 1989

305

Silver, gilding, niello.
H. 8.8cm; wt. 225g.
Elec, obl. Lipeck, Russia.
10th cent. Russian-Scandinavian.
Gosudarstvennyj Ermitaž, St Petersburg, 997/1

Equal-armed brooch *(Illustrated p. 201)*

This fragmentary brooch is a stray find from the Upper Don in the border region between the Early Russian State and the areas of the Steppe Nomads. It was probably deposited as **part of a hoard. It consists of the bow and** one arm of an equal-armed brooch decorated with animal ornament, interlace and a palmette in relief, as well as plastic animal figures and heads both cast in one piece with the brooch and riveted to it. Equal-armed brooches with plastic animals are characteristic of east Scandinavia but no Scandinavian example can compete with the Elec example for magnificence. The palmette in relief is foreign to 10th-cent. east Scandinavian art and probably derives from the Orient or Byzantium. The brooch may have been made by a Scandinavian craftsman active in the early Russian State. **OID/IJ**

Bibl.: Arne 1914a, 50, fig. 39; Arbman 1959, 120–30, Abb. 2–6; Wilson and Klindt-Jensen 1966, 91, pl. XXXId

306
Bronze, gilding, silver, glass, semi-precious stones.
L. of oval brooches 11.0cm; 11.2cm.
Kiev grave 124, Ukraine.
Second half of 10th cent. Scandinavian, Russian, Byzantine, Oriental.
Gosudarstvennyj Istoričeskij Muzej, Moscow, 33602, 1678/1–2, 4–6, 11–12

Female grave from Kiev *(Illustrated p. 75)*

2 double-shelled oval brooches of gilt bronze; 1 Byzantine silver coin (928–944) converted to pendant; necklace of 11 glass, 3 carnelian and 1 rock-crystal beads; silver pendant cross with engraved decoration; 2 silver ear-rings with granulated pendants.

Kiev was the capital of the Early Russian State and centre of the 'Russian land'. Few archaeological remains survive in Kiev from the time of the formation of the state, probably because of the destruction of the pagan cemetery of *c.* 1000. This grave was discovered in building work at the end of the 19th cent. No more details are known. The assemblage, including Scandinavian brooches and ear-rings of west Slav 'Volhynian' type, illustrates the complicated processes of cultural assimilation in the Early Russian capital. **VVM**

Bibl.: Golubeva 1949, 107f., fig. 2; Karger 1958, 209, fig. 45, pl. 28

307
Silver.
Wt. 2.97g.
Sigsarve, Hejde parish, Gotland, Sweden.
c. 1000. Russian (Kiev).
Kungl. Myntkabinettet, Stockholm, SHM 16077

Coin of Vladimir I (978–1015)

Obverse: VLADIMIR AND THIS IS HIS[SILVER] (legend in Russian). Bust looking to front. Reverse: JESUS [CHRIST] (legend in Russian). Christ looking to front.

In the Viking Age Russia was a single state with its centre in Kiev; in 988 Vladimir was converted to Orthodox Christianity. The minting of gold coins (*zlatniki*) began in Kiev *c.* 988, and silver coins (*srebreniki*) were minted soon after. Only 3 of these coins have been found outside Russia but coins issued in Novgorod in 1010s are somewhat more common. Byzantine coins were used as models for the Kiev coins, the Novgorod coins being more novel. **KJ**

Bibl.: Sotnikova and Spasski 1982, 24–2

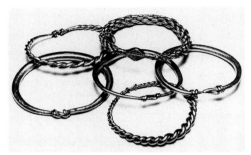

308

309

310

308
Gold.
Kiev, Ukraine.
10th cent. ?Scandinavian.
Gosudarstvennyj Ermitaž, St Petersburg
304/1–6

Six arm-rings

6 gold arm-rings: 3 of a smooth, rounded rod with ends coiled together, 2 double with coiled ends, 1 double with rhomboid ends. The arm-rings were found with almost 3,000 Islamic silver coins (dated 709–906) in a small copper cauldron sealed with wax discovered on Professor Sikorskij's property in central Kiev. Arm-rings of this type are considered to be Scandinavian and probably served as signs of wealth and high social standing. **OID/IJ**

Bibl.: Korzuchina 1954, 83, pl. 5; *1000 Jahre russische Kunst* 1988, no. 221–226

309
Bronze.
H. 4.6cm.
Černaja Mogila, Černigov, Ukraine.
10th cent. Scandinavian.
Gosudarstvennyj Istoričeskij Muzej, Moscow,
76990, inv. 1539/77

Seated male figure

The figure depicts a seated man holding his beard in his right hand and with a broad belt around his waist. It has many parallels in Scandinavia (cf. cat. no. 77), and possibly represents the god Thor. This comes from one of the best known pagan burial mounds in Early Russia, Černaja Mogila, where a high-status member of a princely guard is thought to have been buried. The complicated burial rite and the miscellaneous assemblage (a Scandinavian figure of a god, a ritual horn of possible Khazar manufacture, etc.) suggests that the grave belongs to an ethnically mixed milieu. **VVM**

Bibl.: Samokvasov 1908, 199; Rybakov 1949, 45, 17; Puskina 1984

310
Bronze.
L. 7.3cm.
Korosten, obl. Žitomir, Ukraine.
10th cent. Scandinavian.
Gosudarstvennyj Istoričeskij Muzej, Moscow,
105009, inv. 2575/1

Scabbard chape

The openwork chape is decorated in Borre style. Similar chapes have been found within the area of the Early Russian State and some have been found elsewhere—in the Crimea and by the Lower Volga. This example comes from the region around the town of Korosten—*Iskorosten* of the Chronicles—and has been connected with Prince Igor who was killed near the town in 945 (cf. cat. no. 330).

VVM/IJ

Bibl.: Fechner 1982

311
Iron, bronze.
L. 85.5cm.
Foščevataja, near Mirgorod, obl. Poltava, Ukraine.
First half of 11th cent. Early Russian.
Gosudarstvennyj Istoričeskij Muzej, Kiev, V-2714

Sword

The hilt consists of 4 cast-bronze parts. The rim-mount of the scabbard remains beneath the guard. The grip is decorated with plant and geometric ornament, other bronze parts have animal ornament in relief. On the upper part of the blade the fuller is inscribed in Cyrillic letters inlaid with pattern-welded wires: on one side is the owner's name *Ljudota* or *Ljudoša*, on the other side *koval* (smith).

The animal ornament is a variant of the Scandinavian Ringerike style, thus the sword was originally thought to be the only certain Scandinavian sword from the Early Russian State. The literate early Russian craftsman who manufactured the blade incorporated traits from various parts of Europe: Francia (technique of the inscription), Scandinavia (parts of the decoration), Early Russian State (blade and parts of the decoration). OVB/IJ

Bibl.: Arne 1914a, 57, fig. 42; Kirpičnikov 1966–71, vol. 1, 37, pl. 13–15; Kirpičnikov 1970, 66ff., fig. 6–7

312
Limestone. H. 47cm.
Berezan, mouth of Dnepr, Ukraine.
11th cent. Scandinavian.
Odesskij Archeologičeskij Muzej, Odessa, A-50378

Rune stone

The lower part of the slab is broken. The inscription follows the curved upper edge: 'Grane made this memorial (*hvalf*) after Karl, his comrade (*félagi*)'. The slab was discovered in a secondary position in a stone coffin in a burial mound. It had originally been raised over Karl's grave and was probably part of a gabled Christian cist of a type known in Sweden. The word *hvalf* means 'vault', but in 12th- and 13th-cent. Swedish describes hori-

zontal, flat or cist-shaped grave-stones.

Berezan was an important stopping-place on the route 'from the Varangians to the Greeks', it is not, therefore, surprising that the only rune-stone in E Europe has been found on this island. Grane and Karl may have been on a trading venture; the word *félagi* probably means 'partner'. They may, however, have been part of the troops of a Russian chieftain, or have been on their way south to join the Byzantine emperor's Varangian guard. A fragment of a Finnish penannular brooch has also been found on the island. VPV/IJ

Bibl.: Braun 1907; Arne 1914b; Jansson 1963, 63f.; Melnikova 1977, 154, fig. 84. For some Scandinavian parallels to the Berezan stone see *Sveriges runinskrifter* V, 1940–70, 37ff., pl. 22–26. For the brooch see Cleve 1929, 252ff., Abb. 1

313
Silver, partly gilded.
Diam. at rim 10.6–10.9cm.
Dune, Dalhem, Gotland, Sweden.
11th cent. Byzantine.
Statens Historiska Museum, Stockholm, 6849:5

Cup

The cup comes from a large silver hoard probably deposited at the time of King Valdemar Atterdag's invasion of Gotland in 1361. It was discovered in 1881 when digging a ditch, and contains cup, spoons, drinking bowls, jewellery and silver dress-accessories from the 12th to 14th cent., but no coins.

The surface has chased, chiselled and punched decoration: a broad band with birds, winged lions and palmettes surrounded above and below with foliage; the handle, in the form of a ring, has a palmette-shaped plate on top. The foot is slightly rounded and has a foot ring. A secondary engraving on the bottom contains within a square the magic formula SATOR AREPO TENET OPERA ROTAS in runes, and in a triangle a name in runes UEMNTER (?Vämund). GT

Bibl.: af Ugglas 1936; Andersson 1983

312

311

313

314

314

Bronze.
H. 31.4cm.
Aska, Hagebyhöga, Östergötland, Sweden.
10th cent. Islamic.
Statens Historiska Museum, Stockholm, 16560

Flask

The flask, part of a drinking service from a wealthy female grave, was made by soldering together three bronze sheets which made up the neck, body and base. A heavy iron rivet near the rim suggests that it may originally have had a handle and perhaps a lid. The punched decoration on the shoulder incorporates an Arabic inscription (inlaid with modern chalk) which is so stylized that it is illegible. Many similar flasks, both with and without handles, are known from the eastern Caliphate. Only three have been found in Scandinavia, two of them as containers for hoards (cf. cat. no. 143).   IJ

Bibl.: Arne 1932, 75, 100ff., Abb. 20–1; Graham-Campbell 1980, no. 351; Jansson 1988, 621ff., 646, Abb. 31B

316

316

315

a Willow (*Salix* sp.). *b* Fir
a L. 25cm; *b* L. 13.2cm.
a Argisbrekka, Eysturoy; *b* Kvívík, Streymoy, Faroes.
Viking Age. Local.
Føroya Fornminnissavn, Tórshavn, 4765/1159; 3797

Toy boat and horse *(Illustrated p. 58)*

a The boat is carefully designed and copies clinker-built vessels of the period. The gunwale is marked on the exterior and the two uppermost strakes are decorated with faint, oblique lines. Obvious keel.

b Carved stallion. Both objects were found during excavations of Viking-age settlements. They are comparable with toys found elsewhere (cf. cat. no. 13–14, 73, 279).

                DLM/SVA

Bibl.: Dahl 1979; Mahler 1986; Mahler forthcoming

316

Soapstone.
Spindle-whorl: Diam. 4.2cm. Net sinker:
L. 15.0cm.
Toftanes, Leirvik, Eysturoy, Faroes.
10th cent. Scandinavian.
Føroya Fornminnissavn, Tórshavn, 4666/330; 4666/1567

Spindle-whorl and net-sinker

The spindle-whorl has a convex upper side. The net-sinker has a circular cross-section, perforations at both ends and a groove for the line. Both were found during excavations of a 10th-cent. farm (cf. cat. no. 317–22) and reflect the main occupations of the Faroese—wool production and fishing. Many other soapstone objects were found, including sherds of bowls and some 50 spindle-whorls. Soapstone does not occur naturally on the Faroes and these objects must have been brought to Toftanes by the first settlers, or imported.   SSH

Bibl.: Stummann Hansen 1988; Stummann Hansen 1989; Stummann Hansen forthcoming

317

a Alder (*Alnus*). *b* Larch (*Larix*).
a Diam. 18.1cm. *b* L. 17.5cm.
Toftanes, Eysturoy, Faroes.
10th cent. Scandinavian.
Føroya Fornminnissavn, Tórshavn, 4666/941; 4666/1422

Wooden bowl and spoon

Found during excavations of a farm (cf. cat. no. 316). *a* The bowl is carved and has a lug and handle. Other bowls from Toftanes are also of alder which seems to have been the only wood used for making bowls. It does not grow on the Faroes and was probably brought from Norway. *b* The spoon was probably carved from driftwood. Fragments of other spoons (or dough scrapers) are known from Toftanes, including a spoon-bowl with band decoration.   SSH

Bibl.: as for cat. no. 316

318

Spruce (*Picea abies*).
L. 16.1cm.
Toftanes, Eysturoy, Faroes.
10th cent. Scandinavian.
Føroya Fornminnissavn, Tórshavn, 4666/694, 697

Tally-stick

The stick, which is fragmentary, is of square cross-section and perforated; probably carved from driftwood. This is one of several tally-sticks found from the excavation of a farm (cf. cat. no. 316); they were presumably used for everyday reckoning and keeping accounts.   SSH

Bibl.: as for cat. no. 316

317

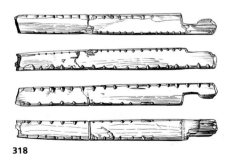

318

319

319 Bronze. Diam. 2.6cm.
Toftanes, Eysturoy, Faroes.
10th cent. Scandinavian.
Føroya Fornminnissavn, Tórshavn, 4666/2076

Disc brooch

This slightly domed brooch was found during the excavation of a farm (cf. cat. no. 316). It is decorated in Borre style with interlace and three heads. Parallels are known from mainland Scandinavia where the brooch was probably made, e.g. from Birka, Hedeby and Trelleborg. **SSH**

Bibl.: as for cat. no. 316

320 Bronze. L. 12.5cm.
Toftanes, Eysturoy, Faroes.
10th cent. ?Irish.
Føroya Fornminnissavn, Tórshavn, 46666/2073

Ring pin

Found during the excavation of a farm (cat. no. 316). This type of dress pin with smooth ring and faceted head with knot and cross motifs occurs almost exclusively in the west of the Viking world. The type is inspired by Irish pins and has parallels in Ireland, the Isle of Man, Scotland and the Isles, Iceland and Newfoundland (cat. no. 346); a few are known from Scandinavia. This is the only example from the Faroes and was probably made in Ireland. **SSH**

Bibl.: as for cat. no. 316; Fanning 1990, 143–6

320

321 Oak (*Quercus*). L. 70.5cm.
Toftanes, Eysturoy, Faroes.
10th cent. Scandinavian.
Føroya Fornminnissavn, Tórshavn, 4666/2250

Gaming board

The gaming board, with handle and a rim about 1cm high, is split longitudinally; about half is preserved. A wheel game is carved in the depression on the upper side and a chequerboard on the under side, probably for the game *hneftafl*. Gaming-pieces probably used in this game are found in Scandinavian burials (cat. no. 71, 123), but few gaming boards are preserved (cat. no. 572); the Faroese example is one of the oldest. Found during excavation of a farm (cat. no. 316). **SSH**

Bibl.: as for cat. no. 316

321

322

322 Juniper (*Juniperus*).
L. 133cm.
Toftanes, Eysturoy, Faroes.
10th cent. Faroese.
Føroya Fornminnissavn, Tórshavn, 4666/1762

Bundle of branches

The bundle is asymmetrical (91 × 34cm). Juniper bushes were the only significant tree-like plants on the Faroes when the Scandinavians arrived. Juniper was used for many purposes in their homeland and was also used in the Faroes. The finds from Toftanes demonstrate that juniper branches were used for repairs, barrel hoops and ropes. More than 100m of rope have been found. This bundle lay at the entrance of the farmhouse (cf. cat. no. 316). **SSH**

Bibl.: as for cat. no. 316; Larsen forthcoming

323

323 *a* H. 14cm; *b* H. 12.5cm.
Ergidalur, Suduroy, Faroes.
Late Viking Age. Faroese.
Føroya Fornminnissavn, Tórshavn, 4050/11;
4050

Two pottery vessels, fragmentary

Both pots are of local clay and hand made. The fabric is reddish/brown, coarse, grogged with small stones. The sides are symmetrical, the rims inturned; *b* has a slightly rounded base. They were found during excavation of a small settlement, probably a shieling. Pottery making seems to have begun on the Faroes in 11th cent. The earliest dated pottery is from Argisbrekka (cat. no. 315). **SVA**

Bibl.: Dahl 1971; Arge 1989, 117–19

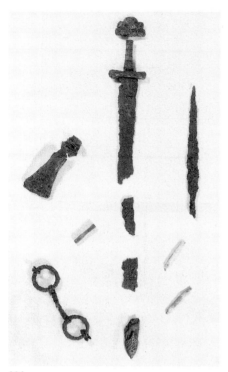

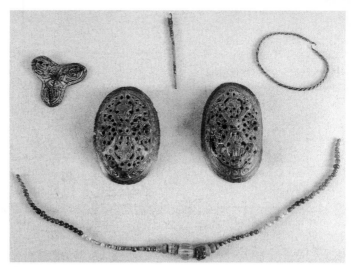

325

326

324

---

324 Iron, bronze, stone, antler.
Hafurbjarnarstaðir, SW Iceland.
Late 10th cent. Scandinavian.
Islands Nationalmuseum, Reykjavík, 557–65,
567

Male grave

a Spearhead. L. 40.5cm (Petersen type K). *b* Sword (Petersen type S), fragmentary with remains of scabbard of thin slivers of wood and chape of bronze with Jellinge-style decoration and traces of gilding. similar chapes are known from England, Denmark, Norway, Sweden, Germany and Russia. L. (hilt) 16.9cm. *c* Axe (Petersen type K). Blade max. w. 8.5. *d* Bridle, l. 26.0cm. *e* Comb, fragments of 4 strips, with band ornament. Max l. 11cm. *f* Pendant whetstone of yellow and brown striped stone, l. 7.3cm.

The grave, discovered in 1868, contained the skeletons of two men. There were also skeletons of a horse and a dog, a fragmentary shield boss, comb, and other small iron objects. This is the richest grave from Viking-age Iceland. Nine pagan graves were found at Hafurbjarnastaðir. **vöv**

Bibl.: Petersen 1919, 142–149; Paulsen 1953; 35–41; Eldjárn 1956, 73–78, 272, fig. 94, 107, 156; Graham-Campbell 1980, no. 273

---

325 Bronze, glass, rock crystal, amber, soapstone.
Dadastaðir, NE Iceland.
10th cent. Nordic.
Islands Nationalmuseum, Reykjavík, 15691

Grave-goods from a female

grave *(Illustrated in part)*

a Two oval brooches, l. 10.9cm; 10.7cm. One is bronze, of Petersen type 51d, the only example of this type from Iceland. The other is Petersen type 51b, the most common type in Iceland. *b* Trefoil brooch with Borre-style decoration, w. 5.9cm. Three other brooches of the same type have been found in Iceland. *c* Necklace of 52 beads, l. 40,8cm. 49 beads are glass, two are rock crystal and one is amber. *d* Ringed pin of bronze with ridge below loop. Ring missing, l. 9.0cm. Common Scandinavian type (Petersen type C). *e* Arm-ring of two twisted bronze wires; diam. 6.0–8.5cm. *f* Strap holder of bronze, l. 2.5cm. Cast, with two stylized animal heads. *g* Two spindle-whorls of soapstone, one fragmentary. Diam. 2.0cm; 3.2cm.

This rich burial also included a sickle, remains of woolcombs, shears, a comb, a knife, a piece of flint, an iron hook, a bronze cylinder, five iron fragments and two dog's teeth. Excavated 1956. **vöv**

Bibl.: Petersen 1928, fig. 51, 97, 238; Eldjárn 1957–1958, 134–44; Gudjónsson 1974, 141–2; Gudjónsson 1979, 209 note 13

---

326 Glass and silver. L. 23.0cm.
Mjóidalur, W Iceland.
10th cent.
Islands Nationalmuseum, Reykjavík, 10913–14

Necklace with Kufic coins

Bead necklace with 25 glass beads and two Kufic coins minted 917–18 and 926–27, in the reign of Caliph Nasr ibn Ahmed. Most of the beads are blue and translucent, but there are larger melon-shaped and segmented beads. The necklace is a stray find, provenance unknown. Iceland did not mint its own coins in the Viking Age and Middle Ages and coins are seldom found, either in hoards or as ornaments. No bead-making workshops are known on Iceland. **vöv**

Bibl.: Eldjárn 1956, 327–30; Rafnsson 1976, 489–501

---

327 Bronze, glass, amber, carnelian.
Kornsá, N Iceland.
10th cent.
Islands Nationalmuseum, Reykjavík, 1780–82

Jewellery from female grave

a Two tongue-shaped brooches of bronze decorated in Jellinge style, l. 6.1cm. *b* Necklace of 33 beads. 31 are glass: blue, yellow, with silver foil, translucent, melon-shaped. One is amber. One bead is carnelian with plastic ornamental knobs, probably oriental. *c* Six-sided bronze bell, l. 3.0cm—two comparable bell amulets are known from pagan graves on Iceland and similar ones have been found in York and at Freswick, Scotland. The type is probably Anglo-Scandinavian.

The finds are from the most richly-furnished female grave from Viking-age Iceland. It also contained fragments of an iron cauldron, shears, a weaving sword, a comb, balance pan and tweezers. The woman may have belonged to one of the foremost families of the settlement period.　**vöv**

Bibl.: Petersen 1928, no. 137, fig. 134; Eldjárn 1956, 95–97, 327–30, fig. 145; Batey 1988; Batey 1989, 101–10

327a

327b

328

> Bronze.
> Diam. (brooch) 3.6cm.
> Vað, E Iceland.
> 10th cent. North Scandinavian.
> Islands Nationalmuseum, Reykjavík, 4340

Brooch with long chains

The cast, circular, domed brooch has cruciform interlace and a raised knob in the middle. On the back is a finely shaped plate to which the pin is soldered. A thin plate impressed in the Borre style is suspended by two chains from the brooch. Three further chains terminate in axe-shaped bronze plates; they suggest E European or Baltic influence. Such brooches occur rarely in west and south Scandinavia, but many examples are known from Iceland and from north Scandinavian and Saami hoards.　**vöv**

Bibl.: Eldjárn 1956, 182, 309–313, fig. 128; Kivikoski 1973, pl. 86, no. 759; Zachrisson 1984, 64, fig. 41

329

> Jet.
> Outer diam. 7.7cm.
> Alaugarey, SE Iceland.
> 10th cent. Insular.
> Islands Nationalmuseum, Reykjavík, 11565

Arm-ring

The arm-ring has a smooth inner and a convex outer face. From a female grave, which also included a bone comb, two oval brooches, shears, a knife and a spit. Arm- and finger-rings of jet are well known in Dublin (cf. cat. no. 396), but jet objects are also known from Denmark, Norway (cf. cat. no. 75, 154, 410), Sweden, and the Faroes (Toftanes). The raw material comes from Whitby, Yorkshire, England (cf. cat. no. 409). Jet objects illustrate the close trading contacts between the west Scandinavian area and the British Isles.　**vöv**

Bibl.: Arbman 1940, pl. 109:7; Shetelig 1944; Eldjárn 1956, 332

330

> Bronze.
> L. 5.7cm.
> Lundur, N Iceland.
> 9th–10th cent. Scandinavian.
> Islands Nationalmuseum, Reykjavík, 5251

Scabbard chape

Cast openwork chape with Borre-style decoration. The type is thought to derive from Gotland or the east Baltic but is also known in the west (cf. cat. no. 217, 263, 310, 324b, 374). In contrast to the few swords found on Iceland there are many scabbard chapes. An exact parallel to this comes from Steigen, Engelöya, north Norway. According to Landnámabók (cat. no. 336), the first settler in the area, Eyvindur, came from Engelöya and settled in Flateyjardalur, near to Fnjóskadalur, where the farm of Lundur lies.　**vöv**

Bibl.: Paulsen 1953, 49; Eldjárn 1956, 273–76; Lund 1965, 323; Johansen 1980, 188

331

> Bronze with niello.
> L. 4.0cm.
> Lundur, SE Iceland.
> 11th cent. East European.
> Skógar museum, S-627

Belt mount

The mount is cast. Its slightly convex decorated surface is inlaid with niello. It was fastened to the belt by two hooks. Stray find, probably from a deserted farm.

It belongs to a group of strap mounts of oriental type well known from east Sweden, in Lappish graves, and in east Europe east of the Urals to the Black Sea. Apart from Iceland, they do not occur in the west Scandinavian area and probably originate in Russia or the east Baltic.　**vöv**

Bibl.: Jansson 1975–77; Zachrisson 1984, 49–55

327c

328

329

330

331

332

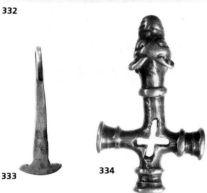

333　　　　**334**

336

332　　　　　Silver. Total weight 304g.
　　　　　　　　　　Sandmúli, N Iceland.
　　　　　　　　　　10th cent.
　　　Islands Nationalmuseum, Reykjavík, 5884

Silver hoard from Sandmúli

The hoard consists of 36 pieces of hack-silver and contains no coins. The largest items are the terminals of a neck-ring plaited from 12 strands and the terminal of a Hiberno-Norse penannular brooch, the back of which carries an incised animal in Jellinge style. Icelandic silver hoards from the Viking age are few and small, only two include coins.　　**VÖV**

Bibl.: Eldjárn 1956, 316–17, 368, fig. 178

333　　　　　　　Silver. L. 3.5cm.
　　　　　　　　　Vatnsdalur, NW Iceland.
　　　　　　　　　10th cent. Scandinavian.
　　Islands Nationalmuseum, Reykjavík, 1964: 122

Thor's hammer

This amulet was clipped and filed from a single sheet of silver. The end of the shaft was bent into a loop. This is the only Thor's hammer known from Iceland and was recovered from a boat-grave with other grave-goods.　　**VÖV**

Bibl.: Magnússon 1966, 5–32; Steffensen 1966, 33–54; Smyth 1984, 163.

334　　　　　　　Silver. L. 5.0cm.
　　　　　　　　　　Foss, S Iceland.
　　　　　　　　10th-11th cent. Scandinavian.
　　Islands Nationalmuseum, Reykjavík, 6077

Pendant cross

The cross is cast; the mouth of the animal head on the longest arm forms a loop. Cruciform perforation in centre. Stray find. The object is often considered to be a combination of cross and Thor's hammer, specific to Iceland of the Conversion Period, but a similar cross without the animal head has been found in a later Iron-age burial mound at Huse in Romedal, Hedemark, Norway.

　　　　　　　　　　　　　　　　　VÖV

Bibl.: Rygh 1886, 109–10, pl. IV, no. 18; Eldjárn 1956, 326–7; Eldjárn 1981, 73–84; Graham-Campbell 1980, no. 526

335　　Bronze with remains of wooden shaft.
　　　　　　　　　H. (with wood) 7.1cm.
　　　　　　　　　Thingvellir, S Iceland.
　　　　　　　　　c. 1100. Scandinavian.
　　Islands Nationalmuseum, Reykjavík, 15776

Tau cross　*(Illustrated p. 155)*

The cast terminal consists of a socket from which a head in Urnes style is produced on each side. The shaft is of dogwood (*Cornus sanguinea L.*) which does not grow in Iceland. The crozier was accidentally found at Thing-vellir in 1957, probably in a floor layer. Europe's earliest 'parliament', Althing, met at Thingvellir. The cross, which probably had an ecclesiastical function, has no direct parallels. Related tau-crosses are known from England and related terminals in wood have been found in Dublin and dated to second half of 10th or 11th cent.　　**VÖV**

Bibl.: Eldjárn 1970, 65–81; Graham-Campbell 1980, no. 540; Lang 1988, 66, 84, fig. 36, 42, 78, 103

336　　　　　　　　　　Paper.
　　　　　　　　　　　30 × 20.4cm.
　　　　　　Iceland. Copy, end of 17th cent.
　　　Stofnun Árna Magnússonar, Reykjavík,
　　　　　　　　　　　AM 104, fol.

Landnámabók

Most of Iceland's settlers came from Norway at the end 9th and beginning 10th cent. The most important are recorded in *Landnámabók*. It informs us of where they came from and where they settled, and their families are traced. The book was originally composed in the first half of the 12th cent., but the extant versions are somewhat changed and expanded. The bare biographical bones are enlivened by many (sometimes moving) tales about the settlers and their descendants, and we can glimpse a primitive Viking community, still without law and justice. *Landnámabók* is a unique document. No other people has such a source for its origins and earliest history. It survives almost only in later copies on medieval vellum. This version, *Skarðsár-bók*, is called after the farm of Skarðsa in northern Iceland where it was written.　　JK

Bibl.: Kålund 1889–94, I, 70; Benediktsson (ed.) 1958, IX–XII; Benediktsson (ed.) 1968; Benediktsson (ed.) 1974, XVIII–XX, 355–562; Pálsson and Edwards (tr.) 1972; Boyer (tr.) 1973; Kristjánsson 1988, 124–27

337　　　　　　　　　Vellum.
　　　　　　　　　　H. 24.3cm.
　　　　Iceland—Norway. Early 14th cent.
　　Den Arnamagnæanske Samling, Copenhagen,
　　　　　　　　　　AM 544, 4to

Hauksbók with the Saga of Erik the Red　*(Illustrated p. 60)*

The displayed page shows part of the Saga of Erik the Red, which tells of the first settlement of Greenland and the Vikings' exploration of the coast of North America. Erik's

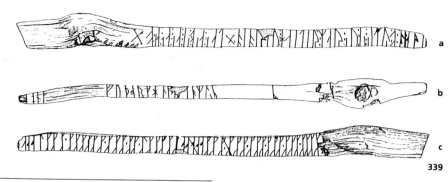

a

b

c

339

son, Leif the Lucky, is on his way home from Norway carrying a commission from King Olaf Tryggvason to bring Christianity to Greenland, but is blown off course and driven west by the wind, which results in his being the first to discover Vinland. The Saga of Erik the Red was probably composed in the 13th cent. Another source for the discovery of Vinland is found in the Saga of the Greenlanders, in the Flatey manuscript (*Flateyjarbók*).

Hauksbók is named after the man who had written it: the Icelandic law-man (*logmaðr*) Haukr Erlendsson (d. 1334) who obtained high office in Iceland and Norway. The original manuscript has been divided into three parts—the middle section is shown here. The varied contents of the book demonstrate the various interests of a private person. They extend from the account of the settlement of Iceland provided in *Landnámabók* (cf. cat. no. 336) to the 12th-cent. Icelandic translation of the widespread didactic work *Elucidarius*; from native histories such as *Fóstbræðra Saga* and the Saga of Erik the Red, to a chronicle about the Trojan war translated from Latin sources, the plan of Jerusalem, geographical and philosophical bits and pieces translated into Icelandic—and much besides.

PS

Bibl.: Kålund 1889–94, I, 683–87; Jónsson (ed.) 1892–96; Helgason (ed.) 1966

338
Soapstone.
L. 8.0cm.
Brattahlid (Qassiarsuk), Ruin group 61V3-III-540
(⌀29), Greenland.
c. 1000. Scandinavian.
Danmarks Nationalmuseum, Copenhagen,
D12213.606

Loom-weight with Thor's hammer

Loom-weight with a Thor's hammer incised on one face. Fragmentary, with remains of 4 perforations. Found in 1932 in the barn of Brattahlid farm which is thought to have been built by Erik the Red, the first colonizer of SW Greenland, and his wife Tjodhilde. The loom-weight is from the earliest period, the transition between paganism and Christianity. A small church, the so-called Tjodhilde's church, was excavated at Brattahlid in the early 1960s. It is of the same period as this loom-weight.

JA

Bibl.: Nørlund and Stenberger 1934, 91, 130, fig. 96; Graham-Campbell 1980, no. 525; Krogh 1982, 27–52

339
Pine. L. about 43cm.
Narsaq, Ruin group 60V1-I-518 (⌀17a),
Greenland.
c. 1000. Scandinavian.
Danmarks Nationalmuseum, Copenhagen,
no number

Rune stick

Square cross-sectioned stick with runic inscription on each face. Stray find 1953. The inscriptions are in short-twig runes which were dominant in the North Atlantic in the colonizing period. These inscriptions are thus older than most Greenlandic runic inscriptions of the Middle Ages. One face, *a*, carries a probably magical inscription with roots in Scandinavian mythology, 'On the sea, the sea, the sea, is the waiting place of the gods; *bibrau* is the name of the maiden who sits in the blue [the arch of the heavens]'. The opposite face, *c*, carries a row of secret runes (not interpreted), and the face between them, *b*, has the 16-character Viking-age runic alphabet, perhaps a key to the inscriptions.

JA/MS

Bibl.: Moltke 1961; Vebæk 1965

340
Reindeer antler.
L. 10.7cm; 6.9cm.
Narsaq, Ruin group 60V1-I-518 (⌀17a),
Greenland.
11th cent. Scandinavian.
Danmarks Nationalmuseum, Copenhagen, no
number

Two arrowheads

Found in the dwelling-house of a farm from the colonizing period. There were archaeological excavations here in 1953, 1958 and 1962, (cf. cat. no. 339).

Hunting and fishing played a great part in the northern Greenland economy. Bones found on the farm show that reindeer were an important source of food and these arrowheads were probably used for hunting them.

JA

Bibl.: Vebæk 1965

338

340

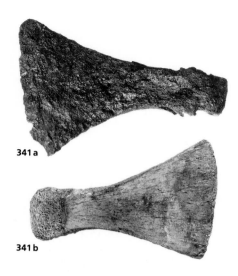

341a

341b

342

343

345

341

Iron, whalebone.
a L. 14.8cm; *b* 13.9cm.
Tunuarmiut, Tunulliarfik, Ruin group 60V2-IV-661 (Ø2O); Sandnæs (Kilaarsarfik), Ameralla, Ruin group 64V2-III-511 (V51), Greenland.
11th–13th cent. Scandinavian.
Danmarks Nationalmuseum, Copenhagen,
D7486, D11706

Two axeheads

The iron axe is a stray-find; the hafting-flange is broken. The whalebone axe was found in the excavations of the midden of Sandnæs farm. It copies contemporary iron axes. Its function is unknown; it may have been a toy, or may simply be evidence of the scarcity of iron in Greenland.　　　JA

Bibl.: Clemmensen 1911; Nørlund 1934b, 68–69; Roussell 1936

342

Walrus ivory.
H. 2.2cm; 3cm.
Sandnæs (Kilaarsarfik), Ameralla, Ruin group 64V2-III-511(V51), Greenland.
11th cent. Scandinavian.
Grønlands Nationalmuseum og Arkiv, Nuuk,
KNK4x400–401

Two gaming-pieces

Both are conical and lathe-turned. They were found in excavations in 1984, at the bottom of a midden of an 11th-cent. stone and turf building. They are examples of the many gaming-pieces and other small artifacts of walrus ivory found on Scandinavian settlements on Greenland. They were probably of native manufacture for the ivory was easily available.　　　JA

Bibl.: Arneborg 1985. For the walrus ivory see cat. no. 591

343

Gold.
Diam. (inner) 1.8cm.
Gardar (Igaliku), Ruin group 60V2-IV-621 (Ø47), Greenland.
11th-12th cent. Scandinavian.
Danmarks Nationalmuseum, Copenhagen,
D11157

Finger-ring

Ring of twisted thick and thin gold wire, broad and round at the front, but tapering off gradually; the back being hammered smooth. Found in the choir of the latest phase of the bishop's church. The ring is clearly older and dates from the first two centuries of Scandinavian occupation in Gardar.　　　JA

Bibl.: Nørlund 1930, 52

344

Walrus ivory, gold.
Crozier: h. 14.1cm. Ring: diam. 2.4cm.
Gardar (Igaliku), Ruin group 60V2-IV-621 (Ø47), Greenland.
End 12th cent. Scandinavian.
Danmarks Nationalmuseum, Copenhagen,
D11154, D11155

Crozier head and finger-ring

(Illustrated p. 61)
Both faces of the crozier are identical. It is made of 2 pieces of walrus ivory, the junction of which lies above the belt of ornament on the neck. The knop has a central band with a wavy line and a circle of leaves above and below. There is a belt of ornament above the knop. A narrow band with wavy line runs lengthways along the crook and ends in a large symmetrical cluster of leaves. The ring is thin, hammered flat on each side and with an oval setting for a stone, now lost. The setting is biconical in cross-section and between it and the ring is a small plate on each side.

The crozier and ring were found during excavations in 1926. They lay together with the skeleton of a middle-aged man in a grave in the north chapel of the bishop's church. He has been identified as Jon Smyrill who died in Greenland *c.* 1209. Only a few of the Greenland bishops visited Greenland or remained there until their death. The crozier was probably made on Iceland or in Trondheim, Norway.　　　JA

Bibl.: Nørlund 1930; 1934b, 32–43; Blindheim (ed.) 1972, no. 19; Krogh 1982, 144–47

345

Soapstone.
Diam. 3.3cm.
L'Anse aux Meadows, Newfoundland, Canada.
c. 1000. Icelandic/Greenlandic.
Canadian Parks Service 4A600A1–97

Spindle-whorl

The whorl is undecorated and shaped like a flattened hemisphere, the hole is cylindrical. The lower side of the whorl is concave and blackened by soot, an indication that it was made from a cooking pot or oil lamp. It was found in a boat-repair shed ('room VI') attached to hall F. The whorl belongs to the type described by Hofseth as existing only in the late Iron Age. It is light (16.9g) and suitable for the spinning of thin thread. The whorl is an indication that women were present on the site.　　　BLW

Bibl.: Ingstad 1970; Ingstad 1977; Hofseth 1985; B.L. Wallace forthcoming

346
Copper alloy.
L. *c.* 8cm (originally longer).
L'Anse aux Meadows, Newfoundland, Canada.
c. 1000. Icelandic/Greenlandic.
Canadian Park Service 4A600A1–169

Ring-headed pin (fragmentary)
(Illustrated p. 61)
The upper part of the shank is circular in cross-section, the lower part square. The slightly enlarged head of the pin is perforated to hold the ring. The ring is circular and decorated with two, possibly three, sets of parallel lines. The pin was found in a forge pit in the smithy (room III) of hall A. The shank was broken into several parts and its point reduced to nothing. It is in poor condition, its metal totally mineralized. To prevent complete disintegration, it has been encased in a polycarbonate box.

The pin is a simple example of the Hiberno-Norse type described by Fanning as distinctive of the Norse settlements in Ireland, the Isle of Man, Scotland, the Faroes and Iceland. The distribution pattern of examples of this ring-headed pin mirrors the northern and western sea routes of the Norse settlers of the late 10th cent. **BLW**

Bibl.: Ingstad 1970; Ingstad 1977; Fanning 1983, 33, fig. 4; Fanning 1990, 144; B.L.Wallace forthcoming

347
Iron, silver, copper. L.89.4cm.
Nantes (Ile de Bièce), France.
c. 800–950. ?Scandinavian.
Musée Dobrée, Nantes, 928.2.1

Sword
The blade has a broad fuller on both sides, corresponding to the flexible damascened core, which is bordered with cutting-edges of hard steel. It is unclear whether there was originally an inscription. The upper and lower hilt and pommel are oval in section; the pommel is attached by two long rivets. The surface is covered with a fine inlay of silver and copper thread. The sword is a good example of Petersen's type H, well-known both in Scandinavia and on the Continent and one of the most common sword types of the Viking Age. Found in 1928 on the small island of Bièce (Beaulieu) in Nantes, together with a number of weapons of various periods. Some may have been lost during one of the Vikings' many attacks on Nantes (the *Chronique de Nantes* mentions six attacks between 843 and 860). **JSa/ER**

Bibl.: Durville 1928, 125, pl.A9; Arbman 1937, 223; Arbman and Nilsson 1966–68, 168f., fig.6; *L'Or des Vikings*, 1969, 255; Müller-Wille 1978, 70–79. Cf. *Kulturhistorisk leksikon for nordisk middelalder* XVII, 1972, *s.v.* 'Sverd'

348

348
Silver.
Diam. 19cm.
Botnhamn, Lenvik, Troms, Norway.
11th cent. Scandinavian.
Tromsø Museum, Ts1649

Neck-ring with runic inscription
(Illustrated also p. 165)
Neck-ring of 5 pairs of twisted rods with twisted wires between. At the ends the rods are hammered into terminal plates with a perforation and hook. On the inner faces of the terminals there is a runic inscription, *Fórum drengja Frislands á vit, ok vigs fotum vér skiptum* (We went to meet the lads of Friesland and split the spoils of war [between us]).

From a hoard (1905) of 2 neck-rings, a crucifix and a pendant with plaited chain. The pendant is of 4 quatrefoil and 3 axe-shaped thin plates, the latter on separate chains. This runic inscription from the northern point of the island of Senja is the most northerly found in Norway and one of the few found within the Arctic circle. The neck-rings are Scandinavian, but two of the other objects are eastern (cf. cat. no. 239). **GSM**

Bibl.: Grieg 1929, 262f.; *Norges Innskrifter med de Yngre Runer* V, 1960, 127–40; Sjøvold 1974, 156, 330–33; Graham-Campbell 1980, no. 303

347

349
Clay daub.
H. 18cm.
La Grande Paroisse, Seine-et-Marne, France.
10th century. French.
Direction des Antiquités d'Ile-de-France, GP23–258TC

Graffito of Viking ship
Fragment of clay daub, on one side of which has been scratched a representation of a Scandinavian ship with curved prow and stern, square sail, a row of shields along the gunwale and one or two steering oars. **MP**

Bibl.: *Archéologie de la France*, 1989, 411, no.256.1

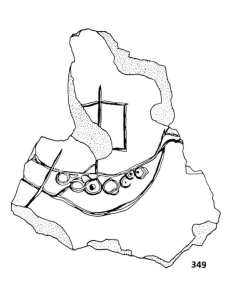
349

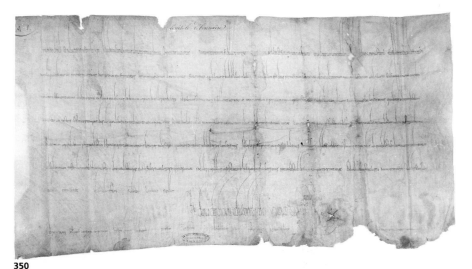

350

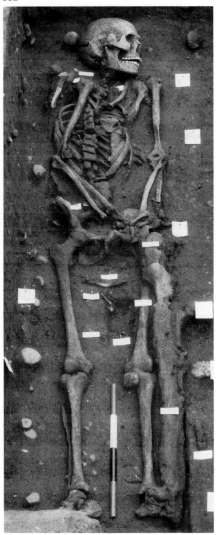

352

liturgical use, and this distinguished specimen, with splendid calligraphy enhanced with gold, belongs to a group of manuscripts produced at the court school of Charles the Bald, which is thought to have been sited in Compiègne or Soissons. On fol. 24 is a prayer for protection against the Normans (here meaning the Vikings/Scandinavians): '...de gente fera Normannica nos libera, quæ nostra vastat, Deus, regna...'. (Grant us freedom, Lord, from the wild Norman people who lay waste our realms...). There are musical notations above the lines. **FA/ER**

Bibl.: Delisle 1890, 17f.; Hesbert 1935; Gamber 1963, 243; Froger 1980, 338–54; Koehler & Mütherich 1982, 9–16, 33, 47, 51, 67–71; McKitterick 1980, 38ff.

350
Vellum.
66.5–66.7cm × 34.5–37.5cm.
Archives de l'abbaye de Tournus, France.
16 March 819. Aix-la-Chapelle.
Archives départementales de Saône-et-Loire,
Mâcon, H177 no.1

Charter of Louis the Pious

Original on vellum; Carolingian minuscule. Emperor Louis the Pious authorizes the Abbot Arnoul to build an aqueduct across a royal road in order to take water from the Boulogne river to supply the new monastery he had built, with the approval and support of the Emperor, at Deas in the region of Herbauges (Deé, now St Philibert de Grandlieu, Loire). The monastery had been moved from the island of Noirmoutier in the Loire estuary '... propter incursiones barbarorum qui frequenter ipsum monasterium depopulantur...' (... because of raids by the barbarians who often laid waste this monastery...). The charter is one of the earliest pieces of evidence concerning Viking raids in western Europe. **DG**

Bibl.: *Musée des Archives départementales*, 1878, 8, pl.III no.4; Lot et Lauer, II, 1936–46, pl.36, no.36 (facsimiles); Lex 1888 (text); *Diplomatarium Danicum*, 1975, no.20

351
Vellum.
H.32.5cm.
Abbaye Saint-Corneille de Compiègne, France.
Third quarter of 9th century. Court of
Charles the Bald.
Bibliothèque nationale, Paris, Ms Latin 17436

Antiphonal *(Illustrated p. 89)*

Illuminated manuscript (painted frameworks on ff.1, 1v, 2, 2v, 31v, 32, 32v). Gilt initial letters. The binding is 19th century. An antiphonal is a collection of pieces of music for

352
Iron, copper alloy, glass, silver.
L. (sword) 89.1cm.
Repton (excavations 1986, grave 511), Derbyshire, England.
c. 873–4. Scandinavian.
Derby Museum, 1989–59: 7113, 7114, 7108, 7126, 7092, 7093.

Viking grave from Repton

The burial of a man aged at least 35–40 who had died (probably while the Vikings wintered at Repton 873–4, cf. cat. no. 353) as a result of a massive cut into the head of his left thigh. He was 1.82m tall and similar in physical type to the male population of the burial deposit in the mass grave cat. no. 353. This is one of the Viking-type burials found near the east end of the church. A post-hole in the east end of the grave suggests a substantial wooden grave marker.

Grave goods: Iron sword with remains of wooden scabbard lined with fleece and covered with leather (the wood had been attacked before burial by the common woodworm); the grip was made of softwood covered by woollen textile; blade: l. 77.3cm. Buckle of copper alloy for the sword suspension-strap; l. 4.5cm. Buckle (probably for the belt) of copper alloy; l. 4.1cm. Necklace of 2 glass beads and a plain silver-alloy Thor's hammer, the loop of which is now in the hole of one of the beads; present l. 1.65cm (original l. c. 2.4cm). The grave also contained an iron folding knife, an iron knife, an iron key, a tusk of an adult boar (between the upper thighs), and the humerus of a jackdaw (also between the thighs). **MB/BKB**

Bibl.: Biddle and Kjølby-Biddle forthcoming; Biddle and Kjølby-Biddle in preparation

353   Human bones: 2 male skulls; four long
bones.
Repton, Derbyshire, England.
c. 873–4. Viking.
The Natural History Museum, London,
R82,8.718NE; skull 7, Box 467; skull 24, Box 682;
31L, Cab 140/10; T31L, Cab 141/90. R82,8.736,
H2R, Cab 140/4; 718SE, U15L, Cab 140/80

Charnel from a burial mound in Repton *(Illustrated p. 98)*

Two skulls, a left femur and a left tibia, a right humerus and a left ulnus: from the charnel in a reused Anglo-Saxon building covered by a burial mound at Repton, where the Viking 'Great Army' wintered 873–4. Excavations 1974–88 showed that the Vikings constructed a D-shaped earthwork on the bank of the River Trent enclosing an area of 1.46ha. The line of the earthwork incorporated the Anglo-Saxon stone church, probably using the N and S doors of the nave as a gateway.

To SW an earlier stone building was cut down to serve as the chamber of the Viking mound. When this was first opened *c.* 1686 it contained the stone coffin of a 'Humane Body Nine Foot long' surrounded by 100 skeletons 'with their Feet pointing to the Stone Coffin'. Re-excavation in 1980–6 revealed the disarticulated remains of at least 249 people whose bones had originally been stacked charnel-wise against the walls. The central burial did not survive, but the deposit contained many objects which may have accompanied it, including part of a sword, tiny gold and silver fragments, and five Anglo-Saxon pennies from the earlier 870s. Anthropological study of the charnel shows that it was 80% male in the age range 15–45, of a massively robust non-local population type parallels for which can be found in Scandinavia. The females were of a different type, possibly Anglo-Saxon.

It is likely that this was a burial of kingly status to which the bodies of those of the 'Great Army' who had died in the season of 873–4 (many probably from an epidemic) and perhaps in the previous years had been gathered from graves elsewhere (cf. cat. no. 352). There is little evidence of battle wounds. The division of the 'Great Army' in the autumn of 874 may have been the occasion for so singular and ritually complex a deposit. **MB/BKB**

Bibl.: Biddle, Kjølby-Biddle et al. 1986; Biddle and Kjølby-Biddle forthcoming; Biddle and Kjølby-Biddle in preparation

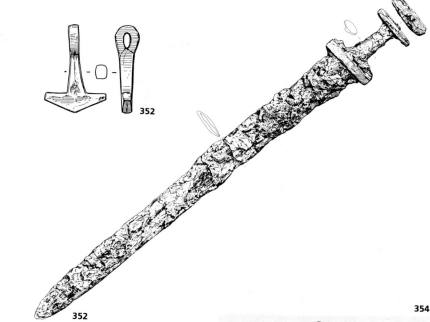

352

352

354   Iron, silver.
L. (sword) 99,0cm.
Kilmainham-Islandbridge, Dublin, Ireland.
9th cent. Scandinavian and Irish.
National Museum of Ireland, Dublin, 1933:7–15

Male grave group

Group of iron weapons consisting of a double-edged sword of Petersen type H with inlaid silver wires on the pointed oval pommel and guard; axe-head with expanded blade and projecting spurs on either side of the head; socketed spearhead of Petersen type K with copper-alloy rivets in the sockets; two iron handles and four bent nails; an elongated spatulate object with tang and central slot.

This group of objects is one of the few excavated grave groups from the Kilmainham-Islandbridge cemetery (cf. cat. no. 355). The sword, axe-head and spearhead are of Scandinavian origin and of types commonly found in Viking graves in western Europe. The iron handles and nails have been interpreted as fittings for a box or casket. The curious slotted and pointed object is one of three from the cemetery. Such objects are common finds on secular sites of 8th–10th cent. in Ireland and Scotland but are otherwise unknown in Scandinavian contexts. They have been variously interpreted as tools for rope-making, sharpening irons, augurs or strike-a-lights. **RÓF**

Bibl.: Bøe 1940, 62–65

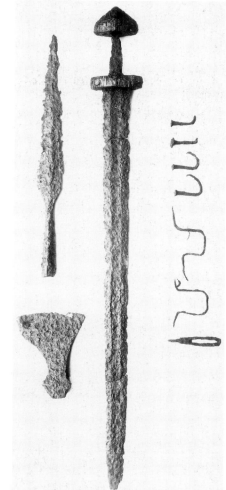

354

355a

355b

356

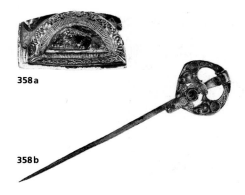

358a

358b

355d

355

Copper alloy, glass, amber.
L. (oval brooch) 10.4cm.
Kilmainham-Islandbridge, Dublin, Ireland.
9th cent. Scandinavian and Irish.
National Museum of Ireland, Dublin, R 2420;
1881:486–494; R 2410; W 122

Group of female grave-goods

Pair of single-shell copper-alloy oval brooches of Petersen type 37. String of nine beads (two of amber, the remainder of glass); needle case of tinned copper-alloy; linen-smoother of glass.

These objects are a selection of unassociated grave-goods from the Viking cemetery at Kilmainham-Islandbridge, located 2km west of the city of Dublin. It is the largest Viking cemetery outside the Viking homelands—the finds represent a minimum of 30 male and 7 female graves. It is of particular importance in that it can be historically dated to the period *c*. 841 to 902 AD. Most of the finds are undocumented and come from quarrying and work associated with the building of a railway line in the late 19th century.

The oval brooches are of the most common Viking form, and the linen smoother, needle case and most of the beads are likely to be Scandinavian imports. Two of the glass beads with cable decoration in blue and white occur on many high-status secular sites in Ireland and are of Irish manufacture. RÓF
Bibl.: Bøe 1940, 39, 45, 49

356

Copper alloy, tinned.
L. 19.0cm.
Kilmainham-Islandbridge, Dublin, Ireland.
9th cent. Scandinavian or Irish.
National Museum of Ireland, Dublin, R 2395

Balance scales

Complete balance-scales of copper alloy with tinned copper-alloy pans suspended on chains. The folding cross-beam pivots on a suspension loop to the top of which is attached by a short chain the figure of a bird. The pans are attached by three chains to cast three-legged elements which in turn are attached to the ends of the beam by short chains. The pans are decorated with rows of concentric lines inside and out.

This is one of four sets of balance scales from the Kilmainham-Islandbridge cemetery complex. This example was acquired with a large group of objects which included the weights (cat. no. 357), but there is no evidence that they were associated. The majority of these balance scales come from graves—mostly male—in Norway but it has not been established whether they are native products or imports (cf. cat. no. 302). Cast figures of birds are found on only a small number, and include examples from a grave on the island of Gigha, Scotland, and from a hoard from Jåtten, Norway (cat. no. 150), in both cases accompanied by decorated lead weights. RÓF
Bibl.: Bøe 1940, 50, cf. Grieg 1940, 29

357

Lead alloy with mounts of gilt copper-alloy, silver, glass, enamel and amber.
H. 1.8cm–3.7cm.
Kilmainham-Islandbridge, Dublin, Ireland.
9th cent. Scandinavian and Irish.
National Museum of Ireland, Dublin, R 2389;
2399–2401; 2413–2417

Nine weights

Nine lead-alloy weights with decorated mounts from the Kilmainham-Islandbridge cemetery complex, not necessarily associated (cf. cat. no. 355–6). *a* Rectangular with a cast animal head of gilt copper-alloy. *b* Circular with a conical base surrounded with geometric cells fitted with enamel and millefiori insets. *c* D-shaped with a herring-bone pattern of silver and copper wires. *d* Circular stud with cast interlace and empty stud-setting. *e* Trapezoidal with cast animal head. *f* Circular stud with cast interlace and central stud-setting. *g* Circular stud with cruciform device set with silver wires and enamel. *h* Rectangular, set with two rods of twisted blue glass. *i* Circular stud with cast interlaced triskele.

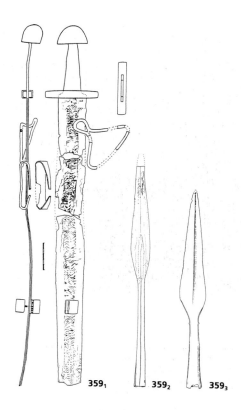

Lead weights set with cut-up pieces of decorated objects are known throughout the Viking world. The decorated mounts used on these weights are all likely to be of Irish origin, except for *c* which uses an inlay technique used on weapons of Scandinavian origin. The circular studs *d* and *f* are likely to have come from small house-shaped shrines.

RÓF

Bibl.: Bøe 1940, 50–52; Graham-Campbell 1980, no. 308

358

Copper-alloy, amber.
L. *a* 5.8cm; l. *b* 13.6cm.
Kilmainham-Islandbridge, Dublin, Ireland.
9th cent. Irish.
National Museum of Ireland, Dublin, 1906:477;
1885:120

Brooch and ringed pin

a Fragment of a decorated object adapted as a brooch consisting of a rectangular mount of gilt copper-alloy cut off at one end; it has a semi-circular boss set with an amber stud, and its sides bear a design of running knots executed in chip-carved technique; at the back is a pin and catch-plate. *b* A copper-alloy ringed-pin consisting of a cast ring and plain pin; the ring takes the form of a pair of animal heads grasping a pair of opposed human heads in their open jaws; a third animal head projects from the base of the ring; there are three empty stud-settings, perhaps originally for amber.

Mount *a* is typical of many fragments of Insular decorated metalwork which have been cut up and adapted as brooches. It may originally have formed the terminal of a cross-shaped shrine mount. The ringed-pin (*b*) is a simplified version of the more elaborate Irish and Pictish brooches of the 9th cent. Norse copies of this particular type are known.

RÓF

Bibl.: Bøe 1940, 40–41; Armstrong 1921–22, pl. 12, fig. 3

359₅

359

Iron, wood, silver.
Camp de Péran, Côtes-d'Armor, France.
10th century. ?French, ?Scandinavian.
Musée, Saint-Brieuc, 1295, 1291, 1211, 1343–4,
1109, 1156, 76

Find from Camp de Péran

It is probable that there is a connection between the severe damage caused by fire at the castle of Camp de Péran (near Saint-Brieuc) and the presence of the Vikings in Brittany in the first half of the 10th century; the dates are compatible. But so far there is no evidence as to whether the Vikings were the attackers or had taken up a defensive position there. In the latter case the destruction of the fortifications may have occurred when Alain Barbetorte attacked the site in 936. A large quantity of objects found during excavations in the 1980s, include: a sword, Petersen type X, pattern-welded blade, with point missing, l. 75cm; two spearheads, iron, l. 47cm, 39.8cm; an axe, iron, l. 20cm; a stirrup, iron, h. 15.2cm; an iron pot made in the same way as a pot from the Viking grave on the Île de Groix (cat. no. 360), diam. 50cm, h. *c.* 16cm; wool comb with teeth and shaft of iron, l. 12.5cm. A silver coin, St Peter penny of York Vikings, *c.* 905–25 with inscription: EBORACE CI, and on the reverse, SCI PE TRI NO.

JPN/ER

Bibl.: Nicolardot 1984; Jaubert 1988; Nicolardot 1989; Price 1989, 54–60, 98 (372–78, 416) and passim.

359₁

359₂

359₃

359₄

359₆

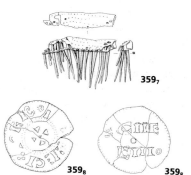

359₇

359₈

359₈

360₁

360₄

360₈

360₂,₉

360₃

360₅

360₆

360₇

360₁₀

360   Iron, wood, gold, silver, bronze, slate,
antler. Île de Groix, Morbihan, France.
First half to mid 10th cent. Scandinavian.
Musée des Antiquités nationales, St. Germain-
en-Laye, 86117.

Viking grave from the Île de Groix   *(Illustrated in part)*

The grave is the only known male Viking grave
in France (cf. cat. no. 366). It was situated in a
mound on the shore of the small island of
Groix just off Brittany. Excavated in 1906. It
was a cremation grave in a ship, with the
skeletal remains of 2 bodies. The arrangement
of the contents and the equipment suggest that
the dead chieftain was of Scandinavian origin
but had lived for some time in western Europe.
The ship and the rich grave goods with both
Scandinavian and western European objects
had been badly damaged by fire. Only the best-
preserved remains are included in the exhibition: *From the ship*: two iron fragments from the
ornament of the sternpost (l. 24cm and 18 cm);
three iron rivets and a piece of wood with an
iron nail (at least 800 of these were found); the
ship is thought to have been at least 14m long.

Jewellery, buckles, etc.: a gold ring; two silver
hooks; a decorated bronze buckle. *Equestrian
equipment*: a double iron buckle from a harness.
Weapons: two fragments of swords, the hilts
with Scandinavian ornament encrusted with
silver (max. l. 9.9cm); guard of another sword;
fragment of a sword blade (l. 23.5cm); scabbard
chape, bronze, with the open-work figure of a
bird (l. 6.2cm) (cf. cat. no. 330, 374); three
shield-bosses, iron (there were fragments of a
total of some 15–20 shield-bosses); fragment of
the cutting edge of an iron axe; fragments of
two spearheads, one with wings. *Tools*: whetstone; spoon-bit, iron; iron anvil; iron smith's
tongs; nail-iron. *Dishes, bowls, caskets*: bronze
plate (diam. 26cm); mount for ?bowl, bronze,
with an animal head (l. 6.8cm); rhomboid
bronze mount; 2 iron mounts for ?casket.
Games: die made of the tusk of a marine mammal (?walrus) (l. 2.8cm); 12 gaming-pieces of
antler and marine-mammal tusk (?walrus).

FV/ER

Bibl.: du Chatellier & le Pontois 1908; Shetelig (ed.) 1940,
IV, 109–14; Müller-Wille 1978; Price 1989, 64–74, 95–97
(382–92, 413–15).

361
Silver.
Cuerdale (near Preston), Lancashire,
England.
Deposited c. 905. Scandinavian-type hoard.
The British Museum, London, M&LA 41, 7–11,
1–741

Cuerdale hoard (*Illustrated p. 97*)

Selection of silver bullion, comprising coins, ingots, rings and other ornaments, with miscellaneous hack-silver from East and West.

The hoard was discovered in 1840 and cannot now be reconstructed in its entirety, but it must have consisted of over 8,500 pieces of silver weighing c. 40kg (five times more than any other such Viking hoard in Scandinavia or western Europe), buried in a leaden chest. It contained some 7,500 coins enabling its deposition to be dated c. 905. Most are contemporary Viking issues of Northumbria and East Anglia, but they also include Anglo-Saxon, Frankish, Italian and Kufic coins, as well as four from Hedeby. The non-numismatic silver also comes from many sources, but seems to be predominantly Hiberno-Viking (Irish) in origin. Altogether, the hoard represents an immediate mixture of wealth from the Viking kingdoms of York and Dublin, buried in a newly occupied area of north-west England. **JGC**

Bibl.: Hawkins 1847, 111–30, 189–99; Shetelig (ed.) 1940, 32–45; Graham-Campbell 1980, no. 301; Graham-Campbell 1987a; Philpott 1990; Graham-Campbell forthcoming

---

362
Gold and silver.
Ballaquayle, Douglas, Isle of Man.
Deposited c. 970. Hiberno-Viking and
Scandinavian.
The British Museum, London, M&LA 1895, 8–9,
1–8

Ballaquayle (Douglas) hoard

Part of a hack-silver hoard: twisted gold arm-ring (diam. 7.8cm), 3 silver arm-rings (2 of 'ring-money' type), 1 silver finger-ring, 1 twisted-wire neck-ring fragment, a pin (bent in ring) and pin head (l. 11.3cm) from a ball-type penannular brooch or brooches.

The hoard, 21 objects and several hundred coins, was found in a slate cist in 1894. With its combination of coins, ingots, complete ornaments and hack-silver, it is a classic example of a mixed silver hoard of the Viking Age. The complete gold arm-ring is an unusual component and emphasizes the wealth of the owner living on what was to become one of the island's most substantial medieval farms. **LW**

Bibl.: Kermode 1911, 437–40; Shetelig (ed.) 1940, IV, 51–3, figs. 17–22; Graham-Campbell 1983b, 57, 74–5, figs. 8–9

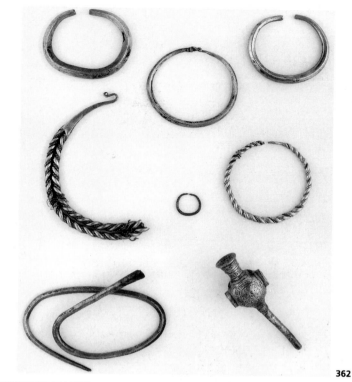

362

363

363
L. 4.5cm–8.1cm.
Ireland, no locality, except a Virginia,
Co. Cavan: h Near Galway. j–k Ballyadams,
Co. Laois.
9th–10th cent. Irish.
National Museum of Ireland, Dublin, a W.34; b
W.63; c W.77; d W.92; e W.98; f P.858; g P.862;
h W.72; i W.76; j W.7; k W.32

Selection of silver objects

a-g: Seven penannular arm-rings of so-called 'Hiberno-Viking' type; they taper from the centre towards the terminals and are decorated with stamped patterns, the saltire being the most common decorative device. *h–i*: Two arm-rings, one made from a coiled rod, the other from a thin ribbon; the ends of both are tightly coiled around the coiled body; they are decorated with stamped devices. *j–k*: An ingot and plain ring, perhaps from a hoard.

Much of the surviving silver of the Viking Age from Ireland occurs in the form of ornaments which are cast or engraved. The most common type is the penannular arm-ring of 'Hiberno-Viking' type of which over 200 examples are known. This form was developed in Ireland, probably from Danish prototypes. The coiled arm-ring is also an Irish development from Scandinavian prototypes and both arm-ring forms are found in coin hoards dating to AD. 850–950. The ribbon arm-ring is much rarer but is also likely to be a Hiberno-Norse type of similar date. The ingot and ring are probably from a hoard of non-numismatic silver of a type common in the southern half of Ireland. **RÓF**

Bibl.: Bøe 1940, 107–127

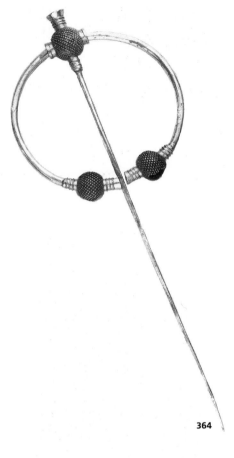

364

365

365

---

364 Silver. L. 51.2cm.
Newbiggin Moor (near Penrith),
Cumbria, England.
First half of 10th cent. Hiberno-Viking.
The British Museum, London, M&LA 1909,
6–24,2

Penannular brooch

Penannular brooch with ball-shaped terminals and pin-head, so-called 'thistle brooch' type. The front of each ball is deeply criss-crossed and punched to give a brambled effect; the backs are decorated with a lightly incised marigold motif. The hollow terminals are socketed onto the brooch hoop, as is the long pin onto the pin-head.

This distinctive type originated in 9th-cent. Ireland but its popularity spread well beyond the Irish Sea area in 10th cent. Early examples are relatively small and simple with solid terminals and pin-head; later versions such as this tend to increase in size and complexity. Their ostentatious appearance indicated wealth and status and their regular occurrence in silver hoards of the period is no surprise. This find (discovered 1785) is now known to be from a scattered hoard of silver brooches further fragments of which were found in 1989 on the same site, known as the Silver Field. **LW**

Bibl.: Shetelig (ed.) 1940, IV, 46, fig. 15; Graham-Campbell 1980, no. 195; Graham-Campbell 1983a

365 Gilded copper-alloy, silver wire.
L. 11.6cm.
Santon Downham, Norfolk, England.
Early 10th cent. Scandinavian.
The British Museum, London, M&LA 1888,
1–3,1 and 3–27,1

Oval brooches from Santon Downham

Pair of double-shelled oval brooches of type P51, gilded on the face and with applied silver wire; cast textile-impressions on the underside.

Although oval brooches were the commonest and most widespread form of Viking brooch, they are rather rare in English Viking-age contexts. The burial represented by this pair is presumably to be seen in the context of the Scandinavian settlements established in East Anglia before c. 900. The suggestion that this may have been a double burial because of the reported association of brooches, sword (Petersen type L) and skeleton should be treated with caution in view of the unscientific nature of the investigation in 1867. **LW**

Bibl.: Shetelig (ed.) 1940, IV, 12–13, fig. 1; Evison 1969, 333, 335, 342, 344, fig. 2; Graham-Campbell 1980, no. 117

366 Bronze, originally gilt. L. 11cm.
Pîtres, Eures, France.
Second half of 9th century. Scandinavian.
Musée départemental des Antiquités de Seine-Maritime, Rouen

Oval brooches from Pîtres *(Ill. p. 89)*

The brooches are cast and of the type P37, cf. cat. no. 101. Small rivets, originally decorated with studs, held in place a now lost framework which outlined the subdivisions of the brooches. In the four rhomboid uppermost spaces are strongly stylized animal motifs. These are repeated in more comprehensible versions in the 6 spaces around the rim. These brooches are unique in that they come from the only female Viking grave known between the Rhine and the Pyrenees, (cf. cat. no. 360). The grave, which was found in 1865, seems to have been in a Christian churchyard, as were a number of Viking graves in England and Ireland. The location near Pîtres is interesting in that it was there that Charles the Bald, in 860–1, decided to build a fortified bridge to prevent the Vikings sailing up the Seine. This fortification was constructed near the present Pont-de-l'Arche, at the confluence of the rivers Seine and Eure. Some years previously, in 855, the Vikings had spent the winter there. **PP**

Bibl.: Cochet 1871, 7; Petersen 1928; Elmqvist 1966–68, 203–24; Périn 1990, 161–88.

---

367 Manx slate. H. 35cm.
Kirk Andreas, Isle of Man.
10th cent. Manx/Scandinavian.
Kirk Andreas parish church, Manx Cross no. 128.

Cross-slab *(Illustrated p. 151)*

Part of a finely-carved cross-slab, found in the Rectory garden about 100m N of the existing burial ground. The two extant scenes on opposing sides of the slab have been interpreted as a scene from Ragnarok, the last great battle of Norse pagan mythology: Odin, one-eyed, with his raven on his shoulder, being devoured by Fenris Wolf. On the opposite side conquering Christianity—represented by a priest with cross and book—tramples the serpent of paganism underfoot, the Christian emblem of a fish alongside. The runic inscription on the surviving narrow edge reads, 'Thorwald raised this cross … '. The cross bears a Manx version of the Borre-style ring-chain. With this Scandinavian stylistic element are combined important elements from Norse mythology in a firm Christian context. **WH/DMW**

Bibl.: Graham-Campbell 1980, no. 452; Hall 1984, 76–8, figs. 82–3.

368   Sandstone.
L. 132.1cm.
Ingleby Arncliffe, North Yorkshire, England.
Early 10th cent. Anglo-Scandinavian.
Durham Cathedral

Hogback tombstone

A complete hogback, a recumbent grave-cover, with large muzzled end-beasts clutching a house-shaped shrine with curved roof-ridge. Three panels of closed-circuit interlace stand above a recessed niche. The decoration is identical on each face. From a hedge bank at Ingleby Arncliffe Hall, found in the 1860s.

This is a fine example of a "Niche Type" hogback, an early form which demonstrates that it is inspired by shrine-tombs: the semi-circular niche is a feature of shrines with openings for the faithful to touch the relics. The confronting end-beasts may derive from small Irish reliquary design. Hogback distribution is confined to areas of Viking settlement in Northern England and Scotland, especially Yorkshire and Cumbria. This example comes from an area of Yorkshire with Hiberno-Norse connections.   JL

Bibl.: Bailey 1980; Lang 1984, 142–43

---

369   Sandstone. L. 63cm.
Sockburn-on-Tees Church, Co. Durham,
England.
Early 10th cent. Anglo-Scandinavian.
Sockburn parish church (lent by Bishop of
Durham)

Hogback tombstone

Large fragment of recumbent tombstone (cf. cat. no. 368) with tegulated roof. The side shows two horsemen with saddles, lances and helmets.

Hogbacks were secular monuments. This area of England was occupied by Christianized Scandinavians, depicted here as warriors. The ornamental knot of the horses' tails is also known in representations of the hair of Scandinavian women (cat. no. 186).   JL

Bibl.: Bailey 1980; Lang 1984, 166, no. 9; Cramp 1984, 140–1, no. 14

---

370   Sandstone. H. 65cm.
10th cent. Anglo-Scandinavian.
St John's Church, Kirkby Stephen,
Cumbria, England

Cross-shaft fragment *(Withdrawn from exhibition)*

Cross shaft showing bound human figure. Identification of the figure is difficult. Sug-

gestions have included the Devil, Loki, and Christ, cf. the Jelling stone (cat. no. 193). Such binding is common in Anglo-Scandinavian designs and may simply be decorative.   JL

Bibl.: Wilson and Klindt-Jensen 1966, 107, pl. XLIIIa; Bailey 1980; Bailey and Cramp 1988, 120–1

---

371   Limestone. H. 63cm.
Newgate, York, England.
10th cent. Anglo-Scandinavian.
The Yorkshire Museum, York

Cross-shaft fragment

Cross shaft with border of angels and panels of animal ornament. The principal face shows Christ. Painted gesso originally covered the carving; construction lines survive.

Stone sculpture is rare in Scandinavia in 10th cent. It is an English and Celtic expression of Christian funerary art. Scandinavian settlers assimilated the tradition, producing hundreds of monuments in northern England, chiefly crosses. This shaft is typical. Its Christ portrait asserts its religion, and the angels are drawn from Carolingian models. Its animal ornament is a mixture of Scandinavian and English styles although here the sculptor (the York Master) prefers the native repertoire.   JL

Bibl.: Bailey 1980; *The Vikings in England*, 1981, 83–94, 138; Lang 1985

368

369

370

371

372

374

373

378

375

372
Magnesian limestone.
L. 23cm.
York (Coppergate), England.
Early 10th cent. Anglo-Scandinavian.
York City Council 1977.7.2115

Grave-slab fragment

Corner of unfinished grave-slab with animal ornament; two interlocked profile beasts and the head of another.

Such slabs covered Christian burials. It is carved by the same hand as cat. no. 371 and its decoration is a mixture of Jellinge-style Scandinavian animals and animals derived from English manuscripts of the period.   JL

Bibl.: Graham-Campbell 1980, no. 455; *The Vikings in England*, 1981, 83–94, 121, 138; Lang 1985

373
Leather. L.34cm.
York (Coppergate), England.
Mid-10th cent. Anglo-Scandinavian.
York City Council 1980.7.8133

Sheath

This sheath for an angle-backed knife was designed to hold both the blade and handle. The decoration on the front face is split into two fields, one representing the blade and the other the handle. They are separated by an animal head viewed from above whose neck develops from a decorative moulding along the back of the sheath. Each field is decorated with a four-strand interlace pattern. The decoration on the reverse is similarly organized. The field representing the knife blade is cross-hatched. That representing the handle is divided into rectangular panels.

Such a sheath was worn parallel to the belt and held by suspension loops at the neck and halfway along its length.   DT

Bibl.: Hall 1984, 83, fig. 88

374
Copper alloy. L. 8.6cm.
York (Coppergate), England.
10th cent. Scandinavian.
The Yorkshire Museum, 551.49.47

Scabbard chape

Chape decorated with openwork Jellinge-style animal enmeshed in multiple-strand interlace.

One of a group of chapes with similar ornament. Most commonly found around the Baltic, they occur as far east as Danilovka on the lower Volga and as far west as Iceland (cf. cat. no. 330). The distribution suggests that the York example is an import from Scandinavia.   DT

Bibl.: Waterman 1959, 72, fig. 6; Graham-Campbell 1980, no. 274

375
York (Coppergate), England.
10th cent. Anglo-Scandinavian.
York City Council 1980.7.8129

Silk cap

Cap in tabby weave of light gold colour. Originally with linen ribbons on either side. A repair patch has been cut from the inside of the dart and stitched over a hole at the back. The seam is stitched with silk thread, the hemming was originally of linen. (From 16–22 Coppergate).

There are similar caps from 5 Coppergate, York, and Saltergate, Lincoln. The plain-weave silk from which they are made is surprisingly similar; the examples from 5 Coppergate and Lincoln are so technically alike that they must have come from the same bolt of cloth.   DT

Bibl.: Hall 1984, 88, fig. 106; Walton 1989, 360–78, figs. 151–2, 154, 158–9, pls. XXVIII–XXIXa, pl. XXXIa–b

376
a: antler; *b*: bone.
L. 12.2cm; 10.7cm.
York (Coppergate), England.
Mid-10th cent; 10th or early 11th cent. Anglo-Scandinavian
York City Council 1980.7.8481; 1979.7.5704

Combs

Two single-sided combs with convex backs made of tooth plates held in place by two connecting plates fixed with iron rivets. The back plates of *a* have incised decoration. The grooving on the ends of *b* may have been filled with black inlay, as on other York combs. Rush seeds were found between its teeth.

There is abundant evidence for the manufacture of antler combs at 16–22 Coppergate. The debris was concentrated on one of the four excavated tenements, tenement B. Comb *b* is one of the few York combs made of bone.   DT

Unpublished

377
Box wood. L. 9.8cm.
York (Coppergate), England.
10th or early 11th cent. Anglo-Scandinavian.
York City Council 1979.7.5083

Pan-pipes

A rectangular piece of wood with five holes of increasing depth (one broken), drilled into one of the ends. A hole for suspension at one corner.

Part of the instrument is probably lost and there may have been another five holes. The remaining holes produce notes ranging from A to E.   DT

Bibl.: Hall 1984, 116, fig. 141

378

Maple.
H. 6.5cm; diam. 4.8–5.7cm.
York (Coppergate), England.
Mid-10th cent. Anglo-Scandinavian.
York City Council 1980.7.8174

Spinning top

Sugar-loaf shaped top with an iron spindle through the long axis. The surface is coloured red with haematite.

The carefully-finished coloured surface and the presence of the iron spindle suggest that this is not a turning core (waste from making wooden bowls or cups) but a functional object. There is another similar spinning top, unpainted, from contemporary levels at 16–22 Coppergate. **DT**

Unpublished

379

Bone. Max. l. 5.1cm; w. 1.6cm.
York (Coppergate), England.
10th or 11th cent. Anglo-Scandinavian.
York City Council 1979.7.5683, 7075

Toggles

Toggles made from immature pig-bones (left 3rd metatarsals), each with a transverse perforation.

Except for the perforation, the bone is unworked. Such objects appear to have been introduced into England by the Scandinavians; they do not occur in earlier levels at York. They may have been used for fastening clothes, but have also been identified as amulets and musical instruments. **DT**

Unpublished

380

Yew, alder.
a diam. 11.5cm; *b* diam. 17.9cm.
York (Coppergate), England.
10th or early 11th cent. Anglo-Scandinavian.
York City Council 1977.7.1384; 1977.7.1383

Wooden cup and bowl

Both are lathe-turned. The cup, of which about half survives, has a shallow foot; the rim is decorated with two incised lines. The bowl has a low foot-ring. A crack was repaired in antiquity with copper-alloy wire.

Excavations in Anglo-Scandinavian York have produced many fragments of lathe-turned wooden vessels including lids, mugs and bowls. In 16–22 Coppergate shallow bowls are the commonest type, many with traces of repair. The site also produced abundant waste from the turning of wooden vessels. The street-name Coppergate probably derives from the Old Norse words *koppari* (a wood turner or cup maker) and *-gata* (street). **DT**

Bibl.: Graham-Campbell 1980, no. 452; Hall 1984, 76–8, figs. 82–3

381

Stone.
L. 15.0cm.
York (Coppergate), England.
10th or early 11th cent. Anglo-Scandinavian.
York City Council 1980.7.9987

Ingot mould

Damaged, but originally of square section. Its four faces have five slots for casting different-sized ingots. **DT**

Unpublished

376a

376b

380b

380a

379

377

381

382

382 Fired clay.
L. 10.7cm.
York (Blake Street), England.
Late 9th or early 10th cent. Anglo-
Scandinavian.
The Yorkshire Museum, York, 1975.6.448

Mould

Incomplete, but obviously for a trefoil brooch; one arm missing. There is an animal mask at the junction of the two surviving arms, and a similar mask in the centre of each arm below a pair of outward-facing but inward-looking winged creatures.

Trefoil brooches were introduced into England from Scandinavia and appear to have been used only briefly before Anglo-Saxon female fashions superseded them. The manufacture of this type of brooch in York suggests the presence of Scandinavian women. The ornament on this brooch combines animal masks derived from the Scandinavian Borre style with birds or winged bipeds whose ancestry is English. No brooch of this sort survives.   DT

Bibl.: MacGregor 1978, 42, fig. 24; Graham-Campbell 1980, no. 437

384

383

383 Micaceous schist.
Max. l. 33.7cm.
York (Coppergate), England.
10th cent. Anglo-Scandinavian.
York City Council 1979.7.6930, 1980.7.7674

Two whetstones

Each hone consists of a naturally-squared length of micaceous schist, dressed roughly square at the ends. The larger one has wear marks on the broad faces.

Micaceous schist is found in Scotland and in the Eidsborg region of Norway. The rocks in the two areas, however, are of different geological ages and Potassium/Argon dating of a sample from the York schist stones confirms that they derive from Norway. The use of schist for whetstones was introduced in the Viking Age and continued into 13th cent.   DT

Unpublished

384 Slate.
L. 4.8cm.
York (Coppergate), England
Mid-10th cent. Anglo-Scandinavian.
York City Council 1980.7.11114

Whetstone

Of square section; tapers towards the upper end which is perforated to take a copper-alloy suspension loop. The slate is obliquely banded in dark grey, purple and pink.

Similar whetstones are known from Birka, Sweden. The York example is of a non-local stone and is almost certainly an import, from Scandinavia or, more probably, from France or Germany.   DT

Bibl.: Hall 1984, 91, fig. 99

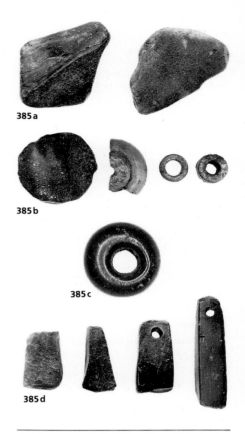

385a

385b

385c

385d

385 York (Clifford Street), England.
10th cent. Anglo-Scandinavian.
The Yorkshire Museum, York, c599a, b. c617a;
c626f, k, l. c625b. c601f, h; c602a, b

Amber: unworked pieces, waste, beads

a Two unworked pieces. Max. l. 4.5cm. *b* Working waste: flat, roughly circular pieces. Max. diam. 3.4cm. Some have central perforation, others are partially-cut rings. Also turned tubular cores. *c* Annular bead, lathe-turned; diam. 1.6cm. *d* 4 wedge-shaped beads or rough-outs; h. 4.2cm.

Amber can be found on east-coast beaches in England, but usually in small pieces. The size of these pieces suggests that this amber came from the coasts of west Jutland or the south Baltic where amber is much more abundant (cat. no. 254). The objects were first roughly shaped with a knife. Perforations were made with a fine drill. Finger-rings and annular beads were further shaped on a lathe. All objects were finally given a burnished surface (cf. cat. no. 189, 395).   DT

Bibl.: *The Vikings in England*, 1981, 97, 137; Hall 1984, 76, fig. 81

386

Gold L. 9.8cm.
Dublin (High Street), Ireland.
Late 10th-early 11th cent. Scandinavian type.
National Museum of Ireland, Dublin, E71:9007

Arm-ring

Arm-ring of two twisted circular-sectioned rods. The rods taper to the ends being at maximum thickness in the centre. The ends of the rods are joined to a polyhedral knob, the outer face of which is decorated with four small circular dots in a lozenge.

This ring is one of two found inside house HS 11/2, one ring on top of the other and both bent out of true. An uncommon Scandinavian type.   **DC/ER**

Bibl.: *Viking and Medieval Dublin*, 1973, no. 10, pl. XVII; Graham-Campbell 1980, no. 220

387

Iron, silver. L. 35cm.
Dublin, Ireland.
9th cent. Viking.
National Museum of Ireland, Dublin, 1979:68

Sword

The blade is broken and badly corroded along the edges. The straight guard is inlaid with thin silver wires. Recovered from a bulldozer dump at Islandbridge, this sword originally came from the John's Lane/Fishamble Street site. Most of the stratified deposits on the Dublin sites date 10th and 11th cent., this is an early type not found elsewhere on excavated urban sites in Ireland.   **DC**

Unpublished

388

L. 11.5cm.
Dublin (Fishamble Street), Ireland.
Early-mid l0th cent.
National Museum of Ireland, Dublin,
E172:13943

Human cranium fragment

The fragment was cut from the back, right-hand side of the skull, behind and to the right of the sagittal suture. The largest cut is a broad chop-mark on the left side. One end of the fragment has been deliberately shaped into a point with five cuts from a knife or saw. It was found outside FS7, a house in Fishamble Street, with no human skeletal remains nearby. It is similar to a missing fragment from another skull, also from Fishamble Street.   **DC**   Unpublished

389

Wood. H. 21.7cm.
Dublin (Fishamble Street), Ireland.
10th cent. Irish.
National Museum of Ireland, Dublin,
E172:11974

Stool

The seat is now trapezoidal; a missing fragment would have made it almost rectangular. There are holes (two of them broken) for six legs, but only two thin and brittle legs plus a number of fragments survive. This is one of two stools found during the Dublin excavations. They are of similar appearance, being roughly carpentered.   **DC**

Unpublished

390

Leather. L. 14cm.
Dublin (High Street), Ireland.
12th cent. Irish.
National Museum of Ireland, Dublin, E71:2093

Child's ankle boot

Wrap-round ankle boot with a thong fastening, for the right foot. Side-seamed with a single-piece upper and a butted seam along the top edge which has been cut away. The top seam may have accommodated a top band. This type of boot has no particular cultural provenance—it was a common type, not only in Dublin, but also on many other sites in medieval Europe. The excavations at High Street were notable for the evidence of leatherworkers' and cobblers' crafts.   **DC**

Bibl.: Philpott 1990, 50 (ill.)

391

Leather (cow).
L. 25cm.
Dublin (High Street), Ireland.
10th cent. ?Irish.
National Museum of Ireland, Dublin, E71:16870

Ankle boot

Wrap-round ankle boot with a thong fastening along the centre of the vamp and instep. It is cut along the top edge. The boot is unique in the Dublin assemblage; only paralleled in Waterford, none are known outside Ireland.   **DC**

Unpublished

392

394a

394b

393

392

H. 21.5cm × 14 cm.
Dublin (Fishamble Street), Ireland.
Late 10th-early 11th cent. Hiberno-Norse.
National Museum of Ireland, Dublin,
E172:10540

Woollen cap

Selvedged cap, woven from worsted yarns with a Z/Z twist. Open, regular, tabby weave. It has a rolled hem at the face edge and a doubled hem at the base. Diagonal seam at the top rear of the cap provides a curve to fit the head. A patch is stitched to the inner side.

Seven such wool caps were identifiable from Fishamble Steet/John's Lane (and five of silk, cf. cat. no. 375). These were possibly produced locally, if not they are more likely of N European/Scandinavian origin than of Near Eastern, where wool and silk were more usually produced with an S/S twist. They were of high quality, fine worsteds. The two selvedges suggest that the wool was produced on a small loom probably specially used for caps and scarves. DC

Unpublished

393

Silk. H. 17.3cm.
Dublin (Fishamble Street), Ireland.
11th cent. ?Byzantine.
National Museum of Ireland, Dublin, E190:3169

Hair net

Fine hair-net; open, loose weave; there are small tied knots at each corner of the lozenges formed by the weave.

The origin of silk hair pieces (several have been found in Dublin) is problematic since silk was imported into Dublin as yarn. It could have been made in Dublin. It is, however, not woven with the characteristic twist of north European weaves (cf. cat. no. 392), and it seems more likely to have come from the Near or Far East. DC Unpublished

394

Wool; silk.
a l. 23cm; b l. 22cm.
Dublin (Fishamble Street), Ireland.
a 10th cent., Irish; b 11th cent. Byzantine.
National Museum of Ireland, Dublin,
E172:10577; E190:1698

Two bands

a Complete woollen band; close tabby weave, as in the silk band; finished at both ends. b Silk selvedged band; finished at one end across its width by a fringe where the warp threads are tied off; there is damage along one side of the band and it is torn at one end.

Such woollen and silk bands could have been head-bands or for edging garments. There are plenty of textile tools such as spindles, whorls, tablets and needles to suggest that either of these pieces could have been woven in Dublin. DC Unpublished

395

Dublin (Fishamble Street and High Street), Ireland.
10th–11th cent. Hiberno-Norse.
National Museum of Ireland, Dublin, a E141:4623; b E172:15109 and E141:5062; c E71:16769 and E172:8078; d E172:10728; e E172:10220

Amber

a Ring fragment; diam. 2.0cm. b Two perforated, trapezoidal pendants (one broken); l. 2.7cm; 2.3cm. c Two beads; diam. 2.6cm; l.3cm. d Bead rough-out, unperforated; diam. l.5cm. e Two nodules; l. 4.0cm; 2.9cm. Amber was imported into Dublin in unworked lumps and then worked into rings, pendants and beads. The amber jeweller had his workshop in plot 2, Fishamble Street, where most of the manufacturing debris was excavated. DC Unpublished

396

Dublin (Fishamble Street and High
Street), Ireland.
10th–11th cent. Hiberno-Norse.
National Museum of Ireland, Dublin, *a*
E172:13939; *b* E71:9981; *c* E172:10554; *d*
E172:7730; *e* E172:10803 and E190:6401; *f*
E172:10219

Jet

a Two fragments of different bracelets; the
small piece is smooth and polished; l. 8.3cm
and 4.6cm. *b* Bracelet fragment, well-
polished; l. 5.4cm. *c* Nodule: lump of unworked jet; l. 6.9cm. *d* Bead, roughly worked,
perforated; diam. 2.7cm. *e* Two rings, the
larger unpolished, the smaller unfinished but
partly polished; diam. 3.0cm; 2.2cm. *f* Bead
rough-out, unpolished, unperforated; diam.
3.9cm.

Jet was probably imported to Dublin in
unworked nodules from Whitby in Yorkshire (cf. cat. no. 408). It was worked into
jewellery in the same workshop as the amber
(cf. cat. no. 395).   DC

Unpublished

397

Bone.
L. 11.4cm; 19.5cm; 22.2cm.
a–b Dublin (High Street); *c* Lagore Crannog, Co.
Meath, Ireland.
a–b 11th cent.; *c* 9th cent. *a–b* Hiberno-Norse,
c Irish.
National Museum of Ireland, Dublin, *a* E71:708;
b E71:3318; *c* W29 (c)

Three motif-pieces

a Central portion of a long bone with
patterns over all four surfaces; the main design is a pair of interlaced snakes in the
Ringerike style (cf. cat. no. 398, 430) with ten
other designs of interlaced animals and
foliate and spiral bands; all surfaces highly
polished. *b* End portion of a rib bone with
main pattern of snake interlace; three other
patterns: sketched outline of main design, a
spiral and a fragment of body loop. *c* End of a
long bone. 29 patterns on one face with
9 further patterns on the other three faces.
The variety of finished patterns include two
single-ribbon bipeds and squared interlace
bands. There are a number of unfinished
bands and scratches including triquetras.

All three motif-pieces show examples of
pattern layout and cutting, particularly *b*,
where the main design can also be seen
scratched. Some of the bands are only
scratches, others are trials and there are also

finished designs. The finished patterns were
transferred onto metal artifacts. Foliate and
interlaced animal designs predominate. The
sites at High Street and Christchurch Place
produced most of the many motif pieces
found in Dublin although there were also
finds at Fishamble Street. Lagore Crannog is
an early historic or Early Christian settlement.   DC

Bibl.: Wilde 1861, 344; Wakeman 1894; *Viking and
Medieval Dublin*, 1973, no. 41, pl.6; Ó Riordáin 1976;
O'Meadhra 1979, cat. nos. 32, 35, 119; Graham-Campbell
1980, no. 477; Fuglesang 1980, no. 102

395

396

397 a

397 a

397 b

397 c

398

Wood.
H. l6.1cm.
Dublin (Fishamble Street), Ireland.
Early 11th cent. Hiberno-Norse.
National Museum of Ireland,
Dublin, E172:5587

Finial or crook

Animal head rising from a plain cylindrical base. Head and neck are decorated with volute tendrils. The design on the sides is made up of three oval panels formed by interlaced trails. On one side the tendrils knot in a loop and fall parallel, ending in volutes; the other side has no final loop. The snout has a lozenge on the top; a bar crossing it joins two tendrils which trail on either side of the snout. A thin tongue protrudes over a curled-back lower jaw. Most of the decorated surface is pelleted.

This is the finest example of the Dublin School of decorated wood: a distinctive Dublin version of the 11th-cent. Ringerike art style (cf. cat. no. 397, 430). The emphasis is on the interlace and loop designs, rather than foliage, as in Scandinavian pieces. The tendrils on the Dublin School pieces lie adjacent and parallel; this feature is also distinctive of contemporary English and Scandinavian decoration.   DC

Bibl.: Wallace 1983, 154–8; Wallace 1985, 81–7; Lang 1987, 174–8; Lang 1988, 18–25, 63, Fig. 17, Pl. XIII

399

400

401

399

Iron.
Diam. 2.8cm; wt. 463g.
York (Coppergate), England.
c. 925. Anglo-Scandinavian.
York City Council 1980.7.9351

Coin die

A die for the obverse of a St Peter penny, second issue with sword. Face: o+o /SCIPE/ /TR IIo / o o; letters retrograde and incuse, above and below a sword to left; Thor's hammer between the lower half of the legend. Collar: only the top one of the four control points is now clearly defined. Body: cylindrical, flaring slightly above a rectangular tang, now broken.

This is a pile or lower die and was the first known complete specimen of a die from the Anglo-Saxon period (cf. cat. no. 427). No coin struck from it is known, although coins are struck from very similar dies. The discovery of this die, a die cap, and three lead trial

pieces at 16–22 Coppergate suggests the presence here of a mint and possibly even a die-cutter's workshop. The distribution of the finds suggests that this was located in either tenement C or D, both of which have also produced abundant evidence for silver working.   EJEP/DT

Bibl.: Hall 1984, 60–3; Pirie 1986, no. 43, 33–43, fig. 6, pls. I,V

400

Silver.
Wt. 1.07g.
York (Coppergate), England.
921-7. Anglo-Scandinavian.
York City Council 1980.7.9539

Penny

Contemporary imitation of the *Sword/Hammer* issue. Obv: SITEI (retrograde) / Я CDIX, above and below sword pointing to left. Rev: +IIEBIΛIIOEIX; inner circle enclosing ?Thor's hammer with a trefoil of pellets on either side.

This is the first certain example of a coin from York of the Norse king Sihtric Caoch. It is now thought that most of Sihtric's regular coins were produced south of the River Humber, and that imitations such as this coin were struck in the king's northern territory.   EJEP

Bibl.: Pirie 1986, no. 44, pl. IV

401

Silver.
Wt. 1.2g.
York (Coppergate), England.
939-41. Anglo-Scandinavian.
York City Council 1980.7.7999

Penny

Obv: +OHLΛFCVNVNC +, raven with outstretched wings, inner circle. Rev: +ODELER·MONETΛ

Hitherto, Æthelferd, striking in York, has been the only moneyer known for the Viking *Raven* issue of the Norse king Anlaf Guthfrithsson. Odeler, whose name is Germanic in origin, has been recorded as a moneyer for Edmund (940–6), but never before for Anlaf. The rendering here of the king's name as ONLAF suggests that the moneyer was striking south of the Humber, probably at Lincoln.   EJEP

Bibl.: Pirie 1986, no. 55, pl. IV

402

402

Lead.
Diam. 3.0cm; wt. 6.2g.
York (Coppergate), England.
c. 928–39. Anglo-Scandinavian.
York City Council 1980.7.8563

Trial piece

Uniface, bearing the reverse die for a penny of the regal moneyer of York, Regnald (type BMC v). Rev: +REGNALD MOEFoRPI. Collar: four pellets, one at each corner.

No coin struck from this die is known. Regnald was the sole moneyer of this type at York, and over 80 of his coins survive, all with the mint signature rendered EFORPWIC. It is possible, therefore, that the die with which this trial piece was struck was rejected from further use because the legend was not wholly correct (cf. cat. no. 399). This was during the reign of King Æthelstan.   **EJEP**

Bibl.: Hall 1984, 60–3; Pirie 1986, no. 50, fig. 6, pl. VIb

403

403

Silver. Wt. 1.23 g.
From the Fécamp hoard,
Seine-Maritime, France. Pre-942. Norman.
Musée départemental des Antiquités de Seine-Maritime, Rouen, 83.2.

Coin of William Longsword

Obverse: +WILELMVZ, cross and four balls. Reverse: +ROTOMA CIVI, cross with rhomboid recess and four crescents. William Longsword (d. 942) was the first Duke of Normandy to have coins struck. They occur in hoards found in Saint-Ours-de-Soleure in Switzerland, in Terslev in Denmark and in Fécamp in Normandy (found in 1963). The coin-type is thought to have been influenced by Anglo-Saxon coins: a cross on each side, the name of the Duke and the place of coinage (Rouen), and a rhomboid recess on the cross. A single example of another type was found in the 18th century in Hertfordshire in England. These coins, which demonstrate the autonomy of Normandy in relation to

the French king, could have been struck during the reign of King Ralph (d. 936), who conceded the peninsula of Cotentin and Avranchin to William in return for an oath of fealty; alternatively they may have been struck after the return of Louis IV from England. William did not pay homage to the latter until 940; two years later William was assassinated at Picquigny by the Count of Flanders.   **MD**

Bibl.: Poey d'Avan 1858, 23, no.115, pl.IV,1; Dumas 1979, 87–88 and note 5; Dumas et Pilet-Lemire 1989; Dhénin 1990, 18–19

404

404

Silver.
Diam. 2.0cm.
Dublin (Fishamble Street), Ireland.
c. 997. Hiberno-Norse.
National Museum of Ireland, Dublin

Two coins of Sihtric Silkbeard

Sihtric Silkbeard (d. 1042) was a Norse king of Dublin and the first Irish mint was established by him, c. 997. English types of Æthelred II were first copied in Dublin, and in Scandinavia at the same time (cf. cat. no. 423). Seventeen of the pre-Norman coins from the Fishamble Street excavations are of English origin and only seven are Hiberno-Norse.   **DC/ER**

Bibl.: Unpublished. For coins of Sihtric cf. Dolley 1965; Graham-Campbell 1980, no. 381

405

405

Copper alloy, silver, niello.
L. 9.8cm.
Greenmount, Co. Louth, Ireland.
c. 1100. Irish.
National Museum of Ireland, Dublin, X 2893

Strap-end

Rectangular copper-alloy mount with concave long sides. One end is split to take the end of a leather strap and is pierced by three rivets, one a secondary repair. One face is decorated with a regular interlace pattern of inlaid silver wires flanked by niello. The re-

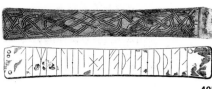

405

verse bears a lightly engraved runic inscription which reads 'Domnall Seal-head owns this sword'.

The inscription identifies this object as a sword fitting, probably a strap end. The owner's name indicates that he may have been of mixed Scandinavian and Irish parentage. The form of the mount is unique although probably derived from earlier 9th- and 10th-cent. strap ends manufactured in the Celtic areas of Britain and Ireland. The interlace and use of silver and niello inlays is of a type found on dated pieces of metalwork of about 1100. The object was found in a souterrain probably associated with a settlement site of early medieval date.   **RÓF**

Bibl.: Lefroy 1870–71, 471–502; Bøe 1940, 85–86

406

Red-deer antler.
L. 59.5cm.
Dublin (Fishamble Street), Ireland.
11th cent. Norse.
National Museum of Ireland, Dublin, E172:9630

Runic inscription

A panel (10.7 × 1.5 cm) has been flattened and smoothed to provide a surface for the inscription. This begins: *hurn:hiartaR* . . . (Hart's horn . . .).

This is one of several runic inscriptions found in Dublin (cf. also cat. no. 405). The antler still has a part the deer's skull attached. This is unusual; most of the antler pins, spoons and combs were made from shed antler. This antler had been cut from the skull.   **DC/ER**

Bibl.: Moltke 1985, 363–65; Page 1987, 54–56. See also Ó Ríordáin 1976, 136–37

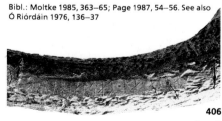

406
Detail

406

407

408
a   b

409

410

411

407

Antler. L. 13.0cm.
Lincoln, England.
10th cent. Anglo-Scandinavian.
The British Museum, London, M&LA 1867,
3–20, 12

Comb case

Antler comb-case of composite construction held together by iron rivets. On the back is a runic inscription in Old Norse: *kamb:kothan: kiari:Thorfastr*, 'Thorfast made a good comb'. Found in 1851.   LW

Bibl.: Shetelig (ed.) 1940, IV, 99; Page 1973, 194; Moltke 1985, 463, 466; Page 1987, 54–5

408

Wood; fossil stone.
a Diam. 3.9cm; *b* Diam. 3.3cm.
Dublin (High Street; Fishamble Street), Ireland.
11th cent. Hiberno/Anglo-Scandinavian.
National Museum of Ireland, Dublin,
E71:5394;E172:4298

Two snake-amulets

The wooden amulet (of ivy or holly), in the shape of a coiled snake with pointed snout and raised circular eyes (*a*), is a treatment in wood of the fossil amonite (*b*).

This type of ammonite (found in Yorkshire) is commonly known as a 'snake stone'. It has a history in folklore as a good luck charm. Snake amulets carved in jet are known from York and Norway (cat. no. 409–10) and also in silver and gold from Scandinavia (cat. no. 26e, 411). There was probably a direct transmission from Yorkshire to Dublin of this type of carving.   DC

Bibl.: Lang 1988, 15–17 (DW21)

409

Jet. L. 5.2cm.
York, Railway Station, England.
10th cent. Anglo-Scandinavian
The Yorkshire Museum, York, H110

Snake pendant

Circular pendant in the form of a coiled snake with the head in the centre. There is a cylindrical suspension-loop round which the snake's tail is coiled twice.

Pendants of this form are known in metal in Scandinavia and in wood from Dublin. A comparable example in jet is known from Norway. Jet for these pendants probably came from near Whitby, 30km NE of York; the only other known European source is in Spain.   DT

Bibl.: Waterman 1959, 94, fig. 53; Graham-Campbell 1980, no. 175

410

Jet.
W. 4.2cm.
Longva, Haram, Sunnmøre, Norway.
9th cent. Anglo-Scandinavian.
Historisk Museum, Bergen, B9471b

Snake pendant

Pendant in the form of a snake curled around a central hole. Head with small snout and suggestion of tongue. From a woman's boat-burial in a mound with other rich and varied grave-goods.

Gold, silver, bronze and jet snake-pendants are known from Scandinavian graves. There is a more highly modelled example from York and wooden examples from Dublin (cf. cat. no. 408). The jet used for the pendants probably came from Whitby, Yorkshire, England.   SK

Bibl.: Shetelig 1944; Graham-Campbell 1980, no. 174

411

Silver wire.
Diam. 2.1cm.
Birka grave 844, Uppland, Sweden.
10th cent. Scandinavian.
Statens Historiska Museum, Stockholm, Bj 844

Snake pendant

From a female grave, with beads and other pendants. Of striated silver wire curled into a spiral, the inner end hammered out to form a head, with eyes. Wire suspension loop secondarily attached; it was probably orginally suspended by a wire through a central hole. Such amulets in varying materials and techniques are known throughout the North (cf. cat. no. 408–10).   IJ

Bibl.: Arbman 1940–43, 317ff., Taf. 98:29; *Kulturhistorisk lexikon för nordisk medeltid* 1956–78: *s.v.* Drake, Ormer, Ormkult, Slanger

412

Vellum.
H. 25.5cm, ff. 69.
Winchester, New Minster, England.
?1031, with additions to 16th cent.
Anglo-Saxon.
The British Library, London, Stowe MS.944

The New Minster *Liber Vitae*
(*Illustrated p. 103*)

A *Liber Vitae*, or Book of Life, contains a record of the members, friends and benefactors of a religious community to be remembered in its prayers. The New Minster *Liber Vitae* was probably begun about 1031; the scribe, who was probably also the artist, being a monk called Ælsin.

The book is prefaced by two tinted drawings, the first showing Knut the Great and his Queen presenting an altar cross to the monastery. This drawing is the only contemporary representation of Knut. The names of the royal couple are written over their heads. The Queen's name is given as Ælfgifu, by which she was generally known in England. She was a Norman by birth and her original name was Imme, often Latinized as Emma. Above the cross is the figure of Christ, flanked by the New Minster's patrons, the Virgin Mary and St Peter. Below, in an arcade, Ælsin has included a group of his fellow monks. The second drawing, extending over two pages, shows the Last Judgment.   JB

Bibl.: Temple 1976, no. 78; *The Vikings in England*, 1981, no. I 16; *The Golden Age of Anglo-Saxon Art 966–1066*, 1984, no. 62

413

---

413   Iron with silver and copper alloy.
L. 87.6cm.
London, (prob. from River Thames at the Temple church), England.
Late 10th cent. Scandinavian.
The British Museum, London, M&LA 1887, 2–9,1

Sword

Sword of Petersen type S with lobed pommel, the pommel and guards inlaid with silver and copper-alloy wire in Mammen-style decoration. The blade was damaged before its deposition.

This is a fine example of a prestige weapon of the later Viking period. Its probable provenance, the River Thames near the City of London, has produced many weapons of the period, reflecting the shift of urban activity from the area of the Strand into the City in the 10th cent. Some of the weapons must have been casual losses but they occur in the river in such quantities as to suggest that they were deliberately cast into the river. LW

Archaeologia L (1887), 530; Shetelig (ed.) 1940, IV, 77–8, fig. 45

---

414   Iron, silver with gilding and niello, gold.
Present I. 52cm.
Dybäck, Östra Vemmenhög, Skåne, Sweden.
Late 10th cent and *c.* 1000. English and south Scandinavian.
Statens Historiska Museum, Stockholm, 4515

Sword

Upper and lower guard and scabbard rim of cast silver with gilding and niello, along the upper edge of the scabbard rim a heavy cord

twisted from two beaded gold wires, the grip (of organic material, not preserved) bound with thin gold wire and a ring twisted from fine gold wires. When the sword was complete, its hilt was crowned by a trefoil pommel, it must have been one of the most magnificent swords in Sweden. The guards were probably made in England *c.* 1000. Their convex sides are decorated with birds, quadrupeds and snakes in high relief, and with stylized foliage on the sides towards the grip. The animal heads and semi-foliate interlace on the scabbard mouth show it to be a product of the end of the Jellinge-Mammen style, probably made in Denmark in the second half of the 10th century.   IJ

Bibl.: Strömberg 1961, vol. 1, 138ff., vol. II, 66f., Taf. 65:2; Wilson 1964, 45f.; Fuglesang 1980a, 144; Graham-Campbell 1980, no. 250

---

415   Stirrups: iron, copper. Fittings: gilt bronze.
H. including ornamental plates 34cm.
Velds, central Jutland, Denmark.
End 10th cent. Anglo-Saxon.
Danmarks Nationalmuseum, Copenhagen, 11519

Two stirrups with decorated fittings

Triangular stirrups with straight tread; a small rounded mount on each side. Orna-

414

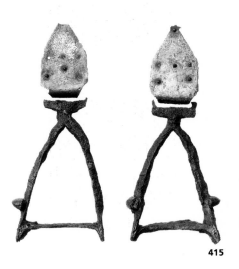

415

mental plates with engraved plant-ornament and 2 interlaced birds.

Found in a male grave; strap mounts, bells, strap distributors and bit also preserved. Decoration closely related to the Winchester style.   HL

Bibl.: Brøndsted 1936, no. 33; Wilson 1964, 50, Pl. IXa; *The Vikings in England*, 1981, 177; *The Golden Age of Anglo-Saxon Art*, 1984, no. 98

416

---

418   Walrus ivory, glass, copper alloy.
L. 23.2cm.
City of London, England.
Mid-11th cent. Anglo-Saxon.
The British Museum, London, M&LA 1870,
8–11, 1

Pen case

Tapering pen-case of walrus ivory with slid-ing lid. It is carved in high relief on the lid and four sides with elaborate figural scenes, animal and plant decoration; there are glass inlays in the eyes of the creatures.

This splendid object is a rare and particu-larly complex example of an object which must have been a frequent sight in *scriptoria*. A lid of a similar (but wooden) box from Lund (cat. no. 419) has been associated with the activities of Christian missionaries in Scandinavia. The lively decoration is of superb quality and shows a close stylistic and thematic relationship with Anglo-Saxon 11th-cent. manuscripts, particularly the calendars.   **LW**

Bibl.: Goldschmidt 1926, IV, no. 28; Beckwith 1972, no. 46; Wilson 1984, 160, 195–6, pl. 198; Backhouse, Turner and Webster (eds.) 1984, no. 132; Williamson and Webster 1990, 195

416	Oolitic limestone. 47 × 57 cm (max).

416   Oolitic limestone. 47 × 57 cm (max).
London (St Paul's churchyard), England.
Early 11th cent. Scandinavian Ringerike style.
Museum of London, London, 4075

St Paul's Stone   *(Illustrated also p. 29)*

End slab from a box-tomb or sarcophagus, carved in relief with incised details, display-ing traces of paint. The ornament consists of a four-legged animal, intertwined with cluster-ing tendrils, one of which terminates in a small-er animal head. There is a Scandinavian runic inscription incised on the narrow left face.

Found in 1852 adjacent to a skeleton; the lower part of the stone has been broken away since discovery. The runic inscription reads in translation, 'Ginna and Toki had this stone set up'. The original colour-scheme is uncertain but its probable appearance has been reconstructed by Wilson (1974). The treatment of its 'great beast' motif is excep-tionally fine and fully characteristic of the 'classic phase' of Scandinavian Ringerike-style art, closely paralleled on the Heggen vane from Norway (cat. no. 417). The St Paul's stone was most probably carved by a Scandinavian craftsman, along with a small group of other sculpture in SE England (in-cluding a newly-discovered painted fragment at Rochester, Kent), a likely context for such a workshop being the reign of Knut the Great (d. 1035).   **JGC**

Bibl.: Wilson and Klindt-Jensen 1966, 135f., pl. LVIIIa; Wilson 1974; Fuglesang 1980a, no. 88; Graham-Campbell 1980, no. 499; Moltke 1985, 322–25

---

417   Gilt copper.
L. 28cm.
Probably from Heggen church, Buskerud,
Norway.
1000–1050. Scandinavian.
Universitetets Oldsaksamling, Oslo, C. 23602

Weather vane   *(Illustrated p. 46)*

Thin copper-plate with large rivets along the edges, the crest a cast lion in brass, all gilt. The framing strip along the curved side is secondary and covers the original lower edge. Regularly placed holes along the curved edge show wear and may have held loose pieces of metal. Many later repairs and several incised dates. The decoration is in rocked lines against a punched background. On one face are 2 lions, on the other a bird struggling with a snake, framed with ten-drils, all in Ringerike style.

Its function is debatable; its sharp angle suggests that it was mounted on the slant, perhaps as a symbol on the prow of a ship. Illustrations of similar ones are known (cf. cat. no. 616). 6 similar vanes are extant, 3 from 11th cent., the others later (cat. no. 3) all of the same general shape with an animal crest.   **EBH**

Bibl.: Brøgger 1925; Wilson and Klindt-Jensen 1966, 136, fig. 61, pl. LIX; Fuglesang 1980a, 45ff.; Blindheim 1982a; Blindheim 1982b

---

419   Wood (maple).
L. 33.4cm.
Lund (Kv Färgaren 22), Sweden.
1000–1050. English.
Kulturen, Lund, KM 53.436:1125

Pen-case lid

The surface of the lid is curved and at one end terminates in a lion's head holding an unidentified animal in its gaping jaws. The skilfully carved decoration on the surface is in Winchester style, so-called after English manuscript illumination. The flat underside of the lid has a recessed area for wax and a damaged inscription in the Latin alphabet: LEOFWINE MY . . .ER.

The lid was part of a narrow box which must have contained pens (*styli*) and possibly extra wax. The inscription has been inter-preted as 'Leofwine moneyer' and the lid may be associated with an English moneyer who worked first in Lincoln and then in Lund during the reigns of Knut the Great and Sven Estridsson.   **CW**

Bibl.: Blomqvist and Mårtensson 1963, 213–16; Andrén 1980; *The Vikings in England*, 1981, no. K20

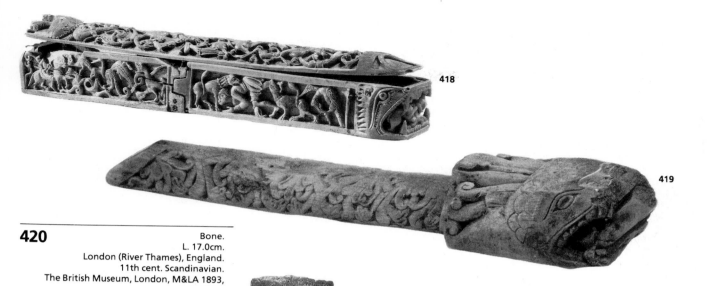

418

419

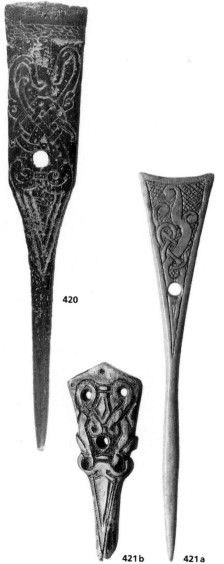

420

421b   **421a**

420

Bone.
L. 17.0cm.
London (River Thames), England.
11th cent. Scandinavian.
The British Museum, London, M&LA 1893,
6–18,72

Pin

Bone pin with flat, splayed head, pierced at
the lower centre by a hole, and decorated
with incised Ringerike ornament. Found in
1837.

A particularly elaborate example of a common type. The pin was secured by a cord or
thong passed through the perforation.   LW

Bibl.: Shetelig (ed.) 1940, IV, 92, fig. 59; Wilson and
Klindt-Jensen 1966, fig. 64; Fuglesang 1980a, no. 101;
Graham-Campbell 1980, no. 209

421

Bone.
L. 13.1cm; 11.0cm.
Trondheim, Norway.
11th cent. Norwegian.
Vitenskapsmuseet, Trondheim, N37383/FF2019,
N37326//FF2019

Two decorated pins

a Head decorated in Urnes-style interlaced
animals. Background emphasized by cross-
hatched lines. A marked outer contour. The
hole in the head is probably adapted to the
decoration. *b* Pin in 2 fragments. Head decorated with 2 symmetrically intertwined
animals in Urnes style; the 3 holes adapted to
the decoration.

Bone and wooden pins are common finds
from Trondheim. Many of them are finely
decorated, as these, but most undecorated.
The variable raw materials, shape, and decorative finish suggest that the pins served
different purposes; most of them being dress
accessories.   AC/EJ

Bibl.: Christophersen 1987, 72 f.; Nordeide 1989, fig. 22 *et
passim*

422

Silver.
Wt: 1.32g, 1.49g, 1.38g, 1.81g, 1.47g.
Found in Denmark.
c. 985–1017. English.
Danmarks Nationalmuseum, Copenhagen,
KM&MS, Sylloge 151, 533, 831, 1107, 1435

Æthelred II of England
(978–1016). Five pennies
(Illustrated p. 338)

Almost all types of coins minted by Æthelred
II are represented in Denmark, mainly
brought there because of the Danegeld. The
least well represented is the 'Hand' type.
Many types were copied in Scandinavia.
a 'Second Hand' (*c.* 985–91), Exeter mint,
moneyer Brun; from the Kulhus hoard 1863.
b 'Crux' (*c.* 991–97), Lincoln mint, moneyer
Colgrim; from Munkegård hoard 1864; the
type is the model for the earliest coins with
kings' names from Denmark, Norway, Sweden (cat. no. 423, 552a) and Ireland.
c 'Long Cross' (*c.* 997–100), Lymne mint,
moneyer Godric; from Tørring hoard 1830;
the type was frequently copied in Scandinavia (cat. no. 424).
d 'Agnus Dei' (*c.* 1009), Nottingham mint,
moneyer Oswold; from Enner hoard 1849;
the type with the Lamb of God and the Holy
Ghost is known in 14 examples, 2 from Denmark; this uncommon type was used as a
model for several Danish coins in the following decades.
e 'Last Small Cross' (*c.* 1009–17), Winchester
mint, moneyer Wulfnod; from Enner hoard
1849; this type, like the Long Cross, had
many Scandinavian copies (cat. no. 425d).   JSJ

Bibl.: Galster 1966; Talvio 1990; Leimus 1990

422 a   b   c   d   e

424 a   b

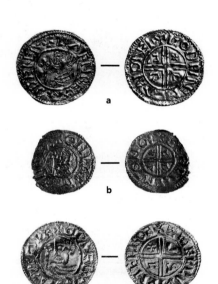

423 a   b   c

423

Silver.
Wt. 1.28g; 0.98g; 1.83g.
Öster Ryftes, Gotland (1871); Igelösa, Skåne (1924); Stora Haltarve, Gotland (1931), Sweden.
c. 995. Danish, Norwegian, Swedish (Sigtuna).
Danmarks Nationalmuseum, Copenhagen, KM&MS, BP1021; Lunds Universitets Historiska Museum, LUHM 28668; Kungl. Myntkabinettet, Stockholm, SHM 19654

Three pennies. Sven Forkbeard, Olaf Tryggvason (copy), Olof Skötkonung

a Sven Forkbeard, Denmark (*c.* 987–1014). Obverse: ZVEN REX AD DENER (Sven king in Denmark). Reverse: GODWINE M⁻AN DNER (Godwine moneyer in Denmark). *b*

Olaf Tryggvason, Norway (*c.* 995–1000). Obverse: ONLAF REX NOR (Olaf king of the Norsemen). Reverse: GODWINE M⁻O NO (Godwine moneyer in Norway). *c* Olof Skötkonung, Sweden (*c.* 994–1022). Obverse: +OLAF RX AON ZTUNE (Olof king in Sigtuna). Reverse: +ZNELLING ME PROF (Snelling made me).

All have left-facing busts with sceptre on obverse; on reverse double cross with CRVX in angles of cross.

The coins are inspired by Æthelred II's 'Crux' type, minted *c.* 991–997 (cf. cat. no. 422b), and are among the earliest coins minted in Norway and Sweden; only in Denmark were coins minted earlier (cf. cat. no. 153). England, because of the coin reform of *c.* 973, had a unified coinage system with regular changes. Æthelred's 'Crux' type was the first to be imported in great quantities to Scandinavia; they were imitated in Denmark, Norway and Sweden in the reigns of these kings. In all three countries English moneyers were at first responsible for the issues; Sven and Olaf had a short-lived and limited coinage (8 coins known from Sven; 4 from Olaf). In contrast, Olof issued many coins over many decades(some 400 coins are known) (cf. cat. no. 552). Only the Swedish coins give the place of minting (Sigtuna). The three coins are the earliest in Scandinavia to carry the names of the kings and the moneyers. **KJ**

Bibl.: Lagerqvist 1970, 3; Blackburn, Dolley and Jonsson 1979; *Corpus Nummorum Saeculorum IX–XI qui in Svecia reperti sunt*, 1, 4 (1982), 17.1927; Blackburn, Dolley and Jonsson 1983; Malmer 1989, 3.72.1

424

Silver.
Wt. 1.93g; 1.64g.
No provenance.
c. 1000. Swedish, ?Danish.
Kungl. Myntkabinettet, Stockholm

Two Scandinavian pennies

a Olof Skötkonung (*c.* 994–1022), minted in Sigtuna, 'Long Cross/Short Cross' hybrid. Obverse: Confused legend. Left-facing bust. Reverse: Confused legend. Small cross. *b* Copy of Æthelred II 'Long Cross' type. The legends are confused with Chester, the moneyer Elewne being the model.

Coin finds from northern Europe contain many thousands of coins with the same motifs as English originals, particularly coins of Æthelred II (978–1016) (cf. cat. no. 422), but diverging in legend, style, weight, etc. The legends are often totally confused and the types are combined in ways quite impossible in England. There are also coins where it is impossible to say whether they are copies of English coins or whether they were actually minted there. Detailed research has shown that some of the coins were minted in Scandinavia, particularly in Denmark and Sweden. In Denmark this type of coin was minted sporadically *c.* 995–1050, in Sweden its minting was concentrated *c.* 1000–1025. **KJ**

Bibl.: Hildebrand 1881, 1515; Blackburn 1981, 102a; Malmer 1989, 251.574.2

426

425

425   Silver.
Wt 1.03g, 1.01g, 0.88g, 1.62g, 0.98g.
a Faroes, *b, e* Denmark, *c* N. Germany,
d no provenance.
c. 1017–1035/36. 3 English, 2 Danish.
Danmarks Nationalmuseum, Copenhagen,
KM&MS, Sylloge 2325, 2276, 2298, Thomsen
9830, FP 79.21

Knut the Great of England (1016–35) and Denmark (c. 1018–35). Five pennies

During the reign of Knut the Great there were 3 English issues, each of 6 years: 'Quatrefoil', 'Pointed Helmet' and 'Short Cross'. They had wide distribution in Scandinavia and were also copied in Denmark (cf. cat. no. 426, 552b).

a 'Quatrefoil' (*c.* 1017–23), London mint, moneyer Eadsigne; Sand hoard, Faroes 1863.
b 'Pointed Helmet' (*c.* 1023–29), London mint, moneyer Bruninc; Enner hoard 1849.
c 'Short Cross' (*c.* 1029–35), London mint, moneyer Corin; Lübeck 1875 (cf. cat. no. 427).
d 'Small Cross'-type (Hauberg 1); Lund, Skåne, Sweden (then Denmark) mint; copy of Æthelred's latest type, minted probably before 1018 (cf. cat. no. 422). This type has been used to argue that Knut's reign in Denmark began earlier than the traditional 1018.
e 'Short Cross'-type (Hauberg 39), with Latin inscription 'In the name of God the Father'; Slagelse, Denmark, mint; Store Valby hoard 1839; copy of Knut's last English issue.
                     JSJ

Bibl.: Hauberg 1900; Galster 1970; Malmer 1986; Posselt 1991

426   Silver.
Wt. 1.33g.
No provenance.
c. 1030. Swedish (Sigtuna).
Kungl. Myntkabinettet, Stockholm, SHM 29856

Anund Jakob, Sweden (c. 1022–1050). Penny

'Short Cross/Small Cross' hybrid. Obverse: +CNVT REX SW (Knut king of the Svear). Left-facing bust with sceptre. Reverse: +THORMOTH IN SIHT (Thormoth in Sigtuna). Small cross.

In 1016 Knut became king of England and 3 coin types were minted there during his reign (cf. cat. no. 425). Knut was also king of Norway 1028–1035 but no coins from his reign are known. The Sigtuna coins, which are attributed to Knut's assumed reign in Sweden after the famous battle of Helgeå in 1026, must be of Anund Jakob, with legends copying the English 'Short Cross' originals.

Coins modelled on English originals were also minted in Denmark (cf. cat. no. 425), but combinations of these or local types dominate. The legends are sometimes legible but most of them are confused. It was not until *c.* 1028 that large-scale minting began when the number of types decrease and they can be associated with known mints. This may perhaps be connected with the (failed) attempt to control coin circulation in Denmark which was dominated in Knut's reign by imported coins from Germany and England.
                     KJ

Bibl.: Lagerqvist 1968, 13/12; Lagerqvist 1970, 12/10; Sawyer 1989

427   Iron.
H. 6.5cm.
London, Thames Exchange, England.
c. 1030–35. Anglo-Saxon.
M.D. O'Hara Collection

Coin die of Knut

Attached to the wrought-iron shaft is a separate hardened iron tip the surface of which is square with rounded corners. Punched in its centre is the circular die, reading in mirror image, +ÐRV[LF]ONORÐ, around a short voided cross. The die was found with a metal detector on soil removed from the Thames Exchange building site on N bank of Thames, in 1989.

This is the earliest of four dies (the others are of the Norman period) from Thames Exchange. It is a reverse, upper, die of Cnut's Short Cross type for use by the moneyer Thurulf at Norwich. No coins struck from it have been traced, and Thurulf was previously known in Knut's reign (King of England 1016–35) only at Stamford. The presence of a Norwich die of this type in London confirms deductions made from the coins that, although coinage dies had been made at a number of regional centres earlier in Knut's reign, by the Short Cross period production was centralized in London.   **MDOH/MMA**

Bibl.: O'Hara forthcoming a; forthcoming b

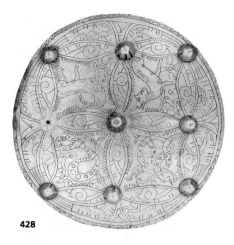

428

429

430

428
Diam. 14.9–16.4cm.
Sutton, Isle of Ely, Cambridgeshire, England.
First half of 11th cent. Anglo-Scandinavian.
The British Museum, London, M&LA 1951,11-1,1

Silver brooch

Silver disc-brooch. Slightly convex, set with bosses and decorated with lightly incised animal and plant decoration. On the back are two incised triquetras, a damaged inscription in pseudo-runes, and around the edge an Old English verse inscription which may be read 'Aedwen owns me, may the Lord own her. May the Lord curse the man who takes me from her unless she gives me of her own free will'. It was ploughed up in 1694 with the remains of a lead casket, coins, and other gold and silver objects. First illustrated in 1705, its whereabouts were thereafter unknown until it reappeared in 1951.

The latest surviving example of a late Saxon bossed silver disc-brooch, it was buried with coins of William I c. 1070. Its coarse and sketchy decoration is an amalgam of Ringerike and late Saxon style elements.

LW

Bibl.: Hickes 1705, III, 187–8; Wilson 1964, no. 83; Fuglesang 1980a, no. 50; Graham-Campbell 1980, no. 146; Backhouse, Turner and Webster (eds.) 1984, no. 105

429
Gilded copper-alloy.
Diam. 3.9cm.
Pitney, Somerset, England.
Second half of 11th cent. Anglo-Scandinavian.
The British Museum, London, M&LA 1979,11-1,1

Pitney brooch

Gilded copper-alloy openwork brooch with Urnes-style design of two animals in combat. Found in the churchyard.

A fine example of the English version of the Urnes style; the animal and snake combat is close to Scandinavian versions of this theme, while the scalloped frame and beaded body of the main animal are Anglo-Saxon features.

LW

Bibl.: Shetelig (ed.) 1940, IV, 57, fig. 24; Wilson 1964, no. 60; Graham-Campbell 1980, no. 147; Backhouse, Turner and Webster (eds.) 1984, no. 110

430
Iron, bronze with various inlays.
H. 30cm.
Cooke Collection; said to have been found near Glankeen, Co. Tipperary, Ireland.
Late 11th cent. Hiberno-Scandinavian.
The British Museum, London, M&LA 1854,7-14,6

Bell-shrine

Bronze-coated iron bell in a sheet-bronze casing, now incomplete, with a cross engraved on one face. An upper mount of cast bronze is elaborately ornamented with two human heads in the round and four stylized animal masks, its surfaces inlaid with copper and silver wires, niello, and bands of silver in Ringerike style. Enamels are set over the apex. Openwork forms an important element in the design.

This enshrined bell, often referred to as St Cuilean's bell, is a fine example of Irish metalworking which under Viking influence absorbed the Scandinavian Ringerike animal-interlace style. The distinctive use of silver ribbons outlined in niello against plain surfaces, the variety of wire inlays and use of enamel place it technically and artistically alongside other fine metalwork associated with north Munster. This implies the concentration of production in a few monastic workshops. The style of decoration is also found in contemporary Irish manuscripts and wood carving.

SY

Bibl.: Henry 1970, 102 ff.; Ó Floinn 1987, 180–2

431
Iron, copper alloy, silver, niello.
L. 20.5cm.
Lough Derg (near Curraghmore), Co. Tipperary, Ireland.
c. 1100. Irish.
National Museum of Ireland, Dublin, 1988:226

Sword hilt

Double-edged iron sword with fullered blade, 78.5cm long: found in five pieces, only the hilt exhibited. During conservation traces of a scabbard of wood, leather and wool were found. The pommel and guard are plain and slightly curved, and the grip is provided with a pair of mounts with scalloped inner edges. These are inlaid with a border of twisted copper and silver wires and an interlaced pattern of silver wires against a niello ground. The interlaced strands terminate in plant scrolls some of which may be debased animal heads.

431

In form, the sword betrays Anglo-Scandinavian influences with its curved pommel and guard and scalloped mounts. The decoration is, however, purely Irish. The inlaid decoration is paralleled on contemporary ecclesiastical metalwork such as the Clonmacnoise crozier and the bell shrine from Glankeen, Co. Tipperary (cf. cat. no. 430), both places not far from where the sword was found. It is a rare survival of a decorated secular object of the period. **ROF**

Bibl.: Ryan (ed.) 1991, 152, 215

---

432   Iron and brass.
L. 10cm.
York (Coppergate), England.
11th or 12th cent. Anglo-Scandinavian.
York City Council 1977.7.1612

Key

Sliding key. The bulbous stem is spirally inlaid with brass wire. At the upper end there is a flat extension perforated to accommodate an iron suspension-loop. The bit is circular, originally perforated with an axial rectangular slot with a circular hole to either side, now broken.

Keys of this type were used with box padlocks with T-shaped slots. Several are known from 16–22 Coppergate and comparable examples come from Lincoln and Northamp-

ton but they are much more common in Scandinavia, and the English examples are probably imports. They are usually found in 11th- or 12th-cent. contexts in England and probably represent continuing contact with Scandinavia after the Norman Conquest (cf. cat. no. 433–5). **DT**

Bibl.: *The Vikings in England*, 1981, 111, no. YDL 18

---

433   Iron, copper alloy.
L. 11.1cm.
Fljótsdalur, S. Iceland.
Prob. 11th–12th cent. Scandinavian.
Islands Nationalmuseum, Reykjavík, 12780

Key

This stray find has a bulbous stem spirally inlaid with copper alloy. The bit is circular with openings to fit into a trapezoidal lock, common in England and Scandinavia in the late Viking Age and early Middle Ages (cf. cat. no. 432). Another Icelandic example was found at Stöng in Thjórsárdálur. **VÖV**

Bibl.: Roussell 1943, 95; Nørlund 1948, pl. XXII:3; Andersen *et al.* 1971, 186–8; Long 1975, 27–8

---

434   Iron, bronze.
L. 7.5cm.
Sandnæs (Kilaarsarfik), Ameralla, Ruin group
64V2-III-511(V51), Greenland.
11th cent. Scandinavian.
Grønlands Nationalmuseum og Arkiv, Nuuk,
KNK4x1109

Key

The key has a loose attachment ring, a swelling shank with circular cross-section, and spiral inlay of bronze wire. The bit has 2 teeth. Found with cat. no. 342. Similar keys are known from Iceland, York, and many sites in Scandinavia (cf. cat. no. 432). It was for a padlock and shows the Greenlanders' close connections with the outside world, even on the level of daily life. **JA**

Bibl.: Arneborg 1985, 7

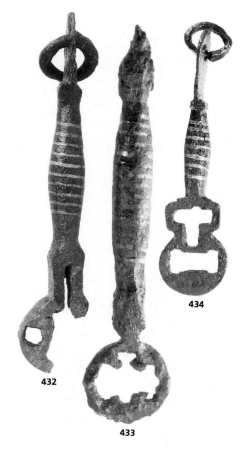

434

432

433

---

435   Iron with bronze inlay.
L. 10.2cm.
Lund (Kv S:t Clemens 8), Sweden.
1100–1150. Scandinavian.
Kulturen, Lund, KM 66.166:1787

Key

The key belongs to a padlock. This type of lock is the predecessor of the padlock and is common in finds from 11th and 12th cent. Many locks are fairly small and must have been used on shrines and caskets. Larger examples may have been used to lock doors.

CW

Bibl.: Andrén and Nilsson 1976, 399–405

435

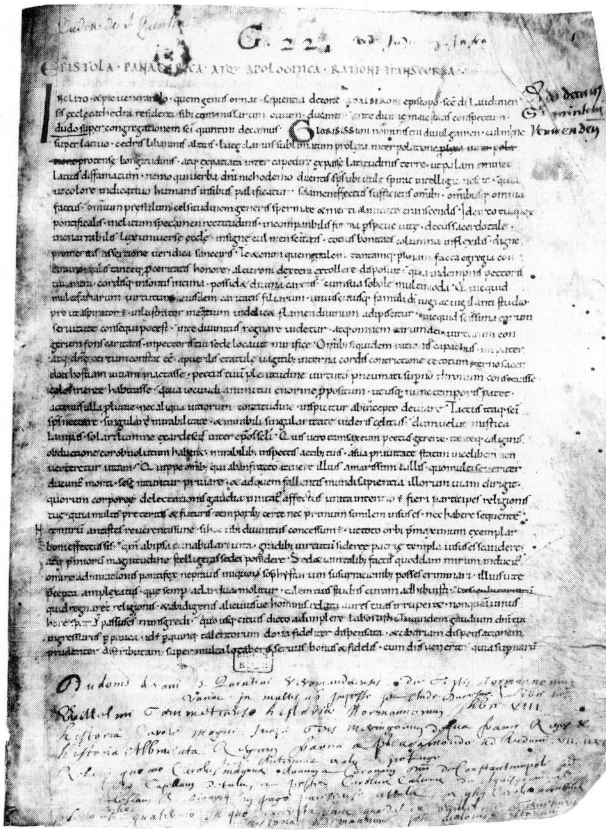

436

436

Vellum.
H. 31cm; 169ff.
Abbaye de Jumièges, Seine-Maritime, France.
Transcripts, respectively from the 11th and 12th
centuries, of two documents. Norman.
Bibliothèque municipale de Rouen, MS. YII
(1173)

Two Norman historical texts

This manuscript contains texts written by
Dudo of St Quentin and William of
Jumièges, who were the first historians to
describe the illustrious Duchy of Normandy,
its Dukes and its Scandinavian antecedents.
Dudo's work *De moribus et actis primorum Normanniae ducum*, from c. 1020, seems to have
been copied in Jumièges in the 2nd half of
the 11th century. Unusually, numerous
blank spaces divide the text, and no satisfac-
tory explanation has been found for this.
After Dudo's text there follows in this volume a manuscript of the work by William of
Jumièges, c. 1070, *Gesta Normannorum ducum*,
which was also transcribed in Jumièges, but
in the 2nd half of the 12th century.   **VN**

Bibl.: Lair 1865; Marx (ed.) 1914; Albrectsen 1979; van
Houts 1983; Huisman 1984

437

Vellum.
19 × 29.5cm.
Abbaye Saint-Ouen de Rouen, France.
c. 1051. Norman.
Archives départementales de la Seine-
Maritime, Rouen, 14H797

Deed of gift to the Abbey of Saint-Ouen

Original document. Robert Bertram and his
wife Suzanne donate to the Abbey several
churches and other property which they own
in Normandy, with the agreement of Duke
William (the Conqueror). Six place-names
are mentioned which are partly or completely Scandinavian: Clarum Beccum (Clarbec),
Ovretoth (Vrétot), Sortinvilla (Surtainville),
Bricebec (Bricquebec), Barnaville (Barnevil-
le), Torgisvilla (Tourgéville). There are also
Scandinavian personal names: Turstinus
(three individuals); Osbernus and Ansfridus
are possibly also Scandinavian. The deed
bears the signature of the Duchess Matilda
along with that of her son Robert, dating it
not earlier than 1051.   **CH/ER**

Bibl.: Fauroux 1961, no. 205

437

438

439
Vellum.
29.5 × 20.4cm; 7ff.
Abbaye Saint-Aubin d'Angers, France.
c. 1100. Anjou.
Bibliothèque nationale, Paris, Ms. Nouv. acq.
Lat. 1390

Life of St Aubin *(Illustrated p. 19)*

Seven sheets of parchment with 14 full-page illustrations of scenes from St Aubin's life. He was Bishop of Angers, an area ravaged by Vikings in the 9th century; on fol. 7 they are depicted in their ships ready to attack. The picture testifies to the fact that the Vikings left a deep impression which survived vividly and for a long time in the popular collective memory.

The manuscript belongs to a small group of illuminated books taking the life of a saint as their theme. The anonymous artist, on account of this manuscript, has been designated the "Master of the Life of St Aubin". He was probably an itinerant layman. He also illustrated two other manuscripts for St Aubin Abbey: a large Bible and a Psalter. He was one of the most lively of the personalities involved in pictorial illustration in the west of France in his time. A period which witnessed a flourishing development in this field, producing, for example, the renowned wall-paintings at Saint-Savin and other works in Poitiers. **FA**

Bibl.: Wormald 1952, 257; *Les manuscrits en peintures en France du VIIe au XIIe siècles*, 1954, no. 221; Herbécourt and Porcher 1959, 182–216; Carrasco 1984

438
Diam. 8.5cm.
Appended to a deed of gift to the
Abbaye de Saint-Denis, 1069.
Archives nationales D9998 et bis (replica). AE III,
no.61 (=K20 no.5) (deed)

William the Conqueror's seal (replica)

Obverse: the King can be seen, full face, sitting on the throne, crowned and dressed in full-length costume. In his right hand he is holding a raised sword and in the left a globe with a cross. Inscription: +HOC.ANGLIS.REGEM.SIG-NO.FATEARIS EUNDEM. Reverse: the Duke is represented on horseback, galloping to the right, with a coat of mail, a conical helmet, a lance with banner at his right shoulder, and in his left hand a shield. Inscription: +HOC.NORMANNORVM WILLELMVM NOSCE. PATRONVM SI(gno).

The double-sided seal, which William used after the conquest of England, is evidence of the new situation created by the formation of the Anglo-Norman kingdom. Like his predecessor Edward the Confessor, he is seen on the obverse as King of England; but on the reverse he is the warlord and prince of the mighty Duchy of Normandy. The English kings who succeeded him maintained this double representation on their seals, with images of seated majesty on one side and equestrian knighthood on the other. In this deed of gift, issued in Winchester on 14 April 1069, William and his wife Matilda present to the Abbey of Saint-Denis near Paris the church of *Derhest* (Deerhurst), Gloucestershire, England. **CD/MDG**

Bibl.: Douët d'Arcq 1868; *Documents impériaux et royaux de l'Europe médiévale*, 1977, no. 203; Dalas-Garrigues 1984

Scandinavia–Tradition and innovation

440
Oak.
L. 309cm; 308cm; 288cm.
Hemse, Gotland, Sweden.
1140s. Swedish.
Statens Historiska Museum, Stockholm, 10232

Three wall planks

Building works in 1896 revealed that the wooden floor of the stone church was made of the remains of wall planks from a stave church. The planks lay on solid beams which had been the sill and wall-plate of the stave church; all, except a pine capital and one plank, are of oak. The front of the planks is convex, the back plain. Their upper ends are decorated with ring-and-dots and trimmed on their convex sides; the transition to full thickness is elegant with curved contours which run together in a sharp point at the middle of the plant. The church has been dated dendrochronologically to the 1140s, contemporary with the wooden churches of Eke and Sproge on Gotland (Th. Bartolin). **GT**

Bibl.: Eckhoff 1914–16; Andersson 1968, 385ff.; Lagerlöf and Stolt 1969

440

441

Pine. H. 390cm.
Ål church, Hallingdal, Norway.
1130–1160. Norwegian.
Universitetets Oldsaksamling, Oslo, C.10590

Portal of stave church *(Illustrated p. 23)*

W. portal of Ål church, demolished 1880. 5 tongue-and-grooved planks with applied capitals above which are three-dimensional lions. The outer faces of the planks are curved and the relief deeply carved. On each side a tendril grows from a lion head, above the doorway are 3 fighting dragons, entwined with 19 small dragons. The doorway is framed by half columns.

It belongs to the 'Sogn-Valdres' type of which 46 examples are preserved, all slightly different but with the same main composition. Various impulses mingle. The motifs are Romanesque: palmette friezes, tendrils, lions and dragons, but the intertwining of the long animal bodies and interest in the combat motif are signs of the origins of the animal ornament. The motif above the columns in which lions devour a man of whom only the head remains is inspired by Rhenish-Lombardic architecture, while the details of the foliage are related to English decoration of the early 12th cent.   EBH

Bibl.: Blindheim 1965; Anker 1969; Hohler 1989

442

Pine. H. 215cm.
Hylestad, Setesdal, Norway.
c. 1200. Norwegian.
Universitetets Oldsaksamling, Oslo, C.4321

Portal of stave church *(Illustrated p. 170 and 223)*

Portal of which the area over the arch and the top of the door frame is missing (its design is not recorded). The broad planks of the jambs are decorated with figural scenes, on one side set in circular frames. The doorway has attached half-columns with bell-shaped capitals and a flat archivolt frieze. The scenes are taken from the Sigurd legend: Sigurd and Regin making a sword; Sigurd slaying the dragon Fafnir; Sigurd roasting Fafnir's heart; Sigurd slaying Regin; and Gunnar in the snake pit. The planks are flat, the relief is firmly modelled and clearly detailed.

Hylestad church was demolished in 1838 and the two portals reused in a private house. This portal belongs to a group in which scenes from the Sigurd legend are depicted in medallions. Several related exam-ples from the same workshop exist, some with tendril ornament which is associated with the late 12th-cent. English-N French "Channel School". The softly-pleated garments on the Hylestad portal support this date.   EBH

Bibl.: Blindheim 1965; Hohler 1971–72; Margeson 1981; Hohler 1989

443

Pine. H. 56cm.
Vinje church, Telemark, Norway.
c. 1200. Norwegian.
Universitetets Oldsaksamling, Oslo, C.1735

Capital with lion

Figure of lion on pilaster capital broken at bottom edge; the lion is carved in flat relief, its head thrust forward. Axe marks and re-mains of trenail on back.

Vinje church can be dated before 1202 by means of a runic inscription naming known people. It was demolished in 1796. Similar lions are known from portals of stave churches (cf. cat. no. 441), but on a different type of capital. This pilaster with its lion was probably loose and nailed onto its background; possibly from a portal or choir screen.   EBH

Bibl.: Kjellberg 1946; *Norges Innskrifter med de Yngre Runer* II, 1951, 264ff.; Blindheim 1965

443

444

Soapstone.
H. 22cm.
Trondheim (church not known), Norway.
Early 12th cent. Anglo-Norwegian.
Nidaros Domkirkes Restaureringsarbeider,
no. 8, Trondheim

Capital *(Illustrated p. 211)*

Badly damaged. Originally softly square. One of the sides is plain, the others decorated with composite flowers. The flowers have large tendrilled calices with smaller stems forming new leaves and small palmettes which hold the 3 sides together. It has a strongly contoured double collar at the base. The relief is low but carefully modelled over a plain background.

The details and relief have close parallels in SE English sculpture and manuscripts 1100–1130, and could have been carved by an Englishman. A number of stone churches were built in Trondheim in 12th cent. and continuing influences from England characterize the school which shows a mixture of direct imports and native features. This capital represents an early phase in this process.   EBH

Bibl.: Blindheim 1965, fig. 27 *et passim*

445

Soapstone.
H. 33cm.
Trondheim (church not known), Norway.
First half of 12th cent. Norwegian.
Nidaros Domkirkes Restaureringsarbeider,
no. 2, Trondheim

Capital *(Illustrated p. 211)*

Capital and jamb stone carved in one, slightly damaged. The jamb is separated from the capital by a keel moulding, and decorated with lion mask with pendant tongue above a bunch of leaves. The relief on the capital is high and strongly modelled, the jamb stone has punched surfaces in several places.

This and the two following capitals were found reused in Trondheim Cathedral, but may not have originated there. Capitals with jambs are a Lombardic type but may, like so many other features, have reached Trondheim by way of England. The lion mask is clearly English, but the style of the whole has distinct Norwegian characteristics. The bunch of leaves beneath the mask is repeated on cat. no. 446.   EBH

Bibl.: Holmqvist 1948; Blindheim 1965, fig. 8 *et passim*; Fischer 1965, 549

446

Soapstone.
H. 38.5cm.
Trondheim (church not known), Norway.
First half of 12th cent. Norwegian.
Nidaros Domkirkes Restaureringsarbeider,
no. 6, Trondheim

Capital *(Illustrated p. 211)*

Capital and jamb stone carved in one in sloppy relief. The capital has a corner volute above reversed conjoined heart-shaped palmettes. On the jamb stone is an inhabited tree-motif which includes a goat. Next to it is an architectural motif consisting of a column flanked by niches. Discovered with cat. no. 445.

The stone shows influences from English sculpture as represented by cat. no. 444 and is probably a second-generation work. The simplified foliage and flowers are typical. The lion, goat and mask are frequent motifs in Trondheim sculpture.   **EBH**

Bibl.: Holmqvist 1948; Blindheim 1965, fig. 2 *et passim*; Fischer 1965, 549

447

Soapstone.
H. 21cm.
Trondheim (church not known), Norway.
First half of 12th cent. Norwegian.
Nidaros Domkirkes Restaureringsarbeider,
no. 1, Trondheim

Capital *(Illustrated p. 211)*

Capital carved in one with jamb stone but standing proud of it. It has corner volutes flanking a chip-carved star above a rope-like collar. An owl-like mask on the jamb stone; on the side a small dragon entwining the owl's legs, with its neck in the owl's beak. The owl is carved in rough pelleted ridges. Found with cat. no. 445.

The volutes and star show English late 11th-cent. influence, while the details of the beasts are typical of the local school (cf. cat. no. 444–6). The stone must come from a small portal or chancel screen where the columns stood proud of the wall. This rare architectural motif may go back to Anglo-Saxon sources and is well known from the portals of Norwegian stave-churches.   **EBH**

Bibl.: Holmquist 1948; Blindheim 1965, fig. 9 *et passim*; Fischer 1965, 549

448

Limestone.
H. 47.5; w. 28.0.
Sønder Kirkeby, Falster, Denmark.
c. 1200. Danish.
Danmarks Nationalmuseum, Copenhagen,
MDCCC

Relief *(Illustrated p. 211)*

Relief of a layman and a cleric who, according to the inscription, are Toste and Conrad. Toste, bearded, is in knee-length clothing and holds a round object (a coin or a symbolic lump of earth) in his right hand, Conrad carries a chalice. Each carries a candle in his left hand.

The relief was placed in the church's south porch with a corresponding relief of *Traditio Legis*. Conrad and Toste were the patrons who paid for the porch (perhaps for the whole church), here they are in procession with their symbolic gifts towards the enthroned Christ in the *Traditio Legis* scene. Walterus, whose name is carved on the latter stone, may have been the artist.   **PGH**

Bibl.: Christiansen 1950; Nyborg 1979, 52

449

Sandstone, traces of paint.
H. of sides from lower edge of
decoration 48cm—50cm.
Ardre church, Gotland, Sweden.
11th cent. Local.
Statens Historiska Museum, Stockholm,
11118:I–II, V–VI

Stone cist *(Illustrated p. 189)*

Found in a secondary context beneath the church floor, traces of red paint survive. Made as a memorial to a mother by her sons. The brothers also erected a rune-inscribed picture stone for their father, thus this inscription can be reasonably supplemented and interpreted. The inscription starts on the side with two symmetrical ribbon-shaped animals and has been reconstructed: 'Liknat's sons [caused to] have raised a good memorial for Ailkni, a good woman, mother [of Aivat and Ottar] and Gairvat and Liknvi. God a[nd the Mother of God be merciful] to her and to those who raised the memorial, [the largest] to be seen . . . in Garda, which is the home of (?)Viv . . .' Garda is the neigbouring parish to Ardre.

The Ardre cist is a good example of the renaissance of picture stones on Gotland at the end of the Viking Age. The shape of the picture stones is preserved but the figural scenes are replaced partly or wholly by

animal ornament, often with runic inscriptions on the ribbon-shaped animals, or on the borders. Here ornamental animals in Urnes style are supplemented by scenes from Gotland pagan mythology; for example, one gable shows a warrior on an eight-legged horse (cf. cat. no. 1, 175). Nevertheless, this monument was probably that of a Christian family, the inscription, if the interpretation is correct, being a Christian prayer. The cist may have been placed over the grave of Ailikni in Ardre churchyard.   **IJ**

Bibl.: Lindqvist 1941–42, vol. 1, *passim*, fig. 159–67, 224f., vol. II, 18ff.; *Sveriges runinskrifter* XI 1962, 199ff., 210ff., pl. 58–61; Lindqvist 1960–62, 10ff., fig. 3–7; Nylén 1978, 81–3

450

Sandstone.
L. 172cm.
Botkyrka church, Södermanland, Sweden.
c. 1130. Swedish.
Statens Historiska Museum, Stockholm, 3841

Grave cover *(Illustrated p. 189)*

The monument is shaped as a church with an apse; the roof ridge is curved. One long side has arcades with figures in low relief: in the middle is Christ with the stigmata; to the left six figures, perhaps apostles, with humbly bowed heads; on the immediate right of Christ an archangel blows a trumpet; next to the right the dead rise from the tomb. At the far right a man rises from his tomb. Above the arcades is an inscription in Latin majuscule, 'He who reads this and is ignorant [must know that] a nobleman lies here. I pray that you, Christ, will say: He, Björn, is cleansed from the corruption [of sin]'. The other long side shows David, with staff in hand, binding the jaws of a lion. There are also three other lions, one winged.

A runic inscription along both sides of the somewhat damaged ridge reads, 'Karl made the stone after Björn, his kinsman, Sven's and Bänkfrid's son in Hammarby, his . . . He lies here beneath this stone. Bänkfrid . . . his son'. Stylistic forerunners to the floral interlace on the roof are found in northern English art of late 11th cent.-early 12th cent. date. The Björn of the inscription may be identified with the brother of the apostle of Södermanland, St Botvid, to whose memory he built the first church at Botkyrka, dedicated 1129. The monument must have been erected shortly afterwards.   **GT**

Bibl.: *Sveriges runinskrifter* III, 1924–36; Andersson 1973

451 Granite.
H. 100cm.
Nørre Snede church, Jutland, Denmark.
c. 1150. Danish.
Nørre Snede kirkes menighedsråd (Parish Council)

Font *(Illustrated p. 210)*

The bowl is carved in high relief with 4 powerful lions' bodies opposed in pairs with conjoined almost human masks. The manes are of interlaced locks. The tails are threaded between the back legs and end in ornamental clusters of leaves. A 4-leaf rosette separates the 2 pairs of lions.

About 180 lion fonts are known from Denmark, almost all from E Jutland. The Nørre Snede font belongs to a small group characterized by the intertwined manes, which includes that in Gellerup church, the construction of which is dated by inscription to 1140. The Nørre Snede font is one of the finest examples and is still in use. **PGH**

Bibl.: Mackeprang 1941, 265ff.; Norn 1968, 22, 53, 59, no. 50

452 Sandstone.
H. 86cm.
Tingstad church, Östergötland, Sweden.
Late 12th cent. Gotlandic.
Statens Historiska Museum, Stockholm, 7983

Font *(Illustrated p. 210)*

The cylindrical bowl is decorated with figural scenes in low, flat relief; it stands on a square foot with flat sides and four figures in relief at the corners. The carvings on the bowl depict scenes from the birth of Christ: the Annunciation, the meeting of Mary and Elizabeth, the birth of Christ, the ?washing of the Christ child, the Magi following the star to Bethlehem, the adoration of the Magi. Between the birth of Christ and the Annunciation is a free-standing depiction of the Archangel Michael's battle with the dragon. On one of the sides of the foot is a church with apse, choir, nave and tower, one of the earliest, and undoubtedly the most detailed, illustration of a church in Scandinavia.

The font was made on Gotland and can be attributed to the mason Sighraf, whose signature is found on the font at Åkirkeby church on Bornholm. About 20 works belong to this group. **GT**

Bibl.: Roosval 1918; Andersson 1968, 136

453

455

453 Wood (pine).
H. 95cm.
Näs church, Jämtland, Sweden.
c. 1200. Scandinavian.
Statens Historiska Museum, Stockholm, 23002:5

Font

Two medieval wooden fonts have been preserved in Sweden, both from Jämtland: Näs (known as Lockne in early references) and Alnö. There were probably more. The bowl, stem and foot of the Näs font are in one piece. A double-palmette frieze runs around the foot. The bowl displays an elegantly rhythmic decoration in high and distinct relief: 6 medallions joined by vegetal fronds containing fabulous beasts and dragons which are produced from the encircling vegetation. One medallion contains a scene from the Volsunga saga—Gunnar in the snake pit. According to the saga, he was thrown into the pit with his hands bound but played so beautifully on his harp with his feet that the snakes fell asleep.

In the Middle Ages Jämtland was part of Norway, where the artistic prototypes of this font are to be found. **GT**

Bibl.: Andersson 1968, 176; Karlsson 1977

454 Pine.
a H. 43cm. *b* h. 74cm. *c* h. 75cm.
Flatatunga, N Iceland.
11th cent. Scandinavian.
Islands Nationalmuseum, Reykjavík, 15296 a–c

Wall panels *(Illustrated p. 56)*

Three of 4 panels, probably from a church wall, perhaps Hólar cathedral. All are carved and trimmed at both ends; there are holes for square-sectioned trenails. They are decorated on the front face in an upper and lower field separated by two horizontal lines; the backs are plain. The upper fields contain Ringerike-style plant decoration, the lower fields show Christ with shepherd's crook (*b*), and apostles or saints. All the figures are haloed. The final use of the planks was as the roof-lining of the last turf-built farm at Flatatunga. They had probably previously been used as building timber. **TM**

Bibl.: Eldjárn 1953, 81–101; Jónsdóttir 1959, 37–57; Wilson and Klindt-Jensen 1966, 138; pl. LX; Magerøy 1967, 153–72; Fuglesang 1980a, 69–70, 197, no. 106; Graham-Campbell 1980, no. 539; Ágústsson 1989, 111–59

455

Wood (oak).
L. 313cm.
Eke church, Gotland, Sweden.
Mid-12th cent. Gotlandic.
Statens Historiska Museum, Stockholm, 15844

Plank, fragmentary wall painting

On the front, a well preserved painting from a scene with many figures. Beneath the paint are traces of carved or engraved interlace, mostly obliterated before the surface was painted. At the top, a large figure turns towards the left. Beneath a curved border many smaller figures gaze upwards and raise their hands.

The plank is probably part of an Ascension, painted on the east wall of the nave of the mid 12th-cent. stave church (cf. cat. no. 440) which preceded the 13th-cent. stone church, some 70 planks of which were reused as flooring in the stone church and survive. The figural style is Russian-Byzantine, with heavy outlines, large almond-shaped eyes, and long, thin expressive hands. The colours are black, dark grey, red and green with traces of yellowish-white. Parallels occur in the paintings from St Sophia's cathedral in Novgorod, probably *c.* 1100. The paintings at Eke are probably mid-12th cent. and show lively contacts between Gotland and Russia in the early Middle Ages. There are similar paintings on wood in the churches of Dalhem and Sundre, and frescoes in Garde and Källunge, all also 12th cent.　**GT**

Bibl.: Andersson 1968, 280f.; Lagerlöf and Stolt 1974; Lagerlöf 1984

456

Fresco on plaster, removed and mounted on wooden board.
H. 160cm.
Jørlunde Church, Sjælland, Denmark.
c. 1150–75. Danish.
Danmarks Nationalmuseum, Copenhagen, no number

Mural

Fragment of an angel and another standing figure. In front of them are various golden objects: a chalice, globe and two neck-rings. The fresco is from the west wall of the choir, south of the chancel arch. It was found in 1964.

The motif is the third of Christ's Temptations in the desert where the Devil (now lost) offers worldly riches. Here the angel comforts Christ. The painting is the product of a Byzantine-inspired school which worked

456

especially on Sjælland in churches associated with the Danish aristocratic family Hviderne.

PGH

Bibl.: Nørlund and Lind 1944, 64–112, no. 4; *Danmarks Kirker* II, *Frederiksborg amt*, 1975, 2251–58; Haastrup 1975; Haastrup 1981; *Danske Kalkmalerier 1080–1175* (1986), 56, no. 34

457

Birch. H. 89cm.
Tyldal church, Østerdalen, Norway.
1150–1200. Norwegian.
Universitetets Oldsaksamling, Oslo, C.9906

Chair

Post construction: the horizontal planks are tenoned into 4 upright posts. All elements are decorated: knots and strapwork in sharp 2-plane relief, fields with tendrils and fighting animals in flat relief. Lions, snakes, dragons, masks, a centaur, and a man struggling with 2 lions and a snake; tendrils and palmettes, ring-chains, knots and ropes cover front and back.

The fund of motifs is taken from the artistic milieu of the 12th-cent. building phase of Trondheim cathedral (cf. cat. no. 444–7, 612) and is perhaps a professional product. The carving is shallow and finely

457

detailed, related to ivory carving rather than stone sculpture. The details are rather mannered, the leaf shapes are some way from the original inspiration and 1150–1200 seems a likely date.　**EBH**

Bibl.: Fischer 1962; Blindheim 1965

458

458 Wood (pine) with decorative ironwork.
L. 146cm.
Voxtorp church, Småland, Sweden.
c. 1200. Swedish.
Statens Historiska Museum, Stockholm, 4094

Chest

In the Middle Ages church doors often had decorative ironwork, made by village smiths or in more specialized workshops. The chest from Voxtorp belongs to a group of chests and doors with elaborate ironwork of high quality which may all have been made in the same workshop; they are preserved in east Småland and Östergötland (chests from Rydaholm, Ryssby and Voxtorp; doors from Roglösa and Voxtorp). The chest is made up of sides, ends, lid and bottom each consisting of a single plank. The pieces have been nailed together and the construction stabilized by strong iron bands decorated with herring-bone pattern. Most of the front is covered with a hunting scene: to the left a bearded man dressed in a mitre-like head-dress grasps the tail of a deer. A snake is by the deer's forelegs and between its legs are a dog and a hawk killing a smaller quadruped. Another man stands on the right, a small winged dragon at his feet. There are various interpretations of these scenes, all relating to medieval legends with hunting motifs: Giles, Eustace, Hubert or Didrik of Bern (Theodoric the Great)—who is represented here is not known. Other products of the workshop have similar motifs.   GT

Bibl.: Andersson 1968, 371; Karlsson 1988

459

460

459 Wood. H. 130cm; 123cm.
Hemsedal church, Hallingdal, Norway.
c. 1200. Norwegian.
Universitetets Oldsaksamling, Oslo, C.11394 a, b

Two bench-ends

Two hewn ends from a bench with rebate for the seat and traces of back. Crowned by dragon's heads, the carving is most detailed on the outer faces. The figures are carved in simple broad lines. The animals have strongly rounded skulls, wrinkled snouts, big teeth and drop-shaped eyes. The front edges of the bench-ends are profiled.

Several examples of this type of bench—a simple seat between two ends often dragon-headed—have been preserved. Similar heads are found on stave-churches and other wooden sculpture.   EBH

Bibl.: *Norges Kirker. Buskerud* I, 1981, 72

460 Gilded copper sheets on oak.
H. 56.7cm.
Åby, Jutland, Denmark.
c. 1100. Danish.
Danmarks Nationalmuseum, Copenhagen,
D629

The Åby crucifix

(Illustrated also back-cover)

The figure is carved in oak and covered with riveted, embossed and gilded copper sheets. *Émail brun* emphasizes the details. Christ, as King Triumphant, stands upright with open eyes, a crown on His head and a collar around His neck. Only the hands have nail holes. The crown is attached by a dowel, it is probably secondary. The figure may derive from the same workshop as the slightly later Lisbjerg altar (cat. no. 467). It came from the church to the museum in 1870.   PGH

Bibl.: Nørlund 1968 (1926), 61–68; *Danmarks Kirker* XVI, Århus amt, 1976, 1443–4; Langberg 1979; Blindheim 1980

461 Wood (aspen, beech).
H. 67cm.
Viklau church, Gotland, Sweden.
Mid-12th cent. Swedish or Rhenish.
Statens Historiska Museum, Stockholm, 18951

Madonna   *(Illustrated p. 209)*

The Madonna—a young girl—sits frontally on a throne with lathe-turned legs; she wears a wooden crown and plaits fall over her shoulders. Her face is long, with large eyes and a naive expression. She is clad in a golden gown with long, capacious sleeves; the crown, the V-shaped neck-ornament and the sleeves have painted representations of jewels. The Christ child must have sat on her left knee, held by her long, slender hands.

This Madonna, with its well-preserved colour, is one of the finest surviving medieval sculptures in Sweden. The same workshop also produced a group of high-quality Gotland crucifixes and a figure of St Michael from Häverö in Medelpad. Aron Andersson has proved a connection with the French-inspired art of Cologne in the middle of the 12th cent. The workshop may have been on Gotland, or the figures may have been imported from Cologne or another north-German workshop under its influence.   GT

Bibl.: Andersson 1962; Andersson 1967; Andersson 1968; *Medieval Wooden Sculpture in Sweden* IV, 1975; Tångeberg 1986

462
Wood (lime). H. 71.5cm.
Mosjö church, Närke, Sweden.
Mid-12th cent. Swedish.
Statens Historiska Museum, Stockholm, 7306

Madonna   *(Illustrated p. 22)*

The Mosjö Madonna is unique in Scandinavia. It is one of the earliest sculptures to have been preserved in Sweden. She has a thin body with a bent head crowned by a plaited crown. The large, slightly slanting, almond-shaped eyes and thin, down-turned lips give her a tragic appearance. The drapery is highly symmetrical with narrow folds; the arms are thin and low slung. The Christ child is missing.

The folds of the drapery and the arms (fashions of the mid-12th cent.), are west-European elements, whereas the interlace and tragic appearance have a different source. The Mosjö Madonna has been seen as an example of a continuing pagan tradition, but has also been related to the English Hereford School, c. 1150.   GT

Bibl.: Andersson 1967; Andersson 1968, 318ff.; *Medieval Wooden Sculpture in Sweden* IV 1975; Tångeberg 1986

463
Wood (willow).
H. 144.5cm.
Tryde church, Skåne, Sweden.
c. 1160.
Statens Historiska Museum, Stockholm, 8282

Crucifix   *(Illustrated p. 208)*

The life-size figure of Christ is depicted as living, hanging fully frontal on the cross, with head bent forward and eyes to the front. The solid body is carved in the round, finely

modelled and with a realism unusual for the time. The loin-cloth is symmetrically draped with a wedge-shaped fold at the front and pendant folds at the sides. The colours under many layers of later over-painting were revealed in 1937. Christ wears a crown of gilt brass with an engraved tendril and the symbols of the evangelists in medallions. The points of the crown are missing, they were probably palmettes. The crucifix, probably installed in the church at the time of its dedication in 1160, has no clear Scandinavian parallels, the closest being a small crucifix from an unknown, but probably Danish, church now in a private collection. There are similarities with the bronze Ottonian crucifix in the cathedral of Minden, Westphalia, and the close connection between the art of Saxony-Westphalia and that of the Lund diocese has been pointed out. Nevertheless, its origin is unknown.   GT

Bibl.: Wåhlin 1921; af Ugglas 1937; Andersson 1966; Andersson 1968; *Medieval Wooden Sculpture in Sweden* IV, 1975; Tångeberg 1986

464
Broad-leaved lime (*Tilia platyphylla Scop.*).
H. 166cm.
Danderyd church, Uppland, Sweden.
Second half of 12th cent. Western German.
Danderyds församling (parish council)

Crucifix   *(Illustrated p. 208)*

Despite its damaged condition, this crucifix is one of the most magnificent Romanesque sculptures in Sweden. The dead Christ has bowed head and half closed eyes. The stylized body, the elongated head and S-shaped curvature of the body are all Byzantine in style, while the symmetrical arrangement of the loin cloth is western in character. The closest parallel is the bronze crucifix in Essen-Werden in Westphalia, where the dead Christ has the same slender proportions, stylized body and symmetrically arranged loin-cloth. It is dated 1060–1080.

The Danderyd crucifix is carved in a species of lime which occurs on the Continent, but in Sweden only in Bohuslän. The type of wood, the high artistic quality of the sculpture and its distinct character suggests that it was probably imported from Westphalia, perhaps intended for another, larger, church.   GT

Bibl.: Andersson 1958; Andersson 1967; Andersson 1968; *Medieval Wooden Sculpture in Sweden* IV, 1975

465
Birch, paint.
H. 24cm.
Urnes church, Sogn og Fjordane, Norway.
Late 12th cent. ?Scandinavian.
Historisk Museum, Bergen, MA77

Saint's head   *(Illustrated p. 209)*

Head with tonsure, remains of oil paint on a thin chalk base; cut off at the neck where a peg of pine is inserted. The neck is narrow and square. In 19th cent. the head formed the finial of a font cover. It is presumably the head of a saint (St Lawrence?) It is often dated c. 1200 but its art-historical context is difficult. There are similarities with the Madonna from the same church (cat. no. 617).   HVA/EBH

Bibl.: Schjetlein Johannessen 1964, no. 2; Andersson 1970a, 326

466

466
Oak.
H. 55.0cm.
Probably from Roskilde Cathedral, Denmark.
1220–30. Danish.
Danmarks Nationalmuseum, Copenhagen, D13676

Relief of The Women at the Tomb   *(Illustrated also p. 209)*

The women at Christ's tomb. Carefully carved on three sides, the back is hollowed. Despite being cleaned in recent times there are traces of five layers of paint, the two oldest being medieval.

The relief is inspired by early French gothic, probably made in a workshop in Roskilde. It is one of many examples of close contact with France at that time (cat. no. 471, 528, 538). Analyses of the early paint shows similarities with that on the head of the chancel-arch crucifix in Roskilde cathedral. The relief was probably part of the cathedral's great Rood.   PGH

Bibl.: *L'Europe Gothique XIIe-XIVe Siècles*, 1968, no. 68; Andersson 1970b, 136 ff.; Nyborg 1991

468

---

467   Gilded copper sheets on oak.
L. 159.5cm.
Lisbjerg church (near Århus), Denmark. To the
National Museum in 1867.
c. 1150; crucifix *c.* 1100–1125. Danish.
Danmarks Nationalmuseum, Copenhagen,
D287

The Lisbjerg altar   *(Ill. pp. 6 and 183)*

Frontal and arched retable of altar. Within the arch an early crucifix has been secondarily inserted. The figure on the crucifix and the altar decoration have a core of oak clad with embossed and chased copper sheets. The sheets are fire-gilt with *émail brun* probably originally worked in different colours to emphasize the decoration. The central figure on the frontal is cast. On the borders were rock crystals laid on vellum or textile, the colour of which provided the appearance of precious stones.

The main motif on the frontal is the Virgin and Child enthroned in the heavenly Jerusalem, surrounded by angels, cherubs and scenes from the life and death of the Virgin. On each side of the central field are six females—6 virtues (defined by inscription), two saints (Brigid and Tekla) and four unidentified women. Medallions in the borders contain the symbols of the four Evangelists, an *Agnus Dei*, and two fighting lions.

On the retable Christ is enthroned between sun and moon, flanked by the Apostles. In medallions at the feet of the arch Abraham sacrifices Isaac, Abraham is represented with the souls in his bosom (alluding to Christ's sacrificial death and salvation in paradise). At the top of the arch Christ as Judge between Mary and John the Baptist, the physician saints Cosmas and Damian, and angels.

The ornament mainly consists of fighting men and animals in plant tendrils. The lowest border of the frontal has animal ornament related to Scandinavian art of the 11th and 12th cent. Learned Latin inscriptions on

the edges of the frontal and the retable arch elaborate the theological message of the altar —on the frontal with allusions to the Day of Judgment, on the retable with allusions to the death of Christ and the salvation which humanity might achieve because of it.

Nine virtually complete golden frontals are known from Denmark, three with retables. There are also many fragments and written sources which indicate that this type of altar was fairly widespread in Denmark in the early Middle Ages. They are probably of local workmanship but foreign inspiration; the inspiration for Lisbjerg probably came from England.   **PGH**

Bibl.: Nørlund 1968 (1926), 73–98; Lasko 1972; *Danmarks Kirker* XVI, Århus amt, 1976, 1400–1412; Langberg 1979; Fuglesang 1981b; la Fuente Pedersen 1988

---

468   Gilded copper.
Max. h. 20.6cm.
Tamdrup church, Jutland, Denmark.
c. 1200. Danish.
Danmarks Nationalmuseum, Copenhagen,
D801

The seven 'historiated' Tamdrup panels   *(Illustrated also p. 212)*

In 1870 the Renaissance pulpit in Tamdrup church was found to have nailed to it 29 trimmed plates, which had been painted over. The plates are made in the technique known from the golden altars (cf. cat. no. 467). 22 plates have biblical motifs, a Majesty and symbols of the Evangelists, which are iconographically comparable with other golden frontals. Seven plates stand out as being illustrations of the account of a cleric, Poppo, who carried a red-hot iron, an action which converted the Danish king to Christianity.

Previously all 29 plates were placed tentatively in a reconstruction of an altar frontal with four rows of depictions of the Majesty. Christiansen has suggested that the seven historiated panels were on a reliquary of Poppo. Some changes were made to the

plates during manufacture. In the scene with the baptism of the king in a large barrel an archbishop with pallium is represented, but this plate has been covered by another where he is shown as bishop.   **PGH**

Bibl.: Nørlund 1968 (1926), 155–76; Christiansen 1968; Langberg 1979, 25–9

---

469   Gilt copper on wood.
L. 40.3cm.
Eriksberg church, Västergötland, Sweden.
Second half of 12th cent. Danish or Swedish.
Statens Historiska Museum, Stockholm, 5561

Reliquary   *(Illustrated p. 212)*

The shrine is rectangular, in the shape of a church; it stands on four three-toed paws. The ridge is crowned by an upright crest terminating in animal heads. The shrine is covered with gilt chased and engraved copper plates. The sides are decorated with figures in round-arched arcades; each long side with six figures, one short side with a bishop with crozier and book, the other with an angel with a halo holding a ?cross in one hand. The main fields are surrounded by broad borders with engraved decoration. The roof is engraved with acanthus fronds and round and square rosettes. The points on the ridge must have terminated in small leaves and there would have been a cross at the centre. Latin inscriptions are engraved along the edges of the roof. Above, '[relics] of St Savina and relics of the [11,000] holy virgins; of the Apostle Andrew and of the Holy Cross; Clement *leder* (?donor ?goldsmith)'. Below, 'of the cloth which was around Christ's head in the grave; of the head [possible lacuna] of St Pancratius; of the blood of St Vincent; of the saintly bishops [continued on short side] Melano and Bobino'.

An almost identical shrine is known from the neighbouring church of Jäla, Västergötland.   **GT**

Bibl.: Nørlund 1968 (1926); Andersson 1968, 340

470 Copper with enamel and remains of gilding.
Shrine: l. 19.5cm. Crucifix: h. 17.0cm.
Frøslev Mose, Jutland, Denmark.
c. 1100–1150. North German or Scandinavian.
Danmarks Nationalmuseum, Copenhagen, D751

The Frøslev shrine

The shrine's original wooden core has dis-appeared and it now consists of five (roof and four side) copper plates with blue, green and white champlevé enamel. At the back an enamelled roundel supports a bronze crucifix. The roof shows the Enthroned Christ in a mandorla surrounded by symbols of the Evangelists. The front plate depicts the Crucifixion; the other plates, saints with haloes; the roundel below the crucifix, an *Agnus Dei*.

The shrine belongs to a group of about 10 shrines in churches and museums in Europe and USA with highly-coloured enamels and knobs around the edges of the plates. The Frøslev shrine differs from these in that its crucifix is preserved. The age and origin of the shrines are not certain. They may also have been used as portable altars. Their rep-resentations of anonymous saints would have made them appropriate for many places. **FL**

Bibl.: Nørlund 1933; Gauthier 1952, 156–7; Svensson 1981; Christiansen 1983; Liebgott 1986, 17–20

471 Enamel and gilded copper on wood.
L. 29.5cm.
1180–1185. French.
Danmarks Nationalmuseum, Copenhagen, 9110

Limoges shrine

The house-shaped shrine is of oak covered with five copper plates with champlevé enamel on a gold vermiculé ground (one plate missing). The enamel is blue, green, purple, yellow and white. One of the gables has an opening for access to the relic; the door is missing. The other gable shows a saint, probably St Paul. On the front is the Adoration of the Magi, with heads cast in high relief. On the back are enamelled quatrefoils on a gold ground.

The shrine was probably brought to Den-mark during the Valdemar period when there were close cultural contacts between Denmark and France. In particular, arch-bishops Absalon and Anders Sunesøn were

471

associated with the University of Paris. The shrine has similarities with one in Uppsala cathedral. **FL**

Bibl.: Marquet de Vasselot 1906, 29; Gauthier 1966, C11, 942–6, 950; Gaborit 1972, 205–11; Liebgott 1986, 36–9; Gauthier 1987, no. 207

472 Silver gilt.
H. 21cm.
Bru, Rennesøy, Rogaland, Norway.
12th cent. (cross); ?9th cent. (Christ).
Universitetets Oldsaksamling, Oslo, C.1968

Altar crucifix

The cross is cast, engraved and touched-up with a chisel: roundels at end of arms and part of foot missing. Front and back have simple tendrils with Byzantine palmettes. A mask with moustache and ears in the centre of the back. The lower roundel depicts a saint with sword, the missing side roundels were probably different. Christ is cast with a flat back and riveted to the cross. Cross and foot are joined to a socket, probably later. The foot is cast in one piece, skewed, and with many small breaks mended with lead, it consists of three twisted dragons in open-work. The whole stands on 3 lion's feet.

Christ's loin cloth and heavy torso are of Carolingian type. The foot with swooping dragons is inspired by Continental candle-sticks and crosses, and the faces of the cross have tendrils with Byzantine palmettes. The work must be modelled on a Byzantine cross, perhaps made in the North. The Christ is probably earlier. **EBH**

Bibl.: Blindheim 1956–57

470

472

474

475

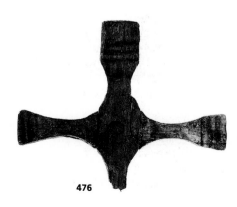

476

473

Copper.
H. 16.3cm.
Veinge church, Halland, Sweden.
c. 1100. South Scandinavian.
Statens Historiska Museum, Stockholm, 26669

Altar cross *(Illustrated p. 151)*

An almost equal-armed cross with the upper arm and lateral arms with fleur-de-lis terminals and engraved interlace. On the front Christ wears a knee-length, long-sleeved tunic with V-neck. The hand of God is seen above. The back is ornamented with engraved palmettes. Christ is not shown nailed to the cross, rather his wrists are shown as being coupled by bracelets. This depiction of Christ is reminiscent of those on the Gåtebo reliquary cross (cat. no. 492) and the Jelling stone (cat. no. 193). The base of the cross is broken, it was probably attached to a foot or a staff.   **GT**

Bibl.: Holmqvist 1963; Andersson 1968, 334; Fuglesang 1981c

474

Gilt bronze.
H. 48cm.
Flädie, Skåne, Sweden.
Early 12th cent. South Scandinavian (Skåne).
Lunds universitets historiska museum, 3157

Processional cross

Processional cross, engraved on both faces. The arms of the cross end in medallions and the stem terminates in a tang beneath the roundel. Openwork decoration in the angles between the arms.

The cross belongs to a group of processional crosses from Skåne of uniform type, all probably of local workmanship. This example differs from the others in its iconography. The front shows Christ on the cross beneath the hand of God, the roundels contain scenes from the life of Christ which relate to the Eucharist. The saint on the reverse has been interpreted as Constantine the Great, the roundels depict a legend where Constantine, afflicted by leprosy, saw a vision of Peter and Paul who told him to visit Pope Silvester. He was baptized and cured of his illness.   **HC**

Bibl.: Nordenfalk 1944

475

Copper with remains of gilding.
H. 55.2cm.
Lundø Church, north Jutland, Denmark.
c. 1100. Scandinavian.
Danmarks Nationalmuseum, Copenhagen, D894

The Lundø cross

The figure of Christ is cast and chased; symbols of the Evangelists in relief are riveted to the ends of the cross (John's eagle and Mark's lion survive). Above the figure is engraved the ascension of Christ's soul, and below is an inscription: AILMAR F[EC]IT PA[R]ARE CRVCEM DNIMI (Ailmar had this cross of the Lord made). On the back is an engraving of the archangel Michael's struggle with the dragon. The crucifix is secondarily mounted on a socketed copper knob, showing that it was carried in processions.

Ailmar is the Anglo-Saxon name Æthelmær, and the engraving is influenced by the Winchester school, whereas the Christ figure seems to be influenced from the Continent. As there is a correspondence between the rendering of the sculpture and the engraving, a Danish origin is probable.   **FL**

Bibl.: Schultz 1957; Nørlund 1968 (1926), 43; Oman 1954; Blindheim 1980; *English Romanesque Art*, 1984, no. 229

476

Wood.
H. 7.7cm.
Trondheim, Norway.
Mid-12th cent. Norwegian.
Vitenskapsmuseet, Trondheim, N77591FG563

Cross

The cross is made up of 2 pieces of wood dowelled together. Part of one arm missing. Each arm is splayed and terminates in 2 simple mouldings. Found on the Public Library Site.

The function of this simple cross is unknown. It may have been an altar cross but there are no indications that it carried a crucifix and it was found in a secular context. Other finds from the same site suggest that the people who lived there were associated with the church.   **AC/EJ**

Unpublished

477
Pewter/silver alloy.
H. 6.3cm.
Skara cathedral, Sweden.
c. 1064. Swedish or N German.
Cathedral chapter, Skara

Funerary chalice *(Illustrated p. 188)*

This small funerary chalice has an egg-shaped bowl, a knop on the stem, and conical foot. An inscription in majuscule round the rim, between two raised borders reads: ADALVVARDVS PECCATOR, 'Adalvard, sinner'. This must refer to Adalvard the Elder, under whose episcopate (1060–64) Skara cathedral was founded. The bishop-list in the early Västergötland law calls him *haelghi* (holy). The chalice first appears in an inventory of 1721. It was probably discovered when a teacher or priest was buried in the choir in the 17th cent.　　　**GT**

Bibl.: *Kulturhistoriskt Lexikon för nordisk medeltid* VIII, 1963: *s.v.* Kalk och patén; Andersson 1968

478

478
Silver. H. 9.0cm.
Svalbard Church, Iceland.
c. 1200. Anglo-Scandinavian.
Danmarks Nationalmuseum, Copenhagen, 9147

Chalice

The chalice has a deep, polished, rounded bowl, a stem with knop and smooth foot. An inscription in majuscule surrounds the rim of the bowl: +SVMMITVR : HINC : MVNDA : DIVINI : SANGVINIS VNDA (From this is taken a wave of the holy blood). Above the knop is DEVS:MEVS (My God).

This small Romanesque chalice belongs to a group of chalices (including one from Grund Church, Iceland) the style of which has roots in Mosan goldsmith's art which probably appeared on both sides of the English Channel before travelling further north. **FL**

Bibl.: Kielland 1927, 88; Blindheim (ed.) 1972, 49–51

479
Bronze. H. 20.0cm.
Fakse Church, Sjælland, Denmark.
c. 1200. North German.
Danmarks Nationalmuseum, Copenhagen, MMXXXVIII

Censer

The lid is decorated with a frieze of pierced triangles, palmettes in circles, and at the top a centralized church with tower, the symbol of the heavenly Jerusalem. Along the edges a majuscule inscription: ASCENDIT FUMOS AROMATUM IN CONSPECTU DNI DE MANU ANGELI ('The smoke from the censer rises from the hand of the angel to the sight of God' (Revelations 8, 4)).　　**PGH**

Bibl.: *Danmarks Kirker* VI, *Præstø amt*, 1933–35, 522

480
Bronze. H. 25.5cm.
Unknown provenance.
c. 1200. Lorraine.
Danmarks Nationalmuseum, Copenhagen, D334/1970

Aquamanile

Aquamanile in the shape of a mounted horse. The rider, who is clad in chain mail with hood, has a sword at his side and reins in his left hand. The shield and lance are missing. On the top of the hood there is a hole through which the vessel could be filled. The horse's head forms a spout. The subject of the aquamanile suggests that is was intended for use at a lord's table. However, most aquamaniles known from Denmark come from churches where they were used for liturgical handwashing.　　**PGH**

Bibl.: Falke and Meyer 1935, 43 f., no. 287, fig. 254

481
Elephant ivory.
H. 23.2cm.
Unknown provenance.
11th. cent. Byzantine with Danish runes.
Danmarks Nationalmuseum, Copenhagen, D12123

Relief with crucifixion

Byzantine relief with crucifix under a vaulted and pierced baldachino carried on pierced columns. Angels above the arms of the cross and the columns. On the foot board *Jesus* is written in runes dated after *c.* 1000. On the reverse is an incised figure of Mary dated *c.* 1100 and probably made in Denmark. Rivet holes in the upper and lower borders indicate that it was attached to a backing, probably a book cover.　　**FL**

Bibl.: Goldschmidt and Weitzmann 1934, II, no. 28; Nørlund 1934a; Jacobsen and Moltke 1942; Liebgott 1985, 30 f.

479

480

481

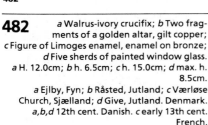

482

482   *a* Walrus-ivory crucifix; *b* Two fragments of a golden altar, gilt copper; *c* Figure of Limoges enamel, enamel on bronze; *d* Five sherds of painted window glass. *a* H. 12.0cm; *b* h. 6.5cm; *c* h. 15.0cm; *d* max. h. 8.5cm.
a Ejlby, Fyn; *b* Råsted, Jutland; *c* Værløse Church, Sjælland; *d* Give, Jutland. Denmark. *a,b,d* 12th cent. Danish. *c* early 13th cent. French.
Danmarks Nationalmuseum, Copenhagen, D3545; D12973; D8384; D5820

Finds from churches and churchyards

The simple crucifix figure (*a*) was found together with a weathered figure of Mary in the floor of the choir; it may originally have embellished a shrine or book. The fragments of the golden altar (*b*), found in the same place, are made in the same technique as, e.g., the Lisbjerg altar (cat. no. 467). The figure in Limoges enamel (*c*) was found in the churchyard. It shows St John and probably comes from a crucifixion group on a reliquary. The sherds of painted glass (*d*) were found in the floor of the choir and probably come from the east window. One of them carries an unintelligible runic inscription: *VURTHIK*.

Archaeological finds from churches are usually fragmentary but provide an important supplement to the preserved ecclesiastical objects from the early Middle Ages. They show, for instance, that glass painting was much more common than the few preserved windows would suggest. Similarly, fragments of golden altars show that this type of altar was not confined to great town churches.

The material was obtained in the course of the Museum's systematic supervision of building work in Danish churches.   **PGH**

Bibl.: Jacobsen and Moltke 1942, no. 45; Christiansen, in Nørlund 1968, 24–5; *Corpus Vitraearum Medii Aevi*, 1964, 299 f., pl. 7:c–d; Moltke 1985, 426; Liebgott 1985, 22; Liebgott 1986, 50 f.; Liebgott 1989, 117–214

483   Silk, gold, silver, linen. *a* Part of stole. L. 106cm. *b* Part of maniple. L. without tassels 88.2cm. *c* Amice apparel. L. 50.3cm. Hólar cathedral, Iceland. Early 13th cent. ?English.
Islands Nationalmuseum, Reykjavík, 6028a, c, e

Gold-embroidered vestments from Hólar   *(Illustrated p. 56)*

Apparel of an amice and parts of stole and maniple from a matched set of vestments. Two other incomplete fragments of stole and maniple are not exhibited. The embroidery is carried out in gold and silver thread and silk (dark brown, green, white and red) on a silk fabric (samite) which on the stole and maniple is reddish brown, purplish red on the amice. The underlying cloth is linen tabby. The gold and silver embroidery is worked in underside couching; the silk in split stitch.

The trapezoidal end panels of the stole enclose St Peter and St Paul, each with his name (the latter exhibited). The band is decorated with four types of pointed ovals with plant ornament. The band of the maniple is decorated with similar pointed ovals and plants but also with roundels. The end panels enclose two of Iceland's three bishop saints, identified by inscriptions: St Thorlákur (bishop of Skálholt 1178–93) and St Jón (bishop of Hólar 1106–1121). (The latter exhibited). On the amice apparel is Christ

surrounded by the symbols of the Evangelists and flanked by four apostles in elaborately detailed arcades. Three apostles are identifiable: Peter, Paul and Andrew.

The decoration, materials and technique suggest that the embroideries are English *opus anglicanum* of the early 13th cent. The two Icelandic bishops were canonized in 1199 and 1200, and, as they were acknowledged only locally, the embroideries must have been made as a special order for Iceland. Bishop Gudmundur Arason of Hólar (1203–1237) was probably the first to use the vestments.   **EEG**

Bibl.: Thórdarson 1911; Thórdarson 1931; Eldjárn 1973, section 48; Guðjónsson 1977; Guðjónsson 1988; Guðjónsson 1989

484   Wool, linen. L. 205cm. Høylandet church, Nord-Trøndelag, Norway. 13th cent. Norwegian. Vitenskapsmuseet, Trondheim, T389

Tapestry

Fragment of 'tapestry' in red extended tabby. Embroidered in blue, yellow and green wool and white linen thread. Outlines in stem stitch in white linen thread.

Depictions of the visit of the Magi: in the centre the adoration of Mary and the Christ Child, fragments of the journey to Bethlehem, and angels with two sleeping kings. The tapestry is thought to be of Norwegian workmanship, probably made in a convent in Trondheim. The figures are related to the English St Alban's school.   **MH**

Bibl.: Wallem 1911; *Kulturhistorisk leksikon for nordisk middelalder* II, 1957, s.v. Broderi; Franzén 1960; Andersson 1970a, 392, pl. 244, colour pl. 12; Geijer 1979

485   Sandstone. L. 8.5cm. Timans, Roma, Gotland, Sweden. Late 11th cent. Gotland. Gotlands Fornsal, Visby, C 9181

Whetstone with runic inscription   *(Illustrated p. 110)*

Two flat polished faces; the broader engraved with a mould for a simple circular ornament, the other with three rows of runes. The narrow sides show traces of wear by sharpening. The runic text: *ormiga:ulfua-r: krikiaR:iaursaliR:islat:serklat* (Ormiga, ?Ulvat, Greekland, Jerusalem, Iceland, Särkland). Ormiga and Ulvat are both men's names. Greekland —or 'the Greeks'—means the Byzantine empire. Särkland (land of the Saracens) is the Islamic world, probably the Caliphate.

484

This inscription may be interpreted in many ways. Some have suggested that Ormiga and Ulvat were two merchants who visited the four places mentioned. Others believe that the inscription is a list of two famous Gotlanders and four legendary destinations. Pilgrimages are mentioned in several 11th-cent. runic inscriptions. **GW**

Bibl.: *Sveriges runinskrifter* XII, 1978, 233ff.; Snædal Brink and Jansson 1983, 435ff.

486

486
Glazed pottery.
H. 4.4cm.
Sigtuna, Kv Ödåker, Uppland, Sweden.
11th cent. Kiev-Russian.
Statens Historiska Museum, Stockholm, 18562

Resurrection egg

The egg has a feather-like pattern in brown and yellow glaze. It is pierced by a small hole in the round end: in the hollow interior is a small, loose ball. The egg, as a symbol of the Resurrection, played an important part in eastern Christianity. At the beginning of the 11th cent. glazed eggs began to be made in the Kiev region and were distributed throughout the Russian state, eastern Germany, Poland, the Baltic and east Scandinavia (Gotland, Lund and, particularly, Sigtuna). The eggs are thought to be connected with Christianity, their wide distribution being the result of the eastern mission. **IJ**

Bibl.: Arbman 1945, 73ff., fig.1; Graham-Campbell 1980, no.343

487
Scallop shell.
W. 10.5cm.
Roskilde Cathedral cemetery, Denmark.
c. 1200. Spanish.
Danmarks Nationalmuseum, Copenhagen,
D3566

Pilgrim badge

The shell is perforated and of the type sold as pilgrim badges at the shrine of St James at Santiago de Compostella, Spain. Found in a brick-lined grave in Roskilde cathedral. Most of the some 200 European finds of medieval pilgrims' shells have been found in graves. **PGH**

Bibl.: Köster 1983, 119–55, no. M 14a

488
Silver.
Cross: h. 9.1cm. Chain: l. 78.5cm.
Gundslevmagle, Falster, Denmark.
1050–1100. Provincial Byzantine.
Danmarks Nationalmuseum, Copenhagen,
11465, 11690

The Gundslevmagle cross
(Illustrated p. 110)

Cast front of reliquary cross. Christ in relief with the gospels in His left hand, gives a blessing with His right. By His sides are the torsos of saints. A roundel at the end of each arm of the cross. Above, a bead-shaped loop with ring for the chain. The back is missing. Found with parts of an Urnes-style brooch, a crystal mounted in silver, beads, and a silver finger-ring.

The cross is probably provincial Byzantine work, possibly from Georgia, where similar representations of the standing Christ are known. It may have come to Denmark with a pilgrim or as an item of trade. **FL**

Bibl.: Skovmand 1942, 151, 153; *Danmarks middelalderlige Skattefund*, 1991

487

489
Silver gilt, amethyst, wood.
H. 7cm.
Tønsberg (Storgaten) Vestfold, Norway.
Prob. 11th cent. Byzantine or German.
Universitetets Oldsaksamling, Oslo, C. 23299

Reliquary cross   *(Illustrated p. 111)*

Walls and base of thin sheet silver, with remains of gilding. The front face is covered with filigree: twisted wires and simple figures-of-eight. Coarse mounts hold amethysts or rock crystal on the arms of the cross; 2 missing. Rosette with filigree beads in centre. Wood shows through the gaps between the filigree bands. A coarsely made and probably later loop and ring were fixed to the top.

A reliquary for a splinter of the True Cross. The open construction with the relic clearly visible is originally a Byzantine form, but similar reliquary crosses were also made in Germany, cf. a triptych from Ste Croix, Liège. In the middle ages Tønsberg was one of the most important royal centres. **EBH**

Bibl.: Westermann-Angerhausen 1974

492

492

Silver.
Gåtebo, Bredsätra, Öland, Sweden.
c. 1100. Swedish.
Statens Historiska Museum, Stockholm,
100,120,123 A–B,124,125

Hoard

The hoard, discovered in 1763, consists of a reliquary cross on a chain, four disc brooches of silver filigree and one with rock crystal. The chain has two animal-head terminals and the cross hangs from two cast, curved loops joined together by two large oval beads. The cross (h. 6cm) is cast in two halves, hinged above and below. The cross type is of Byzantine origin, with rounded ends and knobbed projections. The front depicts Christ, engraved and nielloed, His arms entwined with branches springing from the border of the cross. There is a similar interlace above His head. Five figural medallions embellish the back of the cross (cf. cat. no. 532). The cross is a late 11th-cent. Swedish copy of a Byzantine or Russo-Byzantine original.

Three of the filigree brooches (diam. 9cm) have similar designs with highly stylized animals. The fourth (diam. 7.7cm) has a circular central motif and encircling field defined by 'spokes', each area being filled by backward-looking dragons in chased work. The brooch with the rock crystal (h. 5.5cm) is oval, its brim decorated with 'beehives' of striated wire and standing arches of granulation. The brooches date from the 12th cent.

GT

Bibl.: Holmqvist 1963; Andersson 1967; Andersson 1968, 23; Graham-Campbell 1980, no. 533; Fuglesang 1981c

490

490

Silver with niello.
H. 6.4cm.
Ytings, Othems, Gotland, Sweden.
11th–12th cent. Byzantine or Russian.
Statens Historiska Museum, Stockholm, 3574

Reliquary cross

The cross is made in two halves, hinged at its upper and lower ends, the lower fastened by a rivet, the upper end may have been similarly fastened or held together by a suspension loop. On the front is engraved Christ in tunic and cloak, standing and blessing with his right hand. A cross is above His head, and He is flanked by crosses in the form of four-leaf clovers. On the back Mary stands on a podium in prayer, flanked by palmettes. Some of the fields are filled with niello.

GT

Unpublished

491

491

Gold.
H. 4.2cm.
Stora Bjärge, Vallstena, Gotland, Sweden.
11th–13th cent. Byzantine.
Statens Historiska Museum, Stockholm, 2860

Pendant cross

The cross is cast, with a crucifix of Byzantine type on the front; the stem and arms curve out towards the rounded ends which have knob-shaped projections. On the back a Greek inscription is engraved in the shape of the cross, 'Lord, help the one who wears this'. A silver Byzantine cross without the crucifix but with the same inscription is in the British Museum.

GT

Bibl.: af Ugglas 1933

493

Gold.
Cross: h. 8.3cm. Chain: l. 76.5cm.
Orø, Roskilde Fjord, Denmark.
c. 1100. Scandinavian.
Danmarks Nationalmuseum, Copenhagen,
10861

The Orø cross *(Illustrated p. 191)*

This reliquary cross consists of two parts, joined together at the top by a hinge, at the bottom by loops and a bar. On the edges are double beaded-borders, with filigree palmettes on the hinge and fastening. Riveted on the front and back are engraved plates with the representation of the crucified Christ trampling a dragon, and an inscription: OLAFCVNVnCE (King Olaf); and the Virgin Mary with the Holy Ghost as a dove, and two medallions with saints. At the side of Mary there is S MAI; the other inscriptions are confused. The chain is fastened to the ring of the cross with dragons' heads in Urnes style.

The shape of the cross derives from Byzantium whence it spread to Italy and the rest of Europe. The engraved representations of Christ and the Virgin Mary suggest Scandinavian origin, probably Lund. The Olaf inscription probably refers to the Norwegian royal saint. The chain is Scandinavian. **FL**

Bibl.: Worsaae 1859, no. 510; Skovmand 1942, 179; *Danmarks Middelalder*, 1972, 24; Lindahl 1975, 169–81; Lindahl 1980a; Lindahl 1990

494
Silver.
H. (cross) 10.6cm. L. (chain) 76cm.
Diam. (brooch) 8.2cm.
Kjøpsvik, Tysfjord, Nordland, Norway.
Prob. 12th cent. Eastern.
Tromsø Museum, Ts2714, 2789

Reliquary cross and brooch

Reliquary cross pendant from a ring and plaited chain. All 4 arms expanded. On the front a Crucifixion probably with niello; the hand of God above. On the reverse Mary with an ox's head above. Circular hollow brooch with flat, beaded rim. Niello decoration of palmettes sprouting from an equal-armed cross. A beaded suspension ring is attached to the rim.

Hoard from a stone quarry. A parallel to the brooch comes from the hoard from Skar, Skjerstad, Nordland, decorated with a running lion with raised tail. **GSM**

Bibl.: Kielland 1927, 63; Stamsø Munch 1960

495
Silver.
Ring with crosses l. 10.0cm;
chain l. 73.5cm.
Suotniemi, Käkisalmi (Kexholm), Ladoga-Karelia.
c. 1200. Crosses ?Russian. Chain ?Scandinavian.
Finlands Nationalmuseum, Helsinki, 2487:34

Chain with cross (Illustrated p. 191)

Plaited chain with 3 crosses and 5 spherical beads on a ring. The ends of the arms of the crosses terminate in knobs; nielloed plates are attached to the middle of each cross, that on the central cross is octagonal, the other, circular.

The chain, the ends of which terminate in gilt stylized animal heads, seems to be Scan-

494

dinavian, but the crosses have Byzantine prototypes. The jewellery was discovered in a wooden box in a male grave which also included an axe, a pair of knives, a silver finger-ring and horse equipment. The grave is from no earlier than c. 1200. **PLLH**

Bibl.: Kivikoski 1973, 141; Purhonen 1987, 42–3.

496
Siver, partly gilded and nielloed.
Joensuu in Halikko, Varsinais-Suomi, Finland.
12th cent. German, Scandinavian.
Finlands Nationalmuseum, Helsinki, 2570:1–4

Halikko treasure (Illustrated p. 5)

a Crucifix of silver gilt, l. 10.0cm, on a silver chain with 4 animal-headed terminals. 2 are fastened by a ring at the head of the crucifix, 2 to a circular reliquary the front of which is decorated with a lion in relief. On the crucifix Christ is flanked by the Virgin and St John. The arms of the cross contain angels and human figures which seem to represent the sun and the moon. Other symbols are a cross, a bird and a fish between the terminals; there are also silver beads between the terminals and the chain. An inscription in majuscule on the back. The crucifix seems to be German 11th cent., the chain is Scandinavian 12th cent.

b Chain with animal-headed terminals and a reliquary cross of silver with niello inlay. L. 10.0cm. In the middle of the front of the cross a figure, probably a misunderstood Virgin; the circular fields on the arms contain saints. On the back of the cross is the crucified Christ, beneath a star and a hand, flanked by trees.

c Chain with simple terminals and a reliquary cross of silver and niello. L. 9.7cm. At the head of the cross is a sun, in the arms human male figures with hands in prayer. At the foot is a lion in Scandinavian style. The arms on the back of the cross contain plant ornament and each face has a central ring-cross.

d 36 silver spheres and 1 hemispherical pendant in filigree. Diam. of largest beads 4.0cm.

The hoard was discovered in 1887 in a plain pottery vessel. It has been suggested that it belonged to a bishop and may have been concealed sometime in 12th cent. as loot from a church. **PLLH**

Bibl.: Nordman 1944, 29–62; Holmqvist 1963, 57–8, 157; Purhonen 1987, 34–6, 43–5

497

Granite.
H. 145 (+ about 30cm below ground).
Morby, Lagga, Uppland, Sweden.
11th cent. Scandinavian.
Uppsala universitets museum, U 489

Runestone *(Illustrated p. 164)*

The stone carries the text, 'Gullög made the bridge for her daughter Gillög's soul, who Ulv had as wife. Öpir carved'. The stone is typical of 11th-cent. Uppland rune-stones, but is unusual in that it was raised both by and in memory of a woman (women are mentioned in some 40% of the Uppland stones). The mother's making a bridge for her daughter's soul is a Christian action;

bridge-building was to the glory of God and earned indulgences. The cross also indicates Christianity.

The elegant ornament is a variant of the Urnes style, sometimes called the rune-stone style. Öpir was a prolific rune carver, with about 50 signed carvings and probably the same number of unsigned ones. He was active in second half of the 11th cent. with his products being mainly in S and E Uppland.

ASG

Bibl.: *Sveriges runinskrifter* VII 1943–46, 320–4, pl. 94; Jansson 1987; Gräslund 1989

498

Rib bone.
L. 14.5cm.
Sigtuna (Kv Trädgårdsmästaren 9 and 10),
Uppland, Sweden.
12th cent. Swedish (Sigtuna).
Sigtuna Museums, 5429

Bone with runic *futhark*

Bone with *futhark* (alphabet). The rune row is almost complete with 16 runic characters: *f u þ a r k h n i a s t b m l R*. Damage has obliterated the tops of the *m* and *l* runes; *i* and *n* runes are reversed. The back of the bone has *ba* engraved twice. **MÅ**

Bibl.: Roslund 1990b

499

Animal bone.
L. 10cm.
Gamlebyen, Oslo, Norway.
Second half of 11th cent. Norwegian.
Universitetets Oldsaksamling, Oslo, C.33448/
6097

Bone with runic inscription

Fragment of cattle vertebra, broken at both ends, with runic inscription on one side: *kysmik* (Norse *kyss mik*—kiss me).

Many of the animal bones from Gamlebyen, Oslo, carry runic inscriptions. A runic inscription from Bryggen, Bergen, has almost the same text, *Kjæresten min, kyss meg* (my darling, kiss me). JEK

Bibl.: Liestøl 1977

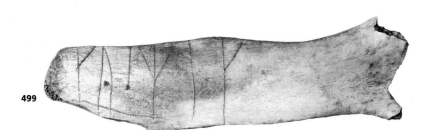

498

499

500

Copper sheet.
Diam. 10.0cm.
Sigtuna, Uppland, Sweden.
11th–12th cent.
Statens Historiska Museum, Stockholm, 14513

Box for scales

Box with domed lid and convex base; a folded hinge for lid on the inside of the base. The box served as a container for scales (cf. cat. no. 150). A runic inscription runs around the edges of lid and base, 'Djärv got these scales from a *semsk* man (a man from Samland or Semgallen) . . . And Värmund carved these runes. May the bird tear at the pale pirate. I noted the corpse cuckoo, how he swelled'.

Samland is the peninsula in the SE corner of the Baltic which was an important trading destination because of its amber deposits. Semgallen is the area south of the bay of Riga and the lower Dvina in Latvia, also an

500

important trading centre. A rune-stone from Södermanland mentions a man who 'often sailed to Semgallen with richly-laden *knarr* (ships) from Domesnäs'.

The end of the inscription is an incantation against thieves. It threatens that the 'corpse cuckoo', a circumlocution for raven, will gorge itself on the thief's corpse in the same way as on the dead in a battlefield. The terrible oath is written in *dróttkvætt*, a verse form well known from scaldic poetry: *Fugl velva slaeit falvan. Fann'k gauk a nas auka.*　IJ

Bibl.: von Friesen 1912; Jansson 1963, 59, 134, fig. 23

501　　　　　　　　　　Wood.
L. 7.1cm.
Trondheim, Norway.
Early 12th cent. Scandinavian.
Vitenskapsmuseet, Trondheim, N91694/FU408

Tally stick/label　*(Illustrated p. 135)*

Stick with runic inscriptions and 4 groups of 6 tally notches. The inscription is secondary to the tally. On one side: *s i k m u n t r a s æ k*; the other side: *th e n a*.

106 runic inscriptions were found during the excavations on the Public Library Site. 23 are unusual in that they are carved on pieces of wood intended to be fastened to parcels of goods. The runic inscriptions on these labels (mostly from 13th cent.) typically give the name of the owner and also the type of goods. Some of the names indicate commercial connections with Iceland.

The object exhibited here is not a typical label as the inscription is carved on a 'tally stick' used for keeping an account of consignments of goods, etc. (cf. cat. no. 318). It is also somewhat older than the typical labels from the same site.　AC/EJ

Bibl.: Hagland 1986; Christophersen 1987, 74f.; Nedkvitne 1989; Seim 1989; Nordeide, in press

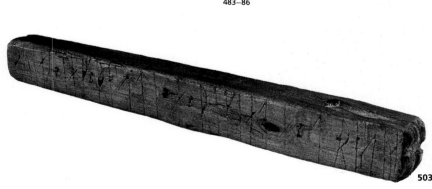

503

502

502　　　　　　　　　　Wood.
L. 10.7cm.
Bryggen, Bergen (Nordre Søstergården),
Norway.
c. 1200. Norwegian.
Historisk Museum, Bergen, BRM29622

Rune stick

Sender's note accompanying a package, written in runes. Dated by fire layers. Inscription reads, 'Thorkjell the moneyer sends you pepper'. This moneyer is otherwise unknown and this is the first time that 'pepper' is mentioned in Norway.　JEK

Bibl.: *Norges Innskrifter med de Yngre Runer* VI, 1980–90, 118–9

503　　　　　　　　　　Wood.
L. 12.8cm.
Schleswig (Old Town), Germany.
End 11th cent. Scandinavian.
Archäologisches Landesmuseum, Schleswig,
SL1.73.13.21

Rune stick

Each of the four smoothed sides is incised with runes. Two sides have the whole area inscribed, one has four-fifths of the area inscribed, the other about one quarter. On the front there is an incised cross and the inscription begins: *runaR iak risti . . .* (I carved the runes . . .).

This is a *rúnakefli*. The inscription is a poem in Old Danish, in the metre *ljóðaháttr*. The meaning is unclear but it seems to be a jocular verse which *c.* 1075 emerged during a drinking party in Schleswig.　VV

Bibl.: Moltke 1975; Moltke 1976, 387–9; Moltke 1985, 483–86

504

504　　　　　　　　Wood, wax, and red paint.
H. 30.0cm.
Trondheim, Norway.
c. 1125–1175. Scandinavian.
Vitenskapsmuseet, Trondheim, N58120/FM230,
N59338/FM230

Diptych writing-tablet with runes

Each tablet has a rim 2mm high and remains of wax, signs of stylus on one tablet. Individual runic letters but no running text preserved. On the backs incomplete ornament of men, animals and foliage and runic texts: *u i s k u r i*. 3 perforations show that the tablets were intended to be held together like a book.

Found in a dwelling on the Public Library Site, with cat. no. 476 and other objects.

A stylus was used to incise runes, symbols, etc. in the soft wax; these could be smoothed out with the flat end of the stylus and the wax reused. The scratches on the wood under the wax show that the runic alphabet had been used. Such writing tablets are rarely found in urban excavations. They indicate the widespread use of writing, particularly runes, among ordinary people in Norwegian medieval towns.　AC/EJ

Bibl.: Hagland 1986; Christophersen 1987, 84f

505

505

506

507

505

Rib bone.
L. 13.3cm.
Sigtuna (Kv Trädgårdsmästaren 9 and 10),
Uppland, Sweden.
12th cent. Scandinavian.
Sigtuna Museums, 2841

Bone with Latin prayer in runes

Found in an occupation deposit in an urban plot. On one side the text runs, '*manas kruks maria matra tomina*'; on the other side, '*kruks markus kruks lukus kruks ma...*'. The prayer, or formula, is an example of the everyday belief of the people in the early-medieval town. The bone may have been carried as an amulet dedicated to the mother of God, the most powerful of all the saints. She and the four Evangelists mentioned would ensure safety in a world of hidden dangers. The prayer must have been devised by someone skilled in both Latin and runes. Most parishioners would have been illiterate, a priest would have been one of the few with this knowledge.   MR

Bibl.: Roslund 1990a; Åhlén 1990

506

Wood. L. 21.7cm.
Bryggen, Bergen (Søndre Engelgården),
Norway.
c. 1220 or early 13th cent. Norwegian.
Historisk Museum, Bergen, BRM18910

Rune stick

Stick with runes on all faces, love poetry in Old Norse and Latin. Dated archaeologically by fire layers.

The inscription begins with a scaldic verse in 'court metre'. The first half reads, 'The troll-woman's ancient burden (i.e. love) for me turned early towards the beautiful, harmful woman'; the end is disputed. A quotation from Virgil, *Omnia vincit amor; et nos cedamus Amori* (Love conquers all; let us yield to love) follows in line 3 after the scaldic verse. The last line, carved by another hand, is an attempt to copy line 3 (cf. cat. no. 507).   JEK

Bibl.: Liestøl, Krause, Helgason 1962; Frank 1978, 179–81

507

Leather.
L. 34cm.
Bryggen, Bergen (Gullskoen), Norway.
End 12th cent. Norwegian.
Historisk Museum, Bergen, BRM 52927

Shoe with runes

Upper embroidered with runes around ankle and down to toe, dated archaeologically by fire-layers. Inscription includes a Latin quotation and reads, *i m u l i l a m o r v i c i t h o m n i a o th*. The first runes are indecipherable. Then follows a variant of the phrase from Virgil, *Amor vincit omnia* (Love conquers all). The 2 last letters may be a distortion of the word *et* (and), and the rest of the sentence *nos cedamus Amori* (let us yield to love) may have been embroidered on the other shoe of the pair (cf. cat. no. 506). **JEK**

Bibl.: *Norges Innskrifter med de Yngre Runer* VI, 1980–90, 228

508
Vellum.
H. 34; w. 22.
Kammararkivet, Landskapshandlingar,
Värmland 1589:12, mantalsregister.
10th–11th cent. English (Winchester).
Riksarkivet, Stockholm Mi, 1

Missal

Fragment of an English missal used as the binding of a Värmland account book in 1589. This fragment is one of 29 surviving leaves; the text includes parts of *Proprium de tempore* and *Proprium de sanctis*. The saints mentioned include bishop Swithun, venerated only in the diocese of Winchester and, later, in Stavanger in Norway. His cult, known in Sweden only in the early Middle Ages, probably arrived by way of Norway. Most of the 29 leaves have been preserved as bindings of account books from Värmland, on the border of Norway (part of the Skara diocese in the Middle Ages). **JBr/CN**

Bibl.: Collijn 1914, 33; Schmid 1944; Schmid 1963

509
Vellum.
H. 21.5 × 15.2cm.
Dalby, Skåne, Sweden.
11th cent. Skåne: ?Dalby.
Kgl. Bibliotek, Copenhagen, Gl. kgl. S. 1325 4°

The Dalby Gospels *(Illustrated p. 217)*

The four gospels in Latin with canon tables (f. 12r–19v) and full-page pictures of the Evangelists (Matthew f.26v; Mark f.84v; Luke 130v; John f.192v). The binding is made of various components of different dates and is covered with fragments of 11th–13th cent. manuscripts.

Additions, including a note dated 1387, indicate that the manuscript belonged to the Augustinian convent in Dalby. The book

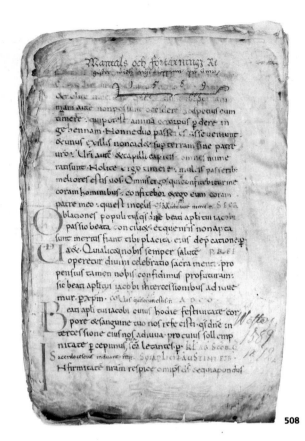

508

may have been written in Skåne, for this is where it was in the late Middle Ages. Influences from England and Bremen respectively, are discernible in the book in the style (pictures of the Evangelists) and cult (pericopes). If so, the book is the earliest extant manuscript from Scandinavia. **EP**

Bibl.: *Greek and Latin Illuminated Manuscripts*, 1921, 10; Jørgensen 1926, 10; *Gyllene Böcker* 1952, 27 no. 17; Petersen 1991

510
Vellum.
31.7 × 21.2cm.
Northern Iceland. c. 1150.
Stofnun Árna Magnússonar, Reykjavík AM 237 a, fol

Icelandic homily *(Illustrated p. 218)*

The first works to be written in the vernular in Iceland were, as was the case among all other Germanic peoples, religious—biblical texts, liturgies, saints' lives, homilies, etc. The earliest of all surviving Icelandic manuscripts is, indeed, this fragment of a homily collection. **JK**

Bibl.: Kålund 1889–94, I, 198; Hægstad 1906; Hermansson 1929; *Kulturhistorisk leksikon for nordisk middelalder*, VI, 1961, *s.v.* Homiliebøker; Benediktsson 1965, p. iii

---

511
Vellum, contemporary binding of
vellum-covered wood.
31 × 21cm.
Skara cathedral, Sweden.
Mid-12th cent. N French or Swedish.
Skara stifts- och landsbibliotek

Skara missal *(Illustrated p. 217)*

Of the few medieval liturgical manuscripts to survive the Reformation, the Skara missal is of particular interest because of its illuminations, rare in Sweden. It is a so-called *missale plenum*, i.e. it contains the eucharistic prayers, psalms with notes, and biblical texts. It originally comprised more than 300 pages in two volumes; 41 pages survive. The preserved illuminations come from the second volume. Two full-page illuminations show Christ in Majesty and the Crucifixion in a primitive figural style with sophisticated colours. There are similarities with Irish and N French book illumination. The latter connection is strengthened by the list of saints in the prayer *Communicantes*. The missal may have been copied in Skara from a mid-12th cent. from a N French model. **GT**

Bibl.: Nordenfalk 1941; *Gyllene böcker*, 1952, no. 21; Johansson 1956

517

512
Vellum.
24.9 × 17cm.
Lund cathedral, Skåne, Sweden.
Early 1140s. Helmarshausen, Germany.
Uppsala Universitetsbibliotek, C 83

Gospel book (Illustrated p. 217)
This magnificent manuscript is one of 3 medieval gospels preserved from Lund. The volume comprises 177 pages, bound in one volume in the 18th cent. to replace a contemporary gold-mounted binding. The book is richly illuminated: 18 canon tables, each with a symbol of the Evangelist in the arcade, 4 full-page initials, and 6 full-page miniatures. The first page shows the dedication where Jerome gives his translation of the Bible to Pope Damasus; above them stand St Lawrence, patron saint of Lund cathedral. The other full-page illuminations show the birth of Christ and the four Evangelists. The codex was commissioned for Lund cathedral, probably from the scriptorium of the Benedictine monastery of Helmarshausen in Hesse where, before 1189, the famous Gospels of Henry the Lion were made. **GT**

Bibl.: *Gyllene böcker*, 1952, no. 22; Krüger 1972; Ekström 1985

513
Vellum.
28.6 × 19.8cm.
Sweden, later Denmark (13th cent.).
12th cent. English.
Kgl. Bibliotek, Copenhagen, Thott 143 2

Folkunga Psalter (Illustrated p. 217)
Latin Psalter, with liturgical calendar (f. 2r–7v) and 16 full-page illuminations (f. 8r–15v) with scenes from the life of Christ, from the Annunciation to the Crucifixion, ending with *Majestas Domini*. Also numerous decorated initials.

In 13th cent. an anonymous nun wrote a prayer in the manuscript, *pro anima byrgeri ducis*, presumably referring to Birger Jarl the Elder, a member of the powerful Folkunga dynasty. The manuscript takes its name from this prayer. An addition in the calendar suggests that the manuscript was later owned by Queen Mechtilde who was first married to King Abel of Denmark and then to Birger Jarl the Younger. The name of the possible first owner has been erased. The Folkunga Psalter is a major example of English Romanesque art and may be seen as an indicator of the increasing respect and significance which came to be given to grandly decorated liturgical books in Scandinavia, as well as elsewhere. **EP**

Bibl.: Jørgensen 1926, 208f.; *Greek and Latin Illuminated Manuscripts*, 1921, 32ff.; *Gyllene Böcker*, 1952, 30f., no. 24; *English Romanesque Art 1066–1200*, 1984, 128, no. 76; Petersen 1991

514
Bronze.
H. 9.6cm.
Unknown provenance.
c. 1162. ?English.
Danmarks Nationalmuseum, Copenhagen, DCXXXIII

Radulf's seal (Illustrated p. 122)
Pointed-oval seal matrix with loop. The seated bishop is encircled by an inscription SIGILLVM:RADULFI:DEI:GRATIA: RIPENSIS:EPISCOPI. Radulf, who may have been of English origin, was bishop in Ribe 1162–1170 and also chancellor to the king. The seal is the earliest preserved matrix from Denmark and is probably of English workmanship. **PGH**

Bibl.: H. Petersen 1886, no. 797

515
Vellum, wax.
40 × 35cm.
Julita Monastery.
1164–67. Swedish.
Riksarkivet, Stockholm, RAperg 1164–1167, DS 51

Sweden's earliest preserved diploma (Illustrated p. 41)
The earliest preserved letter about Swedish affairs. Vellum in a specially designed cover. 2 loose seals of red wax in modern vellum box. Some threads of hemp—remains of the seal attachment—still attached to seal 2. In state ownership since the 16th century.

The letter is a property transaction, one party being the Cistercian house in Viby which was later moved to Julita. It was issued by Stefan, first archbishop of Uppsala (founded 1164). The document is sealed by the archbishop and by king K[arl Sverkersson], died 1167, who is named as the first witness. **CN**

Bibl.: *Diplomatarium Suecanum* 1, 1829–1834, no. 51

516
Vellum.
18 × 22cm.
Probably from Nidaros cathedral archive.
1196 17/3. Papal chancellory.
Riksarkivet, Oslo, NRA dipl. perg. 1196 17/3

Papal bull to Nidaros (Trondheim) cathedral (Illustrated p. 123)
Vellum with lead seal on yellow silk thread. On obverse of seal: 'Celestinvs PP (Papa) III'; on reverse: 'SPASPE' (Sanctus Paulus, Sanctus Petrus) above heads of 2 apostles flanking a cross.

Pope Celestin III supports Nidaros cathedral in its case against lawyers who have usurped its ecclesiastical jurisdiction. The writer forbids the lawyers to do so. The letter shows the Pope intervening on the side of the chapter and archbishop of Nidaros in the conflict between the church and king Sverre, regarding the relationship between spiritual and secular power. **HK**

Bibl.: *Diplomatarium Norvegicum* I, 1849, no. 1; *Norges gamle Love* IV, 1885, 105; Seip 1942, 119–25; Vandvik 1959, 106–9, 203–4, 216 (with translation and facsimile)

517
Birch.
Unknown provenance.
L. 39.5cm.
12th–13th cent. Norwegian.
Universitetets Oldsaksamling, Oslo, C.23306

Document box
Carved from single piece of wood; the lid swivels on a wooden peg at one end. At the other end a man's head with shoulder-length hair, ring-chain pattern on the lid. The relief is low, the detailing simple: deep lines and cuts made with a knife.

The ring-chain and 2-band interlace are both motifs with a long history, known in Norwegian folk-art up to 19th cent. A few simple caskets such as this are known, but are difficult to date. **EBH**

Bibl.: Blindheim 1965; Anker 1985

518

Vellum. 27.2 × 9.7cm.
?Bergen, Norway.
End 12th cent. Norwegian.
Riksarkivet, Oslo, NRA norrøne fragm, 1 B a

Gulating law, fragment *(Illustrated p. 121)*

Fragment of membrane from codex with red initials. Norse hand, influenced by English manuscript tradition.

Excerpt from the district law for SW Norway. Section on Christianity in the Gulating law, from chapt. 28–30, 32: Prohibition against witchcraft, sacrifice and other misdeeds. Replaced by the Law of the Realm of 1274, which itself was replaced by Christian IV's Norwegian Law, printed 1604. A printed law book made the old manuscripts so out of date that many of them were torn up and reused for new administrative purposes. The present fragment was used in the binding of an account book of Nordhordland in the early 17th cent.   **HK**

Bibl.: *Norges Gamle Love* II, 1948, 495–7 (restored transcription); IV, 1885, pl XIII (facsimile); Eken 1963, 2–3 (facsimile); *Kulturhistorisk leksikon for nordisk middelalder* V, 1960, s.v. Gulatingsloven; Robberstad 1969, 42ff.

519

Vellum. 33.5 × 24cm.
West Iceland. *c.* 1260–70.
Stofnun Árna Magnússonar, Reykjavík,
AM 334, fol

Grágás *(Illustrated p. 125)*

When Iceland was almost completely settled at the beginning of 10th cent., the settlers established a state with one common *Thing*, which was held each summer in the open air, in the place later called Thingvellir (p. 54). The laws of the new state had to be established and preserved orally, but when literacy developed after the introduction of Christianity the laws were written down as in other Nordic countries (cf. cat. no. 518). The law of the Icelandic republic in later times acquired the name *Grágás* (grey goose) (probably originally the name of a manuscript now lost). In its extant form *Grágás* is extensive and detailed, and has been called 'the giant bird of all the Germanic law books'. It survives in many fragments, the earliest from 12th cent., and in two complete codices from the years before 1270. One, *Staðarhólsbók*, exhibited here.

Iceland came under the rule of Norway during 1262–64 and soon acquired a new law adapted to that kingdom and new European

520

ideas. But a considerable part of *Grágás* lived on in the new law, and some provisions are valid in Iceland today.   **JK**

Bibl.: Finsen (ed.) 1879; Kålund 1889–94, I, 275–6; Lárusson (ed.) 1936; Dennis, Foote, Perkins (tr.) 1980; Kristjánsson 1988, 117–20

520

Paper. 29.3 × 19.3cm.
Iceland. Copy 1651.
Stofnun Árna Magnússonar, Reykjavík, AM 113a, fol

Íslendingabók

'The priest Ari the Wise Thorgilsson . . . was the first man in this country who wrote down in the Norse language narratives of events both old and new', wrote Snori Sturluson in the introduction to *Heimskringla* (cat. no. 526–7). Ari's manuscript is called *Íslendingabók* (The Book of the Icelanders) and is a short survey of Icelandic history from the settlement to *c.* 1120. It was written 1122–1133 but the gathering of material began some decades earlier. Ari relied almost entirely on oral information and chose his informants carefully from among people who were reliable and had long memories. He laid great stress on chronology and his work forms the basis of all later Icelandic history writing. He dates the first settlement of Iceland to the year when King Edmund of England was murdered, 870. As might be expected he had an incomplete knowledge of the earliest times, but when he reached the discovery and settlement of Greenland (985–86) and the conversion of Iceland (999 or 1000) he had contemporary sources, and dated the events with precision. Vinland is mentioned in a way which shows that it was commonly known in Iceland in Ari's day. The two earliest extant copies (one exhibited here) are from the middle of the 17th cent. The pages shown tell of the establishment of the Althing in the early 10th cent.   **JK**

Bibl.: Kålund 1889–94, I, 74; Hermannsson (ed.) 1930; Jónsson (ed.) 1930; Jóhannesson (ed.) 1956; Benediktsson (ed.) 1968; Kristjánsson 1988, 120–3

521
Vellum.
28.0 × 20.2cm.
Iceland. Mid-14th cent.
Den Arnamagnæanske Samling, Copenhagen,
AM 242 fol

Codex Wormianus *(Illustrated p. 119)*

Codex Wormianus is one of the three main medieval manuscripts of Snorri Sturluson's *Edda* of the 1220s which sought to revive the scaldic poetry of the Viking Age. Beside giving later ages an insight into the sophisticated rules of Scandinavian poetry, the *Edda* contains a multitude of mythological tales; thus it also forms one of the most important sources for pre-Christian religion in the North.

This manuscript also includes 4 treatises on phonology, style and rhetoric. The so-called *First Grammatical Treatise* is thought to have been composed by an Icelander *c.* 1150. It is a pioneering scholarly work which deals with the problems of adapting the Latin alphabet to Icelandic use, and presents an orthographic system for improving the practices which arose when the Icelanders began to write in the vernacular. The treatise is preserved only in this copy, 200 years later than the original.

The manuscript is named after the Danish polymath Ole Worm (1588–1654) who obtained it in 1628 from the Icelandic humanist Arngrímur Jónsson.   PS

Bibl.: Kålund 1889–94, I, 213–5; Nordal (ed.) 1931; Haugen 1972; Faulkes (tr.) 1987; Dillmann (tr.) 1991

522
Vellum.
18.5 × 14.2cm.
Western Iceland. *c.* 1200.
Stofnun Árna Magnússonar, Reykjavík, AM
673 a, 4to

Physiologus *(Illustrated p. 219)*

Physiologus is a work on natural history, originally written in Greek early in the Christian era. It contains a mixture of natural science and superstition. In the Middle Ages the work was used by the Church and, by way of Latin, was translated into many European languages. Many versions have been preserved and the manuscript texts are illustrated with pictures of the various animals and fabulous beasts. Physiologus was translated into Icelandic in 12th cent. and survives in two manuscript fragments of *c.* 1200; one is shown here. On the bottom of the right-

hand page are figures of 3 fabulous peoples: the Cyclops with two blind and one seeing eye (the latter in the middle of the forehead); the Panotii have ears so large that they cover their entire bodies; the Hippopodes have hooves like horses and live in Scythia. The manuscript collector Árni Magnússon got the two connected leaves from north-west Iceland, where they had been perforated and used as a flour sieve.   JK

Bibl.: Kålund 1889–4, II, 90–2; Hermannsson (ed.) 1935; Hermannsson (ed.) 1938; Benediktsson 1965, p. vii; *Romanske stenarbejder* 2, 1984, 25–58

523
Vellum.
21.2 × 14.0cm.
Iceland. End 13th cent.
Den Arnamagnæanske Samling, Copenhagen,
AM 291, 4to

The Saga of the Jómsvikings

The renowned Jómsvikings were based in the mighty stronghold of Jómsborg on the Baltic coast, whence, under the leadership of the chieftain Palnatoke, they operate. They are no friends of the Danish kings Harald Bluetooth and Sven Forkbeard. They considered themselves to be invincible and when on a visit to Sven Forkbeard of Denmark they drunkenly make an ill-starred vow to conquer Norway. During this hazardous venture they suffer ignominious defeat in the sea battle of Hjorungavágr, but some of the survivors have the opportunity of displaying their legendary heroism before being executed.

An introductory, and largely historical, account of the relationship between Norway and Denmark forms the background for the more more fanciful portrayal of the rumbustious exploits of the Jómsvikings. Partly based on historical sources, it is preserved in several versions, thought to stem from one text composed *c.* 1200.   PS

Bibl.: Kålund 1889–94, I, 538; Blake (ed. and tr.) 1962; Bätke (tr.) 1966; Degnbol and Jensen (tr.) 1978

524
Vellum.
22 × 16cm.
Iceland. Copy *c.* 1400.
Stofnun Árna Magnússonar, Reykjavík, AM
162A E, fol

Egils saga Skalla-Grímssonar
(Illustrated p. 175)

Egils saga was composed in the early 13th cent., based on earlier oral tradition and on

Egil's poems. Egil was the son of one of Iceland's mightiest settlers who arrived at the end of 9th cent. He himself was a chieftain in Borgafjörður in western Iceland. At the same time he was one of the greatest poets of the North and moved among kings and nobles in other countries. He came into conflict with the Norwegian Viking king Erik Bloodaxe, and when the king took him prisoner and wanted to execute him in York, Egil saved his life by, in the course of one night, composing a prose-poem about King Erik in a resounding metre never before used in Scandinavian poetry. When Egil had recited the poem before the king, queen and their retinue the king rewarded him by sparing his life. Thus the poem acquired the name *Hǫfuðlausn*, 'Head-ransom'. This manuscript includes one of the earliest known versions of the poem.   JK

Bibl.: Kålund 1889–94, I, 115–6; Jónsson (ed.) 1886–88, XVII; Nordal (ed.) 1933, XCVI; Fell (tr.) 1975; Pálsson and Edwards (tr.) 1976; Kristjánsson 1988, 98–103, 265–70

525
Vellum.
21 × 16.5cm.
Iceland. *c.* 1300.
Den Arnamagnæanske Samling, Copenhagen,
AM 325 I, 4to

Orkneyinga saga

The Orkney Islands were colonized from Norway and an earldom was established there. The history of the earldom from *c.* 900 to end 12th cent. is the subject of this history, written in Iceland in the early 13th cent.

One of the main figures in the chronicle is Earl Rǫgnvald Kali (d. 1158) who was also an eminent poet. He sets out for the Holy Land, on the way he and his retinue pass Narbonne, and there, at the court of Countess Ermingard, the Vikings from the Atlantic come across a truly courtly environment. Ermingard is known from other sources as a courtly lady who enjoys the adoration of troubadours. Rǫgnvald and two Icelandic scalds who accompany him each compose a verse about her and thereby show that they know how to adapt to the style of troubadour poetry. The manuscript fragment here tells of this visit.   PS

Bibl.: Kålund 1889–94, I, 552; Meissner 1925; Guðmundsson (ed.) 1965; Pálsson and Edwards (tr.) 1978

526

Vellum. 26.5 × 24.6cm.
Iceland. *c.* 1260.
Landsbókasafn Íslands, Reykjavík, Lbs. fragm. 82

Heimskringla (Kringla) *(Ill. p. 18)*

Kringla is a leaf from the oldest and best
manuscript of *Heimskringla*, a history of
Norwegian kings to 1177, composed by the
famous Icelander Snorri Sturluson
(1179–1241) (cf. cat. no. 527). The text of
this leaf is from Olaf the Holy's saga. *Kringla*,
which originally consisted of *c.* 180 pages,
was written on Iceland, sent to Norway in
the Middle Ages, brought from there to
Denmark, and belonged to the University
Library in Copenhagen where it burned in
1728. This leaf, which had been taken to
Sweden before the fire, is the only one extant
and was given to Iceland by the king of
Sweden on a state visit in 1975. **FG**

Bibl.: Jónsson (ed.) 1895; Karlsson 1976

527

Vellum. 31.0 × 24.0cm.
Iceland. Early 14th cent.
Den Arnamagnæanske Samling, Copenhagen,
AM 45 fol.

Heimskringla—Codex Frisianus *(Illustrated p. 174)*

In *c.* 1230 the Icelander Snorri Sturluson
(1179–1241) wrote his great chronicle of the
Norwegian kings from the legendary age to
1177. The chronicle has been named *Heimskringla*, 'The Circle of the World' (cf. cat. no.
526). Its style and psychological insight make
it the masterwork of kings' sagas and it later
came to have great significance for the concept of national identity in Norway. The
book is constructed with St Olaf (d. 1030),
'Norway's eternal king', as its central figure.
This page tells of the famous sea battle near
the island of Svöld in the Baltic in the year
1000, when the Norwegian king Olaf Tryggvason was defeated by two Norwegian earls,
the Swedish king Olof and the Danish king
Sven Forkbeard.

Codex Frisianus is one of the most beautiful
Icelandic books from the Middle Ages. It
came to Norway soon after its composition
and the vellum has, therefore, not discol-
oured. The central part about St Olaf is
omitted, probably because the Norwegian
who commissioned it already owned a manuscript of this. Two chronicles about kings
after 1177 have been added. The manuscript
is named after the Danish nobleman Otto
Friis, in whose possession it was *c.* 1600. **PS**

Bibl.: Unger (ed.) 1871; Kålund 1889–94, I, 32–3; *Codex
Frisianus*, 1932

523

525

528

---

528 Vellum.
29 × 21.8cm.
Monastery of St Mary in Sorø.
12th cent. French.
Kgl. Bibliotek, Copenhagen, Gl. kgl. S. 450 2

Justinus manuscript

Justinus's Latin *Epitoma historiarum Phillicarum Pompei Trogi*; on the last page of the manuscript there is an appendix with a series of annalistic records 1202–1347. The manuscript's attribution to Archbishop Absalon and the Sorø monastery results from a note added to the end of the book.

Absalon's clerk, Saxo Grammaticus (cf. cat. no. 529), used Justinus as one of his stylistic models and borrowed this codex from Absalon. In his will, Absalon instructed Saxo to return two manuscripts to the Monastery of St Mary in Sorø. One was later destroyed in the fire of Copenhagen in 1728; this manuscript found its way to the Royal Library as a gift to Christian V in 1691. **EP**

Bibl.: Jørgensen 1926, 325; Munk Olsen 1982–1989, 1, 542f; 3.1, 296

---

529 Vellum.
21.6 × 16.1cm.
Angers, France; acquired by Royal Library through exchange, 1878.
c. 1200. Danish.
Kgl. Bibliotek, Copenhagen, Ny kgl. S. 869g 4

Saxo's Gesta Danorum: the Angers fragment *(Illustrated p. 168)*

Four leaves (1 double and 2 single leaves) found in 1863 in the binding of a 15th-cent. book in Bibliothèque Publique, Angers.

The Angers fragment of Saxo Grammaticus's great Latin chronicle *Gesta Danorum* (the history of the Danes from ancient times to c. 1200) is unique as a textual and codicological source. It was probably written by Saxo himself, and the corrections and additions in the fragment give an idea of how Saxo worked with his text. Apart from a few other fragments of a later date, the Angers fragment is the only surviving manuscript of Saxo's work (cf. cat. no. 530). **EP**

Bibl.: Jørgensen 1926, 403f.; Olrik-Ræder 1931, XIIIff.; Boserup 1981

---

530 Paper.
27.5 × 20cm.
Kgl. Bibliotek, Copenhagen, LN 240 ex. 4

Saxo's Gesta Danorum, Paris 1514

First edition of Saxo's chronicle, published by the Danish humanist Christiernus Petri and printed by Jodochus Badius Ascensius, Paris 1514.

Written in a flawless and highly elaborate Latin, Saxo's history of Denmark deserved the international readership and fame which the work obtained through being published by the great printer in Paris. The title page includes an idealized picture of 'the King of the Danes' with the Danish coat of arms before him and warriors behind. The 1514 Paris edition is the primary source for Saxo's text since no medieval manuscript has been preserved in its entirety (cf. cat. no. 529). The edition is an early and important work of Danish humanism and is characteristic of the discovery of the past which came to be a distinctive feature of the Renaissance, in Scandinavia as well as elsewhere. **EP**

Bibl.: Renouard 1908, 249ff.; Nielsen 1919, no. 240; Olrik-Ræder, XIff.; Petersen 1985; Friis-Jensen 1989

530

532

531

531

531
L. 24.4cm.
Sigtuna (Kv Trädgårdsmästaren
9 and 10), Uppland, Sweden.
Early 12th cent. Scandinavian.
Sigtuna Museums, 22145

Bone with runic inscription

Found in occupation layer on an urban plot. Runes on both sides, carved by two people with different styles. On the concave side, '*Kongungr iæR matar bæstr. Hann (?)gaf mest. Hann iæR thækkili(gr)*' (The king is most hospitable. He (?)gave most. He is popular).

These words are also found on rune stones in Uppland, Småland and Skåne and show what was appreciated—a groaning board was expected from the man whom one served. The Sigtuna bone praises the king with superlatives. As a *primus inter pares* it was necessary for him to prove his supremacy by being lavish with food. The inscription gives a clear picture of how royal power was exercised in the early Middle Ages. **MR/MÅ**

Bibl.: Roslund 1990b

532
Silver.
Gamla Uppsala, Kungsgården,
Uppland, Sweden.
11th–12th cent. Swedish, Russian.
Statens Historiska Museum, Stockholm, 8889

Hoard

The hoard was found in 1891 in a field belonging to a royal farm, near the mounds and church (previously cathedral) of Gamla Uppsala. It consists of five fluted silver bowls with a punched decorationn of vines around the rim (rim diam. 12.5–13.5cm), a Russian or Byzantine silver-gilt reliquary cross, three chains with animal-head terminals, one of the chains supporting a simple annular brooch in silver, four chains, three with their original pendants. The hoard contained no coins. The bowls are decorated in Romanesque style, one with a basal roundel of a lion in niello bordered by an angular twist. The bowls are of the same type as that from Lilla Valla, Rute, Gotland, but of poorer quality. **GT**

Bibl.: Andersson 1983

533

Marble.
H. 32cm.
?Munkeliv monastery, Bergen, Norway.
2nd quarter of 12th cent.
Historisk Museum, Bergen, MA76

King's head *(Illustrated p. 40)*

Bearded head with moustache. The crown is
a high ring with pendilia-like attachments
and crosses. On the ring : eYsTEIN REX.
The head is severed at the neck.

The stone's broken surfaces suggest its
possible original situation as a column statue
in a portal. The Benedictine monastery of
Munkeliv was founded by King Eystein
Haraldson (1103–22), and the stone was
found near the ruins in 1853, but its connection with the original building is problematic. The Eystein head is different from all
known Norwegian works. The crown is
Byzantine/German. It has been assumed to
be an import, but the type of stone has not
been determined. Epigraphy and style date it
to first half of 12th cent.; it is an exceptionally early sculptural representation of a king,
even in a pan-European context. **HVA/EBH**

Bibl.: Blindheim 1965, 22f., fig. 80; Anker 1981, 151; Lidén 1990, 161

535

534

Bronze.
Diam. 5.8cm.
Trondheim (provenance not known), Norway.
Second half of 13th cent. Scandinavian.
Vitenskapsmuseet, Trondheim, T1504

Seal matrix

Encircling legend: +SIGILL CAPITVLI
ECLIE SCIOLAWI REGIS ET MAR-
TIRIS+. In the centre St Olaf enthroned
with an orb in his left hand, a lily-headed
sceptre in his right; a rose on each side of his
head. Loop on the reverse.

The oldest known seal of Nidaros (Trondheim) cathedral chapter. The church housed
the grave of St Olaf and was the centre of his
cult. Impressions of this seal are known from
1263–1281 but the roses are secondary, impressions with roses being known from
1307–1448. The iconography of this seal
matrix is unusual in that St Olaf is shown
holding a sceptre. He is usually depicted with
an axe, as on the later seal of the chapter.

KS/EBH

Bibl.: Trætteberg 1953

534

534

535

Gilt brass, glass.
Diam. of original, 19.8–20.3cm.
Original in Uppsala cathedral, Sweden.
?1160. Swedish.
Statens Historiska Museum, Stockholm, 24168

Replica of St Erik's funerary crown *(Original illustrated p. 39)*

Scientific investigation of the contents of St
Erik's shrine in Uppsala cathedral, carried
out in 1946, allowed the crown (which is still
kept in the shrine) to be recorded. It is
documented back to the late 17th cent. The
crown consists of a broad circlet of copper
gilded on the outside, now broken in 15
pieces, held together by a secondary band of
copper around the inside and the upper and
lower edges. The upper edge has 7 small
projections, some of which carried elements
of unknown appearance. Contemporary
crowns and depictions show many possible
reconstructions: cross and lily, or various
leaf, cross or spherical terminals. The outer
surface is decorated with engraved lines and
ornamental squares, with coloured glass held
in place by copper sheet riveted to the inside
of the crown. Its shape suggests that it was
probably not worn by King Erik in his
lifetime, but was made for his burial. **GT**

Bibl.: Thordeman 1954

536

Bone, linen, silk.
L. 18.3cm.
Turku (Åbo) cathedral, Finland.
Finlands Nationalmuseum, Helsinki, 52090:3

Head reliquary *(Illustrated p. 71)*

The major portion of the relic is a lower jaw wrapped in linen. The upper part of the framework is built up of many bones, including many skull bones each sewn in white linen, thus supporting each other. The whole wrapped in a white linen cloth to hold the whole together. The reliquary is covered with 2 layers of silk, the inner light red, the outer of wine-red Chinese silk-damask from 2nd half of 13th cent. At the eyes and on the top of the head is a segmental opening in the silk through which the linen is visible.

On the front is a scene of a martyrdom embroidered in silk and gold thread; a man dressed in a clinging garment of gold thread and gold armour, with drawn sword, confronts a kneeling decapitated man in a light blue cloak. The head, surrounded by a nimbus of gold thread, lies on the ground.

The lower jaw is probably that of the Swedish royal saint, St Erik, who according to legend tried to convert the Finns, and whose relics are preserved in Uppsala cathedral (cf. cat. no. 537). An anatomical examination of the jaw in 1946 in connection with the opening of St Erik's reliquary in Uppsala, neither confirmed nor denied this theory. But there are many indications that it is so: the embroidery (which was probably done in Uppsala using the famous cope of Bishop Fulco as a model) must depict the execution of St Erik on 18 May 1160. In any event, the preparation of the reliquary, which must have been given to the cathedral of Turku *c.* 1400, means that the jaw was then regarded as a true relic of St Erik. The scene depicted cannot be connected with any other saint with associations with Turku cathedral.   **TE**

Bibl.: Rinne 1932; Nordman 1954

537

537

Vellum in covers of leather-bound wood. 33 × 22cm.
Vallentuna church, Uppland, Sweden.
Calendar *c.* 1198; binding 16th cent. Swedish (?Mälar valley).
Statens Historiska Museum, Stockholm, 21288

Calendar, included in Liber ecclesiae Vallentunensis

The earliest part of the volume is a missal with calendar, written *c.* 1198. Ten pages of the missal, for *proprium de tempore* and 3 pages of the calendar survive. The text is written in dark-brown ink, the initials outlined in red, green, blue and yellow; red is used for the rubrics, annotations, and the major festivals in the calendar. Musical notation is of square notes on 4 red lines. The calendar—the earliest known from Sweden—includes the months March to December. Festivals are marked in red. This page-spread shows May to August with the three Scandinavian royal saints—St Erik (18/5) in left column of left-hand page, and St Knut (10/7), St Olaf (29/7) in left column of right-hand page.   **GT**

Bibl.: Schmid 1945

538

Original: vellum. 30.4 × 20.4cm.
c. 1200. Northern France.
Original in the Musée Condé, Chantilly, ms.1695.

Ingeborg's Psalter (facsimile)

This manuscript, a masterpiece of French manuscript-illustration of *c.* 1200, is illuminated with 27 miniatures and with ornamental letters. The illustrations depict the principal figures, who stand out from the gilded background in impeccable elegance; Byzantine influence is clear.

It was made for Ingeborg (1176–1236), the daughter of King Valdemar the Great of Denmark. In 1193 she married the King of France, Philip August, but was repudiated the following day. She remained in France but did not regain her title until 1213, after many years of strenuous Danish diplomatic efforts and intervention by the Pope. The manuscript was produced between 1195 and 1215. Stylistically it is closely related to contemporary illuminations from Noyon or Soissons in the circle of Aliénor, Countess of Vermandois. The picture shows Abraham's sacrifice (fol.11).   **DGC**

Bibl.: Deuchler 1967; Grodecki 1969, 73–78; Hausherr 1977, 231–50; Liebman 1985, 65–77; Avril 1987, 16–21. On the facsimile see *Codices Selecti*, vol. LXXX, 1985

538

540

Silver. Wt. 0.71g.
No provenance.
c. 1043. Danish (Hedeby).
Danmarks Nationalmuseum, Copenhagen,
KM&MS, Ramus & Devegge, Tillægstavler IV, 16

Magnus the Good in Denmark (1042–47). Penny

Minted in Hedeby; moneyer Ioli (Hauberg 37). Obverse shows a ruler with sceptre and battle-axe. It may be the earliest representation of Norway's patron saint, St Olaf (died 1030 in the battle of Stiklestad). The axe is his attribute (he was killed with an axe). The coin may be a memorial of the great victory over the Slavs at Lyrskov Hede in 1043, when Olaf appeared to his son Magnus in a vision.

JSJ

Bibl.: Hauberg 1900; Becker 1983

542

542

Silver.
Wt. 0.73g.
Holsteinsborg, Sjælland, Denmark (1730s).
Danish.
Danmarks Nationalmuseum, Copenhagen,
KM&MS, Ramus & Devegge 4

St Knut (1080–86). Penny

Minted in Roskilde by Arcil. The coin belongs to a series with individual motifs: king with sword on obverse, cross on reverse, which was minted east of Lille Bælt, somewhere between Odense and Lund (Hauberg 7). After Harald Hen's (or Sven Estridsen's) coinage reform it was customary to use only Danish coins, thus many coins were struck; in Roskilde alone there were more than 10 moneyers. Most of the coins from this period derive from the hoard found in Holsteinsborg.

JSJ

Bibl.: Hauberg 1900; Galster 1937

539

539

Silver.
St Jørgensbjerg church, Roskilde,
Denmark.
Deposited c. 1030–1035. English, Danish,
German.
Danmarks Nationalmuseum, Copenhagen,
KM&MS, FP 2374a

Coin hoard from Knut or Hardeknut's reigns (Illustrated in part)

Found during the excavation of a demolished church in 1953: it is interpreted as an offering. There were 34 English coins and imitations (Æthelred II and Knut the Great), 6 Danish coins of Knut, 61 coins of Hardeknut, some with new iconography; and 9 German coins (80 of 110 exhibited).

The hoard was first thought to have been deposited c. 1040, during the reign of Hardeknut (1035–42), but it is now thought that Hardeknut minted coins as early as c. 1026–8, i.e. during Knut's reign. The slightly earlier dating of the hoard is supported by a number of die-linked coins of Knut's last English issue c. 1029–35 (cf. cat. no. 425). Thus the church in which the coins were found, the earliest stone building in Denmark, must be dated a little earlier than previously assumed.

JSJ

Bibl.: Galster 1954; Olsen 1960; Galster 1977b; Glob (ed.) 1980, no. 38; Becker 1981, 154f. et passim

541

a   b

541

Silver. Wt 1.14g, 1.11g.
No provenance.
Danish (Lund).
Danmarks Nationalmuseum, Copenhagen,
KM&MS, Ramus & Devegge 194; KP 1715.1000

Sven Estridsen (1047–74). Two pennies

Both coins are of types minted in great numbers in Lund; each represents one end of Sven's long reign. The earlier coin shows strong Byzantine influence (cf. cat. no. 586). a The very popular motif, an angel and an emperor (Hauberg 8), is taken from a rare gold coin minted in 1041 in Thessaloniki. Such coins may have been brought home by Harald Hardråde who served the Byzantine emperor before he became king of Norway. b Coin minted c. 1065 with runic legends. They were peculiar to their time and probably attempted to support ancient Scandinavian traditions. The mint master was Azur Pai (Hauberg 30).

JSJ

Bibl.: Hauberg 1900; Moltke 1950; Grierson 1966; Hendy 1970; Steen Jensen 1975; Moltke 1985, 391–7

a   b

543

543

Silver.
Wt. 0.86g, 0.88g.
Lund Cathedral, Sweden (1835); Haraldsborg,
Denmark (1853).
Danish.
Danmarks Nationalmuseum, Copenhagen,
KM&MS, BP10, FP139

Niels (1104–34). Two pennies

During the long reign of Niels two types of coin were struck at his main mint Lund. a Obverse shows the king with a specifically royal attribute: a falcon. Reverse influenced by Germany, with Latin inscription PAX PORTU (Hauberg 1).

b Only this Scandinavian coin-type from the Middle Ages carries a legend for both king and queen. The queen was the powerful Margrethe Fredkulla. Only some of this series carry her name, perhaps because she died before the king. **JSJ**

Bibl.: Hauberg 1900; Ernst 1946; Lindahl 1979; Kiernsowski 1988; Steen Jensen 1990

a

b

544

c

544 Silver.
Wt. 0.21g. 0.66g, 0.64g.
a Øster Tranders; *b* Klarup church; *c* no provenance.
Danish (Viborg; Schleswig; Roskilde).
Danmarks Nationalmuseum, Copenhagen, KM&MS, Ramus & Devegge 9; FP3209,5;
Thomsen 10,374

Sven Grathe (1146–57). Valdemar the Great (1157–82). Three pennies *(b also illustrated p. 111)*

These coins illustrate aspects of minting in 12th-cent. Denmark.

a Sven Grathe (Hauberg 5). Small bracteate. Minting of fine quality and clearly inspired by Germany, probably because of Sven's German marriage and his subsequent homage to Frederic Barbarossa in 1152. *b* Valdemar the Great (Hauberg 61) or Knut VI (1182–1202). Obverse with majestic profile; reverse with cross-emblazoned banner, probably the earliest representation of the Danish flag. The coin has no legend but was probably struck in Schleswig. *c* Valdemar the Great and Absalon (Hauberg 8). Representation of the king on one side, the bishop on the other; legend: Valdemar and Absalon (bishop of Roskilde, closely related to the king, founder of Copenhagen, active in the Baltic crusades, later archbishop). This is one of the first Roskilde coins on which the bishop is portrayed. **JSJ**

Bibl.: Hauberg 1906; Galster 1935; Galster 1977; Glob (ed.) 1980, no. 42

545

545 Silver (90.2% Ag).
Wt. 1.01g.
Stein (in ruins of St Olaf's church), Hole, Buskerud, Norway.
1015/19–28. Norwegian.
Universitetets Myntkabinett, Oslo, Skaare 2a

Penny of Olaf Haraldsson (1015–1030)

Obverse: +OLEFRE+NORMANORV. Bare-headed bust looking left, with sceptre. Reverse: Illegible legend. *En face* bird with spread wings and head turned upwards towards left. Found 1924.

The 14 known examples of Olaf Haraldsson's minting fall into 3 types, 2 of them struck from square blanks. All have Anglo-Saxon models. 2 moneyers' names are known from the legends: Asthrith and Liafa. 4 of the coins have been found in Norway, the rest in Skåne, Gotland, south Finland, Poland and north Germany. The finds and the known number of dies suggest that the Norwegian royal saint had an extensive minting mechanism. **KS**

Bibl.: Fonahn 1926; Skaare 1976, 60–4, 137 no. 139, 191–2, no. 2a; Graham-Campbell 1980, no. 397

546

546 Silver (85.7% Ag).
Wt. 0.82g.
From O. Chr. Bjørnstad's Collection, Oslo.
1047–55. Norwegian.
Universitetets Myntkabinett, Oslo, Skaare 13a

Harald Hardråde (1047–1066) Penny

Obverse: +HARALDE+NAO. Triquetra. Reverse: Illegible legend. Double cross in inner circle, 3 points in 2 crosses.

Harald Hardråde established a national mint in Norway after Olaf Tryggvason (995–1000) and Olaf Haraldsson issued

pennies which were closely related to Anglo-Saxon types, and he continued this line (cat. no. 423, 545). King Harald's main type was a three-quarter figure modelled on Danish pennies. The weight of the Norwegian three-quarter pennies, 0.90g, corresponds to Norwegian weight and coinage systems. These pennies were gradually devalued through an increasing alloying with copper.

Extensive metal analyses have confirmed the description given in the *Morkinskinna* of the payment made by Harald to his men on New Year's Day, 'It was called *Haraldsslåten*, was largely copper, at the best only half silver' (cat. no. 547). Nevertheless, finds of coins from this time show that Harald's poor coinage did circulate and was in use. **KS**

Bibl.: Skaare 1976, 65–113, 193 no. 13a

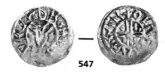

547

547 Silver (33.0% Ag).
Wt. 0.89g.
Helgelandsmoen, Hole i Buskerud, Norway.
c. 1055–65. Norwegian.
Universitetets Myntkabinett, Oslo, Skaare 8a

Harald Hardråde (1047–1066). Penny

Obverse: +HAROLD RE (retrograde). Triquetra in circle. Reverse: +OLAFRAHAM. Double cross in inner circle, 3 points in alternate angles of cross, 1 point in the others.

From a coin hoard found 1892. The reverse legend comprises the moneyer's name in Norse: *Olafr á Ham(ri)*, Olaf in Hamar. Other Harald Hardråde's coins name Nidarnes (Nidaros/Trondheim) as the mint place with the moneyers Geirfinn and Ulf. The Hamar coins must belong to the later phase of king Harald's minting (cf. cat. no. 546). The style and epigraphy suggest that a large group of anonymous triquetra pennies claimed Nidarnes as their mint. **KS**

Bibl.: Stenersen 1895; Skaare 1976, 98–100, 137 no. 38, 193 no. 8a

548

551

548	Silver (31.1% Ag). Wt. 1.14g. Gresli, Tydal, Sør-Trøndelag, Norway. *c.* 1065–80. Norwegian. Universitetets Myntkabinett, Oslo, Stenersen N8

Olaf Kyrre (1067–1093). Penny

Obverse: Illegible legend. Bare-headed bust with sceptre, looking to left. Reverse: Illegible legend. Double-cross in circle. From a large hoard found 1881.

The penny belongs to a type and variant group recognizable by its highly barbarized design, developed—under the influence of ?native animal ornament—from the kings' heads on Anglo-Saxon pennies. Silver content fluctuates around *c.* 37% Ag. A penny related to this was found in 1957 during the excavation of a large Indian hunting site on Naskeag Point, Penobscot Bay, Maine, USA. The excavation produced no other Scandinavian material but the penny is probably genuine and best explained as the result of indirect contact in early times. KS

Bibl.: Stenersen 1881; Malmer 1961, 260f.; Skaare 1985

549

549	Silver (92.4% Ag). Wt. 0.42g. 'From Nordlandene' (according to Schive). *c.* 1095–1100. Norwegian. Universitetets Myntkabinett, Oslo, Schive III 44

Magnus Barefoot (1093–1103). Penny

Obverse: Illegible legend. Left-facing bust with helmet and pyramidal shoulder. Reverse: illegible legend. In inner circle a double cross with a circle around centre of cross; half moon in one angle of cross.

A coin reform took place in Norway after a long period of issuing coins with low silver content (cf. cat. no. 547–8). This involved halving the weight, to *c.* 44g, and restoring the silver content to the high, international level of 90% Ag or more. This reform, for which the coins themselves are the only evidence, was originally attributed to the reign of Olaf Kyrre (1067–1093), but has now been redated to Magnus Barefoot. KS

Bibl.: Schive 1965, Tab. III:44; Malmer 1961, 345, 361; Skaare 1969

550

550	Silver (95.9% Ag). Wt. 0.44g. Dæli, Stavsjø, Nes (near Ringsaker), Hedmark, Norway. *c.* 1180. Norwegian. Universitetets Myntkabinett, Oslo, UM 20

Sverre (1177–1202). Penny

Obverse: +REXSVERVSMAGNVS. Crowned head *en face* within beading. Reverse: NI/NI/NI/NI. Large double cross with fleur-de-lis in the angles, circle beaded. Found 1840.

The coin hoard from Dæli (5,000 coins, *c.* 4,500 of which Norwegian), deposited after 1194, gives a good insight into Norwegian minting in Sverre's reign. The issuing of whole pennies began again for the first time since Magnus Barefoot. They were minted according to the half-penny standard. Design and epigraphy reflect English sterling types. The letters NI on the reverse is thought to stand for Nidaros (Trondheim), probably the mint place. A moneyer, Hagbart, mentioned in *Sverres Saga* chapter 62, celebrated his wedding in the town in 1181. It seems that Sverre gradually abandoned minting pennies and instead issued large quantities of half- and, particularly, quarter-pennies as leaf-thin bracteates (cat. no. 551), the latter being only about 0.06g average weight. They are some of the smallest coins known in the history of coinage. KS

Bibl.: Holmboe 1841; Skaare 1979/80

551	Silver (83.1% Ag). Weight 0.16g. Lom church, Oppland, Norway. *c.* 1180–1200. Norwegian. Universitetets Myntkabinett, Oslo, UM 62

Sverre (1177–1202). Half-penny bracteate

Obverse: +BERGIS. Crowned head *en face* in circle. No impression on reverse. Found 1973.

The design and epigraphy connect this bracteate to Sverre's issues, although his name does not appear on the coin. A penny, minted as a bracteate and with only reverse impression, has the legend BV/BV/BV/BV (cf. cat. no. 550). Probably from Bergen (Bjorgvin). KS

Bibl.: Skaare 1978; Skaare 1979/80

a

b

552

552	Silver. Wt. 2.22g; 1.40g. No provenance. *c.* 995, *c.* 1025. Swedish (Sigtuna). Kungl. Myntkabinettet, Stockholm

Olof Skötkonung (c. 994–1022), Anund Jakob (c. 1022–1050). Two pennies

a Olof Skötkonung, 'Crux' type. Obverse: +VLVAF REX ZVENO (Olof king of the Svear). Right-facing bust with sceptre. Reverse: +IN NOMINE DNI MC (In the name of God, creator of the world). Double cross with CRVX (cross) in the angles. *b* Anund Jakob. 'Pointed Helmet' type.

Obverse: +ANVND REX SI (Anund king in Sigtuna). Left-facing bust with sceptre and helmet.
Reverse: THORMOTH ON SIHTV (Thormoth in Sigtuna). Double cross with spheres in the angles.

The earliest Sigtuna coins of Olof Skötkonung copy English models (cf. cat. no. 422–3) but with differences. In this example the reverse has an obviously Christian motif combined with a Christian legend which must have been inspired by north German coins. Olof's coinage lasted until his death in 1022, and more than 1,000 coins are known. Anund Jakob issued fewer coins although many coins with confused legends have been attributed to him. Some 100 coins have been preserved from his reign, i.e. less than 10% of the coins of Olof. His issues were certainly limited to a short period, c. 1025–1030 (cf. cat. no. 426), but the impression is that they were of a lower quality. After his reign no coins were issued in Sweden until c. 1140. KJ

Bibl.: Lagerqvist 1968, 8; Lagerqvist 1970, 7; Malmer 1989, 15.51.3

553

Lead.
Sigtuna (Kv Urmakaren 1), Uppland, Sweden.
Early 11th cent. Swedish (Sigtuna).
Sigtuna Museums, 225

Trial-piece for coin die

(Illustrated p. 221)

Discovered in a building which seems to have been a dwelling (not simply a workshop) although one corner of the house contained a forge surrounded by many crucibles, suggesting that the place was occasionally used as a workshop. This was the area in which the trial-piece was discovered. Each side of the lead strip shows impressions of an upper and lower stamp, with a schematic king's portrait on one face and a large cross on the other. They associate it with the Anglo-Saxon 'Long Cross' coin type which the Swedish king Olof Skötkonung imitated in Sigtuna 1000–1005 (cf. cat. no. 423–4, 552). When a coin die of steel, was engraved, trial-pieces were struck in lead to check the results, and then the die was tempered (cf. cat. no. 399, 402, 427). Several thousand coins could then be struck before the die needed to be re-engraved or before it

shattered and needed to be renewed. The neighbouring area of Sigtuna (Kv Trädgårds-mästaren) has produced a lead trial-piece showing that some of Knut Eriksson's coinage of the 1180s was struck in Sigtuna. ST

Bibl.: Malmer 1989; Lagerqvist 1990; Svensson 1990; Tesch 1990

554a

554b

554

Silver. Wt. 0.25g; 0.12g.
No provenance.
c. 1180, c. 1190. Swedish (Sigtuna, Lödöse).
Kungl. Myntkabinett, Stockholm

Knut Eriksson (1167–1196). Two pennies

a Bracteate (single sided). Sigtuna. Royal bust looking forward with sceptre and banner. *b* Bracteate (single sided). Lödöse. KANVTVS REX S (Knut king of Sweden). Crowned *en face* head with sword.

The medieval minting of coins on the Swedish mainland began in Lödöse in west Sweden just before 1150, i.e. at much the same time as on Gotland. The earliest coins were inspired by Norwegian coins and have a cross as motif but no legend. The first time that a king's name appeared on coins was c. 1190 (Knut Eriksson) when the model was English double-sided coins. The coinage standard followed the Gotland model (384 pennies = 1 mark) and was used in an area equivalent to the Skara diocese.

In central Sweden coining began c. 1180 in the reign of Knut Eriksson, after a break of c. 150 years. The coins were minted in Sigtuna and used the Svea standard (192 pennies = 1 mark). KJ

Bibl.: Lagerqvist 1970, I:A:2a, XI:A:1a

555

555

Silver.
Wt. 0.47g.
Burge, Lummelunda, Gotland, Sweden (1967).
c.1140. Swedish (?Visby).
Kungl. Myntkabinettet, Stockholm, SHM 28830

Gotland. Penny

Obverse: Confused legend. Wheel-cross. Reverse: Church gable.

When the Viking-age import of coins to Gotland ceased c. 1140, local coining began. Gotland formally belonged to Sweden but there was no royal minting there in the early Middle Ages. Instead there was some form of local organisation which controlled the coinage; the standard differed from the mainland system, using 288 pennies = 1 mark, there was no royal name, and a single type was current for a long period. Until c. 1250, Gotland coins also dominated south-east Sweden (the area equivalent to the Linköping diocese) and went further afield. The Gotland coins also served as models for Baltic coins which began to be minted in Riga in 1211. KJ

Bibl.: Lagerqvist 1970, XX:A:1

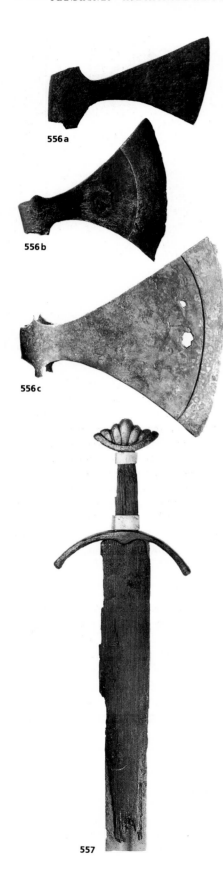

556a

556b

556c

557

556

Iron.
Width of edge: *a* 9.1cm; *b* 14.5cm;
c 21.8cm.
a–b Grathe Hede, Thorning, Jutland;
c Værebro, Gundsømagle, Sjælland, Denmark.
11th cent. Danish.
Danmarks Nationalmuseum, Copenhagen,
D3298; D2199; D8524

Three battle-axes

The shapes of the axes are typical of the early
Middle Ages. Axes *b* and *c* have edges of
hardened steel. All have winged sockets.
They represent a development of late Viking-
age axes (cf. cat. no. 111–2). These examples
were found on battlefields mentioned in
written sources: *a–b* a battle of 1157 where
king Valdemar the Great defeated king Sven
Grathe; *c* a battle of 1133.   **PGH/ER**

Bibl.: la Cour 1959; *Kulturhistorisk leksikon for nordisk
middelalder* XX, 1976, *s.v.* Öks; Liebgott 1976, 15–20

557

Iron, bronze sheet, wood.
L. 105.5cm.
Korsødegården, Stange, Hedmark, Norway.
c. 1100–1150. Scandinavian.
Universitetets Oldsaksamling, Oslo, C.9981

Sword

The guard strongly curved, thickened at both
ends, expands to a point in the middle. Five-
lobed pommel. The grip has remains of wood
and 2 bronze mounts, one with runic inscription 'AMUND MADE ME, ASLEIK
OWNS ME', the other with a simple tendril
in Romanesque style. The blade has a deep
and narrow fuller. Found with remains of a
wood-and-leather scabbard and shield
mounts.

The combination of 5-lobed pommel and
curved guard with central point has its best
parallels on 14th–15th gravestones from the
West Highlands of Scotland which probably
have earlier prototypes. The tendril on the
Norwegian grip-mount seems to be 12th
cent. The inscription appears to be the oldest
known swordsmith's signature in Scandinavia.   **EBH**

Bibl.: Grieg 1933, 268; *Norges Innskrifter med de Yngre
Runer* I, 1941, 66; Hoffmeyer 1954, I, 35, II, pl. IIIa

b

c

558a

d

558

Iron.
Marikkovaara in Rovaniemi, Lappland,
Finland.
12th cent. West European, Finnish.
Finlands Nationalmuseum, Helsinki, 3631:1–4

Weapons of a Lappland traveller

a Sword with discoid pommel and long
guard; one face of the blade inscribed GISE-
LIN ME FECIT, the other INNOMINE DO-
MINI. L. 97.5cm. *b* Spearhead with socket
and rhomboid blade; the central part of the
blade is skilfully pattern-welded. L. 40.9cm.
c Spearhead with tang and 2 barbs. L.
22.3cm. *d* Finnish working-axe with curved

back and shaft lappets, decorated with a simple groove around the neck. L. 15.9cm.

The objects were discovered just below ground surface on Marikkovaara mountain, Lappland, probably left by a traveller to Lappland who lost his way in the wilderness sometime in 12th cent. **PLLH**

Bibl.: Leppäaho 1964, 58–9, 122–3; Tomanterä 1978, 31–2

559

Beech.
Stakes: H. 336cm; 295cm. Floater:
L. 390cm.
Helnæs, Fyn, Denmark.
Second half of 11th cent. Danish.
Vikingeskibshallen, Roskilde, 3215/3216, 3410,
3411

Timbers from sea blockade

Two stakes and a floater. The stakes have a rectangular cross-section in the upper 2m and a point *c.* 1.3m long cut like a double cone. The floater has pointed ends and a thickening around the stake holes.

The timber forms part of a blockade between Helnæs and Illumø on Fyn, which consisted of a series of single elements: 2 stakes and a floater placed *c.* 1.25m apart, lengthways to the direction of the fairway. This prevented the passage of ships and may have stretched for 500–700m. It was probably erected as a defence against the Wends. **JSM**

Bibl.: Crumlin-Pedersen 1973; 1985

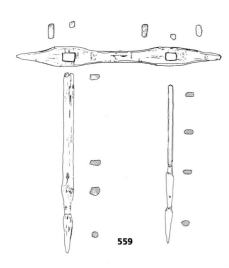

559

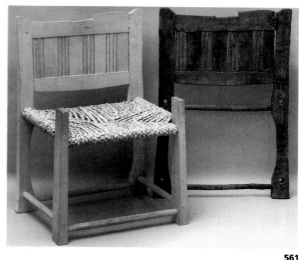

561

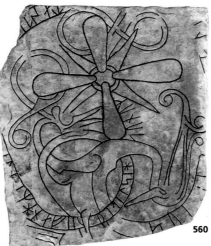

560

560

Red sandstone. H. 92cm.
Sigtuna, Uppland, Sweden.
Second half of 11th cent. Scandinavian
(Sigtuna).
Sigtuna Museums, U395

Rune stone

The earliest information about this stone is from the beginning of 17th cent. when it lay in front of the high altar in the ruined church of St Per. Even then it was fragmentary. Despite its damaged state, the inscription is of great interest, ' ... Sven ... raised the stone ... who brought her to Sigtuna ...'. Sven presumably brought his female relative (?wife) to Sigtuna for Christian burial, where the stone originally stood in St Per's churchyard. Apart from the abbreviated forms on the coins of Olof Skötkonung and Anund Jakob, this is the earliest local mention of the town's name. **TS**

Bibl.: *Sveriges runinskrifter* VII, 1943–46; Åneman 1989

561

Wood (maple and beech).
H. 75cm.
Lund (Kv Färgaren 22), Sweden.
1000–1050. Scandinavian.
Kulturen, Lund, KM 53.436:1065

Chair back and reconstruction

The chair back is of maple apart from the cross pieces which are of beech. The parts are jointed together by mortise-and-tenon and in the upper cross-pieces the tenons are secured by trenails. The chair has been reconstructed using the same types of wood as used in the original, with a straw seat (although the seat could have been made of other materials). In the Viking Age such luxurious chairs were unusual and this must have belonged to a person of high rank. A chair symbolized power; ordinary people would have sat on the floor, on raised earth benches, on whatever came to hand, or on stools (cat. no. 70). The chair back has been interpreted as part of a bishop's throne but this has since been discounted for the find context is essentially secular. Its method of construction has its origins in the Classical world. **CW**

Bibl.: Blomqvist and Mårtensson 1963, 218–21; Graham-Campbell 1980, no. 28

562

564
Wood.
H. 56.0cm.
Trondheim, Norway.
c. 1100–1150. Scandinavian.
Vitenskapsmuseet, Trondheim, N30000/FH415

Decorated plank (*Illustrated p. 139*)

Plank decorated in Urnes style. A rebate and a slot for another plank on left edge. Decorated in flat relief. It shows an animal head with gaping jaws, mane and almond-shaped eye. Probably part of an elaborately decorated chest, bench or chair. The head entwined with knots and loops. From an excavated timber building on the Public Library Site. Similar decorated planks, once parts of pieces of furniture were found in other houses on the site. They show that the small timber buildings not only had the spartan furnishings of a hearth and earth benches along the walls, but were often provided with free-standing pieces of furniture. They demonstrate a highly developed tradition of wood carving. **AC/EJ**

Bibl.: Graham-Campbell 1980, no. 454; Fuglesang 1981d; Christophersen 1987, 52 f.

562
Wood (beech).
L. 46.5cm.
Lund (Kv Färgaren 25), Sweden.
c. 1050. Scandinavian.
Kulturen, Lund, KM 71.075

Child's chair

Only the back and one side were found but they have enabled a convincing reconstruction of the whole object to be made: five pieces joined by mortise-and-tenon. Children's chairs were used throughout Europe until modern times and numerous variants are known in 19th-cent. They were chairs in which children could be confined so that they would need little attention. This is the earliest known example; the earliest illustration of one is Swiss (1601). **CW**

Bibl.: Lindström 1979; Wahlöö 1986

565
Wood.
L. 39cm.
Sandnæs (Kilaarsarfik), Ameralla, Ruin group 64V2-III-511(V51), Greenland.
?11th cent. Scandinavian.
Danmarks Nationalmuseum, Copenhagen, D12016

?Arm of a chair

Rectangular cross-section with rounded corners; it tapers towards one end where it terminates in a three-dimensional animal head with gaping mouth and large teeth. Behind the left jaw is an incised runic inscription *halki*, probably the man's name Helge. On its upper surface are 3 animal heads in low relief. Found during excavations 1930–32 of an 11th-cent. house built of stone and turf. The function of the object is uncertain, perhaps the arm of a chair or a tiller. **JA**

Bibl.: Moltke 1936; Roussell 1936; Krogh 1982, 158

563

563
Pine (pinus sylvestris).
H. 68.3cm.
Gaulverjabær, S. Iceland.
11th cent. Scandinavian.
Islands Nationalmuseum, Reykjavík, 1974: 217

Decorated plank

The plank is part of a composite object, probably a piece of furniture (chair or bench). The original length survives, rounded at the top. Ringerike-style plant decoration is carved on the front. Four secondary, triple concentric rings are scratched above the original design. The plank is a stray find (1974) from a recently demolished outhouse; it may have been part of its roof-lining. **TM**

Bibl.: Magnússon 1974

565

566

566

Wood.
H. 53cm.
Schleswig (Old Town), Germany.
End 12th cent. Scandinavian.
Archäologisches Landesmuseum, Schleswig,
SL1.73.11.17

Cradle

The narrow end of a cradle with rockers.
Legs and side have a zig-zag pattern. The
side, dowelled into the legs, has an opening
at the top to serve as a handle. The outer face
decorated with carving. The runner of oak;
the legs and side of ash.

The cradle is the earliest example of a
long-lived type. It is known from illustrations *c.* 1300 and was in use in the countryside until the 20th cent. This is the earliest
extant example.   **VV**

Bibl.: Zglinicki 1979

567

Wood.
Diam. 13.7cm.
Trondheim, Norway.
c. 1100. Scandinavian.
Vitenskapsmuseet, Trondheim, N38082/FF2025

Decorated bowl

Bowl with relief decoration on exterior. The
decoration consists of a band with 3 (originally 4 or 5) two-looped union knots. Parts
of the rim missing.

From a dwelling on the Public Library
Site. Probably a drinking vessel.   **AC/EJ**

Bibl.: Nordeide 1989

567

568

Wood.
H. 17.7cm.
Trondheim, Norway.
End 10th cent. Scandinavian.
Vitenskapsmuseet, Trondheim, N40837/FA740

Decorated hook

Carved from a flat piece of wood. The hook
is decorated on both faces as an animal with
mouth, eyes, mane, hip, etc. It has a hole for
suspension. Found in one of the oldest dwellings on the Public Library Site, dated 1004
by dendrochronology.

The hook is in a form of the Ringerike
style in which curves and foliage are atypical.
Its function is unknown, possibly a yoke.

AC/EJ

Bibl.: Fuglesang 1981d; Nordeide 1989

569

Wood.
L. 18.7cm.
Trondheim, Norway.
c. 1075–1150. Norwegian.
Vitenskapsmuseet, Trondheim, N36697/Fe1043

Decorated spoon

Little of the bowl is preserved. The handle is
complete and decorated in Urnes style with
interlaced animals with double contour. The
background is engraved with fine parallel
lines.

This spoon belongs to a group of some 20
decorated in the Urnes style, found by excavations on the Public Library Site. Some of
the spoons, including this, display a sophisticated carving technique suggesting that they
were made by a professional craftsman.
Others are simpler and smaller, indicating
attempts to copy professional examples. **AC/EJ**

Bibl.: Fuglesang 1981d; Christophersen 1987, 50f.

570

Bone.
L. 17.5cm.
Trondheim, Norway.
c. 1075–1150. Norwegian.
Vitenskapsmuseet, Trondheim, N93241/Fu433

Decorated spoon

Decorated in basketwork pattern with incised background (cf. cat. no. 571).

This (from the Public Library Site) is one
of the few early bone spoons. Most contemporary spoons are of wood. The accomplished angular interlace decoration is also
unusual, most contemporary spoons being
decorated in Urnes style. Heavy wear on the
bowl shows that the spoon was well used.

AC/EJ

Bibl.: Christophersen 1987, 50f.

568

569

570

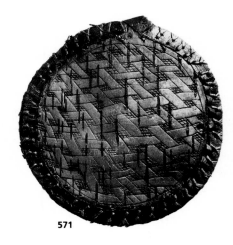

571

573

571
Birch bark.
Diam. 17.5cm.
c. 1025–1075. Norwegian.
Vitenskapsmuseet, Trondheim, N39662/FF2060

Decorated lid

Around the edge a band is sewn to the lid with birch-root fibres. On the underside the remains of a flange to fit the box.

Norway has a long tradition of boxes made of birch bark or wood shavings. They were used for transporting or preserving food, seed, etc. This lid from the Public Library Site fitted a round box. It is competently made and decorated with a basket-work pattern against a hatched background, unusual at this date. **AC/EJ**

Bibl.: Christophersen 1987, 88f.

573
Earthenware (A ware).
H. 11.0cm.
Lund (Kv Färgaren 22, Kv Gyllenkrok), Sweden.
1000–1050. Scandinavian.
Kulturen, Lund, KM 53.436:848, KM 76.420:164

Pottery vessels

The pots are not wheel-thrown and were fired at a fairly low temperature (400–600°). They represent a west Slav pottery tradition which dominated the household wares of south Scandinavia in the 11th and 12th cent. This small pot may have been a cooking pot, the larger one a storage vessel. Found buried in the floor of a mid 11th-cent. building. Its lid remains, which makes it unique. **CW**

Bibl.: Wahlöö 1976, no. 23

572

572

572
Wood; walrus ivory.
Board: l. 25.6cm. Piece: h. 3.3cm.
c. 1100–1150. Scandinavian.
Vitenskapsmuseet, Trondheim, N29723/FH414,
N38256/FE1043

Gaming board and gaming-piece

Little over half of a gaming board, now in 3 pieces. The field is divided into squares by incised parallel lines. A bordering rim, 7–8mm high, is fastened to the board with dowels. The board had been damaged and broken into two pieces and repaired by wedges on the back. The turned gaming-

piece is pear-shaped with flat base; the top broken. A hole in the base. Polished on upper surface. Both found on the Public Library Site.

The board was originally divided into 11x11 squares and was used for the game *hneftafl*, in which pieces were moved by casting a die (cf. cat. no. 71, 342, 360). In Trondheim *hneftafl* was replaced by chess in the mid-13th cent. Another game (tric-trac) is incised on the back of the board. **AC/EJ**

Bibl.: Christophersen 1987, 54f.; McLees 1990

574
Clay.
a H. 9.0cm.; *b* h. 6.0cm.
Bryggen, Bergen, Norway.
End 12th/early 13th cent. Rhenish.
Historisk Museum, Bergen, BM10004, BM9496

Two imported pots

a Beaker of Pingsdorf ware, neck decorated with red-brown lines. *b* Paffrath-ware handled ladle.

Little pottery was made in Norway and N Sweden during the Viking Age. Domestic vessels were made of wood, soapstone or metal. But pottery was imported alongside other more important materials into coastal centres. Pingsdorf pottery from the Rhineland was brought to Scandinavia mainly in 11th and 12th cent., mainly as table wares following the import of wine. Paffrath pottery was produced in the Rhineland with imitations elsewhere. The pots are cooking pots or ladles of highly-fired, white fabric with grey surfaces. Paffrath-ware pots are among the commonest imports into W Scandinavia in 12th cent. **PM**

Bibl.: Molaug 1977; Carlsson 1982; Davey and Hodges (ed.) 1983; Lüdtke 1985; Lüdtke 1989

575   Earthenware, glazed, red ware.
a H. 24.5cm; *b* H. 24.5cm.
Schleswig (Schild excavation), Germany.
13th cent. Scandinavian.
Archäologisches Landesmuseum, Schleswig

Two jugs

Two wheel-turned jugs with handles and external lead glaze. The glaze is brown-green and does not cover the whole surface. One has plastic decoration with floral motifs.

Glazed red wares first occur around the coast of S Scandinavia *c.* 1200, and from then make up some 10% of the pottery found. Most are wheel-turned jugs with plastic decoration, designed as table ware, the rest is kitchen ware. The lead glaze, usually covering only the upper part of the pots, must have been purely decorative. This pottery belongs to the group of highly decorated wares which were dominant along the NW coast of Europe in 13th cent. and widely traded. These jugs were probably produced locally in Schleswig. **HLü**

Bibl.: Lüdtke 1985

574a

574b

575

576   Volhynian schist (2); glass (2);
amber (1); pottery (1).
Sigtuna (Kv Trädgårdsmästaren 9 and 10),
Uppland, Sweden.
End 10th cent.—12th cent. Russian, W.
European, Sigtuna.
Sigtuna Museums, 7641, 9358; 5851, 7991;
9936; 27187

Spindle-whorls

Discovered during the excavation of a dwelling house. The same excavation also produced some 50 biconical spindle-whorls of Volhynian schist, a light-red stone found NW of Kiev, imported during 11th cent. Diam. 2.2cm; 2.9cm. A smaller group of imported glass spindle-whorls are conical, and of W European type; they occurred in 12th-cent. layers. Diam. 3.1cm; 2.5cm. Amber spindle-whorls are rare; they were probably lathe-turned in Sigtuna. Diam. 3.1cm.

576

The black pottery spindle-whorl came from a late 10th cent. dwelling, together with an upright loom, and lay by a carbonized wooden spindle and thread. Diam. 2.8cm.

BP

Bibl.: Deutgen 1990; Roslund 1990c

577

577

	Bone.
	L. 15.3cm.
	Lund (Kv S:t Clemens 8), Sweden.
	1000–1050. Scandinavian.
	Kulturen, Lund, KM 66. 166:885

Mount

Mount in form of a stylized dragon. The surface is polished. It may have embellished a scabbard and is an example of the rich bone and horn manufactures in Lund in the 11th and 12th cent. and distributed thence into the countryside: most of the its products were combs. **CW**

Bibl.: *Uppgrävt förflutet för PKbanken i Lund*, 1976, Pl.VII

578

	Elk antler.
	L. 23.8cm.
	Sigtuna (Kv Kyrkolunden), Uppland, Sweden.
	11th cent. Scandinavian.
	Sigtuna Museums, 432

Composite single-sided comb

(Illustrated p. 202)

The back plate is decorated with T-shaped perforations through which silver or bronze sheet could be seen. The comb's size and well-designed appearance suggest that it was a prestige object. There are engravings on each side, including the Christ child. Earliest Sigtuna (*c.* 970-first half of 11th cent.) had no established comb makers, the craftsmen were probably itinerant. Workshops were established in 11th cent. and have been found on Stora gatan. **JR**

Bibl.: Tesch 1987; Ros 1990. For comb-making cf. Christophersen 1980; Ambrosiani 1981

579

	Wood.
	H. 17.2cm; 20.0cm.
	Trondheim, Norway.
	c. 1175–1225; 12th cent. Scandinavian.
	Vitenskapsmuseet, Trondheim, N30304/FF810c,
	N5092/E399a

Two carved heads *(Illustrated also p. 142)*

a Stick terminating in head, from the Public Library Site. The head is 3-dimensional and shows either a face partly concealed by a mask with almond-shaped eyes and pro-

580

nounced ears, or a a lion with a man's head between its jaws. *b* Head at top of a pointed stick; oval eyes, a simple nose and mouth indicated by a thick line.

Figures with a head/face at the end of a short, straight stick are frequent finds in Trondheim and other medieval towns in Scandinavia. They must have had a specific purpose, perhaps as dolls (cf. cat. no. 580). **AC/EJ**

Bibl.: Long 1975; Christophersen 1987, 94f.

580

	Juniper.
	L. 13.5cm.
	Svendborg, Fyn, Denmark.
	c. 1100. Slav.
	Svendborg & Omegns Museum, Svendborg,
	10764

Peg with human heads—Svantevit

Pointed at one end, the other end terminating in 4 identical human heads with mouth, nose, eyes and pointed beard, all crowned with a single hat. It may be a traveller's souvenir of the Slav god Svantevit whose cult on Rügen is described by the historian Saxo *c.* 1200. Many-headed cult figures are known from the Slav area. Various other objects found in Svendborg and elsewhere in SE Denmark are of Slav origin or illustrate contacts with Slav lands. Slav settlement is indicated by place-names in the area. **HMJ**

Bibl.: Jansen 1988; 1989; 1990. Cf. Filipowiak 1985, 126f.

581

	Wood (box).
	L. 20.5cm.
	Lödöse, S Peder, Västergötland, Sweden.
	mid-12th cent. ?Danish.
	Statens Historiska Museum, Stockholm,
	27600:61:KA 152

Calendar stave

The stave has an entasis, rounded ends and rectangular cross-section. The four sides have 657 incised different symbols: straight lines, rune-like signs, crosses, etc. 631 single signs, 26 composite. There are 365 lines on the broad sides, i.e. the days in a year, with the winter months November-April on one side, and the summer months on the other. The signs are arranged in two rows and read from left to right and (below) right to left. The narrow sides carry groups of lines and dots. The dots indicate *dies Ægyptiaci* or *dies mali*, unlucky days—two in each month. Saints' days and their degree of sanctity are

581

also marked, as are concurrents (the numbers 1–7 which correspond to later calendars' Sunday letters), the phases of the sun and moon, i.e. everything necessary to work out the festivals of the year.

The calendar is unique in the North, its closest equivalent being a calendar in the lost manuscript *Hortus deliciarum* by Herrad von Landsperg of the 1170s.   **GT**

Bibl.: *Sveriges runinskrifter* V, 1940–70; Svärdström 1963

582

| 582 | Glass (5); amber (1). Sigtuna (Kv Trädgårdsmästaren 9 and 10), Uppland, Sweden. 12th cent. Polish or Russian. Sigtuna Museums, 4253, 3758, 2810, 3287, 5242; 2837 |

Finger-rings

a Glass: complete, plain, yellow, diam. 1.8cm. Late 11th-early 12th cent. *b* Glass: fragment, 'signet-ring shaped', yellow, diam. *c*. 2.7cm. 12th cent. *c* Glass fragment, plain, green, l. 2.0cm. *d* Glass: fragment, plain, blue-green with flecked surface, l. 2.1cm. 12th cent. *e* Glass: fragment, plain, blue-green, l. 1.6cm. Late 11th-early 12th cent. *f* Amber: complete, 'signet-ring shaped' with concentric circles and a cross on inner face, orange/translucent, diam. 2.7cm. 12th cent.

In the early Middle Ages rings were made of many materials other than metal. Sigtuna's occupation deposits sparkle with yellow and green glass rings and amber rings of shades of warm red. Their size suggests that many were worn by children. Glass-making was little practised in Sigtuna. We know that glass factories were at work in Poland and the Kiev region at this time and that these types of rings were made there.

The amber ring has many parallels in Novgorod and other places in the Kiev region. Raw material in the form of lumps of amber has been found together with finished products.   **MR**

Bibl.: Roslund 1990c

583

| 583 | Pewter/lead alloy and glass. Diam. *c*. 2cm. Sigtuna (Kv Trädgårdsmästaren 9 and 10), Uppland, Sweden. First half of 11th cent. Slav. Sigtuna Museums, 29504 |

Finger-rings

44 more or less complete finger-rings of pewter/lead alloy with polished, thin glass bezels. They were found during excavation and lay together, buried in the floor beside a long wall in one of the dwellings from first half of 11th cent. The rings may be divided into three types : with large round bezels, small round bezels, and rectangular bezels. The rings with small round bezels have plant ornament around the outside of the rings. All are cast and soldered, and the rings in their respective groups are virtually identical. The rarity of pewter/lead alloy objects of this date suggest that these were precious items. Their origin is uncertain but as no pewter is known from 11th-cent. Scandinavia they must be imports.   **BP**

Bibl.: Drenzel and Henriksson 1990

584

584 Sigtuna (Kv Trädgårdsmästaren 9 and 10), Uppland, Sweden. 12th cent. Sigtuna Museums, 765, 2604; 303, 1112, 1472, 2763, 7313; 5267

Rock crystal: raw material, crystals for mounting, bead

9 unpolished crystals; 5 polished crystals, ready for mounting (2 convex, 2 round convex, 1 flat faceted); 1 gadrooned bead with perforation.

The working of rock crystal into beads and mounts has left few traces. Finds from Sigtuna suggest that polishing took place there in the mid and late 12th cent. Products of rock crystal were probably made for an aristocrat. The mounts may have been intended for crucifixes, reliquaries, book covers or pendants; the smaller ones for signet rings. The bead, dated 11th cent., was probably from a necklace. JR

Bibl.: Dock 1990

585 Lilla Rone, Lye, Gotland, Sweden. 11th–12th cent. Gotland and ?eastern. Statens Historiska Museum, Stockholm, 8315

Rock-crystal pendants and silver beads

a 3 pendants of rock-crystal with stamped and embossed mounts of silver-gilt foil and omega-shaped silver-foil loops; diam. of spheres 2.6cm—4.2cm; *b* 11 round or oval lenses of rock-crystal with silver-foil frames of granulation, and silver-foil loops with stamped decoration, diam. 2.1cm—3.0cm; *c* 10 silver-foil beads with granulation or, in one case, filigree, l. 0.8cm—2.3cm.

Rock-crystal pendants with silver mounts are often found in Gotland hoards. The rock-crystal is of high quality and usually shaped into lenses with a pronounced convex front and flat back. Similar rock crystals are known from jewellery and book-bindings in western Europe but are never mounted in the same way as those from Gotland. The granulation on the mounts is Slav in character, but no similar pendants are known from Slav hoards. They have been found only in Finland, Estonia, and Latvia. Gotland silversmithing displays many signs of eastern contacts (cf. cat. no. 143), and these pendants

585

may have been made on Gotland. The beads with granulation are of mainly Russian character but were probably also made on Gotland. **IJ**

Bibl.: Stenberger 1947–58, vol. 1, 214ff., 201ff., vol. 2, 143f., Abb. 248:1–3, 5; Graham-Campbell 1980, no. 157; Duczko 1983, 347ff., fig. 23

587

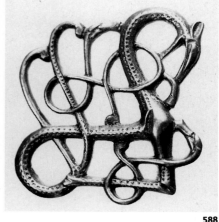

588

586

586

586
Bronze.
Diam. 3.2cm; 2.6cm.
Lund (Kv S:t Clemens 8, Kv Färgaren 22), Sweden.
1000–1050; 1040–1050. Scandinavian.
Kulturen, Lund KM, 53.436:621; KM 53.436:549

Two brooches

By the mid-11th cent. Byzantine coins were very influential on minting in Lund and the picture of two angels flanking a flag is derived from a coin minted under Emperor Michael IV (1034–41). The moneyers in Lund were often also goldsmiths and so the rather distorted pictures on coins were also used to decorate brooches. The brooch with the interlaced cross was probably made in Lund and has its roots in native style. The brooches demonstrate the importance of the goldsmith's trade in 11th-cent. Lund. **CW**

Bibl.: Blomqvist and Mårtensson 1963, 192–4; Mårtensson 1968

587
Gold, stones.
Diam. 5.2cm.
Gran, Hadeland, Norway.
Late 12th cent. Scandinavian or German.
Universitetets Oldsaksamling, Oslo, C.968

Brooch

Rosette-shaped brooch with domed centre cast in one with lower rim. Centre decorated with alternating stones and filigree spirals with granulated beads, an oval amethyst, keeled cut, in the middle. The rim has settings for 4 precious stones, interspaced by groups of 3 hemispheres decorated with filigree.

The type is common in 11th–13th cent. The large, dense filigree spirals place this brooch at end 12th cent. Gran was a power centre in the early Middle Ages. **EHB**

Bibl.: Meyer 1935

588
Silver.
B. 4.6cm.
Tröllaskógur, S Iceland.
c. 1100. Scandinavian.
Islands Nationalmuseum, Reykjavík, 6524

Urnes-style brooch

The openwork brooch is formed as a sinewy stylized animal entwined by two snakes. Two parallel rows of dots with niello embellish the animal's body and legs. The brooch is one of the finest of the many Urnes-style brooches from Scandinavia (cf. cat. no. 38, 589). It is a stray find from a deserted farm. One other Urnes-style brooch in copper alloy is known from Iceland. **VÖV**

Bibl.: Eldjárn 1956, 415–6; Eldjárn 1973, no. 52; Graham-Campbell 1980, no.151

589
Baked clay (mould) and bronze.
H. (brooch) 2.5–2.7cm.
Lund (Kv S:t Clemens 8), Sweden.
1100–1150. Scandinavian.
Kulturen, Lund, KM 66.166:2627, 2613, 2612, 2626

Mould and three Urnes-style brooches *(Illustrated p. 199)*

The objects come from the site of a workshop. The brooches are not finished. The animal is in Urnes style. There are other examples of the production of Urnes-style brooches in Lund and the area of distribution was wide (cf. cat. no. 588). **CW**

Bibl.: Bergman and Billberg 1976, 206–12; Graham-Campbell 1980, no.440

590a

590d

591

590b

590c

590e

590f

590g

590
Iron, bronze, pottery, antler, stone. Stöng, S Iceland. 11th–13th cent. Islands Nationalmuseum, Reykjavik, *a* 1356; *b* Stöng 1983:25; *c* 13880; *d* 13829; *e* 1.7.1971; *f* 13878; *g* Stöng 1984:15

Stöng in Thjórsárdalur: selected finds

a Ard or plough-share of iron. L. 38.5. The type was commonly used to plough hillside fields in the high Middle Ages. Limited arable farming took place in Iceland in the Viking Age and Middle Ages but deteriorating climate led to its total abandonment in the 16th cent. *b* Needle case. L. 4.5cm. Cast cylinder with ribs and three 'teeth' with ring-and-dot decoration. No exact parallels known, but it resembles 11th–12th-cent. east-Scandinavian needle cases. *c* Potsherd. L. 3.0cm. Hard-fired grey sherd, horizontally ridged surface and olive-green glaze. Grimston ware from East Anglia, England; early 13th cent. *d* High-backed single-sided comb of ivory. L. 19.1cm. The type dates from mid-12th and early 13th cent. *e* Spindle-whorl of soapstone. Diam. 5.1cm. Imported stone, probably from Norway. *f* Lamp of local volcanic tufa. L.10.3; b. 4.9. *g* Grindstone, fragment. L. 4.5cm. The stone (sandstone) probably came from Ireland where similar examples have been found in Dublin and dated 11th–12th cent.

The objects come from the farm of Stöng in the deserted valley of Thjórsárdalur, excavated 1939 and 1983–6. Stöng was long considered to have been destroyed by the eruption of Mt Hekla in 1104. Recent investigations suggest that the farm was abandoned at the beginning of the 13th cent. because of climatic deterioration, erosion and repeated volcanic eruptions of Hekla. Before the catastrophe, Stöng was a comparatively large and rich farm. **VöV**

Bibl.: Roussell 1943, 72–97; Vilhjálmsson 1988; Vilhjálmsson 1989

591
L. 16cm. Igaliku (Gardar), Ruin group 60V2-IV-Ø47), Greenland. Medieval. Zoologisk Museum, Copenhagen, ZMK9/1926

Fragment of walrus skull

The skull has signs of chopping to remove the tusks. It is one of the 20–30 fragments of walrus skull and 4–5 narwhal skulls found in 1926 in the church and churchyard at Gardar (20 skulls lay in a heap by the E gable of the church). The site is probably an indication of the great significance of walrus for the economy of the Norse Greenlanders.

Medieval written sources mention tusks of walrus and narwhal among the most important exports of Greenland; through this trade they maintained contact with the outside world. Walrus, and particularly narwhal, live off northern Greenland; the hunters had to sail north along the west coast to Disco Bay and even further in order to find them. They must also have obtained them through barter with the Inuit. Narwhal bones are rare in farm middens and probably only the tusks were brought home from the hunting trips, but cranial bones of walruses have ben found on many farms in Greenland, as in towns in Scandinavia and in Dublin (cat. no. 593). The tusks were probably brought back in pairs, still attached to the skull. **JA**

Bibl.: Degerbøl 1929, 183–92; Nørlund 1934b, 90–8

Detail 592

592 L. 48cm; 30.5cm.
Rømmen, Åfjord, Sør-Trøndelag, Norway.
Prob. *c.* 1100–1300. Scandinavian.
Vitenskapsmuseet, Trondheim, T2383a+b

Two walrus tusks

One tusk incomplete, cut at one end, with a runic inscription: *Ketil(l) á* (Ketill owns this). The other carries *OSSK* in Latin letters. Found in a crevice in the hillside a little above Rømmen farm, on the coast slightly N of the mouth of Trondheim fjord. Probably deposited for safekeeping as the runic inscription shows ownership. Walrus tusks were obtained from N Norway, the White Sea or Greenland and used for fine carving in Scandinavia and many places in W Europe. **KSo**

Bibl.: *Norges Innskrifter med de Yngre Runer* V, 1960, no. 451

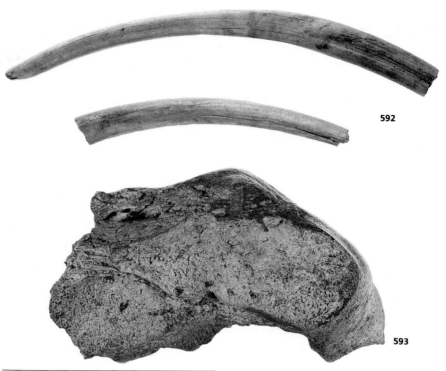

592

593

594 L. 9.4cm.
Dublin (Fishamble Street), Ireland.
11th cent. Hiberno-Norse.
National Museum of Ireland, Dublin, E172:9314

Walrus tusk fragment

Curved, cut section of walrus ivory. Two smoothed flattened edges were made by cutting pin roughouts. The underside is partly smoothed but still displays many chop marks. This fragment is similar in section to the piece cut from the skull and tusk fragment (cat. no. 593). Sections like this were cut and roughly worked from complete tusks and rough-outs were then cut for pins. **DC**
Unpublished

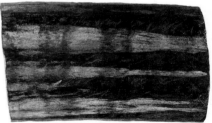

594

593 H. 14.3cm.
Dublin (Fishamble Street), Ireland.
11th cent. Hiberno-Norse.
National Museum of Ireland, Dublin, E172:4311

Walrus skull and tusk fragment

A number of chop and cut marks show where the ivory was removed and where there has been subsequent working and polishing. Part of the ivory is still attached to the skull. A small drill hole cuts into the ivory at one side.

Such material suggests that the skull frontal was hacked off the walrus with the tusks still intact. The polishing and working visible on this piece would have been done in Dublin. Walrus-ivory pins are relatively common in the excavated material here (cf. cat. no. 594), most of the finished pieces having highly decorated, zoomorphic heads. **DC**
Unpublished

595 Walrus ivory. H. 3.0cm; 2.5cm.
Dublin (Fishamble Street), Ireland.
11th cent. Hiberno-Norse.
National Museum of Ireland, Dublin

Gaming-piece and rough-out

The rough-out is of a conical gaming-piece; the surface has a number of cut marks and is split in two places; the edges around the base are flat. The finished gaming-piece is well rounded at the base and polished to a smooth surface; there are polishing marks and one cut mark. Both pieces are pierced at the base; they may have been intended for use on a peg board with the hole in the base holding a metal peg. **DC**
Unpublished

595

595

596

596

Walrus ivory.
L. 5.3cm.
Lund (Kv Glambeck 4), Sweden.
12th cent. ?Scandinavian.
Kulturen, Lund, KM 59.126:768

Comb

The comb is made from one piece, the central field on one side is decorated with a dragon whose body is formed by a plant tendril. It may come from the Rhenish area where similar combs are known, but equally, may have been made in Lund, as the type of ivory and the comparatively poor standard of carving indicate.   CW

Bibl.: Mårtensson and Wahlöö 1970, no. 82

598

Elephant ivory.
Sigtuna (Kv Trädgårdsmästaren 9 and
10), Uppland, Sweden.
c. 1100—early 12th cent. Byzantine—East
Mediterranean.
Sigtuna Museums, 8287, 14057

Two liturgical combs

a Single-sided comb with decoration in relief. On each side a backward-looking bird of prey. A secondary perforation at one edge. L. 8.8cm. *b* Double-sided comb with decoration in relief. On one side a backward-looking lion and secondary runic inscription *kunt*. Two heraldically opposed birds of prey on the other side, one backward-looking. L. 7.9cm.

The combs were found in two neighbouring urban plots. The same excavation also produced 2 fragmentary ivory combs. The plots lie 50m NE of the church of St Gertrud, probably the bishop's church. Another ivory comb has been found W of the church. Sigtuna was the seat of a bishop from at least the 1060s until the see moved to Gamla Uppsala at some time between 1134 and 1164.

Apart from one example from Lund (cat. no. 597) these are the only combs of this type found in Sweden. Frequent motifs, sometimes in a barbarized or misunderstood form, are lions, eagles and peacocks, and the tree of life. The creatures are often heraldically opposed and backward-looking. The double-sided comb is almost identical to one in the Louvre and also to combs discovered at Caravec, Bulgaria, and Corinth, Greece. The single-sided comb is of the same type as two others found in Sigtuna and the comb from Lund. They are assumed to be designed for liturgical use and formed part of altar furnishings. When Christianity was introduced into Scandinavia the usual practice was for the officiating priest to comb his hair before mass, using a special comb, whereby all thoughts of sin and everyday life were cleansed away. *Missale Lundense* from the beginning of 12th cent. states that while the priest combed his hair he should pray 'Corripe me, Domine, in misericordia tua'. ST

Bibl.: Roslund 1990c; cf. Ferté 1961, 127; Slavcev 1990, 56–60

597

597

Elephant ivory.
L. 11.8cm.
Lund (Kv Färgaren 22), Sweden.
1000–1050. East Mediterranean.
Kulturen, Lund, KM 53.436:781

Comb

The comb is made in one piece and is decorated with a duck and, on the other face, two lions. This is a luxury object which reached Europe from the eastern Mediterranean (cf. cat. no. 598). Originally interpreted as a foreign intrusion into its find context, it was mistakenly considered to be simple and poor. Such combs are frequently described as liturgical.   CW

Bibl.: Blomqvist & Mårtensson 1963, 216–8; Andrén 1980

598b

598b

598 a

598 a

599

Walrus ivory.
H. 4.8cm.
L'Office des Biens privés.
c. 870–80. From the court of Charles the Bald.
Paris, Museé du Louvre, Paris, OAR 369 A,B.

Two panels from a casket or portable altar *(Illustrated p. 205)*

Both panels have representations of two apostles standing in mountainous terrain. They come from the same object (?casket or portable altar) as three corresponding panels now in the musée Vivenel at Compiègne. All have been trimmed and were originally taller. The 'dancing' posture of the figures, their relatively slim proportions and the undulating landscape are features of work in the 'Liuthard style' characteristic of many ivories carved for Charles the Bald. The panels could be compared with the Virgin and the St. John of the Missal of St.-Denis, or possibly with the carved apostle-figures on caskets in Quedlinburg, Berlin and Munich. The panels from the Louvre and Compiègne are among the earliest surviving reliefs of high quality carved walrus-tusk of the Carolingian period. **DGC**

Bibl.: Rademacher 1942. Cf. Goldschmidt 1914, I, nos. 49–51, 58–62; Goldschmidt 1918, II, no.194

600

Walrus ivory.
H. 9.1cm.
Unknown provenance.
Last quarter of 10th cent. Anglo-Saxon.
The British Museum, London, M&LA 1974,10-2,1

Panel fragment *(Illustrated p. 205)*

Walrus-ivory openwork carving of the Baptism of Christ, in part cut down from a larger panel.

The panel is an outstanding example of the late Saxon Winchester style; the exaggerated gestures and fluttering draperies of the Baptist give a nervous animation to the piece which strongly recalls the great illuminated manuscripts of the Benedictine Re-

form Movement, such as *The Benedictional of St Ethelwold*. Indeed, the ivory may well have been mounted on the cover of such a book. **LW**

Bibl.: Goldschmidt 1926, IV, no. 18; Beckwith 1972, no. 14, pl. 35; Wilson 1984, 190, 193, pl. 266; Backhouse, Turner and Webster (eds.) 1984, no. 117; Williamson and Webster 1990, 185

601

Walrus ivory.
H. 9.6cm.
Unknown provenance.
c. 1000. Anglo-Saxon.
Danmarks Nationalmuseum, Copenhagen, D13324

Relief with crucifixion

Relief of Christ on the cross between Mary and John within an eight-lobed frame. Above the cross is the hand of God between two angels. Two rivet holes for attachment, probably to a book cover.

The colour is dark brown due to oxidation, suggesting that the piece was found in the ground. **FL**

Bibl.: Beckwith 1972, 144, no. 17a; *Ivory Carvings in Early Medieval England 700–1200*, no. 12; Liebgott 1985, 15

602

Walrus ivory.
H. 4.6cm.
Lund (Kv Kulturen 25), Sweden.
11th cent. Scandinavian.
Kulturen, Lund, KM 38.252

Gaming-piece

The gaming-piece depicts a bearded man sitting on a stool, holding his beard in both hands (cf. cat. no. 77). Ten ring-and-dots decorate his spine. The quality of the carving is poor. It may have been intended as a statuette of a god, the configuration of the ring-and-dots is vaguely reminiscent of a Thor's hammer. The simple chair on which he sits is of art-historical interest as similar chairs hewn from a single, massive, piece of wood are known from the Middle Ages. **cw**

Bibl.: Lindqvist 1962; Graham-Campbell 1980, no.99

601

602

603

603

604

605a

605b

603
Walrus ivory.
H. 4.8cm.
Jumièges, Seine-Maritime, France.
11th century. Anglo-Norman.
Musée départemental des Antiquités de Seine-
Maritime, Rouen, R90-96

Head of a Tau crozier

In the centre is a half-length figure of a man
with a book in one hand and a crozier in the
other; on the other side the figure of a
woman. The figures are flanked by circular
fields containing inhabited foliage. It is
strongly influenced by the Winchester style
and can be compared with the tau cross
from Le Mans in the Victoria and Albert
Museum, but differs in showing less precision of execution and being probably of
slightly earlier date.   **LF**

Bibl.: Goldschmidt 1926, IV, no.45; Gaborit-Chopin 1978,
94, no.120; *Trésors des abbayes normandes*, 1979, no.
269; *English Romanesque Art 1066–1200*, 1984, no.181.

604
Walrus ivory.
Diam 6.5cm.
Roskilde cathedral, Denmark.
c. 1150–1200. Danish.
Danmarks Nationalmuseum, Copenhagen, 9099

Seal matrix

Circular seal matrix with loop, showing the
bust of Pope Lucius, patron saint of Roskilde
cathedral, tonsured, without halo, with palm
branch and book in his hands. He is behind a
semicircular crenellated wall in front of the
two-towered west facade of the cathedral.
The inscription reads SIGIL.S.TRINITATIS
DOM(VS). On each side of the church
facade is LVCIVS and PAPA.

The seal was probably made in Roskilde.
The workshop of the bishopric must have
influenced many of the French-inspired
ivory objects of this period.   **PGH**

Bibl.: H. Petersen 1886, no. 192; Goldschmidt 1926, IV, no.
57; Liebgott 1985, 40

605
Walrus ivory.
a Diam. 5.6cm; *b* Diam. 5.9cm.
Vordingborg, S Sjælland, Denmark.
12th cent. *a* Scandinavian; *b* from Cologne or
England.
Danmarks Nationalmuseum, Copenhagen,
7139; D444/1978

Two gaming-pieces

a In relief, a bearded man grips two dragons
which curl their tails around his legs. Plain
edge. Presumably Scandinavian. *b* In high
relief, a monster with three bearded male
heads with Phrygian caps; it has 2 legs with
hoofs and a scaly twisted tail ending in an
acanthus leaf. Another acanthus in front of
the monster. Border with palmettes. Foreign
workmanship. Liebgott attributes it to Cologne; Lindahl to St Alban's, *c.* 1125–50. **FL**

Bibl.: Goldschmidt 1918, III, no. 246 *et passim*; Beckwith
1972; Lindahl 1980b; Liebgott 1985

606
Walrus ivory. L. 9.5cm.
c. 1150. Danish.
Danmarks Nationalmuseum, Copenhagen, 9113

Belt buckle

The buckle is decorated with three small roll-
mouldings of a type otherwise known from
goldsmiths' work (e.g. the Dagmar cross).
The workmanship is reminiscent of the
Gunhild cross (cat. no. 607) and the belt-
buckle from Lewis (cat. no. 614).   **FL**

Bibl.: Langberg 1982, 49, 71; Liebgott 1985, 26–7

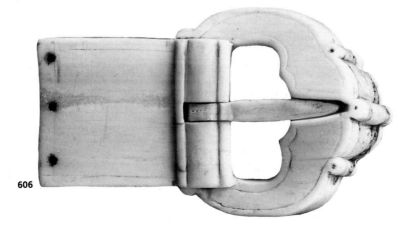
606

607   Walrus ivory. H. 28.4cm.
Owned by Sophie Brahe (d. 1646).
c. 1150. Danish, influenced by Continental art.
Danmarks Nationalmuseum, Copenhagen, 9087

The Gunhild cross *(Illustrated p. 203)*

Cross with roundels in relief. The figure of Christ on the front is missing but the halo is carved on the cross. The reliefs represent personifications of Life and Death, Church and Synagogue, with Latin inscriptions. On the back: Christ as Judge on a rainbow, with the Just and the Damned in the fields at the ends of the arms. Above: Lazarus in Abraham's bosom; below: the Rich Man in the embrace of the Devil.

Latin inscriptions refer to biblical texts from which the motifs are taken. On the sides of the cross are Latin inscriptions with prayers for 'Helena, daughter of the great King Sven' who had the cross made, and for 'Liutger who carved me at the request of Helena, also called Gunhild'. Thus the princess had both a Latin and a Danish name, the latter also being written in runes. There are traces of red and gold on the cross which must have been gilded all over. According to Langberg, Gunhild was the daughter of Sven Grathe (d. 1157) and not, as previously thought, the daughter of Sven Estridsen (d. 1074); a date which accords with the style of the cross.   **FL**

Bibl.: Goldschmidt 1918, III, no. 124; Jacobsen and Moltke 1942, no. 413; Christiansen 1976; Gaborit-Chopin 1978, 114 f.; Moltke 1985, 454–6; Langberg 1982; Liebgott 1985, 23 f.

608   Walrus ivory. H. 18.5cm.
No provenance.
c. 1130–50. Mosan (Liège) or North France
(Saint-Omer). Musée du Louvre, Paris OA2593

The Sibylle Cross

The cross is composed of several assembled pieces of walrus ivory (the body of Christ and the stem of the cross; the horizontal arms; and the end-sections of the stem). Christ, fastened to the cross with four nails, is surrounded by allegorical depictions: at the ends of the arms, the Sun and the Moon; above, the hand of God; below, a female figure, kneeling, and an inscription including the name Sibylle, who has been identified as Sibylle the daughter of Count Fulco of Anjou, who was married to Dietrich of Alsace, Count of Flanders. In 1157 she withdrew into the convent of St. Lazarus in Jerusalem, where she became abbess (d. 1163). The cross was fixed on a book-cover. Originally there were probably four symbols of the Evangelists in the corners of the cover (now in museums in Leningrad, Berlin and Munich). The cross is related to reliefs in walrus ivory thought to have been produced in the Meuse region or N. France. As with the reliefs from the portable altar with Saint-Denis (cat. no. 609), the Sibylle cross shows that walrus ivory was extensively used in these regions in the 12th century, even for extremely refined objects.   **DGC**

Bibl.: Molinier 1896, no.26; Goldschmidt 1918, III, no.18 (cf. nos. 19–22); Beckwith 1927, no. 87, fig.141; *Rhein und Maas*, 1972, 189, no. J15; Gaborit-Chopin 1978, 99

609   Walrus ivory (repaired with elephant ivory). H. 4.6cm.
Mid–12th cent. Ile de France.
Musée du Louvre, Paris, OA 2008, 2009

Two panels from a portable altar
(Illustrated p. 205)

The two openwork panels, of exceptional quality, formed the long sides of a rectangular object; a third, shorter panel which made up one of the other sides is also in the Louvre. The iconography indicates that it was a portable altar. On the long sides are two groups, each of six apostles, standing in arcades supported by pillars. The names of the apostles are carved in the arches of the colonnade, which are ornamented with beading. The ends of each panel are bordered by a vertical band of palmettes; monsters and fantasy animals disport themselves in the spandrels. The third panel (not exhibited) has similar ornament apart from the end-borders, where the palmettes are replaced by foliated scrolls. This panel has three figures: St Denis in the centre, the only figure with a halo, flanked by two companions in martyrdom, Rusticus and Eleutherius. The prominence given to St Denis and his companions suggests an association with the Abbey of Saint-Denis. None of the objects described in inventories of the Abbey's treasury, however, correspond to this portable altar. The style of the figures, strongly influenced by the art of the Meuse, and the English influences observable in the ornamentation, have parallels in the art of the Ile-de-France and particularly in Saint-Denis around the middle of the 12th century; this permits an attribution to the entourage of the Abbey, towards the end of Suger's abbacy (d. 1152).   **DGC**

Bibl.: Molinier 1896, nos. 38–40; Goldschmidt 1926, IV, no. 61; McCrosby 1970; Arquié-Bruley 1981, 88; *The Royal Abbey of Saint-Denis*, 1981, no. 28.

608

610

610   Walrus ivory. H. 15.5cm.
c. 1150. English or Danish.
Danmarks Nationalmuseum, Copenhagen, 10366

Figural group

Two figures in high relief. That in front, carrying a scroll, is probably Christ; that at the rear may be an apostle (or they may both be apostles). The figures are influenced by Byzantine and Continental styles of 11th cent. but seem to have been carved in England or Denmark. Rivet holes show that the mount was attached to a flat base, probably a book cover.   **FL**

Bibl.: Goldschmidt 1918, III, no. 40; Nørlund 1963; Liebgott 1985, 30 f.

611   Walrus ivory, copper, crystal.
L. 44cm.
Walrus tusk: 3rd quarter of 12th cent. Norwegian. Metal mounts: 14th cent. Scandinavian.
The British Museum, London, M&LA 1959,12-2,1

Reliquary   *(Illustrated p. 204)*

Walrus tusk carved on four faces with inhabited foliage scrolls, one end hollowed out for a relic; gilt-copper mounts set with a crystal added on the ends and a third crystal mounted in centre of one face.

It has been suggested that this was the leg of a throne, but it is more likely always to have been a reliquary; the 14th-cent. mounts replace earlier copper mounts (traces of green stains near each end). The tusk was no doubt selected to contain a relic because of its exceptional quality and size. Lasko showed how closely the inhabited foliage scrolls relate to the ornamental thrones of the Lewis Chessmen (cat. no. 615) whose artistic origin in western Norway seems reasonably assured. Parallels for the engraved grotesques and animals on the metal mounts exist in Norway and Sweden, perhaps an indication that the reliquary was in Scandinavia during the Middle Ages. **NS**

Bibl.: Lasko 1960; Taylor 1978; Gaborit-Chopin 1978, 113–4, 200, no. 164; *English Romanesque Art 1066–1200*, 1984, no. 211

613

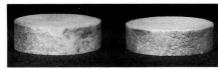

614

614

612

612   Walrus ivory. L. 9.4–12.5cm.
Found 1715, Munkholm, Trondheim fjord, Norway. End 12th cent. Norwegian.
Danmarks Nationalmuseum, Copenhagen, 9101

Mount

In relief on both sides is an inhabited vine scroll with lions in profile. The piece is trimmed at one end and has a square hole at the bottom; it may have been attached to a crozier. The plants and animals have parallels in stone carving and stave-churct stone carving and stave-church carvings in Trøndelag and other parts of Norway (cf. cat. no. 457, 611, 615).   **FL**

Bibl.: Goldschmidt 1918, III, no. 143; Kielland 1925; Lasko 1960, 12 f.; Blindheim (ed.) 1972, no. 47

613   Walrus ivory.
H. 2.8cm.
Lund (Kv Billegården), Sweden.
12th cent. Scandinavian.
Kulturen, Lund, KM 72.250:45

Chess piece, fragmentary

The fragment is a sawn-off part of a playing-piece (knight) with the front leg of the horse and the rider's feet in stirrups. It is similar to the Lewis pieces (cat. no. 615) which are attributed to Scandinavia. This fragment was found in the debris of a bone and antler workshop which specialized in combs.

There are a few other signs that walrus ivory was worked in Lund, but in this case the object is more likely to have come from a Norwegian workshop.   **CW**

Bibl.: Ryding and Kriig 1985

614   Walrus ivory.
Tablemen: diam. 5.2cm. Buckle:
l. 6.4cm.
Isle of Lewis, Outer Hebrides, Scotland.
Third quarter of 12th cent. Norwegian.
The British Museum, London, M&LA 1831,
11-1,68/70/76

Two tablemen and a belt buckle

Two undecorated tablemen, and a belt-buckle with incised foliage ornament.

The 14 tablemen found with the Lewis chessmen (cat. no. 615) are undecorated except for a circle finely incised with a pair of compasses around the edge; it is possible that they are in a roughed-out state for eventual carving. The belt buckle (cf. cat. no. 606) has foliage ornament similar to that on the chessmen but cut in shallow relief. This walrus-ivory carver did not specialize exclusively in gaming pieces.   **NS**

Bibl.: Dalton 1909, nos. 145, 147, 153, pl. XLVIII; Taylor 1978

615   Walrus ivory.
Max. h. 10.2cm.
Isle of Lewis, Outer Hebrides, Scotland.
Third quarter of 12th cent. Norwegian.
The British Museum M&LA 1831,11-1,1/7/13/37/
38/41/47/50/56

Nine chessmen   *(Illustrated also p. 104)*

King, queen, bishop, two knights, two warders and two pawns, from the deposit of 93 ivory chessmen, tablemen and a single belt-buckle (cf. cat. no. 614). These nine pieces give an idea of the variety of the Lewis chessmen, of which 78 survive in The British Museum and The National Museum of

Antiquities of Scotland (the remains of four nearly complete sets). The find, discovered in 1831 from a sandbank on Uig Bay, was poorly documented. It seems that the hoard was part of the stock of a merchant or walrus-ivory carver, either based in the Outer Hebrides or in transit; some pieces appear unfinished.

Stylistically the figures are without parallel in English art but the foliage ornament on the backs of the thrones is related to certain stone sculpture at Trondheim (cat. no. 444) and to early stave-church portals (p. 206, fig. 1) in western Norway. These monuments were influenced by English art of the early 12th cent. but in the Lewis find western Norway seems to have returned the compliment; Trondheim is documented as a centre of the walrus-ivory trade. A few similar walrus-ivory foliage carvings, including cat. no. 611, have no known provenance, but one (cat. no. 612) comes from Munkholm near Trondheim and a queen, recorded in an old drawing and virtually identical to the Lewis queens, was dug up in Trondheim in 1890 (cf. cat. no. 613).

The Outer Hebrides were politically part of the kingdom of Norway during 12th cent. and the Lewis hoard provides unique evidence of cultural links between the Western Isles and western Norway, as well as being the largest and most important series of chessmen to have survived from the Middle Ages. **NS**

Bibl.: Dalton 1909, nos. 78–144, pls. XXXVIII-XLVIII, particularly nos. 78, 84, 90, 114, 115, 118, 124, 127, 133; Goldschmidt 1926, IV, nos. 182–239, pls. LXIV-LXIX; Lasko 1960, 12–6, pls. VIII-X; Taylor 1978; *English Romanesque Art 1066–1200*, 1984, no. 212; McLees & Ekroll 1990

615

615

616

Iron.
L. 71.5cm.
Dale church, Sogn og Fjordane, Norway.
12th cent. ?Norwegian.
Historisk Museum, Bergen, MA58

Boat-shaped candlestick

Three-pronged candlestick in the shape of a long-ship standing on riveted legs. Vanes at stem and stern (cf. cat. no. 3, 417), red paint with white half-moons.

A similar candlestick is known from Urnes church. The type was not confined to churches; a boat-shaped candlestick is mentioned in a will of 1360s. **HVA/EBH**

Bibl.: Wallem 1907; Bendixen 1909, 37, no. 16

617

Willow, paint.
H. 119cm.
Urnes church, Sogn og Fjordane, Norway.
Second half of 12th cent. Scandinavian.
Historisk Museum, Bergen, MA46

Virgin   (Illustrated pp. 209, 392)

Hollowed out at back. Face with oil painting on thin chalk base, tunic and cloak in imitation gold (silver foil covered by yellow glaze). Hands have been mortised on separately (the left hand rather lower than the right). Christ child missing. The Virgin sits on a folding chair with dragon heads. She has plaited hair over her shoulders, conspicuous cloak, and crown with large fleurs-de-lis (partly restored). The tunic falls in oval shapes over the knees and spreads out fanwise between the legs.

The Virgin with plaits and cloak is not uncommon in the North; this figure is among the oldest. It has been placed stylistically with mid 12th-cent. French sculpture, but the striking coat-motif is primarily found on English Madonnas, as on seals from the same period. The type of wood suggests Scandinavian work. The saint's head from the same church (cat. no. 465) shows some similarities but is made of a different wood. **HVA/EBH**

Bibl.: Bendixen 1911, no. 12, 7; Hauglid 1940; Schjetlein Johannessen 1964; Andersson 1970a, 318; Heslop 1978

616

617

Dates 800–1200

Niels Lund

Scandinavia | | ## Europe

Scandinavia		Europe
The monastery of Lindisfarne sacked by Vikings on 8 June.	793	
	796	The Franks defeat the Avars between the Danube and Tisza.
	800	Imperial coronation of Charlemagne on Christmas morning in Rome.
Godfred, king of Denmark, destroys the Slav town of Reric and transfers the merchants to his own town of Schleswig.	808	
Murder of King Godfred.	810	
Danish royal expedition to Vestfold in South Norway to re-establish Danish overlordship.	813	
Harald Klak, ousted pretender to royal power in Denmark, takes	814	Death of Charlemagne. He is succeeded by his son Louis the Pious.
service with Louis the Pious, emperor of the Franks.	822/23	Pope Paschal I authorizes Ebo, archbishop of Rheims, to evangelize
Ebo, archbishop of Rheims, visits Denmark to evangelize.	823–24	"in the northern parts".
Danish coinage in Hedeby begins.	c. 825	The Irish monk Dicuil mentions the remote "Thule" (possibly
Harald Klak is baptized in Mainz and sent to Denmark with the missionary Ansgar in his following.	826	Iceland) and Irish hermits there, in his *De mensura orbis terrarum*.
Ansgar's first visit to the *Svear* in Birka.	829–31	The sons of Louis the Pious rise against him.
The monastery of Armagh in Ireland sacked by Vikings.	832	Ansgar consecrated to the newly created archdiocese of Hamburg.
Annual Viking attacks on Dorestad in Frisia.	834–37	New rising against Louis the Pious who is taken prisoner by his son Lothar. Viking raids on western Europe increase.
Intensive Viking activity in Ireland.	840	Death of Louis the Pious, who is succeeded by Lothar. The Vikings
Lothar, emperor of the Franks, grants Walcheren, an island in the	841	begin to penetrate the rivers of France.
Rhine estuary, to Harald Klak. In Ireland the harbours of Dublin and Annagassan are fortified.	843	Tripartition of the Carolingian empire agreed at Verdun. First recorded wintering of Danish Vikings in Francia.
	845	Sack of Hamburg and Paris. Ansgar's archbishopric is moved from Hamburg to Bremen. First Danegeld paid out by the Franks.
Ansgar with royal permission builds churches in Schleswig and Ribe.	850	
	851	First recorded wintering of Vikings in England, on Thanet.
Ansgar's second visit to Birka.	852–54	Olaf the White and Ivar control the Vikings in Ireland (853).
Horik I of Denmark dies in a civil war.	854	
	856–57	Paris is sacked by Vikings, and taken again in 861.
Horik II of Denmark sends gifts to Pope Nicholas I.	864	
The sons of Ragnar Lothbrok attack England.	865	Ansgar dies, and Rimbert succeeds to the archbishopric of Hamburg.
The Vikings conquer York.	866–67	Salomon, duke of Brittany, with Viking mercenaries, defeats the
The colonization of Iceland.	c. 870–930	Franks in the battle of Brissarthe.
The voyages of the north Norwegian chieftain Ohthere to the White	871–99	Alfred the Great king of Wessex.
Sea and to Hedeby; the Englishman Wulfstan's voyage in the Baltic.	876–79	The Vikings in England settle permanently.
	885–	Siege of Paris. Beginning of Danish coinage in England.
	886	Alfred the Great takes London from the Vikings.
The Olaf dynasty in Denmark. The battle in Hafrsfjord and Harald	890–	
Finehair's attempt to unite Norway.	891	Arnulf, king of the East Franks, defeats a Viking force near Louvain, on the river Dyle in Belgium.
	910	Foundation of the Cluniac order.
	911	Foundation of Normandy by Viking chieftain Rollo.
	c. 920	The Arab envoy Ibn Fadhlan meets Vikings on the Volga. The Danes in England submit to Edward the Elder 912–20.
Institution of the Althing on Iceland.	930	The Vikings expelled from Brittany in the 930s.
Henry the Fowler, German king, defeats the Danes.	934	
	936	Archbishop Unni of Hamburg-Bremen dies in Birka. Otto the Great
Bishops are appointed to Schleswig, Ribe and Århus, all in Jutland.	948	German king 936–73.
Fortification of Hedeby, Ribe and Århus. Hakon the Good, king of Norway, attempts to convert Norway.	c. 950	
	954	Expulsion of Erik Bloodaxe, formerly king of Norway, from York.
	955	Otto the Great defeats the Hungarians decisively at Lechfeld, south of Augsburg, on 10 August.
Gorm the Old, king of Denmark, is buried in Jelling.	958/59	Edgar king of England 957/59–75.
Harald Bluetooth king of Denmark 958–987.		
Harald Bluetooth restores Danish influence in Norway.	960–	
	962	Imperial coronation of Otto the Great.
Harald Bluetooth converts Denmark.	c. 965	
	966	Mieszko, duke of Poland, converts Poland.

Scandinavia

Europe

Scandinavia		Europe
Refortification of Danevirke by Harald Bluetooth.	968	
Foundation of Sigtuna.	c. 970	
Danes defeated by Emperor Otto II.	974	
	978–1016	Æthelred the Unready king of England.
Construction of the Ravning Enge bridge and the Danish circular fortresses.	c. 980	Vladimir the Great king of Russia 980–1015. The Irish conquer Dublin.
	982	Otto II, German emperor, is defeated badly by the muslims at Capo Colonne, south of Crotone in Calabria.
Harald Bluetooth reconquers the Danish borderland.	983	
Erik the Red settles in Greenland.	c. 985	
Death of Harald Bluetooth and burial in Roskilde; bishops consecrated in Hamburg expelled from Denmark. Sven Forkbeard king of Denmark 987–1014.	987	
	988	Conversion of Russia. Foundation of the Varangian guard in Constantinople by Basil II "the Bulgar-slayer", Byzantine emperor.
The first church in Lund in Skåne.	before 990	
	991	The battle of Maldon; the English are defeated and make the first in a long series of increasing payments of Danegeld.
Olaf Tryggvason takes service with Æthelred the Unready.	994	
Olaf Tryggvason unites Norway. Olof Skötkonung king of Sweden c. 995–c. 1022). Coinages of Norway, Sweden, Denmark and Dublin modelled on English types.	995–	
	999	A Polish archbishopric is created at Gniezno.
The Battle of Svold. The conversion of Iceland. Voyages from Greenland to Vinland (in America). Thjodhild's church at Brattahlid.	c. 1000	The Conversion of Hungary.
Conquest of England by Sven Forkbeard.	1013	Æthelred the Unready seeks refuge in Normandy at Christmas.
Death of Sven Forkbeard in Gainsborough on 3 Feb. His elder son Harald succeeds to Denmark (1014–18).	1014	The English recall Æthelred the Unready. Basil II blinds 15,000 Bulgarians. Brian Boru, king of Dál Cais and 'high-king of all Ireland', defeats an alliance of his Irish enemies with Vikings at Clontarf but looses his own life.
Olaf Haraldsson, future St Olaf, conquers Norway. Olof Skötkonung, king of Sweden, has bishops for Sweden consecrated in Hamburg.	1015–	
Conquest of England by Knut the Great, son of Sven Forkbeard.	1016	
Olaf Haraldsson, with the support of the English bishop Grimkell, has a Christian code passed at the Moster Thing.	1022	
	1024–1125	The Salian dynasty in Germany.
Knut the Great faces the kings of Norway and Sweden and Ulf, his regent in Denmark, at the battle of the Holy River.	1026	
Murder of Earl Ulf in Roskilde. The first stone church in Scandinavia is built in Roskilde.	1027	Knut the Great visits Rome and witnesses the imperial coronation of Konrad II.
Olaf Haraldsson, king of Norway, is expelled.	1028	
Olaf Haraldsson is killed in the Battle of Stiklestad 29. July.	1030	
Olaf Haraldsson, Saint Olaf, is enshrined.	1031	Dissolution of the Caliphate of Cordova.
Knut the Great dies and is succeeded in Denmark by Harthaknut 1035–42, in Norway by Magnus the Good 1035–47.	1035	Harald Harefoot king of England 1035–40. In Spain the *Reconquista* begins.
Ingvar's disastrous expedition to the east.	c. 1040	
Magnus the Good reunites Denmark and Norway 1042–47.	1042	Edward the Confessor king of England 1042–66.
Magnus defeats the Slavs near Schleswig.	1043	
Magnus the Good is succeeded in Denmark by Sven Estridsen, in Norway by Harald Hardråde 1047–66.	1047	Imperial coronation of Henry III, king of Germany, in Rome. Pope Clement II confirms the rights of the archbishopric of Hamburg-Bremen in Scandinavia.
A bishop from Hamburg is appointed to Orkney.	c. 1050	
Earl Thorfinn of Orkney visits Rome.	1054	Mutual excommunication of the pope in Rome and the patriarch of Constantinople.
Creation of the first bishopric of Iceland, at Skálholt.	1056	
Division of Denmark into 8 dioceses: Schleswig, Ribe, Århus, Viborg, Vendsyssel, Odense, Roskilde and Lund; Sigtuna is made a bishopric.	c. 1060	In 1059 a Lateran council banned lay investiture and thereby started the Investiture Struggle. Philip I king of France 1060–1108.
Olaf Kyrre king of Norway 1066–93.	1066	Harald Hardråde, king of Norway, falls at Stamford Bridge; William, duke of Normandy conquers England.
	1071	The Normans capture Bari from the Byzantines. Alp Arslan defeats the Byzantines at Manzikert. The Turks conquer Jerusalem.
Sven Estridsen dies and is succeeded by five sons in turn.	1076	Pope Gregory VII excommunicates Henry IV, king of Germany and Roman emperor.
The oldest known diploma in Scandinavia: Grant of land and immunities to St Lawrence at Lund, by Knut, king of Denmark.	1085	Knut, king of Denmark, and Robert, count of Flanders, prepare to attack England. Toledo is captured from the muslims.
Knut, king of Denmark (St Knut), is killed in St Alban's, Odense.	1086	The making of *Domesday Book* in England.
	1091	Norman conquest of Sicily.
	1095	Alexios Komnenos, Byzantine emperor, appeals to the West for help against the Turks. Pope Urban II preaches the crusade at Clermont.
Erik Ejegod king of Denmark 1096–1103.	1096	The first crusade 1096–99.
	1099	The conquest of Jerusalem. Foundation of the Cistercian order 1098.
King Magnus Barefoot asserts the Norwegian overlordship of the Western Isles and conquers Dublin.	c. 1100	El Cid, the Spanish national hero, dies.

Scandinavia   ## Europe

Scandinavia	Date	Europe
Enshrinement of St Knut, king of Denmark, killed 1086, in Odense.	1100	Henry I king of England 1100–1135.
Foundation of the first monasteries in Norway: Selje, Nidarholm and Munkeliv near Bergen.	1100–10	
Lund in Skåne is made the metropolis of all Scandinavia.	1103	
Niels king of Denmark 1104–34.	1104	
Hólar becomes the second bishopric of Iceland.	1106	
Crusade of Sigurd Jorsalfar, king of Norway.	1107–11	
	c. 1110	The *Russian Primary Chronicle* is compiled in Kiev.
The *Florence-List* mentions the first diocesan division of Sweden, and Finland occurs under the name *Findia*.	c. 1120	The Cistercian *Carta Caritatis* 1119.
	1122	Settlement of the Investiture Struggle through the Concordat of Worms.
Ari Thorgilsson composes *Íslendingabók*.	1122–33	
Stavanger is made a bishopric. A bishop for Greenland is consecrated in Lund.	c. 1125	
	1127	Charles the Good of Flanders, son of St Knut, king of Denmark, is murdered in Bruges. Roger II unites Sicily and Apulia.
Prolonged succession disputes begin in Norway.	1130	
The Danish pretender Knut Lavard is murdered.	1131	
The first Icelandic monastery is founded on Thingeyrar.	1133	
The battle of Fodevig. Niels, king of Denmark, is killed in Schleswig.	1134	
	1138–1254	The Hohenstaufens in Germany.
The bishopric of Sigtuna is transferred to Gamla Uppsala.	1140	Gratian compiles canon law in his *Decretum*.
Cistercian monasteries are founded in Scandinavia.	1143	
Danish succession disputed between Sven, Knut and Valdemar.	1146–57	
Danish crusade against the Slavs on Rügen.	1147	The second crusade.
Cardinal Nicholas Breakspear, papal legate, visits Norway and Sweden. Trondheim is elevated to metropolitan status for Norwegian lands, Iceland and Greenland.	1152–53	
	1152	Frederick Barbarossa emperor of Germany 1152–90.
	1153	Death of St Bernard of Clairvaux.
Crusade of St Erik, king of Sweden, and bishop Henrik to Finland.	1155	
End of succession wars in Denmark; Valdemar the Great sole king 1157–82.	1157	
	1158	Henry the Lion, duke of Bavaria and Saxony, founds Lübeck.
Death of St Erik (Jedvardsson), king of Sweden.	c. 1160	
Karl Sverkersson becomes king of *Svear* and *Götar*.	1161	
	1162	Frederick Barbarossa destroys Milan.
Magnus Erlingsson is crowned king of Norway, the first coronation in Scandinavia; a Norwegian law of succession introduces sole kingship; Archbishop Øystein revises the Christian code.	1163–64	
Uppsala is made archdiocese for Sweden.	1164	
First mention of Copenhagen. Karl Sverkersson is killed.	1167	Formation of the Lombard League.
The Danes conquer Rügen.	1169	Beginning of the Norman conquest of Ireland. Conquest of Dublin.
Coronation of Knut VI and the enshrinement of his grandfather Knut Lavard at Ringsted.	1170	Thomas à Becket, archbishop of Canterbury, is murdered.
The pope advises the archbishop of Uppsala how to convert Tavastia. Knut Eriksson king of *Svear* and *Götar*.	1171/72	
Eskil, archbishop of Lund, retires to Clairvaux and is succeeded by Absalon.	1176	Frederick Barbarossa defeated by the Lombard League at Legnano.
	1177	
Rudolf, bishop of Finland, is taken prisoner and killed in Curland.	1178	
Birth of the Icelandic author Snorri Sturluson (1179–1241). In Norway Sverre defeats Erling Skakke and his son Magnus. Start of conflict between Monarchy, represented by Sverre, and Church.	1179	
	1180	Philip II August king of France 1180–1223.
Knut VI, king of Denmark, conquers Pomerania.	1185	
Pagan pirates, probably Estonians, ravage the Mälar area, kill the Swedish archbishop and set Sigtuna on fire.	1187	Saladin conquers Jerusalem from the crusaders.
Danes and Frisians fit out 50 ships for participation in the third crusade and take part in the siege of Acre.	1188	
	1189–92	The third crusade. Richard the Lionheart king of England 1189–99.
The archbishop of Trondheim seeks refuge in Lund.	1190	Frederick Barbarossa is drowned in Asia Minor.
Danish expedition to Finland. Danish and Norwegian joint participation in crusade to Jerusalem.	1191	
Sverre, king of Norway, is crowned and excommunicated.	1193	Philip II August marries Ingeborg of Denmark and immediately rejects her.
	1194	
Danish crusade against Estonia.	1197	
Thorlákr Thórhallsson, bishop of Skálholt (died 1193) is sanctified by the Althing.	1198	Foundation of the order of Teutonic Knights.
King Sverre's "Speech against the bishops". Sverre dies 1202 and his successor seeks reconciliation with the church.	c. 1200	Salt-making in Lüneburg begins.
	1204	The fourth crusade captures Constantinople. Philip II August seizes Normandy from England.

Information on illustrations

Photographs
Photographs of objects in the exhibition are, unless otherwise stated, provided by the lender.

Black-and-white photographs of objects in the exhibition—private photographs
Vilhjálmur Örn Vilhjálmsson: all objects in the National Museum of Iceland, except cat. nos. 71, 324–25, 335, 454, 483, 563.
Evgenij N. Nosov, IIMK, St. Petersburg: 284, 288–90.
Martin Biddle, Hertford College, Oxford: 352.
James T. Lang, English Heritage: 368–70.

Other photographs, including colour photographs, not from lenders, where the owner is not named in the caption.
pp. 18–23: Fig. 4, G. P. Skachkov, Gosudarstvennyj Ermitaž, St. Petersburg.
pp. 24–29: Fig. 2, Svend Tougaard, Fiskeri- og Søfartsmuseet, Esbjerg. Fig. 3, Sigrid Christie, Oslo. Fig. 4, Giuseppe Kier, Venezia; foto på Danmarks Nationalmuseum.
pp. 32–41: Fig. 1, Lantmäteriverket, Gävle. Fig. 2 og 6, Nordam-Ullitz & Balslev, Hjørring. Fig. 3, Karsten Kristiansen/Tromsø Museum. Fig. 4, Universitetets Oldsaksamling Oslo. Fig. 5, Knud J. Krogh, Danmarks Nationalmuseum. Fig. 7, Karsten Kristiansen, Mørke.
pp. 42–51: Fig. 1, Grete Schantz, Viking Ship Museum, Roskilde. Fig. 2, 5, 10, Universitetets Oldsaksamling, Oslo. Fig. 6, Kjell Winnér, RAÄ, Stockholm. Fig. 7–9, Mogens Schou Jørgensen, Copenhagen.
pp. 52–61: Fig. 2, Else Roesdahl, Aarhus Universitet. Fig. 3, Litbrá hf, Reykjavík. Fig. 6–7, Símun V. Arge, Føroya Fornminnissavn. Fig. 9, Knud J. Krogh, Danmarks Nationalmuseum.
pp. 62–71: Fig. 2 og 5, Matti Bergström/Museiverket. Fig. 3 og 8, Matti Huuhka/Museiverket. Fig. 4, Pirkko-Liisa Lehtosalo-Hilander, Åbo universitet. Fig. 6, M. Rikkonen/Museiverket. Fig. 9, P.O. Welin/Museiverket.
p. 73: Gert Magnusson, RAÄ, Stockholm.
pp. 74–83: Fig. 1, Ingmar Jansson, Stockholms universitet. Fig. 4–5, G. P. Skachkov, Gosudarstvennyj Ermitaž, St. Petersburg. Fig. 9, Annette Trolle, Ålborg Historiske Museum.
pp. 84–87: Fig. 1 og 4, Klaus Hamann, Berlin. Fig. 2, Römisch-Germanisches Zentralmuseum, Mainz. Fig. 3, Flemming G. Rasmussen, Roskilde Museum.

pp. 88–95: Fig. 5, François Dugue, Musées départementaux de Seine-Maritime, Rouen. Fig. 6–7, via Musée des Antiquités Nationales, St.-Germain-en-Laye.
pp. 96–105: Fig. 2, Martin Biddle, Hertford College, Oxford. Fig. 4, York Archaeological Trust. Fig. 5 and 8, David M. Wilson, The British Museum.
pp. 106–09: Fig. 1, York Archaeological Trust. Fig. 2, Anne Jaubert, Paris. Fig. 3, Else Roesdahl, Aarhus Universitet.
p. 113: Nidaros Domkirkes Restaureringsarbeider.
pp. 116–19: Fig. 2, Berit Jansen Sellevold, Oslo.
pp. 126–35: Fig. 1, Jan Norrman, RAÄ, Stockholm. Fig. 5, Vejle Museum.
pp. 136–43: Fig. 3, Else Roesdahl, Aarhus Universitet. Fig. 8, Kulturen, Lund.
pp. 144–51: Fig. 3, Bengt A. Lundberg, RIKfoto, Stockholm.
pp. 152–61: Fig. 2, Knud J. Krogh, Danmarks Nationalmuseum. Fig. 3, Nordam-Ullitz & Balslev, Hjørring. Fig. 5, Carl Johan Billmark 1857–59, foto Uppsala universitetsbibliotek. Fig. 6, B. Lindstad/A. Kjersheim, N-Riksantikvaren. Fig. 7 and 9, Jens-Jørgen Frimand, Copenhagen.
pp. 162–65: Fig. 2, G. P. Skachkov, Gosudarstvennyj Ermitaž, St. Petersburg. Fig. 3, Anne-Sofie Gräslund, Uppsala universitet. Fig. 4, Bengt A. Lundberg, RIKfoto, Stockholm.
pp. 166–71: Fig. 1–2, Bengt A. Lundberg, RIKfoto, Stockholm.
pp. 172–75: Fig. 1, Bengt A. Lundberg, RIKfoto, Stockholm.
pp. 176–83: Fig. 5, Universitetets Oldsaksamling, Oslo. Fig. 6, Per Jonas Nordhagen, Universitetet i Bergen.
p. 186: Fig. 1, Birkagrävningen/Björn Ambrosiani, Stockholm.
p. 188: Fig. 2, Lars Ekelund, Vreta kloster. Sweden.
p. 191: Fig. 6, Matti Huuhka/Museiverket. Helsinki.
p. 193: Fig. 2–3, Danmarks Nationalmuseum.
p. 195: Fig. 5, Kunstindustrimuseet, Oslo.
p. 197: Fig. 2, G. P. Skachkov, Gosudarstvennyj Ermitaž, St. Petersburg. Fig. 3, Gert Magnusson, RAÄ, Stockholm.
p. 201: Fig. 3, G. P. Skachkov, Gosudarstvennyj Ermitaž, St. Petersburg.
p. 202: Fig. 2, Bildarchiv Marburg.
pp. 206–07: Fig. 1–4, Universitetets Oldsaksamling, Oslo. Fig. 5, Lennart Karlsson, Statens Historiska Museum, Stockholm.
p. 210: Fig. 2, Ole Schiørring, Horsens Museum.
pp. 212–15: Fig. 5, Ebbe Nyborg, Danmarks Nationalmuseum. Fig. 4, 6–8, Jens-Jørgen Frimand, Copenhagen.

Drawings

Maps drawn by Jørgen Mührmann-Lund, Forhistorisk Museum Moesgård.

Drawings other than those which are provided by lender:

p. 29 fig. 5: Eva Wilson, Castletown, Isle of Man.

p. 31: Brita Malmer, Stockholms universitet.

p. 40 fig. 10: After J.J.A. Worsaae og C. F. Herbst: *Konge-gravene i Ringsted Kirke*, 1858.

p. 11 and p. 45 fig. 3: Morten Gøthche, Viking Ship Museum, Roskilde.

p. 100 fig. 3: National Museum of Ireland.

p. 109 fig. 4: After P. Sawyer: *Da Danmark blev Danmark.* Gyldendal og Politikens Danmarkshistorie bd. 3, 1988.

p. 115: After E. Nylén: *Bildstenar*, 1978.

p. 129 fig. 3: Flemming Bau, Århus. After Stig Jensen: *Ribes vikinger*, 1991.

p. 133 fig. 6: Steen Hvass, Vejle Museum; redrawn by Jørgen Mührmann-Lund.

p. 137 fig. 1: Lone Hvass, Vejle Museum.

p. 162 fig. 1: Raymond Page, Corpus Christi College, Cambridge.

p. 187 fig. 2: After *Ny Illustrerad Tidning*, 21 december 1889; fig. 3: After H. Arbman: *Birka I. Die Gräber. Text*, 1943.

p. 192 fig. 1: Torkil Oxe, Forhistorisk Museum, Moesgård, based on information provided by Pirkko-Liisa Lehtosalo-Hilander and Ingmar Jansson.

p. 196 fig. 1: Gert Magnusson, RAÄ, Stockholm.

pp. 198–99 fig. 1: Flemming Bau, Århus. After Stig Jensen: *Ribes vikinger*, 1991.

p. 213 fig. 3: Morten Aaman Sørensen. After *Strejflys over Danmarks Bygningskultur* (ed. R. Egevang), 1979.

p. 221 fig. 3: Brita Malmer, Stockholms universitet.

p. 223: Jørgen Mührmann-Lund.

Cat. no. 331: Ingmar Jansson, Stockholms universitet.

Cat. no. 352: Judith Dobie, Repton Excavation Project.

Literature

For the purposes of this bibliography the letters å, ä, ø, ö—although typographically distinguished—have been treated as a, a, o and o; æ is treated as ae. They have *not* been placed after the letter z and treated—as in Scandinavia—as separate letters of the alphabet.

General works

Almgren, B. *et al.* 1967: *The Viking.* Gothenburg (dansk og svensk udg.: *Vikingen.* Gothenburg 1967; éd. française: *Les Vikings.* Paris 1968).

Andersen, P.S. 1977: *Samlingen av Norge og kristningen av landet 800–1130.* Oslo.

Anker, P. & A. Andersson 1968–69: *L'art scandinave* 1–2. La Pierre-qui-Vire (Engl. ed.: *The Art of Scandinavia* 1–2. London, New York 1970).

Arbman, H. 1955: *Svear i österviking.* Stockholm.

Foote, P. & D.M. Wilson 1980: *The Viking Achievement,* 2nd ed. London.

Graham-Campbell, J. 1980: *The Viking World.* London.

Graham-Campbell, J. 1980: *Viking Artefacts. A Select Catalogue.* London.

Graham-Campbell, J. & D. Kidd 1980: *The Vikings.* London.

Helle, K. 1974: *Norge blir en stat 1130–1319,* 2. ed. Oslo.

Herrmann, J., (ed.) 1982: *Wikinger und Slawen. Zur Frühgeschichte der Ostseevölker.* Berlin, Neumünster (Russian edition: *Slavjane i skandinavy.* Moscow 1986).

Jansson, I., (ed.) 1983: *Gutar och vikingar.* Stockholm.

Jones, G. 1986: *The Norse Atlantic Saga,* 2nd ed. Oxford, New York.

Kivikoski, E. 1964: *Finlands förhistoria.* Helsinki (Engl. ed.: *Finland.* Ancient Peoples and Places 53. London 1967).

Kivikoski, E. 1973: *Die Eisenzeit Finnlands.* Bildwerk und Text. Neuausgabe. Helsinki.

Kristjánsson, J. 1988: *Eddas and Sagas. Iceland's Medieval Literature.* Reykjavík.

Kulturhistorisk leksikon for nordisk middelalder = Kulturhistoriskt lexikon för nordisk medeltid, vol. I–XXII, 1956–78, reprint 1980–82.

Liebgott, N.-K. 1989: *Dansk middelalderarkæologi.* Copenhagen.

Magnusson, M. 1987: *Iceland Saga.* London.

Musset, L. 1951: *Les peuples scandinaves au Moyen Age.* Paris.

Musset, L. 1971: *Les Invasions: Le second assaut contre l'Europe chrétienne (VIIe–XIe siècles).* Paris (1. ed. 1969).

Norges Kunsthistorie 1–2 (ed. K. Berg *et al.*). Oslo 1981.

Page, R.I. 1987: *Runes.* London.

Reallexikon der Germanischen Altertumskunde, Bd. 1 ff. Berlin, New York 1973 ff.

Roesdahl, E. 1980: *Danmarks vikingetid.* Copenhagen (Engl. ed.: *Viking Age Denmark.* London 1982).

Roesdahl, E. 1987: *Vikingernes verden.* Copenhagen (Engl. ed.: *The Vikings.* London 1991).

Sawyer, P. 1982: *Kings and Vikings.* London, New York.

Sawyer, P. 1991: *När Sverige blev Sverige.* Alingsås (Engl. ed.: *The Making of Sweden.* Alingsås 1988).

Skovgaard-Petersen, I., A.E. Christensen, H. Paludan 1977: *Danmarks historie,* bd. 1 (Gyldendal). Copenhagen.

Steinsland, G. & P. Meulengracht Sørensen 1992: *Kultur og religion i vikingtid.* Oslo (Engl. ed.: *Viking Age Man.* Oslo 1992).

Thorsteinsson, B. 1985: *Island.* Politikens Danmarkshistorie. Copenhagen.

Tuulse, A. 1968: *Romansk konst i Norden.* Stockholm (deutsche Ausg.: *Scandinavia Romanica. Die hohe Kunst der romanischen Epoche in Dänemark, Norwegen und Schweden.* Vienna, Munich 1968).

Wilson, D.M., (ed.) 1980: *The Northern World.* London (éd. française: *Les Mondes Nordiques.* Paris 1980; deutsche Ausg.: *Kulturen im Norden.* Munich 1980; svensk utg.: *Vikingarna och folken i norr.* Stockholm 1980).

Chapters

The Scandinavian kingdoms (pp. 32–41)

Andersen, P.S. 1977: *Samlingen av Norge og kristningen av landet 800–1130.* Oslo.

Bagge, S. 1989: State Building in Medieval Norway. The Origin of the State, *Forum for utviklingsstudier* 1989 nr. 2. Oslo.

Christiansen, E. 1980: *The Northern Crusades. The Baltic and the Catholic Frontier 1100–1525.* London.

Gyldendal og Politikens Danmarkshistorie bd. 3 (P. Sawyer: *Da Danmark blev Danmark*); bd. 4 (O. Fenger: *"Kirker rejses alle vegne"*), ed. O. Olsen. Copenhagen 1988, 1989.

Helle, K. 1974: *Norge blir en stat 1130–1319,* 2. ed. Oslo.

Hyenstrand, Å. 1989: *Sverige 989. Makt och herravälde I.* Stockholm.

Musset, L. 1951: *Les peuples scandinaves au Moyen Age.* Paris.

Sawyer, P. 1982: *Kings and Vikings.* London.

Sawyer, P. 1991: *När Sverige blev Sverige.* Alingsås (Engl. ed.: *The Making of Sweden.* Alingsås 1988).

Skovgaard-Petersen, I, A.E. Christensen, H. Paludan 1977: *Danmarks historie,* bd. 1 (Gyldendal). Copenhagen.

Ships and travel (pp. 42–51)

Seafaring and ships.

Andersen, B. & E. 1990: *Råsejlet – Dragens Vinge.* Roskilde.

Brøgger, A.W. & H. Shetelig 1950: *Vikingeskipene. Deres forgjengere og etterfølgere.* Oslo (Engl. ed.: *The Viking Ships. Their Ancestry and Evolution.* Oslo 1951).

Crumlin-Pedersen, O. 1986: Aspects of Viking-Age Shipbuilding, *Journal of Danish Archaeology,* vol. 5. Odense.

Crumlin-Pedersen, O. 1989: Schiffstypen aus der frühgeschichtlichen Seeschiffahrt in den nordeuropäischen Gewässern, *Untersuchungen zu Handel und Verkehr der vor- und frühgeschichtlichen Zeit in Mittel- und Nordeuropa.* Teil V. Abhandlungen der Akademie der Wissenschaften in Göttingen, Philol.-Historische Klasse, 3. Folge, Nr. 180. Göttingen.

Ellmers, D. 1972: *Frühmittelalterliche Handelsschiffahrt in Mittel- und Nordeuropa*. Neumünster.

Olsen, O. & O. Crumlin-Pedersen 1969: *Fem vikingeskibe fra Roskilde Fjord*. Roskilde (deutsche Ausg.: *Fünf Wikingerschiffe aus Roskilde Fjord*. Kopenhagen 1978; Engl. ed.: *Five Viking Ships from Roskilde Fjord*. Copenhagen 1978).

Schnall, U. 1975: *Navigation der Wikinger*. Schriften des Deutschen Schiffahrtsmuseums 6. Oldenburg/Hamburg.

Skamby Madsen, J. 1990: Fribrødre – a shipyard site of the late 11th century, *Aspects of Maritime Scandinavia AD 200–1200* (ed. O. Crumlin-Pedersen). Roskilde.

Land transport

Ambrosiani, B. 1987: Vattendelar- eller Attundalandsvägen, *Runor och runinskrifter,* KVHAA Konferenser 15. Stockholm.

Jørgensen, M. Schou 1988: Vej, vejstrøg og vejspærring, *Fra Stamme til Stat i Danmark*, 1 (ed. P. Mortensen & B. Rasmussen). Jysk Arkæologisk Selskabs Skrifter 22. Højbjerg (English Summary).

Sawyer, B. 1990: Women as bridge-builders, *People and Places in Northern Europe 500–1600* (ed. I. Wood & N. Lund). Woodbridge.

Smedstad, I. 1988: *Etableringen av et organisert veihold i Midt-Norge i tidlig historisk tid*. Varia 16. Oslo.

Winter transport

Berg, G. 1935: *Sledges and wheeled vehicles*. Nordiska museets handlingar 4. Stockholm.

Easton, C. 1928: *Les hivers dans L'Europe occidentale*. Leyden.

Kulturhistoriskt lexikon för nordisk medeltid, vol. XV, 1971, *s.v.* "Skidor"; vol. XVI, 1972, *s.v.* "Släde".

Luho, V. 1948: Über steinzeitliche Winterverkehrsmittel in Finnland, *Acta Archaeologica* XIX.

New lands in the North Atlantic (pp. 52–61)

Iceland

Ágústsson, H. 1968: Islands byggeskik i fortiden, *Nordisk byggedag* 10. Copenhagen.

Bruun, D. 1928: *Fortidsminder og Nutidshjem paa Island*. Ny omarb. og forøget Udg. Copenhagen.

Eldjárn, K. 1956: *Kuml og haugfé úr heinum si á Íslandi*. Akureyri.

Jóhannesson, J. 1956: *Íslendingasaga* I. Reykjavík (norsk utg.: *Islands historie i mellomalderen*. Oslo 1969; Engl. ed.: *A History of the Old Icelandic Commonwealth: Islendinga Saga*. Winnipeg 1974).

Meulengracht Sørensen, P. 1977: *Saga og Samfund*. Copenhagen (Engl. ed.: *Saga and Society*. Marburg 1992).

Stenberger, M., (ed.) 1943: *Forntida gårdar i Island*. Copenhagen.

Thorsteinsson, B. 1985: *Island*. Copenhagen.

The Faroe Islands

Arge, S.V. 1991: The Landnam in the Faroes, *Arctic Anthropology*, vol. 28, no. 2.

Dahl, S. 1970: The Norse Settlement of the Faroe Islands, *Medieval Archaeology*, vol. XIV.

Stummann, Hansen S., in press: A Faroese Viking Age Farm from the 9th–10th Century, *Acta Archaeologica*.

Thorsteinsson, A. 1981: On the development of Faroese Settlements, *Proceedings of the Eighth Viking Congress* (ed. H. Bekker-Nielsen *et al.*). Odense.

Greenland and America

Arneborg, J., in press: The Roman church in Norse Greenland, *Acta Archaeologica*.

Jones, G. 1986: *The Norse Atlantic Saga*, 2. ed. A new and enlarged edition with contributions by Robert McGhee, Thomas H. McGovern & colleagues, and Birgitta Linderoth Wallace. Oxford, New York.

Krogh, K.J. 1967: *Viking Greenland*. With a Supplement of Saga Texts, The Greenlanders' Saga & The Story of Einar Sokkason, by H. Bekker-Nielsen. Copenhagen.

Krogh, K.J. 1982: *Erik den Rødes Grønland*. Sagatekster ved H. Bekker-Nielsen, 2. rev. og stærkt udvidede udgave (1. udgave 1967). Copenhagen (tekst på dansk og grønlandsk).

McGovern, T.H. 1983: Contribution to paleoeconomy of Norse Greenland, *Acta Archaeologica*, vol. 54.

Finland (pp. 62–71)

Gallén, J. 1984: Länsieurooppalaiset ja skandinaaviset Suomen esihistoriaa koskevat lähteet (Summary: Western European and Scandinavian sources concerning Finnish prehistory). *Suomen väestön esihistorialliset juuret. Bidrag till kännedom av Finlands natur och folk*. Utgivna av Finska Vetenskaps-Societeten, hft. 131. Helsinki.

Kivikoski, E. 1963: *Kvarnbacken. Ein Gräberfeld der jüngeren Eisenzeit auf Åland*. Helsinki.

Kivikoski, E. 1965: Magisches Fundgut aus finnischer Eisenzeit, *Finskt Museum* 1965. Helsinki.

Kivikoski, E. 1973: *Die Eisenzeit Finnlands*. Bildwerk und Text. Neuausgabe. Helsinki.

Lehtosalo-Hilander, P.-L. 1982: *Luistari – A Burial-Ground Reflecting the Finnish Viking Age Society* I-III. Suomen Muinaismuistoyhdistyksen Aikakauskirja 82:1–3. Helsinki.

Lehtosalo-Hilander, P.-L. 1984: *Ancient Finnish Costumes*. Vammala.

Lehtosalo-Hilander, P.-L. 1990: Le Viking finnois, *Finskt Museum* 1990. Helsinki.

Strandberg, R. 1938: Les broches d'argent caréliennes en forme de fer à cheval et leur ornements, *Eurasia Septentrionalis Antiqua* XII. Helsinki.

Tolonen, K., A. Siiriäinen, A.-L. Hirviluoto 1979: Iron Age Cultivation in SW Finland, *Finskt Museum* 1976. Helsinki.

Vahter, T. 1932: Les "kaatteris" chez les peuples finnois pendant l'âge récent du fer, *Eurasia Septentrionalis Antiqua* VII. Helsinki.

Zachrisson, I. 1984: *De samiska metalldepåerna år 1000–1350 i ljuset av fyndet från Mörtträsket, Lappland. (The Saami Metal Deposits A.D. 1000–1350 in the light of the find from Mörtträsket, Lapland)*. Archaeology and Environment 3. Umeå (Engl. summary).

The Saami in Scandinavia (pp. 72–73)

Ruong, I. 1982: *Samerne i historien och nutiden*, 4. uppl. Stockholm.

Storli, I. 1991: *"Stallo"-boplassene. Et tolkningsforslag basert på undersøkelser i Lønsdalen, Saltfjellet*. Institutt for samfunnsvitenskap, Universitetet i Tromsø.

Zachrisson, I. 1984: *De samiska metalldepåerna år 1000–1350 i ljuset av fyndet från Mörtträsket, Lappland. (The Saami Metal Deposits A.D. 1000–1350 in the light of the find from Mörtträsket, Lapland)*. Archaeology and Environment 3. Umeå (Engl. summary).

Zachrisson, I. 1987: Arkeologi och etnicitet. Samisk kultur i mellersta Sverige ca 1–1500 e Kr, *Bebyggelseshistorisk tidsskrift* 14.

Zachrisson, I. 1988: Archéologie et Ethnologie, *Boréales. Revue du Centre de Recherches Inter-Nordiques* 34–35.

The way to the East (pp. 74–83)

Arbman, H. 1955: *Svear i österviking*. Stockholm.

Ģinters V. 1981: *Tracht und Schmuck in Birka und im ostbaltischen Raum. Eine vergleichende Studie*. Antikvariskt arkiv 70. Stockholm.

Herrmann, J., (ed.) 1982: *Wikinger und Slawen. Zur Frühgeschichte der Ostseevölker*. Berlin, Neumünster (Russian edition: *Slavjane i skandinavy*. Moscow 1986).

Nerman, B. 1958: *Grobin-Seeburg. Ausgrabungen und Funde*. Stockholm.

Nosov, E.N. 1990: *Novgorodskoe (Rjurikovo) gorodišče*. Leningrad (Engl. summary: The Ryurik Gorodishche near Novgorod).

Oldenburg – Wolin – Staraja Ladoga – Novgorod – Kiev. Handel und Handelsverbindungen im südlichen und östlichen Ostseeraum während des frühen Mittelalters. Internationale Fachkonferenz, Kiel 1987. *Bericht der Römisch-Germanischen Kommission 69*, 1988. Frankfurt.

Les Pays du Nord et Byzance. Actes du colloque 1979. Acta Universitatis Upsaliensis. Figura, Nova series 19. Uppsala 1981.

Srednevekovaja Ladoga. Novye otkrytija i issledovanija (ed. V.V. Sedov). Leningrad 1985.

Thompson, M.V. 1967: *Novgorod the Great. Excavations at the medieval city directed by A.V. Artsikhovsky and B.A. Kolchin*. London.

Untersuchungen zu Handel und Verkehr der vor- und frühgeschichtlichen Zeit in Mittel- und Nordeuropa IV. Der Handel der Karolinger- und Wikingerzeit. Bericht über die Kolloquien 1980 bis 1983 (ed. K. Düwel, H. Jankuhn, H. Siems, D. Timpe). Abhandlungen der Akademie der Wissenschaften in Göttingen, Philol.-Historische Klasse, 3. Folge, Nr. 156. Göttingen 1987.

Varangian problems. Report on the first international symposium on the theme "The Eastern Connections of the Nordic Peoples in the Viking Period and Early Middle Ages", Moesgaard 1968. Scando-Slavica, supplementum 1. Copenhagen 1970.

The West Slav lands and the North (pp. 84–87)

Herrmann, J. 1980: The Northern Slavs, *The Northern World* (ed. D.M. Wilson). London (deutsche Ausg.: *Kulturen im Norden*. Munich 1980; éd. française: *Les Mondes Nordiques*. Paris 1980; svensk utg.: *Vikingarna och folken i norr*. Stockholm 1980).

Herrmann, J., (ed.) 1982: *Wikinger und Slawen. Zur Frühgeschichte der Ostseevölker*. Berlin, Neumünster (Russian edition: *Slavjane i skandinavy*. Moscow 1986).

Leciejewicz, L. 1989: *Słowianie Zachodnie z dziejów tworzenia się średniowieczej Europy*. Wrocław u.a.

Oldenburg – Wolin – Staraja Ladoga – Novgorod – Kiev. Handel und Handelsverbindungen im südlichen und östlichen Ostseeraum während des frühen Mittelalters. Bericht der Römisch-Germanischen Kommission 69, 1988. Frankfurt.

Ralswiek und Rügen. Landschaftsentwicklung und Siedlungsgeschichte der Ostseeinsel (ed. J. Herrmann). Teil I, 1986: Die Landschaftsgeschichte der Insel Rügen seit dem Spätglazial. Von E. Lange, L. Jeschke, H.D. Knapp. Berlin.

Die Slawen in Deutschland. Geschichte und Kultur der slawischen Stämme westlich von Oder und Neiße vom 6.–12. Jahrhundert. Ein Handbuch (ed. J. Herrmann). Berlin 1985.

The Scandinavians and the Western European continent (pp. 88–95)

Barbarani, F. 1979: *L'espansione dei vichinghi. Aspetti culturali, economici e sociali*. Verona.

d'Haenens, A. 1967: *Les invasions normandes en Belgique au IXe siècle. Le phénomène et sa répercussion dans l'historigraphie Médiévale*. Louvain.

Musset, L. 1971: *Les Invasions* II. *Le second assaut contre l'Europe Chrétienne*, 2. ed. Paris.

Roesdahl, E. 1987: *Vikingernes verden*. Copenhagen (Engl. ed.: *The Vikings*. London 1991).

Sawyer, P.H. 1971: *The Age of the Vikings*, 2. ed. London.

Sawyer, P.H. 1982: *Kings and Vikings*. London.

Settimane di Studio del centro italiano di Studi sull'alto medievo XVI. *I Normanni e la loro espansione in Europa nell'alto medioevo*. Spoleto 1969.

Vogel, W. 1906: *Die Normannen und das fränkische Reich bis zur Gründung der Normandie (799–911)*. Heidelberg.

Zettel, H. 1977: *Das Bild der Normannen und der Normanneneinfälle*. Munich.

The Scandinavians in Britain and Ireland (pp. 96–105)

The Archaeology of York (ed. P.V. Addyman), vol. 1 ff. London 1976 ff.

Bailey, R.N. 1980: *Viking Age Sculpture in Northern England*. London.

Clarke, H. 1990: *Medieval Dublin, the Making of a Metropolis*. Dublin.

Crawford, B.E. 1987: *Scandinavian Scotland*. Leicester.

Fell, C. *et al.*, (ed.) 1983: *The Viking Age in the Isle of Man*. London.

Graham-Campbell, J. 1989: The Archaeology of the Danelaw: an introduction, *Les Mondes Normands (VIIIe-XIIe s.)*, (ed. H. Galinié). Caen.

Hall, R.A. 1984: *The Viking Dig*. London.

Loyn, H.R. 1977: *The Vikings in Britain*. London.

Ó Corráin, D. 1972: *Ireland before the Normans*. Dublin.

The Vikings in England (ed. E. Roesdahl *et al.*). London 1981 (exhibition catalogue).

Scandinavian names and words in Europe (pp. 106–9)

Adigard des Gautries, J. 1954: *Les Noms De Personnes Scandinaves En Normandie De 911 À 1066*. Lund.

Baecklund, A. 1956: Les Prénoms Scandinaves Dans La Tradition Médiévale De Velikij Novgorod, *Revue des Études Slaves* 33.

Fellows-Jensen, G. 1968: *Scandinavian Personal Names in Lincolnshire and Yorkshire*. Navnestudier 7. Copenhagen.

Fellows-Jensen, G. 1985: *Scandinavian Settlement Names in the North-West*. Navnestudier 25. Copenhagen.

Fellows-Jensen, G. 1988: Scandinavian place-names and Viking settlement in Normandy. A review, *Namn och Bygd* 76.

Fellows-Jensen, G. 1990: Scandinavian Personal Names in Foreign Fields, *Cahier Des Annales De Normandie* 23.

Gorog, R.P. de 1958: *The Scandinavian Element in French and Norman*. New York.

Greene, D. 1978: The Evidence of Language and Place-Names in Ireland, *The Vikings* (ed. T. Andersson and K.I. Sandred). Uppsala.

Hofmann, D. 1955: *Nordisch-Englische Lehnbeziehungen der Wikingerzeit*. Bibliotheca Arnamagnæana XIV. Copenhagen.

Thörnqvist, C. 1948: *Studien über die nordischen Lehnwörter im Russischen*. Uppsala-Stockholm.

Pilgrimages and crusades (pp. 110–11)

Andersson, L. 1989: *Pilgrimsmärken och vallfart*. Lund Studies in Medieval Archaeology 7. Lund.

Christiansen, E. 1980: *The Northern Crusades. The Baltic and the Catholic Frontier 1100–1525*. London.

Jónsson, F. & E. Jørgensen 1923: Nordiske Pilegrimsnavne i Broderskabsbogen fra Reichenau, *Aarbøger for nordisk Oldkyndighed og Historie* 1923.

Köster, K. 1983: Pilgerzeichen und Pilgermuscheln von mittelalterlichen Santiagostraßen. *Ausgrabungen in Schleswig* 2. Neumünster.

Kulturhistorisk leksikon for nordisk middelalder bd. VII, 1962: *s.v.* "Itinerarier"; bd. XIII, 1968: "Pilegrim", "Pilegrimsveier", "Pilgrimsmärken".

Liebgott, N.-K. 1981: *Hellige mænd og kvinder*. Højbjerg.

People and language (pp. 116–19)

Almenningen, O. *et al.* 1985: *Språk og samfunn gjennom tusen år*, 2. utg. Oslo.

Haugen, E. 1976: *The Scandinavian Languages. An Introduction to their History*. London.

Sellevold, B.J. 1988: Iron Age inhumation burials in Denmark and Norway, *Supplemento della Rivista di Antropologia*, Vol. LXVI. Rome.

Sellevold, B.J., U. Lund Hansen & J. Balslev Jørgensen 1984: *Iron Age Man in Denmark (Prehistoric Man in Denmark*, Vol. III). Nordiske Fortidsminder, Series B, Vol. 8. Copenhagen.

Wessén, E. 1979: *De nordiska språken*, 11. utg. Stockholm.

Scandinavian society (pp. 120–25)

Fenger, O. 1971: *Fejde og mandebod* (über die kollektive Verantwortlichkeit der Verwandten im mittelalterlichen Recht). Aarhus (Deutscher Zusammenfassung).

Fenger, O. 1981: L'influence du droit romain dans la Scandinavie médiévale. *Jus Romanum Medié Aevi*, pars V, 14. Milan.

Hastrup, K. 1985: *Culture and History in medieval Iceland*. Oxford.

Hvass, S. 1986: Vorbasse – Eine Dorfsiedlung während des 1. Jahrtausends n. Chr. in Mitteljütland, Dänemark, *Von der Eisenzeit zum Mittelalter. Bericht der Römisch-Germanischen Kommission* 67.

Sawyer, P.H. 1982: *Kings and Vikings. Scandinavia and Europe AD 700–1100* (Chapter 4: Scandinavian society). London.

Resources and settlements (pp. 126–35)

Andrén, A. 1985: *Den urbana scenen. Städer och samhälle i det medeltida Danmark*. Bonn & Malmö.

Clarke, H. & B. Ambrosiani 1991: *Towns in the Viking Age*. Leicester.

Graham-Campbell, J. 1980: *The Viking World*. London.

Hvass, S. 1984: Wikingerzeitliche Siedlungen in Vorbasse, *Offa* 41.

Nedkvitne, A. 1983: *Utenrikshandelen fra det Vestafjelske Norge 1100–1600*. Bergen.

Ottar og Wulfstan. To rejseberetninger fra vikingetiden (ed. N. Lund). Roskilde 1983 (Engl. ed.: *Two voyagers at the court of King Alfred* (ed. N. Lund, trans. C. Fell). York 1984).

Proceedings of the Tenth Viking Congress, Larkollen, Norway, 1985 (ed. J. Knirk). Universitetets Oldsaksamlings Skrifter. Ny rekke, nr. 9. Oslo 1987.

Sawyer, P.H. 1982: *Kings and Vikings. Scandinavia and Europe AD 700–1100*. London.

Society and Trade in the Baltic during the Viking Age (ed. S.-O. Lindquist). Visby 1985.

Untersuchungen zu Handel und Verkehr der vor- und frühgeschichtlichen Zeit in Mittel- und Nordeuropa. Teil 4 (ed. K. Düwel *et al.*). Abhandlungen der Akademie der Wissenschaften in Göttingen, Philologisch-Historische Klasse, 3. Folge, Nr. 156. Göttingen 1987.

Urbaniseringsprosessen i Norden 1. Middelaldersteder (ed. G. Authén Blom). Oslo, Bergen, Tromsø 1977.

House and home (pp. 136–43)

Almgren, B., (ed.) 1967: *Vikingen*. Gothenburg (Engl. ed.: *The Viking*. Gothenburg 1967. Ed. française: *Les Vikings*. Paris 1968).

Graham-Campbell, J. 1980: *Viking Artefacts. A Select Catalogue*. London.

Hus, gård og bebyggelse (ed. G. Ólafsson). Reykjavík 1983.

Liebgott, N.-K. 1989: *Dansk middelalderarkæologi*. Copenhagen.

Roesdahl, E. 1980: *Danmarks vikingetid*. Copenhagen (Engl. ed.: *Viking Age Denmark*. London 1982).

Roesdahl, E. 1987: *Vikingernes verden*. Copenhagen (Engl. ed.: *The Vikings*. London 1991).

Tesch, S., (ed.) 1990: *Makt och människor i kungens Sigtuna. Sigtunautgrävningen 1988–1990.* Sigtuna (Engl. ed. in preparation).

Scandinavian paganism (pp. 144–51)

Ahlbäck, T. 1987: *Saami Religion.* The Donner Institute for Research in Religious and Cultural History. Åbo, Uppsala.

Bäckman, L. and Å. Hultkrantz 1978: *Studies in Lapp Shamanism,* Acta Universitatis Stockholmiensis 16. Stockholm.

Davidson, H.R.E. 1977: *Gods and Myths of Northern Europe.* London.

de Vries, J. 1970: *Altgermanische Religionsgeschichte* I-II. Berlin (reprint of 2. ed., 1956–57).

Dumézil, G. 1959: *Les Dieux des Germains. Essai sur la formation de la religion scandinave.* Paris. (Engl. ed.: *Gods of the Ancient Northmen,* ed. E. Haugen. Berkeley 1973).

Meulengracht Sørensen, P. & G. Steinsland 1990: *Før kristendommen. Digtning og livssyn i vikingetiden.* Copenhagen.

Munch, P.A. 1963: *Norse Mythology. Legends of Gods and Heroes* (tr. S.B. Hustvedt). New York.

Ström, Å. & H. Biezais 1975: *Germanische und Baltische Religion.* Die Religionen der Menschheit, Bd. 19,1. Stuttgart, Berlin.

Turville-Petre, E.O.G. 1977: *Myth and Religion of the North. The Religion of Ancient Scandinavia.* Connecticut (1. ed. London 1964).

Vorren, Ø. & E. Manker 1975: *Samekulturen. En kulturhistorisk oversigt.* Tromsø, Bergen.

Christianity and churches (pp. 152–61)

L'art scandinave 1 (P. Anker) og 2 (A. Andersson). La Pierre-qui-Vire 1969, 1968 (Engl. ed.: *The Art of Scandinavia* 1–2. London 1970).

The Christianization of Scandinavia (ed. B. Sawyer, P. Sawyer and I. Wood). Alingsås 1987.

Krins, H. 1968: *Die frühen Steinkirchen Dänemarks.* Dissertation zur Erlangung der Doktorwürde der Philosophischen Fakultät der Universität Hamburg. Hamburg.

Musset, L. 1967: La pénétration chrétienne dans l'Europe du Nord et son influence sur la civilisation scandinave, *La conversione al cristianesimo nell'Europa dell'alto medioevo.* Settimane di Studio del centro italiano di Studi sull'alto medioevo XIV. Spoleto.

Olsen, O. 1981: Der lange Weg des Nordens zum Christentum, *Frühe Holzkirchen im nördlichen Europa* (ed. C. Ahrens). Hamburg.

Tuulse, A. 1968: *Romansk konst i Norden.* Stockholm (deutsche Ausg.: *Scandinavia Romanica. Die hohe Kunst der romanischen Epoche in Dänemark, Norwegen und Schweden.* Vienna, Munich 1968).

Runes and rune-stones (pp. 162–65)

Danmarks Runeindskrifter I-II (ed. L. Jacobsen & E. Moltke). Copenhagen 1941–42.

Düwel, K. 1983: *Runenkunde,* 2. ed. Stuttgart.

Jansson, S.B.F. 1963: *Runinskrifter i Sverige.* Stockholm (English ed.: *Runes in Sweden,* transl. P. Foote, 2. ed. Stockholm 1987).

Liestøl, A. 1963: Runer fra Bryggen, *Viking* 1963 (reprint of article: *Runer fra Bryggen.* Bergen 1964).

Moltke, E. 1976: *Runerne i Danmark og deres oprindelse.* Copenhagen (English ed.: *Runes and their origin. Denmark and elsewhere,* rev. text, transl. P. Foote. Copenhagen 1985).

Musset, L. 1965: *Introduction à la runologie,* based on collections by Fernand Mossé. Paris.

Norges innskrifter med de yngre runer. Oslo 1941 ff.

Page, R.I. 1987: *Runes.* London.

Sawyer, B. 1988: *Property and inheritance in Viking Scandinavia: the runic evidence.* Alingsås.

Sveriges Runinskrifter. Stockholm 1900 ff.

From oral poetry to literature (pp. 166–71)

de Vries, J. 1964–67: *Altnordische Literaturgeschichte* I-II, 2. ed. Berlin.

Foote, P. 1985: Skandinavische Dichtung der Wikingerzeit, *Neues Handbuch der Literaturwissenschaft,* Bd 6, Europäisches Frühmittelalter. Wiesbaden.

Hallberg, P. 1962: *Den fornisländska poesien.* Stockholm (American ed.: *Old Icelandic Poetry: Eddic Lay and Scaldic Verse.* Lincoln, Nebr. 1975; dansk udg.: *Den norrøne digtning.* Copenhagen 1982).

Holm-Olsen, L. 1975: *Middelalderens litteratur i Norge. Norges litteraturhistorie,* bd. 1. Oslo.

Kristjánsson, J. 1988: *Eddas and Sagas.* Reykjavík.

Meulengracht Sørensen, P. 1982: Die skandinavischen Sprachen und Literaturen, *Propyläen Geschichte der Literatur,* Bd. 2, Die mittelalterliche Welt. Berlin.

Nordal, S., (ed.) 1942, 1953: *Litteraturhistorie* A: Danmark, Finland og Sverige, B: Norge og Island. *Nordisk Kultur* VIII: A og B. Stockholm, Oslo, Copenhagen.

Schier, K. 1981: Die Literaturen des Nordens. *Neues Handbuch der Literaturwissenschaft,* Bd. 7. Wiesbaden.

Teilgård Laugesen, A. 1972: *Introduktion til Saxo.* Copenhagen.

Turville-Petre, G. 1953: *Origins of Icelandic Literature.* Oxford.

Scaldic poetry (pp. 172–75)

Frank, R. 1978: *Old Norse Court Poetry.* Ithaca and London.

Hallberg, P. 1962: *Den fornisländska poesien.* Stockholm (American ed.: *Old Icelandic Poetry: Eddic Lay and Skaldic Verse.* Lincoln, Nebr. 1975; dansk udg.: *Den norrøne digtning.* Copenhagen 1982).

Helgason, J. 1953: Norges og Islands digtning. *Nordisk Kultur* VIII B. Stockholm, Oslo, Copenhagen.

Heusler, A. 1941: *Die altgermanische Dichtung,* 2. neubearb. und verm. Ausg. Handbuch der Literaturwissenschaft (ed. O. Walzel). Potsdam.

Hollander, L.M. 1968: *The Skalds,* 2. udg. Ann Arbor.

Jónsson, F. 1912–15: *Den norsk-islandske Skjaldedigtning.* A I-II, Tekst efter håndskrifterne. B I-II, Rettet tekst. Copenhagen.

Jónsson, F. 1920–24: *Den oldnorske og oldislandske Litteraturs Historie* I-III, 2. udg. Copenhagen.

Kristjánsson, J. 1988: *Eddas and Sagas.* Reykjavík.

See, K. von 1980: *Skaldendichtung. Eine Einführung.* Munich, Zürich.

Turville-Petre, E.O.G. 1976: *Scaldic Poetry.* Oxford.

Art (pp. 176–83)

Andersson, A. 1966: *Medieval wooden sculpture in Sweden*, vol. 2. Stockholm.

Anker, P. and A. Andersson 1968–69: *L'art scandinave* 1–2. La Pierre-qui-Vire (Engl. ed.: *The Art of Scandinavia* 1–2. London 1970).

Blindheim, M. 1965: *Norwegian Romanesque Decorative Sculpture*. London.

Fuglesang, S.H. 1980: *Some Aspects of the Ringerike style*. Odense.

Fuglesang, S.H. 1981: Vikingtidens kunst, *Norges Kunsthistorie* 1 (ed. K. Berg). Oslo.

Fuglesang, S.H. 1986: Ikonographie der skandinavischen Runensteine der jüngeren Wikingerzeit, *Zum Problem der Deutung frühmittelalterlicher Bildinhalte* (ed. H. Roth). Sigmaringen.

Hohler, E.B. 1981: Stavkirkene. Den dekorative skurd, *Norges Kunsthistorie* 1 (ed. K. Berg). Oslo.

Lindqvist, S. 1941–42: *Gotlands Bildsteine*. Stockholm.

Schetelig, H. 1920: *Osebergfundet* III. Kristiania.

Wilson, D.M. & O. Klindt-Jensen 1966: *Viking art*. London, repr. 1980 (dansk udg.: O. Klindt-Jensen & D.M. Wilson: *Vikingetidens kunst*. Copenhagen 1965).

Burial customs in Scandinavia during the Viking Age (pp. 186–87)

Brøndsted, J. 1936: Danish inhumation graves of the Viking Age, *Acta Archaeologica* VII.

Gräslund, A.-S. 1980: *Birka IV. The burial customs. A study of the graves on Björkö*. KVHAA. Stockholm.

Hyenstrand, Å. 1979: *Ancient monuments and prehistoric society*. Stockholm.

Müller-Wille, M. 1968–69: Bestattung im Boot. Studien zu einer nordeuropäischen Grabsitte, *Offa* 25/26.

Steuer, H. 1984: Zur ethnischen Gliederung der Bevölkerung von Haithabu anhand der Gräberfelder, *Offa* 41.

Christian graves and funerary monuments (pp. 188–89)

Gardell, S. 1945: *Gravmonument från Sveriges medeltid*. Stockholm.

Kieffer-Olsen, J. 1990: Middelalderens gravskik i Danmark – en arkæologisk forskningsstatus, *Hikuin* 17. Højbjerg (Engl. summary).

Kulturhistoriskt lexikon för nordisk medeltid, vol. V, 1960: *s.v.* "Gravmonument".

Löffler, J.B. 1889: *Danske Gravstene fra Middelalderen*. Copenhagen.

Madsen, P.K. 1990: Han ligger under en blå sten. Om middelalderens gravskik på skrift og i praksis, *Hikuin* 17. Højbjerg (Engl. summary).

Nilsson, B. 1989: *De sepulturis. Gravrätten i Corpus iuris canonici och i medeltida nordisk lagstiftning*. Bibliotheca Theologiæ practicæ. Kyrkovetenskapliga studier 44. Uppsala.

Thor's hammers, pendant crosses and other amulets (pp. 190–91)

Arwidsson, G., (ed.) 1984: *Birka II:1. Systematische Analyse der Gräberfunde*. Kap. 12 Kreuzanhänger, Kruzifix und Reliquiar-Anhänger (A.-S. Gräslund); Kap. 15 Thorshammerringe und andere Gegenstände des heidnischen Kults (K. Ström). Stockholm.

Fuglesang, S.H. 1981: Crucifixion iconography in Viking Scandinavia, *Proceedings of the Eighth Viking Congress* (ed. H. Bekker-Nielsen *et al.*). Odense.

Fuglesang, S.H. 1989: Viking and medieval amulets in Scandinavia, *Fornvännen* 84.

Purhonen, P. 1987: Cross pendants from Iron Age Finland, *Byzantium and the North. Acta Byzantina Fennica*, vol. 3, 1987. Helsinki.

Skovmand, R. 1942: De danske Skattefund fra Vikingetiden og den ældste Middelalder indtil omkring 1150. *Aarbøger for nordisk Oldkyndighed og Historie* 1942. Copenhagen (Resumé français).

Stenberger, M. 1947, 1958: *Die Schatzfunde Gotlands der Wikingerzeit* I-II. Stockholm.

Dress (pp. 192–93)

Bender, Jørgensen L. 1986: *Forhistoriske textiler i Skandinavien*. Copenhagen.

Graham-Campbell, J. 1980: *Viking Artefacts. A select Catalogue*. London.

Groenman van Waateringe, W. 1984: *Die Lederfunde von Haithabu. Berichte über die Ausgrabungen in Haithabu* 21. Neumünster.

Hägg, I. 1974: *Kvinnodräkten i Birka. Livplaggens rekonstruktion på grundval av det arkeologiska materialet*. Uppsala.

Hägg, I. 1984: *Die Textilfunde aus dem Hafen von Haithabu. Berichte über die Ausgrabungen in Haithabu* 20. Neumünster.

Kulturhistorisk leksikon for nordisk middelalder, vol. III, 1958: *s.v.* "Drakt".

Lehtosalo-Hilander, P.-L. 1984: *Ancient Finnish costumes*. Helsinki.

Weapons and their use (pp. 194–95)

Kulturhistoriskt lexikon för nordisk medeltid, vol. I-XXII, 1956–1978: *s.v.* "Ambrøst"; "Båge"; "Spjut"; "Sverd"; "Øks".

Lehtosalo-Hilander, P.-L. 1985: Viking Age spearheads in Finland, *Society and trade in the Baltic during the Viking Age*. Acta Visbyensia VII. Visby.

Leppäaho, J. 1964: *Späteisenzeitliche Waffen aus Finnland. Schwertinschriften und Waffenverzierungen des 9–12. Jahrhunderts*. SMYA-FFT 61. Helsinki.

Müller-Wille, M. 1985: Westeuropäische Import der Wikingerzeit in Nordeuropa, *Society and trade in the Baltic during the Viking Age*. Acta Visbyensia VII. Visby.

Petersen, J. 1919: *De norske vikingesverd. En typologisk-kronologisk studie over vikingetidens vaaben*. Kristiania.

Iron (pp. 196–97)

Clarke, H., (ed.) 1979: *Iron and Man in Prehistoric Sweden*. Stockholm.

Hyenstrand, Å. 1977: *Hyttor och järnframställningsplatser*. Jernkontorets forskning, Serie H 17. Stockholm.

Magnusson, G. 1986: *Lågteknisk järnhantering i Jämtlands län*. Berghistorisk Skriftserie Nr 22. Stockholm.

Martens, I. 1988: *Jernvinna på Møsstrond i Telemark. En studie i bosetning og økonomi*. Oslo (English summary).

Medieval Iron in Society I-II. Jernkontorets forskning, Serie H 34 och 36. Stockholm 1985.

Mass production in the Viking Age (pp. 198–99)

Fuglesang, S.H. 1987: The personal touch. On the identification of workshops, *Proceedings of the Tenth Viking Congress* (ed. J.E. Knirk). Universitetets Oldsaksamling, Skrifter. Ny rekke 9. Oslo.

Jansson, I. 1985: *Ovala spännbucklor*. Uppsala.

Madsen, H.B. 1984: Metalcasting. Techniques, production and workshops, *Ribe Excavations 1970–76*, bd. 2 (ed. M. Bencard). Esbjerg.

Thunmark-Nylen, L. 1983: *Vikingatida dosspännen*. Uppsala.

Zachrisson, I. 1960: De ovala spännbucklornas tillverkningssätt, *Tor* 6. Uppsala.

Gold- and silver-smithing (pp. 200–01)

Duczko, W. 1985: *Birka V. The filigree and granulation work of the Viking Period*. Stockholm.

Grieg, S. 1929: Vikingetidens skattefund, *Universitetets Oldsaksamlings Skrifter* 2. Oslo.

Hårdh, B. 1976: *Wikingerzeitliche Depotfunde aus Südschweden. Katalog und Tafeln*. Bonn/Lund.

Oldeberg, A. 1966: *Metallteknik under vikingatid och medeltid*. Stockholm (English summary).

Skovmand, R. 1942: De danske Skattefund fra Vikingetiden og den ældste Middelalder indtil omkring 1150, *Aarbøger for nordisk Oldkyndighed og Historie* 1942. (Resumé français).

Stenberger, M. 1947, 1958: *Die Schatzfunde Gotlands der Wikingerzeit* I-II. Stockholm.

Bone, antler, amber and walrus ivory (pp. 202–03)

Goldschmidt, A. 1918, 1926: *Die Elfenbeinskulpturen aus der Romanischen Zeit* III-IV. Berlin.

Langberg, H. 1982: *Gunhildkorset. Gunhild's Cross*. København/Copenhagen.

Liebgott, N.-K. 1984: *Elfenben – fra Danmarks middelalder*. Copenhagen.

Lund, N., (ed.) 1983: *Ottar og Wulfstan. To rejseberetninger fra vikingetiden*. Roskilde (Engl. ed.: *Two voyagers at the Court of King Alfred* (ed. N. Lund, trans. C. Fell). York 1984).

Ulbricht, I. 1984: *Die Verarbeitung von Knochen, Geweih und Horn im mittelalterlichen Schleswig. Ausgrabungen in Schleswig. Berichte und Studien* 3. Neumünster.

Ulbricht, I. 1990: Bernsteinverarbeitung in Haithabu, *Das archäologische Fundmaterial V. Berichte über die Ausgrabungen in Haithabu* 27. Neumünster.

Walrus ivory in Western Europe (pp. 204–05)

The Carver's Art. Medieval Sculpture in Ivory, Bone and Horn (ed. S. St. Clair & E. Parker McLachlan). New Brunswick, New Jersey 1989. Exhibition catalogue.

Gaborit-Chopin, D. 1978: *Ivoires du Moyen Age occidental*. Fribourg.

Goldschmidt, A. 1914–1926: *Die Elfenbeinskulpturen* I-II, *Aus der Zeit der Karolingischen und Sächsischen Kaiser*; III-IV, *Aus der Romanischen Zeit*. Berlin.

Liebgott, N.-K. 1985: *Elfenben – fra Danmarks middelalder*. Copenhagen.

Randall, R. 1985: *Masterpieces of Ivory from the Walters Art Gallery of Baltimore*. New York.

Wood-carving (pp. 206–07)

Fridstrøm, E. 1985: The Viking Age woodcarvers. Their tools and techniques, *Universitetets Oldsaksamlings skrifter* 5. Oslo.

Hohler, E. B. 1989: Norwegian stave church carving: An introduction, *Arte Medievale* 1, 1989.

Karlsson, L. 1976: *Romansk träornamentik i Sverige*. Acta Universitatis Stockholmiensis 27, 1976.

Schetelig, H. 1920: *Osebergfundet* III. Kristiania.

Twelfth-century wooden sculpture (pp. 208–09)

Andersson, A. 1966: *Medieval Wooden Sculpture in Sweden* II. *Romanesque and Gothic Sculpture*. Stockholm.

Andersson, A. 1968: *L'art scandinave* 2. La Pierre-qui-Vire (Engl. ed.: *The Art of Scandinavia* 2. London 1970).

Anker, P. 1981: Høymiddelalderens skulptur i stein og tre, *Norges Kunsthistorie* 2 (ed. K. Berg). Oslo.

Tuulse, A. 1968: *Romansk konst i Norden*. Stockholm (deutsche Ausg.: *Scandinavia Romanica. Die hohe Kunst der romanischen Epoche in Dänemark, Norwegen und Schweden*. Vienna, Munich 1968).

Stone sculpture (pp. 210–11)

Blindheim, M. 1965: *Norwegian Romanesque Decorative Sculpture 1090–1210*. London.

Blomqvist, R. 1929: *Studier i Smålands romanska stenkonst*. Lund.

Mackeprang, M. 1941: *Danmarks middelalderlige Døbefonte*. Copenhagen.

Mackeprang, M. 1948: *Jydske granitportaler*. Copenhagen.

Roosval, J. 1918: *Die Steinmeister Gottlands*. Stockholm.

Rydbeck, M. 1936: *Skånes stenmästare före 1200*. Lund.

Church treasures and wall decoration (pp. 212–15)

Andersson, A. 1968: *L'art scandinave* 2. La Pierre-qui-Vire (English ed.: *The Art of Scandinavia* 2. London 1970).

Nørlund, P. 1926: *Gyldne Altre*. Copenhagen. 2. ed., med Appendix af T.E. Christiansen, Århus 1968 (Engl. summary).

Nørlund, P. 1944: *Danmarks Romanske Kalkmalerier*. Copenhagen (Résumé français).

Norn, O. & S. Skovgaard Jensen 1990: *The House of Wisdom. Visdommen i Vestjylland.* Copenhagen (Text in Danish and English).

Tuulse, A. 1968: *Romansk konst i Norden.* Stockholm (deutsche Ausg.: *Scandinavia Romanica. Die hohe Kunst der romanischen Epoche in Dänemark, Norwegen und Schweden.* Vienna, Munich 1968).

Manuscripts and Latin literary culture (pp. 216–17)

Brøndum-Nielsen, J., (ed.) 1943, 1954: *Palæografi.* A: Danmark og Sverige. B: Norge og Island. *Nordisk Kultur* vol. 28 A & B. Stockholm, Oslo, Copenhagen.

Ekström, P. 1985: *Libri Antiquiores Ecclesiæ et Capituli Lundensis. Lund domkyrkas äldsta liturgiska böcker.* Lund (Text in Swedish and English).

Kulturhistorisk leksikon for nordisk middelalder, vol. I-XXII. Copenhagen 1956–1978 (reprint 1982).

Nielsen, L. 1937: *Danmarks Middelalderlige Håndskrifter.* Copenhagen.

Icelandic manuscripts (pp. 218–19)

Hermannsson, H. 1929: *Icelandic Manuscripts.* Islandica XIX. Ithaca.

Hermansson, H. 1934: *Icelandic illuminated manuscripts of the Middle Ages.* Corpus Codicum Islandicorum Medii Aevi VII. Copenhagen.

Kristjánsson, J. 1980: *Icelandic Sagas and Manuscripts,* 2. ed. Reykjavík (dansk og norsk udg.: *Islandske sagaer og håndskrifter,* 1970; deutsche Ausgabe: *Isländische Sagas und Handschriften,* 1980).

Palæografisk Atlas 1. Copenhagen 1905.

Seip, D. Arup 1954: *Palæografi.* B: Norge og Island. *Nordisk Kultur* 28 B. Stockholm, Oslo, Copenhagen.

Scandinavian coins (pp. 220–21)

Bendixen, K. 1976: *Danmarks mønt,* 2. ed. (Engl. ed.: *Denmark's money.* Copenhagen 1967).

Hauberg, P. 1900: *Myntforhold og Udmyntninger i Danmark indtil 1146.* Det Kgl. Danske Vidensk. Selsk. Skr., 6. Række, hist. og filos. Afd. V:1. Copenhagen (Resumé en français).

Lagerqvist, L.O. 1970: *Svenska mynt under vikingatid och medeltid.* Stockholm.

Malmer, B. 1966: *Nordiska mynt före år 1000.* Acta Archaeologica Lundensia, series in 8:0, 4. Lund.

Malmer, B. 1989: *The Sigtuna Coinage c. 995-1005.* Commentationes de nummis saeculorum IX-XI in Suecia repertis, nova series 4. Stockholm.

Schive, C.I. 1865: *Norges Mynter i Middelalderen.* Christiania.

Sigtuna Papers. Proceedings of the Sigtuna Symposium on Viking-Age Coinage 1-4 June 1989 (ed. K. Jonsson and B. Malmer). Commentationes de nummis saeculorum IX-XI in Suecia repertis, nova series 6. Stockholm 1990.

Skaare, K. 1975: *Coins and Coinage in Viking-Age Norway.* Oslo.

Catalogue nos. 1–617

1000 Jahre russische Kunst. Ausstellungskatalog Schleswig-Wiesbaden 1988–89 (ed. H. Spielmann & J. Drees). Hamburg 1988.

Admoni, V. & T. Silman 1957: Predvaritelnoe soobščenie o runičeskoj nadpisi iz Staroj Ladogi, *Soobščeni ja Gosudarstvennogo Ermitaža* 11. Leningrad.

Ágústsson, H. 1989: *Dómsdagur og helgir menn á Hólum.* Reykjavík.

Åhlén, M. 1990: Runfynd 1988, *Fornvännen* 1990:1.

Ahrens, D. 1964: Die Buddhastatuette von Helgö, *Pantheon* 1964.

Albrectsen, E., (ed.) 1979: *Dudo. Normandiets historie under de første Hertuger.* Odense.

Almgren, B. 1955: *Bronsnycklar och djurornamentik vid övergången från vendeltid till vikingatid.* Uppsala.

Ambrosiani, B. 1980: Båtgravarnas bakgrund i Mälardalen, *Vendeltid* (ed. A. Sandwall). Stockholm.

Ambrosiani, K. 1981: *Viking Age Combs, Comb Making and Comb Makers in the light of finds from Birka and Ribe.* Stockholm.

Andersen, H.H., P.J. Crabb, H.J. Madsen 1971: *Århus Søndervold. En byarkæologisk undersøgelse.* Aarhus (deutsche Zusammenfassung).

Andersson, A. 1958: *Kristusbilden i Danderyd och de äldsta uppländska triumfkrucifixen.* Antikvariskt arkiv 11. Stockholm.

Andersson, A. 1962: *Viklaumadonnans mästare.* Antikvariskt arkiv 18. Stockholm (deutsche Zusammenfassung).

Andersson, A. 1966: *Medieval Wooden Sculpture in Sweden. II. Romanesque and Gothic Sculpture.* Stockholm.

Andersson, A. 1967: Relikkorset från Gåtebo, *Nordisk medeltid. Konsthistoriska studier tillägnade Armin Tuulse.* Uppsala (English summary).

Andersson, A. 1968: *L'Art Scandinave* 2. La Pierre-qui-Vire (English ed.: Andersson, 1970a).

Andersson, A. 1970a: *The Art of Scandinavia* 2. London (éd. française: Andersson, 1968).

Andersson, A. 1970b: The Holy Rood of Skokloster and the Scandinavian Early Gothic, *The Burlington Magazine* vol. 22. London.

Andersson, A. 1973: Gravstenen från Botkyrka och korset från Granhammar, *Fornvännen* 1973.

Andersson, A. 1983: *Mediaeval drinking bowls of silver found in Sweden.* Stockholm.

Andrén, A. 1980: Biskopen som försvann ... ... eller att tolka fynd, *Meta* 1980:1.

Andrén, A. & T. Nilsson 1976: Lås och nycklar, *Uppgrävt förflutet för PKbanken i Lund* (ed. A.W. Mårtensson). Lund.

Åneman, C. 1989: Runbelägget til Sihtunum, *Studia Onomastica. Festskrift till Thorsten Andersson den 23. februari 1989.*

Anker, P. 1969: *L'Art Scandinave* 1. La-Pierre-qui-Vire (English ed.: *The Art of Scandinavia* 1. London 1970).

Anker, P. 1981: Høymiddelalderens skulptur i stein og tre, *Norges Kunsthistorie* 2. Oslo.

Anker, P. 1985: Retardering eller renessanse, *By og Bygd*. Norsk Folkemuseums Årbok 30. Oslo.

Appelgren, Hj. 1905: *Die vielreihigen silbernen Gliederketten in finnländischen Funden*. SMYA-FFT XXIII. Helsinki.

Arbman, H. 1933: En släktgrav från vikingatiden, *Från Gästrikland*. Gävle.

Arbman, H. 1937: *Schweden und das karolingische Reich*. Stockholm.

Arbman, H. 1940: *Birka I. Die Gräber. Tafeln*. Stockholm.

Arbman, H. 1943: *Birka I. Die Gräber. Text*. Uppsala.

Arbman, H. 1940–43: *Birka I. Die Gräber. Tafeln. Text*. Stockholm, Uppsala.

Arbman, H. 1945: "Uppståndelseägg" av glaserad lera, *Situne Dei* 1945. Sigtuna.

Arbman, H. 1955: *Svear i österviking*. Stockholm.

Arbman, H. 1959: Skandinavisches Handwerk in Russland zur Wikingerzeit, *Meddelanden från Lunds Universitets Historiska Museum* 1959.

Arbman, H. & N.O. Nilsson 1966–68: Armes scandinaves de l'époque viking en France, *Meddelanden från Lunds Universitets Historiska Museum* 1966–1968.

Archaeologia L, 1887. London.

Archéologie de la France. 30 ans de découvertes, 1989 (Catalogue d'exposition, Grand-Palais). Paris.

Arcichovskij, A.V. & V.L. Janin 1978: *Novgorodskie gramoty na bereste (iz raskopok 1962–1976)*. Moscow.

Arge, S.V. 1989: Om landnamet på Færøerne, *Hikuin* 15, 1989. Højbjerg (English summary).

Armstrong, E.C.R. 1921–22: Irish Bronze Pins of the Christian Period, *Archaeologia* LXXII.

Arne, T.J. 1914a: *La Suède et l'Orient*. Uppsala.

Arne, T.J. 1914b: Den svenska runstenen från ön Berezanj utanför Dnjepr-mynningen, *Fornvännen* 1914.

Arne, T.J. 1915: Nya bidrag till Södermanlands förhistoria, *Bidrag till Södermanlands äldre kulturhistoria* 16. Strängnäs.

Arne, T.J. 1932: Ein bemerkenswerter Fund in Östergötland, *Acta Archaeologica* III.

Arne, T.J. 1934: *Das Bootgräberfeld von Tuna in Alsike*. Stockholm.

Arneborg, J. 1985: Nordboarkæologiske undersøgelser ved Kilaarsarfik i nordboernes vesterbygd, *Forskning-Tusaat* 1985. nr. 2 (text in Danish and Greenlandic).

Arquié-Bruley, F. 1981: Les commissaires-priseurs parisiens avant 1870, *Revue de l'Art*.

Arrhenius, B. 1961: Vikingatida miniatyrer, *Tor* 7. Uppsala.

Arrhenius, B. 1989: Arbeitsmesser aus den Gräbern von Birka, *Birka II:3* (ed. G. Arwidsson). Stockholm.

Arwidsson, G. 1977: *Valsgärde 7*. Uppsala.

Arwidsson, G. 1984: Die Silberkapsel aus dem Sarggrab Bj 464, *Birka II:1* (ed. G. Arwidsson). Stockholm.

Arwidsson, G. 1989: Verschiedene Schmuckgegenstände, *Birka II:3* (ed. G. Arwidsson). Stockholm.

Arwidsson, G. & G. Berg 1983: *The Mästermyr find. A Viking Age tool chest from Gotland*. Stockholm.

Avril, F. 1987: L'atelier du psautier d'Ingeburge: problèmes de localisation et de datation, *Mélanges en hommage à H. Landais. Art, objets d'Art, collections*. Paris.

Backhouse, J., D. H. Turner and L. Webster, (ed.) 1984: *The Golden Age of Anglo-Saxon Art 966–1066*. London.

Bäcksbacka, Chr. 1975: *Föremålsbeståndet i 1000-talets finska myntförande skattfynd*. Helsingin yliopiston arkeologian laitos. Moniste 11. Helsinki.

Bailey, R. 1980: *Viking Age Sculpture in Northern England*. London.

Bailey, R. and R. Cramp 1988: *Corpus of Anglo-Saxon Sculpture* II. London.

Bakka, E. 1963: Some English decorated metal objects found in Norwegian Viking graves, *Årbok for Universitetet i Bergen*. Humanistisk serie 1963:1.

Balodis, F. 1934: Ein Denkmal der Wikingerzeit aus Semgallen, Lettland *Eurasia Septentrionalis Antiqua* IX. Helsinki.

Batey, C.E. 1988: A Viking-Age Bell from Freswick Links, Caithness, *Medieval Archaeology* XXXII.

Batey, C.E. 1989: Bjalla frá söguöld, fundin á Skotlandi, *Árbók hins Íslenzka fornleifafélags* 1989. Reykjavík.

Bätke, W. (tr.) 1966: Die Geschichte von den Orkaden, Dänemark und der Jomsburg, *Thule* XIX, 1966 (1924).

Baumgartner, E. & I. Krueger 1988: *Phönix aus Sand und Asche. Glas des Mittelalters*. Munich.

Becker, C. 1980: Untersuchungen an Skelettresten von Haus- u. Wildschweinen in Haithabu, *Berichte über die Ausgrabungen in Haithabu* 15. Neumünster.

Becker, C.J. 1981: The Coinages of Harthacnut and Magnus the Good at Lund c. 1040–c. 1046, *Studies in Northern Coinages of the Eleventh Century* (ed. C.J. Becker). Copenhagen.

Becker, C.J. 1983: Magnus den Godes Hedeby-mønter og slaget på Lyrskov hede, *Nordisk Numismatisk Unions Medlemsblad* 1983 nr. 3.

Beckwith, J. 1972: *Ivory Carvings in Early Medieval England*. London.

Behre, K.-E. 1983: *Ernährung und Umwelt der wikingerzeitlichen Siedlung Haithabu*. Die Ausgrabungen in Haithabu 8. Neumünster.

Bencard, M. 1979: Wikingerzeitliches Handwerk in Ribe, *Acta Archaeologica* 49.

Bender Jørgensen, L. 1986: *Forhistoriske textiler i Skandinavien*. Copenhagen.

Bendixen, B.E. 1909: Aus der Mittelalterlichen Sammlung des Museums in Bergen, *Bergen Museums Årbok* 1909.

Bendixen, B.E. 1911: Aus der Mittelalterlichen Sammlung des Museums in Bergen, *Bergen Museums Årbok* 1911.

Bendixen, K. 1976: *Danmarks mønt*, 2. ed. Copenhagen (English ed.: *Denmark's Money*. Copenhagen 1967).

Bendixen, K. 1981: Sceattas and other coin finds, *Ribe Excavations 1970–1976* (ed. M. Bencard), vol. I. Esbjerg.

Benediktsson, H. 1965: *Early Icelandic Script*. Íslenzk handrit, Ser. in fol. II. Reykjavík.

Benediktsson, J., (ed.) 1958: *Skarðsárbók*. Reykjavík.

Benediktsson, J., (ed.) 1968: *Íslendingabók. Landnámabók*. Íslenzk fornrit I. Reykjavík.

Benediktsson, J., (ed.) 1974: *Landnámabók*. Reykjavík (Engl. tr. of introduction).

Bergman, K. & I. Billberg 1976: Metallhantverk, *Uppgrävt förflutet för PKbanken i Lund* (ed. A.W. Mårtensson). Lund.

Biddle, M. and B. Kjølbye-Biddle in the press, *Investigations at Repton 1974–88*, vol. I (ed. H.W. Grenville).

Biddle, M. and B. Kjølbye-Biddle in the press, *Investigations at Repton 1974–88*, vol. II. *Monastery, Fortress and Church.*

Biddle, M. and B. Kjølbye-Biddle et al. 1986: A Parcel of Pennies from a Mass-burial Associated with the Viking Wintering at Repton 873–4, *Anglo-Saxon Monetary History* (ed. M.A.S. Blackburn). Leicester.

Björkman, T. 1957: Kuusamon Lämsän hopea-aarre, *Suomen Museo 1957*. Helsinki (Referat: Der Silberschatz von Lämsä in Kuusamo).

Blackburn, M. 1981: An imitative workshop active during Æthelræd II's Long Cross issue, *Studies in Northern Coinages of the Eleventh Century* (ed. C.J. Becker). Copenhagen.

Blackburn, M., M. Dolley & K. Jonsson, 1979: Nyt eksemplar af Svend Tveskægs mønt, *Nordisk Numismatisk Unions Medlemsblad 1979* nr. 4.

Blackburn, M., M. Dolley & K. Jonsson 1983: A new specimen of Svend Tveskæg's Coinage, *Seaby Coin and Medal Bulletin.*

Blake, N.F., (ed. and tr.) 1962: *The Saga of the Jomsvikings.* London.

Blindheim, C. 1959: Osebergskoene på ny, *Viking 23*. Oslo (English summary).

Blindheim, C. 1963: Smedgraven fra Bygland i Morgedal, *Viking 26*. Oslo (English summary).

Blindheim, C. 1981: Slemmedal-skatten. En liten orientering om et stort funn, *Viking 45*. Oslo (English summary).

Blindheim, C., B. Heyerdahl-Larsen & R.L. Tollnes 1981: *Kaupang-funnene* I. Universitetets Oldsaksamling. Norske Oldfunn XI. Oslo (English summary).

Blindheim, M. 1956–57: Brukrusifikset – et tidligmiddelaldersk klenodium, *Universitetets Oldsaksamling. Årbok*. Oslo (English summary).

Blindheim, M. 1965: *Norwegian Romanesque Decorative Sculpture 1090–1210*. London.

Blindheim, M. 1980: En gruppe tidlige, romanske krusifikser i Skandinavia og deres genesis. Kristus fremstillinger, *5. nordiske symposium for ikonografiske studier 1976* (ed. U. Haastrup). Copenhagen (English summary).

Blindheim, M. 1982a: The gilded Viking Ship Vanes. Their use and technology, *The Vikings* (ed. R.T. Farrell). London.

Blindheim, M. 1982b: De gylne skipsfløyer fra sen vikingetid. Bruk og teknik, *Viking 46*. Oslo (English summary).

Blindheim, M. 1983: De yngre middelalderske skipsfløyer i Norge, *Imagines Medievales*. Acta Universitatis Upsaliensis, Ars Suetica vol. 7. Uppsala (deutsche Zusammenfassung).

Blindheim, M. 1984: A house-shaped Irish-Scots reliquary in Bologna, and its place among the other reliquaries, *Acta Archaeologica 55*.

Blindheim, M., (ed.), 1972: See: *Middelalderkunst fra Norge i andre land.*

Blomqvist, R. & A.W. Mårtensson, 1963: *Thulegrävningen 1961*. Lund (English summary).

Bø, O. 1966: *Norsk skitradisjon*. Oslo (English ed.: *Skiing traditions in Norway*. Oslo 1968).

Bøe, J. 1934: A hoard from Western Norway, *The Antiquaries Journal* XIV. London.

Bøe, J. 1940: Norse Antiquities in Ireland, *Viking Antiquities in Great Britain and Ireland*, Part III (ed. H. Shetelig). Oslo.

Boserup, I. 1981: The Angers Fragment and the Archetype of Gesta Danorum *Saxo Grammaticus. A Medieval Author Between Norse and Latin Culture* (ed. K. Friis-Jensen). Copenhagen.

Boyer, R. (tr.), 1973: *Le Livre de la Colonisation de l'Islande (Landnámabók)*. Paris.

Braathen, H. 1989: *Ryttergraver. Politiske strukturer i eldre rikssamlingstid*. Universitetets Oldsaksamling, Varia 19. Oslo (English summary).

Brade, C. 1975: *Die mittelalterlichen Kernspaltflöten Mittel- und Nordeuropas*. Neumünster.

Braun, F. A. 1907: Švedskaja runičeskaja nadpis, najdennaja na o. Berezani, *Izvestija imperatorskoj archeologičeskoj kommissii 23*. St. Petersburg.

Brinch Madsen, H. 1976: Specialist i spænder, *Skalk 1976:6*. Højbjerg.

Brinch Madsen, H. 1984: Metal-Casting. Techniques, Production and Workshops, *Ribe Excavations 1970–1976* (ed. M. Bencard), vol. 2. Esbjerg.

Brøgger, A.W. 1916: *Borrefundet og Vestfoldkongernes graver*. Videnskapsselskapets Skrifter, Hist. Fil. Kl. II, No. 1. Kristiania.

Brøgger, A.W. 1921: *Ertog og øre*. Videnskapsselskapets Skrifter, II, Hist. Fil. Kl. No. 3. Kristiania.

Brøgger, A.W. 1925: Bronsefløien fra Heggen kirke, *Norske Oldfunn* V. Oslo.

Brøgger, A.W. & H. Shetelig, 1950: *Vikingskibene*. Oslo (English ed.: *The Viking Ships*. Oslo 1951).

Brøgger, A.W., Hj. Falk & H. Schetelig, (ed.), 1917–28: *Osebergfundet* I–III, V. Kristiania, Oslo (some copies with a German summary, others with an English one).

Brøgger, A.W., J. Holmboe & H. Schetelig, 1917: *Osebergfundet* I (ed. A.W. Brøgger, Hj. Falk & H. Schetelig). Kristiania.

Brøndsted, J. 1920: Nordisk og fremmed Dyreornamentik i Vikingetiden med særligt Henblik paa Stiludviklingen i England, *Aarbøger for nordisk Oldkyndighed og Historie 1920*. Copenhagen.

Brøndsted, J. 1936: Danish Inhumation Graves of the Viking Age, *Acta Archaeologica* VII.

Brøndsted, J. 1960: *Danmarks Oldtid* III. Jernalderen. Copenhagen (Deutsche Ausg.: *Nordische Vorzeit*, Bd. 3. Neumünster 1963).

Bugge, A. 1925: Bronsefløien fra Tingelstad kirke, *Norske Oldfunn* V. Oslo.

Buisson, L. 1976: *Der Bildstein Ardre VIII auf Gotland*. Abhandlungen der Akademie der Wissenschaften in Göttingen, Phil.-hist. Kl. 3. Folge, Nr. 102. Göttingen.

Callmer, J. 1988a: Slawisch-skandinavische Kontakte am Beispiel der slawischen Keramik in Skandinavien während des 8. und 9. Jahrhunderts, *Oldenburg-Wolin-Staraja Ladoga-Novgorod-Kiev* (ed. M. Müller-Wille). *Bericht der Römisch-Germanischen Kommission 69*.

Callmer, J. 1988b: De åländska lertassgravarna, *Gravskick och gravdata*. University of Lund, Institute of Archaeology, Report series No. 32.

Carlson, K. 1982: *Importkeramik i Gamla Lödöse*. Stockholm.

Carlsson, A. 1988: *Vikingatida ringspännen från Gotland*. Stockholm Studies in Archaeology 8. Stockholm (English summary: Penannular brooches from Viking Period Gotland).

Carrasco, M. 1984: Notes on the Iconography of the Romanesque illustrated Manuscripts of the Life of Saint Albinus of Anger, *Zeitschrift für Kunstgeschichte* 1984.

Chatellier, P. du & L. le Pontois 1908: La sépulture scandinave à barque de l'île de Groix, *Bulletin de la Société Archéologique du Finistère* 35.

Christensen, A.E. 1988: Ship Graffiti and Models, *Medieval Dublin Excavations 1962–81*, Ser. B, vol. 2. *Miscellanea* 1. Dublin.

Christensen, A.E. & G. Leiro 1976: Klåstadskipet, *Vestfoldminne*. Tønsberg.

Christensen, K. & K.J. Krogh 1987: Jelling-højene dateret, *Nationalmuseets Arbejdsmark* 1987. Copenhagen.

Christensen, T. 1987a: Lejrehallen, *Skalk* 1987:3. Højbjerg.

Christensen, T. 1987b: Nye udgravninger i Lejre, *Beretning fra sjette tværfaglige vikingesymposium* (ed. G. Fellows-Jensen & N. Lund). Højbjerg.

Christiansen, T.E. 1950: Sønder Kirkeby-Reliefferne, *Nationalmuseets Arbejdsmark* 1950. Copenhagen.

Christiansen, T.E. 1968: De gyldne altre I. Tamdrup-pladerne, *Aarbøger for nordisk Oldkyndighed og Historie* 1968. Copenhagen.

Christiansen, T.E. 1976: Gundhildkorset og Ribe Domkirke, *Fra Ribe Amt*. Esbjerg.

Christiansen, T.E. 1983: Anmeldelse af P. Svensson: Frøslevskrinet (1981), *Fortid og Nutid* XXX:3. Copenhagen.

Christophersen, A. 1980: *Håndverket i forandring. Studier i horn- og beinhåndverkets utvikling i Lund ca 1000–1350*. Lund.

Christophersen, A. 1987: *Trondheim – en by i middelalderen*. Trondheim. (English, Norwegian and German text).

Cinthio, E. 1948: Två medeltida människotyper, *Situne Dei* 1948. Sigtuna.

Cinthio, M. 1976: Isläggar, *Uppgrävt förflutet för PKbanken i Lund* (ed. A.W. Mårtensson). Lund.

Cinthio, M. 1990: Myntverk och myntare i Lund, *Kulturen* 1990.

Clemmensen, M. 1911: Kirkeruiner fra Nordbotiden m.m. i Julianehaab Distrikt, *Meddelelser om Grønland* XLVII. Copenhagen.

Cleve, N. 1929: Jüngereisenzeitliche Funde von der Insel Berezan, *Eurasia Septentrionalis Antiqua* IX. Helsinki.

Cleve, N. 1941: Ett i Finland funnet tistelspänne, *Finskt Museum* 1941. Helsinki.

Coblenz, W. 1975: Wikingerzeitliches Ortband in einer slawischen Siedlung von Nimschütz, Kr. Bautzen, *Ausgrabungen und Funde* 20. Berlin.

Coblenz, W. 1978: Zur Handelsausstrahlung des Ostens, *Zeitschrift für Archäologie* 12, 1978:2. Berlin.

Cochet, Abbé 1871: Notice sur deux fibules scandinaves trouvées à Pîtres (Eure) en 1865 et entrées au Musée de Rouen (extrait du *Précis de l'Académie de Rouen pour l'année 1869–1870*). Rouen.

Codex Frisianus, with an introduction by H. Hermannsson, 1932, *Corpus Codicum Islandicorum Medii Aevi* IV. Copenhagen (Facsimile).

Collijn, I. 1914: *Redogörelse för... undersökning angående äldre arkivalieomslag*. Stockholm.

Corpus archäologischer Quellen zur Frühgeschichte auf dem Gebiet der DDR (7.–12. Jahrhundert), 1979, (ed. J. Herrmann und P. Donat) 2. Lieferung. Berlin.

Corpus Nummorum Saeculorum IX–XI qui in Suecia reperti sunt, vol. I, Gotland, 2. Stockholm 1977.

Corpus Nummorum Saeculorum IX–XI qui in Suecia reperti sunt, vol. I, Gotland, 4. Stockholm 1982.

Corpus Vitrearum Medii Aevi, Skandinavien, 1964, (A. Andersson *et al.*). Stockholm.

Cramp, R. 1984: *Corpus of Anglo-Saxon Stone Sculpture* I. London.

Crumlin-Pedersen, O. 1973: Helnæs-spærringen, *Fynske Minder* 1973. Odense (English summary).

Crumlin-Pedersen, O. 1985: Ship Finds and Ship Blockages AD 800–1200, *Archaeological Formation Processes* (ed. K. Kristiansen). Copenhagen.

Cubbon, A.M. 1983: *The Art of the Manx Crosses*. Manx Museum.

Dahl, S. 1971: Recent Excavations on Viking Sites in the Faroes, *Proceedings of the Sixth Viking Congress 1969* (ed. P. Foote and D. Strömbäck). London.

Dahl, S. 1979: Forn barnaleiku í Føroyum, *Mondul* 1979 nr. 3. Tórshavn.

Dalas-Garrigues, M. 1984: Guillaume le Conquérant, *Le Club français de la Médaille* nr. 85 (deuxième semestre 1984).

Dalton, O.M. 1909: *Catalogue of the ivory carvings of the Christian era in The British Museum*. London.

Danmarks Kirker, II Frederiksborg amt. Copenhagen 1964–75; VI Præstø amt. Copenhagen 1933–35; XVI Århus amt. Copenhagen 1976 ff.

Danmarks Middelalder, 1972. Copenhagen (Nationalmuseets vejledninger).

Danmarks middelalderlige Skattefund, 1991. Af J. Steen Jensen, K. Bendixen, N.-K. Liebgott, F. Lindahl under medvirken af G. Posselt og K. Grinder-Hansen. Copenhagen (English summary).

Danske kalkmalerier. Romansk tid 1080–1175, 1986 (ed. U. Haastrup & R. Egevang). Copenhagen.

Davey, P. & R. Hodges, (ed.) 1983: *Ceramics & Trade*. Sheffield.

Davidan, O.I. 1962: Grebni Staroj Ladogi, *Archeologičeskij sbornik Gosudarstvennogo Ermitaža* 4. Leningrad.

Davidan, O.I. 1970a: Contacts between Staraja Ladoga and Scandinavia, *Varangian Problems*, Scando-Slavica, supplementum 1. Copenhagen.

Davidan, O.I. 1970b: O vremeni pojavlenija tokarnogo stanka v Staroj Ladoge, *Archeologičeskij sbornik Gosudarstvennogo Ermitaža* 12. Leningrad.

Davidan, O.I. 1976: Stratigrafija nižnego sloja Staroladožskoj gorodišča i voprosy datirovki, *Archeologičeskij sbornik Gosudarstvennogo Ermitaža* 17. Leningrad.

Davidan, O.I. 1982: Om hantverkets utveckling i Staraja Ladoga, *Fornvännen* 1982:3.

Davidan, O.I. 1986: Etnokulturnye kontakty Staroj Ladogi, *Archeologičeskij sbornik Gosudarstvennogo Ermitaža* 27. Leningrad.

Davidson, H.R.E. 1967: *Pagan Scandinavia*. London.

Davidson, H.R.E. 1969: *Scandinavian Mythology*. London.

The Dawn of art. Palaeolithic, Neolithic, Bronze Age and Iron Age remains found in the territory of the Soviet Union, 1974. The Hermitage Collection (ed. M. Artamonov). Leningrad (English and Russian text).

Degerbøl, M. 1929: Animal Bones from the Norse Ruins at Gardar, Greenland, *Meddelelser om Grønland* 76. Copenhagen.

Degnbol, H. og H. Jensen (tr.), 1978: *Jomsvikingernes saga*. Copenhagen.

Delisle, L. 1890: *Instructions adressées par le comité des traveaux historiques et scientifiques... Litterature latine et histoire du moyen age*. Paris.

Dennis, A., P. Foote, R. Perkins (tr.) 1980: *Laws of Early Iceland. Grágás* I. Winnipeg.

Der Ingeborgpsalter 1985. Chantilly, musée Condé, ms 9 olim 1695, Graz, *Codices Selecti*. vol. LXXX (commentaires par Fl. Deuchler).

Deuchler, Fl. 1967: *Der Ingeborgpsalter*. Berlin.

Deutgen, L. 1990: Textilhantverk I – spinning och vävning, *Makt och människor i kungens Sigtuna. Sigtunautgrävningen 1988–90* (ed. S. Tesch). Sigtuna.

Dhénin, M. 1990: Les monnaies normandes, *Le Domfrontais médiéval* 7, IX, 1990.

Dillmann, F.-X. (tr.) 1991: *L'Edda. Récits de mythologie nordique par Snorri Sturluson*. Paris.

Diplomatarium Danicum 1. rk. 1. bd. Regester 789–1052, ved C.A. Christensen og H. Nielsen. Copenhagen 1975.

Diplomatarium Norvegicum I, 1849. Christiania.

Diplomatarium Suecanum I, 1829–1834. Stockholm.

Dock, B. 1990: Bergkristall – som råvara och färdig produkt, *Makt och människor i kungens Sigtuna. Sigtunautgrävningen 1988–90* (ed. S. Tesch). Sigtuna.

Documents impériaux et royaux de l'Europe médiévale, 1977. Paris (catalogue d'exposition).

Dolley, M. 1965: *Viking Coins of the Danelaw and of Dublin*. London.

Douët d'Arcq, M. 1868: *Inventaires et documents publiés par ordre de l'Empereur sous la direction de M. le Marquis de Laborde. Collection de sceaux*, T. III. Paris.

Dreijer, M. 1956: Die Ziernadel von Syllöda, *Suomen Museo* 1956. Helsinki.

Drenzel, L. & L. Henriksson 1990: Dräktens tillbehör, *Makt och människor i kungens Sigtuna. Sigtunautgrävningen 1988–90* (ed. S. Tesch). Sigtuna.

Drescher, H. 1984: Glockenfunde aus Haithabu, *Das archäologische Fundmaterial IV. Berichte über die Ausgrabungen in Haithabu* 19. Neumünster.

Drescher, H. 1989: Zeichnerische Konstruktion plastischer Figuren durch 'Magdeburger' Giesser im 12. Jahrhundert, *Der Magdeburger Dom*. Symposiumsbericht. Leipzig.

Drescher, H. 1991: Gussformen früher Glocken aus Mainz, *Mainzer Jahrbuch* (in preparation).

Drescher, H. in the press in: *Berichte über die Ausgrabungen in Haithabu*. Neumünster.

Drescher, H. & H.G. Rincker 1986: Die Technik des Glockengusses in Geschichte u. Gegenwart, *Frankfurter Glockenbuch* (ed. K. Bund). Mitt. a.d. Frankfurter Stadtarchiv 4.

Drescher, H. & K. Hauck 1972: Götterthrone des heidnischen Nordens, *Frühmittelalterliche Studien* 16. Berlin, New-York.

Duczko, W. 1983: Slaviskt och gotländskt smide i ädla metaller, *Gutar och vikingar* (ed. I. Jansson). Stockholm.

Duczko, W. 1985: *Birka V. The filigree and granulation work of the Viking period*. Stockholm.

Duczko, W. 1989: Østlig kontakt, *Skalk* 1989:4. Højbjerg.

Duisburg und die Wikinger, 1983. Begleitheft zur Ausstellung 16.1–10.4 1983 (ed. T. Bechert). Duisburg.

Dumas, F. 1979: Les monnaies normandes (X^e–XIIe siècles), avec un répertoire des trouvailles, *Revue Numismatique* 1979.

Dumas, F. et J. Pilet-Lemière 1989: La monnaie normande X^e–XIIe siècle. Le point de la recherche en 1987, *Les Mondes Normands* (ed. H. Galinié). Caen.

Durville, G. 1928: Les épées normandes de l'Ile de Bièce, *Bull. Soc. Arch. et Hist. de Nantes et de Loire-Inférieure* 68.

Eckhoff, E. 1914–1916: *Svenska stavkyrkor*. Stockholm.

Edgren, T. 1987: Kring ett graverat bronsfat från Vilusenharju i Tavastland, *Museerna och forskningen. Festskrift tillägnad Knut Drake på 60-årsdagen 6.3.1987*. Åbo.

Edgren, T. 1988: Om leksaksbåtar från vikingatid och tidig medeltid, *Festskrift til Olaf Olsen* (ed. A. Andersen et al.). Copenhagen (Summaries in English, French or German).

Eken, T. 1963: *Gammalnorske membranfragment i Riksarkivet*. Oslo (English Introduction).

Ekström, P. 1985: *Libri Antiquiores Ecclesiæ et Capituli Lundensis. Lunds domkyrkas äldsta liturgiska böcker*. Lund (also English text).

Eldjárn, K. 1953: Carved Panels from Flatatunga, Iceland, *Acta Archaeologica* vol. XXIV.

Eldjárn, K. 1956: *Kuml og haugfé. Úr heiðnum sið á Íslandi*. Akureyri.

Eldjárn, K. 1957–58: Þrjú kuml norðanlands, *Árbók hins Íslenzka fornleifafélags 1957–1958*. Reykjavík (English summary).

Eldjárn, K. 1970: En Tau-stav fra Island, *Kuml* 1970. Højbjerg (English summary).

Eldjárn, K. 1973: *Hundrad ár i Þjóðminjasafni*. Reykjavík (English summary).

Eldjárn, K. 1981: The bronze image from Eyrarland, *Speculum Norroenum, Norse Studies in Memory of Gabriel Turville-Petre* (ed. U. Dronke et al.) Odense.

Elmqvist, B. 1966–68: Les fibules de Pîtres, *Meddelanden från Lunds Universitets Historiska Museum 1966–1968*.

English Romanesque Art 1066–1200, 1984, (ed. G. Zarnecki, J. Holt, T. Hillard). London.

Ernst, A. 1946: Om møntfundet fra Lunds domkirke 1835, *Nordisk Numismatisk Årsskrift* 1946.

Evison, V.I. 1969: A Viking Grave at Sonning, Berks., *Antiquaries Journal* XLIX.

Falke, O. von & E. Meyer 1935: *Bronzegeräte des Mittelalters* I. Berlin.

Fanning, T. 1983: The Hiberno-Norse pins from the Isle of Man, *The Viking Age in the Isle of Man* (ed. C. Fell et al.). London.

Fanning, T. 1990: Die bronzenen Ringkopfnadeln aus der Ausgrabung im Hafen von Haithabu, *Berichte über die Ausgrabungen in Haithabu* 27. Neumünster.

Farbregd, O. 1972: *Pilefunn på Oppdalsfjella*. Det kgl. norske Videnskabers selskab, Museet. Miscellanea 5. Trondheim (English summary).

Faulkes, A. (tr.) 1987: *Snorri Sturluson. Edda*. London and Melbourne.

Fauroux, M. 1961: *Recueil des Actes des ducs de Normandie, 911–1066*. Caen.

Fechner, M.V. 1965: O "skramasakse" iz Gnezdova, *Novoe v sovetskoj archeologii*. Moscow.

Fechner, M.V. 1967: Šejnye grivny, *Očerki po istorii russkoj derevni X–XIII vv*, Trudy Gosudarstvennogo Istoričeskogo Muzeja 43. Moscow.

Fechner, M.V. 1982: Nakonečnik nožen meča iz kurgana bliz Korostenja, *Sovetskaja Archeologija* 1982:4.

Fechner, M.V. & N.G. Nedosivina 1987: Etnokulturnaja charakteristika Timerevskogo mogilnika po materialam pogrebalnogo inventarja, *Sovetskaja Archeologija* 1987:2.

Fell, C. 1975: Old English beor, *Leeds Studies in English*. New Series VIII.

Fell, C. (tr.) 1975: *Egils Saga*. London and Melbourne 1975, 1985.

Ferté, C. de la 1961: *La Revue du Louvre et des Musées de France* No. 3. Paris.

Filipowiak, W. 1985: Die Bedeutung Wolins im Ostseehandel, *Society and Trade in the Baltic during the Viking Age* (ed. S.-O. Lindquist). Acta Visbyensia VII. Visby.

Filipowiak, W. 1986: *Wolin-Vineta*. Rostock-Stralsund.

Filipowiak, W. 1988: Handel und Handelsplätze an der Ostseeküste Westpommerns, *Oldenburg-Wolin-Staraja Ladoga-Novgorod-Kiev* (ed. M. Müller-Wille). *Bericht der Römisch-Germanischen Kommission 69*.

Filipowiak, W. 1991: *Wolin-Jomsborg*. Roskilde.

Finsen, V., (ed.) 1879: *Grágás, Staðarhólsbók*. Copenhagen.

Fischer, D. 1962: Tyldalstolen, *Viking* 25. Oslo (English summary).

Fischer, D. 1965: Tidlig-romanske stenfunn, in: G. Fischer: *Trondheims Domkirke*, Vol. II. Oslo (English summary).

Fonahn, A. 1926: Note on a hoard of medieval coins found at Stein, Ringerike, Norway, *Numismatic Chronicle*, Fifth Series, Vol. VI.

Fornnordiska klanger (The sounds of prehistoric Scandinavia). Swedish Music Anthology. Musica Sveciæ (MS 101). Redigerad och producerad av C. Lund. Gramophone record, EMI 1361031.

Forsåker, A.L. 1986: Zaumzeug, Reiterausrüstung und Beschirrung, *Birka* II:2 (ed. G. Arwidsson). Stockholm.

Forsell, H. 1983: Fynd av sydda båtar i Finland, *Båtar* 1. Skrifter utgivna av Skärgårdsmuseet. Lovisa.

Forsell, H. 1985: The reconstruction of a sewn boat find from Lake Mekrijärvi, *World Archaeology* 16 No. 3.

Fraenckel-Schoorl, N. 1978: Carolingian jewellery with plant ornament, *Berichten van de Rijksdienst voor het Oudheidkundig Bodemonderzoek* 28.

Frank, R. 1978: *Old Norse Court Poetry: The Dróttkvætt Stanza*. Islandica XLII. Ithaca and London.

Franzén, A.M. 1960: Høylandsteppet, *Det kgl. norske Videnskabers selskab, Museet. Årbog* 1960. Trondheim.

Friesen, O. von 1912: Runinskrifterna på en koppardosa, funnen i Sigtuna, *Fornvännen* 1912.

Friis-Jensen, K. 1989: Humanism and Politics. The Paris edition of Saxo Grammaticus' Gesta Danorum 1514, *Analecta Romana Instituti Danici* vol. 17/18. Rome.

Froger, J. 1980: Le lieu de destination et de provenance du "Compendiensis", *Ut mens concordet voci*. Festschrift E. Cardine (ed. J. Berschmans Göschl). St. Ottilien.

Fuglesang, S.H. 1980a: *Some Aspects of the Ringerike Style. A phase of 11th century Scandinavian art*. Odense.

Fuglesang, S.H. 1980b: Vikingtidens ristninger – Dekorasjonsteknikk, skisse og tidstrøyte, *Ristninger i forhistorie og middelalder* (ed. D.S. Hjelvik & E. Mikkelsen). Universitetets Oldsaksamling. Varia 1. Oslo.

Fuglesang, S.H. 1981a: Vikingtidens kunst, *Norges Kunsthistorie* 1 (ed. K. Berg et al.). Oslo.

Fuglesang, S.H. 1981b: Stylistic groups in late Viking and early Romanesque art, *Acta ad archaeologiam et artium historiam pertinentia*, ser. alt. in 8, vol. I. Rome.

Fuglesang, S.H. 1981c: Crucifixion iconography in Viking Scandinavia, *Proceedings of the Eighth Viking Congress* (ed. H. Bekker-Nielsen et al.). Odense.

Fuglesang, S.H. 1981d: Woodcarvers – professionals and amateurs – in eleventh-century Trondheim, *Economic aspects of the Viking Age. British Museum Occasional Paper No. 30* (ed. D.M. Wilson and M.L. Caygill). London.

Fuglesang, S.H. 1982: Early Viking Art, *Acta ad archaeologiam et artium historiam pertinentia*, ser. alt. in 8°, vol. II. Rome.

Fuglesang, S.H. 1989: Viking and medieval amulets in Scandinavia, *Fornvännen* 1989:1–2.

Fuglesang, S.H. 1990: Ågerup – kvinnemasker på ovalspenner, *Oldtidens Ansigt/Faces of the Past* (ed. P. Kjærum & R.A. Olsen). Copenhagen (Danish and English text).

Fuglesang, S.H. 1991: The axehead from Bjerringhøj and the Mammen style, *Mammen. Grav, kunst og samfund i vikingetid* (ed. M. Iversen, U. Näsman & J. Vellev). Højbjerg.

Fuglesang, S.H. in the press: Vikings II:1, Scandinavia, *The Dictionary of Art*.

Gaborit, D. 1972: Deux émaux limousins, *Revue du Louvre* 17–3.

Gaborit-Chopin, D. 1978: *Ivoires du Moyen Age occidental*. Fribourg.

Gabriel, I. 1988: Hof- und Sakralkultur sowie Gebrauchs- und Handelsgut im Spiegel der Kleinfunde von Starigard/Oldenburg, *Bericht der Römisch-Germanischen Kommission 69*.

Galster, G. 1935: Møntfundet fra Vraabjerg, *Aarbøger for nordisk Oldkyndighed og Historie* 1935.

Galster, G. 1937: Møntfund i Danmark og Norge 1739–1780, *Nordisk Numismatisk Årsskrift* 1937.

Galster, G. 1954: Årsberetning for Den kgl. Mønt- og Medaillesamling 1953, *Nordisk Numismatisk Årsskrift* 1954.

Galster, G. 1964: *The Royal Danish Collection, Copenhagen. Part I. Ancient British and Anglo-Saxon Coins. Sylloge of Coins of the British Isles*, no. 4. London.

Galster, G. 1966: *The Royal Danish Collection, Copenhagen. Part II. Anglo-Saxon Coins. Æthelred II. Sylloge of Coins of the British Isles*, no. 7. London.

Galster, G. 1970: *The Royal Danish Collection, Copenhagen.* Part III. *A, B and C. Cnut. Sylloge of Coins of the British Isles,* no. 13–15. London.

Galster, G. 1977a: Uttrup-møntfund 1696 og 1708, *Aarbøger for nordisk Oldkyndighed og Historie* 1977 (English summary).

Galster, G. 1977b: Treenighedssymbol på mønt, *National-museets Arbejdsmark* 1977.

Gamber, K. 1963: *Codices liturgici latini antiquiores.* Freiburg.

Gauthier M.-M. 1952: *Émaux du moyen âge occidental.* Brussels and Paris.

Gauthier, M.-M. 1966: Une châsse limousine du dernier quart du XIIe siècle: thèmes iconographiques, composition et essai de chronologie. *Mélanges R. Crozet.* Poitiers.

Gauthier, M.-M. 1987: *Émaux méridionaux. Catalogue international de l'œuvre de Limoges.* 1. L'époque romane. Paris.

Geijer, A. 1938: *Birka III. Die Textilfunde aus den Gräbern.* Stockholm.

Geijer, A. 1979: *A History of Textile Art.* London.

Gestsson, G. 1961: Billedstenen fra Snaptun, *Kuml* 1961. Århus (English summary).

Ginters, V. 1944: Wikinger im Ostbaltikum, *Deutsche Monats-hefte in Norwegen* 5:3. Oslo.

Ginters, V. 1981: *Tracht und Schmuck in Birka und im ostbaltischen Raum.* Stockholm.

Ginters, V. 1984: Der Ursprung der Ringspangen von öst-lichem Typ, *Birka II:1* (ed. G. Arwidsson). Stockholm.

Gjærder, P. 1964: The beard as an iconographic feature in the Viking period and early Middle Ages, *Acta Archaeologica* XXXV.

Glob, P.V. 1959: Avlsten, *Kuml* 1959. Århus (English summary).

Glob, P.V. 1977: Et vikingeskib af bronze og et af guld. *Anti-kvariske studier tilegnet Knud Thorvildsen* (ed. S.E. Albrethsen). Copenhagen.

Glob, P.V., (ed.) 1980: *Danefæ. Til Hendes Majestæt Dronning Margrethe II.* Copenhagen (text in Danish and English).

The Golden Age of Anglo-Saxon Art 966–1066, 1984 (ed. J. Back-house *et al.*). Exhibition Catalogue. London.

Goldschmidt, A. 1914, 1918: *Die Elfenbeinskulpturen aus der Zeit der Karolingischen und Sächsischen Kaiser VIII.–XI. Jahrhundert.* I–II. Berlin (Neuaufl. Berlin 1969–70).

Goldschmidt, A. 1918, 1926: *Die Elfenbeinskulpturen aus der Romanischen Zeit XI.–XIII. Jahrhundert.* III–IV. Berlin (Neuaufl. Berlin 1972–75).

Goldschmidt, A. und K. Weitzmann 1930, 1934: *Die Byzantinis-chen Elfenbeinskulpturen des X.–XIII. Jahrhunderts.* I–II. Berlin. (Neuauflage Berlin 1979).

Golubeva, L.A. 1949: Kievskij nekropol, *Materialy i issledovanija po archeologii SSSR,* vol. 11. Moscow-Leningrad.

Graham-Campbell, J. 1975: Bossed pennanular brooches, review of recent research, *Medieval Archaeology* XIX.

Graham-Campbell, J. 1980: *Viking Artefacts. A Select Catalogue.* London.

Graham-Campbell, J. 1983a: Some Viking-Age Penannular Brooches from Scotland and the Origins of the "Thistle Brooch", *From the Stone Age to the Forty-Five: essays presented to R.B.K. Stevenson* (ed. A. O'Connor and D.V. Clarke). Edinburgh.

Graham-Campbell, J. 1983b: The Viking Age Silver Hoards of the Isle of Man, *The Viking Age in the Isle of Man* (ed. C. Fell *et al.*). London.

Graham-Campbell, J. 1987a: Some archaeological reflections on the Cuerdale hoard, *Coinage in Ninth-Century Northumbria* (ed. D.M. Metcalf). Oxford, B.A.R.

Graham-Campbell, J. 1987b: Western Penannular Brooches and Their Viking Age Copies in Norway: a new classifica-tion, *Proceedings of the Tenth Viking Congress* (ed. J.E. Knirk). Oslo.

Graham-Campbell, J. in the press: *The Cuerdale Hoard and related Viking-age Silver from Britain and Ireland in the British Museum.* London.

Graham-Campbell, J. & D. Kidd 1980: *The Vikings.* London.

Gräslund, A.-S. 1984: Kreuzanhänger, Kruzifix und Reliquiar-Anhänger, *Birka II:1* (ed. G. Arwidsson). Stockholm.

Gräslund, A.-S. 1989: "Gud hjälpe nu väl hennes själ". Om runstenskvinnorna, deras roll vid kristnandet och deras plats i familj och samhälle, *Tor* 22. Uppsala (English summary).

Grieg, S. 1928: *Osebergfundet* II (ed. A.W. Brøgger & H. Schetelig). Oslo.

Grieg, S. 1929: Vikingetidens skattefund, *Universitetets Oldsak-samlings Skrifter* II. Oslo.

Grieg, S. 1933: *Middelalderske byfund fra Bergen og Oslo.* Oslo.

Grieg, S. 1940: Viking Antiquities in Scotland, *Viking Antiquities in Great Britain and Ireland,* Part II (ed. H. Shetelig). Oslo.

Grieg, S. 1947: *Gjermundbufunnet. En høvdinggrav fra 900-årene fra Ringerike.* Universitetets Oldsaksamling. Norske Oldfunn VIII. Oslo.

Grierson, P. 1966: Harald Hardrada and Byzantine Coin Types in Denmark, *Byzantinische Forschungen* 1 (Repr. P. Grierson: *Later Medieval Numismatics.* London 1979).

Grodecki, L. 1969: in: *Revue de l'Art,* No. 5.

Groenman van Waateringe W. 1984: Die Lederfunde aus Haithabu, *Berichte über die Ausgrabungen in Haithabu* 21. Neumünster.

Guðjónsson, E.E. 1974: "Formálsorð" og "tilvitnanir", in: Jónasson K.: Að kemba i togkömbum, *Árbók hins Íslenzka fornleifafélags* 1974. Reykjavík (English summary).

Guðjónsson, E.E. 1977: "Inskrifter", Island (Tekstiler), *Kul-turhistorisk leksikon for nordisk middelalder,* vol. XXI.

Guðjónsson, E.E. 1979: Togcombs in the National Museum of Iceland with some notes on Icelandic woolcombs in general, *Textile History* 10.

Guðjónsson, E.E. 1988: Romanesque Gold Embroidered Vest-ments from the Cathedral Church at Hólar, *Opera Textilia Variorum Temporum. To honour Agnes Geijer on her Ninetieth Birthday.* Stockholm.

Guðjónsson, E.E. 1989: Biskupsskrúði Guðmundar góða? Gullsaumadur messuskrúði frá dómkirkjunni á Hólum í Hjaltadal, *Skagfirðingabók* 18. Reykjavík (English summary).

Guðmundsson, F., (ed.) 1965: *Orkneyinga saga.* Íslenzk fornrit 34. Reykjavík.

Guščin, A.S. 1936: *Pamjatniki chudožestvennogo remesla Drevnej Rusi X–XIII vv.* Moscow-Leningrad.

Gyllene Böcker. Illuminerade medeltida handskrifter i dansk och svensk ägo, 1952, (ed. K. Olsen och C. Nordenfalk). Stockholm. (Catalogue). (Dansk udg.: *Gyldne Bøger: illuminerede middelalderlige håndskrifter i Danmark og Sverige.* Copenhagen 1952).

Haastrup, U. 1975: Fristelsen i Jørlunde, *ICO* 1975: 2–3. Copenhagen.

Haastrup, U. 1981: Byzantine Elements in Frescoes in Zealand in the Middle of the 12th Century, *Les Pays du Nord et Byzance. Actes du colloque nordique et international de byzantinologie tenu à Upsal 20–22 avril 1979* (ed. R. Zeitler). Uppsala.

Hægstad, M. 1906: *Vestnorske maalføre fyre 1300.* Kristiania.

Haevernick, T.E. & W. Haberey 1963: Glättsteine aus Glas, *Jahrbuch des Römisch-Germanischen Zentralmuseums Mainz X.*

Hagen, A. 1953: *Studier i jernalderens gårdssamfunn.* Universitetets Oldsaksamlings Skrifter 4. Oslo (English summary).

Hägg, I. 1983: Birkas orientaliska praktplagg, *Fornvännen* 1983:3–4 (English summary).

Hägg, I. 1984: Textilfunde aus dem Hafen von Haithabu – Aspekte und Interpretation, *Offa* 41.

Hägg, I. 1985: *Die Textilfunde aus dem Hafen von Haithabu. Berichte über die Ausgrabungen in Haithabu 20.* Neumünster.

Hägg, I. 1986: Die Tracht, *Birka II:2* (ed. G. Arwidsson). Stockholm.

Hägg, I. 1991: Textilfunde aus der Siedlung und aus den Gräbern von Haithabu. Materialbeschreibung und -gliederung, *Berichte über die Ausgrabungen in Haithabu 29.* Neumünster.

Hagland, J.R. 1986: Runefunna. Ei kjelde til handelen si historie, *Fortiden i Trondheim bygrunn: Folkebibliotekstomta. Meddelelser nr. 8.* Trondheim.

Hald, M. 1980: *Ancient Danish Textiles from Bogs and Burials. A Comparative Study of Costume and Iron Age Textiles.* Copenhagen (dansk udg.: *Olddanske Tekstiler.* Copenhagen 1950).

Hall, R. 1984: *The Viking Dig.* London.

Hällström, O. af 1947–48: Lisiä suomalaisten soikeiden kupurasolkien syntyhistoriaan, *Suomen Museo* 1947–1948. Helsinki (Deutsche Zusammenfassung: Beiträge zur Entstehungsgeschichte der finnischen ovalen Buckelfibeln).

Hatz, G. 1974: *Handel und Verkehr zwischen dem Deutschen Reich und Schweden in der späten Wikingerzeit.* Stockholm.

Hauberg, P. 1900: *Myntforhold og Udmyntninger i Danmark indtil 1146.* København (Résumé français). Reprint, se Hauberg 1965.

Hauberg, P. 1906: *Danmarks Myntvæsen i Tidsrummet 1146–1241.* Copenhagen (Résumé français). Reprint, se Hauberg 1965.

Hauberg, P. 1965: *Danmarks Mønter c. 870–1241* (fotografisk genoptryk af Hauberg 1900 og 1906). Copenhagen.

Haugen, E. 1972: *First Grammatical Treatise. The Earliest Germanic Phonology. An edition, translation and commentary.* London (2nd rev. ed.).

Hauglid, R. 1940: Chartres Trends in the Former Northern Medieval Plastic Art, *Det kgl. norske Videnskabers selskabs Skrifter 1932*, 2. Trondheim.

Hauglid, R. 1973: *Norske Stavkirker. Dekor og utstyr.* Oslo.

Haussherr, R. 1977: Der Ingeborgpsalter. Bemerkungen zu Datierungs und Stilfragen, *The Year 1200: a Symposium.* New York (Metropolitan Museum of Art).

Hawkins, E. 1847: An account of coins and treasure found in Cuerdale, *The Archaeological Journal IV*, 1847.

Helgason, J., (ed.) 1966: *Hauksbók. The Arnamagnæan Manuscripts 371 4to, 544 4to, and 675 4to.* Manuscripta Islandica vol. 5. Copenhagen (Facsimile).

Hendy, M. 1970: Michael IV and Harald Hardrada, *The Numismatic Chronicle.*

Henry, F. 1954: *Early Christian Art.* Dublin.

Henry, F. 1956: Irish enamels of the Dark Ages and Their Relation to the Cloisonnée Techniques, *Dark Age Britain* (ed. D.B. Harden). Dublin.

Henry, F. 1970: *Irish Art in the Romanesque Period 1020–1170 A.D.* London.

Herbécourt, P. & J. Porcher 1959: *Anjou roman* (English summary; deutsche Zusammenfassung). La Pierre-qui-Vire.

Herfert, P. 1973: Ralswiek. Ein frühgeschichtlicher Seehandelsplatz auf der Insel Rügen, *Greifswald-Stralsunder Jahrbuch* 1972/1973.

Hermannsson, H. 1929: *Icelandic Manuscripts.* (Islandica XIX). Ithaca, N.Y.

Hermannsson, H., (ed.) 1930: *The Book of the Icelanders.* (Islandica XX). Ithaca, N.Y.

Hermannsson, H., (ed.) 1935: *Icelandic Illuminated Manuscripts of the Middle Ages.* Corpus Codicum Islandicorum Medii Aevi VII. Copenhagen.

Hermannsson, H., (ed.) 1938: *The Icelandic Physiologus* (Islandica XXVII). Ithaca, N.Y.

Herrmann, J. 1978: Ralswiek und Rügen – ein Handelsplatz des 9. Jahrhunderts und die Fernhandelsbeziehungen im Ostseegebiet, *Zeitschrift für Archäologie* 12, 1978:2. Berlin.

Hesbert, Dom R. 1935: *Antiphonarium missarum sextuplex.* Brussels.

Heslop, T.A. 1978: The Romanesque seal of Worcester Cathedral, *Medieval Art and Architecture at Worcester Cathedral, Brit. Arch. Ass. Conference Transactions* 1975.

Heyerdahl-Larsen, B. 1981: "Gnostiske" amulettgjemmer i skatten fra Hon, *Viking* 45.

Hickes, G. 1705: *Linguarum Vett. Septentrionalium Thesaurus Grammatico-criticus et Archæologicus.* Oxford.

Hildebrand, B.E. 1881: *Anglosachsiska mynt i Svenska Kongl. Myntkabinettet, funna i Sveriges jord.* Stockholm.

Hildebrand, B.E. & H. 1878: *Teckningar ur Svenska statens historiska museum 2.*

Hirviluoto, A.-L. 1956: Laitilan suksilöytö, *Osma* 1956. Helsinki.

Hodges, R. 1981: *The Hamwih pottery: the local and imported wares from 30 years' excavations at Middle Saxon Southampton and their European context.* CBA Research Report 37. London.

Hoffmeyer, A.B. 1954: *Middelalderens tveæggede sværd.* Copenhagen.

Hofseth, E.H. 1985: *Det går i spinn. Forsøk på en klassifikasjon av spinnehjul i Rogaland.* AmS, Skrifter 11. Stavanger.

Hohler, E. 1971–72: Hylestadportalen og dens forbilder, *Aust-Agder Arv* 1971–72. Arendal (English summary).

Hohler, E. 1989: Norwegian Stave Church Carving: An Introduction, *Arte Medievale* 1. Rome.

Holmboe, C.A. 1841: *De prisca re monetaria Norvegiae et de numis seculi duodecimi nuper repertis*. Christianiae.

Holmqvist, W. 1948: Sigtunamästaren och hans krets, *Situne Dei 1948* (English summary).

Holmqvist, W. 1955: *Germanic art during the first millennium A.D.* Stockholm.

Holmqvist, W. 1956: *Valöfyndet*. Stockholm.

Holmqvist, W. 1959: The Syllöda Silver Pin – an English Element in the Art of the Viking Age, *Suomen Museo 1959*. Helsinki.

Holmqvist, W. 1961: Bronze, *Excavations at Helgö* 1 (ed. W. Holmqvist). Stockholm.

Holmqvist, W. 1963: *Övergångstidens metallkonst*. Kungl. Vitterhets Historie och Antikvitets Akademiens Handlingar. Antikvariska Serien II. Stockholm (English summary).

Houts, E. van 1983: *Gesta Normannorum ducum: een studie over de handschriften, de tekst, het geschiedwerk en het genre*. Groningen.

Huisman, G.H. 1984: Notes on the manuscript tradition of Dudo of St Quentin's *Gesta Normannorum, Anglo-Norman Studies* (ed. R.A. Brown), vol. VI.

Humbla, P. 1934: Äskekärrsbåten, *Göteborgs och Bohusläns Fornminnesförenings tidskrift*.

Hüster, H. 1990: Untersuchungen an Skelettresten von Rindern, Schafen, Ziegen und Schweinen aus dem mittelalterlichen Schleswig. Ausgrabung Schild 1971–1975, *Ausgrabungen in Schleswig* 8. Neumünster.

Hvass, S. 1979: Vorbasse. The Viking-age Settlement at Vorbasse, central Jutland, *Acta Archaeologica* vol. 50.

Hvass, S. 1984: Årtusinders landsby, *Skalk* 1984: 3. Højbjerg.

Hvass, S. 1986: Vorbasse – Eine Dorfsiedlung während des 1. Jahrtausends n. Chr. in Mitteljütland, Dänemark, *Bericht der Römisch-Germanischen Kommission* 67.

Ingstad, A.S. 1970: The Norse Settlement at L'Anse aux Meadows, Newfoundland. A Preliminary Report from the Excavations 1961–1968, *Acta Archaeologica* XLI.

Ingstad, A.S. 1977: *The Discovery of a Norse Settlement in America: Excavations at L'Anse aux Meadows, Newfoundland, 1961–1968*. Oslo.

Iversen, M., U. Näsman & J. Vellev, (ed.) 1991: *Mammen. Grav, kunst og samfund i vikingetid*. Højbjerg.

Ivory Carvings in Early Medieval England 700–1200, 1974. Victoria & Albert Museum, London.

Jacobsen, L. og E. Moltke 1941–42: *Danmarks Runeindskrifter* I–II. Copenhagen.

Jansen, H.M. 1988: Svendborg-udgravningerne, *Fynske Minder* 1988. Odense (Deutsche Zusammenfassung).

Jansen, H.M. 1989: Svantevit fra Svendborg, *Årbog fra Svendborg & Omegns Museum* 1989 (deutsche Zusammenfassung).

Jansen, H.M. 1990: Svendborgs Svantevit, *Skalk* 1990:2. Højbjerg.

Jansson, I. 1975–77: Ett rembeslag av orientalisk typ funnet på Island. Vikingatidens orientaliska bälten och deras eurasiska sammanhang, *Tor* 17. Uppsala.

Jansson, I. 1985: *Ovala spännbucklor*. Uppsala (English summary).

Jansson, I. 1986: Gürtel und Gürtelzubehör vom orientalischen Typ, *Birka II:2* (ed. G. Arwidsson). Stockholm.

Jansson, I. 1987: Communications between Scandinavia and Eastern Europe in the Viking Age, *Untersuchungen zu Handel und Verkehr der Vor- und frühgeschichtlichen Zeit in Mittel- und Nordeuropa IV* (ed. K. Düwel et al.). Abhandlungen der Akademie der Wissenschaften in Göttingen, Philol.-hist. Klasse, 3. Folge, Nr. 156. Göttingen.

Jansson, I. 1988: Wikingerzeitlicher orientalischer Import in Skandinavien, *Bericht der Römisch-Germanischen Kommission* 69.

Jansson, S.B.F. 1963: *Runinskrifter i Sverige*. Stockholm (English rev. ed.: see S.B.F. Jansson 1987).

Jansson, S.B.F. 1987: *Runes in Sweden*. Stockholm.

Jaroslavskoe Povolže X–XI vv, 1963, (ed. A.P. Smirnov). Moscow.

Jaubert, A.N. 1988: Betragtninger over Camp de Péran, *Hikuin* 14. Højbjerg (English summary).

Jensen, S. 1986: En lille viking rejste, *Skalk* 1986:5. Højbjerg.

Jensen, S. 1990: Odin fra Ribe, *Oldtidens ansigt/ Faces of the Past* (ed. P. Kjærum & R.A. Olsen). Copenhagen (Text in Danish and English).

Jensen, S. og L.B. Frandsen 1987: Pre-Viking and Early Viking Age Ribe, *Journal of Danish Archaeology* 6. Odense.

Jóhannesson, J., (ed.) 1956: *Íslendingabók Ara fróða*. Reykjavík (English tr. of introduction).

Johannson, F. 1982: Untersuchungen an Skelettresten von Rindern aus Haithabu (Ausgrabung 1966–1969), *Berichte über die Ausgrabungen in Haithabu* 17. Neumünster.

Johansen, O.S. 1973: Bossed pennanular brooches, *Acta Archaeologica* XLIV.

Johansen, O.S. 1980: The Chronology of the court sites of North Norway, *Studien zur Sachsenforschung*, vol. 2 (ed. H.-J. Hässler). Hildesheim.

Johansson, H. 1956: *Den medeltida liturgien i Skara stift*. Lund.

Jondell, E. 1974: *Vikingatidens balansevågar i Norge*. Uppsala.

Jónsdóttir, S. 1959: *An 11th Century Byzantine Last Judgement in Iceland*. Reykjavík.

Jónsson, F., (ed.) 1886–88: *Egils saga Skallagrímssonar*. Copenhagen.

Jónsson, F., (ed.) 1892–96: *Hauksbók*. Copenhagen.

Jónsson, F., (ed.) 1895: *De bevarede brudstykker af skindbøgerne Kringla og Jöfraskinna*. Copenhagen.

Jónsson, F., (ed.) 1930: *Íslendingabók*. Copenhagen.

Jørgensen, E. 1926: *Catalogus codicum latinorum medii ævi Bibliotheca Regiæ Hafniensis*. Hafniæ.

Jungner, H. 1930: Den gotländska runbildstenen från Sanda, *Fornvännen 1930*.

Jungner, H. 1979: *Radiocarbon Dates I*. Radiocarbon Dating Laboratory. University of Helsinki. Report No 1. Helsinki.

Kålund, K. 1882: Islands fortidslævninger, *Aarbøger for nordisk Oldkyndighed og Historie 1882*.

Kålund, K. 1889–94: *Katalog over den Arnamagnæanske Håndskriftsamling* I–II. Copenhagen.

Karger, M.K. 1958: *Drevnij Kiev*, vol. I. Moscow-Leningrad.

Karlsson, L. 1977: *Romansk träornamentik i Sverige*. Stockholm (English summary).

Karlsson, L. 1988: *Medieval Ironwork in Sweden*. Kgl. Vitterhets

Historie och Antikvitets Akademien. Stockholm.

Karlsson, S. 1976: Kringum Kringlu, *Landsbókasafn Íslands. Árbók* 1976. Reykjavík (English summary).

Kermode, P.M.C. 1911: The Woodbourne Treasure-Trove, 1894, *Proceedings of the Isle of Man Natural History and Antiquarian Society* 1:6.

Keskitalo, O. 1969: Suontaka-svärdet, *Finskt Museum* 1969. Helsinki.

Kielland, T. 1925: Kunsthåndverket i Middelalderen, *Norsk Kunsthistorie* I. Oslo.

Kielland, T. 1927: *Norsk guldsmedkunst i middelalderen*. Oslo.

Kiersnowski, R. 1988: *Moneta w kulturze wieków srednich*. Warsaw.

Kiil, V. 1964: Runepinnen fra Gamle Ladoga, *Arkiv för nordisk Filologi* 79. Lund.

Kirpičnikov, A.N. 1966–71: *Drevnerusskoe oružie* vol. 1–3. Moscow-Leningrad.

Kirpičnikov, A.N. 1970: Connections between Russia and Scandinavia in the 9th and 10th centuries, as illustrated by weapon finds, *Varangian problems*, Scando-Slavica, supplementum 1. Copenhagen.

Kirpičnikov, A.N. 1973: *Snarjaženie vsadnika i verchovogo konja na Rusi IX–XIII vv*. Leningrad.

Kirpičnikov, A.N. 1988: Staraja Ladoga/Alt-Ladoga und seine überregionale Beziehungen im 8.–10. Jahrhundert, *Bericht der Römisch-Germanischen Kommission* 69.

Kivikoski, E. 1934: Eisenzeitliche Tontatzen aus Åland, *Eurasia Septentrionalis Antiqua* IX. Helsinki.

Kivikoski, E. 1965: Magisches Fundgut aus finnischer Eisenzeit, *Finskt Museum* 1965. Helsinki.

Kivikoski, E. 1970: Zu den axtförmigen Anhängern der jüngsten Eisenzeit, *Studia archaeologica in memoriam Harri Moora*. Tallinn.

Kivikoski, E. 1973: *Die Eisenzeit Finnlands. Bildwerk und Text*. Neuausgabe. Helsinki.

Kjellberg, R. 1946: Djevelen fra Vossestrand, *Fataburen* 1946. Stockholm.

Klindt-Jensen, O. & D.M. Wilson 1965: *Vikingetidens kunst*. Copenhagen (English ed.: see Wilson, D.M. & O. Klindt-Jensen 1966).

Koehler, W. & F.P. Mütherich 1982: *Die Hofschule Karls des Kahlen*. Berlin.

Kolčin, B.A. 1989: *Wooden artefacts from Medieval Novgorod*. British Archaeological Reports, International Series 495. Oxford (Russian edition: B.A. Kolčin, *Novgorodskie drevnosti. Reznoe derevo*. Moscow 1971).

Kornerup, J. 1875: *Kongehøiene i Jellinge*. Copenhagen.

Korzuchina, G.F. 1954: *Russkie klady*. Moscow-Leningrad.

Köster, K. 1983: Pilgerzeichen und Pilgermuscheln von mittelalterlichen Santiagostrassen, *Ausgrabungen in Schleswig, Berichte und Studien* 2. Neumünster.

Kristjánsson, J. 1988: *Eddas and Sagas*. Reykjavík.

Krogh, K.J. 1980: Kongelige smykker?/ Royal Ornaments?, *Danefæ. Til Hendes Majestæt Dronning Margrethe II* (ed. P.V. Glob). Copenhagen.

Krogh, K.J. 1982: The Royal Viking-Age Monuments of Jelling in the Light of Recent Archaeological Excavations. A Preliminary Report, *Acta Archaeologica* 53.

Krogh, K.J. 1982: *Erik den Rødes Grønland/Qallunaatsiaaquarfik Grønland*. Copenhagen (tekst på dansk og på grønlandsk).

Krogh, K.J. og O. Voss 1961: Fra hedenskab til kristendom i Hørning, *Nationalmuseets Arbejdsmark* 1961. Copenhagen.

Krongaard Kristensen, H. 1988: A Viking-Period and Medieval Settlement at Viborg Søndersø, Jutland, *Journal of Danish Archaeology* 7.

Krongaard Kristensen, H. 1988–89: Spor efter guldsmede fra vikingetiden i Viborg, *Kuml* 1988–89. Højbjerg (English summary).

Krüger, E. 1972: *Die Schreib- und Malerwerkstatt der Abtei Helmarshausen bis in die Zeit Henrich des Löwen*. Darmstadt and Marburg.

Kulturhistorisk leksikon for nordisk middelalder vol. I–XXII, 1956–78, reprint 1980–82. Copenhagen, Helsinki, Reykjavík, Oslo, Malmö.

Kulturhistoriskt lexikon för nordisk medeltid, se *Kulturhistorisk leksikon for nordisk middelalder vol. I–XXII*.

Kyhlberg, O. 1980: *Vikt och värde*. Stockholm (English summary).

L'Europe Gothique XII e–XIVᵉ Siècles. (Council of Europe Exhibition. Musée du Louvre, 1968). Paris.

L'Or des Vikings, 1969 (catalogue d'exposition). Musée d'Aquitaine, Bordeaux.

la Cour, V. 1959: Havnebondens våben, *Våbenhistoriske Årbøger* X. Copenhagen.

la Fuente Pedersen, E. de 1988: Majestas Mariae I. Lisbjergalterets ikonografi og motiviske forbilleder, *ICO* 1988:2. Stockholm (English summary).

Lagerlöf, E. 1984: Bysantinskt måleri från en gotländsk stavkyrka, *Den ljusa medeltiden. Studier tillägnade Aron Andersson*. Statens historiska museum. Studies 4. Stockholm.

Lagerlöf, E. & B. Stolt 1969: *Hemse kyrkor. Sveriges kyrkor* vol. 131. Stockholm.

Lagerlöf, E. & B. Stolt 1974: *Eke kyrka. Sveriges kyrkor* vol. 156. Stockholm.

Lagerqvist, L.O. 1968: The coinage at Sigtuna in the names of Anund Jacob, Cnut the Great and Harthacnut, *Commentationes de nummis saeculorum IX–XI in Suecia repertis*, vol. II (ed. N.L. Rasmusson & B. Malmer). Stockholm.

Lagerqvist, L.O. 1970: *Svenska mynt under vikingatid och medeltid samt gotländska mynt*. Stockholm.

Lagerqvist, L.O. 1990: Sensation igen i Sigtuna, *Svensk numismatisk tidsskrift* 8/1990.

Lair, J. 1865: *De moribus et actis primorum Normanniae ducum auctore Dudone Sancti Quintini decano*. Mém. de la Soc. des Antiquaires de Normandie, 3e série, t. III. Caen.

Lamm, C.J. 1941: *Oriental glass of mediaeval date found in Sweden and the early history of lustrepainting*. Stockholm.

Lang, J. 1984: The Hogback: A Viking colonial monument, *Anglo-Saxon Studies in Archaeology and History*, vol. 3.

Lang, J. 1985: The compilation of design in colonial Viking sculpture, *Festskrift til Thorleif Sjøvold. Universitetets Oldsaksamlings Skrifter*, ny rekke nr. 5, 1984. Oslo.

Lang, J. 1987: Eleventh-century style in decorated wood from Dublin, *Ireland and Insular Art A.D. 500–1200* (ed. M. Ryan). Dublin.

Lang, J.T. 1988: *Viking-Age Decorated Wood. A Study of its Ornament and Style*. Medieval Dublin Excavations 1962–81. Ser. B 1. Royal Irish Academy. Dublin.

Langberg, H. 1979: *Gyldne billeder*. Copenhagen.

Langberg, H. 1982: *Gunhildkorset – Gunhild's Cross and Medieval Court Art in Denmark*. Copenhagen (Text in Danish and English).

Larsen, A.-C. (in print): Norsemen's use of Juniper in Viking Age Faroe Islands, *Acta Archaeologica*.

Lárusson, Ó., (ed.) 1936: *Corpus Codicum Islandicorum Medii Aevi* IX. Copenhagen.

Lasko, P. 1960: A Romanesque ivory carving, *British Museum Quarterly* XXIII.

Lasko, P. 1972: *Ars sacra 800–1200*. Harmondsworth.

Latvijas PSR arheologija, 1974 (ed. A. Birons, E. Mugurevics, A. Stubavs, E. Snore). Riga (deutsche Zusammenfassung).

Lefroy, J.H. 1870–71: On a bronze object bearing a runic inscription found at Greenmount, Castle-Bellingham, County Louth, *Journal of the Royal Society of Antiquaries in Ireland* 11.

Lehtosalo, P.-L. 1966: Rapukoristeisten solkien ajoituksesta, *Suomen Museo 1966*. Helsinki (Referat: Zur Datierung der Krebsverzierten Schalenspangen).

Lehtosalo, P.-L. 1973: *Luistarin hopeasolki*, SMYA-FFT 75. Helsinki.

Lehtosalo-Hilander, P.-L. 1982 a: *Luistari I. The Graves*. SMYA-FFT 82:1. Helsinki.

Lehtosalo-Hilander, P.-L. 1982 b: *Luistari II. The Artefacts*. SMYA-FFT 82:2. Helsinki.

Lehtosalo-Hilander, P.-L. 1982 c: *Luistari III. An Inhumation Burial-Ground Reflecting the Finnish Viking Age Society*. SMYA-FFT 82:3. Helsinki.

Lehtosalo-Hilander, P.-L. 1984: *Ancient Finnish Costumes*. Vammala.

Lehtosalo-Hilander, P.-L. 1985 a: Viikinkiajan aseista. Leikkejä luvuilla ja lohikäärmeillä, *Suomen Museo 1985*. Helsinki (English summary: About Viking Age Weapons – a play with numbers and dragons).

Lehtosalo-Hilander, P.-L. 1985 b: Viking Age Spearheads in Finland, *Society and Trade in the Baltic during the Viking Age*. Acta Visbyensia VII. Visby.

Lehtosalo-Hilander, P.-L. 1988: Suur-Savon suuruuden alku – uusi sukellus hopeasolkien salaisuuksiin. *Baskerilinja. Unto Salo 60 vuotta*. Vammala (English summary: The beginning of prosperity in Suur-Savo – a new approach to the secrets of the silver penannular brooches).

Lehtosalo-Hilander, P.-L. 1990: Le Viking finnois, *Finskt Museum 1990*. Helsinki.

Leimus, I. 1990: A Fourteenth Agnus Dei penny of Æthelred II, *Studies in Late Anglo-Saxon Coinage in memory of Bror Emil Hildebrand*. Numismatiska Meddelanden 35.

Leppäaho, J. 1964: *Späteisenzeitliche Waffen aus Finnland. Schwertinschriften und Waffenverzierungen des 9.–12. Jahrhunderts. Ein Tafelwerk*. SMYA-FFT 61. Helsinki.

Les manuscrits à peintures en France du VIIe au XIIe siècle, 1954, (Exposition). Paris.

Lex, L. 1888: *Documents originaux antérieurs à l'an mille des archives de Saône-et Loire*. Chalon-sur-Saône. – Tiré à part de *Mémoires de la Société d'Histoire et d'Archéologie de Chalon-sur-Saône*, t. VII, 6e partie, 1888.

Lid, N. 1930: Skifundet fra Øvrebø, *Universitetets Oldsaksamling. Årbok 1930*. Oslo.

Lidén, H.E. 1990: *Norges Kirker*. Bergen 3. Oslo (English summary).

Liebgott, N.-K. 1976: *Middelalderens våben*. Copenhagen.

Liebgott, N.-K. 1985: *Elfenben*. Copenhagen.

Liebgott, N.-K. 1986: *Middelalderens emaljekunst*. Copenhagen (English summary).

Liebgott, N.-K. 1989: *Dansk Middelalderarkæologi*. Copenhagen.

Liebman, Ch. S. 1985: Paleographical Notes on Ms. Morgan 338 of the Old French Psalter Commentary, *Codices manuscripti*, Jahrg. 11. Vienna.

Liestøl, A. 1970: Runic inscriptions, *Varangian Problems*. Scando-Slavica, Supplementum 1. Copenhagen.

Liestøl, A. 1977: Runeinnskriftene frå "Mindets tomt", in: H.I. Høeg et al.: *De arkeologiske utgravninger i Gamlebyen, Oslo. I. Feltet "Mindets tomt": Stratigrafi, topografi, daterende funngrupper*. Oslo (English summary).

Liestøl, A. 1981: Runerne i Slemmedal-skatten, *Viking* 45. Oslo (English summary).

Liestøl, A., W. Krause & J. Helgason 1962: Drottkvætt-vers fra Bryggen i Bergen, *Maal og Minne 1962*. Bergen.

Lindahl, F. 1975: Orøkorset, *Guld fra Nordvestsjælland* (ed. M. Schou Jørgensen). Holbæk (English summary).

Lindahl, F. 1979: Haraldsborg-skatten, *Strejflys over Danmarks Bygningskultur. Festskrift til Harald Langberg* (ed. R. Egevang). Copenhagen.

Lindahl, F. 1980 a: *Dagmarkorset, Orø- og Roskildekorset*. Copenhagen.

Lindahl, F. 1980 b: Spillelidenskab, *Hikuin 6*. Højbjerg.

Lindahl, F. 1982: Roskildedyret – en dyreslyngsfibula, *Historisk årbog fra Roskilde amt 1982*.

Lindahl, F. 1990: Om nogle relikviekors og fingerringe i Danmarks ældre middelalder, *Synligt og usynligt. Studier tilegnede Otto Norn* (ed. H. Johannsen). Herning.

Lindqvist, I. 1962: Två vikingatida gudabeläten, *Kulturen 1962*.

Lindqvist, S. 1941–42: *Gotlands Bildsteine* I–II. Stockholm.

Lindqvist, S. 1960–62: Forngutniska altaren och därtill knutna studier, *Kungl. Humanistiska vetenskapssamfundet i Uppsala, Årbok 1960–62* (deutsche Zusammenfassung).

Lindström, U. 1979: *Småbarns tillsyn och träning : en etnologisk studie av äldre redskap och metoder i Europa med särskild hänsyn till Sverige*. Stockholm (Deutsche Zusammenfassung).

Long, C.D. 1975: Excavations in the medieval city of Trondheim, Norway, *Medieval Archaeology* XIX.

Lot, F. & Ph. Lauer, (ed.) 1936–46: *Diplomata Karolinorum. Recueil de reproductions en fac-similé des actes originaux des souverains Carolingiens . . . II*. Paris.

Lüdtke, H. 1985: *Die mittelalterliche Keramik von Schleswig. Ausgrabung Schild 1971–1975. Ausgrabungen in Schleswig 4*. Neumünster.

Lüdtke, H. 1989: The Bryggen pottery I. Introduction and Pingsdorf ware, *The Bryggen Papers* (ed. A.E. Herteig), Supplementary Series No. 4. Bergen.

Lund, H.E. 1965: Hålöygske hövdinge-gårder og tunanlegg av Steigentypen fra eldre og yngre jernalder, *Norsk tidsskrift for Sprogvidenskap* XX.

MacGregor, A. 1978: Industry and Commerce in Anglo-Scandinavian York, *Viking Age York and the North* (ed. R.A. Hall). CBA Research Report 27. London.

Mackeprang, M. 1941: *Danmarks middelalderlige Døbefonte.* Copenhagen (English summary).

Mackeprang, M., V. Madsen & C.S. Petersen, (ed.) 1921: *Greek and Latin Illuminated Manuscripts, X–XIII Centuries, in Danish Collections.* Copenhagen, London, Oxford.

Madsen, H.J. 1990: Loke fra Snaptun, *Oldtidens Ansigt/Faces of the Past* (ed. P. Kjærum & R.A. Olsen). Copenhagen (Danish and English text).

Magerøy, E.M. 1967: *Planteornamentikken i islandsk treskurd. En stilhistorisk studie.* Bibliotheca Arnamagnæana. Supplementum, vol. V. Copenhagen.

Magnusson, G. 1986: *Lågteknisk järnhantering i Jämtlands län.* Jernkontorets Bergshistoriska Skriftserie No 22. Stockholm.

Magnússon, Th. 1966: Bátskumlið í Vatnsdal, *Árbók hins Íslenzka fornleifafélags* 1966. Reykjavík (English summary).

Magnússon, Th. 1974: Hringaríkisútskurðir frá Gaulverjabæ, *Árbók hins Íslenzka fornleifafélags* 1974. Reykjavík.

Mahler, D.L.D. 1986: Hvatt eitt rekapetti eisini kann brúkast til, *Mondul* 1986 nr. 1. Tórshavn.

Mahler, D.L.D. in the press: Shielings and their role in the Viking Age Economy – New Evidence from the Faroe Islands, *Proceedings of the 11th Viking Congress 1989* (ed. C.E. Batey and J. Jesch).

Malm, V.A. 1966: Podkovoobraznye i kolcevidnye zastežki-fibuly, *Očerki po istorii russkoj derevnij*, Trudy Istoričeskogo Muzeja 43. Moscow.

Malmer, B. 1961: A contribution to the numismatic history of Norway during the eleventh century, *Commentationes de nummis saeculorum IX–XI in Suecia repertis*, vol. I. Lund.

Malmer, B. 1966: *Nordiska mynt före år 1000.* Lund-Bonn.

Malmer, B. 1986: On the Danish coinage of Cnut, Hauberg type 1, *Nordisk Numismatisk Unions Medlemsblad* 1986 nr. 9.

Malmer, B. 1989: *The Sigtuna Coinage c. 995–1005.* Commentationes de nummis saeculorum IX–XI in Suecia repertis. Nova Series 4. Stockholm.

Malmer, B. og K. Jonsson 1986: Sceattas och den äldsta nordiska myntningen, *Nordisk Numismatisk Unions Medlemsblad* 1986 nr. 4.

Manker, E. 1938, 1950: *Die lappische Zaubertrommel. Eine ethnographische Monographie*, Bd 1–2. Acta Lapponica 1,6. Stockholm.

Margeson, S. 1981: Saga-Geschichten auf Stabkirchenportalen, *Frühe Holzkirchen im nördlichen Europa* (ed. C. Ahrens). Hamburg.

Margeson, S. 1983: On the iconography of the Manx Crosses, *The Viking Age in the Isle of Man* (ed. C. Fell *et al.*). London.

Marquet de Vasselot, J.-J. 1906: Émaux à fond vermiculé, *Revue Archéologique* VI. Paris.

Marstrander, S. 1950: Antikvarisk avdelings tilkvekst 1950, *Det kongelige Norske Videnskabers Selskab. Museet. Årsberetning* 1950. Trondheim.

Martens, I. 1979: Jerndepotene – noen aktuelle problemstillinger, *Jern og jernvinne som kulturhistorisk faktor i jernalder og middelalder i Norge.* AmS-Varia 4. Stavanger (deutsche Zusammenfassung).

Martens, I. 1988: *Jernvinna på Møsstrond i Telemark*, med bidrag af A.M. Rosenqvist. Universitetets Oldsaksamling, Norske Oldfunn XIII. Oslo (English summary).

Mårtensson, A.W. 1968: Aus dem frühmittelalterlichen Lund – ein Stock und eine Spange, *Res mediaevales* (ed. A.W. Mårtensson). Lund.

Mårtensson, A.W. & C. Wahlöö 1970: *Lundafynd. En bilderbok.* Lund.

Marx, J., (ed.) 1914: *Guillaume de Jumièges. Gesta Normannorum Ducum.* Rouen.

McCrosby, S. 1970: *The Apostle Bas-relief at Saint-Denis.* New York.

McKitterick, R. 1980: Charles the Bald and his Library, *English Historical Review* no. 95.

McLees, C. 1990: Games people played. Gaming-pieces, boards and dice from excavations in the medieval town of Trondheim, *Fortiden i Trondheim bygrunn: Folkebibliotekstomten. Meddelelser* nr. 24. Trondheim.

McLees, C. and Ø. Ekroll 1990: A drawing of a medieval ivory chesspiece from the twelfth century church of St. Olav, Trondheim, Norway, *Medieval Archaeology* XXXIV.

Medieval Wooden Sculpture in Sweden. IV, 1975. The museum collection. Catalogue (Museum of National Antiquities, Stockholm). Stockholm.

Meinander, C.F. 1973: Brobackan pyöreä solki, *SMYA-FFT* 75. Helsinki.

Meissner, R. 1925: Ermengarde, Vicegräfin von Narbonne, und Jarl Rögnvald, *Arkiv för nordisk filologi* XLI. Lund.

Melnikova, E.A. 1977: *Skandinavskie runičeskie nadpisi.* Moscow.

Melnikova, E.A. 1986: Amulety s runičeskoj nadpisju s Gorodišče pod Novgorodom, *Drevnejšie gosudarstva na territorii SSSR* 1986. Moscow.

Melnikova, E.A. 1987: New finds of Scandinavian runic inscriptions from the USSR, *Runor och runinskrifter.* Kungliga Vitterhets Historie och Antikvitets Akademien, Konferenser 15. Stockholm.

Metcalf, D.M. 1985: Danmarks ældste mønter, *Nordisk Numismatisk Unions Medlemsblad* 1985 nr. 1.

Meulengracht Sørensen, P. 1986: Thor's Fishing Expedition, *Words and objects. Towards a Dialogue Between Archaeology and History of Religion* (ed. G. Steinsland). Oslo.

Meyer, E.A. 1935: Zur Geschichte des hochmittelalterlichen Schmuckes, *Festschrift für A. Goldschmidt.* Berlin.

Middelalderkunst fra Norge i andre land/Norwegian Medieval Art Abroad, 1972 (ed. M. Blindheim). Oslo.

Minasjan, R.S. 1980: Četyre gruppy nožej Vostočnoj Evropy epochi rannego srednevekovja, *Archeologičeskij sbornik Gosudarstvennogo Ermitaža* 21. Leningrad.

Moeck, H. 1954: Die skandinavischen Kernspalt-flöten in Vorzeit und Tradition der Folklore, *Svensk tidskrift för musikforskning* 1954.

Molaug, P. B. 1977: Leirkarmaterialet fra "Mindets tomt", in: H. I. Høeg et al.: De arkeologiske utgravninger i Gamlebyen, Oslo, bd. 1. Oslo.

Molinier, E. 1896: Catalogue des ivoires du musée du Louvre. Paris.

Moltke, E. 1936: Greenland Runic Inscriptions IV, Meddelelser om Grønland 88,2. Copenhagen.

Moltke, E. 1950: De danske runemønter og deres prægere, Nordisk Numismatisk Årsskrift 1950.

Moltke, E. 1961: En grønlandsk Runeindskrift fra Erik den Rødes Tid, Grønland nr. 11.

Moltke, E. 1975: Runeninschriften aus der Stadt Schleswig, Beiträge zur Schleswiger Stadtgeschichte 20.

Moltke, E. 1976: Runerne i Danmark og deres oprindelse. Copenhagen (English ed.: see Moltke 1985).

Moltke, E. 1985: Runes and their Origin. Denmark and elsewhere. Copenhagen (Dansk udg.: see Moltke 1976).

Muhl, A. 1988: Der Bamberger Schrein und der Camminer Schrein. Zwei im Mammenstil verzierte Prunkkästchen der Wikingerzeit. Diss. Würzburg.

Müller, S. 1900: Drikkehornsbeslag fra Oldtidens Slutning, Aarbøger for nordisk Oldkyndighed og Historie 1900.

Müller-Wille, M. 1970: Bestattung im Boot. Studien zu einer nordeuropäischen Grabsitte, Offa 25/26. Neumünster.

Müller-Wille, M. 1976a: Das Bootkammergrab von Haithabu. Berichte über die Ausgrabungen in Haithabu 8. Neumünster.

Müller-Wille, M. 1976b: Das wikingerzeitliche Gräberfeld von Thumby-Bienebek (Kr. Rendsburg-Eckernförde) Teil I. Offa-Bücher 36. Neumünster.

Müller-Wille, M. 1978: Das Schiffsgrab von der Ile de Groix (Bretagne). Ein Exkurs zum Bootkammergrab von Haithabu, Das archäologische Fundmaterial III der Ausgrabung Haithabu. Berichte über die Ausgrabungen in Haithabu 12. Neumünster.

Müller-Wille, M. 1984: Opferplätze der Wikingerzeit, Frühmittelalterliche Studien 18.

Müller-Wille, M. 1985: Westeuropäischer Import der Wikingerzeit in Nordeuropa, Society and Trade in the Baltic during the Viking Age (ed. S.-O. Lindqvist). Acta Visbyensia VII. Visby.

Müller-Wille, M. 1987: Das wikingerzeitliche Gräberfeld von Thumby-Bienebek (Kr. Rendsburg-Eckernförde). Teil II. Offa-Bücher 62. Neumünster.

Munk Olsen, B. 1982–1989: L'étude des auteurs classiques latins aux XIe et XIIe siècles. Paris (Tome 1, Catalogue des manuscrits classiques latins copiés du IXe au XIIe siècle, Apicius-Juvénal 1982; Tome 3.1, Les classiques dans les bibliothèques médiévales, 1987).

Munksgaard, E. 1962: Skattefundet fra Duesminde, Aarbøger for nordisk Oldkyndighed og Historie 1962 (English summary).

Munksgaard, E. 1977: En guldhalsring fra Nordvestsjælland, Fra Holbæk amt 1977.

Munksgaard, E. 1978: Justerede ringe af ædelmetal fra germansk jernalder og vikingetid, Aarbøger for nordisk Oldkyndighed og Historie 1978 (English summary).

Munksgaard, E. 1984: The embroideries from Bjerringhøj, Mammen, Festskrift til Thorleif Sjøvold på 70-årsdagen. Universitetets Oldsaksamlings skrifter. Ny rekke 5. Oslo.

Munksgaard, E. 1987: Vor ældste Kristus-figur, Nyt fra Nationalmuseet nr. 34. Copenhagen.

Munksgaard, E. 1988: Kongens klær, Skalk 1988:3. Højbjerg.

Murray, H.J.R. 1952: A history of board games other than chess. Oxford.

Musée des Archives départementales, 1878: Recueil de fac-similé héliographiques de documents tirés des Archives des Préfectures, Mairies et Hospices. Texte et Atlas. Paris.

Nallinmaa-Luoto, T. 1978: Tampere-Vilusenharju. Nuoreman rautakauden kalmisto Pirkanmaalla, Karhunhammas 3. Turku (English summary: The Cemetery of Vilusenharju, Tampere).

Naskali, E. 1989: Suksi muinaislöytöjen valossa, Hiihtomuseon julkaisuja I. Lahti (English summary).

Näsman, U. 1984: Vendel period glass from Eketorp-II, Öland, Sweden, Acta Archaeologica 57.

Näsman, U. 1991a: Ett vikingatida depåfynd, Mammen. Grav, kunst og samfund i vikingetid (ed. M. Iversen, U. Näsman & J. Vellev). Højbjerg.

Näsman, U. 1991b: Grav og økse. Mammen og den danske vikingetids våbengrave, Mammen. Grav, kunst og samfund i vikingetid (ed. M. Iversen, U. Näsman & J. Vellev). Højbjerg.

Nedkvintne, A. 1989: Runepinner og handelshistorie, [Norsk] Historisk Tidsskrift bd. 68.

Nerman, B. 1929: Die Verbindungen zwischen Skandinavien und dem Ostbaltikum. Stockholm.

Nerman, B. 1958: Grobin-Seeburg. Ausgrabungen und Funde. Stockholm.

Nerman, B. 1969–75: Die Vendelzeit Gotlands. Stockholm.

Nicolardot, J.-P. 1984: Eléments de datation du Camp de Péran, Plédran (Côtes-du-Nord), Actes des VIe Journées Nationales de l'Association Française d'Archéologie Mérovingienne, sous la direction de X. Barral i Altet. Paris.

Nicolardot, J.-P. 1988: Pledran (Côtes-du-Nord) Camp de Péran. Chronique des fouilles médiévales, Archéologie Médiévale XVIII.

Nicolardot, J.-P. 1989: Résultats des fouilles exécutées en 1989 au Camp de Péran, Plédran, Côtes-d'Armor, Centre Archéologique de Péran.

Nicolaysen, N. 1882: Langskibet fra Gokstad ved Sandefjord. Kristiania.

Nielsen, B.H. 1991: Langbladsøksen, Skalk 1991:2. Højbjerg.

Nielsen, L. 1919: Dansk Bibliografi 1482–1550. Copenhagen.

Nielsen, L.C. 1986: Omgård. The Viking-age Water-mill complex, Acta Archaeologica 57.

Nilsson, T. 1976: Något om hushållet och dess inventarium, Uppgrävt förflutet för PKbanken i Lund (ed. A.W. Mårtensson). Lund.

Nordahl, E. 1988: Reykjavík from the Archaeological Point of View. Aun 12. Uppsala.

Nordal, S., (ed.) 1931: Codex Wormianus. Corpus Codicum Islandicorum Medii Aevi II. Copenhagen (Facsimile).

Nordal, S., (ed.) 1933: Íslensk fornrit II. Reykjavík.

Nordeide, S.W. 1989: "... De beste bønder i kiøbstæden...", Fortiden i Trondheim bygrunn. Folkebibliotekstomten. Meddelelser nr. 20. Trondheim (English summary).

Nordeide, S.W. in the press: Activity in an Urban Community, Acta Archaeologia 60.

Nordenfalk, C. 1941: Romanska bokmålningar i Skara stifts-bibliotek, *Göteborgs högskolas årsskrift* 1941.

Nordenfalk, C. 1944: Konstantin den store i Skåne. Vad ett skånskt processionskors har att berätta, *Meddelanden från Lunds universitets historiska museum* 1944 (= *Kungl. humanistiska vetenskapssamfundet i Lund. Årsberättelse* 1943/44 (deutsche Zusammenfassung).

Nordisk Tidsskrift for Oldkyndighed I, 1832. Copenhagen.

Nordman, C.A. 1931: Nordisk ornamentik i Finlands järnålder, *Nordisk Kultur* XXVII. Kunst. Stockholm.

Nordman, C.A. 1944: Gotländisch oder deutsch – ein Silber-kruzifix von Halikko im Eigentlichen Finnland, *Acta Archaeologica* XV.

Nordman, C.A. 1945: Smyckefyndet från Sipilänmäki i Sakkola, *SMYA-FFT* XLV. Helsinki.

Nordman, C.A. 1954: En relik av Erik den Helige i Åbo dom-kyrka, *Erik den Helige. Historia – Kult – Reliker* (ed. B. Thordeman). Stockholm.

Norges Gamle Love II, 1848. Christiania (restored transcription).

Norges Gamle Love IV, 1885. Christiania (Facsimile).

Norges Innskrifter med de Yngre Runer I, 1941 (M. Olsen). Oslo.

Norges Innskrifter med de Yngre Runer II, 1951 (M. Olsen). Oslo.

Norges Innskrifter med de Yngre Runer III, 1954 (M. Olsen). Oslo.

Norges Innskrifter med de Yngre Runer IV, 1957 (M. Olsen). Oslo.

Norges Innskrifter med de Yngre Runer V, 1960 (M. Olsen). Oslo.

Norges Innskrifter med de Yngre Runer VI, 1980–90 (I. Sanness Johnsen & J.E. Knirk). Oslo.

Norges Kirker. Buskerud I, 1981 (S. Christie & H. Christie). Oslo.

Nørlund, P. 1930: Norse Ruins at Gardar, *Meddelelser om Grøn-land* LXXVI. Copenhagen.

Nørlund, P. 1933: An Early Group of Enamelled Reliquaries, *Acta Archaeologica* IV.

Nørlund, P. 1934a: To byzantinske Elfenbensreliefter med nor-diske Runer, *Aarbøger for Nordisk Oldkyndighed og Historie* 1934.

Nørlund, P. 1934b: *De gamle Nordbobygder ved Verdens Ende.* Copenhagen (several Danish eds.; English ed.: *Viking Settlers in Greenland and their Descendants during Five Hundred Years.* London 1936; deutsche Ausg.: *Wikingersiedlungen in Grönland.* Leipzig 1937).

Nørlund, P. 1948: *Trelleborg.* Nordiske Fortidsminder IV, 1. Copenhagen (English summary).

Nørlund, P. 1963: To efterladte Småstykker, *Aarbøger for Nordisk Oldkyndighed og Historie* 1963. Copenhagen (English summary).

Nørlund, P. 1968: *Gyldne altre* (1926). 2. udgave med Appendix af Tage E. Christiansen. Århus (English summary)

Nørlund, P. & M. Stenberger 1934: Brattahlid, *Meddelelser om Grønland* 88,1. Copenhagen.

Nørlund, P. og E. Lind 1944: *Danmarks romanske kalkmalerier.* Copenhagen (Res. français).

Norn, O. 1968: *Jydsk granit.* Copenhagen (English summary; deutsche Zusammenfassung).

Nosov, E.N. 1984: Historical ties between the population of the Novgorod Land centre and the Baltic countries in the 9th–10th centuries, *Iskos* 4. Helsinki.

Nosov, E.N. 1987: New data on the Ryurik Gorodishche near Novgorod, *Fennoscandia Archaeologica* 4. Helsinki.

Nosov, E.N. 1988: Neue Forschungen über das Rjurikovo Gorodišče bei Novgorod, *Das Altertum* 34, Heft 3.

Nosov, E.N. 1990: *Novgorodskoe (Rjurikovo) Gorodišče.* Leningrad.

Nyborg, E. 1979: Enkeltmænd og fællesskaber i organiseringen af det romanske sognekirkebyggeri, *Strejflys over Danmarks Bygningskultur. Festskrift til Harald Langberg* (ed. R. Egevang). Copenhagen.

Nyborg, E. 1991: The Holy Rood of Roskilde Cathedral and the Scandinavian Early Gothic, *Hafnia. Copenhagen papers in the history of art.* Copenhagen.

Nylén, E. 1973: Finskt, gotländskt eller nordiskt. Kring ett ovanligt exempel på sen runstensornamentik, *SMYA-FFT* 75. Helsinki.

Nylén, E. 1978: *Bildstenar.* Stockholm (2. uppl.: E. Nylén & J.P. Lamm: Bildstenar. 1987; deutsche Ausg.: E. Nylén & J.P. Lamm: *Bildsteine auf Gotland.* Neumünster 1981; Engl. ed.: E. Nylén & J.P. Lamm: *Stones, Ships and symbols. The picture stones of Gotland from the Viking Age and before.* Stockholm 1988).

Ó Floinn, R. 1987: Schools of Metalworking in eleventh- and twelfth-century Ireland, *Ireland and Insular Art A.D. 500–1200* (ed. M. Ryan). Dublin.

Ó Floinn, R. 1989: See *"The Work of Angels"* (ed. S. Youngs).

O'Hara, M.D. in the press: A recently discovered die of Cnut (*Proceedings of International Conference on Cnut, Manchester University, March 1990*).

O'Hara, M.D. in the press: An Iron Reverse Die of King Cnut, *British Numismatic Journal.*

Ojateva, E.I. 1965: Obuvi drugie kožannye izdelija Zemljanogo gorodišča Staroj Ladogi, *Archeologičeskij sbornik Gosudar-stvennogo Ermitaža* 7. Leningrad.

Oldeberg, A. 1966: *Metallteknik under vikingatid och medeltid.* Stockholm.

Olsen, O. 1960: St. Jørgensbjerg kirke, *Aarbøger for nordisk Oldkyndighed og Historie* 1960 (English summary).

Olsen, O. & O. Crumlin-Pedersen 1969: *Fem vikingeskibe fra Roskilde Fjord* (English ed.: *Five Viking Ships.* Copenhagen 1978; deutsche Ausg.: *Fünf Wikingerschiffe.* Roskilde 1990).

Olsen, O. & O. Crumlin-Pedersen 1967: The Skuldelev Ships, *Acta Archaeologica* 38.

Oman, C. 1954: An Eleventh-century English Cross, *The Bur-lington Magazine* 96. London.

O'Meadhra, U. 1979: *Motif-pieces from Ireland.* Stockholm.

O'Meadhra U. 1988: Skibe i Ranveigs skrin, *Skalk* 1988:5. Højbjerg.

Ó Ríordáin, B. 1976: The High Street Excavations, *Proceedings of the Seventh Viking Congress* (ed. B. Almqvist and D. Greene). London.

Osebergfundet I–III, V, see: A.W. Brøgger, H.J. Falk & H. Schetelig, (ed.) 1917–28.

Otčet Archeologičeskoj komissii 1906. St. Petersburg.

Oxenstierna, E. Graf, 1959: *Die Wikinger*, 2. Aufl. Stuttgart.

Page, R.I. 1973: *An Introduction to English Runes.* London.

Page, R.I. 1983: The Manx rune-stones, *The Viking Age in the Isle of Man* (ed. C. Fell *et al.*). London.

Page, R.I. 1987: *Runes*. London.

Pálsson, H. and P. Edwards (tr.) 1972: *The Book of Settlements. Landnámabók*. Winnipeg.

Pálsson, H. and P. Edwards (tr.) 1976: *Egil's Saga*. Harmondsworth.

Pálsson, H. and P. Edwards (tr.) 1978: *Orkneyinga Saga. The History of the Earls of Orkney*. London.

Paulsen, P. 1933: *Studien zur Wikingerkultur*. Neumünster.

Paulsen, P. 1936: *Der Goldschatz von Hiddensee*. Leipzig.

Paulsen, P. 1937: *Der Wikingerfund von Leckhus*. Kiel.

Paulsen, P. 1953: *Schwertortbänder der Wikingerzeit. Ein Beitrag zur Frühgeschichte Osteuropas*. Stuttgart.

Paulsen, P. 1956: *Axt und Kreuz in Nord- und Osteuropa*. Bonn.

Périn, P. 1990: Les objets vikings du musée des antiquités de la Seine-Maritime à Rouen, *Recueil d'études en hommage à Lucien Musset*. Cahier des Annales de Normandie nr. 23.

Petersen, E. 1985: Humanism and the Medieval Past: Christiernus Petri as a Humanist Scholar, *Acta Conventus Neo-Latini Bononiensis. Proceedings of the Fourth International Congress of Neo-Latin Studies 1979 (= Medieval & Renaissance Texts & Studies*, vol. 37). Binghamton, New York.

Petersen, E. 1991: Illuminatio. Texts and Illustrations of the Bible in Medieval Manuscripts in the Royal Library, Copenhagen, *Transactions of the XVth Congress of the International Association of Bibliophiles* (Copenhagen 1987). Copenhagen.

Petersen, H. 1886: *Danske gejstlige Sigiller fra Middelalderen*. Copenhagen.

Petersen, J. 1919: *De norske vikingesværd*. Kristiania.

Petersen, J. 1928: *Vikingetidens smykker*. Stavanger.

Petersen, J. 1951: *Vikingtidens redskaper*. Skrifter utgitt av Det Norske Vitenskapsakademi i Oslo. Hist. Fil. Kl. 1951. No. 4. Oslo.

Petersen, J. 1955: *Vikingetidens smykker i Norge*. Stavanger.

Petruchin, V.J. 1975: Ritualnye sosudy iz kurganov Gnezdova i Černigova, *Vestnik Moskovskogo Universiteta, Istorija*, 1975 No. 2. Moscow.

Philpott, F.A. 1990: *A Silver Saga. Viking Treasure from the North West*. Liverpool.

Pirie, E.J.E. 1986: *Post Roman Coins from York Excavations 1971–81*. The Archaeology of York 18/1. York.

Poey d'Avant, F. 1858: *Monnaies féodales de France*. Paris.

Polubojarinova, M.D. 1972: Raskopki na Rjurikovom Gorodišče v 1965 g, *Novoe v archeologii*. Moscow.

Posselt, G. 1991: Vikingetidsskatten fra Enner, *Tamdrup. Kirke og gård* (ed. O. Schiørring). Horsens.

Price, N.S. 1989: *The Vikings in Brittany*. London (= *Saga-Book* XXII:6, London, pp. 319–440).

Purhonen, P. 1987: Cross Pendants from Iron Age Finland, *Byzantium and the North. Acta Byzantina Fennica* III. Helsinki.

Puskina, T.A. 1984: Bronzovyj idol iz Černoj Mogily, *Vestnik Moskovskogo Universiteta, Istorija*, 1984 No. 3. Moscow.

Rademacher, F. 1942: Unbekannte karolingische Elfenbeine, *Pantheon 1942*.

Rafnsson, S. 1976: Mjóidalsfundurinn, *Minjar og Menntir. Afmælisrit helgað Kristjáni Eldjárn* (ed. G. Kolbeinsson). Reykjavík.

Ramskou, T. 1950: Viking Age cremation graves in Denmark, *Acta Archaeologica* 21.

Ramskou, T. 1980: Vikingetidsbroen over Vejle Ådal, *Nationalmuseets Arbejdsmark 1980*. Copenhagen.

Raudonikas, W.J. 1930: *Die Normannen der Wikingerzeit und das Ladogagebiet*. Stockholm.

Raudonikas, V.I. & K.D. Lauškin 1959: Ob otkrytii v Staroj Ladoge runičeskoj nadpisi na dereve v 1950 g, *Skandinavskij sbornik* 4. Tallinn.

Renouard, Ph. 1908: *Bibliographie des impressions et des oeuvres de Josse Badius Ascensius, imprimeur et humaniste 1462–1535*, tome III. Paris.

Resi, H. G. 1979: *Die Specksteinfunde aus Haithabu. Berichte über die Ausgrabungen in Haithabu* 14. Neumünster.

Resi, H. G. 1991: *Die Wetz- und Schleifsteine aus Haithabu. Berichte über die Ausgrabungen in Haithabu* 28. Neumünster.

Rhein und Maas. Kunst und Kultur 800–1400, 1972. Cologne (éd. française: *Rhin-Meuse, 800–1400*. Liège 1972).

Riga-Katalog 1896 = *Katalog der Ausstellung zum X. archäologischen Kongress in Riga 1896*. Riga.

Ringquist, P.-O. 1969: Två vikingatida uppländska människofigurer i brons, *Fornvännen 1969*.

Rinne, J. 1932: *Pyhä Henrik, piispa ja marttyyri*. Helsinki.

Rispling, G. 1987: Coins with crosses and bird heads – Christian imitations of Islamic coins?, *Fornvännen* 1987:2–3.

Rjabinin, E.A. 1980: Skandinavskij proizvodstvennyj kompleks VIII v. iz Staroj Ladogi, *Skandinavskij sbornik* 25. Tallinn.

Rjabinin, E.A. 1985: Novye otkrytija v Staroj Ladoge, *Srednevekovaja Ladoga* (ed. V.V. Sedov). Leningrad.

Robberstad, K. 1969: *Gulatingslovi*. Oslo (translation).

Roesdahl, E. 1974: The northern mound: burial chamber and grave goods, in: Jelling Problems. A discussion (ed. K.M. Nielsen), *Mediaeval Scandinavia* 7. Odense.

Roesdahl, E. 1976: Otte vikingetidsgrave i Sdr. Onsild, *Aarbøger for nordisk Oldkyndighed og Historie 1976* (English summary).

Roesdahl, E. 1977: *Fyrkat. En jysk vikingeborg II. Oldsagerne og gravpladsen*. Copenhagen (English summary).

Roesdahl, E. 1980: *Danmarks vikingetid*. Copenhagen (English ed.: *Viking Age Denmark*. London 1982).

Roesdahl, E. 1981 a: En tusindårig guldfugl, *Hikuin* 7, 1981. Højbjerg.

Roesdahl, E. 1981 b: Aggersborg in the Viking Age, *Proceedings of the Eighth Viking Congress* (ed. H. Bekker-Nielsen et al.). Odense.

Roesdahl, E. 1986: Vikingernes Aggersborg, *Aggersborg gennem 1000 år* (ed. F. Nørgaard et al.). Herning (English summary).

Roesdahl, E. 1989: Prestige, Display and Monuments in Viking Age Scandinavia, *Les Mondes Normands* (ed. H. Galinié). Caen.

Roesdahl, E. 1990 a: At bygge bro – om det ældste brobyggeri i Norden, *Gulnares hus* (ed. A. Bistrup et al.). Copenhagen.

Roesdahl, E. 1990 b: Spil eller tro, *Oldtidens Ansigt/Faces of the Past* (ed. P. Kjærum & R.A. Olsen). Copenhagen (Danish and English text).

Roesdahl, E. 1990c: Viking i Høm, *Oldtidens ansigt/Faces of the Past* (ed. P. Kjærum & R.A. Olsen). Copenhagen (Danish and English text).

Romanske Stenarbejder 2, 1984 (ed. J. Vellev). Højbjerg.

Roosval, J. 1918: *Die Steinmeister Gottlands*. Stockholm.

Ros, J. 1990: Horn- och benhantverk, *Makt och människor i kungens Sigtuna. Sigtunautgrävningen 1988–90* (ed. S. Tesch). Sigtuna.

Roslund, M. 1990a: Tidig kristen tro, *Makt och människor i kungens Sigtuna. Sigtunautgrävningen 1988–90* (ed. S. Tesch). Sigtuna.

Roslund, M. 1990b: Runor – magi och meddelanden, *Makt och människor i kungens Sigtuna. Sigtunautgrävningen 1988–90* (ed. S. Tesch). Sigtuna.

Roslund, M. 1990c: Kulturkontakter och varuutbyte 970–1200, *Makt och människor i kungens Sigtuna. Sigtunautgrävningen 1988–90* (ed. S. Tesch). Sigtuna.

Roussell, Aa. 1936: Sandnes and the Neighbouring Farms, *Meddelelser om Grønland* 88,2. Copenhagen.

Roussell, Aa. 1943: Stöng, *Forntida gårdar i Island* (ed. M. Stenberger). Copenhagen.

The Royal Abbey of Saint-Denis, 1981. Exhibition Catalogue, The Cloisters. New York.

Ruonavaara, L. 1989: Kuhmoisten "hansavati", *Suomen Museo* 1989. Helsinki (English summary).

Ryan, M., (ed.) 1991: *The Illustrated Archaeology of Ireland*. Dublin.

Rybakov, B.A. 1949: Drevnosti Černigova, *Materialy i issledovanija po archeologii SSSR*. Moscow-Leningrad.

Ryding, O. & S. Kriig 1985: Kammakeri i medeltidens Lund, *Populär arkeologi* 4. Lund.

Rygh, O. 1885: *Norske Oldsager/Antiquités Norvégiennes*. Christiania.

Rygh, O. 1886: Fortegnelser over de til Universitetets Samling af Nordiske oldsager i 1886 indkomne sager fra tiden før Reformationen, *Foreningen til Norske Fortidsmindesmerkers bevaring, Aarsberetning for 1886*. Kristiania.

Salin, B. 1913: Några ord om en Fröbild, *Opuscula archaeologica Oscari Montelio septuagenario dicata*. Holmiæ.

Salin, B. 1922: Fyndet från Broa i Halla, Gotland, *Fornvännen* 1922.

Salmo, H. 1938: *Die Waffen der Merowingerzeit in Finnland*. SMYA-FFT 42:1. Helsinki.

Salmo, H. 1956: *Finnische Hufeisenfibeln*. SMYA-FFT 56. Helsinki.

Samokvasov, D. J. 1908: *Mogily russkoj zemli*. Moscow.

Sarvas, P. 1966: Kaiser und Jungfrau Maria. Barbarische Darstellungen auf einigen in Finnland gefundenen Nachahmungen byzantinischer Münzen, *Suomen Museo* 1966. Helsinki.

Sarvas, P. 1972: *Länsi-Suomen ruumishautojen raha-ajoitukset*. Helsingin yliopiston arkeologian laitos. Moniste 6. Helsinki.

Sawyer, P. 1989: Knut, Sweden and Sigtuna, *Avstamp – för en ny Sigtunaforskning* (ed. S. Tesch). Sigtuna.

Saxonis Gesta Danorum, 1931 (ed. J. Olrik & H. Ræder), tom. I. Hauniæ.

Schetelig, H., see also Shetelig.

Schetelig, H. 1917: *Osebergfundet* I (ed. A.W. Brøgger, Hj. Falk, H. Schetelig). Kristiania.

Schetelig, H. 1918: To danske pragtskrin fra vikingetiden, *Kunst og Haandverk, Nordiske Studier*.

Schetelig, H. 1920: Vestfoldskolen, *Osebergfundet* III (ed. A.W. Brøgger Hj. Falk & H. Schetelig). Kristiania.

Schietzel, K. 1970: Hölzerne Kleinfunde aus Haithabu (Ausgrabung 1963–1964), *Berichte über die Ausgrabungen in Haithabu* 4. Neumünster.

Schietzel, K. & O. Crumlin-Pedersen 1980: Havnen i Hedeby, *Skalk* 1980:3. Højbjerg.

Schiørring, O. 1978: Korset i øksen, *Skalk* 1978:6. Højbjerg.

Schive, C. I. 1865: *Norges Mynter i Middelalderen*. Christiania.

Schjetlein Johannessen, A. 1964: Urnesgruppen i Historisk Museum, *Bergen Museums Årbok* 1964 nr. 2.

Schmid, T. 1944: Smärre liturgiska bidrag VIII. Om Sankt Swithunusmässan i Sverige, *Nordisk tidskrift för bok- och biblioteksväsen* 31. Uppsala.

Schmid, T. 1945: *Liber ecclesiæ vallentunensis*. Stockholm (deutsche Zusammenfassung; Résumé français).

Schmid, T. 1963: Problemata, *Fornvännen* 1963 (deutsche Zusammenfassung).

Schmidt-Lornsen, J. 1986: Bilddarstellungen auf wikingerzeitlichen Mähnenstuhlpaaren, *Zum Problem der Deutung frühmittelalterliche Bildinhalte* (ed. H. Roth). Sigmaringen.

Schmidt-Lornsen, J. 1990: Skikkelse og ansigt på mankestole, *Oldtidens Ansigt/Faces of the Past* (ed. P. Kjærum & R.A. Olsen). Copenhagen (Danish and English text).

Schönbeck, B. 1980: *Båtgravskicket, Vendeltid* (ed. A. Sandwall). Stockholm.

Schou Jørgensen, M. 1975: Oldtidsguld, *Guld fra Nordvestsjælland* (ed. M. Schou Jørgensen). Holbæk (English summary).

Schou Jørgensen, M. 1988: Vej, vejstrøg og vejspærring. Jernalderens landfærdsel, *Fra Stamme til Stat i Danmark* (ed. P. Mortensen & B. Rasmussen). Århus (English summary).

Schuldt, E. 1956: *Die slawische Keramik in Mecklenburg*. Berlin.

Schultz, C.G. 1952: Jellingbægeret – vor ældste kristne kalk?, *Kuml* 1952. Århus (English summary).

Schultz, C.G. 1957: Two English Crosses, *The National Museum of Denmark* (ed. Aa. Roussell). Copenhagen (dansk udg.: *Danmarks Nationalmuseum*, ed. Aa. Roussell. Copenhagen 1957).

Schvindt, Th. 1893: *Tietoja Karjalan rautakaudesta*. SMYA-FFT XIII. Helsinki (Referat: Aus dem Eisenalter Karelens).

Seim, K.F. 1989: Runeinnskrifter fra Trondheim og Bergen som kilder til Islandshandelens historie? Et innfløkt proveniens-spørgsmål, *[Norsk] Historisk Tidsskrift*, bd. 68.

Seip, J.A. 1942: *Sættargjerden i Tunsberg og kirkens jurisdiksjon*. Oslo.

Selirand, J. & E. Tõnisson 1984: *Through past millennia. Archaeological discoveries in Estonia*. Tallinn.

Selling, D. 1955: *Wikingerzeitliche und frühmittelalterliche Keramik in Schweden*. Stockholm.

Serning, I. 1956: *Lappska offerplatsfynd från järnålder och medeltid i de svenska lappmarkerna*. Stockholm.

Shetelig, H., see also Schetelig.

Shetelig, H., (ed.) 1940: *Viking Antiquities in Great Britain and Ireland* I–V. Oslo.

Shetelig, H. 1944: Smykker av jet i norske vikingefunn, *Bergens Museums årbok* 1944 (English summary).

Sizov, V.I. 1897: Drevnij železnyj toporik iz kollekcii Istoričeskogo Muzeja, *Archeologičeskie izvestija i zametki* 5. Moscow.

Sizov, V.I. 1902: *Gnezdovskij mogilnik bliz Smolenska.* Materialy po archeologii Rossii 28. St. Petersburg.

Sjøvold, T. 1941–42: Studier i Vestfolds vikingetid, *Universitetets Oldsaksamling. Årbok* 1941–1942. Oslo.

Sjøvold, T. 1974: *The Iron Age settlement of Arctic Norway*, II. Tromsø Museums Skrifter X,2. Tromsø, Oslo, Bergen.

Sjøvold, T. 1985: *Vikingskipene i Oslo.* Oslo (also in English, German, French, Italian).

Skaare, K. 1969: "Olav Kyrres" myntreform, *Nordisk Numismatisk Årsskrift* 1969 (English summary).

Skaare, K. 1976: *Coins and coinage in Viking-Age Norway.* Oslo-Bergen-Tromsø.

Skaare, K. 1978: Myntene fra Lom kirke, *Foreningen til norske fortidsminnesmerkers bevaring. Årbok* 1978.

Skaare, K. 1979/80: Kong Sverres utmyntning, *Nordisk Numismatisk Årsskrift* 1979/80 (English summary).

Skaare, K. 1981: Mynterne i Slemmedal-skatten, *Viking* 45. Oslo (English summary).

Skaare, K. 1985: An eleventh century Norwegian penny found on the coast of Maine, USA, *Nummus et Historia.* Warsaw.

Skaare, K. 1988: Der Schatzfund von Hon und seine Münzen, *Commentationes Numismaticae* 1988. Hamburg.

Skaarup, J. 1976: *Stengade 2. En langelandsk gravplads med grave fra romersk jernalder og vikingetid.* Rudkøbing (deutsche Zusammenfassung).

Skamby Madsen, J. 1984: Et skibsværft fra sen vikingetid/tidlig middelalder ved Fribrødre å på Falster, *Hikuin* 10. Højbjerg (English summary).

Skamby Madsen, J. 1987: Dänish-wendische Beziehungen am Schluss des 11. Jahrhunderts vom Fund einer Schiffswerft bei Fribrødreå auf Falster aus beleuchtet, *Bistum Roskilde und Rügen* (ed. B. Wiberg). Roskilde.

Skamby Madsen, J. 1991: Fribrødre – a shipyard site from the late 11th century, *Aspects of Maritime Scandinavia A.D. 200–1200* (ed. O. Crumlin-Pedersen). Roskilde.

Skjølsvold, A. 1961: *Klebersteinsindustrien i vikingetiden.* Oslo, Bergen.

Skovgaard-Petersen, I. 1977: Oldtid og vikingetid, *Danmarks Historie* 1, I. Skovgaard-Petersen, A.E. Christensen, H. Paludan. Copenhagen (Gyldendal).

Skovmand, R. 1942: De danske Skattefund fra Vikingetiden og den ældste Middelalder indtil omkring 1150, *Aarbøger for nordisk Oldkyndighed og Historie* 1942 (Résumé français).

Slavcev, P. 1990: Peigne en os de Caravec, *Archeologija* 32, 1990:1. Sofia.

Slavjane i Skandinavy, 1986 (ed. E.A. Melnikova). Moscow (revised Russian version of J. Herrmann (ed.): *Wikinger und Slaven.* Berlin 1982).

Smyth, A.P. 1984: *Warlords and Holy Men. Scotland AD 800–1000.* London.

Snaedal-Brink, T. & I. Jansson 1983: Gotländska runinskrifter 900-talets slut – ca 1100, *Gutar och vikingar* (ed. I. Jansson). Stockholm.

Sognnes, K. 1988: Iron Age Arrow-heads from Hordaland, Norway. Testing a classification system, *Gunneria* 60. Trondheim.

Sotnikova, M.P. & I.G. Spasski 1982: *Russian coins of the X–XI centuries A.D.* British Archaeological Reports (Int. Ser.) 136. Oxford.

Speake, G. 1989: *A Saxon bed-burial on Swallowcliffe Down.* English Heritage Archaeological Report no. 10. London.

Spicyn, A.A. 1905: Gnezdovskie kurgany v raskopkach S.I. Sergeeva, *Izvestija archeologičeskoj komissii* 15. St. Petersburg.

Stamsø Munch, G. 1960: Skattefunnet fra Skar i Misvær, *Viking* 1960. Oslo (English summary).

Stamsø Munch, G. 1967: Funnene fra Eiterjord i Beiarn og Vestvatn i Misvær, *Viking* 30. Oslo (English summary).

Stamsø Munch, G. and O.S. Johansen 1988: Borg in Lofoten – An Inter-Scandinavian Research Project, preliminary report, *Norwegian Archaeological Review*, Vol. 21, No. 2. Oslo.

Stamsø Munch G., O.S. Johansen and I. Larssen 1987: Borg in Lofoten, A Chieftain's farm in arctic Norway, *Proceedings of the Tenth Viking Congress, Larkollen, Norway* (ed. J. Knirk). Universitetets Oldsaksamlings Skrifter, Ny rekke, Nr. 9. Oslo.

Steen Jensen, J. 1975: Svend Estridsens byzantinske mønt, *Den kgl. Mønt og Medaillesamling. Møntsamlernyt* 1975.

Steen Jensen, J. 1990: The Lund coinage of king Niels (1104–1134) as illustrated by the hoard from Sct. Drotten (1984). A preliminary report, *Sigtuna Papers* (ed. K. Jonsson & B. Malmer). *Commentationes de nummis saeculorum IX–XI in Suecia repertis.* Nova Ser. 6. Stockholm.

Steffensen, J. 1966: Lysing mannabeina, *Árbók hins Íslenzka fornleifafélags* 1966. Reykjavík (English summary).

Stenberger, M. 1947–58: *Die Schatzfunde Gotlands der Wikingerzeit* I–II. Stockholm.

Stenersen, L.B. 1881: *Myntfundet fra Græslid i Tydalen.* Christiania.

Stenersen, L.B. 1895: Om et myntfunn fra Helgeland i Hole, *Videnskabs-Selskabet i Christiania. Skrifter* II. *Historisk-filosofisk klasse*, nr. 3.

Stolpe, H. & T.J. Arne 1912: *Graffältet vid Vendel.* Stockholm.

Strandberg, R. 1938: Les broches d'argent caréliennes en forme de fer à cheval et leur ornements, *Eurasia Septentrionalis Antiqua* XII. Helsinki.

Ström, K. 1984: Thorshammerringe und andere Gegenstände des heidnischen Kults, *Birka II:1* (ed. G. Arwidsson). Stockholm.

Strömberg, M. 1961: *Untersuchungen zur jüngeren Eisenzeit in Schonen* I–II. Lund.

Stummann Hansen, S. 1988: The Norse Landnam in the Faroe Islands in the Light of recent Excavations at Toftanes, Leirvik, *Northern Studies* 25. Edinburgh.

Stummann Hansen, S. 1989: Toftanes – en færøsk landnamsgård fra 9.–10. århundrede, *Hikuin* 15. Højbjerg.

Stummann Hansen, S. in the press: Toftanes. A Faroese Viking Age Farm from the 9th–10th Century, *Acta Archaeologica.*

Svärdström, E. 1963: *Kalenderstickan från Lödöse.* Antikvariskt arkiv 21. Stockholm (deutsche Zusammenfassung).

Svensson, E. 1990: Myntfynd i Sigtuna, *Makt och människor i kungens Sigtuna. Sigtunautgrävningen 1988–90* (ed. S. Tesch). Sigtuna.

Svensson, P. 1981: *Frøslevskrinet.* Padborg

Sveriges runinskrifter III, 1924–36. *Södermanlands runinskrifter* (E. Brate & E. Wessén).

Sveriges runinskrifter V, 1940–70. *Västergötlands runinskrifter* (H. Jungner & E. Svärdström).

Sveriges runinskrifter VII, 1943–46. *Upplands runinskrifter* (E. Wessén & S.B.F. Jansson).

Sveriges runinskrifter XI, 1962. *Gotlands runinskrifter* (S.B.F. Jansson & E. Wessén).

Sveriges runinskrifter XII, 1978. *Gotlands runinskrifter* (E. Svärdström).

Swarzenski, H. 1954: *Monuments of Romanesque Art.* London.

Talvio, T. 1978: Coin Imitations as Jewellery in Eleventh Century Finland, *Finskt Museum* 1978. Helsinki.

Talvio, T. 1990: Agnus Dei: Mynt och Myntsmycken, *Nordisk Numismatisk Unions Medlemsblad* 1990.

Tångeberg, P. 1986: *Mittelalterliche Holzskulpturen und Altarschreine in Sweden. Studien zu Form, Material und Technik.* Stockholm.

Taylor, M. 1978: *The Lewis Chessmen.* London (British Museum Publications).

Temple, E. 1976: *Anglo-Saxon Manuscripts 900–1066.* A survey of manuscripts illuminated in the British Isles, vol. 2. London.

Tesch, S. 1987: Kyrkolunden – en historisk och arkeologisk tillbakablick, *Sigtunahem.* Sigtuna.

Tesch, S. 1990: Stad och stadsplan, *Makt och människor i kungens Sigtuna. Sigtunautgrävningen 1988–90* (ed. S. Tesch). Sigtuna.

Thålin-Bergman, L. 1983 a: Järn och järnsmide för hemmabruk och avsalu, *Gutar och vikingar* (ed. I. Jansson). Stockholm.

Thålin-Bergman, L. 1983 b: Der wikingerzeitliche Werkzeugkasten vom Mästermyr auf Gotland, *Das Handwerk in Vor- und Frühgeschichtlicher Zeit* II (ed. H. Jankuhn *et al.*). Gothenburg.

Thålin-Bergmann, L. 1986: Übersicht der Speerspitzen von Birka, *Birka* II:2 (ed. G. Arwidsson). Stockholm.

Thórðarson, M. 1911: Biskupskápan gamla, *Árbók hins Íslenzka fornleifafélags* 1911. Reykjavík.

Thórðarson, M. 1931: Islands middelalderkunst, *Nordisk Kultur* XXVII. Copenhagen.

Thordeman, B. 1954: Erik den heliges gravkrona, *Erik den Helige. Historia, kult, reliker* (ed. B. Thordeman). Stockholm (deutsche Zusammenfassung).

Thorvildsen, K. 1950: En Tylvt Økser fra Vikingetiden, *Aarbøger for nordisk Oldkyndighed og Historie* 1950 (English summary).

Thunmark-Nylén, L. 1983: *Vikingatida dosspännen – teknisk stratigrafi och verkstadsgruppering.* Uppsala (English summary).

Tillväxten 1913 = Statens historiska museum och K. Myntkabinettet, tillväxten under år 1913, *Fornvännen* 1913.

Tomanterä, L. 1978: *Kaksi Köyliön miekkahautaa. Vanhankartanon C-kalmiston haudat XVI ja XVII.* Helsingin yliopiston arkeologian laitos. Moniste 16. Helsinki.

Tomanterä, L. 1980: The Disc-Pommelled Swords from Kekomäki in Kaukola, *Fenno-ugri et slavi* 1978 (ed. The University of Helsinki. Department of Archaeology. Stencil no. 22). Helsinki.

Tomanterä, L. 1984: Braid, Weave and "Foxtail", *Fenno-ugri et slavi* 1983. *Iskos* 4. Helsinki.

Tõnisson, E. 1962: Eesti aardeleiud 9.–13. sajandist, *Muistsed kalmed ja aarded II.* Tallinn.

Trætteberg, H. 1953: Geistlige segl i Nidaros, *Den norske kirkeprovins 1153–1953* (ed. S. Marstrander). Trondheim (Exhibition catalogue).

Trésors des abbayes normandes, 1979 (Catalogue de l'exposition de Rouen et de Caen).

Ugglas, C.R. af 1933: *Kyrkligt guld- och silversmide.* Ur Statens historiska museums samlingar 2. Stockholm.

Ugglas, C.R. af 1936: *Gotländska silverskatter från Valdemarstågets tid.* Ur Statens historiska museums samlingar 3. Stockholm.

Ugglas, C.R. af 1937: Trydekrucifixet och Lund, *Från stenålder till rokoko. Studier tillägnade Otto Rydbeck.* Lund.

Ulbricht, I. 1978: *Die Geweihverarbeitung in Haithabu.* Die Ausgrabungen in Haithabu 3. Neumünster.

Ulbricht, I. 1984: Bernsteinfunde aus Haithabu, *Offa* 41. Neumünster.

Ulbricht, I. 1990: Die Bernsteinverarbeitung in Haithabu, *Berichte über die Ausgrabungen in Haithabu* 27. Neumünster.

Unger, C.R., (ed.) 1871: *Codex Frisianus. En samling af norske konge-sagaer.* Christiania.

Uppgrävt förflutet för PKbanken, 1976 (ed. A.W. Mårtensson). Lund.

Vaage, J. 1979: *Skienes verden.* Oslo.

Vaage, J. 1981: Våre eldste ski datert etter C14-klokken, *Foreningen til Ski-Idrettens Fremme, Årbok* 1981. Oslo.

Vahter, T. 1932: Les "kaatteris" chez les peuples finnois pendant l'âge récent du fer, *Eurasia Septentrionalis Antiqua* VII. Helsinki.

Valonen, N. 1972: Euran suksilöytö, *Satakuntaa ja satakuntalaisia* III. Pori.

Valonen, N. 1980: Varhaisia lappalais-suomalaisia kosketuksia, *Ethnologia Fennica. Finnish Studies in Ethnology* 10. (English summary: Early contacts between the Lapps and the Finns). Helsinki.

Vandvik, E. 1959: *Latinske dokument til norsk historie.* Oslo.

Vebæk, C.L. 1965: An Eleventh-Century Farmhouse in the Norse Colonies in Greenland, *The Fourth Viking Congress* (ed. A. Small). Aberdeen.

Vebæk, C.L. 1980: Guldhalsring fra Vestsjælland, *Danefæ. Til Hendes Majestæt Dronning Margrethe II* (ed. P.V. Glob). Copenhagen (Danish and English text).

Vedel, E. 1878: Nyere Undersøgelser angaaende Jernalderen paa Bornholm, *Aarbøger for nordisk Oldkyndighed og Historie* 1878.

Vedel, E. 1886: *Bornholms Oldtidsminder og Oldsager.* Copenhagen.

Vendel Period Studies, 1983 (ed. J.P. Lamm & H.-Å. Nordström). Stockholm.

Vendeltid, 1980 (ed. A. Sandwall). Historia i fickformat. Stockholm.

Vierck, H. 1983: Ein Schmiedeplatz aus Alt-Ladoga und der präurbane Handel zur Ostsee vor der Wikingerzeit, *Münstersche Beiträge zur antiken Handelsgeschichte* II:2.

Viking and Medieval Dublin 1973 = *Viking and Medieval Dublin. National Museum Excavations, 1962–1973. Catalogue of Exhibition.* Dublin.

Vikingerne i England, 1981 (ed. E. Roesdahl *et al.*). London. Udstillingskatalog (English ed.: *The Vikings in England.* London 1981).

The Vikings in England, 1981 (ed. E. Roesdahl *et al.*). Exhibition Catalogue. London (Dansk udg.: *Vikingerne i England.* London 1981).

Vilhjálmsson, V.Ö. 1988: Dateringsproblemer i Islands arkæologi, *Hikuin 14.* Højbjerg (English summary).

Vilhjálmsson, V.Ö. 1989: Stöng og Thjórsárdalur-bosættelsens ophør, *Hikuin 15.* Højbjerg (English summary).

Vilkuna, K. 1964: Das Kauharz, ein uraltes Genussmittel, *Studia ethnographica upsaliensia XXI.* Uppsala.

Voss, O. 1991: Hørninggraven, *Mammen. Grav, kunst og samfund i vikingetid* (ed. M. Iversen, U. Näsman & J. Vellev). Højbjerg.

Vuolijoki, H. 1972: *Suomen rautakauden silmäkirveet.* Helsingin yliopiston arkeologian laitos. Moniste 4. Helsinki.

Wåhlin, H. 1921: Några prov på skånsk metallkonst i Skåne, *Äldre kyrklig konst i Skåne. Studier utgivna med anledning av kyrkliga utställningen i Malmö 1914 genom Otto Rydbeck och Evert Wrangel.* Lund.

Wahlöö, C. 1976: *Keramik 1000–1600 i svenska fynd.* Lund.

Wakeman, W.F. 1894: *Catalogue of Specimens in the Collection of the Royal Irish Academy 1–2.* Dublin.

Wallace, B.L. in the press: L'Anse aux Meadows, Gateway to Vinland, *Acta Archaeologica.*

Wallace, P.F. 1983: Wooden objects from Fishamble Street, Dublin, *Treasures of Ireland. Irish Art 3000 B.C.–1500 A.D.* (ed. M. Ryan). Dublin.

Wallace, P.F. 1985: The survival of wood in tenth to thirteenth century Dublin, *Waterlogged Wood-Study and Conservation.* Grenoble, Centre d'étude de traitement des bois gorges d'eau.

Wallem, F.B. 1907: *Lys og lysstel.* Oslo.

Wallem, F.B. 1911: *La broderie de l'église de Hölandet en Norvège et son rapport avec la tapisserie de Bayeux.* Kristiania (Oslo).

Walton, P. 1989: *Textiles, Cordage and Raw Fibre from 16–22 Coppergate.* The Archaeology of York 17/5. York.

Wamers, E. 1981: Ein karolingischer Prunkbeschlag aus dem Römisch-Germanischen Museum, Köln, *Zeitschrift für Archäologie des Mittelalters 9.*

Wamers, E. 1984: Eine Zungenfibel aus dem Hafen von Haithabu, *Berichte über die Ausgrabungen in Haithabu 19.* Neumünster.

Wamers, E. 1985: *Insularer Metallschmuck in wikingerzeitlichen Gräbern Nordeuropas.* Neumünster.

Wamers, E. 1991: Pyxides imaginatae. Zur Ikonographie und Funktion karolingischer Silberbecher, *Germania 69.*

Waterman, D.M. 1959: Late Saxon, Viking and Early Medieval Finds from York, *Archaeologia 97.*

Wegraeus, E. 1986: Die Pfeilspitzen von Birka, *Birka II:2* (ed. G. Arwidsson). Stockholm.

Westermann-Angerhausen, H. 1974: Das ottonische Kreuzreliquar, ein Reliquentriptychon von Ste. Croix, Liège, *Wallraf-Richartz-Jahrbuch XXXVI.*

Wilde, K.A. 1953: *Die Bedeutung der Grabung Wolin 1934.* Hamburg.

Wilde, W. 1861: *A Descriptive Catalogue of the Antiquities of animal materials and bronze in the Museum of the Royal Irish Academy.* Dublin.

Williamson, P. & L. Webster 1990: The decoration of Anglo-Saxon ivory carvings, *Early Medieval Wall Painting and Painted Sculpture in England* (ed. S. Cather *et al.*). Oxford, B.A.R.

Wilson, D.M. 1960: The Fejø Cup, *Acta Archaeologica 31.*

Wilson, D.M. 1964: *Anglo-Saxon Ornamental Metalwork 700–1100 in the British Museum.* London.

Wilson, D.M. 1974: "Men de ligger i London", *Skalk 1974:5.* Højbjerg.

Wilson, D.M. 1983: The Art of the Manx crosses of the Viking Age, *The Viking Age in the Isle of Man* (ed. C. Fell *et al.*). London.

Wilson, D.M. 1984: *Anglo-Saxon Art.* London.

Wilson, D.M. 1985: *The Bayeux Tapestry.* London.

Wilson, D.M. and O. Klindt-Jensen 1966: *Viking Art.* London. Reprint 1980 (Dansk udg.: Klindt-Jensen, O. og D.M. Wilson: *Vikingetidens kunst.* Copenhagen 1965).

Wojtasik, J. 1957: Znaleziska bursztynowe ze stanowiska 4 w Wolinie (Bernsteinfunde aus Fundstelle 4 in Wolin). *Materialy Zachodniopomorskie*, III, Szczecin (deutsche Zusammenfassung).

"The work of Angels". Masterpieces of Celtic Metalwork, 6th–9th centuries AD, 1989 (ed. S. Youngs). Exhibition Catalogue, The British Museum. London.

Wormald, F. 1952: Some illustrated Manuscripts of the Lives of the Saints, *Bulletin of the John Rylands Library 1952.*

Worsaae, J.J.A. 1859: *Nordiske Oldsager i Det Kongelige Museum i Kjøbenhavn.* Copenhagen

Worsaae, J.J.A. 1869: Om Mammenfundet, *Aarbøger for nordisk Oldkyndighed og Historie 1869.*

Zachrisson, I. 1984: *De samiska metalldepåerna år 1000–1350 i ljuset av fyndet från Mörtträsket, Lappland* (English summary: The Saami Metal Deposits A.D. 1000–1350 in the light of the find from Mörtträsket, Lapland). Archaeology and Environment 3. Umeå.

Zariņa, A. 1988: *Lībiešu apgērbs.* Riga (deutsche Zusammenfassung).

Zglinicki, F. von 1979: *Die Wiege, volkskundlich-kulturgeschichtlich-kunstwissenschaftlich-medizinhistorisch.* Regensburg.

Index of places—catalogue nos. 1–617

Else Roesdahl

Index of exhibits—catalogue nos. 1–617 *Göran Tegnér*

References are to catalogue numbers

Acknowledgements

The Nordic Council of Ministers wishes to express its warmest gratitude for the invaluable help and support from many sources which has made this exhibition and catalogue possible.

In addition to the people and institutions named elsewhere in this book we should like to acknowledge with deep gratitude the contribution made to the initiation of the exhibition by the late Carl Tomas Edam, Special Projects Director of the Nordic Council of Ministers, who died in 1991.

Thanks are particularly due to the Department of Medieval Archaeology, Aarhus University, and the Prehistoric Museum, Moesgård, for the use of premises and for many other kinds of assistance, and especially to Bodil Bjerring, Lene Larsen and Annemette Kjærgård for the preparation of texts and organization of a formidable amount of material. Further, we would wish to thank Preben Meulengracht Sørensen, Aarhus University, for much sound advice and guidance; Jørn Street-Jensen, Statsbiblioteket, Århus, for help with the bibliography; Maj Stief of Danmarks Nationalmuseum for advice on conservation and transport. We would also like to thank Thora Fisker, of Copenhagen, who laid the foundations for the design of the book, as well as Christina Wikblad of Bohusläningens Boktryckeri.

ICELAND
Hólar
Reykjavík
Thingvellir
Skálholt

Polar Circle

Hålogaland

ATLANTIC OCEAN

Faroe Islands

Shetland

Trondheim
(Nidaros)

NORWAY

SWEDE

Bergen

Lewis
Hebrides
Orkney

Oslo

Oseberg

Uppsala

Birka

St
ho

G
la

SCOTLAND

Lindisfarne

NORTH SEA

DENMARK

Copenhagen

Lund

BALT

IRELAND
Isle
of Man
Dublin

Stamford Bridge
York

Ribe
Hedeby/
Schleswig
Danevirke

Rügen

ENGLAND
Danelagen

London

Southampton

Hastings

Flanders

Rouen

Dorestad

Cologne

Hamburg
Bremen
Saxony

Lübeck

Wolin

Tru

Berlin

Oder

Gniez

Frisia

Rhine

Weser

Elbe

Normandy

Brittany

Nantes

Noirmoutier

Tours

Loire

Paris
Rheims

Seine

Clairvaux

Mainz

Bamberg

Prag

Danube

Limoges

Bordeaux

Garonne

Santiago de
Compostela

Toulouse

Rome

Cordova

Seville

Gibraltar

MEDITERANEAN SEA

Sicily

North Cape

Lappland

WHITE SEA

URAL MOUNTAINS

FINLAND

LADOGA

Turku/Åbo

FINNISH BIGHT

Volchov

Staraja
Ladoga

Beloozero

Tallinn

Novgorod

Gorodišče

Volga

Bolšoe
Timerevo
Jaroslavl

Volga *Kama*

Bulgar

Daugmale

Dyna/Daugava

Curland *Semgallen*

Grobiņa

Gnezdovo

Elec

Don

Wisla

Černigov

Kiev

Dnepr

Foščevataja

Volga

Itil

Danube

Berezan

Caucasus

CASPIAN SEA

BLACK SEA

Constantinople
/Byzantium

Athens

Bagdad

Polar Circle — North Cape

ICELAND

Hólar
Mývatn
Reykholt
Borg
Thingvellir
Þjórsárdalur
Reykjavík
Skálholt
Hekla
Vatna-jökull

FAROE ISLANDS

Kirkjubøur
Tórshavn

Polar Circle

Lofoten
Senja
Troms
Borg
Rautasjaure
Nordland
Lappland/Lappi
Ukonsaari
Rovaniemi
Kuusamo
Lappland
Vindelgransele

GULF OF BOTHNIA
Pohjanmaa/Österbotten

Stiklestad
Trondheim
(Nidaros)
Trøndelag
Tyldal

Mikkeli/
St. Michel
Laatokan Karjala/
Ladoga Karel
Savo/
Savolax
Tampere/
Tammerfors
FINLAND
Satakunta
Eura
Häme/
Tavastland
Varsinais-Suomi
Türku/Åbo
Halikko

Sogn og
Fjordane
Urnes

NORWAY
Bergen
Buske-rud
Ringerike
Ål
Hamar
Dalarne
Bergslagen
Hon
Oslo
Eidsborg
Vestfold
Borre
Oseberg
Gokstad
Kaupang
Telemark
Stavanger
Roga-land
Hylestad
Byg-land

Vendel
Uppland
Uppsala
Sigtuna
Birka
SWEDEN
MÄLAR
Helgö
Stockholm

ÅLAND
FINNISH BIGHT
Kostivere
Tallinn

Skara
VÄNERN
Lödöse
Göta älv
Väster-götland
Öster-götland

Visby
Broa
Gotland

Öland

BALTIC SEA

Ösel/
Saarema

Daugmale
Semgallen
Dyna/Daugava

Aggersborg
Fyrkat
DENMARK
Viborg
Jutland
Århus
Jelling
Vor-basse
Ribe
Odense
Fyn
Trelle-borg
Roskilde
Skåne
Lund
Dalby
Sjæl-land
Copenhagen
Ringsted

Curland
Grobiņa

Visnevo
Samland

Schleswig
Danevirke
Hedeby
Hamburg
Lübeck
Ralswiek
Arkona
Rügen
Kamień
Wolin
Truso